M000224199

# Georgia Women

# Georgia Women

## *THEIR LIVES AND TIMES*

*Volume 1*

EDITED BY

*Ann Short Chirhart and Betty Wood*

The University of Georgia Press   *Athens and London*

© 2009 by the University of Georgia Press

Athens, Georgia 30602

www.ugapress.org

All rights reserved

Set in Minion by Graphic Composition, Inc.

Printed and bound by Thomson-Shore

The paper in this book meets the guidelines for permanence and durability of the Committee on
Production Guidelines for Book Longevity of the Council on Library Resources.

Printed in the United States of America

09 10 11 12 13   P   5 4 3 2 1

Library of Congress Cataloging-in-Publication Data

Georgia women : their lives and times / edited by Ann Short Chirhart and Betty Wood.

v. cm.

Includes bibliographical references and index.

Contents: Introduction / Ann Short Chirhart with Betty Wood—Mary Musgrove (ca. 1700–1765) :
maligned mediator or mischievous malefactor / Julie Anne Sweet—Nancy Hart (ca. 1735–
ca. 1830) : "Too good not to tell again" / John Thomas Scott—Elizabeth Lichtenstein Johnston (1764–
1848) : "Shot round the world but not heard" / Ben Marsh—Ellen Craft (ca. 1826–1891) : the fugitive
who fled as a planter / Barbara McCaskill—Fanny Kemble (1809–1893) and Frances Butler Leigh
(1838–1910) : becoming Georgian / Daniel Kilbride—Susie King Taylor (1848–1912) : "I gave my services
willingly" / Catherine Clinton—Eliza Frances Andrews (1840–1931) : "I will have to say Damn! yet,
before I am done with them" / Christopher J. Olsen—Amanda America Dickson (1849–1893) : a wealthy
lady of color in nineteenth-century Georgia / Kent Anderson Leslie—Mary Gay (1829–1918) : sin, self,
and survival in the post–Civil War South / Michele Gillespie—Rebecca Latimer Felton (1835–1930) :
the problem of protection in the new South / LeeAnn Whites—Mary Latimer McLendon (1840–1921) :
"Mother of suffrage work in Georgia" / Stacey Horstmann Gatti—Mildred Lewis Rutherford (1851–
1928) : the redefinition of new South White womanhood / Sarah Case—Nellie Peters Black (1851–1919) :
Georgia's Pioneer Club woman / Carey Olmstead Shellman—Lucy Craft Laney (1855–1933) and Martha
Berry (1866–1942) : lighting fires of knowledge / Jennifer Lund Smith—Corra Harris (1869–1935) :
the storyteller as folk preacher / Donald Mathews—Juliette Gordon Low (1860–1927) : late-blooming
daisy / Anastatia Hodgens Sims.

ISBN-13: 978-0-8203-3336-6 (hardcover : alk. paper)   ISBN-10: 0-8203-3336-0 (hardcover : alk. paper)
ISBN-13: 978-0-8203-3337-3 (pbk. : alk. paper)   ISBN-10: 0-8203-3337-9 (pbk. : alk. paper)

1. Women—Georgia—Biography. 2. Women—Georgia—History. 3. Georgia—Biography.

I. Chirhart, Ann Short. II. Wood, Betty.

CT3262.G4 G46 2009

975.8092'2—dc22

[B]   2009008552

British Library Cataloging-in-Publication Data available

# Contents

# Acknowledgments

As in any collection of essays, this book owes its achievements to the scholars who contributed their research. We would like to thank all of them for their patience and substantial work. At an early stage, Sarah Gardner provided some assistance. Betty Wood graciously agreed to serve as coeditor at a vital time. Indiana State University provided funding to Ann Short Chirhart through an Indiana State University Research Grant that allowed her to complete portions of the editing. From the beginning of this collection, John Inscoe, with his love of Georgia history, provided valuable assistance. We would like to express our deep appreciation to Nancy Grayson of the University of Georgia Press for all the support she has given to this project. She ushered the completion of this book in more ways than we can enumerate.

Special thanks to the Girl Scouts of the USA for research assistance and permission to use materials located at the Juliette Gordon Low Birthplace in Savannah, Georgia, and the National Historic Preservation Center, GSUSA Headquarters in New York. The *Journal of Southern History* and the University of Georgia Press kindly permitted reprints of portions of works published by Sarah Case, Catherine Clinton, Kent Anderson Leslie, and Barbara McCaskill. LeeAnn Whites's article, "Rebecca Latimer Felton: The Problem of Protection in the New South," from *Visible Women: New Essays on American Activism* copyright 1993 from the Board of Trustees of the University of Illinois, is used with permission of the University of Illinois Press.

Finally, we would like to thank George, Emma, Ruthie, and, as always, to Ken Chirhart who always believed in the success of this collection.

*Ann Short Chirhart and Betty Wood*

• Rome

• Cartersville

Athens•

ELBERT
COUNTY

*Broad River*

Atlanta •   • Decatur

Washington •

HANCOCK
COUNTY

Augusta •

Macon •

• Coweta

Savannah •

St. Simons Island

# Georgia Women

# Introduction

ANN SHORT CHIRHART WITH BETTY WOOD

This is the first of two volumes that together explore the diverse and changing patterns of Georgia women's lives. Volume 1 focuses on eighteen Georgia
women between the founding of the colony in 1733 and the end of World War I.
What has it meant for women of different social classes and ethnicities to be a
Georgia woman? Does identification with a particular state shape a woman's
identity in any significant way? Do women's experiences cast a new light on the
first two centuries of Georgia's history, as the colony became one of the United
States and part of the South? These are the questions that are at the heart of
essays included in these volumes, essays that are devoted to those who for so
very long were either marginalized or ignored by the men who compiled their
histories of the "Peach State."

As the essays included here make clear, during the eighteenth and nineteenth
centuries, some of the preoccupations of Georgia women, like those in other
states, were shaped by men and remained largely unchallenged by women,
while others were not. This was true regardless of class, legal status, and ethnicity. From the very beginning, even before the first European colonists landed
in 1733, women were instrumental in shaping the multifaceted history of Georgia even as Georgia shaped their lives. Albeit in often very different ways, the
women included in this volume also provide a unique lens through which the
lives of all Georgia women, whatever their background, may be examined.

For contemporary readers, identifying with a state denotes little more than
a geographical location. Yet, whether rich or poor, black or white, enslaved or
free, women in the eighteenth and nineteenth centuries saw themselves as part
of a local community. Living in a colony or a state meant far more to them than
a physical location. Fanny Kemble and her daughter Frances Butler Leigh, each
of whom spent only a little time in Georgia, grasped their claim to the state by
choice. Some women implicitly construed themselves as Georgians, donning or

putting off its beliefs and values as easily as the garments they wore, while others struggled with Georgia's history and southern values.

During the era of the American Revolution women of European ancestry such as Elizabeth Lichtenstein Johnston had to determine whether being a Georgian was, or could be, synonymous with being an "American"; a century later, as a bitter civil war broke out, the issue had become the extent to which being a Georgian might or might not also be synonymous with being a "southerner." From 1751, when slavery was first introduced to Georgia, women and men of color found that over time identities and attachments that had been forged in West and West Central Africa were modified, and sometimes completely transformed, by new cultural possibilities and imperatives. How white and black, male and female, grappled with the many constraints, as well as with the possibilities, involved in forging and articulating their Georgian identity varied, often dramatically so, yet all shared a connection to the state through their imaginations, geographical locations, cultural beliefs, family connections, and historical participation.

The biographies that follow attest to the processes by which women of different social ranks and ethnicities constructed their particular Georgian identity as they sifted through the meanings of local, state, national, and even international events. The stories related here evoke each woman's experiences with interlocking communities, including those of other women, religious denominations, national identities, class, and race. Unsurprisingly, the modes of expression that shaped their notions of place changed over time, contributing to the diverse ways in which women saw themselves as participants in Georgia's evolving history. Key events, such as the introduction of slavery, the American Revolution, and the dramatic upheaval associated with the Civil War, Reconstruction, and Jim Crow, struck at the core of women's lives and their understanding of themselves as women.[1]

As was true of all the British North American colonies, Georgia and its residents experienced historical events unique to the colony while sharing other aspects common to colonial life. James Edward Oglethorpe and the other British-based Trustees envisaged a colony that would provide land and work for Britain's poor. Chartered in 1732, the Trustees promoted small-scale agriculture, and banned slavery and hard alcohol as well as Roman Catholics and lawyers. These restrictions set Georgia apart from all the other southern colonies that allowed slavery and promoted monoculture, as well as from the northern colonies that also tolerated slavery. But by 1750 the Trustees' utopian vision had collapsed, and slavery was permitted in the colony. Two years later, Georgia became a Royal colony.

As a Royal colony, Georgia's landholders imitated South Carolina and cultivated rice and indigo on larger farms worked by ever-increasing numbers of slaves. Commercial agriculture, with the rapid emergence of large landholders and their attendant social privileges, created growing socioeconomic divisions in the colony. The slave codes drafted by eminent planter-politicians gave slaveholders more authority over those they held in bondage. In contrast to the changes for enslaved Africans, Mary Musgrove's biography reveals that the Creeks managed to preserve their diplomatic and trade relations with the British Crown. Mary Musgrove herself proved most adept at learning how to navigate the shifting limitations on the landholding claims of the Creek people.

Unlike the other mainland American colonies, Georgia's political role was minimal during the years leading up to the American Revolution. In fact, Georgia was the only colony that complied with the Stamp Act of 1765, something about which Elizabeth Lichtenstein Johnston, who rejected an identity rooted in an independent Georgia and United States of America, would surely have approved. The significance of the Revolution and Revolutionary War lay more in their consequences for Georgia and, not least, for its female populations. Legends about the uncompromising stance taken by Nancy Hart against Loyalists helped to establish Georgia's allegiance to the new republic.

During the immediate postwar years, economic development and land speculation thrived as white families benefited from generous public land grants of up to two hundred acres each. Other land claims, the U.S. governmental policies toward Native Americans, and defeat at the hands of General Andrew Jackson sealed the fate of the Creeks and Cherokees, who were forced to leave Georgia for Oklahoma in 1838.

The greater availability of land, along with the perfection of the cotton gin by the early 1790s, set the future of Georgia for the next one hundred years. In most respects, all Georgian lives came to revolve around cotton culture. During the antebellum period, cotton production meant the expansion of slavery for the simple reason that slaves provided the cheapest and most productive form of labor. In 1820 African American slaves constituted 44 percent of Georgia's population, a fact that by the 1840s and 1850s, albeit for different reasons, women like Fanny Kemble and Ellen Craft found intolerable. For Kemble, slavery encouraged idleness and inculcated the habit of command in whites over blacks. Moreover, in her opinion it also encouraged wretched habits, including adultery and dishonesty, among slaves. Even more significant, particularly in the present context, was Kemble's sensitivity to slave women's oppression. For Craft, an enslaved African American, slavery meant something very different: bondage and an inability to claim her children as her own. To declare and to assert her respectability as a woman, Craft, along with her husband, fled from Georgia in 1848. Susie King Taylor, another African American woman, remained in Georgia and took a different course. She defied a southernwide system that denied African Americans' intellectual abilities by setting up a secret school in which she taught as many of them as she possibly could to read.

Most slaveholders and enslaved people lived in the Plantation Belt, or in central Georgia, that included Augusta and the state capital of Milledgeville or in the coastal region that included Savannah. More numerous yet less influential were the yeomanry, who grew crops for domestic consumption together with some cotton for trade. Most yeoman households were located in the Upcountry, the mountains, and there were also some in the Plantation Belt. For thirty-five hundred white Georgians, those who owned twenty or more slaves on five hundred or more acres, the system of slavery afforded wealth and privilege. Combined with the twenty thousand additional households that owned more than five slaves and over one hundred acres of land, 21 percent of free, white households, but particularly those of large slaveholders, dominated Georgia's social, political, and economic policies. These were the estates on which white women such Eliza Andrews, the Latimer sisters (Rebecca Latimer Felton and Mary Latimer McLendon), Mary Gay, and Mildred Rutherford no doubt envisaged a future in which judicious marriages and slave labor would preserve Georgia's paternalistic and patriarchal social hierarchy. Women like Amanda America Dickson, Susie King Taylor, and Lucy Craft Laney, on the other hand, who were born and raised on similar estates, longed for freedom, for the chance to assert their rights as both women and as Americans.

Regardless of their social class and ethnicity, in antebellum Georgia few women received a formal education. This was mainly because the Georgia government, like most other southern governments, saw little need to fund a public education system for boys, let alone for girls. Formal education was a matter reserved for elite women in private academies, and unsurprisingly it was they, rather than lower rank white or enslaved women, who penned most of the journals and diaries that have survived from the antebellum period and the Civil War years.

By the 1850s slavery was stratifying Georgia's white hierarchy to an even greater extent than had been the case during the previous century. Now, as slave prices rose and fertile land was becoming less available, fewer small farmers found themselves able to purchase slaves and produce cotton on a commercial scale. A few Georgians, like Nellie Peters Black's father, made their money not in the countryside but in the new city of Atlanta or in the older cities of Savannah and Augusta. Nevertheless, slaveholders and slaves had created a social, economic, and political order that stabilized relations, notwithstanding occasional acts of defiance from slaves. Then came the Civil War.

Secession from the United States was a controversial decision for white Georgians, but on January 19, 1861, the state convention approved secession, making Georgia the fourth of the original seven states that formed the Confederate States of America in February 1861. Beginning with the famous shots fired at South Carolina's Fort Sumter on April 12, 1861, until Confederate general Robert E. Lee surrendered the Army of Northern Virginia on April 9, 1865, all southerners faced a war that augured dramatic transformations in their lives. For African American women in Georgia, the war became a war for freedom, notably after the Emancipation Proclamation, and even more so after Sherman's March, which meant the possibility of receiving an education, reassembling families, owning property, and possibly even participating in the political process. Within two years after the end of the war, white women, especially those from elite families, confronted a very different reality: the end of almost every facet of women's lives and roles as they had known them.

The Civil War had taken husbands, fathers, brothers, and other male relatives and friends from farms and plantations to battlefields, leaving white women to preserve families, crops, and belongings, including the slaves they owned. To be sure, black and white women viewed Confederate and Union victories differently. Regardless of their rank and ethnicity, however, by 1863 women and men alike who remained on the home front were experiencing serious shortages of food and other basic supplies. White women yearned for the return of their loved ones to care for the land that lay fallow, to protect them from the Union troops who were drawing ever closer to Georgia, or to discipline African American women and men who were beginning to assert their independence. Daughters, mothers, and wives nursed wounded soldiers or prayed for their safe return from war; some even encouraged their menfolk to desert and return home. Other white women maintained their loyalties to the Union. Some enslaved black women looked for ways to leave their plantations; others chose to stay with their mistresses and masters, not necessarily out of affection but perhaps in the hope of thereby securing some protection against rape and theft by northern soldiers. A few owners gave black women their freedom before the Emancipation Proclamation; others left their owners with their families. Across Georgia, black and white women alike hoped for the end of the war, but they longed for different outcomes.

Many Georgia women witnessed a facet of the war that few other southern women did, unless they happened to live in Virginia or Vicksburg, Mississippi, Tennessee, or South Carolina. Beginning in May 1864 General William T. Sherman began the Union drive to conquer Atlanta, the first stage of a campaign that would cut across central Georgia and end in Savannah on December 21, 1864. Thus, the war came to Georgia women's front porches. Thousands of black women joined the crowd of African American refugees who followed Sherman and his troops as they marched across Georgia. White women watched angrily as Union troops destroyed property, ate their scarce food supplies, and killed livestock in keeping with General Grant's order for a scorched-earth policy. At the same time, Confederate president Jefferson Davis ordered those living in Atlanta to burn supplies in advance of Union troops, something that few of them were willing to do.

Numerous women, such as Eliza Frances Andrews, who found themselves in the path of the Union army quickly packed and, leaving their homes behind, dashed for safety. Andrews, one of the most vocal diarists of Sherman's March to the Sea, unleashed her fury at the Yankees as she described her family's flight from Washington, Georgia. Nellie Peters Black, Mary Gay, and Mary Latimer fled their homes in Atlanta. Homes, slaves whom they believed to be loyal, loved ones, and belongings all disappeared, or seemed to disappear. Caught in the swirl of destruction and death, white women recognized their vulnerability. Historians debate whether the experience of the Civil War or the hardships of Reconstruction marked the profound change in women's lives as they began to seek out wage-earning opportunities. The fear, shock, and anger that most white women who remained in Georgia felt when they realized that the paternalistic protection that they had counted on for so long had evaporated cannot be ignored.

In sharp contrast, although some historians speculate that some of Sherman's soldiers raped African American women as the troops advanced to Savannah, most black women welcomed the northern army as liberators. Some, like Susie King Taylor, and later Ellen Craft, taught freed people. Others attended schools, searched for family members who had been sold away, began to farm land on the coastal areas of Georgia, organized churches, and began to meet with one another to discuss how they might best go about gaining their objective of securing equal rights.

White women's disgust toward Yankee soldiers, along with their recognition of paternalism and patriarchy's flaws, opened cracks in the southern hierarchy as emancipation created opportunities, albeit temporary, for black women. While Susie King Taylor taught African Americans, she married a black Union officer. Lucy Craft Laney attended a school for African Americans in Macon, her first formal educational opportunity. White women, including Mildred Rutherford and Eliza Andrews, quickly used whatever education they had to teach and earn money for their families. Schools established or taught by white women soon proliferated across the state and offered more educational opportunities for white Georgia women. Andrews, Rutherford, Mary Gay, and Rebecca Latimer Felton published journals or historical accounts of the South, many of which were instrumental in the creation and, later, the preservation of the Lost Cause, a post–Civil War belief that the South was a superior and distinct social and cultural system. Women's publications broke new ground in the southern social system that had restricted elite white women's role within the household, in contrast to numerous northern women who had been publishing both fiction and nonfiction for several decades. Corra Harris drew from the legacy of these women when she published numerous works of fiction and autobiography that garnered national attention.

Publications were not the only evidence of a fundamental change in southern women's roles in the late nineteenth century. Black and white women's contributions to political discussions and their diverse means of earning incomes revealed that public and private domains for women no longer split but were permeable. Mary Gay sold her memoir from door to door in order to earn money for her family. Mildred Rutherford's histories became textbooks in numerous schools for white girls. Eliza Andrews not only taught school, she also became a botanist and traveled on expeditions to look for specimens.

The fierce commitment of women like Mary Latimer McLendon, her sister Rebecca Latimer Felton, Nellie Peters Black, and Mildred Lewis Rutherford to the United Daughters of the Confederacy (UDC), organized in Nashville, Tennessee, in 1894, connected them to middling and upper-class women elsewhere in the South. In their home state, in virtually every town of any size, they played a crucial role in erecting monuments to various Confederate heroes. At their meetings, as well as in their writings, they went to great lengths to promote the notion that the South went to war for entirely honorable reasons, notably for states' rights, to fight northern aggression, and to defend the region from what they depicted as the evils of capitalism. They worked as hard as men to maintain the Lost Cause myths about the nobility of white supremacy and the need to preserve the remnants of southern honor and culture. Mocking the UDC in her writings, Corra Harris remained ambivalent about women's organizations and suffrage, although she benefited from their groundbreaking ventures into public work.

During the latter part of the nineteenth century, southern women's actions connected them not only inter- and intra-regionally but also, in some spheres, to other middling and upper-class women elsewhere in the nation. During the rise of Populism and Progressivism, as reform movements mushroomed,

Georgia women like Mary Latimer McLendon, Rebecca Latimer Felton, Mildred Rutherford, Nellie Peters Black, and Martha Berry became tireless advocates for numerous local and national campaigns, including those focusing on education and agriculture. They were also to be found on both sides of the growing debate on woman suffrage.

Southern white women's activism during the late nineteenth and early twentieth century both paralleled that of, and brought them into close connection with, middle-class reformers across the nation. Yet Georgia women's commitment to white supremacy, combined with their lingering desire for male protection, allegiance to local communities, membership in conservative evangelical Protestant churches, and family ties, often differentiated them from northern settlement house workers, members of the National American Woman Suffrage Association (NAWSA), General Federation of Women's Clubs (GFWC), and the Women's Christian Temperance Union (WCTU). They understood themselves as different from men, as did northern maternalists, but their gendered construction drew from Lost Cause notions of protection and honor as opposed to their perceptions of late nineteenth-century materialism, and the aggressive individualism embodied in corporate America. Modernity's opportunities for individual accomplishments compelled them, even as they looked behind them at their treasured heritage of agrarian values. These women from the Progressive Era were intrigued by some ideas of modernity, like the benefits of industry and assistance for education, but they balked at other forms of modernity, such as secularization, urban growth, federal legislation, and individualism. Theirs was rather like a Janus-faced perception of the national scene, and it was this, more than anything else, that differentiates them from the white women whose lives will be explored in our second volume of essays.

During the last twenty years of the nineteenth century, African American women like Lucy Craft Laney, Susie King Taylor, Amanda America Dickson, and Ellen Craft grabbed whatever opportunities they could, and created others, in order to advance their education or solidify their position as property owners. As signs of Jim Crow laws and practices began to appear in the 1880s Laney capitalized on her position as founder of the Haines Institute to push for equal opportunities for blacks and economic backing for her institute. Still, the promises of emancipation remained elusive. Black women gained little from white women's reforms and organizations. Like some African Americans who despaired of gaining equality, Taylor left for the North. Laney remained in Augusta, but found she could do little to prevent white supremacists' success in denying black men the right to vote guaranteed in the Fifteenth Amendment.

More the exception than the rule was Craft, who decided to return to Georgia from England.

White supremacy, including the lynching of black men by white mobs, ruled the state of Georgia, and many, perhaps most, white women supported it. Organizations like the Georgia WCTU, GFWC, NAWSA, and the Georgia Association Opposed to Women's Suffrage frequently campaigned for temperance, education, suffrage, or anti-suffrage as the means to enforce white supremacy. Often, activism was perceived as an extension of white women's household duties, a way to educate, convert, and extol southern values. Martha Berry became an advocate for the poor, yet her greatest success lay in her work for children. Combining traditional and modern roles for white girls, in Savannah Juliette Gordon Low looked to the English example set by Sir Robert Baden-Powell and his sister Agnes and founded the Girl Scouts.

After the end of World War I, the event that also marks the end of the Progressive Era, Georgia women attained the right to vote, and their perspectives on race and modernity began to shift. More black and white women entered professions and occasionally found ways to work together in cities such as Atlanta for common goals such as school reform and anti-lynching campaigns. Still bound by Jim Crow, women expressed their authority in more public ways after 1920 and contributed significantly to reform movements of the twentieth century such as the New Deal and the civil rights movement. These women's stories are the subject of volume 2.

The Georgia women's biographies in this volume attest to the variety of women's lives. From the colonial period to the Progressive Era, these black and white women's stories do not always conform to the depictions of women in countless monographs about U.S. women's history. Yet southern—and indeed northern—history is full of broadly similar stories. Drawn to the possibilities of the era in which they lived, some women's ambitions vaulted them beyond expectations of what women should do. Some never married, others purposefully sought new opportunities, and many pursued sweeping changes in the local, regional, and national societies in which they found themselves.

The lives of the women included in this volume tell us much, but by no means all, about the range and dynamics of female experiences in Georgia between the mid-eighteenth and the early twentieth century. For Georgia, like the other southern states, remained a predominantly rural state mired in cotton production based on sharecropping. Out of over 2.5 million Georgians, more than 2 million lived in rural areas. Atlanta, the "Gate City" of the South, numbered little more than 150,000 people, compared to over 560,000 in Cleveland and over 2 million in Chicago. No woman sharecropper's voice, black or white, appears in this volume because these women simply lacked the skills, time, or materials to write accounts of their lives. Their lives were governed by often grueling farm labor, with few consumer goods. Socializing came from church gatherings or harvests rather than from club meetings.

These biographies from the Peach State are, necessarily, partial. Yet even though contemporary circumstances dictated that many women's voices would be lost to future historians, those exceptional women whose voices have survived provide us with tantalizing glimpses of the lives and experiences of all Georgia women during the first century and a half of the state's existence.

### NOTE

1. For further reading on the central themes and topics in the history of Georgia between 1733 and the early twentieth century, see Kenneth Coleman, *History of Georgia* (Athens: University of Georgia Press, 1977); Numan V. Bartley, *The Creation of Modern Georgia* (Athens: University of Georgia Press, 1990); and the New Georgia Encyclopedia at http://www.georgiaencyclopedia.org (accessed December 20, 2008). See also the special issues on Georgia women in the *Georgia Historical Quarterly* 76 (Summer 1992) and 82 (Winter 1998). More-specialized studies are to be found in the bibliography to this volume.

# Mary Musgrove

## (ca. 1700–1765)

*Maligned Mediator or Mischievous Malefactor?*

JULIE ANNE SWEET

Coosaponakeesa, also known as Mary Musgrove Matthews Bosomworth, represents one of the few women from colonial Georgia about whom any records survive.[1] Unfortunately, the documents of her bitter and constant battles with British officials at home and abroad paint her as a discontented and bothersome female who incessantly pestered the authorities with her petitions for land and financial compensation. In these accounts, she comes across as a selfish Indian trader who epitomized the stereotypically negative attributes of that occupation. In late twentieth-century scholarship, however, sympathetic scholars portray her as a mixed-blood woman maligned by white English aristocrats and exploited for her interpretive skills without receiving any form of gratitude. Her gender and racial heritage combined to make her an apparent victim in a world dominated by white men. Both of these interpretations have a grain of truth to them, and both point to similar conclusions: Mary stood up for herself and suffered the consequences of her assertiveness. That tenacity should receive applause instead of jeers, and she should be remembered for her diplomatic contributions that helped make Georgia a success. Mary was truly a friend to the early colony and worked to protect its security and advance its status, yet when she applied the same resolve to her personal circumstances, she reaped scorn instead of praise.

The simplest explanation is that Mary fought the law and, for the most part, the law won. She happened to be in the right place at the right time when James Oglethorpe arrived with the first settlers of Georgia, and she made the most of the opportunity both as a trader and a translator. She benefited from this partnership for years as Oglethorpe came to rely upon her services more and

MARY MUSGROVE

Detail from "The Bosomworths Invade
Savannah," Georgia Historical Society
collection of etchings, silhouettes, and other
prints, 1800s–1900s, MS 1361-PR, Georgia
Historical Society, Savannah, Georgia.

more. But when she expected the Trustees to make exceptions to their regulations regarding land transactions and ownership and they refused, she overestimated her importance and crossed the line from friend to foe. Neither gender nor race played a role in the Trustees' stance against her; they simply upheld the law despite her previous contributions to their colony. Mary only made her situation worse by calling upon her Creek relatives to support her claim and causing a scene that has made her infamous and that continues to attract the most attention. Few look past this episode and realize that Mary learned an important lesson from this incident. She changed tactics again, returned to the good graces of colonial authorities, and persisted with her fight to obtain what she believed was rightfully hers. After over twenty years of appeals, she finally reached a compromise and withdrew from public life. Although her inability to acquire all of her demands may technically constitute a failure, her perseverance as well as her diplomatic efforts should earn her a prominent place in the history books.

Because of her gender and race, little documentation exists about Mary's early life. Born around 1708 in Coweta, a leading Creek town near present-day Columbus, Georgia, she received the name Coosaponakeesa, meaning "little fawn."[2] Her father, Edward Griffin, served as an Indian trader for South Carolina, and her mother remains unnamed, although it is known that she was a Tuckabatchee Creek woman with ties to the native hierarchy. Supposedly, Mary's mother was the sister of Chekilli, the older brother of Brims, one of the most significant Creek chiefs of the early eighteenth century. Since women occupied a prominent place in the matrilineal Creek society, this association with leadership usually resulted in special privileges. Kinship terms did not necessarily reflect bloodlines, however, so the family connection appears vague.[3]

Mary's upbringing included exposure to both Creek and British customs. At a young age she moved to Ponpon, South Carolina, where she received baptism into the Anglican faith and the name "Mary" by which she was more commonly known. She also obtained a basic education, which provided her with the language skills that would make her so valuable to the Georgia colony. Mary was among the South Carolinians when the Yamasee War broke out in 1715, but she returned to Coweta, possibly to avoid hostility from white British settlers who might have ostracized Mary because of her Creek heritage. Brims, leader of Coweta, later made several overtures for peace with certain British traders to resume the commerce that the war had interrupted. To secure these agreements, Brims set up exclusive deals with a number of people, one of whom was John Musgrove Sr., who had a mixed-blood son, also named John. In 1716 young John and Mary married to seal the treaty of peace and trade between their older relatives, and they remained in Coweta until 1723, when they relocated back to Ponpon to open their own business. Once they established a dependable reputation and made necessary contacts with British and Creek traders, they moved again in 1732, this time to Yamacraw on the bluffs of the Savannah River. There, Tomochichi, an elderly yet dubious Creek headman, had built a village with about two hundred followers, and the Musgroves took advantage of the opportunity to serve this community as well as provide a meeting place for Indians and merchants who traversed the region.[4]

Their decision proved most providential. Less than a year after their relocation, James Oglethorpe and his band of approximately one hundred settlers arrived to found the colony of Georgia, and he chose those same bluffs for his town of Savannah. Thus, Indians and English people alike recognized the value of this place but for different reasons, and the Musgroves immediately demonstrated their many services by offering to translate discussions, host activities, and supply provisions. While Tomochichi appeared receptive to the idea of an additional British outpost in order to improve his position within the Creek confederacy, not all headmen welcomed the newcomers. At a conference in May 1733 the two parties met at Savannah and asked for terms with the help of the Musgroves. Oglethorpe acquired his Treaty of Friendship and Commerce, which included a land grant for his colony, the Creeks received promises of fair trade, and the Musgroves earned a permanent place in the new world of international diplomacy.[5]

John Musgrove even accompanied an entourage of Indians to England in 1734, acting as their interpreter while Mary remained behind to manage the store and maintain peaceful relations with neighboring Indian nations. She reported in July that a delegation of Choctaws had visited to seek trade with Georgia and declared that "they have received great favours from . . . the colony, and a great deal of respect showed them, which they are wonderfully pleased at."[6] Local circumstances, however, became complicated due to the mischief of Joseph Watson. A recent immigrant, Watson joined the Musgrove operation and planned to develop his own outpost and plantation. Instead, he became a nuisance because of his corrupt business practices and drunken revelries with nearby Indians. Perhaps he believed that he could take advantage of Mary while her husband traveled abroad. If so, he tangled with the wrong woman. She brought him to court on several occasions for various misdemeanors, including calling her a witch and threatening her with a gun. The magistrates ruled in Mary's favor each time and awarded her monetary damages for the injustices. These positive outcomes proved to Mary that she could get a fair trial among British officials, regardless of her race or gender, and gave her at least temporary faith in the system. Watson's troubles had only just begun, how-ever. A drinking binge with an Indian warrior named Skee resulted in Skee's death, an event for which Watson brazenly took credit. Skee's relative Esteeche came to the store to avenge the murder, but Watson escaped and Mary's servant was killed in the confusion. Colonial officials confined Watson to house arrest, but the complicated state of affairs caused tension between natives and new-comers and required Mary's assistance to keep the peace. The event tested her abilities as a mediator to see that all sides received justice as well as challenged her personal convictions as she defended her livelihood against a greedy rogue. Once her husband returned, the couple continued their many services, but John died in June 1735, leaving Mary a wealthy widow and an important player within the arena of Indian-white relations in early Georgia.[7]

Despite her widowed state, her mixed heritage, and her gender, Mary re-mained an influential figure throughout the Southeast. In particular, James Oglethorpe regularly sought her opinion on matters involving the nearby Indians. He knew that his situation remained tenuous, so he strengthened his Indian alliances and called on Mary to translate conferences. Although he did not approve of the Musgroves' disregard for the prohibition of hard liquor in Georgia, he explained that "I did not care to disoblige them, because they are the only interpreters we have to the Indians."[8] Mary's work earned Oglethorpe's gratitude on many occasions, and his frequent correspondence requesting and praising her assistance testify to her invaluable role.

Other colonists also noticed Mary's prominent position within the colony. Thomas Causton, storekeeper and magistrate, noted that "The Presants for the Indian Nation are all now delivered and Mrs [John] Musgrove has behaved very well. I have been much obliged to her in that matter."[9] John Martin Bol-zius, pastor and administrator of the nearby Salzburger community of Ebenezer, wrote often to his superiors in Germany and the Trustees in England and men-tioned Mary's efforts to preserve peace. He, too, relied on Mary's diplomatic skills when he feared trouble with his native neighbors, and he even hoped to learn the Creek language from her because "she has a special talent for express-ing Indian terms in English."[10] When Anglican missionaries Benjamin Ingham and John Wesley arrived in February 1736, they sought Mary's advice about how to proceed with their plans to convert the Indians to Christianity, and they retained her services to teach them the Creek language, although only Ingham followed through with this desire.[11] Mary's estate remained open to Indians and Englishmen alike, making it a center for commerce and exchange on many levels. Above all, she maintained a respected reputation as a trusted negotiator who worked to find a common ground that benefited all involved parties.

Mary expanded her entrepreneurial enterprises at Oglethorpe's request and built a second outpost, called Mount Venture 150 miles up the Altamaha River, to fulfill the colony's economic and defensive motives. The location afforded Mary additional trade opportunities with her Creek kinsmen, and it gave Oglethorpe an excuse to send a company of twenty rangers to protect the site while also keeping an eye on the Spanish threat to the south. Moreover, it demonstrated Mary's growing influence within the colony, since she enjoyed profitable commerce with traders of many nations and special privileges from Oglethorpe.[12]

A widowed, wealthy woman attracted attention of all kinds, and in March 1737, she married Jacob Matthews, a former indentured servant. Her decision to marry may seem strange, and her choice of husbands even stranger, but Matthews was a full-blooded Englishman, and perhaps she believed that she could dominate the marriage because of his lowly status. If that was the case, it did not happen. Matthews promptly put on the airs of an English gentleman and became an outspoken member of the Malcontents, critics of the Trustees' administration. Despite her husband's antipathy toward the colonial authorities, however, Mary continued to fulfill her chosen duties as interpreter and hostess whenever conditions required.[13]

Her negotiating and peacekeeping skills earned her praise from Indians as well as Englishmen, so Tomochichi decided to reward her loyalty with a generous gift of land. In December 1737 he entrusted her with the region reserved for Indian use in the treaty that he and the other Creek headmen had made with Oglethorpe, namely the Yamacraw tract along the Savannah River as well as the three sea islands of Ossabaw, St. Catherine's, and Sapelo.[14] Mary appreciated this extravagant present but realized that she needed more than just Tomochichi's word to verify this transaction. She had enough experience with English law to know that without sanction from the proper British authorities, her claims to the property would mean nothing, regardless of the stature of the Indian who granted them.[15]

Mary wasted no time pursuing that approval. She attempted to enlist the aid of James Oglethorpe, who deflected the question to his Trustee colleagues in London. Even though he needed her assistance more than ever as he began to shore up alliances and defenses against an impending war with Spanish Florida, he still chose not to support her cause. The Trustees also understood the dangerous position of their fledgling colony and the important influence that Mary had over neighboring Indian allies, but they could not approve the deal because it violated several unalterable regulations. No individual could engage in a transfer of land with an Indian, and no individual could own more than five hundred acres. The first rule allowed the Trustees to maintain control and accuracy when it came to acquiring land from its original owners, and the second sought to avoid the creation of a new aristocracy and to offer more opportunities to the indigent colonists for whom the administrators had designed the province.[16] The Trustees had already denied several claims that violated one or both of these rules, so they were not inclined to make an exception for Mary. Rather than risk alienating her at this precarious moment, though, the Trustees shelved the matter and turned their attention to war with Spain.[17]

Mary, too, became distracted with international affairs occurring in her regional domain. She traveled to Frederica often to help Oglethorpe communicate with his Indian allies, mostly Creek warriors looking for a moment of glory and an opportunity to collect a bounty and other trophies. She attempted to keep her two outposts open so that Indians and Englishmen had a safe place to do business and she could cover her living expenses and make a profit. Her husband, Jacob Matthews, offered little help, however; he carried on with the local Malcontents who criticized the colonial and imperial administration and persisted with his wife's land claims in order to further improve his own status. The Trustees, weary of Matthews's pestering, ruled against his petition, citing their regulations regarding property transactions. His death in June 1742 after a lengthy illness prevented a response, and he left his estate to Mary. Meanwhile, Mary shuttled from place to place working for Oglethorpe, caring for her dying husband, and maintaining two trading posts. Unfortunately, she spread herself too thin. Besides losing Matthews that year, she suffered the ruin of Mount Venture when marauding Yamasee Indians seized the fort, killed many inhabitants, destroyed the buildings and stock, and captured several Creek allies. Nevertheless, she continued to support the British cause despite the costs.[18]

Her generosity had its limits, though, and Oglethorpe realized the hardships that she had endured on his behalf. Before leaving the colony in July 1743 to answer charges of misconduct and to report current events, he rewarded her loyalty with a diamond ring and the sum of two hundred pounds, with promises of more money to follow. He later declared, "Because She is of Consequence, and in the Kings Interest. Therefore it is the Business of the King's friends to Support her; besides which, I shoud always be Desirous to serve her, out of the good will, and Friendship She has at all times Shewed to me, as well as the Interest of the Colony."[19] Mary appreciated the tokens and the sentiments, and with Oglethorpe's departure, she obtained some release from her interpretive duties and turned her attention from imperial matters to rebuilding her personal assets. Mary had spent years courting Oglethorpe's favor to acquire her influential position within colonial society, but after his return to England, she had to fend for herself. She still hosted Indians and whites at her estate and served as translator for the military authorities in Frederica, but she realized that she needed to find another way to maintain her status.

As Mary assessed her losses and started to reconstruct her reputation and business, she met and married her third husband, Thomas Bosomworth. He wanted all the luxuries that life had to offer—wealth, power, prestige—but refused to exert any effort to obtain them. The Trustees had sent Bosomworth to Georgia at their expense at the end of 1741, intending him to serve as a clerk to William Stephens, the colony's appointed secretary. Upon arrival, however, Bosomworth rejected such a lowly position, so the Trustees made him the Secretary of Indian Affairs, which also did not suit his fancy. Instead, he returned to England, received Holy Orders, and requested appointment as minister to Savannah. That office fulfilled his personal goals since it included the use of land, servants, and a furnished house as well as a salary of fifty pounds a year. He lacked only one item to complete his entourage, and once back in Georgia, he wasted no time courting the richest woman in town—Mary Musgrove Matthews.[20]

The two married on July 8, 1744, in Frederica, much to everyone's surprise. William Stephens recorded that the event "appeared so incredible to some of our Neighbours in Savannah, that 'twas looked on as a piece of Merriment . . . till night put an end to the Dispute."[21] While the residents of Savannah loved gossip as much as any small town, there appears to have been more to it than that. The participants represented two well-known names, since all colonists had frequent contact with the minister and most had crossed paths with Mary financially, diplomatically, or personally at some point. Beyond mere celebrity lay the politics of the match. Thomas and Mary could have chosen anyone as their mates, yet they found each other and created one of the most powerful couples in the colony. Both spouses benefited from the arrangement: Thomas increased his wealth, while Mary significantly improved her social status by marrying an English gentleman. Mary's mixed heritage apparently did not bother Thomas, and in fact, he would later urge her to exploit it for their private gain.

Of the two, however, Mary stood to gain more from the match. Her previous marriages had enhanced her reputation, but by wedding Thomas, she took a significant leap up the social ladder. Her earlier activities as an Indian-British mediator made her an important player in the colony but did not necessarily result in respect from ordinary citizens. Her livelihood as a trader, an occupation associated with corruption and vice, marred her public image, and her association with men, white and Indian, further damaged her integrity.[22] Success and influence did not translate into appreciation. Therefore, to better integrate herself into colonial society, she did what any enterprising woman would do and married above her station.

To confirm their nuptials and dispel the rumors, the newlyweds hosted a celebration in Savannah on August 20, 1744, for their neighbors.[23] Afterward, Mary returned to her previous professions as merchant and translator, while Thomas flitted from one post to another, incurring debt and searching for schemes that he hoped would lead to quick riches. To those ends, Thomas decided to build cattle plantations on Mary's landholdings, specifically St. Catherine's Island and possibly other locations. Mary reminded her husband that although she had applied for the property, her grant had not yet received recognition from the Trustees, making her claim tenuous at best. So, to solidify her assertion and to enhance her wealth in order to cover debts and finance the cattle-raising enterprise, in December 1745 Mary once again petitioned the overseas administration to recognize her ownership of the Yamacraw tract and the three sea islands and to pay her 1,200 pounds for her years of service. Once again, the Trustees denied her memorial, citing the size and nature of the transaction and stating that they had never agreed to give her any compensation for her work.[24]

Unlike her response to her previous rejections, however, Mary did not resume her regular activities with her usual alacrity. Her change in outlook at this moment requires consideration. Mary had received the lands in question from Tomochichi in December 1737 and had requested official British approval several times without success. Usually, she had gone back to work as a trader and interpreter and refiled her appeal years later, depending on her personal circumstances and the international situation. This time, though, she not only resubmitted her claim, but she sent it further up the chain of command.

Several possibilities exist as to why she chose this course of action. Perhaps her ambitious husband Thomas Bosomworth pushed her to persist with the matter. After all, he wanted to advance in society quickly and effortlessly, and what better way to accomplish that goal than to ride his wife's fortune straight to the top? Mary also may have entertained ideas of promotion, however, or at least retribution. She had sacrificed much for the colony over the past decade but received little in return. A few military officials recognized the importance of her translating and trading services but only paid her with words of gratitude, and most colonists ignored and dismissed her. Her background and her profession held her back from full acceptance in Savannah. Perhaps the time had come for Mary to take a stand. She may have felt that she had not only earned but deserved the land and salary that she demanded, and she planned to use her skills of persuasion to assert her rights to both of them.

Mary continued her interpretive and commercial services to the colony, but instead of delaying her claim again, she retooled her petition and sent it in August 1747 to a higher power: the King of England. If she could not convince the Trustees to acknowledge her point of view, perhaps a greater authority might force them to do so. Her lengthy memorial outlined her many contributions to the colony throughout its early years, especially in the arenas of diplomacy and business, and she made it clear that Georgia might not exist at all without her assistance. To bolster her claim, she included copies of letters from Oglethorpe reiterating the important role that she had played in his negotiations with various Indians, and letters from William Horton, one of the commanding officers at Frederica who also had employed Mary's translating skills to communicate with native warriors.[25] Alexander Heron soon replaced Horton, and he too wrote in support of Mary's claim, since he understood the precarious situation in the Southeast and her influential position in maintaining peace.[26] Despite her efforts to achieve recognition, though, King George II neither acknowledged nor accepted her plea for fairness.

In order to strengthen her title even further, Mary turned to her Creek relatives for assistance and traveled to Coweta at that same time. This move made sense because of her mixed heritage and the power that women wielded in a matrilineal culture, but it did little to advance her claim among British magistrates at home and abroad who came from a strongly patriarchal background. If she sought acceptance by colonial officials, this decision represented a step in the wrong direction, since the British rarely allowed Indian testimony about any issue. Although the Creeks dominated the region, they were hardly ever consulted about British expansion until white settlers intruded on native lands. Mary used this argument as well as reminders about countless trade abuses to rally her kin to her side in hopes that fear of potential destruction at the hands of a "savage" enemy might compel the British to recognize her grant.

Spoken pledges of support may have satisfied other Indian nations respectful of an oral culture, but Mary knew from her many years of diplomacy that the British would want more. To convince the colonists of her determination, she had Malatchi, the headman of Coweta and a distant relative, accompany her with about one hundred warriors to Frederica in December 1747 to give an extensive speech that explained and affirmed Mary's property claims as well as her prominent status within native society. After summarizing Creek-British relations and Mary's indispensable role in maintaining their friendship, he concluded: "There is Mary our Sister, in whom the whole Nation confides, because She is of my own Blood, a friend to us as well as the English, and whatever she says we shall always be determin'd by, because She has more Sense than we, and knows what is for our good."[27] Although the impressive oration made many important points, it failed to have the intended effect, because the settlers did not realize its significance or heed its warning. The Indians could say whatever they wanted, but the British recognized only written documents that they had authorized and transcribed.

Mary understood that fact and played on that tradition when she negotiated a formal purchase of the land in question the following month. Malatchi received "Ten Peices of strouds twelve Peices of Duffles two Hundred weight of Powder two Hundred weight of Bulletts twenty Guns twelve Pair of Pistols One Hundred weight of Vermillion and thirty Head of Breeding Cattle" in exchange for the three islands of Ossabaw, St. Catherine's, and Sapelo as well as all their resources including "Timber . . . Mines Fossils Minerals precious Stones or Metals."[28] With this transaction, she bought the property and received a bill of sale, two moves that used European practices to legitimize the gift made by Tomochichi over a decade earlier.

In addition, Thomas urged his wife to assume a royal Indian title to demonstrate her kinship ties to Creek leadership and to gain more respect from the British officials. Even though women occupied a dominant role in southeastern Indian society, no ceremonial terms existed to reflect that respect. Similarly, however, the concept of "king" or "emperor" represented an honorific imposed by Europeans in order to carry out diplomacy with chosen individuals. By calling herself "queen" and "empress," Mary blended cultural conventions in hopes of earning the recognition necessary to resolve the property dispute in her favor.[29]

These actions had little influence, however. If anything, colonial and overseas authorities became more rigid in their stance against her claims because she sought to incite neighboring natives to rebellion. All levels of British administration denied her right to own that land, and their decision had nothing to do with her race or gender. The regulations regarding property transactions and quantities, dating back to the charter, protected colonists from fraud and abuse, and they applied to all citizens, including Mary because of her marriages and profession. In fact, the Trustees kept a strict eye on land grants throughout their tenure, having denied similar requests from white male immigrants who sought to expand their holdings above the stated limits, and they weathered intense criticism about this issue from the Malcontents. From their perspective, the Trustees had upheld the letter of the law for more than a decade, and they were not about to make any exceptions or accommodations now no matter how much Mary had aided them in their times of need.

Mary did not agree. These foreign aristocrats had exploited her abilities and influence to their advantage and refused to compensate her accordingly. The land remained an important aspect of her claim, but she also felt exploited by their lack of payment for her services and resented their general disrespect toward her place in their society. She wanted rightful recognition for her many years of assistance.

The summer of 1749 saw all her frustrations come to the breaking point. If the colonial magistrates ignored a speech and a land deed from Malatchi, she must take other measures. The headman arrived at her estate in late July with a contingent of warriors and the expectation that more would arrive in the near future. She notified William Stephens, now president of Georgia, about the gathering and explained that since "it had been reported for two Years past among her People in the Nation, That She was to be sent Home in Irons," she and her husband Thomas had invited them down to witness her voluntary departure.[30] The president and his assistants expressed concern, but Mary assured them that the group had no business with them. They still worried that if they denied her land claims once more in the presence of a hundred or so warriors who followed and supported their kinswoman, they would face severe consequences.[31]

A few days later, an ominous letter arrived from Mary expressing Malatchi's displeasure for his treatment thus far. Although he and his attendants had arrived unannounced, they still expected to enjoy the usual arrangements prepared for all visiting Indian delegations, and they had yet to receive any recognition. She warned the president that "some Indians are come and the rest expected very soon Therefore he hopes you have provided Provisions and other Necessaries for their Reception and when the Head Men come together . . . he hopes that all Talks will be Streight and good."[32] Mary knew exactly why these chiefs had appeared, and she wanted to use their presence as leverage to push her property claims through the colonial administration once and for all. Her letter served as a warning of future conflict as well as an invitation for Stephens to make the first move, and he did so with a dinner at his home.

Mary's challenge had just begun, however. As more Indians assembled, tensions and troubles increased. Stephens scheduled a meeting for Friday, August 11, to discern the true meaning of this gathering and ordered a path cut from the forest to facilitate travels between Savannah and Mary's trading post and to prevent ambush by either side. When they reached Mary's property line, however, the workers kept felling trees without her permission. Although this oversight might seem minor, the men continued chopping after the Bosomworths had warned them to stop, which incensed Mary even further. It was bad enough that the magistrates refused to recognize her claims to distant lands, but to damage her immediate acreage represented a rude affront as well as a bold assertion of their power. After repeatedly ordering the laborers off her territory, she "threatned them at their Peril to go any farther, and immediately the Indians seized their Tools, and carried them without their Line, and threw them down."[33] The work ceased, and President Stephens reassured the visiting delegation that he meant no harm and that the wide, clear path signified their prestige. He did not apologize to Mary, the injured party, however, nor did she attend that evening's festivities.

She occupied a prominent position in the subsequent meeting, though. On Friday morning the Bosomworths and the Indians processed into town led by the colonial militia on horseback. Mary stood at the front of the column but behind her husband and next to Malatchi, openly demonstrating her affiliation with the Creeks. Once at the meeting place, she took a seat with Malatchi and the other headmen. Stephens asked why they had arrived in town at this time, and Malatchi replied that "they had been informed, that Mary . . . was to be sent Home in Irons, and he was come to See, and if it was so, he would untie her."[34] Stephens replied "that no such design was known here, but if She had done any thing to deserve it, as we looked upon her as a Subject of the King of Great Britain, we should tie her, and send her home without asking their Liberty."[35] Malatchi countered that Mary was the "Empress and Queen of the Upper and Lower Creeks," meaning that she gave orders rather than received them. Stephens finally asked Mary directly "if she was not a Subject of the King of Great Britain? She answered, She owed him no Allegiance otherwise, than in Alliance, being herself a Sovereign."[36]

Mary's comment complicated the situation greatly. She not only acknowledged her Creek heritage, but she also asserted that her native lineage trumped her European background, making her unaccountable to English law. This affiliation may have legitimized her land claim, since it now involved two Indians, not an Indian and an Englishwoman, but it did little to improve her standing with the local officials. Her use of matrilineal terms of royalty in a patriarchal society did not help her case either. Furthermore, she declared that she possessed connections to the elite line of Brims and Malatchi among others. She set herself up as an equal with King George II, and with that remark, she overplayed her hand and immediately lost credibility among the colonial magistrates.

Mary sensed this change in atmosphere and acted promptly. Just as dinner was served, "She abruptly rose up and Spoke to the Indians to follow her, upon which Malatchee and five other did, and Six remained, two of which are allowed to be of equal esteem and authority with Malatchee in the Nation."[37] She made this move to prove her authority over her people, but it backfired when only half of the delegation left with her. All southeastern Indian nations allowed individuals to make their own decisions regarding political matters, and this instance was no different.[38] Such division weakened her position, however, and further damaged her cause.

That same afternoon, another disturbance rocked Savannah. A few Indians paraded through town to the beat of a drum, but the frayed nerves of the colonists resulted in the assembly of the militia to suppress the uprising. Fortunately, the magistrates arrived upon the scene to pacify the situation and rebuke both parties. All seemed well until Mary suddenly appeared and "like a Mad and Frantick Woman came running in among them, endeavouring all she could to irretate the Indians afresh."[39] She became so enraged that she "repeatedly . . . threaten[ed] the Lives of some of the Magistrates, and the destruction of the Colony, through her influence with, and command over the Indians, and . . . said you talk of your White Town, your General and his Treaties, a fig for your General, you have not a Foot of Land in the Colony, and Stamping with her Foot on the Ground imprudently said, That very Ground was hers."[40] Her outburst did not have the desired effect, however, and militiamen threatened to detain her for disturbing the peace. Realizing that she would have no influence from jail, she quieted and submitted to a verbal reprimand by Stephens, who called for a conference the following morning once all tempers had cooled.

Mary's fight had escalated drastically. Her land claims seemed secondary after these two encounters that had resulted in disrespect and contempt from the colonial magistrates. They had refused to take her seriously, let alone treat her with the dignity that she deserved as a former mediator and as an elite Indian. This latest offense required further action. Clearly, Mary needed to ease and neutralize their animosity and gain command of the situation.

The next day's events complicated matters even further. That morning, Thomas Bosomworth sent word that the headmen could not attend the planned meeting because they were still drunk from the night before. The administrators insisted that Thomas ascertain the Indians' condition to determine if further guards were necessary to contain any mischief, and Mary arrived to apologize for the delay and asked to reschedule the conference for that afternoon. The appointed time came and went, but no visitors appeared to discuss terms.[41] Perhaps Mary used this opportunity to humiliate the officials, but in fact, she only angered them more and gave them the chance to make diplomatic inroads with other members of the native party. By avoiding the magistrates, she could not keep an eye on them and, therefore, could not control their actions.

Stephens wasted no time summoning Malatchi under various threats and informing him of the Bosomworths' scheme. They planned to keep one-third of all presents for themselves and to develop the Indian lands for personal gain. Stephens, on the other hand, promised that the Indians would receive all of their gifts as intended by the king and would retain use of the sea islands for generations to come. Malatchi responded that he now understood the deception by the Bosomworths and refused to have any more contact with them. Stephens pressed him on the title that Mary claimed as "Empress and Queen of the Creek-Nation, and whether he thought She or himself was Chief there" to which he replied "with some warmth, that He did not before understand, that He was Ranked with an Old Woman, and he was Chief."[42] Stephens successfully drove a wedge between Mary and Malatchi despite their kinship ties and hoped that it would hold until the completion of the conference. The two men spent the following day, a Sunday, together attending Anglican religious services and walking about town. The president and his assistants also agreed among themselves to distribute presents soon without Mary in order to prevent her from taking some and to establish another block to her influence.

If Stephens believed that he had triumphed, he had seriously underestimated his enemy. On Wednesday afternoon, a large delegation of Indians arrived to collect their payment. Before the ceremony could commence, however, Malatchi delivered a lengthy speech in which "He declared that it was by Mary's . . . permission, that we Lived here, for that she was here before the Squire (meaning General Oglethorpe) brought any White People; that She gave them liberty to Settle; that the Lands they now lived on were held under her; that all the Lands they should Settle on, should be held from her, for that She was the Queen and Head of their Nation."[43] To affirm this title, Malatchi presented a written document signed by all the Creek headmen making Mary "rightful and lawful Princess and Chief of their Nation (descended in a Maternal Line from their Lawful Emperor) by an Indian Name; and investing of her with a sole power and Authority to transmit all Matters, Causes or things whatsoever relating to Lands or otherwise with the Great King and his Beloved Councillors over the great Waters, as well as with his Beloved Men on this side the Water."[44] Thus, Mary claimed all land that comprised the colony of Georgia, accepted a royal title, and equated herself with the King of England for all diplomatic matters, and she used both oral and written as well as Creek and European traditions to solidify her stance.

Stephens refuted this entire declaration and recast Mary in a much less favorable light. He claimed that Oglethorpe had done Mary a favor by using her as an interpreter because "She then appeared to be in mean and low Circumstances, being only Cloathed with a Red Stroud Petticoat and Osnabrig

Shift" but since that time, he improved her reputation and status throughout the region, paid for her services with money and presents, and "made her the Woman she now appears to be."[45] In fact, colonists appreciated her efforts until she married Bosomworth, whereupon she lost their trust. As for Mary's connection to royalty, Stephens reminded Malatchi that Mary "is not of your Family, being a Daughter of a Woman of the Tuckabachee Town (of no Note or Family) by a White Man" and that Oglethorpe made his treaty for Georgia with the Creek leadership, not Mary.[46] Finally, the president threatened not to distribute presents but to give them all to Mary instead, since she apparently ruled their nation. With that last comment, the other headmen reacted with such uproar that even Malatchi changed sides again and burned the questionable document. To seal the deal, the Indians went to the courthouse and received their gifts, except for ammunition to avoid adding any more fuel to an already unstable situation.

Curiously, Mary remained absent from this entire proceeding. Possibly, she knew that she could not hold her temper, so she allowed her relative Malatchi to represent her. Perhaps she thought it would be better if the male native leaders spoke to the male administrators without her presence to disrupt or distract from the business at hand. She believed that she had finally won Malatchi's unconditional support, which she confirmed through both oral and written traditions. She trusted her kinsman to protect her interests, but she miscalculated the strength of his loyalty.

Once Mary heard about the outcome of the meeting, she took matters into her own hands. That evening, as chiefs and magistrates celebrated in a local tavern, she stormed into the room to present her case. Unfortunately for her, they had settled the matter earlier, and they dismissed her as "a Woman Spirited up with Liquor, Drunk with Passion, and disapointed in her Views."[47] Mary proclaimed "that these People (meaning the Indians) were her's and that She would be, where they were, and that they should follow her, whereever she should command them . . . She was the Empress and Queen of the Upper and Lower Creeks . . . and that She could command every Man in those Nations to follow her, and We should soon know it to our Cost."[48] Stephens and the other magistrates tried repeatedly to send her away, but she refused to leave. They had ignored and abused her for the last time, and she would not surrender without a fight. Several Indians, including Malatchi, verbally supported her, but most sat quietly and watched idly. Finally, peace officers arrived and removed her to the guardhouse until her temper cooled.

There Mary sat for the rest of the night to contemplate her situation. She had finally pushed too far, and her unseemly behavior did little to help her cause among the British officials. The next day, she attempted to save face by having her husband apologize and promise to "prevent his Wife creating any more disturbance, and that She should behave as a prudent Woman ought."[49] When brought before the magistrates, Mary likewise asked forgiveness and hoped that all mistakes would be forgotten. To prove the sincerity of her repentance, Stephens required Mary and Thomas to hold a public audience with the Indian delegation at the courthouse the following day where they admitted their error and blamed Mary's unseemly behavior on her intoxication. All accepted the talk and enjoyed an evening of entertainment before the Indians began to head home the next day.[50]

Mary's self-humiliation might seem like capitulation, but it was hardly that. As an experienced diplomat, Mary understood that she had lost this battle, so she retreated in order to regroup and fight another time. She satisfied the colonial officials by going through the motions of repentance and allowing them to put her back in her place, so to speak. In her speech to her native followers, she wisely attributed her behavior to overindulgence in alcohol, because Indians believed that they could not be held responsible for their actions while under the influence. Thus, her actions make it appear as if she had given up and returned to the traditional subservient female role, but in actuality, she had attempted a calculated move to rectify the current chaos and make peace with both parties as best she could.

Despite this major setback, Mary did not abandon her claims. She still believed that the islands belonged to her, and she wanted her title recognized by British authorities to make it official. She maintained her strong ties to her Creek kin so that she did not lose their support in the continuing battle, and she spent much of 1750 in Coweta convincing her kinsmen of her royal title and her property rights. She also understood, however, that without proper documentation from the British command, her claims meant nothing. Realizing that she had little chance of success within Georgia, she again decided to disregard local governance and take her case straight to the Board of Trade and even the king himself if necessary.[51]

In early 1752 Mary and Thomas went to Charlestown, South Carolina, to book passage to London to press their demands. Events there delayed their departure, however. Governor James Glen needed assistance mediating a tense conflict in the far regions of his colony where the Cherokees and Creeks were waging war. Mary's reputation as an interpreter and her status as a relative of Malatchi preceded her, but some hesitated to entrust her with such a weighty matter because of her gender. Nonetheless, Glen sent Mary and Thomas west in July to settle the dispute. Officials in Georgia complained that their northern brethren had opened the possibility for additional disturbances because of her previous quarrel, but those events did not concern the people of South Carolina, who simply employed the most capable person for the job.[52]

The Bosomworths crossed through Georgia en route to Coweta to mediate the situation. After discussion with Malatchi and other Creek headmen, she convinced them to impose a death sentence on Acorn Whistler, an Upper Creek warrior who had instigated much of the recent conflict between the Creeks and Cherokees. Mary and Thomas hoped to prevent further hostilities by blaming Whistler's death on clan vengeance and removing the troublemaker from the scene. After issuing the decision, Mary helped recover stolen property for certain Carolinian traders and negotiated peace between the two Indian nations. To solidify the renewed friendship with South Carolina, Malatchi accompanied the Bosomworths to Charlestown and met with Governor James Glen in May 1753. Malatchi mentioned Mary's land claims, but Glen explained that he had no authority over matters in Georgia. Despite this setback, Mary reaffirmed her skills as a mediator by resolving major issues to the satisfaction of all involved parties.[53]

Upon this successful conclusion, Mary and Thomas submitted a bill for their services for a sizeable yet reasonable sum, especially considering the danger and importance of their mission. Glen balked and paid only a fraction of their desired amount, much to their dismay. They did not sue for the difference, however, choosing instead to focus on the real reason for their trip to Charlestown in the first place. Although her reputation as an intermediary had spread to other colonies, Mary still lacked the material trappings that proved her importance within British society. While she occupied a high-profile position, she did not possess the wealth that legitimized that status. She aspired to achieve complete recognition for her actions during the past two decades, and she refused to surrender. To fulfill that objective, she pressed her land claims through the South Carolina courts and assembly, but to no avail. Therefore, Mary and Thomas followed through with their original plan and departed for England in the summer of 1754 to present her petition in person.[54]

Mary resubmitted her memorial to the Board of Trade and waited for an answer. Circumstances in Georgia, however, had seriously altered the situation. During her time in South Carolina, the Trustees who oversaw the colony relinquished their charter to the king in June 1752, leaving Parliament to create another administration for the region. After two years of bureaucratic dealings, they established a royal government with an appointed governor and council to complement the small representative assembly already in place. The first governor, John Reynolds, had already departed for his assignment, and the

Board of Trade informed Mary that she would have to send her claims to him since he now had authority over the province. Moreover, with the new regime in Georgia came the formation of new regulations regarding land distribution, so she needed to check with colonial authorities to determine what laws applied to her situation and how to proceed in obtaining approval for what she believed rightfully belonged to her. Although this latest sequence of events further postponed resolution of her case, the demise of the Trustees significantly improved the possibility of success since it was their rules that had blocked her claims all along.[55]

In the fall of 1755 Mary returned to Savannah. Despite her last disastrous encounter there, she insisted on going back to the city and pursuing her property claim. By this time, she had dedicated over twenty years of her life to Georgia, and she refused to let anyone forget that fact. Not only had she received the land as a gift from Tomochichi, but she firmly believed that she had earned some sort of recompense for all her efforts. Moreover, she had worked so hard and gambled so much to make her title valid with British authorities that to stop now would admit a terrible defeat. Mary brought her proposal to Governor John Reynolds and his advisors and received the same denial as always. Reynolds's days as governor of Georgia were numbered, however. He routinely annoyed important local officials, and he exacerbated tensions with the neighboring Creeks by not following their cultural customs. The current situation required someone of ability, diplomacy, and strength to take charge of the disorganized colony after its many years of neglect, and Reynolds was not the man for the job.[56]

Fortunately, under the leadership of the next governor, Henry Ellis, Georgia not only found its footing but began to succeed and flourish. In February 1757, he took charge of the factionalized administration and broke the deadlock between the assembly and the council. He contacted the Creeks, reestablished peaceful relations, and obtained the three sea islands in question for so many years. Not only did he regain an important ally in the Creeks, but this move also served as his first step toward resolving the property dispute with Mary, much to the relief of everyone involved. In July 1759 Ellis made a compromise: he offered to grant Mary the island of St. Catherine's and to sell the other two, Sapelo and Ossabaw, as well as the tract along Pipemaker's Creek, in order to pay her 2,000 pounds for her service. After years of conflict, a British official finally resolved the controversy, and Mary accepted the deal. It did not include all that she sought, but of the properties in question, St. Catherine's offered the most lucrative possibilities. In June 1760 she received the deed to St. Catherine's, and in the following month, the other two islands were auctioned to finance her settlement. Ellis received praise as a hero from local residents and overseas administrators for concluding the deal in a fair, efficient manner, and Mary acquired the legal paperwork and monetary reward for which she had worked so hard and struggled so long. With this transaction, she became Georgia's largest landholder and wealthiest colonist, and she retired to the island with her husband Thomas to spend the rest of her days in peace until her death in mid-1765.[57]

Although Mary had achieved the material benefits of a member of the colonial elite, she never broke into that class or gained acceptance. She had labored at uncouth professions to obtain her fortune and fought the law to receive recognition. She had rejected the place of a traditional colonial woman who ruled the private domain but rarely entered the public one. Her mixed heritage served as another mark against her and, even worse for Mary, as a reminder of her awkward position within two societies but never completely embraced by either. Rather than allow this flaw to prevent her from enjoying certain opportunities, she chose a different path, one that required strength and determination as she made her way through a world that, despite its changing circumstances, remained dominated by men. She refused to submit, and because of that refusal, contemporaries portrayed her negatively as an unruly rebel or simply a troublemaker. Only recently have scholars begun to appreciate her true contributions to several colonial themes, including law, diplomacy, and identity studies.[58] Thus, Mary was neither the maligned mediator nor the mischievous malefactor; instead, she should be remembered as a woman who refused to settle for anything less than what she deserved. For that, she should receive commendation as one of the first notable Georgia women.

## NOTES

Many thanks to Joshua Piker and Sarah E. Gardner for their recommendation to write this piece and to Kimberly R. Kellison, T. Michael Parrish, and Thomas W. Riley for their editorial assistance.

1. Mary has received more attention from historians lately. See E. Merton Coulter, "Mary Musgrove, 'Queen of the Creeks': A Chapter of Early Georgia Troubles," *Georgia Historical Quarterly* 11 (March 1927): 1–30; John Pitts Corry, "Some New Light on the Bosomworth Claims," *Georgia Historical Quarterly* 25 (September 1941): 195–224; Marion E. Gridley, *American Indian Women* (New York: Hawthorne Books, 1974), 33–38; Helen Todd, *Mary Musgrove: Georgia Indian Princess* (Chicago: Seven Oaks, 1981); Doris Behrman Fisher, "Mary Musgrove: Creek Englishwoman" (PhD diss., Emory University, 1990); Rodney M. Baine, "Myths of Mary Musgrove," *Georgia Historical Quarterly* 76 (Summer 1992): 428–35; Clara Sue Kidwell, "Mary Musgrove," in *Native American Women: A Biographical Dictionary,* ed. Gretchen M. Bataille (New York: Garland Publishing, 1993), 180–81; Michael Morris, "The Peculiar Case of Mary Musgrove Matthews Bosomworth: Colonial Georgia's Forgotten Leader, 1733–1759," *International Social Science Review* 71 (1993): 14–23; Michael P.

Morris, *The Bringing of Wonder: Trade and the Indians of the Southeast, 1700–1783* (Westport, Conn.: Greenwood Press, 1999), 39–53; Michele Gillespie, "The Sexual Politics of Race and Gender: Mary Musgrove and the Georgia Trustees," in *The Devil's Lane: Sex and Race in the Early South*, ed. Catherine Clinton and Michele Gillespie (New York: Oxford University Press, 1997), 187–201; Michael D. Green, "Mary Musgrove: Creating a New World," in *Sifters: Native American Women's Lives*, ed. Theda Perdue (New York: Oxford University Press, 2001), 29–47. Despite her multiple names, most biographers simply refer to her as "Mary," as is the case throughout this essay.

2. Todd, *Mary Musgrove*, 18.

3. Baine, "Myths of Mary Musgrove," 428–434; Gillespie, "Sexual Politics of Race and Gender," 187–89; Fisher, "Mary Musgrove," 51–52; Green, "Mary Musgrove," 30; Charles Hudson, *The Southeastern Indians* (Knoxville: University of Tennessee Press, 1976), 184–96.

4. David H. Corkran, *The Creek Frontier, 1540–1783* (Norman: University of Oklahoma Press, 1967), 57–82; Fisher, "Mary Musgrove," 50–53; Hudson, *Southeastern Indians*, 234; Todd, *Mary Musgrove*, 32–41.

5. Corkran, *Creek Frontier*, 83–84; Fisher, "Mary Musgrove," 55–65; Todd, *Mary Musgrove*, 43–48.

6. Mills Lane, ed., *General Oglethorpe's Georgia, Colonial Letters, 1733–1743* (Savannah: Beehive Press, 1975), 1:44–45.

7. Allen D. Candler, et. al. eds., *The Colonial Records of the State of Georgia*, 39 volumes, hereafter cited as CRG (Atlanta: Chas. P. Byrd, 1904–1916; Athens: University of Georgia Press, 1976–1989; Savannah: Georgia Historical Society), 20:87–88, 122, 172–76, 197–98, 439.

8. Lane, *General Oglethorpe's Georgia*, 1:20.

9. CRG, 20:439.

10. George Fenwick Jones, ed., *Detailed Reports on the Salzburger Emigrants Who Settled in America . . .* vol. 2, *1734–1735*, ed. Samuel Urlsperger (Athens: University of Georgia Press, 1969), 106–7, quotation on 107.

11. Luke Tyerman, *The Oxford Methodists: Memoirs of the Rev. Messrs. Clayton, Ingham, Gambold, Hervey, and Broughton, with Biographical Notices of Others* (New York: Harper and Brothers, Publishers, 1873), 75, 80; *The Journal of John Wesley* (London: J. M. Dent and Sons Ltd., 1906), 1:23.

12. CRG, 4:511; Corkran, *Creek Frontier*, 100; Todd, *Mary Musgrove*, 56–57.

13. CRG, 4:517–19; CRG, 23:219; Fisher, "Mary Musgrove," 109–10; Todd, *Mary Musgrove*, 63, 66.

14. CRG, 4:49–50.

15. Green, "Mary Musgrove," 35–36; Todd, *Mary Musgrove*, 67–68.

16. CRG, 1:12, 22.

17. Ibid., 30:226–27, 234.

18. Ibid., 5:590, 654; E. Merton Coulter, ed., *The Journal of William Stephens, 1741–1743* (Athens: University of Georgia Press, 1958), 142–43; Baine, "Myths of Mary Musgrove," 434; Corkran, *Creek Frontier*, 110; Fisher, "Mary Musgrove," 129–30, 136–44; Todd, *Mary Musgrove*, 73–81.

19. CRG, 36:290.

20. Corry, "Some New Light," 198–200; Coulter, "Mary Musgrove," 9–11; Fisher, "Mary Musgrove," 158–66; Green, "Mary Musgrove," 36–37; Todd, *Mary Musgrove*, 86.

21. E. Merton Coulter, ed., *The Journal of William Stephens, 1743–1745* (Athens: University of Georgia Press, 1959), 127.

22. Gillespie, "Sexual Politics of Race and Gender," 189, 195–99.

23. Coulter, *Journal of William Stephens, 1743–1745*, 136–37.

24. CRG, 1:487–88; CRG, 31:44–45, 79.

25. CRG, 36:256–97.

26. Ibid., 36:310–11.

27. Ibid., 36:315–25, quotation on 324–25.

28. "Deed From Malatchi to the Bosomworths for Three Coastal Islands," in *Early American Indian Documents: Treaties and Laws, 1607–1789,* vol. 11, *Georgia Treaties, 1733–1763,* ed. John T. Juricek (Frederick, Md.: University Publications of America, 1989), 157–61.

29. Corkran, *Creek Frontier,* 126, 135–36; Hudson, *Southeastern Indians,* 185–190; Todd, *Mary Musgrove,* 96–97.

30. CRG, 6:252.

31. Ibid., 6:253.

32. Ibid., 6:257.

33. Ibid., 6:260.

34. Ibid., 6:262.

35. Ibid.

36. Ibid., 6:263.

37. Ibid.

38. Hudson, *Southeastern Indians,* 223–26.

39. Ibid., 264.

40. Ibid.

41. Ibid., 266.

42. Ibid., 268.

43. Ibid., 270–71.

44. Quotation on CRG, 6:271; statement on CRG, 27:207–9.

45. CRG, 6:272.

46. Ibid.

47. Ibid., 6:274.

48. Ibid., 6:275.

49. Ibid., 6:277.

50. Ibid., 6:277–79.

51. CRG, 25:412–23; "Confirmation Deed from Malatchi and Other Creek Headmen to the Bosomworths for the Yamacraw Tract and the Three Coastal Islands" in Juricek, *Early American Indian Documents: Georgia Treaties,* 205–10.

52. William L. McDowell, ed., *Colonial Records of South Carolina: Documents relating to Indian Affairs, May 21, 1750–August 7, 1754* (Columbia: South Carolina Archives Department, 1958), 264–68, 343–47; CRG, 26:404–5.

53. Ibid., 268–342, 347–51, 387–458.

54. Ibid., 369, 376–77, 385–87, 495–98.

55. CRG, 26:465–502.

56. Corkran, *Creek Frontier,* 170–71; Corry, "Some New Light," 218–19.

57. Edward J. Cashin, *Governor Henry Ellis and the Transformation of British North America* (Athens: University of Georgia Press, 1994), 65–94.

58. Corry, "Some New Light," 224; Coulter, "Mary Musgrove," 30; Gillespie, "Sexual Politics of Race and Gender," 187–201; Fisher, "Mary Musgrove," 537–51; Green, "Mary Musgrove," 46; Todd, *Mary Musgrove,* 137.

# Nancy Hart

## (ca. 1735–ca. 1830)

### *"Too Good Not to Tell Again"*

JOHN THOMAS SCOTT

Georgians love a good story, and Georgia has produced numerous skilled story-tellers and many marvelous stories, some fictional, some historical. Georgia has also produced stories that seem to hang in a mythical realm somewhere between fiction and history. The stories of Nancy Hart rest in just such an ambiguous place. Hart, nicknamed Georgia's War Woman, is herself no historical fiction. The stories of Nancy Hart's Revolutionary War exploits, however, have a much more tenuous hold on historical reality. They did not appear in print until at least fifty years after the Revolution, and many Georgia historians of the nineteenth century either didn't know of them or chose not to include them in their texts. As for Georgia's people, despite naming a county after her in 1853, Georgians during their first century of statehood little recognized or exploited the stories of her heroic deeds. Only at the middle of the nineteenth century did the stories begin to circulate widely in print and only at the turn of the twentieth century did Nancy Hart and her stories become entrenched in both the historical renderings and the public fabric of the state. Curiously enough, the Nancy Hart stories owe their prominence to several sociopolitical movements of the nineteenth and early twentieth centuries unrelated to either the American Revolution or to the cold, academic pursuit of historical truth.

More than sufficient documentary evidence proves Nancy Hart's existence. Born Nancy Morgan either in Pennsylvania or North Carolina in the mid-1730s, she eventually married Benjamin Hart, a North Carolinian, and the two of them moved first to South Carolina and then to Georgia sometime in the early 1770s. They settled in the Broad River region along the upper Savannah River and lived there during the Revolutionary years before moving to Brunswick on the

## NANCY HART

Sarah Habersham, *Nancy Hart and Her Captives.* Courtesy of Georgia
Archives, Georgia Capitol Museum Collection, 2003-30-4089.

lower Georgia coast in the early 1790s. After her husband died, Nancy Hart moved with her son, John, first to Athens, Georgia, and then later to Henderson, Kentucky, where she died in the early decades of the nineteenth century.[1] The public and newspaper records that attest to her life, however, provide no information about her exploits contained in the stories that form her legend.

The stories themselves are marvelously entertaining and genuinely inspiring. By the mid-nineteenth century, seven stories of Nancy Hart's Revolutionary War exploits had made it into print.[2] All of them are set in Elbert County in north Georgia along the Savannah River during the latter years of the war when the British occupied Savannah and a "savage guerrilla warfare raged in the Georgia-Carolina backcountry" between those forces and settlers loyal to the crown—the Tories—and those forces and settlers loyal to the new American government. The fighting included the murder in his home of the American Whig Colonel John Dooly, an action later connected to one of the Nancy Hart stories.[3] In this kind of brutal and deadly context, the stories of Nancy Hart's exploits fit perfectly.

Two of the stories center on Nancy Hart's ability to provide the rebels with valuable intelligence about the movements and intentions of Tory forces. In one story she braved the dangers of the Savannah River to collect information about Loyalist actions on the Carolina side of the river.[4] A second intelligence-gathering story runs parallel in highlighting the intrepid nature of Hart's character and the obvious coldness of her nerves. During the British occupation of Augusta, American troops under the command of Elijah Clarke were "very anxious to know something of the intentions of the British." To obtain the information, Hart "assumed the garments of a man," traveled to Augusta, and "went boldly into the British camp, pretending to be crazy." The act worked. Hart, so the story goes, obtained "much useful information, which she hastened to lay before" Colonel Clarke.[5] These two stories, taken together, illustrate Hart's willingness to expose herself voluntarily to bodily harm, even death, for the sake of the American cause and to do so when the men of the area were apparently too timid or slow for her taste.

Three additional brief stories display a number of Nancy Hart's other qualities: her quick thinking, her lack of fear of Tory men—or even men in general—and her willingness to capture or fight them when necessary. One story began with her walking along a road. On this walk, she met an armed Tory and fell into conversation with him, "so as to divert his attention." Having successfully distracted him, she "seized his gun, and declared that unless he immediately took up the line of march for a fort not too far distant, she would shoot him." The soldier ("dastard" in the original story), "intimidated" by Hart, willingly complied. Another story found Hart and a group of women and children guarding a fort, "the men having gone some distance, probably for provisions." A band of "Tories and savages" attacked the fort, but "at this critical period, when fear had seized the women and children, to such an extent as to produce an exhibition of indescribably confusion, Mrs. Hart called into action all the energies of her nature." She attempted to move the fort's single cannon into position to fire it at the enemy. Unable to do so, she began looking around for some tool to help her move it. While searching the fort, she found a "young man hid under a cow-hide." Hart "immediately drew him from his retreat, and threatened him with immediate death unless he instantly assisted her with the cannon." The frightened boy, "who well knew that Nancy would carry her threats into execution unless he obeyed," helped her move the cannon. Having trained it on the attackers, she fired it and "so frightened the enemy that they took to their heels."[6] The third story placed Hart "at home with her children, sitting round the log fire, with a large pot of soap boiling over the fire." While she stirred the soap she enthralled the family with the latest stories of the war. In the midst of this pacific, domestic scene, one of the family members noticed someone "peeping through the crevices of the chimney, and gave a silent intimation of it to Nancy." Unrattled, Hart proceeded to tell even more "exaggerated accounts of the discomfiture of the Tories," all the while stirring the soap and waiting for the reappearance of the snooping eye. Upon its reappearance, "with the quickness of lightning, she dashed the ladle of boiling soap through the crevice full in the face of the eavesdropper." Scalded by the hot soap, the offender "screamed and roared," but "the indomitable Nancy went out, amused herself at his expense, and with gibes and taunts, bound him fast as her prisoner."[7]

The final two Revolutionary War stories are intertwined, and the latter story is the most famous of all of the Nancy Hart stories. According to the second story, Nancy Hart herself told the first story to a band of Tories who had "unceremoniously entered" her cabin "to learn the truth of a story in circulation, that she had secreted a noted rebel" from a group of pursuing "king's men." Hart "undauntedly avowed her agency in the fugitive's escape" and went on to tell the tale. She had heard a horse approaching her cabin and looked out to see "a whig flying from pursuit." She motioned to the rider to pass through the front and back doors of her cabin and "take to the swamp, and secure himself as well as he could." Soon thereafter, a party of Tories arrived and called loudly into the cabin. Hart dressed herself up as a "sick, lone woman" and asked why they bothered such a poor soul. They explained their hunt for a rebel horseman and inquired whether she had seen the man. Upon telling them that she had

seen a horseman turn into the woods several hundred yards back, they gal-
loped away. "Well fooled," they were, bragged Hart to the band now sitting in
her cabin. They went off "in an opposite course to that of my whig boy; when,
if they had not been so lofty minded—but had looked on the ground inside the
bars, they would have seen his horse's tracks up to that door, as plain as you
can see the tracks on this here floor, and out of t'other door down the bath to
the swamp."[8] Her impudent telling of this tale "did not much please the tory
party," who did not immediately "wreak their revenge upon the woman who so
unscrupulously avowed the cheat she had put upon the pursuers of a rebel" but
instead "contented themselves with ordering her to prepare them something to
eat." The cockiness of the Tories marked the beginning of the final story and
proved their eventual doom.

Hart neither immediately gave in to the Tory demands nor turned the tables
on them. She initially answered their demand for food by informing them that
she "never fed traitors and king's men if she could help it," because the king's
supporters had stolen or killed all of her animals except for one old turkey
poking about the yard. The leader of the band demanded she cook the bird and
to help matters along "shot down the turkey" himself while another "brought
[it] into the house and handed [it] to Mrs. Hart to be cleaned and cooked without delay." Hart "stormed and swore awhile" but soon, looking to "make a merit
of necessity," she "began with alacrity" to cook, assisted by her young daughter, Sukey, and one of the party "with whom she seemed in a tolerably good
humor." The Tories, apparently satisfied with her new attitude and grown comfortable with the strength of their position, made their fatal (literally) mistake:
they began consuming alcohol and even invited Hart to imbibe as well, "an
invitation which was accepted with jocose thanks."

Having lulled these supporters of the crown into a relaxed repose, she then
began to spring her trap. She started by sending her daughter into the swamps
ostensibly to retrieve water from the spring, but in reality to blow a conch shell
placed there for just such a situation. She instructed Sukey to blow it "for her
father in such a way as should inform him there were tories in the cabin." Once
the "party had become merry over their jug, and sat down to feast upon the
slaughtered gobbler," they stacked their weapons. Hart continued the deception
by nonchalantly passing several times between the weapons and the men. Soon
more water was needed, and Hart sent Sukey back to the swamp to retrieve
water and blow the conch again to signal her father to advance to the cabin
immediately. While Sukey was gone, and while the Tory party continued to
make merry, Hart commenced passing their weapons one by one through a
chink in the cabin wall. At her attempt to pass the third, the Tories detected

her and "sprang to their feet." With no time to think or otherwise react, Hart
leveled the musket in her hands directly at the party and warned them that she
would shoot the first one who menaced her. Eventually, one of them "made a
movement to advance upon her; and true to her threat, she fired and shot him
dead!" She instantly grabbed another musket and leveled it at the remaining
Tories. By this time, Sukey had returned, taken the remaining gun out of the
cabin, and informed her mother that help would soon be on the way. Now realizing their desperate situation, the Tories chose to rush Hart, who promptly shot
another one of them dead. Grabbing another weapon from the hands of her
daughter, Hart posted herself in the doorway, and "called upon the party to surrender 'their d—— carcasses to a whig woman.'" Soon her husband and several
other men arrived at the cabin and prepared to shoot the captured men. Nancy
objected, saying that "'shooting was too good for them,'" and immediately the
men dragged the Tories from the house, took them out into the woods and
hanged them. This "capture" story, more than any of the others, later became
the foundation of Nancy Hart's reputation.[9]

In addition to the stories themselves, descriptions of Nancy Hart herself
and visual depictions of the Tory capture story added to her legend. Early
nineteenth-century accounts described her as a large and powerful woman.[10]
They also portray her as a "vulgar and illiterate" woman—"ungainly in figure, rude in speech, and awkward in manners"—who "could boast no share of
beauty." The accounts describe her as a woman who possessed a violent temper,
especially toward weak men and Tories. Indeed, the Tories reportedly "stood
somewhat in fear of her vengeance for any grievance or aggressive act."[11] Some
reports pictured her as cross-eyed and gave credit to that defect for stymieing
the Tories in the capture story. Apparently they did not rush her, because they
did not know at whom she was aiming owing to the crossing of her eyes.[12] In
addition to cowing the Tories, she reportedly over-awed her husband as well.
One report compared her to the Wife of Bath, who ruled over her "tongue-
scored husband," while another claimed she labeled him as a "poor-stick" for
not taking a "decided and active part with the defenders of his country."[13] In
sum, Nancy Hart was described as "a honey of a patriot—but the devil of a
wife!"[14]

These marvelous stories and vivid descriptions, however, did not come immediately into print in Georgia or anywhere else in the United States. Later
accounts cite two 1825 newspaper stories, but most of the credit for bringing
the Nancy Hart stories into regional and national prominence must rest with
author, poet, and critic, Elizabeth F. Ellet.[15] Owing to the work of her husband,
a college professor, Ellet lived for a time in South Carolina and apparently came

across the capture story during her sojourn in the South.[16] In 1848 she published the Nancy Hart capture story in two locations: *Godey's Lady's Book* and a two-volume work entitled *The Women of the American Revolution*.[17]

Ellet never commented directly on her reasons for publishing the Hart story specifically, but as a leader in the first American women's rights movement, putting forward ideas about a revised version of gender relationships appears to have been at the center of her historical writing. Ellet "took an interest in women's concerns throughout her lifetime," and in writing *The Women of the American Revolution*, she apparently hoped to show that during the Revolution "at least two wars, a men's war and a women's war" took place.[18] By "highlighting and labeling such traits as heroism, courage, and intelligence," Ellet kept "the reader always aware that women endured incredible hardships—rapine, violence, hunger, lack of basic essentials," while at the same time she portrayed "women's heroic deeds that enabled colonists to overthrow their oppressors."[19] Ellet hoped to "create a past that advances a new and radically altered set of cultural assumptions" about gendered roles. She "rebelled against the very notion of a separate woman's sphere," and used her historical writing to argue for a world in which "men and women interacted freely and gender did not determine individual worth."[20]

In addition to these gender-related motivations, Ellet also hoped to forward a particularly patriotic vision of American women. As part of a collection of authors known as the Young Americans, Ellet wanted to use her stories as "a useful medium through which to examine the American 'character,' extol the country's values, and inspire national allegiance." Throughout her book, she offered "a portrait of women engaged in the world continuously, actively, and aggressively and wholly willing to sacrifice their lives for the good of the American people."[21] The Nancy Hart capture story fit both of her models perfectly. Here was a wife and mother—the keeper of her home—who did not hesitate to invade a man's sphere—warfare—and display supposedly manly characteristics: courage, marksmanship, and deceptive intelligence. At the same time, Hart in her story displayed unswerving patriotism and endured hardship and sacrifice for the good of her country.

Ellet's publications spawned a fairly quick and broad reaction in print, in picture, and in law in the 1850s and in imitation during the Civil War. Two famous Georgians over the next several years picked up and even added to the Nancy Hart legend. George White, a Methodist and later Episcopalian minister and educator, followed first.[22] In 1849 White published *Statistics of the State of Georgia* and included in it Ellet's sketch "with some slight alteration."[23] He followed up that work with a broader treatment of Hart in his 1855 *Historical*

*Collections of Georgia.* In that work he added biographical, bibliographical, and genealogical information as well as several new stories: the boiling soap story, the raft story, the walking along the road story, the fort story, and the crazy male spy story, thus rounding out the seven early stories of Hart's Revolutionary exploits.[24] George Gilmer, former Georgia congressmen and governor, further added to her reputation.[25] First in an 1851 address delivered at the University of Georgia and then in his 1855 publication, *Sketches of Some of the First Settlers of Upper Georgia*, Gilmer related the capture story, several additional non-Revolutionary stories, and some (as it later turned out) false biographical information about Hart. Gilmer also claimed to have known about Hart long before Ellet's piece appeared in print. In both works he related how when he had been a congressman in 1829 he had drafted a resolution to fill one of the "vacant niches" of the Capitol rotunda "with a painting of Nancy Hart wading Broad River, her clothes tucked up under one arm, a musket under the other, and three Tories ahead, on her way to the camp of the Whigs, to deliver them up to the tender mercies of Col. Elijah Clark."[26] No congressional record of his submitting this resolution exists, and certainly the painting never was made; as a later historian pointed out, Gilmer only claimed to have "prepared" a resolution, never to have submitted one.[27] White and Gilmer probably were attracted to the stories primarily through their love of interesting people and of the state of Georgia and saw the stories as proof of the basic strength and goodness of its people.[28] They may also have been tapping into a desire by many southerners in the 1850s to proclaim themselves as the true heirs of the American Revolution in the midst of the rising sectional crisis.[29]

Ellet's story of Nancy Hart also apparently caught the attention of one of America's most popular and most prolific illustrators, Felix O. C. Darley.[30] An 1853 lithograph by Darley shows a resolute and fairly attractive Nancy Hart wielding a musket toward three frightened Tories while another lies dead on the floor and a fifth is either wounded or has been knocked on the floor. Sukey hides safely behind her mother while the recently cooked meal remains partially eaten on the table. The caption below tells the story of the capture and attributes the information to Ellet's *The Women of the American Revolution*.[31] No circulation records for Darley's lithograph remain, but having an artist of his stature produce a wash drawing of Nancy Hart certainly added credence and weight to the stories.[32]

Ellet's stories, combined with White's and Gilmer's retellings, also caught the attention of the Georgia legislature in the early 1850s. In 1853 the legislature moved to create a new county out of Franklin and Elbert counties and name it Hart County after Nancy Hart.[33] No record of the debates surrounding the passage of the act remains, but two newspaper accounts of the time indicate the intent to honor Hart's memory. The *Savannah Morning News* commented that the creation of a county named after her seemed a "fit tribute for such a brave-hearted woman."[34] The *Augusta Chronicle* additionally noted that one member of the legislature even proposed the county be named "Nancy Hart"; a voice vote seemed to carry the amendment, but it lost on a division. In any event, naming a county after this "celebrated heroine of the Revolution" seemed suitable to all.[35]

By the time of the Civil War, the name Nancy Hart seems to have been accepted in Georgia as symbolic of women willing to defend hearth and home against oppressive foreign invaders. Two incidents in that war led to the use of that moniker to describe armed Georgia women. The first occurred in northeastern Georgia in the early summer of 1863. Apparently a report of a large Union force operating near Hart and Elbert counties in early June 1863 sent the locals into a panic. Despite having no idea how such a force could have appeared suddenly in the heart of the Confederacy, town and country folk alike began meeting to organize resistance. Soon the report proved false and the *Augusta Chronicle* explained the entire farce: "It appears that some ten or twelve ladies—all white women are ladies—in Hart or Madison counties, for the sake of a frolic, or perhaps for a more serious cause, undertook to play soldiers, or 'Nancy Harts,' and so had put on men's clothes—'mounted the imminent deadly *breeches*,' as Shakspeare [*sic*] says—and with corn-stalks, had invaded an old gentlemen's plantation. . . . At the sight of the Amazonian cohort [the planter] stampeded his negroes and spread the alarm that ten thousand Yankees were coming." The whole affair, the writer commented, had been "caused by the above mentioned freak of the feminine gender," but at least, he noted, "the late feminine fracas" showed that people were willing to defend their own homes.[36] The second use of the name "Nancy Harts" occurred nearer to the end of the war and closer to the Alabama line than the South Carolina border. Not long after the start of the war, roughly forty women residents of LaGrange, Georgia, armed themselves and organized a militia company to defend the town. When it faced invasion in the spring of 1865 by a detachment of Brigadier General James Wilson's cavalry, the women, led by "Captain" Nancy Morgan, turned out to defend the town. Combat was averted when the commander of the Union forces "promised to spare the city from looting and destruction."[37] Neither set of "Nancy Harts," then, suffered any casualties in the Civil War.

By 1865, in Georgia at least, the stories about and the character of Nancy Hart first brought to light by the writings of Elizabeth Ellet had clearly become embedded in the culture. The stories about her and her reputation seemed destined to become a central part of the state's Revolutionary historical fabric along with remembrances about Button Gwinnett and Elijah Clarke. Instead, over the next forty years Nancy Hart and her stories received very little recognition and sometimes considerable skepticism.

The inattention and skepticism about Hart and her stories, in fact, appeared even in the first heyday of her reputation, the 1850s, and it continued to the turn of the century. In 1859 William Bacon Stevens, formerly a professor of history at the University of Georgia, wrote a two-volume comprehensive history of the state of Georgia from its discovery to 1798 but made absolutely no mention of Hart or her exploits.[38] The next year, Adiel Sherwood, one of the founders of Mercer University, produced the fourth edition of his *Gazetteer of Georgia*.[39] In it he mentioned Nancy Hart but cautioned that "the stories related in fancy sketches ought to be taken with some grains of allowance."[40] The diffidence continued in the postbellum period when Charles Colcock Jones Jr., Georgia's preeminent historian of the day, gave Nancy Hart only a scant footnote mention in his *Revolutionary Epoch*.[41] Between 1863 and 1901 the *Augusta Chronicle*, the largest newspaper near Hart County, mentioned her only once in a brief notice about an 1886 congressional race.[42] A locomotive named after her in 1879 seems to have been the only commemorative naming of the period.[43]

The skepticism reached its height in 1901 when the *Macon Telegraph* quoted the minister-historian George G. Smith as saying, "This is a story of fiction. There was no such person as Nancy Hart in real life."[44] Smith had published a history of Georgia the year before but had only mentioned Hart in the section on pioneer life, calling her a "woman of substance and family and integrity." In that work he had chided Gilmer for "somewhat overstat[ing] things about her."[45] Four days later he softened and clarified his remarks (which had been picked up by the *Atlanta Journal*) by confessing the reality of the person but maintaining that the Revolutionary Hart saga "lacks foundation." He criticized White for publishing stories about Hart that "have no sufficient support" and cited Stevens's and Jones's skepticism.[46] By 1901, however, the Nancy Hart stories were already in the process of being rescued from the historical back lot by Georgia's preeminent postbellum storyteller, Joel Chandler Harris, and by the period's most active national historical remembrance organization, the Daughters of the American Revolution (DAR).

Joel Chandler Harris rose to national and even international fame in the late nineteenth century as the author of the Uncle Remus stories as well as the author of many other tales. Along the way, he helped rescue the Nancy Hart stories from oblivion and inadvertently began a second Nancy Hart craze in Georgia.[47] As early as 1887 Chandler had been asked by E. J. Brooks, editor of the D. Lothrop Corporation, to write a history of Georgia to be a part of a series of state histories. Brooks sketched out the "plan of the series": "to tell the real story of each state in brisk, entertaining, and stirring narrative—the story of the people for the people—connected, historical, and picturesque—with a dash of fiction if need be to give it thread."[48] Chandler did not immediately take to the task, but by the mid-1890s had produced a manuscript that appeared first in 1896 as *Georgia: From the Invasion of DeSoto to Recent Times* and later that year as *Stories of Georgia*. In the preface to the latter work, he explained he wrote the book because he "had in view the desirability of familiarizing the youth of Georgia with the salient facts of the State's history in a way that shall make the further study of that history a delight instead of a task." He regretted that despite Charles C. Jones's efforts, "there is no history of Georgia in which the dry bones of facts have been clothed with the flesh and blood of popular narrative."[49] In the book itself, he retold all seven of White's Nancy Hart stories and described her as "the most remarkable woman in some respects that the country has produced." He gave central focus to the capture story, he said, because it "brought into play all the courage and devotion of her strong nature, and all the tact and audacity that belonged to her character."[50]

Harris not only redeemed Hart historically, he also used her literarily. In 1899 he published the short story "The Kidnapping of President Lincoln" in a collection entitled *On the Wing of Occasions*. "Universally admired" among all of the ones in *Wing*, the fictional story centered on a Confederate twosome's attempt during the Civil War to kidnap Lincoln and hold him hostage to effect a southern victory.[51] The lead Confederate character that Harris created, Billy Sanders, was cast as the proud grandson of Nancy Hart, and he embodied her plainspoken, down-to-earth, but crafty persona.[52] The Sanders character proved so popular with the public and so well liked by Harris himself that he used Sanders in three later novels and as his public spokesman in his own publishing enterprise, *Uncle Remus's Magazine*.[53] In many ways, Harris used Sanders as an updated (but male) version of Hart—plainspoken and honest, courageous and crafty, loyal and patriotic, a savvy commoner though not "properly" educated.[54] Harris also used Hart as a central figure in the unfinished novel *Qua*, which he penned in 1900 but was not published until 1946.[55]

The Hart and Sanders characters appealed to Harris because they embodied the worldview that Harris had dedicated most of his life to forwarding. Harris was a close friend of fellow Atlantan Henry Grady, although unlike Grady, Harris was never a true believer in the New South movement, but rather "more of a traditionalist" who "hoped the New South would remain the middle class agrarian democracy he believed much of the Old South had been."[56] Harris most closely identified with the "'frontier' plantation ideal that united all landed whites in democratic harmony," and he used the literary character of Billy Sanders, and by extension the historical figure of Nancy Hart, "as a mouthpiece" to express his doubts and fears of the emerging New South.[57] The Hart/Sanders characters fit his model well.

Harris's historical work on Nancy Hart might have receded into the background had it not been picked up and extended by the young journalist-historian Lucian Lamar Knight. A cousin and admirer of Henry Grady, Knight had been introduced as a nine-year-old to Harris and he maintained a close relationship with him until Harris's death in 1908.[58] Harris wrote a glowing introduction to Knight's first historical work, *Reminiscences of Famous Georgians*, published in 1907. In it Harris directly addressed the Nancy Hart legend, saying "Another State had its Moll Pitcher . . . but where, save in Georgia, will you find a Nancy Hart, who was active in killing and capturing the enemies of liberty?" Harris admitted that the stories were "doubted by sober historians," but maintained that "every story that is told of her prowess and patriotism has a basis in solid fact." "Tradition," he continued, "is often truer than written history."[59] Knight's renowned oratorical skills, crafted as a complement to Grady's own prowess, and his love of stories, gained literally at the knee of Harris, combined in *Reminiscences* to produce dynamic, if sometimes melodramatic, historical writing, and Knight treated Hart much more like Harris than Jones, or even White or Gilmer for that matter.

Knight had become interested in history as an undergraduate at the University of Georgia in the late nineteenth century, but apparently had been unimpressed by Charles C. Jones's "dull" renderings.[60] Knight certainly crafted *Reminiscences* more like Grady spoke and Harris wrote than Jones, and he described Nancy Hart in the most glowing terms possible. He called her the "Boadicea of the Revolution" and "one of the most courageous masterpieces of her sex." Her exploits had "electrified the whole tragic theater of war," and her capture of the Tories "surpassed anything in the entire Revolutionary annals" and "challenged the prowess of the Maid of Orleans." Hart had possessed the "elements of Spartan courage," combined with the "dare-devil spirit of the enraged lioness." Knight suggested Westminster Abbey "might sue to enshrine the ashes of this homely heroine of the Georgia backwoods," because she shares the "austere company of sceptered sovereigns and receives the kneeling vows of subject princes from afar."[61] Knight later wrote three other histories of Georgia, all of which described Hart in similar glowing terms.[62]

Knight's *Reminiscences* was well-received in many quarters, and his recognition and depiction of Nancy Hart became the standard in the field for the next several decades.[63] Knight's treatment of Hart also guaranteed her a prominent place in histories of Georgia for the next five decades and left little room for skepticism about the veracity of the stories.[64] Coming at the end of a half-century of historical writing about Nancy Hart, Edna Copeland's 1950 *Nancy Hart the War Woman* provided the most comprehensive and elaborate telling of all the Nancy Hart stories, including several not present in the mid-nineteenth-century sources, and marked the apex of historical writings on Nancy Hart in the first half of the twentieth century.[65]

By the time Knight had written and published *Reminiscences*, a newly formed patriotic group—the Daughters of the American Revolution—had latched onto the Nancy Hart legend. From the turn of the century to the mid-1930s, the DAR expended considerable effort in publicizing, memorializing, and defending the Nancy Hart stories. Like Harris, the ladies of the DAR were traditionalists at heart, and they selected history as "their chosen medium for preserving and transmitting their values." Through a variety of public projects, the DAR "attempted to cast their rendition of the lessons of American history in stone—sometimes literally." Honoring local and state heroes by marking graves, reading papers, collecting relics, founding museums and archives, erecting monuments, and designating certain spots as national historic sites occupied much of their time. The DAR also supported history writing, although their accounts often "more closely resembled hagiography than biography." The DAR, like several other women's remembrance organizations created at the same time, such as the United Daughters of the Confederacy, were looking to the past for "a documented heritage of feminine strength and achievement [that] would inspire women and silence critics of their expanding role in public life." They were searching for "models they and their contemporaries could emulate. They used history to transmit a set of values and a code of behavior."[66] The figure of and the stories about Nancy Hart proved very useful to the Georgia chapters of the DAR.

Founded in 1891, the DAR soon established chapters throughout the nation, including Georgia, and Georgia DAR members quickly moved to elevate Nancy Hart and her stories to a more prominent place in the state's history and the public's view. In 1900 a Milledgeville, Georgia, chapter organized with the name Nancy Hart under the leadership of Ella Kincaid Chappell. Chappell's husband, Joseph Harris Chappell, then president of Georgia Normal and Industrial School (now Georgia College and State University) read the stories of Nancy Hart from his upcoming book at the first meeting. The new chapter moved quickly to partner with the Stephen Heard Chapter to purchase a five-acre tract of land believed to encompass Nancy Hart's cabin as well as the spring nearby where Sukey would have gone to blow the conch shell in the capture story. The chapter also received a wooden gavel said to be made from "the very limb on which the Tories were hanged!"[67] Other chapters and other DAR members joined in the celebration of all things Nancy Hart. Some wrote histories, such as Foster's *Revolutionary Reader* and Cook's *History of Baldwin County*.[68] Several members joined with others to respond to George Smith's aspersions on Hart rendered in the *Macon Telegraph* and the *Atlanta Journal* in October 1901.[69] Having obtained the land around Nancy Hart's original homestead, they rebuilt the cabin and opened Nancy Hart Memorial Park, later conveyed to the state and renamed Nancy Hart State Park.[70] Other chapters and members over the next several decades moved to organize writing contests about Nancy Hart for sixth graders in Richmond County, hold a commemoration of the Battle of Kettle Creek, fought in Wilkes County in 1779, complete with a "live" Nancy Hart, have a highway in northeast Georgia named after her, and place markers signifying her importance around the state.[71] Others made efforts to chronicle her later life and find her burial place, which they did, surprisingly enough in Henderson, Kentucky.[72]

Perhaps the high point of DAR activity came in 1916 with the presentation by the Piedmont Chapter of a new painting by Sarah Habersham of the capture story. The chapter donated the painting, to be hung in the state capitol, at an elaborate ceremony in the capitol on November 25 with the governor in attendance. As the primary speaker for the event, the DAR found the perfect orator— Lucian Lamar Knight—who gladly extolled the glories and legacy of Nancy Hart.[73] The marriage of the DAR to Knight was an ideal match for both partners, for both clearly admired, even worshiped Nancy Hart. Additionally, Knight was at the time pushing for the founding of a department of state archives, while the DAR was undoubtedly pleased to get someone of Knight's stature to recognize their memorializing efforts.[74] The state legislature played along willingly, noting in its 1916 acceptance resolution that "it is just and proper that the memory and deeds of one of Georgia's most noted Revolutionary citizens should thus be perpetuated by the State," and ordered that the painting be "hung upon the walls of the Capitol."[75]

Others besides the DAR and Knight honored and memorialized Nancy Hart during the first half of the twentieth century. Rebecca Latimer Felton, wife of a former congressman and the country's first woman senator, gave speeches in churches and other public venues around Georgia, and later published an interview about Nancy Hart as part of a book on Georgia women.[76] Newspapers published stories about Hart and retold her tales time and again.[77] Others named schools, hotels, and even racehorses after Georgia's Revolutionary heroine.[78]

Many in Georgia seemed quite pleased in 1912 when workers for the Elberton and Eastern Railroad discovered six human skeletons not far from the supposed site of the Hart cabin. Many assumed these skeletons to be the ones of the hapless Tories in the capture story.[79] In 1952 Hart was the subject of a popular national radio program called *Cavalcade of America*, while others wrote poems, and some spoke of making a movie of her life.[80] In 1953 the town of Hartwell, to celebrate the centennial of the founding of Hart County, put on a six-day historical festival that included a pageant, the "Centurama," that retold the story of Nancy Hart.[81] By the early 1950s Nancy Hart had become a hero and a popular icon in the state of Georgia and had attracted the attention of Georgia's preeminent professional historian, E. Merton Coulter. Coulter set out to separate fact from fantasy, but in doing so ironically marked the decline of the second Nancy Hart frenzy and marked the beginning of a second period of disinterest, academically anyway, in the Nancy Hart stories.

By the early 1950s Coulter had established himself not only as one of the leading historians living in Georgia but also as one of the foremost historians of Georgia and the South.[82] In his biographies, Coulter seemed to have been particularly attracted to second-tier or relatively unknown figures.[83] He turned his attention to Hart and her legend in 1954. Coulter set out to separate fact from fiction on the subject of Nancy Hart, and his treatment remains the most exhaustive and comprehensively documented analysis of her person. Through the use of a variety of public records he easily established the existence of a real person named Nancy Hart who had lived in northeastern Georgia during the time of the Revolution, had later moved to the Brunswick area, and had later in her life, moved west to Henderson, Kentucky, where she died sometime in the early nineteenth century. In addition to establishing the reality of the person, Coulter also explored the rise of the stories and identified the location of the earliest stories in print. Coulter concluded that the Hart stories "were undoubtedly current" in northeast Georgia soon after the Revolution, but for unknown reasons were not put into print until much later. As for the veracity of the stories themselves, Coulter could only remark that, "Yes, there was a Nancy Hart and there will always be a Nancy Hart tradition."[84]

The Nancy Hart tradition continued to live during the latter half of the twentieth and into the early twenty-first century, especially locally in Hart County, but also elsewhere. Numerous newspaper and magazine articles appeared about Hart to keep the stories in front of the public.[85] The Nancy Hart DAR chapter continued its work to keep alive the stories of Nancy Hart, and she also played a major part in a work of historical fiction that centered mostly on the experiences of Elijah Clarke during the American Revolution.[86] Artwork depicting

Hart continued to be created, some of it displayed locally, and some of it distributed internationally in *National Geographic*.[87] Popular histories, or portions of popular histories, also included Hart's stories, and the Society of the Cincinnati featured the Darley lithograph as part of a 2003–4 exhibition entitled "Georgia in the American Revolution" at their library and museum in Washington, D.C.[88] Hart County certainly did not forget the Nancy Hart tradition. In 1983, to celebrate the 250th anniversary of Georgia's founding, the local chamber of commerce sponsored a yearlong depiction of Nancy Hart by a local citizen, Ruby Nell Heaton Bannister.[89] Modern technology has also been kind to Nancy Hart; a Google search of the World Wide Web will produce a variety of hits referencing Nancy Hart, including several Web pages dedicated strictly to her and her stories.[90] Coulter's assertion that there will always be a Nancy Hart tradition seems as true in the early twenty-first century as it did in the middle of the twentieth century.

Professional historians, however, have paid very scant attention to Hart and her stories in the intervening decades and have often treated the stories with considerably more skepticism than did their early twentieth-century predecessors. The next great historian of Georgia history, Kenneth Coleman, gave her only brief mention in his 1958 work, *The American Revolution*. Coleman relegated Hart to one paragraph and simply called the capture story "the best known and most interesting legend of the Revolution in Georgia."[91] James Bonner, in a book published in the same year, gave two sentences to Hart in a paragraph on backwoods folk heroes in Georgia's history, saying she belonged "both to history and legend."[92] Three histories of Georgia produced in the 1970s either made no mention, little mention, or very skeptical mention of the stories.[93] Three Georgia histories produced late in the century and aimed primarily at high school students continued the trend.[94] The standard collegiate text on Georgia history notes that Hart took revenge on Tory murderers, at least, "if legends about Nancy can be believed."[95] A recent scholarly treatment of Georgia women in the American Revolution, by Ben Marsh, gives Hart and her stories scant attention or credence, describing the stories as "hardly grounded in verifiable historical evidence."[96]

Professional historians turned away from Hart and her stories in the last half of the twentieth century for a variety of reasons. Ironically, the thoroughness and authoritativeness of Coulter's article itself may have deflated interest in Hart and her stories in the academic world. His meticulous research and thorough documentation seems both to have closed off debate and discouraged further inquiry; no scholarly article dealing exclusively with Hart has appeared since 1954. Additionally, the increased professionalization of the discipline of history, especially the rising emphasis on evidentiary documentation, after World War II probably contributed to the decline in interest except as a subject of folklore, as in the current essay. Ironically as well, the rise of modern women's history in the 1960s probably contributed to professional disinterest in Hart. The new women's history, like much of the new social history of which it was a part, aimed its focus less on the famous and heroic women of the past such as Abigail Adams or Nancy Hart, and more on the lives and experiences of common, ordinary women and the gendered roles they were often forced to play. Marsh described Hart as "the most famous exception to the notion of female vulnerability," one of the dominant notions of women in the late eighteenth century. The Revolution, as a political and military venture, "fell in theory outside of the woman's sphere," and so the intrusions of Nancy Hart into that sphere violated social norms, especially the "resilient social prescriptions of gender" known as "republican motherhood" that dominated American culture in the post-Revolutionary period.[97] Perhaps these gendered proscriptions even contributed to the absence of Nancy Hart stories in print until 1825, or especially 1848, when stories of strong women were more acceptable at least in some citizens' eyes, and they caught the attention of one Elizabeth Ellet.

Stories that have become part of American folklore—from Paul Revere's ride to Daniel Boone's adventures to Nancy Hart's exploits—originate from many and varied sources and owe their survival and popularity to many later re-tellings in prose, poetry, and art, and in commemorations through speeches, namings, and living history. Hart's stories have their own unique and peculiar background, a provenance filled with irony and populated by some of Georgia's leading historical and literary figures. They arose thanks primarily to the efforts of Elizabeth Ellet, who put them forward as part of a larger work aimed at questioning and even reconfiguring the gendered roles of the mid-nineteenth century. Despite being included in some of the most widely read historical works on Georgia in the 1850s, and despite having a county named after her, Hart and her stories receded in the popular and academic mind during the latter half of the nineteenth century. The stories resurfaced with a vengeance around the turn of the twentieth century when Joel Chandler Harris included them as part of an effort to hail the yeoman past of his beloved state and when the DAR used them to promote their efforts to praise the female patriotism of the American past. After five decades of Nancy Hart celebration and commemoration in the popular and academic worlds, the stories declined in power, at least in the academic world, ironically because a professional historian gave her more attention than she had ever previously received and because she did not fit the bill of interest for a new wave of historians of women. In a certain sense, then, the work of Elizabeth Ellet, "the mother of American women's history," was undone by a later generation of historians of women. In between, the stories rose and grew in the public's mind, so that "however finely the boundaries between legend and historical fact may have been drawn, the Nancy Hart story is too good not to tell again."[98]

## NOTES

1. For the most thorough examination of the documentary record of Nancy Hart, see E. Merton Coulter, "Nancy Hart, Georgia Heroine of the Revolution: The Story of the Growth of a Tradition," *Georgia Historical Quarterly* 39 (1955): 118–25.

2. Other stories of Nancy Hart not related to the Revolution had also been printed by the mid-nineteenth century, but this essay examines only those stories connected to the Revolutionary War. For a brief retelling of the non-war-related stories see Coulter, "Nancy Hart," 144–46.

3. Kenneth Coleman, "Part Two: 1775–1820," in *A History of Georgia*, ed. Kenneth Coleman, 2nd ed. (Athens: University of Georgia Press, 1991), 85. See also Kenneth Coleman, *The American Revolution in Georgia* (Athens: University of Georgia Press, 1958), 132.

4. George White, *Historical Collections of Georgia* (New York: Pudney & Russell, 1855), 446.

5. Ibid., 447.

6. Ibid.

7. Ibid., 441–42.

8. Elizabeth F. Ellet, *The Women of the American Revolution* (New York: Baker and Scribner, 1848; Williamstown, Mass.: Corner House Publishers, 1980), 2:228–29. Essentially the same account appeared in E. F. Ellet, "Heroic Women of the Revolution," *Godey's Lady Book* 37 (1848): 201–2; and George White, *Statistics of the State of Georgia* (Savannah: W. Thorne Williams, 1849), 235.

9. This story appeared in largely similar versions in both Ellet publications (*Women of the American Revolution*, 2:229–32 and *Godey's*, 201–2), and in both White publications (*Historical Collections*, 444–46, and *Statistics*, 234–38). In *Historical Collections*, 442–43, White attributed a similar but shortened story to the *Yorkville (S.C.) Pioneer* newspaper of date unknown. A later historian, George Gillman Smith, claimed to have seen an 1825 story in the *Milledgeville (Ga.) Recorder* with essentially the same story. See "The Original Story of Nancy Hart," *Atlanta Journal*, October 12, 1901. Neither newspaper article apparently still exists; see Coulter, "Nancy Hart," 129–30, 130n28.

10. White, *Historical Collections*, 441–42.

11. Ellet, *Women of the American Revolution*, 2:228.

12. The *Yorkville (S.C.) Pioneer* account, quoted in White, *Historical Collections*, gave multiple possible explanations for their timidity, including the possibility that "the incongruity between Nancy's eyes caused each to imagine himself her immediate object." See White, *Historical Collections*, 443. Ellet was more convinced; she wrote, "All were terror-struck; for Nancy's obliquity of sight caused each to imagine himself her destined victim." See Ellet, *Women of the American Revolution*, 2:232.

13. White, *Historical Collections*, 443; and Ellet, *Women of the American Revolution*, 2:227–28.

14. Ellet, *Women of the American Revolution*, 2:233.

15. See note 9 above for information about the two 1825 newspaper articles, and see Coulter,

"Nancy Hart," 126–31, for both a bibliographical review of pre-Ellet histories of Georgia in which Nancy Hart did not appear and an explanation of the 1825 articles. For information about Ellet's literary career, see Carol Mattingly, "Elizabeth Fries Lummis Ellet (1818–1877), *Legacy* 18, no. 1 (2001), 101–3.

16. In Ellet, "Heroic Women," 201, she cited her source as "a gentleman resident in Georgia."

17. Ellet, "Heroic Women," 201–2; and Ellet, *Women of the American Revolution*, 2:227–33.

18. Mattingly, "Elizabeth Fries Lummis Ellet," 103; Linda Kerber, "'History Can Do It No Justice': Women and the Reinterpretation of the American Revolution," in *Women in the Age of the American Revolution*, ed. Ronald Hoffman and Peter J. Albert (Charlottesville: United States Capitol Historical Society by the University of Virginia Press, 1989), 4–5. See also Loretta Valtz Mannucci, "Four Conversations of Future Directions in Revolutionary War Historiography," *Storia Nordamericana* 2, no. 1 (1985): 105–19.

19. Mattingly, "Elizabeth Fries Lummis Ellet," 104.

20. Gretchen Ferris Schoel, "In Pursuit of Possiblity: Elizabeth Ellet and *The Women of the American Revolution*" (master's thesis, College of William and Mary, 1992), 96, 62, 45, 102, 90.

21. Ibid., 78, 96.

22. For biographical information about White see Harryotte F. Burgess, "George White: Georgia Historian, Educator, Priest," *Georgia Magazine* 15, no. 4 (1971): 18–19; and David G. Hewitt, "George White," in *Dictionary of Georgia Biography*, ed. Kenneth Coleman and Charles Stephen Gurr, 2:1054–55 (Athens: University of Georgia Press, 1983).

23. White, *Statistics*, 234–38; quotation, 234.

24. White, *Historical Collections*, 441–47.

25. For biographical information about George Gilmer see Carl Vipperman, "George Rockingham Gilmer," in *Dictionary of Georgia Biography*, 1:347–48; and "Randolph Thigpen, "The Public Life of George R. Gilmer" (master's thesis, University of Georgia, 1936).

26. George Gilmer, *Sketches of Some of the First Settlers of Upper Georgia* (1855; repr. of 1926 ed., Baltimore: Geneological Publishing Company, 1970), 90. See also George R. Gilmer, *The Literary Progress of Georgia* (Athens, Ga.: Wm. N. White and Brother, 1851), 36–37.

27. Coulter, "Nancy Hart," 134.

28. See particularly, Gilmer, *Sketches*, 5–6. One other known book from the 1850s picked up the Ellet account and published a portion of it; no later figures ever referenced this work, however, indicating that it must have had little impact in shaping the Georgia perspective on the stories. See T. S. Arthur and W. H. Carpenter, *The History of Georgia from its Earliest Settlement to the Present Time* (Philadelphia: J. B. Lippincott, 1858), 201–4.

29. See, for instance, John McCardell, *The Idea of a Southern Nation* (New York: W. W. Norton, 1979), 261, 331; and Charles S. Watson, "Simms and the Civil War: The Revolutionary Analogy," *The Southern Literary Journal* 24, no. 2 (1992): 76–89.

30. For information about F. O. C. Darley's popularity in the nineteenth century, see Theodore Bolton, "The Book Illustrations of Felix Octavius Carr Darley," *Proceedings of the American Antiquarian Society* 61 (1951): 137–82; John C. Ewers, "Not Quite Redmen: The Plains Indian Illustrations of Felix O. C. Darley," *American Art Journal* 3, no. 2 (1971): 88–98; and Frank Weitenkampf, "F. O. C. Darley, American Illustrator," *Art Quarterly* 10, no. 2 (1947): 100–113.

31. Felix O. C. Darley, *Nancy Hart*, lithographed by Regnier, printed by Lemercier, Paris, published by Groupil & Co., Paris, London, Berlin, and New York, 1853. The two known extant copies of this lithograph are in the Special Collections of the University of Georgia Library, Athens, and the Library and Museum of the Society of the Cincinnati, Washington, D.C. Because the University of

Georgia Copy is cut off at the bottom, the entirety of the caption, story, and publication information may only be read on the Society of the Cincinnati copy.

32. In *Historical Collections* White included a much cruder, though similar, sketch of the scene. In the Darly lithograph Hart appears fairly young, in her thirties, and with smooth, fair skin. In the White sketch she appears with a pointed nose and wrinkled skin. The Darly lithograph makes her look like a young but determined woman while the White sketch makes her look like a tough, older woman. See White, *Historical Collections*, 440.

33. *Acts of the General Assembly of the State of Georgia, Passed in Milledgeville, at a Biennial Session, in November, December, January, and February. 1853–1854*, compiled and annotated by John Rutherford, 1:302–4, available from the Galileo Scholar database, http://neptune3.galib.uga.edu/ssp/cgi-bin/legis-idx.pl?sessionid=a2fcf9e1-c2aa17df35-0637&type=law&byte=28076508 (accessed November 24, 2008).

34. "Notices from Milledgeville, *Savannah Daily Morning News*, November 22, 1853.

35. *Augusta Chronicle*, November 24, 1853, p. 2, col. 4.

36. *Augusta Chronicle*, June 13, 1863, p. A2, cols. 2–3.

37. T. Conn Bryan, *Confederate Georgia* (Athens: University of Georgia Press, 1953), 185. See also Clifford L. Smith, *History of Troup County* (Atlanta: Foote and Davies Company, 1933), 75; and Chris R. Cleaveland, "Georgia's Nancy Harts," *Civil War Times Illustrated* 33, no. 2 (1994): 44–45. For a much more melodramatic telling of the story, see "'Nancy Harts' of the Confederacy" *Confederate Veteran* 30, no. 12 (1922): 465–66.

38. See William Bacon Stevens, *A History of Georgia*, 2 vols. (Philadelphia: E. H. Butler, 1859).

39. Sherwood first published his *Gazetteer of Georgia* in 1827; see Adiel Sherwood, *A Gazateer of the state of Georgia* (facsimile ed., Athens: University of Georgia Press, 1939). Neither it nor the second or third editions made any reference to Hart.

40. Adiel Sherwood, *A Gazetteer of Georgia*, 4th ed. (Macon: S. Boykin, 1860), 79.

41. Charles C. Jones Jr., *Revolutionary Epoch*, vol. 2 of *The History of Georgia* (Boston: Houghton, Mifflin and Company, 1883), 463. For biographical information on Jones see Vicki G. Proefrock, "Historical Sketch of Charles Colcock Jones, Jr.," *Richmond County History* 15, no. 1 (1983): 9–18.

42. *Augusta Chronicle*, June 25, 1886, p. 4, col. 1.

43. See Coulter, "Nancy Hart," 139.

44. "Was Nancy Hart a Creature of Romance?" *Atlanta Journal*, October 9, 1901.

45. George Gillman Smith, *The Story of Georgia and The Georgia People* (Macon: G. G. Smith, 1900), 190–91.

46. "Was Nancy Hart a Creature of Romance?"; "The Original Story of Nancy Hart," *Atlanta Journal*, October 12, 1901.

47. The journalist Bill Osinski first suggested this connection in a May 11, 1997, article in the *Atlanta Journal-Constitution*, G3.

48. E. J. Brooks to Joel Chandler Harris, November 24, 1887, Joel Chandler Harris Collection, Subseries 1.2, Box 2, Folder 9, Robert W. Woodruff Library, Emory University, Decatur, Georgia.

49. Joel Chandler Harris, *Stories of Georgia* (New York: 1896; Atlanta: Cherokee Publishing Company, 1971), 3–4. See also Joel Chandler Harris, *Georgia: From the Invasion of De Soto to Recent Times* (New York: D. Appleton and Company, 1896). The minimally edited, longhand manuscript of these identical works may be found in the Joel Chandler Harris Collection, Series 2, Box OP10, Folders 6–13, Robert W. Woodruff Library, Emory University, Decatur, Georgia.

50. Harris, *Stories of Georgia*, 69, 73. The entire section on Hart runs from pages 69 to 83.

51. Paul M. Cousins, *Joel Chandler Harris* (Baton Rouge: Louisiana State University Press, 1968), 176.

52. Joel Chandler Harris, "The Kidnapping of President Lincoln," in *On the Wing of Occasions* (Curtis Publishing Company, 1899; New York: Doubleday, Page and Company, 1904), 136, 138–39.

53. Cousins, *Joel Chandler Harris*, 208–16.

54. Ibid., 208.

55. Joel Chandler Harris, *Qua: A Romance of the Revolution*, ed. Thomas H. English (Atlanta: The Library, Emory University, 1946). In the novel, Harris has one scene at "Aunt Nancy's cabin" (63) and originally included a four-paragraph tribute to Hart, but later cut it, thinks English, for narrative purposes (67n).

56. Michael E. Price, *Stories with a Moral: Literature and Society in Nineteenth-Century Georgia* (Athens: University of Georgia Press, 2000), 248; and Wayne Mixon, "Joel Chandler Harris, the Yeoman Tradition, and the New South Movement," *Georgia Historical Quarterly* 61, no. 4 (1977): 309–10.

57. Price, *Stories with a Moral*, 243, 248, 262.

58. For connections between Harris, Grady, and Knight, see Evelyn Ward Gay, *Lucian Lamar Knight, the Story of One Man's Dream* (New York: Vantage, 1967), 17, 51, 58–66, 98, 252, 253.

59. Lucian Lamar Knight, *Reminiscences of Famous Georgians* (Atlanta: Franklin-Turner, 1907), 1:vi.

60. A third-hand remembrance given in the 1960s put Knight's opinion of Jones's work this way: "There was something lacking in each book he read. The realm of human interest stories interwoven into the dull galaxy of cold historical fact had scarcely been touched upon. Many interesting little personal experiences, small details of momentous events in the past life of the state" were waiting to be uncovered and "spread upon the written page for their children and grandchildren and great-grandchildren to enjoy and retell with each succeeding generation." See Gay, *Lucian Lamar Knight*, 79, 493n23.

61. Knight, *Reminiscences*, 2:37–42.

62. See Lucian Lamar Knight, *Georgia's Landmarks, Memorial, and Legends* (Atlanta: For the Author by the Byrd Printing, 1914), 1:671–74, 674n; Knight, *A Standard History of Georgia and Georgians* (Chicago: Lewis Publishing, 1917), 1:295–97, 3:1448, 4:2254; Knight, *Georgia's Bi-Centennial Memoirs and Memories* ([Atlanta]: Published by the Author for Private Distribution, 1932), 120–23.

63. Thomas E. Watson, Hoke Smith, and Joseph M. Brown, all contemporary Georgia politicians of Knight's time, as well as Professor Joseph S. Stewart, chair of the committee that recommended books to state schools, among others, all praised the book. See Gay, *Lucian Lamar Knight*, 240, 244–47.

64. Two histories written after Harris's *Georgia Stories* but before Knight's *Reminiscences* included fairly mild retellings of the capture story and some of the other stories. See Lawton Evans, *A History of Georgia for Use in Schools* (1898; New York: American Book Company, 1908), 117–19; and Frances Letcher Mitchell, *Georgia Land and People* (Atlanta: Franklin Printing and Publishing, 1900), 104–408. Evans gave Hart a somewhat more prominent place in an updated version of *A History of Georgia* in 1913 and in a 1932 Georgia bicentennial tribute entitled *All about Georgia*. See Evans, *First Lessons in Georgia History* (New York: American Book Company, 1913), 173–77; and Evans, *All About Georgia* (New York: American Book Company, [1933]), 34–35. Both of the former two also included a visual rendering of the capture story. G. G. Smith had, of course, also presented his mild rendering of Hart in 1900. The only significant rendering of Nancy Hart after Harris but

before Knight was produced by Joseph Harris Chappell but most likely for reasons to do more with the work of DAR than the writings of Joel Chandler Harris. After *Reminiscences* almost every work for the next four decades gave the Hart stories a prominent place and few expressed any skepticism. See the following: J. E. D. Shipp, *Giant Times or The Life and Times of William H. Crawford* (Americus, Ga.: Southern Printers, 1909), 17–21; William J. Northen, *Men of Mark in Georgia* (Atlanta: A. B. Caldwell), 2:111–19; Sophie Lee Foster, *Revolutionary Reader: Reminiscences and Indian Legends* (Atlanta: Byrd Printing, 1913), 252–55; Anna Maria Green Cook, *History of Baldwin County* (Anderson, S.C.: Keys-Hearn Printing, 1925), 153–66; Clark Howell, *History of Georgia* (Chicago: S. J. Clarke Publishing, 1926), 404; Margaret Davis Cate, *Our Todays and Yesterdays*, rev. ed. (Brunswick, Ga.: Glover Bros., 1930), 184–86; John William Baker, *History of Hart County* (Atlanta: Foote and Davies, 1933), 24–31; Walter G. Cooper, *The Story of Georgia* (New York: American Historical Society, 1938), 2:33–40 (the sketch of Hart in Cooper's work was written by Juanita Helm Floyd, great-great-granddaughter of Nancy Hart); Amanda Johnson, *Georgia as Colony and State* (Atlanta: Walter W. Brown Publishing, [1938]), 160–61; John H. McIntosh, *The Official History of Elbert County, 1790–1935* (1940; Atlanta: Cherokee Publishing, 1968), 17–22; and Louise Frederick Hays, *Hero of Hornet's Nest: A Biography of Elijah Clark[e]* (New York: Stratford House, 1946), 82–85.

65. Edna Arnold Copeland, *Nancy Hart the War Woman* (Elberton, Ga.: Published by the Author, 1950). Copeland had previously written many newspaper articles about Hart. See, for instance, Edna Arnold Copeland, "The Nancy Harts of LaGrange," *Atlanta Constitution Magazine*, August 24, 1930. In her book, Copeland provided no citations and no bibliography; she retold the stories complete with elaborate, but clearly invented, dialogue.

66. Anastatia Sims, *The Power of Femininity in the New South: Women's Organizations and Politics in North Carolina, 1880–1930* (Columbia: University of South Carolina Press, 1997), 130–36.

67. Cook, *History of Baldwin County*, 153–55. See also *Centennial Year Celebration, 1900–2000* (Milledgeville, Ga.: Nancy Hart Chapter of the National Society Daughters of the American Revolution, 2000).

68. See note 64.

69. Loula Kendall Rogers, "A True History of Nancy Hart," and Mrs. J. M. Bosworth, "Story of Nancy Hart Is Pure Fiction, Says Man Who Hunted Her Home," *Atlanta Journal*, October 14, 1901; Mrs. T. M. Green, "Did Bacon Write Shakespeare? and Is Nancy Hart a Myth?" and Kate Robson, "Nancy Hart Not a Myth" and "Nancy Hart's Spinning Wheel," *Atlanta Journal*, October 19, 1901; Mrs. W. H. Felton, "Was Nancy Hart a Myth?" *Atlanta Journal*, October 30, 1901. Smith replied, largely unrepentant, on October 28 to these attacks. He acknowledged the reality of the person of Hart, but largely blamed White for making her so heroic ("Historian Smith Talks of Nancy Hart Again," *Atlanta Journal*, October 28, 1901).

70. "Was Nancy Hart a Creature of Romance?" See also *Acts and Resolutions of the General Assembly of the State of Georgia, 1976*, 1:1502, available from the Galileo Scholar database, http://neptune3.galib.uga.edu/ssp/cgi-bin/legis-idx.pl?sessionid=a2fcf9e1-c2aa17df75-0492&type=law&byte=367161452 (accessed November 24, 2008).

71. *Augusta Chronicle*, October 28, 1913, p. A5, cols. 5–6, December 21, 1913, p. B4, col. 6, and February 12, 1911, p. B4, col. 4. In *Atlanta Constitution*, see "Nancy Hart Boulder Unveiled by D.A.R.," March 29, 1928; "D.A.R. Co-Chairmen Stress Work Done on the Nancy Hart Highway," December 30, 1928; "U.S. Senate Passes Bill for Tablet to Nancy Hart," February 20, 1929; "Nancy Hart Marker Contract Awarded," June 7, 1931; Mrs. Stewart P. Colley, "Marking of Nancy Hart Highway Is Completed by Georgia D.A.R.," September 27, 1931; "Nancy Hart Shaft Will Be Unveiled," November 8,

1931; "Nancy Hart Marker," November 10, 1931; "Georgians to Honor Nancy Hart Today," November 11, 1931; "Nancy Hart, Heroine of Revolutionary War, Is Eulogized at Unveiling of Monument," November 12, 1931. The DAR even managed to get Senator Richard Russell to speak at the November 11 unveiling of the marker. For legislative actions relating to the highway and the markers see *Congressional Record: Proceedings and Debates of the Third Session of the 71st Congress of the United States of America* (Washington, D.C.: Government Printing Office, 1931), 74: pt. 5, 5068–70; and *Senate Documents, Miscellaneous*, 71st Congress, Third Session, Document No. 290 (Washington, D.C.: Government Printing Office, 1931). For other markers and DAR activities see "Home Site of Nancy Hart Presented to State D.A.R.," March 31, 1932, and "Bronze Marker to Nancy Hart to Be Unveiled," June 1, 1941, both in *Atlanta Constitution*; and *Chapter Histories, Daughters of the American Revolution in Georgia*, comp. Mrs. Herbert Fay Baker and Mrs. Bun Wylie (Augusta, Ga.: Ridgely-Tidwell Company, 1932), 155–58. See also *History of the Georgia State Society of the National Society of the Daughters of the American Revolution, 1899–1981*, ed. and comp. Mrs. Leonard G. DeLamar and Mrs. Jerido Ward (Roswell, Ga.: Georgia State Society, DAR, 1982).

72. See Coulter, "Nancy Hart," 140–41.

73. For accounts of the ceremony see "D.A.R. Gives Historic Painting to the State," *Atlanta Constitution*, November 27, 1916, and "Historic Painting Presented to State," *Atlanta Constitution*, December 3, 1916. For Knight's speech see Knight, *Memorials of Dixie-land* (Atlanta: Byrd Printing Company, 1919), 260–70.

74. Gay, *Lucian Lamar Knight*, 308–10.

75. *Acts and Resolutions of the General Assembly of the State of Georgia, 1916*, pt. 4, *Resolutions*, 1:1049, available from the Galileo Scholar database, http://neptune3.galib.uga.edu/ssp/cgi-bin/legis-idx.pl?sessionid=acf1fee2-ceab15d206-1027&type=law&byte=127134459 (accessed November 24, 2008).

76. *Augusta Chronicle*, July 12, 1902, p. A1, cols. 1–2, September 3, 1902, p. A4, col. 3, and July 5, 1903, p. A2, col. 4. For biographical information about Felton see John Erwin Talmadge, *Rebecca Latimer Felton, Nine Stormy Decades* (Athens: University of Georgia Press, 1960). For Felton's interview about Hart, see Rebecca Felton Latimer, *The Romantic Story of Georgia Women* (Atlanta: Atlanta *Georgian and Sunday American*, 1930), 8–9.

77. J. T. Hudson, "From Old Methods in Farming to New Agricultural Plans," *Augusta Chronicle*, January 9, 1918. In *Atlanta Constitution*, see Stiles A. Martin, "Nancy Hart, Heroine of 1776, Not 'Cross-eyed and Lanky,'" March 18, 1928; Bernice Brown M'Culler, "Great-Great-Granddaughter of Nancy Hart, Dr. Juanita Floyd, Teacher in Georgia College" and "Nancy Hart in Action, and Her Great-Great Granddaughter, Dr. Floyd," March 16, 1930; Edna Arnold Copeland, "The Nancy Harts of Georgia," August 24, 1930. In *Atlanta Journal Magazine*, see Annie Laurie Fuller Kurtz, "Exploits of Nancy Hart," December 8, 1935, and Herbert Wilcox, "Nancy Wasn't Cross-Eyed," c. 1937. R. C. Brooks, "Nancy Hart—Heroine of the Revolution," *Savannah Morning News*, July 14, 1924. The articles from the *Atlanta Journal Magazine* and the *Savannah Morning News* are available in the Biographical File on Nancy Hart at the Georgia Historical Society, Savannah.

78. Ruby Nell Heaton Bannister, *A Portrayal of Nancy Hart*, ed. Wassie Vickery (Hartwell, Ga.: Sun Press, 1985), 46–47. The hotel opened in 1922 and was closed and demolished in 1964; see Shirley Kaufheld and Tony Bryant, eds., *The Hart of Georgia: A History of Hart County* (Alpharetta, Ga.: Savannah River Genealogical Society, 1992), 623. For the horse, see the *Augusta Chronicle*, September 26, 1906 p. A10, col. 4.

79. *Atlanta Constitution*, December 22, 1912.

80. See Coulter, "Nancy Hart," 138. After extensive efforts, no recording of the Nancy Hart program could be located; it may no longer exist.

81. *Hartwell Sun*, May 1, 8, 15, 22, and 29, June 5, 12, and 19, 1953. See also *Atlanta Constitution*, June 2, 3, 4, 5, and 8, 1953.

82. E. Merton Coulter's books include *William G. Brownlow, Fighting Parson of the Southern Highlands* (Chapel Hill: University of North Carolina Press, 1937), *Thomas Spalding of Sapelo* (University: Louisiana State University Press, 1940), and *John Jacob Flournoy, Champion of the Common Man in the Antebellum South* (Savannah: Georgia Historical Society, 1942).

83. See Michael Vaughan Woodward, "E. Merton Coulter and the Art of Biography," *Georgia Historical Quarterly* 64, no. 2 (1980): 160; and Michael Vaughan Woodward, "Ellis Merton Coulter and the Southern Historiographic Tradition" (PhD diss., University of Georgia, 1982), 37.

84. Coulter, "Nancy Hart," 150–51.

85. See, for instance, Marjory Rutherford, "Nancy Hart's Musket and Tongue Took Toll," *Atlanta Constitution*, April 18, 1961; and Milton Ready, "Is It True What They Say about Nancy?" *Atlanta Journal Constitution Magazine*, October 21, 1973. In *Atlanta Journal and Constitution*, see Helen C. Smith, "Nancy Hart: Bane of the British," April 11, 1976; Mike Christensen, "Nancy Hart Legend," May 30, 1976; Myra Vanderpool Gormley, "Some Yankee Doodle Mandys," July 4, 1984; Bob Harrell, "Hart County Native Protects the History of Nancy Hart," May 5, 1985; Donna Lorenz, "Remarkable Georgia Women," March 1, 1994; Kent Mitchell, "News for an Active Lifestyle Go for It! Weekend Getaway Hart Offers Access to Camping, Boating," May 20, 1994; Bill Osinski, "Main Street," May 11, 1997; Joe Murray, "Traversing the South: Harwell a Gold Mine of Stories," March 25, 1998; and Gabriella Boston, "DeKalb's History Comes to Life at Society's Log Cabin Hour," July 2, 1998. See also "Atlanta Weekly," *Atlanta Journal and Constitution*, October 21, 1973. The *Augusta Chronicle* and the *Hartwell Sun* during this period have extensive articles on and references to Nancy Hart as well. See also Edna Arnold Copeland, "Nancy Hart—a Revolutionary Heroine," *Georgia Magazine* 8, no. 5 (1965): 30–31; Janet Harvill Standard, *Georgians of Distinction* (Washington, Ga.: Published by the Author, 1966); Howell Lee, "Fryer in Tradition of Strong Women Leaders," *Georgia Trend* 13, no. 6 (1998): 36; and Criselda Valdez Villarreal, "History-Making Performance," *Brownsville Herald*, March 3, 2004.

86. See, respectively, *Centennial Year Celebration*, and Janet Harvill Standard, *This Man, This Woman* (Washington, Ga.: Wilkes Publishing, 1968).

87. For the local artwork, See Bannister, *Portrayal*, 46–47. The General Assembly of Georgia designated a set of twelve historical plates in 1974 to commemorate the two-hundredth anniversary of the founding of the state. Among these twelve was one showing "Nancy Hart capturing the Tories." See *Acts and Resolutions of the General Assembly of the State of Georgia, 1974*, 1:13, available from the Galileo Scholar database, http://neptune3.galib.uga.edu/ssp/cgi-bin/legis-idx .pl?sessionid=acf1fee2-ceab15d297-8693&type=law&byte=343324059 (accessed November 24, 2008). *National Geographic* featured Hart as part of bicentennial story: Lonnelle Aikman, "Patriots in Petticoats," *National Geographic* 148, no. 4 (1975): 474–93. Aikman took a driving tour of a variety of sites associated with famous Revolutionary women, including Nancy Hart. The Hart part of her trip brought her to Hart County, where she was given a tour by E. Merton Coulter. Aikman, commenting on the capture story she was about to tell, wrote that it had "chilling credibility as an example of the civil strife that ravaged the South late in the war" (488). Pages 490–91 consist of a dramatic color drawing of the capture story by Louis S. Glanzman, who provided original illustrations for the entire article. The caption of the drawing also makes mention of the crazy spy and the river crossing stories.

88. See, for instance, Bernice McCullar, *This Is Your Georgia* (Northport, Ala.: American Southern Publishing, 1966), 264–84 (McCuller had a television show entitled *This Is Your Georgia*, out of which this book grew, meaning she probably did a television spot on Nancy Hart); Robert S. Davis Jr. and Kenneth H. Thomas Jr., *Kettle Creek: The Battle of the Cane Brakes* ([Atlanta]: State of Georgia Department of Natural Resources, Office of Planning, Research, and Historic Preservation Section, 1974), 76–77; Robert Scott Davis, *Kettle Creek Battle and Battlefield* (Washington, Ga.: Wilkes Publishing, 1978), 22–23; *Historic Georgia Mothers, 1776–1976* (n.p.: Georgia Mothers Association, 1976), 42–43; Webb Garrison, *A Treasury of Georgia Tales* (Nashville: Rutledge Hill Press, 1987), 41–43; Pam Wilson, "Nancy Morgan Hart," in Kaufheld and Bryant, *The Hart of Georgia*, 17–20; Vickie Lewis, *Side-by-Side: A Photographic History of American Women in War* (New York: Stewart, Tabori, and Chang, 1999), 12, 14, 16–17; and *Georgia in the American Revolution: An Exhibition from the Library and Museum Collections of the Society of the Cincinnati* (Washington, D.C.: Society of the Cincinnati, 2003), 16–17.

89. Bannister, *Portrayal*, passim. Bannister as "Nancy Hart" even received an autograph from the then Atlanta Braves manager Joe Torre at Atlanta Fulton-County Stadium; see p. 59 for the Torre picture. See also *Hartwell Sun*, 23 December 23, 1982, and January 6, 20, and 27, 1983.

90. See, for instance, "Nancy Morgan Hart," http://www.geocities.com/Heartland/Meadows/6651 (accessed November 24, 2008).

91. Kenneth Coleman, *The American Revolution in Georgia* (Athens: University of Georgia Press, 1958), 132.

92. James C. Bonner, *The Georgia Story* (Oklahoma City: Harlow Publishing Corporation, 1958), 116–17.

93. Harold H. Martin, *Georgia: A Bicentennial History* (New York: W. W. Norton, 1977); Stephen Gurr, *Military History, 1776–1782* ([Atlanta]: Georgia Commission for the National Bicentennial and Georgia Department of Education, 1974), 14; and Ronald Killion and Charles T. Waller, *Georgia and the Revolution* (Atlanta: Cherokee Publishing, 1975), 56, 77–79. Killion and Waller used such qualifying statements as "tradition records" and acknowledged that Georgia's backcountry war "gave rise to a treasure trove of legends."

94. Edwin L. Jackson, Mary E. Stakes, Lawrence R. Hepburn, and Mary A. Hepburn, eds., *The Georgia Studies Book* (Athens: University of Georgia, Carl Vinson Institute of Government, 1992), 124–25; Bonita Bullard London, *Georgia: The History of an American State* (Atlanta: Clairmont Press, 1999), 140–41; and Albert B. Saye, *Georgia: History and Government*, rev. ed. (Austin, Tex.: Steck-Vaughn Company, 1982), 57; Saye devoted one sentence to Hart.

95. Kenneth Coleman, "Part Two: 1775–1820," in *A History of Georgia*, ed. Kenneth Coleman, 2nd ed. (Athens: University of Georgia Press, 1991), 85.

96. Ben Marsh, "Women and the American Revolution in Georgia," *Georgia Historical Quarterly* 88, no. 2 (2004), 171.

97. Ibid., 178.

98. *Atlanta Journal Constitution*, May 11, 1997.

# Elizabeth Lichtenstein Johnston

## (1764–1848)

## *"Shot Round the World but Not Heard"*

BEN MARSH

❀ ❀ ❀

"No one could possibly claim," explained Rev. Arthur Wentworth Eaton in his 1901 preface, that Elizabeth Johnston and her *Recollections* "are of very wide historical or even biographical interest." She did not fire any cannons or act heroically, did not enter into personal correspondence with great figures, did not influence the course of political events, or in any other way stake a claim to historical significance. Indeed, Eaton felt the need to justify her significance through her progeny, reeling off a long chain of her descendants who had subsequently held weighty positions in Canada—chief justices and Supreme Court judges, reverends, senators, and physicians "of the highest professional and social standing."[1] Now, more than a century after Eaton's pronouncement, scholars have successfully challenged the kinds of assumptions and biases in his definition of what constitutes "interesting" history. Reaching out beyond the high-profile powerful men has brought immense rewards in better understanding the everyday workings of societies in the past: their organization, their interior values, their evolution—in short, their history. The rich rewards to be gained from this widening of historical and biographic "interest" are often hard earned and contested, mined, as they must be, from limited deposits in the historical record. Historians of women, gender, families, and households in the colonial South first struck on quantitative sources to explore social relationships and have since been meticulously panning and filtering qualitative sources—diaries, letters, and wills, among others—in search of answers to a host of questions about the nature of early southern family life, women's roles in society, and the significance of gender and sexuality to individual and communal identities.[2] Placed in the context of this new scholarship, Elizabeth Johnston's *Recollections* can tell us much about the shifting social boundaries of life in colonial and revolutionary Georgia.

Johnston was seventy-two years old in 1836 when, principally for her grand-children, she wrote her memoirs, which comprised a loose narrative inter-spersed with retrospective observations and memorable vignettes. To these eleven chapters, three of which were devoted to her youth in Georgia, she ap-pended a set of precious family letters dated between 1769 and 1784. She chose the title *Recollections of a Georgia Loyalist,* a notable statement of identity in light of her residency in Nova Scotia from 1806 until her death in Halifax in 1848.[3] This indicated that Johnston carried with her for the rest of her life, like thousands of her contemporaries, the physical and psychological traumas of the American Revolution. Of all the groups touched by the Revolution, migrant Loyalist women (whether white or black) arguably experienced the most radi-cal transformation in their life prospects. On top of the widespread dislocation wrought by war, Loyalists were more likely than others to experience periods as fugitives or forced migration, to endure close association with a transient military (complete with physical, sexual, and epidemiological dangers), to come under legal pressures about their status and rights, and to suffer separation from family and institutional support mechanisms.[4] Had the Revolution never hap-pened, Elizabeth Johnston might have reasonably expected, given her back-ground, to go on to become a plantation mistress, socialite, and slave owner in Georgia. But things were different in Nova Scotia, with many more free blacks than slaves, courtesy of the manumission and relocation policies adopted by self-interested British authorities during the War for Independence. When Johnston alighted at Annapolis Royal in the 1800s, the baggage carters working at the dock included one such freed black, a Rose Fortune, who reportedly held a monopoly in the local trucking business, charged modest prices, and wore "a white cap with the strings tied under her chin, surmounted by a man's hat . . . a man's coat, a short skirt and high legged boots."[5] For better or worse, some thirty thousand Loyalists, including the Fortunes and the Johnstons, would ul-timately have to start lives afresh as "pioneers" in Nova Scotia, a long way from the homes and the futures that might have been theirs.

Elizabeth Johnston, née Lichtenstein (or anglicized as Lightenstone), was born ten miles or so from Savannah, on the Little Ogeechee River, on May 28, 1764. Her parentage reflected the diverse origins of Georgia's fledgling population, for since the colony's founding and in spite of its problematic infancy during the trusteeship (1732–52), immigrants had been arriving from across the Atlantic world. In the year of her birth, the population was only around fifteen thousand, but it would double in size by the time she reached her teens, as newcomers

ELIZABETH LICHTENSTEIN JOHNSTON
Courtesy of Hargrett Rare Book and Manuscript
Library, University of Georgia Libraries.

poured in—most of them now from other British American colonies—seeking cheap, profitable, and fertile lands either for plantation agriculture along the low country or for subsistence farming further west.[6] Elizabeth's father, Johann Lichtenstein (hereinafter John Lightenstone), was himself born half a world away in the Russian seaport town of Kronstadt, where his father, a Protestant minister, ran an academy.[7] This seafaring background served Lightenstone well, enabling him to gain employment as a scout-boat pilot for the royal government that took over the administration of Georgia in 1752.[8] Elizabeth's mother was Catherine Delegal, a woman of French Huguenot stock whose father, Philip Delegal, had left South Carolina in 1736 as an ensign in a company under the command of James Oglethorpe that established a fort at the southern tip of St. Simons Island.[9] Elizabeth's bloodline was thus an odd commingling of peoples set in motion by upheavals in Europe, but converging on the rich prospects of British America's southern frontier.

The common connection between these peoples was their strong, shared commitment to devout Protestantism, an influence that subsequently dominated Elizabeth's worldview throughout her life, and that she herself characterized as her "knowledge of the truth of His Holy Word."[10] When aged just seven, Elizabeth received a letter from her grandparents in Peterhof recommending to her "thy blessed Saviour" for a "pretty companion and a true friend," and urging her to trace his footsteps. Two years earlier, in 1769, the pair had written a warm letter to her mother, imploring her that "Betsey . . . be bred up in the fear and love of God." The grandparents had obviously been hugely moved by the short letters they had received from their unknown new family in Georgia, and, delighted at the "Christian-like sentiments" of Catherine Delegal, responded expressively in the language of affection and tenderness. Elizabeth's maternal grandparents were more visible presences in her life in Georgia, and equally supportive of her early quest for spiritual literacy: she recalled that Philip Delegal in particular was "extremely fond of reading."[11]

The fact that Elizabeth's relatives were literate, enlightened transatlantic correspondents reflected their professional backgrounds and respectable social status—she was born into a genteel world that celebrated bonds of kinship, learning, and the Protestant faith. Few of the early white settlers who had been sent over "on the charity," and none of the enslaved Africans whose presence had been authorized since 1751, enjoyed such advantages upon their arrival to the province. Moreover, John Lightenstone was able to ascend the socioeconomic pyramid of late colonial Georgia with relative speed, thanks to the patronage and influence of both his father-in-law, Philip Delegal, and Georgia governor James Wright, whom Lightenstone ferried around the low country in fulfillment of his government duties as commander of the scout boat. Lightenstone's responsibilities were quite varied. Besides transporting public officers, they apparently included protecting remote families from Indian attack and enforcing quarantine regulations by confining incoming slave ships suspected of infectious diseases (such as smallpox) to Tybee Island, about seventeen miles downriver of Savannah. His expanding responsibilities and frequent absences prompted the Lightenstones to move from Elizabeth's birthplace on the Little Ogeechee—where the Delegal family held considerable lands—to suburban Yamacraw when Elizabeth was an infant. John Lightenstone was awarded a land grant of two hundred acres on the Sapelo River (in the south of the province) in March 1767, but Elizabeth saw little if any of these lands, for he shortly relocated his family to a plantation on Skidaway Island, "a very pleasant place upon the water."[12]

Such migrations were common among settlers as they adapted to changing conditions in the colony, jostling for opportunities and acreage in an unfamiliar environment. Like many of their contemporaries of middling to high status, the Lightenstones also came to maintain a house in the growing market center of Savannah, probably residing there according to season. But they spent most of their country residence on Skidaway, an island largely owned by Philip Delegal. Elizabeth had fond memories of being a young girl enjoying the idyllic delights of Skidaway in the 1760s, with its abundant figs, peaches, pomegranates, plums, mulberries, nectarines, and oranges. She also recalled that the finest varieties of fish and shellfish were "easily procured in plenty," and that, as an only child, she occupied her leisure hours among the trees, the rivers, and the animals.

From an early age, Elizabeth was also surrounded by slaves. Her father apparently owned three bondspeople outright according to his land grant application of 1766, but, thanks to his marital connections, was soon more heavily involved in slave ownership and plantation management. The fertile lands on Skidaway were used partly to raise provisions "for his family and people," chiefly Indian corn and sweet potatoes. Land was also devoted to the production of the dye indigo—one of the key products of the slave economy of the mid-eighteenth century low country.[13] An advertisement posted by John Lightenstone in the *Georgia Gazette* during the spring of 1767 provided evidence of the continuing connections between the Lightenstones' slaveholding and the Delegal family in Elizabeth's formative years:

> Taken or lost, for the Subscriber, about the 14th February last, off or near the plantation of Philip Delegal, Esq. A NEW NEGROE WENCH

Stout and tall, about 30 years old, speaks no English, has her country marks upon her body, had on when she went away white negroe cloth cloaths. Whoever takes her up, or can give any intelligence of her to the subscriber, so that he may have her, shall have 20s. reward.—There is a great reason to think the Indians have carried her off.

The period of Elizabeth's childhood was a significant turning point in Georgia's involvement in the Atlantic slave trade, as Savannah merchants graduated from purchasing a minority of their slaves directly from West Africa (ca. 1755–67) to purchasing an overwhelming majority (ca. 1768–71) from there. But immersion in the complex world of exploitative race relations appears to have made little impression on Elizabeth—or at least, little impression that she wanted to share. Only rarely, and casually, did she engage with the subject of slavery in her *Recollections*. These passing references largely overlooked the traumas and depredations of the institution, and incidents such as the above escape (or kidnapping) reported by her father. Instead, when Johnston dealt with bondspeople, she characterized them as "servants" and described them as "greatly attached to the family."[14]

But while Johnston retrospectively sanitized her *Recollections,* allowing slavery to fade into the black-ground, at the time she must have been acutely conscious of the significance of bondspeople to her life in Georgia, Jamaica, and beyond. In her correspondence she openly discussed her father-in-law's sale of his "negroes" in 1784, commenting that he had received many inquiries from Charleston in the aftermath of the Revolutionary War, as opportunistic developers sought to do business with emigrants.[15] Contemporary letters also made clear that her onerous childcare responsibilities were shared with an enslaved nurse named Hagar, something that Elizabeth left hazy in the *Recollections* themselves.[16] In spite of these conscious efforts to marginalize the influence of bondspeople on her history (and vice versa), Elizabeth Johnston inadvertently offered up evidence that the institution of slavery gnawed at the subconscious worlds of elite white women: when her daughter Catharine was given eighty drops of laudanum to quiet an illness, Elizabeth described the violent delirium that was induced as "a dreadful state, thinking that there was an insurrection of the slaves, that they had set fire to the house, and that the bed she lay on was in flames." She also drew attention, indirectly, to the more leisurely and luxurious lifestyle that Georgia plantation mistresses could afford, by having slaves perform everyday chores. Beyond the slave societies of the low country and the Caribbean, Elizabeth and her daughters had to develop new skills and new strategies, for "it was thought a great indulgence if the mistress had no more labor than to have the fag [supervision] of all the children" on the grand event of the fortnightly wash day; gone were the "habits and comforts of a lady."[17]

That Elizabeth Johnston developed and sustained these views about Africans and African American slaves is testament to the speed and the power with which social models were implanted into the cultural fabric of late colonial Georgia. With the arrival of bondspeople in large numbers from the 1750s, and the legal and economic framework of plantation slavery, came a whole host of societal controls that instilled new behavioral expectations upon the low country population—black or white, wealthy or poor. Elizabeth Johnston was among the first generation of Georgians born into such a system, but its formula was well tested, and had already proved tragically effective, in older colonies—and especially in South Carolina, where many of Georgia's new settlers originated, including Elizabeth's maternal family. Plantation societies were able to be remarkably resilient, in spite of their structural weaknesses, because they relied heavily on the conditioning of ideas about race and gender. Indeed, until relatively recently, historians took few pains to separate the colonial from the antebellum eras in their considerations of American slavery, because the institution, its regions, and its products seemed somehow timeless and amorphous.[18] So it is worth remembering that Elizabeth Johnston's views on slavery were closer to most elite white Georgians' views a century *after* her birth than they were a decade or so *before* it. What were their hallmarks? Put bluntly: that it was ladylike to own slaves but not to discuss them; that blacks were predominantly labor-saving devices; that they were ostensibly loyal but potentially insidious; that they were capable of limited independent agency. Significantly lacking in Johnston's views, though arguably more apparent among southern slaveholders in the antebellum era, were any emphasis on paternalism or "benevolent" slave ownership, any consideration of the religiosity of slaves, and any semblance of "gender affinity" with African American females. For Johnston, a common biological sex could never straddle the differences embodied in color, for gender was always racialized: "I was much exhausted in mind and body," she complained about life as a young mother, "having no female . . . with me, only black servants."[19]

Elizabeth Johnston's cold, emotionless depiction of those outside of her recognized social orbit contrasted dramatically with the warmth she expressed and devotion she showed to those inside it, particularly her family. In her childhood, she recalled that both of her parents read to her and stimulated her interests, though the literature that she apparently enjoyed, which included Gilbert West's 1747 *Observations on the history and evidence of the resurrection of Jesus Christ,* was some way removed from the more romantic mainstream titles being digested by her contemporaries. An only child, Elizabeth was extremely close to her mother, and at age seven "Betsey" protested at being separated to such an extent that she was allowed, at the very last minute, to depart with her on a trip to Philadelphia. Unbeknownst to Elizabeth this would be the first of dozens of oceangoing voyages over the course of her life, though in none other was her wardrobe quite so improvised, courtesy of kind "ladies offering to assist in cutting over some of my mother's clothes for me."[20] Catherine Delegal Lightenstone's summer voyage to cooler climes was intended to alleviate her poor health, but her malaria-style afflictions continued, and, "much regretted" in the *Georgia Gazette,* she died on Skidaway in August 1774 when Elizabeth was aged ten.[21] Motherhood was fragile, even for those of relatively high status, in a colony that had become internationally renowned for its orphans, and where black children were routinely separated from their parents.[22] Elizabeth felt her "beloved and tender" mother's loss keenly, for it heralded a transformation in her upbringing. Gone were the idyllic days on Skidaway Island, as she was sent to live with a great-aunt at her plantation on the mainland, ominously named Mount Piety.

With hindsight, Elizabeth saw some divine purpose in her mother's death, implying that as a child she might have been overindulged and underdisciplined. But by contemporary standards her early education was robust, and the Lightenstone parenting was significantly a team affair. On one occasion, Betsey remembered that she defied her mother by trying to beat their cat, because it had opportunistically eaten her bird. The misbehavior spread: when Catherine threatened to "correct" Betsey, the little girl evaded her and took refuge up a large tree, refusing to come down. Any smugness quickly evaporated, however, when Betsey witnessed (from presumably an excellent vantage point) her father returning home, and she remembered that "I was soon out of the tree and seated in the parlor."[23] Elizabeth's upbringing coincided with a wider shift in Anglo-American parenting that some have characterized as a transition from "patriarchy" to "paternalism," or from a rawer form of authoritarian power to a more reasoned, consensual style of authority.[24] Johnston's writings about the family resounded with the themes of discipline *with* affection, of duty *with* love. As Elizabeth remarked of her fond father, John: "I loved him, yet I always from a child had an awe of him."[25] Such pairings of virtues complicated familial relationships, but also strengthened them. Strict generational deference helped underwrite the low country elite's claims to wider authority, and in Georgia the American Revolution would challenge both.[26]

Three influences shaped Elizabeth's education as a young girl in the 1770s: her father, her great-aunt, and formal classes at the finest schools that Savannah offered. The extent and the quality of private schooling for young females in late colonial Savannah varied.[27] Supply in the form of specialist tutors was initially rather eclectic and peripatetic, but the demand side of the equation was soon large enough to attract enterprising teachers to advertise their subjects, methods, and institutions to wealthy parents. Schoolmistress Elizabeth Bedon, for instance, listed her charges in 1769 at twenty shillings per quarter for day scholars or twenty-five pounds per annum for full boarders.[28] All children at such schools were taught reading, writing, and arithmetic, but beyond those rudimentary skills the curriculum became more gendered. For the young girls of prosperous families, specialization could be pursued in needlework (practical and ornamental), dancing, music, and languages (principally Latin, French, and less commonly Greek).[29] Elizabeth did not enjoy her sewing, to the frustration of her guardian, who cruelly declared her a "botcher at it." But, perhaps unsurprisingly in light of her early start, she excelled in other branches of education and was "always ambitious to be at the head of my class at school." This last comment, in conjunction with her observation that "[o]ur teachers became officers in the rebel army," suggests she may have attended one or the other of the larger schools in Savannah—possibly the mixed academy of Alexander Findlay and James Seymour on Broughton Street, which promised to "bring the rising generation in Georgia to great proficiency in the several branches of literature which they profess to teach" and was examined approvingly by the governor, councilmen, and several prominent scholarly gentlemen in 1770.[30]

Elizabeth Johnston's placid life, divided between the rustic austerity of Mount Piety and her competitive Savannah schooldays, was radically transformed by the onset of the American Revolution. The significance of the event for her was largely social rather than political, and she displayed little interest in the competing ideologies or finer points of constitutional friction. This apparent disinterest reflected her age (just twelve at the signing of the Declaration of Independence) in conjunction with her gender. The intellectual Revolution was held to be a matter for grown-ups and for men, a belief that John Adams articulated in response to his wife Abigail's provocative call to remember the ladies: "their Delicacy renders them unfit for . . . the arduous Cares of State."[31] But a third factor explaining Elizabeth's lightweight treatment of the political conflict was common to a large segment of colonial Americans in the early 1770s, especially outside the northeastern seaboard—described by Benjamin Rush in 1777 as "a great number of persons who were neither Whigs nor Tories."[32] Robert M. Calhoon has estimated that approximately half the colonists of European ancestry tried to avoid involvement in the struggle, most of them "simple apolitical folk."[33] Like many Georgians, Elizabeth's future husband was cautioned by his father, in a letter from Savannah dated August 20, 1774, against "taking any part in the unhappy political disputes . . . be silent on the subject . . . while matters of such consequence are agitating."[34] Leslie Hall has argued that Georgia settlers were only really consistent in their desire for property rights and civil authority, and that many chose to swear allegiance to any politicized group that asked them to do so if it secured their holdings—including lands and, notably, slaves.[35] Elizabeth herself never really explained what motivated the "rebels" to take action in Georgia, falling back on rather vague, passive references to "the spirit of the times" afflicting otherwise "amiable" and "fine" young men such as John Milledge.[36] But through the refracting prism of her memoirs it is possible to discern elements of regionalism and elitism. She felt that people in Georgia were "inflamed" as outside conflicts "began to spread to the southward" after 1774. Moreover, although these "people" included her teachers and the likes of Milledge, she deliberately disparaged them as a "ragged corps," as "the scum [that] rose to the top," an interpretation that was shared even by other Patriots such as the merchant Joseph Clay, who reported in 1777 that Georgia "Government has got into the Hands of those whose ability or situation in Life does not intitle them to it."[37] If there exists a faint suggestion in Johnston's comments that Georgia's revolution was fomented by the lower orders being swept up by New England radicalism, far more apparent is Elizabeth's own bitterness at her family's subsequent victimization. Her American Revolution, like that of thousands of her contemporaries', was not about noble ideas but about hard realities.

By 1776 the actions of local "committees" in Georgia, who monitored adherence to the Continental Association (a trade boycott against the British), were having some effect in polarizing the white population—especially in the backcountry where they had famously tortured and humiliated Thomas Brown.[38] Elizabeth Johnston remembered that armed mobs gathered in Savannah to exact public oaths from everybody, "gentle and simple," and that the consequences of declaring against the association, or for the king, were grave. At one point she preferred to stand away from the window rather than watch a Tory British pilot suffering the indignity of being tarred and feathered and "carried all over the town."[39] As elsewhere, Georgia's Revolutionary movement soon matured beyond traditional crowd protests and economic boycotts, and by the late spring the new faction meeting in Augusta had drafted a rudimentary frame of government, just in time to send delegates to the Philadelphia convention and the signing of the Declaration of Independence (having missed out on the Continental Congress's first two years). By then, most of Georgia's royal governing elites had been arrested or had fled to the British warships that had arrived in the Savannah River in January. Elizabeth's father, John Lightenstone, though surprised while half-shaved and half-dressed, apparently made a dramatic escape by evading a party of Patriot soldiers and sailing his skiff to Tybee Island and the safety of the man-of-war *Scarborough*. Strangely, Lightenstone's bondspeople did not choose to advertise *his* escape from Skidaway. Indeed, Elizabeth reported that one slave, a "sensible, plausible black man, who had been brought up as a pet in my grandfather's house," deliberately engaged the soldiers to delay their search, while Lightenstone grabbed his sails and oars.[40] Lightenstone testified to a British commission investigating Loyalists' claims that he had earlier refused an offer from the rebels to continue as commander of the Georgia scout boat (which they had sequestered), "if he would follow their measures."[41] Lightenstone's unrivalled knowledge of the Georgia seaboard and navigable rivers, his naval and military expertise, his loyalty to the governor who had given him his commission in 1768, and especially this spirited refusal were evidently enough to make him a candidate for arrest.

Georgia remained independent for more than two years, as the Patriots—in spite of the factionalism that pervaded their new republican government—desperately fended off incipient threats from Florida and the backcountry, and sought to maintain control over precarious relations with slaves and Indians. One recurring thorny problem was how to deal with the lands, slaves, and the families of Loyalist émigrés, which could occasion harsh solutions.[42] In August 1778 the Patriot Council of Safety took the radical step of ordering the area along the Ogeechee River cleared of small settlements established by Loyalist wives, because they were providing asylum for their husbands during raids from Florida, passing on intelligence, and giving them "great assistance and help in their plundering schemes."[43] The Patriots employed several methods, including popular harassment, imprisonment, and oaths of neutrality, to control suspected Loyalists and to pressure them to leave Georgia. More common, and less radical, than the breaking up of settlements and the forcible banishment of suspected enemies, was the straightforward confiscation of Loyalists' lands and possessions. An act of attainder in March 1778 allowed the state to sell off the real and personal property of 117 Loyalists attainted of high treason, including that of John Lightenstone. But at some point later in 1778 Philip Delegal, Elizabeth's grandfather, stepped in to protect his family's assets. Against Elizabeth's wishes, for she was still smarting at the humiliating treatment of her father, he drew up a petition on her behalf and had her take it to the Board of Commissioners, whose task it was to assess the confiscated lands. Delegal played his cards effectively: Elizabeth's was an all-female delegation (she was accompanied by an unidentified lady), and the petition emphasized the "orphan condition" that the fourteen-year-old was left in. Georgia authorities, unsure whether or not to impute Loyalist sentiments to the wives, widows, and children of bona fide Loyalist men, and treat them in like fashion, seem to have been rather inconsistent when presented with this paternalistic dilemma. It was one thing to prevent troublesome adult wives from openly abetting Florida Rangers, but when presented with charity cases such as Elizabeth Lightenstone, the commissioners sometimes responded benevolently. "Our property was not sold as was that of many other Loyalists" recalled Elizabeth, noting that "[o]ne or two cases besides mine show that they did give the property to wives and children whose husbands and fathers had been forced away."[44] As enumerated by John Lightenstone in 1784, this property consisted of 381 cultivated acres complete with buildings, indigo vats, crops (corn, peas, and potatoes), fifty-six head of livestock (cattle, sheep, and hogs), and four horses, along with 150 acres of uncultivated land in the northwest of the colony, in Wrightsborough, that had been granted him in 1774.[45] The reason that Lightenstone knew these specifics was that he became reacquainted with his lands when Georgia became the only rebellious state to be officially restored to royal allegiance. Indeed, between December 23 and 28, 1778, Lightenstone actually helped to guide the British army (an assortment of Scottish, Hessian, and Loyalist regiments) up the Savannah River, landing them at an unguarded bluff from which they were able to recapture the city abruptly, and with virtually no casualties, before the New Year.[46]

Largely because of her political alignment, Elizabeth Johnston's account of life in Georgia during the Revolutionary War has been little used by historians, but it offers an invaluable counterpoint to Whiggish historical narratives or popular accounts that tend to foreground the role of white, male Patriots—bolstered by occasional deputy-males such as Nancy Hart. The numbers alone indicate that the story was more complicated, and more interesting, than conventionally assumed.[47] Georgia probably had a higher proportion of Loyalists than any other colony. Almost half of the colony's population was black at the start of the Revolution, and almost half of the whites were female. As we have already established, Johnston was by no means a spokesperson for all of the silent majority on the "wrong" side of political, racial, or gendered divides, but she did provide wide evidence of "the violence with which civil wars are entered upon," and the peculiar dangers and opportunities that were opened up to subaltern groups during the conflict. During the French and American siege of British-held Savannah in October 1779, she remarked on the bravery of "colored children" who ran to snuff out enemy shells' fuses by covering them with sand from the town streets, and who helped to redress the depletion of British ammunition by delivering the spent balls up, receiving "for them seven-pence apiece." People of color had probably also done much of the backbreaking work of digging out the trenches and throwing up the works that protected the British and Loyalist defenders from substantial bombardment during the month-long siege. For Johnston, white female heroics did not manifest themselves in the occasional shooting of Tories, or even Patriots, but in adapting to new circumstances, coping with hardships, and above all protecting the family and its honor—something she described as "the heroism of the mother."[48]

So what was life like for a Loyalist Georgia girl during the messy period of British control in the low country (1779–82)? Elizabeth's memoirs place a strong emphasis on the militarization of society—of a martial transformation in the dynamic of everyday life. The story is a depressingly familiar one at the start of the twenty-first century: British and American troops trying desperately to build on a successful invasion, to pacify a semi-armed and highly mobile civilian population, and to politically unify a disinterested and internally riven society. Elizabeth noted that after the recapture of Savannah, the inhabitants were exposed "to the fury of the British soldiers," who evidently struggled to differentiate friend from foe, and committed much outrage, despite the best efforts of commanders such as Archibald Campbell who had issued clear orders to counter plundering.[49] On the one hand, rebels and fearful neutral refugees streamed away with what goods and belongings they could carry. On the other, Loyalists and neutrals who had tolerated the administrative breakdown under the Patriot government were now infused with a new confidence and hopeful that economic order could be restored. Elizabeth, now fifteen, traveled from her great-aunt's isolated plantation, passing nervously through Hessian officers' checkpoints, to a Savannah whose streets were still littered with feathers, papers, and belongings. There, she was emotionally reunited with her father, whom she had not seen since his flight.[50] Though Elizabeth returned to Mount Piety, over the course of subsequent months John Lightenstone permitted her to spend prolonged periods in Savannah with various guardians.

The coincidence of Elizabeth's adolescence with the British occupation and Loyalist hegemony in the low country heralded a notable change in her socialization patterns. It is probable that the Revolutionary War, like most wars, generally decelerated courtship cycles and slowed marriage across the American colonies. A high proportion of young males were temporarily or permanently removed due to military service, additional adult female contributions within existing families and households became less dispensable, and key determinants of new marriages and households were destabilized—such as inheritance, economic security, and landholding. But the concentration of Loyalists into towns, regions, and migration streams as a result of British campaigning was a countercurrent that acted to create tight circles of association and often stimulated courtship and intermarriage. In a letter to her own new husband dated March 15, 1780, Elizabeth reported "[t]hat a spirit of matrimony has got among" Loyalist families, and claimed that people were "following our example in the matrimonial way."[51]

Elizabeth's sudden immersion in the complicated sexual politics of Savannah society was a rude awakening for the book-loving, pious, bucolic teenager who described herself as "a young unsophisticated girl, quite new to the world, its customs and usages."[52] It might have been ruder. She remembered feeling an "affection . . . for a short time that I can hardly define" toward a friend of her father's, whom she described as "a very handsome man for his time of life," and also feeling rather overwhelmed and bashful when dining with British officers who had been invited by her guardian because "he thought they could not show too much attention to those who had rescued us from rebel power."[53] The man who really swept Elizabeth off her feet, however, was William Johnston, a dashing twenty-five-year-old captain of the New York Volunteers (a Loyalist regiment), whose father, Dr. Lewis Johnston, ranked among the most prominent Savannah residents, was president of the royal governor's council, and newly appointed commissioner of the Loyalist bureau of police.[54] Elizabeth's sentimental recollection of their first meeting, when she turned William's head despite being clad in a simple homemade dress, thereby epitomizing the "romance of the olden times!" was no doubt exaggerated. But her description of their courtship reveals much about contemporary gendered expectations among the elite, as well as the limits of conformity to feminine and masculine models. John Lightenstone, suspicious that William Johnston had no intention of marriage and that his attentions were therefore inappropriate, ordered Elizabeth tearfully and reluctantly back to her great-aunt's plantation.[55] Johnston contrived to speak to her on her last night in Savannah, without her father's knowledge, and she later wept abundantly out of guilt at her filial transgression, even though she had neither said nor done anything. Shortly afterward, the persistent Johnston sought to engineer an encounter in the country by prevailing upon a mutual friend, probably Eliza Houstoun, to invite Elizabeth to stay at the Houstouns' for a couple of days. But Elizabeth's great-aunt's "stiff notions of female decorum" prevented the rendezvous, and she then had the unenviable task of trying to explain to the exasperated teenager that such a trip would "not be delicate," as it would look as if Elizabeth were just going because Johnston was there—which, of course, she was. Though at the time Elizabeth was not persuaded, looking back as a mother (and grandmother) she believed that her great-aunt "was right and had proper ideas of female reserve."[56] The contest between romantic machinations and proscriptive authoritarian influence took new forms in the reconfigured social worlds of Revolutionary Georgia, a development that influenced black conjugal and familial relationships as well as white ones.[57]

Aged fifteen, Elizabeth was engaged to William Johnston some time in the summer of 1779, and the pair were married on November 21.[58] The period between the two events saw Elizabeth move socially from her previous orbit, defined by the Delegals and Lightenstones, to a closer association with the Johnston family—a family as large in number as they were in influence in late colonial Georgia. With no siblings of her own, Elizabeth was soon describing her numerous future in-laws as "brothers" and "sisters," and became the protégée of the matriarch Laleah Johnston, for whom she had immense respect. The head of the family, Dr. Lewis Johnston, was a former navy surgeon educated in Edinburgh, who had moved to Georgia from St. Kitts in 1753 with a substantial number of slaves and set up a merchant house (Johnston & Wylly), a medical practice, and a rice plantation named Annandale after the clan's famous Scottish estate in Dumfriesshire.[59] Before the Revolution intervened, their eldest son, William, had also been training to become a physician, receiving glowing reports from his tutor, Dr. Benjamin Rush, in Philadelphia, much to the gratification of his parents.[60] The Johnston connection allied Elizabeth Lightenstone to a group of people who had profoundly influenced the development of late colonial Georgia and the Atlantic world more generally: Scottish merchants and planters.[61] Their connections would primarily go on to shape the boundaries of her post-Revolutionary life.

Besides moving under the wing of the Johnstons, between her engagement and her marriage Elizabeth also endured the frightening experience of the French and American siege of Savannah in October 1779. Most civilians were removed from the town before the shelling began, to Hutchinson Island, where they crowded into barns with whatever bedding, livestock, and furniture they had managed to transport across the river. Elizabeth remembered that some fifty-eight Loyalist women and children occupied her barn, "all intimate friends," and that every other house and structure was similarly divided into portions and "full of females."[62] Elizabeth's guardian, Laleah Johnston, remained in the town even after her daughters and elderly husband had crossed to the safety of the island, for she had two adult sons in the Tory lines, and two younger boys pleading to be involved, whom she refused to leave. Elizabeth chose to remain with her, not wanting to pass up on the opportunity of being close to William, with the end result that both women were late to embark, and had to leave after the heavy cannonade had started. Though frightened at the shots that were "whistling about our ears" and ducking her head, Elizabeth carried with her en route to the wharf the lasting memory of her "heroic mother-in-law" relenting suddenly and releasing her ten- and fifteen-year-old boys to fight alongside their brothers.[63] From Hutchinson Island, Elizabeth and her fellow refugees could only watch as the Patriots attempted to storm the works at sunrise on October 9, and she remembered that "every heart in our barn was aching, every eye in tears" at the prospect of defeat with no quarter given. But thanks to what she perceived as the intervention of a "merciful" and "Gracious God" the attack was repulsed, and despite the devastation of Savannah's streets and houses, royal authority and Loyalist domination would continue for a time in the low country. Upon hearing of the outcome at around ten o'clock, Elizabeth reported that the relieved women themselves "made war on the poultry and animals," sending a hearty dinner across to their fatigued relatives, including her father and fiancé.[64]

If the siege of Savannah was the first time that Elizabeth Johnston came face to face with the trauma of civil war, and feared for her future husband's life, it was certainly not the last. William Johnston and his regiment had been involved in the British victories at Long Island (August 1776), the White Plains (October 1776), and the storming of Fort Montgomery on the Hudson (October 1777), and besides their action at Savannah he would continue to be heavily involved in the bitter fighting in the southern colonies during 1780–82. The 130-mile corridor between Savannah and Augusta was particularly hazardous, and William suffered fatigue and a nervous condition following his high-speed ride to bring intelligence to the British garrison in the northwest in early 1780. Reading between the lines that Elizabeth penned to venerate her husband's wartime performance, we can learn something more about her own experiences and responsibilities. When she was informed at very short notice that she could accompany him to New York in June 1780 rather than remain, "very disconsolate in my own room, in tears" in Savannah, she leapt into action, which involved packing in half an hour, and getting her husband's linen ready and her own (which was lying wet). Escorted by the convoy of Sir Henry Clinton, which was returning north after the successful reduction of Charleston, the voyage took only eight days, was accompanied by fine weather and music, "and the whole trip was very delightful." Elizabeth was soon expecting her first child.[65]

Before baby Andrew was born, back in Savannah, on March 22, 1781, Elizabeth's wartime experiences had deteriorated. She witnessed firsthand the anti-British disaffection of abandoned Chesapeake Loyalists, suffered a rough, tedious, and mosquito-plagued passage confined in a transport ship, discovered that her widowed sister-in-law's vessel had been captured by a privateer, and found that her brother-in-law—after whom her first child would be named—had been shot in the back near Augusta. Elizabeth was pleased when her husband and father were both appointed to command local troops of dragoons raised by Georgia's royal governor James Wright, but soon she realized that the bonus of having them nearby was not worth the associated risk. On every third night, and when any alarm was raised, Elizabeth watched her husband ride out into the menacing darkness, the city gates locked behind him. Such circumstances reaffirmed her dependence on prayer, though she remembered that frequently "the thought of the danger he had been in overpowered my mind."[66] Perhaps the most traumatic incident was not recorded in her memoirs, but reported by her grandson William Almon. Almon teased out of his reluctant grandmother that William Johnston's youngest brother, Jack, had been taken prisoner and hanged during the vicious skirmishing in Georgia toward the end of the war. Though Elizabeth reminded her grandchild that "we should love our enemies," such Christian thoughts were a long way from their minds during the conflict. William Johnston avenged his brother's death, gathering a posse of about twenty men, for whom Elizabeth provided supper at eleven o'clock, recalling that she told "the negroes to have food also for their horses" and that while some of the men were "gentlemen I knew," others were "bad-looking men, not gentlemen." Some twenty-eight hours later, the sleepless Elizabeth embraced her returned husband. When she asked him where he had been, William apparently replied "Bet, never ask me where I have been or what I have done, but we don't owe the rebels anything for Jack."[67] Elite mothers and wives like Elizabeth Johnston may have been partly insulated from the depredations of war in Georgia, but they still experienced profound dislocation, uncertainty, and trauma that influenced their relationships with partners, family, and outsiders.[68]

Naturally, it is difficult to gauge how far Elizabeth's *Recollections* were accurate or exaggerated, and to what extent the many moments of high drama, heroism, and mystique were embellished for effect. But an important supplementary source is the extant correspondence between Elizabeth and William Johnston, comprising some thirty letters between 1780 and 1784. These letters corroborate the deep frustrations born of war and separation, and chart a sad drift from the excitement and exhilaration of newlyweds to a harder, earthier, though still affectionate relationship. Besides their insight into the Johnstons' relationship, the letters remind us of the daily preoccupations of denizens of the late eighteenth-century Atlantic world. The problems of shipping and irregular correspondence, the little luxuries like sweetmeats and buckles, butter and melons, the sharp increase in the price of horses, the difficulty of getting miniature portraits made, and the cheer to be found in greyhounds.[69]

Elizabeth's pain at William's departures was almost a physical one, and in early letters she frequently described lonely evenings, wandering around empty rooms with a "heart weighed down with grief," and pledging that she would rather inhabit "the meanest hovel in the world" than be apart from him.[70] She apologized for her rapturous expressions, acknowledging them to be unfeminine and overtly passionate, and "not so becoming in my sex," and retreated to idealized, submissive assertions: "I have no wish but to please you in everything."[71] For his part, William responded with poems and assurances, finding "exquisite pleasure" in her letters and fretting when they were delayed or missing, wishing that it were more frequently possible to travel to Savannah without impropriety.[72] Though he continued to put his military career first, he wanted to know how she spent her time, and who was being friendly and attentive to her when she was seven months pregnant with their first child. Both were acutely conscious of gender in their interactions, and Elizabeth often dealt with this by being self-deprecating, acknowledging that her request for several Charleston purchases was something "your sex have no business with" and commenting, wryly, that "[y]ou'll probably think it encroaching beyond the privileges of a wife."[73]

Elizabeth's letters also revealed that the balance of power in their relationship was not as one-sided as it appeared superficially, something also owing to her transition from a fifteen-year-old bride to a more experienced mother. She saw it as her responsibility to monitor William's "impatient disposition," and kept her eyes peeled for civil opportunities that William might accept outside of the military, trying to persuade him to quit the army. On numerous occasions, Elizabeth's more devout Protestantism found expression, as she cautioned her husband about gambling, commenting "I should hope you will not act contrary to my wishes in a matter so easily to be complied with."[74] She called him to account not just with reference to her own happiness but also their children's livelihood, for William was highly expressive about his transition to fatherhood, and had requested a locket with both Elizabeth's and their newborn's hair in it in April 1781.[75] Nor was she above mocking him for his behavior and his devotion to the political and military cause: in 1782 Elizabeth pointedly compared him to the ancient Romans, "who were so disinterested as to sacrifice wives & children and every other consideration for the welfare of their country."[76] The last letter Elizabeth sent from Savannah was on November 3, 1781, and in later years her tone was more assertive, warning that "should you refuse this request I never will forgive your cruelty," and stating that "I hope I need say no more on this subject in future."[77] Increasingly frustrated at their prolonged separation, as they waited for William's regiment to disband at the close of the war,

Elizabeth signed off a letter from St. Augustine, Florida, in 1783 as "your once truly happy, tho' now afflicted wife."[78]

The Loyalist diaspora carried Elizabeth Johnston oceans away from the life she had expected to lead in Georgia, and beyond the remits of this paper. Seven of her ten children survived beyond infancy, and their places of birth pay testament to her repeated upheavals: Savannah (March 1781); Charleston, South Carolina (August 1782); St. Augustine, Florida (March 1784); Edinburgh, Scotland (May 1785); and Liguana and Kingston, Jamaica (six births between 1787 and 1794).[79] At the end of the war William Johnston completed his medical training in Scotland, and he went on to establish his family in Jamaica, thanks in large part to social networks cemented during the Revolutionary War. In contrast to Georgia, Elizabeth found Jamaica to be distasteful, for "[m]orals there were at the lowest ebb," and she referred to blacks practicing degenerate "habits of life" and even well-to-do whites indulging themselves in various ways, including dinner parties and card games on the Sabbath. In an effort to protect the rectitude of her own family from such "dreadful examples," Elizabeth taught her own children at home, reading each morning, conducting family prayers, and instructing her girls in sewing, only consenting to their attending school after they had been in Jamaica for ten years, when she was aged thirty-two. For his part, William agreed not to have company on Sunday, and never interfered with Elizabeth's discipline or mode of child raising, as she noted that "he highly respected my religious principles."[80] For reasons of health as well as disenchantment with the moral dynamics of life in the Caribbean, the family eventually relocated to the less infectious and less dissolute province of Nova Scotia, a long-established Loyalist haven. There, Elizabeth settled into life as the matriarch of a growing dynasty and caught up with old friends, including classmates from her school years in Savannah.[81]

Over the course of her life, Elizabeth Lichtenstein Johnston upheld a set of core values that reflected her background and upbringing in Georgia: the ethnocentricity of the dominant race, the conservatism of the planter class, the conviction of the Protestant faith, and the public deference of the subordinated sex. Race, class, religion, and gender manifested themselves most overtly in Elizabeth Johnston's devotion to education, to (white) family, to health care, and to parenthood. In some respects, her response to the traumas around her—to the effects of slavery, revolution, war, migration, and disease—was to turn inward and focus on those issues over which she could exert some control: her intellect, her children, her relationships, her household. This introspective and spiritual impulse she shared with several elite contemporaries, such as Martha Laurens Ramsay, who showed remarkable similarities in her responses to war and upheaval, despite her prominent Patriot alignment and connections.[82] Even

Johnston's loyalism was more social than political, more emotional than ideological, for much of her fierce partisanship was born out of perceived injustice at the treatment of her family by others, and she showed plenty of disaffection with the British war effort when it fell short. Elizabeth Johnston was catapulted around the British Atlantic world as a result of the American Revolution coming to Georgia, and her memoirs of her life before, during, and afterward remind us that the Revolution was more complex than it is sometimes portrayed. Her social conditioning, her experiences and viewpoints, though beneath the radar of grand historical narratives, help explain how larger, more visible structures have endured. Elizabeth Johnston fought in a long series of internal conflicts—including battles over parental authority, the use of slaves, education, the nature of marriage, the gendering of heroism and political alignment, and the meaning of divine providence. In the context of her patriarchal era the odds were firmly stacked, and the outcome of most of these conflicts saw her reach conclusions that reinforced the social order. She marginalized the significance of slavery and upheld inequities between the sexes, perpetuating conformity to an idealized model of female deference—albeit with a deft amount of practical self-assertion from time to time. But among the trivia and loaded value-judgments of her recollections, there *is* much to interest those exploring the gendered "pursuit of happiness" in the Revolutionary era. Elizabeth Lichtenstein Johnston had made a dramatic journey from the rebellious little girl up a tree on Skidaway Island to the Georgia wife and, ultimately, the Nova Scotian widow who proclaimed that, "like all human enjoyments, mine was not full and satisfactory."[83]

## NOTES

1. Elizabeth Lichtenstein Johnston, *Recollections of a Georgia Loyalist,* ed. A. W. Eaton (New York: M. F. Mansfield and Company, 1901; repr., Spartanburg, S.C.: Reprint Co., 1972), 9–10.

2. For an excellent recent survey essay on the historiography of colonial southern women, see Cynthia A. Kierner, "Women, Gender, Families, and Households in the Southern Colonies," *Journal of Southern History* 73 (August 2007): 643–58.

3. Obituary, *Halifax Church Times,* September 29, 1848.

4. For the classic treatment of Loyalists, see Mary Beth Norton, *The British Americans: The Loyalist Exiles in England, 1774–1789* (Boston: Little, Brown, 1972).

5. Frederick Wheelock Harris quoted in Charlotte I. Perkins, *The Romance of Old Annapolis Royal* (Halifax: Historical Association of Annapolis Royal, 1934), 92–93.

6. Figure derived from Governor Wright's population estimates in 1762 and 1766. A. D. Candler, et al., eds., *The Colonial Records of the State of Georgia* (Atlanta and Athens: various printers, 1904–16, 1976–89), 28:pt. 1, 309, pt. 2, 185. (Hereinafter cited as *Col. Recs.*)

7. Kronstadt was the seat of the Russian Baltic fleet, and the city guards the approaches to St. Petersburg. Johnston records the names of her paternal grandparents as Gustavus Philip Lichten-

stein (of German descent but born in England) and Beatrice Elizabeth Lloyd (English or Irish). Johnston, *Recollections*, 37.

8. From various sources it is likely that Johann Lichtenstein settled in Georgia between 1755 and 1757. According to his testimony to a royal commission (see below) he went to America in 1755, while his daughter recalled that he knew John Milledge (born in 1757) from infancy.

9. Egmont Papers, University of Georgia Library, 14201, p. 208; "A Voyage to Georgia begun in the Year 1735 by Francis Moore," *Collections of the Georgia Historical Society,* 22 vols. (Savannah: Georgia Historical Society, 1840–1996), 1:90, 104, 132; Margaret Davis Cate, *Our Todays and Yesterdays: A Story of Brunswick and the Coastal Islands* (Brunswick, Ga.: Glover Bros., 1930), 58, 118.

10. Johnston, *Recollections*, 39.

11. Peterhof was Tsar Peter the Great's magnificent imperial estate and cultural project overlooking the Gulf of Finland. Quotes and letters listed in Johnston, *Recollections*, 38, 39, 40.

12. Ben Marsh, *Georgia's Frontier Women: Female Fortunes in a Southern Colony* (Athens: University of Georgia Press, 2007), 225n117; Johnston, *Recollections*, 41.

13. Johnston, *Recollections*, 41.

14. Ibid., 45, 73, 76, 85. The term "servant" was commonly used in the eighteenth century to classify black slaves.

15. Ibid., 215, 218, 221. Lewis Johnston ultimately "disposed of your negroes" for £450 according to a letter from St. Augustine, Florida, dated February 12, 1784 (222).

16. Letter from Elizabeth Johnston to her husband, St. Augustine, Florida, February 12, 1784, in Johnston, *Recollections*, 222.

17. Ibid., 108–9, 123.

18. See discussion in Peter Kolchin, *American Slavery, 1619–1877* (New York: Hill and Wang, 1993), 28–29.

19. Johnston, *Recollections*, 85. For a wider discussion of the limited extent to which the low country female population shared and expressed a common gender identity, see Betty Wood, *Gender, Race, and Rank in a Revolutionary Age: The Georgia Lowcountry, 1750–1820* (Athens: University of Georgia Press, 2000).

20. Johnston, *Recollections*, 41–42, 43.

21. Obituary, *Georgia Gazette,* August 24, 1774.

22. For an account of the internationally sponsored orphanage project spearheaded by George Whitefield in Georgia, see Edward J. Cashin, *Beloved Bethesda: A History of George Whitefield's Home for Boys, 1740–2000* (Macon, Ga.: Mercer University Press, 2001). See also Marsh, *Georgia's Frontier Women,* 87–89, 91 (orphans); 122–23, 167–74 (slave families).

23. Johnston, *Recollections*, 50.

24. Daniel Blake Smith, "The Family in Early American History and Culture," *William and Mary Quarterly* 39 (1982): 3–28, esp. 18–19. For a wider discussion of changes in legal and cultural understandings of childhood and authority, see Holly Brewer, *By Birth or Consent: children, law, and the Anglo-American revolution in authority* (Chapel Hill: Published for the Omohundro Institute of Early American History and Culture, Williamsburg, Virginia, by the University of North Carolina Press, 2005), esp. 4–8. The breakdown of older, patriarchal models of authority is addressed at length in Carole Shammas, "Anglo-American Household Government in Comparative Perspective," *William and Mary Quarterly* 52 (1995): 104–44.

25. Johnston, *Recollections*, 50. See also her tribute to him upon his death, aged seventy-nine years. Ibid., 127.

26. Several historians have commented on the generational split among prominent families in

Georgia, whereby the revolutionary leaders were "often the younger sons of the colony's leaders, [and] must have found it difficult to break with their fathers and friends" (Kenneth Coleman, *Colonial Georgia: A History* [New York: Scribner, 1976], 271). See also Frank Lambert, *James Habersham: Loyalty, Politics, and Commerce in Colonial Georgia* (Athens: University of Georgia Press, 2005), 160, 167–78.

27. For a wider discussion of education in colonial Georgia, see Harold E. Davis, *The Fledgling Province: social and cultural life in colonial Georgia, 1733–1776* (Chapel Hill: University of North Carolina Press, 1976), 233–50.

28. Advertisement, *Georgia Gazette,* August 2, 1769.

29. For examples of such schools in the period of Elizabeth Johnston's youth, see the *Georgia Gazette,* August 30, 1764 (taught by Timothy Cronin), September 26, 1765 (taught by Medley D'Arcy Dawes), April 22, 1767 (taught by James Whitefield), May 25, 1768 (taught by Peter Gandy), September 28, 1768 (taught by James Cosgreve).

30. Johnston, *Recollections,* 44–5, 51. *Georgia Gazette,* April 20, 1768, April 18, 1770.

31. Letter from John Adams to James Sullivan, Philadelphia, May 26, 1776, in *Adams Family Correspondence,* ed. L. H. Butterfield et al. (Cambridge, Mass.: Harvard University Press, 1963), 1:401.

32. Benjamin Rush, *The Autobiography of Benjamin Rush: His "Travels Through Life" Together with His Commonplace Book from 1789–1813,* ed. George W. Corner (Princeton: American Philosophical Society, 1948), 119.

33. Robert M. Calhoon, "Loyalism and Neutrality," in *A Companion to the American Revolution,* ed. Jack P. Greene and J. R. Pole (Malden, Mass.: Blackwell Publishers, 2000), 235.

34. Letter from Dr. Lewis Johnston to William Johnston, Savannah, August 20, 1774, in Johnston, *Recollections,* 27–8.

35. Leslie Hall, *Land and Allegiance in Revolutionary Georgia* (Athens: University of Georgia Press, 2001), 30.

36. Johnston, *Recollections,* 45–46.

37. Johnston, *Recollections,* 44–46. Letter from Joseph Clay to Brith and Pechin, Savannah, July 2, 1777, in *Letters of Joseph Clay, Merchant of Savannah 1776–1793,* vol. 8 of *Collections of the Georgia Historical Society* (Savannah: Georgia Historical Society, 1918).

38. Edward J. Cashin, *The King's Ranger: Thomas Brown and the American Revolution on the Southern Frontier* (Athens: University of Georgia Press, 1989).

39. Johnston, *Recollections,* 44.

40. Ibid., 45.

41. Daniel P. Coke, *Royal Commission on the Losses and Services of American Loyalists,* ed. Hugh E. Egerton (New York, Arno Press, 1969), 66–67.

42. For a comprehensive consideration of landholding and political alignment during the Revolution, see Hall, *Land and Allegiance.*

43. A. D. Candler, ed., *The Revolutionary Records of the State of Georgia* (Atlanta: Franklin-Turner, 1908), 2:97. For a fuller discussion of this measure and similar Tory actions during the war, see Ben Marsh, "Women and the American Revolution in Georgia," *Georgia Historical Quarterly* 88 (2004): 157–78.

44. Johnston, *Recollections,* 47.

45. Coke, *Royal Commission,* 67. That John Lightenstone did not make a claim for his slaves suggests that he had either sold them or carried them with him when he abandoned Georgia in 1782. Elsewhere in the commission's reports he vouched for a fellow Loyalist resident on the Georgia coast, George Barry of Tybee Island, swearing that he "[s]aw part of his property in flames it was

burnt by the Rebels on account of his principles & they carried him Prisoner at the same time to Savannah. . . . Has heard that the Rebels shot one of his Negroes" (208).

46. For a discussion of the taking of Savannah, see Hall, *Land and Allegiance,* 74–76; and Johnston, *Recollections,* 47–48.

47. For an excellent recent summary of the prejudicial historiography of Loyalism and Loyalist numbers, see Edward Larkin, "What Is a Loyalist?" *Common Place* 8, no. 1 (2007), available at http://www.common-place.org/vol-08/no-01/larkin/ (accessed December 8, 2008). He writes, "[e]ven at the more conservative (probably too conservative) 20 percent figure favored by some historians, the idea that such a significant proportion of the population may have opposed the independence movement is a staggering fact—a fact that remains virtually unaccounted for in our reckoning of the Revolution."

48. Johnston, *Recollections,* 46 (quote on civil wars), 57–58 (quote on black children—Johnston gave most of the credit for the successful repulse to Colonel Moncrief's "ardour, skill, and industry"), 14 (quote on heroism).

49. Ibid., 48. Archibald Campbell, *Journal of an Expedition against the Rebels of Georgia in North America under the Orders of Archibald Campbell Esquire Lieutenant Colonel of His Majestys Regiment 1778,* ed. Colin Campbell (Darien, Ga.: Ashantilly Press, 1981), December 22, 1778, 15.

50. Johnston, *Recollections,* 49.

51. Ibid., 184.

52. Ibid., 52.

53. Ibid., 49, 53.

54. Coke, *Royal Commission,* 246–47. Lewis Johnston, as president of the Upper House of the restored royal assembly, signed the contentious Georgia Disqualifying Act of July 1780, effectively placing 151 prominent rebels under house arrest. Only in April 1781 did James Wright persuade the assembly to attaint a smaller number for high treason, though the act apparently never became law (Hall, *Land and Allegiance,* 101–2).

55. John Lightenstone had good reason to be wary of Johnston's conduct, for he knew him well from their shared campaigning during the war. Moreover, William Johnston's youth had been rather tempestuous: he was partial to gaming, guilty of "repeated acts of folly and indiscretion" (in his own father's words), and had wounded a night watchman in an altercation in Philadelphia in 1773 (ibid., 25–26, 167–72).

56. The intervention was also fortuitous as far as Johnston's military record was concerned, for it ensured he was able to leave for Carolina with his regiment (ibid., 55–56).

57. For the most comprehensive discussion to date of the impact of the Revolutionary War on black livelihoods in the South, and the triagonal nature of the conflict, see Sylvia R. Frey, *Water from the Rock: Black Resistance in a Revolutionary Age* (Princeton: Princeton University Press, 1991).

58. Johnston, *Recollections,* 15.

59. Ibid., 10–12; Coke, *Royal Commission,* 246–47.

60. Letter from Dr. Lewis Johnston to William Johnston, Savannah, July 17, 1773, in Johnston, *Recollections,* 165–67. Such connections helped to prompt Benjamin Rush to mount a public campaign to restore property and political rights to most former Loyalists, and thanks to this and other pressures, most states began repealing anti-Tory legislation by 1787.

61. For an excellent recent consideration of the impact of Scots merchants on the development of colonial Georgia, see Paul M. Pressly, "Scottish Merchants and the Shaping of Colonial Georgia," *Georgia Historical Quarterly* 91 (2007): 135–68.

62. Johnston, *Recollections,* 58.

63. Ibid., 15–16, 60.

64. Ibid., 61, 62, 17.

65. Ibid., 65–66.

66. Ibid., 66–69, 70, 72.

67. Ibid., 32–33.

68. For a concise, wider consideration of the impact of the Revolutionary War on women, see Carol Berkin, *First Generations: women in colonial America* (New York: Hill and Wang, 1996), 165–94; and on southern white women, see Cynthia A. Kierner, *Beyond the Household: Women's place in the Early South, 1700–1835* (Ithaca: Cornell University Press, 1998), 69–101.

69. For an account of these kinds of everyday influences in the context of a woman's life in revolutionary America, see Joy Day Buel and Richard Buel Jr., *The Way of Duty: A Woman and Her Family in Revolutionary America* (New York: Norton, 1984).

70. Letter from Elizabeth Johnston to William Johnston, Savannah, March 3, 1780 (Johnston, *Recollections,* 181).

71. Letter from Elizabeth Johnston to William Johnston, Savannah, March 10, 1780 (ibid., 183, 184 [March 15]).

72. Letter from William Johnston to Elizabeth Johnston, St. Augustine, Florida, March 27, 1780 (ibid., 187).

73. Letter from Elizabeth Johnston to William Johnston, Savannah, January 16, 1781 (ibid., 196).

74. Ibid., 195.

75. Letter from William Johnston to Elizabeth Johnston, Charlestown, S.C., April 29, 1781 (ibid., 202).

76. Letter from Elizabeth Johnston to William Johnston, Charlestown, S.C., August 15, 1782 (ibid., 208).

77. Letter from Elizabeth Johnston to William Johnston, St. Augustine, Florida, February 12, 1784 (ibid., 223).

78. Letter from Elizabeth Johnston to William Johnston, St. Augustine, Florida, January 2, 1784 (ibid., 215).

79. The birth dates, names, and potted biographies of her children are provided in Johnston, *Recollections,* 34–36. The closeness of the births strongly suggests that Elizabeth Johnston used a wet nurse, an occasional practice among elites in eighteenth-century British America, though not as common as popularly held (Mary Beth Norton, *Liberty's Daughters: The Revolutionary Experience of American Women, 1750–1800* [repr., Ithaca: Cornell University Press, 1996], 90–93).

80. Ibid., 85–86.

81. A childhood friend, Mrs. Thomson, had settled in Halifax (ibid., 111–12).

82. Joanna Bowen Gillespie, *The Life and Times of Martha Laurens Ramsay, 1759–1811* (Columbia: University of South Carolina Press, 2001).

83. Ibid., 70.

# Ellen Craft

## (ca. 1826–1891)

---

## *The Fugitive Who Fled as a Planter*

### BARBARA MCCASKILL

The fugitive slave Ellen Craft (ca. 1826–1891), and her husband William (1824–1900), achieved prominence in their day for a daring and audacious escape from bondage. Not sheltered under cloak of darkness, but instead concealed by a clever disguise and the distractions of holiday revelries, the Crafts tell of fleeing from slavery in Macon, Georgia, in December 1848. To reconstruct Ellen Craft's story is to rely considerably on secondhand accounts rather than primary ones. With the exception of her jointly written memoir, *Running a Thousand Miles for Freedom* (1860), and letters that more closely resemble copybook exercises than intimate reflections, she has not left behind an archive of manuscripts.[1] Nevertheless, what the documentary record does reveal is that Craft pursued a trajectory of political, social, and educational activism commonplace to "doers of the word," as the scholar Carla L. Peterson has christened charismatic early black women writers and speakers.[2]

The conventional fugitive's story—a flight from miserable bondage to a provisional, if somewhat satisfactory, freedom—does not apply to Craft.[3] Instead, the opening paragraph of her narrative with William confides to readers that "It is true, our condition as slaves was not by any means the worst."[4] In the South, Craft certainly was a slave, and she certainly suffered her share of slavery's traumas and deprivations. Yet, owing to both the circumstances of her birth and the schemes of a humiliated mistress, she also occupied a privileged, albeit circumscribed, position that proved key to her escape with William from southern bondage. First in the North and then in England, she quickly fashioned a public image as a conventional wife, daughter, and mother, as virtue and domesticity perfected. She also unraveled this persona, rejecting a constrained and exclusive identity as the companion and helpmeet to William, and complicating this identity by asserting her voice and body in order to subdue the antislavery movement's detractors and to demonstrate success as a speaker, social reformer, teacher, wife, and mother.

Craft's story of slavery and freedom is a messy one. As she matured together with William, she chafed against the paternalism and condescension of reform organizations. Together they strove to cultivate more economic independence and social autonomy, and Craft stretched the norms of her gender through her antislavery activism. This, ironically, may have prevented her and her husband from achieving iconic status in their old age, and from earning the same degree of recognition in historical memory as a Frederick Douglass (1818–95) or a Harriet Tubman (1820?–1913). For those of us who study the lives of nineteenth-century women, Craft's story may ultimately assist in the project of understanding and uncovering how we remember—and why we forget—stories of particular African American women born in and escaped from slavery.

Craft's famous journey from southern enslavement to nominal northern freedom is but one of many flights that she and William would enact during their adventurous lifetimes. It began not with her marriage to him in bustling Macon, but with her birth to a slave mother in the crucible and core of Maconites' prosperity: a cotton plantation. It was in such a household in Clinton, Jones County, Georgia, that Craft was born sometime around 1826 to Major James P. Smith, her white master, and his house slave Maria, who herself was half-white. In such a household Craft avoided in childhood the harsher working conditions and physical deprivations that accompanied field labor, yet she did encounter the inevitable barbs and stings that "the greatest indignity" of slavery—rape—imposed upon slave women and their families.[5] Her mother Maria's sexual relationship with her master Major Smith augured a bleak future for Craft that might consist of sexual assault by her master and/or other white males; resentment, "incessant cruelty," and abuse at the hands of her white mistress; and self-blame or even contempt on the part of her black husband, slave or free, who would be helpless to protect her so long as she remained some white person's property.[6]

Fortunately for Craft, this nettling and dangerous relationship to her master, as his daughter and his slave, precipitated the sequence of events—her removal from Clinton to Macon, her marriage to William, and her scheme with him to light out for the North—that would climax with her ringing in the new year of 1849 with Pennsylvania Quakers and abolitionists on the freedom side of the Mason-Dixon line. "[S]o annoyed, . . . at finding [Craft] frequently mistaken for a child of the family," the "tyrannical" Mrs. Smith discovered a better balm

**ELLEN CRAFT, DISGUISED**
Courtesy of Manuscripts, Archives, and Rare Books Division,
Schomburg Center for Research in Black Culture, the New York
Public Library, Astor, Lenox, and Tilden Foundations.

for her wounded pride than the "incessant cruelty" she directed toward her slave girl: she removed Craft completely from her service, scorn, and sight.[7] Instead of being sold outright, Craft was presented as a wedding present to her half-sister Eliza Cromwell Smith (1819–79). Ellen Craft was eleven years old.

Eliza Smith had married a man who had established himself as a scion of Macon business and society: the physician, financier, and entrepreneur Dr. Robert Collins. Providentially located smack dab in the middle of Georgia, the town of Macon, where Eliza removed in 1837 with Collins and with Ellen her sister/ slave, would gain commercial prominence by the eve of the Civil War. In the 1830s, 1840s, and 1850s it thrived as a center of transportation that served the central and western portions of the state, and as a hub of education and business, thanks in good part to Collins's investments and civic-mindedness. He had earned his money through speculation and finance (he was a cofounder of the Monroe and Bibb [Counties] Railroad and Banking Company), in addition to his medical practice. This enabled him to help initiate railroad service in Macon during the 1830s. The trains linked cotton and other raw materials and crops produced in the interior of the state to the thirsty cities ringing its edges—and especially to the cosmopolitan city of Savannah, a former destination for the ships of the slave trade that was then the busiest commercial seaport on the southeastern coast.[8]

The author of an essay in 1852 on the effective control of slaves (reprinted in London in 1853),[9] Collins owned sixty-two of them in the early 1840s, and over ten thousand acres of land.[10] As if this property were not measure enough of his wealth and status, his city estate commanded a respectable view of Macon's downtown. Here Ellen and Eliza, like the home and grounds where they lived, were as much external indicators of Collins's social and financial success as they were essential ingredients to the running of his household and the rearing of his heirs. In part because of Collins, Craft's life intersected with that of her future husband, William. In quick succession, William's first master had run up gambling debts, declared financial insolvency, auctioned off William's parents and siblings, and sold him to a Macon bank clerk, Ira E. Taylor, who paid half his purchase price—Collins paid the other.[11]

Craft's primary duties were as "a ladies' maid" to her sister, Eliza,[12] which probably included such responsibilities as assisting her mistress and other white women in the household in bathing, dressing, grooming, and maintaining their linens and wardrobe; straightening, cleaning, and organizing the female bedchambers and their contents; accompanying the ladies of the house to the shops and on other errands; escorting them and other family members to visit neighbors; sewing, mending, and quilting; and supervising the mistress's children.[13]

"[A] favourite slave in the family," Craft was even granted "a little room to herself"[14]—an astonishing privilege in a culture where sleeping quarters for a female house slave usually meant a corner in the kitchen, a niche near the doorway, or a pallet at the foot of the mistress's bed.

Looking back decades later on this life, the Crafts pronounced Eliza Smith Collins as "decidedly more humane than the majority of her class." She protected her enslaved half-sister from punishments like imprisonment in the sugar house, where black women would be subject to rape as well as flogging and other tortures.[15] It may therefore be appropriate to consider the similarity between Craft's first name, Ellen, and that of her white sister Eliza as more than an acknowledgment of their mutual bloodline, and as a similarity that also reflects a genuine, if guarded, affection that may have incubated during their childhood and intensified as both became women.[16] For example, the Collinses subscribed to the customary practice of not permitting their slaves to indulge in the Christian sacrament of marriage vows witnessed by a minister. Yet they granted the Crafts permission in 1846 to commemorate their union with the slave's traditional ceremony of "jumping the broomstick."[17] Perhaps Eliza played no small part in the decision to confer this privilege.

It was her marriage to William, according to Ellen Craft, that precipitated forbidden thoughts of escape. Later, in freedom, she would admit to anxieties about the Collinses snatching up her children and selling them, to shame at engaging in a carnal relationship, acceptable by slavery's standards, that was immoral, vile, and promiscuous in Christians' eyes. Like the fugitive slave Harriet Ann Jacobs (1813–97), in freedom Craft would speak of the unique demands that slavery made on black women forced to share their masters' beds. However, instead of accusing Collins directly of sexual overtures, and spotlighting her own vulnerability and exploitation, she would emphasize the dreams of a Christian marriage and children that invigorated her decision to escape. She would focus on cultivating a public image of herself as a decent and respectable woman, overcome with mortification and remorse for the immoral, anti-Christian choices regarding marriage and children that slavery heaped upon its victims.[18]

In 1848, when she and William were in their early twenties, they decided to escape. Since restrictions on the movements of slaves between plantations were often lifted or overlooked, since slaveholders were more genial about granting passes to visit family and friends on neighboring plantations, since slave patrols were likely to be distracted from their duties by the season's revelries, the Christmas holidays would prove to be an ideal time for them to flee. And they chose a bold, risky, calculated method of flight. Craft suggested to her husband that she parlay, for once, her white skin to advantage by masquerading as an infirm and invalid southern gentleman planter.[19] "He" would say that he was traveling from Georgia to Philadelphia by the usual assorted conveyances—rail, carriage, steamship—in order to seek medical treatment for various rheumatic ailments. To complete this ruse, Craft would wear a hat and suit, cut her hair, tie bandages around her smooth face, hide her eyes behind green spectacles, and entwine a sling and a poultice around her right arm and hand. The darker William would dissemble as well, by pretending to be the devoted slave of his "master."[20]

As Donnie D. Bellamy writes, antiliteracy laws for slaves instituted by the Black Codes were not always strictly enforced in pre–Civil War Macon, so that "a number of Macon's bondspersons were able to get some education before the Civil War."[21] The historian Steven Hahn estimates that likely 10 percent of southern slaves could read and write by the eve of the Civil War.[22] Yet Craft and William had managed "by stratagem" only to learn the alphabet, and not to read or spell, so the final touch of a sling would serve the added purpose of preventing her recapture.[23] Otherwise, her preliterate inability to write her name in registers would alert the suspicions of hotel clerks and other authorities on the lookout for runaways.

There is much left unsaid in this daring, romantic version of events that reveals the reality of Craft's enslavement. How did she and William obtain the money to purchase enough clothing and provisions for several days' worth of travel and lodging on the way to the Free States—even more if there were unforeseen delays caused by adverse weather conditions, suspicious fellow travelers, and unreliable transportation? How did they know the most efficient route from Georgia to the North, and where to go and who to see when they got there? What loved ones did they leave behind?

Ellen Craft's movements as a house slave in and around Macon offer tentative answers to these questions. They endow her with a mutually powerful decision-making role within the marriage partnership that *Running a Thousand Miles for Freedom* and other antislavery publications at times would later downplay. For example, William accumulated money because his master allowed him to save a portion of his wages earned from being hired out to do carpentry work for Macon's white community.[24] As Steven Hahn writes in his *A Nation under Our Feet*, by the mid-nineteenth century

In sections of the upper South that had made the transition from tobacco to grains, in nonplantation districts near mines or transportation projects, and in rural areas that came within the orbit of larger towns and scattered manufacturing centers, the hiring of slaves on both short- and long-term bases became increasingly common, and slaveholders frequently allowed the slaves to retain a very small share of their wages as incentive and reward. In cities like Baltimore, Richmond, New Orleans, and to a lesser extent, Charleston—or in agricultural processing towns like Danville, Lynchburg, and Farmville, Virginia, slaves usually fed and lodged themselves, bargained with prospective employers, and might receive payments for "overwork."[25]

For her part, Ellen was an expert seamstress who designed and sewed the pants to complete the black broadcloth suit that she would wear. Abolitionists report that she and William together "procured the necessary articles, buying one at one place, and another at another,"[26] and as Hahn writes, "we may well have underestimated the extent to which slaves in a great many locales—with or without their owners' approval—may have bought, sold, and bargained with merchants, shopkeepers, peddlers, and neighboring whites."[27] Garments, table linens, quilts, and bed coverings that she may have stitched for Macon's white elites also may have brought in additional funds to squirrel away to facilitate their scheme. Her duties in and proximity to their bedrooms and parlors may have presented opportunities for her to steal a few coins or bills during unsupervised moments, and to conceal them right under the white folks' noses in "a chest of drawers" that William had made for her private room.[28] Hired out at jobs in and around Macon, William very likely would have taken advantage of his precious mobility by extracting information about escape routes from free blacks and sympathetic whites he may have encountered, as well as acquiring additional garments to complete Ellen's disguise. On the other hand, Ellen, though rooted, was just as likely to have picked up knowledge of rail lines to take, places to stay, and other important information from eavesdropping on the Collinses' mealtime conversations and listening to guests they hosted. "On individual holdings," Hahn concludes, "women and children were particularly well placed to overhear discussions in the parlors, dining rooms, and immediate environs of their owners' residence."[29]

On the question of loved ones left behind, besides her grandmother and her mother remaining in slavery, as well as the members of her husband's family—his father, brother, and sisters—auctioned on the block and scattered to the four winds, Ellen Craft presented a unified front with her husband by maintaining a public silence. Craft's status as a favored house slave, her own resistance to sexual exploitation,[30] and the protective stances taken toward her by her sister and mistress, may have shielded her from being raped and producing children from this violence, or from being ordered to breed more slaves with other black men, even after she had "married" the man she loved. Yet two white male abolitionist colleagues, Reverend Theodore Parker (1810–60), an eloquent Unitarian minister, and his fellow Bostonian James Freeman Clarke (1810–88), would write that Craft had confided to them about having had a child in slavery who died because she was commanded to abandon it until she completed chores and errands elsewhere in the house and in town.[31]

If Craft's recollections about her kind mistress are sincere, this scenario seems unlikely, and the abolitionists' stories do not ring true. Further evidence debunking these accounts is the differing details each man gives. Finally, reams of abolitionist poems, hymns, and anecdotes feature an aggrieved slave mother whose demanding, imperious mistress forces her to abandon her infant in the fields. Hours later, the slave mother returns, only to discover her little one succumbing from exposure, or suffering death throes after a snake or wild animal has mortally wounded it.[32] Contrived though these fictional episodes may be, it would be consistent with the realities and traumas of slave mothers that Craft may have actually lost a child to miscarriage, malnutrition, auction, or disease by the time she lit out for the North. Nevertheless, in the face of contradictory reports, she and William publicly insisted that they had abstained from having children until they had secured their freedom. By holding to this script of sexual abstinence during her years as a fugitive from the South, Craft could position herself as an acceptable and respectable Victorian woman who presided over a disciplined Christian household, while launching a multipronged assault against the lies that underpinned southern slavery: against the alleged promiscuity of all slave women, against the insisted upon bestiality of all slave men, against the supposed chastity of every elite white woman, against the implied chivalry and gentlemanly behavior of every elite white man.

Another example of where Craft's imagination and agency became integral to the success of the couple's escape is in the use of her pseudonym, "Mr. William Johnson," during their terrifying journey over land and water.[33] A common surname that would have camouflaged Craft by deflecting undue notice, "Johnson" also surfaces in code names devised by abolitionists assisting runaway slaves through the system of safe houses and personal connections that made up the Underground Railroad (UGRR). For example, in March 1849 the fugitive slave Henry Box Brown (1815–?) shipped himself from Richmond to Philadelphia in a box that his friend Samuel Smith addressed to "James Johnson, 131 Arch Street." "James Johnson" was a signal to antislavery friends who had been notified of Brown's plans, and who were waiting to receive the "shipment" at the warehouse of the Philadelphia, Wilmington, and Baltimore Railroad.[34] This combination of a generic surname, Johnson, with her husband's first name may thus reflect both the urgency of Craft's decision making and the sophisticated networks behind many successful escapes devised by fugitive slaves.

Working in the Big House, Craft also might have heard accounts of Colonel

William Ransom Johnson (1782–1849), an affluent Virginia planter and gambler. During Craft's childhood in the 1820s and 1830s, Johnson, affectionately dubbed "The Napoleon of the Turf," was a national figure notorious for his devotion to horses, horse races, and horsemanship, and known nationally as well for the money he lavished on these passions. He helped establish horse races as the first national sport, and he popularized what came to be known as the "intersectional match." In this civil war fought symbolically from the saddle, a horse bred up North and one raised down South raced against each other. The honor and bragging rights of North or South rested on the jockey and animal who won.

On May 17, 1823, a few years before Craft was born, Johnson wagered a horse, Sir Henry, against an undefeated nemesis, American Eclipse, owned by the New Yorker Cornelius W. Van Ranst. In front of a mammoth Long Island crowd of over sixty thousand people, the Yankee's steed won two of three heats, and true to its name, it eclipsed its southern opponent.[35] So, by christening her alter ego "William Johnson," Craft may have intended to accomplish more than protecting her true identity. The name of "William Johnson" she assumed—of a southerner, a white man, and a loser—may also have been meant to mock the alleged superiority of white Americans that underpinned justifications of slavery.[36] Whereas fugitives like Frederick Douglass renamed themselves after landing on free soil (in his case, he selected the surname "Douglass" after a character in Sir Walter Scott's popular 1810 narrative poem *The Lady of the Lake*),[37] Craft's alias finally illustrates how renaming could be a crucial part of initiating escape, in addition to commemorating when the runaway's ordeal was over.

On Christmas Day 1848, after a few close calls, Craft and her husband state that they arrived safely in relatively free Philadelphia. By January 1849 they had settled in Boston, the center of the American antislavery movement. They were mentored by Lewis Hayden (1815–89), a fugitive from Kentucky whose home at 66 Phillips Street was a station on the UGRR and, along with the African Meeting House in nearby Smith Court, a favorite gathering place for abolitionists.[38] On the north slope of Beacon Hill, the denizens of Boston's free black community worked on the waterfront as ship builders and sailors, or they were employed by white families and businesses as servants and laborers, or they pursued entrepreneurial enterprises. By the mid-1840s a full one-fourth of black Boston's approximately two thousand residents owned their own businesses, such as gaming houses, barber shops, boarding houses, and stores.[39]

Inspired by this collective success, and by the individual prosperity of their benefactor Hayden, who sold used clothing, William opened a "New and Second Hand" furniture and restoration business at 62 Federal Street. His establishment prospered, and he advertised it widely in the pages of the *Liberator*, the nation's largest circulating antislavery newspaper. William Lloyd Garrison (1805–79) published the *Liberator* only a few blocks away at 21 Cornhill.[40] With Reverend Parker officiating, the Crafts took their marriage vows in the Christian ceremony that for so long had been their dream.[41] They began night school to obtain their long-delayed educations, Ellen took up sewing again to supplement William's income, and they accompanied another new friend, William Wells Brown (1815–84), on speaking tours throughout New England. Subscribing to Victorian taboos against women public speakers, William did most of the talking. Usually, Ellen politely stood, smiled, and curtsied when his talk ended and the audience members were ready to acknowledge her. Contemporaneous accounts of the couple in Boston make it clear that they meant to agitate actively for an end to slavery, even as they crafted public identities as a responsible husband and breadwinner and a respectable wife and lady.[42]

Although Ellen Craft's voice was largely muted in the lecture hall, her image as a "fugitive, fleeing as a planter," scandalized white viewers even before the "Reform Costume" of the women's rights advocate Amelia Jenks Bloomer (1818–94) rocked gender constructions in 1850s America. Sometime between her arrival in Boston in early 1849 and her departure in late 1850, Craft sat in this masculine disguise for a daguerreotype, a photograph produced on a copper plate surface. She and other abolitionists recognized a new technology, the camera, and a new kind of reformer, the photographer, as tools to serve their arguments for the slaves' immediate emancipation. According to the art historian Deborah Willis, "fifty . . . black daguerrotypists [including Jules Lion of New Orleans (1810–66), James Presley Ball of Cincinnati (1825–1904/05?), and Augustus Washington of Hartford (1820–75)] . . . operated successful galleries in American cities" during the 1840s.[43]

In 1848, in addition to its stature as an antislavery center, Boston was rivaled only by New York City, where Mathew Brady (1822–96) kept his studio, as the photography capital of the nation.[44] By the Civil War, which brought Brady recognition for his images of battleground carnage, mass-produced pictorial magazines such as *Harper's Weekly* and *Frank Leslie's* circulated nationally, their healthy circulations driven in large part by a combination of hand-drawn illustrations and the occasional introduction of eye-grabbing prints made from the new medium of photography.[45] This daring, nervy, fledgling technology nevertheless was not immune to gendered and racialized politics and policies. As the historian Nell Irvin Painter writes, for public photographs featuring African American men, the place to go in the 1840s was neither a gallery's opulent rooms nor a periodical's lush pages, but rather "the files of metropolitan police, where photography had taken its place as a tool of law enforcement."[46]

The scholarship of Kim Sichel and Gwendolyn DuBois Shaw confirms that a few African American photographers did shoot dignified pictures of black community members in mid-nineteenth-century Boston. Sichel states, "[D]aguerrotypist John B. Bailey (active in Boston during the 1840s) . . . taught James P. Ball the art of photography. [And] the painter Edward Mitchell Bannister (1820–1901) was photographing in Boston in about 1840."[47] In addition to making a livelihood, it was to effect "subversive resistance," writes Willis, to replace "negative representations" of black people in white America's literature and art with flattering, humanizing portraits, that many early African American photographers plied their trade.[48] Douglass, who shared the dais with William Craft and William Wells Brown at an 1849 antislavery meeting, immediately gauged the enormousness of the photograph's influence on abolition, and of photography's influential ability to subvert southern slavery. Complaining in the *Liberator* during 1849 of white artists who painted as if all black people looked alike, and made "the likeness of the negro, rather than of the man," Douglass himself posed for numerous photographs over his lifetime, in addition to sitting for artists who painted or sculpted his image following the current fashion.[49] Perhaps he additionally meant to imply that the new visual medium gave a more authentic and dignified rendering of the uniqueness, beauty, and authority of individual African Americans than did other artistic forms. In her book *Portraits of a People*, art historian Gwendolyn DuBois Shaw reminds us that non-black artists during Douglass's day did produce "portraits of African American sitters . . . that are dignified, distinct, and far from stereotypical." Yet, she insisted that "until African Americans began to represent themselves they would not find artists capable or interested in portraying them with the sensitivity that the serious representation of individuals required."[50]

Craft's daguerreotype displayed her in the disguise of masculinity and whiteness that enabled her escape, yet the woman and the black underneath her garments subverted stereotypical meanings associated with this gender and race, audaciously confronting white audiences with her humanity, her intellect, and the ease of her adjustment to freedom. Her decision to sit for the picture may have been inspired by Douglass, William Wells Brown, and other famous runaways. Fugitives who passed muster with the white abolitionist organizations (it was this leadership that typically selected ex-slaves whose lectures or autobiographies would verify the humanity of the race) would recast their public speeches into written narratives, in order to raise money for abolition, and to provide themselves and their families an independent means of support.[51] In his study *Blind Memory*, Marcus Wood finds that fugitive slaves inserted powerful and assertive visual representations of themselves into their published memoirs, in order to undermine the power of conventional illustrations depicting runaways as pitiful, suffering victims.[52] Craft's direct gaze, cleft chin, and refined masculine clothes—her literal transfiguration into a wealthy, albeit sickly, white man—would have shocked and threatened white British and American audiences. As the critic and scholar Teresa C. Zackodnik writes, the complexities invoked by her visual rendering—a man who was really a woman, a white who was really a black, an affluent gentleman who was a dependent invalid who was really an illiterate slave—"unsettled more than it comforted her audiences with the reassuringly familiar," challenging assumptions about the fixity of gender, race, normalcy, and class that those readers viewing her picture may have uncritically accepted.[53]

Craft's daguerreotype survives in the form of a steel engraving reproduced opposite *Running a Thousand Miles for Freedom*'s title page. Like the title page, the fugitive slave woman whose running is represented reflects the complex networks that supported ex-slaves as they strove to attain liberated lives. The inscriptions "After Hale's dag." and "S. A. Schoff and J. Andrews" in the bottom left and right of the engraving of Ellen Craft offer clues to a hidden history. Instead of a black photographer, at least three white Bostonians were involved in the production of Craft's daguerreotype, and in the composition of the steel engraving for her slave narrative's customary frontispiece illustration.

Hale, Schoff, and Andrews were members of the Massachusetts Charitable Mechanic Association (MCMA), an influential group of urban tradesmen. Founded in 1799, the venerable MCMA had named the patriot Paul Revere (1795–98) its first president, and it chiefly held educational programs for its members and competitive exhibitions of their work.[54] Luther Holman Hale (1823–?), who made the daguerreotype of Craft, occupied a studio at 109 Washington Street, near the *Liberator*'s office. Here William submitted business notices for the weekly issue, and two blocks down stood the shop of bookbinder and bookseller Bela Marsh (1797–1869), who specialized in antislavery literature and regularly advertised his inventory in the *Liberator*. One block from Hale on 228 Washington Street was Stephen Alonzo Schoff (1818–1905), who engraved Craft's image and was nationally respected for the quality of his work. Joseph Andrews (1806–73), Schoff's collaborator, had toured European studios and museums in the 1840s with him, and also lived downtown, on 66 State Street.[55] While I have not found Schoff's and Andrews's names in the membership rolls or subscription lists of local antislavery societies, other evidence, in addition to their geographical proximity to each other and the Crafts' haunts, suggests that they were sympathetic to abolition. Schoff had made an engraving of the minister Theodore Parker, who in the parlor of Hayden's house gave the Crafts the legal Christian marriage they had longed for. Andrews's work graced the pages of the antislavery annual the *Liberty Bell*, edited by Maria Weston Chapman (1806–85);[56] he illustrated books by abolitionists John Greenleaf Whittier (1807–92) and Lydia Maria Child (1802–80); and he would engrave 1852 and 1853 editions of *Uncle Tom's Cabin*.

Hale's role in producing Craft's daguerreotype and engraving may suggest the paucity of black photographers in Boston during the early years of this new technology. Additionally, it was commonplace in the antebellum, urban North for black men to find themselves barred from competing with white men like Hale, Schoff, and Andrews for employment and apprenticeships in highly skilled trades, and locked out of memberships in trade organizations or guilds that would set them alongside white men. Or Hale, Schoff, and Andrews may have been recommended to the Crafts by antislavery friends. And whether the Crafts first approached them out of their own initiative to market Ellen's story, or whether they were encouraged to do so by Hayden, William Wells Brown, the Rev. Theodore Parker, or other New England abolitionists they had met is uncertain. It is difficult to determine the extent of the Crafts' agency and decision making in this process.

Perhaps what is knowable is that the couple maneuvered between the good intentions of northern abolitionists to point them down safe and remunerative paths, and their willfulness and determination to chart their own directions in life. Craft and her husband may no longer have been required to jump at Collins's commands, but in the precariousness of nominal northern freedom they relied considerably on Boston's abolitionists to give them a leg up financially until they could stand on their own, to groom them as writers and public speakers, to manage their appearances in the antislavery press, and to protect them from kidnappers and other harm. The cultural historian Ann Fabian reminds us, "[T]he stories told by former slaves did not always end with the narrators' incorporation into a free society; they ended with narrators on the lecture circuit—no longer enslaved, but suspended somewhere between slavery and freedom."[57] On the other hand, as Teresa C. Zackodnik cautions, it is important to balance interpretations of how an ex-slave woman like Craft may have been victimized and commodified by the activists and audiences who eagerly sought her story, with the evidence that she and other fugitives did actively exercise "agency or choice" in deciding how their bodies and writing would gain them attention, earn them a living, and provide them with at least a modicum of security and safety.[58]

The logical follow-up to the production and circulation of Craft's daguerreotype and engraving was the publication of an actual narrative. Her book with

William would not come to fruition until over one decade later, due in part to the growing sectarianism within the American Congress and its compromises to preserve the Union with slavery's expansionists. At no other time since her escape from Georgia did Craft dangle so precipitously between freedom and servitude than in the months following Congress's passage of the Fugitive Slave Law of 1850. This legislation entitled all slave owners to recapture their "property" that had escaped to the Free States. It obligated federal judges, commissioners, and other authorities to marshal all their resources and come to the aid of any southerners who wished to recommit their wayward slaves to manacles and chains. It punished anyone harboring fugitives with stiff fines and prison sentences.[59] As hundreds of former slaves who had found refuge in the North packed their bags and headed for the security of Canada or England, William and Ellen Craft found themselves at the center of a three-week-long cat-and-mouse chase. In November 1850, seeking to make a national example of them, their owner Robert Collins paid two bounty hunters, Willis H. Hughes and John Knight, to recapture the couple and return them to Macon. A biracial group of Boston's black and white men, the Vigilance Committee, formed to shield the Crafts from recapture. They devised a strategy consisting of constant harassment of the bounty hunters, including pelting them with eggs and rotten food, arresting them for driving their carriages too quickly through the streets, and detaining them for smoking in public.[60]

Vigilance Committee members coordinated safe houses for fugitives such as the Crafts. They separated the famous pair and, like pieces on a chessboard, moved them from safe house to safe house in Boston and its suburbs of Brookline and Cambridge, and then further north in the state to the port town of Marblehead. Lewis Hayden sheltered William at 66 Phillips Street, and, rather than surrender to slave catchers, he brandished a match and threatened to blow up his house and everyone in it with two kegs of gunpowder. Meanwhile, Ellen stayed alone one week at the 1 Exeter Place home of Theodore Parker; she also was separated from William and sequestered at the Brookline residences of the antislavery lawyer Ellis Gray Loring (1803–58), and of local politician William Ingersoll Bowditch (1819–1909) and his family at 9 Toxteth Street. Finally, like their journey out of Georgia, both were spirited upstate from Boston by the UGRR. Recalling the cramped attic space where the fugitive slave Harriet Jacobs hid, they were concealed at 236 Washington Street in the Marblehead, Essex County, home of Betsy Dodge (1815–?) and her carpenter husband, Simeon (1819–?), a UGRR "conductor" who had built a tiny room under the floor accessible by a hidden trap door. There, they awaited the all-clear to leave for Portland, Maine, in preparation for crossing over the Canadian border.[61]

Once again, Craft was called upon to present an outward appearance that might not necessarily have revealed her actual feelings. Evading Hughes and Knight—evading reenslavement—became her primary task. She must have been upset by this turn of events that cut short William's profitable business, postponed her plans to publish a narrative with him (and perhaps to sell copies of her engraving), and, in so doing, slowed down the process of weaning them both from economic dependence upon the abolitionists. Where she must have been secretly terrified of losing her husband, her freedom, and possibly even her life, and worried about burdening or exposing to danger black and white activist friends who sheltered her, observers note that she projected an air of tranquility and calm.[62] In freedom she crafted the public persona of submissive wife and quiet helpmeet, while partnering with William behind the scenes, as she had in slavery, in planning their future and supporting their household.[63]

The Vigilance Committee's tactics worked, and a defeated Hughes and Knight fled its wrath back to Macon. However, Craft and her husband understandably desired permanence and peace. Funded by the Boston abolitionists, they traveled secretly from the Portland safe house of Mrs. Oliver Dennet to Halifax, Nova Scotia, where they booked passage on the *Cambria*, a steamship captained by John Leitch of the British and North American Rail line. After embarking on their transatlantic voyage during the final week of November, they arrived in Liverpool on December 11, 1850.[64] Craft would divide the remaining two-thirds of her life between the home she and William eventually made at 12 Cambridge Court, in Hammersmith, a suburb of west London, and, once again, the cotton fields of her early Georgia home.

In England, Craft would continue a pattern of both participating in the quiet domesticity of home and motherhood and entering the limelight, especially when personal outrage or public scandal necessitated her opinions. For example, in her narrative composed with William, which the Irish Quaker William King Tweedie (1803–63) at last published in London in 1860,[65] her husband's first-person voice dominates the text and suggests his sole authorship. Recently, however, scholars have become skeptical about designating William as the solitary creator of *Running*, and they have offered nuanced arguments in support of reinstating Ellen Craft as William's active collaborator and coauthor. Sarah Brusky, for example, relies on documentary evidence that Craft attended and answered questions at antislavery lectures, and at one time even delivered a lecture on her own, to speculate on the likelihood of Craft's continuing this pattern of collaboration through the authorship of the narrative.[66] Additionally, Daneen Wardrop proposes that the discussion of legal issues facing slave women at the beginning of the memoir, "so marked in *Running* as to distinguish it from any [antebellum] text authored by a male writer," verifies Ellen's participation as "a driving and creative force in the pair." Comparing Ellen to other nineteenth-century black American women writers, Wardrop observes that the details and silences evident in *Running*'s "manifold cases" of sexual abuse, and the book's attention to slave mothers, suggest the intervention and "delicacy" of a woman like Craft who observed and perhaps experienced such situations firsthand.[67]

On other occasions, Craft is quite visible. Once ensconced in England, Craft and her husband had the good fortune of being initially supported and advised by a group of wealthy and internationally known abolitionists, including Lady Byron (1792–1860), widow of the famed Romantic poet, and Harriet Martineau (1802–76), the famous philosopher, travel writer and feminist, who spirited them further south to Ockham School, Surrey, for two years of intensive education.[68] Quickly mastering the skills of reading and writing, in December 1852 Ellen published and appended her signature to an open letter, widely circulated in the British and American antislavery press, that intended to silence the "erroneous report" that she wanted to abandon William, and return to southern slavery in the company of a white gentleman whom she had met in London. "I had much rather starve in England," she wrote, "than be a slave for the best man that ever breathed upon the American continent,"[69] and she reported herself to be happily married and a new mother. She may have been sassing back to someone more specific than anonymous rumor-mongers accusing her of her infidelity. In the thick of the November 1850 bounty hunt, her former master, Collins, had written a public letter to President Millard Fillmore, to complain how the Bostonians had harassed Hughes and Knight and defied the Fugitive Slave Law.[70] His correspondence and the president's reply had been printed in the transatlantic antislavery press. To readers, Craft's words, by affirming domesticity, by attesting to her literate ability to imagine, organize, and execute a letter to the nation she had escaped, may have registered as a bold challenge to the institution of slavery that Collins and the Fugitive Slave Law symbolized, and as a victory over a system that was supposed to treat her merely as a beast of burden. Craft's letter thus epitomizes her outspoken position as a critic of racial prejudice and prejudiced white people, slave owning or not. We can understand it as a politically and culturally activist moment that inflected and deepened her domestic roles as a free wife and mother in the North and in Great Britain. As P. Gabrielle Foreman writes, "[D]espite her nearly universal acceptance on both sides of the Atlantic by those of a wide range of castes and colors, Ellen articulates her racial politics clearly."[71]

In England Craft consistently balanced the conventional gender roles of wife and mother with unorthodox, outspoken public activism. She followed her public letter of 1852 with a silent protest of the American exhibit at the London World's Fair, which the transatlantic newspapers also traced.[72] She hosted abolitionist guests in her Hammersmith home and attended meetings of such reform organizations as the London Emancipation Committee, the Women's Suffrage Organization, and the women's arm of the British and Foreign Freedmen's Aid Society.[73] To Craft personally, the most memorable example of this confluence of private and public behavior may have occurred in the fall of 1865, when she relocated her mother, Maria, after Georgia fell to the Union troops and raised money to bring her from America to England.[74]

After nineteen years in England, the historian R. J. M. Blackett writes, she and William were beset by the financial woes that often hounded American fugitives abroad, culminating in "no reliable source of income" and their reluctant sale of their house in order to settle debts.[75] With three of their five children in tow, they returned in August 1869 to the reunited States, where their longtime abolitionist friends in Massachusetts triumphantly welcomed them. Craft was greeted by the famous fugitive and activist Harriet Jacobs and her daughter Louisa at a talk on William's mission work in Africa that he had been invited to present to the New England Women's Club.[76] The couple had publicly announced their intention to move back home to Georgia so that they could instruct the recently emancipated slaves and inculcate within them lessons of self-sufficiency, tailored to the South's struggling postwar economy, that would end their dependence on the contract-labor system.[77] Craft's pre–Civil War success in liberating her mother from bondage also hints at a private motive for their homecoming: perhaps, traumatically, they wished to scour the South with William for other lost relatives; perhaps, unspeakably, to search for a child of their own left behind or sold downriver.

The Crafts rented land and started teaching in Hickory Hill plantation, South Carolina. When vigilantes burned them out, they resettled outside Savannah in Bryan County, to found in 1871 the Woodville cooperative farm and school plantation, a forerunner of the industrial schools. Here former slave children and their parents would attend classes for half of the day, while financing their education and feeding themselves by cultivating crops during the other half.[78] The Crafts had joined the ranks of hundreds of teachers, one-fourth of whom were black, who had set out to educate Georgia's ex-slaves. In their typical spirit of independence, wife and husband operated outside the auspices of the federal government and the missionary societies that were aiding in this enterprise, choosing instead to raise their own funds from Boston's former abolitionists.[79] They also met with other setbacks and disappointments that followed the torching of their first farm/school experiment by white supremacists. For example, Woodville ended in bankruptcy due to crop failures and when the couple's backers, who included old Vigilance Committee allies such as James Freeman Clarke, Edward Everett Hale (1822–1909), and George Hilliard (1808–79), pulled out of the experiment in response to allegations that William was misspending the thousands of dollars in donations they had raised for him.[80] The Crafts' return to post–Civil War Georgia, like their brief residency in pre–Civil War Boston, from this perspective could be said to have been troubled by unfulfilled promises and unrealized dreams.

Such events should not diminish the significance of Ellen Craft's personal and political triumphs. She did attain her youthful vow to raise free children—Charles Estlin Phillips (b. 1852); William Jr.; Brougham; Alfred; and her namesake, Ellen. Before she died in 1891, she would be able to see beyond the looming grave to a legacy of teaching, community reform, government service, and civic activism that she had bequeathed to subsequent generations of the Craft family. She had demonstrated how ex-slave women could participate both publicly and privately in the antislavery movement, and she had stretched meanings of gender, class, race, disability, and other social constructs.[81] Her narrative with William had accomplished complicated work, including blasting the paradigm of a single-authored text that described a single fugitive's flight to freedom without diminishing or downplaying the issues at stake in the perpetuation of southern slavery. Because her life presents a former slave woman's experience of the South both before and after the Civil War, she continues to capture readers' imaginations. Preparing ex-slaves in her twilight years for the education, self-determination, institution building, and civic participation she only could imagine as a youth, Craft stands as a symbol of both the bright sky of Emancipation and the rocky road of the post-Reconstruction South, of public advocacy and progressive social change.

### NOTES

To conduct the research on Ellen Craft appearing in this essay, and to contribute to the mosaic of her life, I would like to thank the following institutions for their generous support: the W. E. B. Du Bois Institute for African and African American Studies, Harvard University, where I was a Fellow during fall semester 1999; the Gilder Lehrman Institute for the Study of Slavery and Abolition, which supported my research at Columbia University during the summer of 1999; and the Radcliffe Institute for Advanced Study, Harvard University, where I was a 2004–5 Augustus Anson Whitney Fellow. I also extend much appreciation to Greg French of Early Photography in Jamaica Plain, Mass.; to Catherina Slautterback, Associate Curator of Prints and Photographs at the Boston Athenæum; and to Jacalyn Blume, Visual Resources Reference Librarian, the Arthur and Elizabeth Schlesinger

Library on the History of Women in America, for their unstinting advice and generous assistance as I have investigated the production history of Ellen Craft's engraving. I finally extend warm thanks to Sarah Robbins for her perceptive comments on an earlier draft of this manuscript.

1. William and Ellen Craft, *Running 1,000 Miles for Freedom, or the Escape of William and Ellen Craft from Freedom* (1860; repr., Athens: University of Georgia Press, 1999).

2. Carla L. Peterson, *"Doers of the Word": African American Women Speakers and Writers in the North, 1830–1880* (New Brunswick: Rutgers University Press, 1995).

3. James Olney, "'I was Born': Slave Narratives, Their Status as Autobiography and as Literature," in *The Slave's Narrative*, ed. Charles T. Davis and Henry Louis Gates Jr. (New York: Oxford University Press, 1991), 148–74.

4. William and Ellen Craft, *Running*, 3.

5. Ibid., 7.

6. Ibid., 3.

7. Ibid., 3.

8. Donnie D. Bellamy, "Macon, Georgia, 1823–1860: A Study in Urban Slavery," *Phylon* 45, no. 4 (1984): 298, 303; Allen D. Candler and Clement A. Evans, *Georgia: Comprising Sketches of Counties, Towns, Events, Institutions, and Persons, Arranged in Cyclopedic Form* (1900; repr., Atlanta, Ga.: State Historical Association, 1906), 3:543.

9. See "The Craft-Naylor Suit: The Third Day of the Georgia Libel Case," *Boston Daily Advertiser*, June 8, 1878.

10. Robert Collins, *Essay on the Treatment and Management of Slaves. Written for the Seventh Annual Fair of the Southern Central Agricultural Society, October, 1852* (Macon, Ga.: B. F. Griffin, 1852). In 1853, perhaps to capitalize on the notoriety of Collins's recent entanglements with the Crafts and the members of the Vigilance Committee, Eastburn's Press of Boston published a second edition.

11. William and Ellen Craft, *Running*, 8–10.

12. Ibid., 21.

13. For information on slaves' daily activities, see, for example, Jacqueline Jones, *Labor of Love, Labor of Sorrow: Black Women, Work, and Family from Slavery to Freedom* (New York: Basic Books, 1985); Brenda Stevenson, *Life in Black and White: Family and Community in the Slave South* (New York: Oxford, 1996); Deborah Gray White, *Aren't I a Woman?: Female Slaves in the Plantation South* (New York: Norton, 1985); David R. Goldfield, "Black Life in Old South Cities," in *Before Freedom Came*, eds. D. C. Campbell Jr. with Kym S. Rice.

14. William and Ellen Craft, *Running*, 21.

15. Ibid., 7.

16. Elizabeth Fox-Genovese, *Within the Plantation Household: Black and White Women of the Old South* (Chapel Hill: University of North Carolina Press, 1988), 34–35, 308–15.

17. Elredge J. McReady, "Wedding Feast in N.Y. Celebrates 1850 Marriage of Macon Slave Couple," *Macon Metro Times*, November 13–19, 1991, 1. Darlene Clark Hine and Kathleen Thompson, *A Shining Thread of Hope: The History of Black Women in America* (New York: Broadway Books, 1998), 80.

18. William and Ellen Craft, *Running*, 19, 21. See also Barbara McCaskill, "'Yours Very Truly': Ellen Craft—The Fugitive as Text and Artifact," *African American Review* 28, no. 4 (1994): 513–15; Jean Fagan Yellin, *Harriet Jacobs: A Life* (New York: Basic Civitas Books, 2004), 22–29; Fox-Genovese, *Within the Plantation Household*, 378–87.

19. In *Running*, their memoir, William claims that he proposed the idea of escaping in this way

to a very reluctant Ellen. "After I thought of the plan," he says, "I suggested it to my wife, but at first she shrank from the idea." However, Josephine Brown, a fugitive slave and friend of the Crafts, asserts in the 1856 biography of her father, William Wells Brown, that it actually was Ellen Craft who initially came up with the idea. If Josephine Brown's story is correct, then William's silencing of Ellen and revision of the facts in the 1861 narrative may stand as an example of how abolitionist literature represented fugitive slave women as meek, submissive Victorian mothers and wives, not the castrating, controlling figures of proslavery propaganda. See William and Ellen Craft, *Running*, 21; McCaskill, "'Yours Very Truly,'" 526nn2–4.

20. Armistead Wilson, *Five Hundred Thousand Strokes for Freedom: A Series of Anti-Slavery Tracts of which Half a Million are Now First Issued by the Friends of the Negro* (London: W. and F. G. Cash and William Tweedie, 1853), 5; William Wells Brown, "Singular Escape," *Liberator*, January 12, 1849, 7; "William and Ellen Crafts [*sic*], The Fugitive Slaves from Boston," *Liverpool Mercury*, January 8, 1851, 6; "The Fugitive Slaves from Boston," *Patriot*, January 16, 1851, 4.

21. Bellamy, "Macon," 307.

22. Steven Hahn, *A Nation under Our Feet: Black Political Struggles from Slavery to the Great Migration* (Cambridge, Mass.: The Belknap Press of Harvard University, 2003), 43; and class discussion with Hahn, "African American Struggles for Civil Rights in the Twentieth Century," NEH Summer Institute, W. E. B. Du Bois Institute for African and African American Research, Harvard University, June 30, 2008.

23. William and Ellen Craft, *Running*, 53.

24. "The Autobiography of Craft," *The Boston Daily Advertiser*, June 7, 1878.

25. Hahn, *Nation under Our Feet*, 22.

26. Wilson, *Five Hundred Thousand Strokes*, 5.

27. Hahn, *Nation under Our Feet*, 27.

28. William and Ellen Craft, *Running*, 21.

29. Hahn, *Nation under Our Feet*, 41.

30. Hine and Thompson, *Shining Thread of Hope*, 93–100.

31. Theodore Parker, *The Trial of Theodore Parker for the "Misdemeanor," or a Speech in Faneuil Hall against Kidnapping, Before the Circuit Court of the United States, at Boston, April 3, 1855* (Boston: For the Author, 1855), 146–47; James Freeman Clarke, *Anti-Slavery Days: A Sketch of the Struggle Which Ended in the Abolition of Slavery in the United States* (1883; repr., New York: AMS Press, 1972), 83–84.

32. See, for example, the following: *Appalling Features of Slavery: Leeds Anti-Slavery Series No. 46* (London: W. and F. G. Cash and William Tweedie, 1853), 1–2; Charlotte Elizabeth, "The Slave and Her Babe," in *The Liberty Minstrel*, comp. George W. Clark (New York: Leavitt and Alden, 1845), 13.

33. "An Incident at the South," *Liberator*, February 9, 1849; "William and Ellen Craft: Fugitives from Slavery," *Non-Slaveholder* 4, no. 3 (1849): 69–70.

34. Jeffrey Ruggles, *The Unboxing of Henry Box Brown* (Richmond: Library of Virginia, 2003), 27–32.

35. John Eisenberg, *The Great Match Race: When the North Met the South in America's First Sports Spectacle* (Boston: Houghton Mifflin, 2006); "The Legacy of the Horse: The Horse in 19th Century American Sport: Intersectional Match Racing," The International Museum of the Horse, http://www.imh.org/museum/history.php?chapter=83 (accessed December 30, 2008).

36. Born one year after the great race, William Craft, in name only, recalls Billy Crafts, the jockey

for Van Ranst who lost the first heat riding American Eclipse against his southern opponent (Eisenberg, *Great Match Race*, 187–97).

37. Frederick Douglass, *The Narrative of Frederick Douglass: An American Slave* (Boston: Anti-Slavery Office, 1845), in *Shadowing Slavery: Five African American Autobiographical Narratives*, ed. John Ernest (Acton, Mass.: Copley Publishing Group, 2002), 109.

38. Archibald H. Grimké, "Anti-Slavery Boston," *New England Magazine* 3, no. 4 (1890): 458; Allen Chamberlain, "Old Passages of Boston's Underground Railroad," in *Beacon Hill: Its Ancient Pastures and Early Mansions* (Boston: Houghton Mifflin, 1925), 221; Robert C. Hayden and the staff of the Museum of Afro-American History, *The African Meeting House in Boston: A Celebration of History* (Boston: Companion Press Book, 1987), 18–25; Thomas H. O'Connor, "Lewis Hayden," in *Eminent Bostonians* (Cambridge, Mass.: Harvard University Press, 2002), 133–34; Jaci Conry, "The Other Beacon Hill," *American Legacy* (Winter 2005): 66.

39. Robert C. Hayden, *African Americans in Boston: More Than 350 Years* (Boston: Trustees of the Public Library of the City of Boston, 1991), 76–77, 104; Conry, "Other Beacon Hill," 62, 63–64.

40. Lewis Hayden, Advertisement, *Liberator*, July 13, 1849, 111; William Craft, Advertisement, *Liberator*, July 27, 1849, 119.

41. See "Theodore Parker," *Liberator*, October 7, 1864, 164.

42. "Runaway Slaves," *[Macon] Georgia Telegraph and Messenger*, February 13, 1849; Lyman Allen, "William and Ellen Craft," *Liberator*, March 2, 1849, 35; "Welcome to the Fugitives," *Liberator*, April 6, 1849, 54.

43. Deborah Willis, *Reflections in Black: A History of Black Photographers, 1840 to the Present* (New York: W. W. Norton, 2000), 4, 5.

44. Pamela Hoyle, *The Development of Photography in Boston, 1840–1875* (Boston: Boston Athenaeum, 1979), 6, 8–11.

45. David Tatham, *Winslow Homer and the Pictorial Press* (Syracuse: Syracuse University Press, 2003), 19–47.

46. Nell Irvin Painter, *Sojourner Truth: A Life, A Symbol* (New York: W. W. Norton, 1996), 196.

47. Kim Sichel *Black Boston: Documentary Photography and the African American Experience* (Boston: Boston University Gallery, 1994); Gwendolyn DuBois Shaw, "Landscapes of Labor: Race, Religion, and Rhode Island in the Painting of Edward Mitchell Bannister," in *Postbellum, Pre-Harlem: African American Literature and Culture, 1877–1919*, ed. Barbara McCaskill and Caroline Gebhard, 59–73 (New York: New York University Press, 2006).

48. Deborah Willis, "The Sociologist's Eye: W. E. B. Du Bois and the Paris Exposition," in *A Small Nation of People: W. E. B. Du Bois and African American Portraits of Progress*, 51–78 (New York: Amistad Press and the Library of Congress, 2003).

49. Frederick Douglass, "Negro Portraits," *Liberator*, April 20, 1846, 62; Frederick S. Voss, *Majestic in His Wrath: A Pictorial Life of Frederick Douglass* (Washington, D.C.: Smithsonian Institution Press, 1995), 22, 70, 71, 79, 88, 95, 97.

50. Gwendolyn DuBois Shaw, *Portraits of a People: Picturing African Americans in the Nineteenth Century* (Andover, Mass.: Addison Gallery of American Art, Phillips Academy, 2006), 13, 14.

51. Ann Fabian, "Slaves," chapter 3 of *The Unvarnished Truth: Personal Narratives in Nineteenth-Century America* (Berkeley: University of California Press, 2000), 80.

52. Marcus Wood, "Rhetoric and the Runaway: The Iconography of Slave Escape in England and America," in *Blind Memory: Visual Representations of Slavery in America and England, 1780–1865*, 78–142 (New York: Routledge, 2000). In addition to mobilizing public opinion against slavery and

replenishing the coffers of the antislavery cause, as William Craft implies in the preface to *Running a Thousand Miles for Freedom*, the Crafts sought to finance the education of their growing brood of children through the sale of their 1861 narrative. That they planned to enlist the engraving of Ellen in this fundraising scheme is obvious, since her picture stands opposite the title page of *Running*'s first edition, and since, years before the narrative's publication, the English abolitionists advertised copies of Ellen's portrait for sale, alongside notices of *Uncle Tom*, in their publications. See Leeds Anti-Slavery Association, Leeds Anti-Slavery Series (London: W. and F. G. Cash and William Tweedie, 1857).

53. Teresa C. Zackodnik, *The Mulatta and the Politics of Race* (Jackson: University Press of Mississippi, 2004), 58.

54. See the "Fine Arts" sections in the following: *The Fourth Exhibition of the Massachusetts Charitable Mechanic Association at Quincy Hall, in the City of Boston, September 16, 1844* (Boston: Crocker and Brewster, 1844), 25; *The Fifth Exhibition of the Massachusetts Charitable Mechanic Association, at Faneuil and Quincy Halls, in the City of Boston, September, 1847* (Boston: Dutton and Wentworth, 1847), 24; *The Sixth Exhibition of the Massachusetts Charitable Mechanic Association, at Faneuil and Quincy Halls, in the City of Boston, September, 1850* (Boston: Eastburn's Press, 1850), 147; *The Seventh Exhibition of the Massachusetts Charitable Mechanic Association, at Faneuil and Quincy Halls, in the City of Boston, September, 1853* (Boston: Damrell & Moore and George Coolidge, 1853), 103, 105.

55. Ronald Polito, *A Directory of Boston Photographers: 1840–1900*, 2nd ed. (Boston: University of Massachusetts, 1983), 37; *The Boston Directory: Containing the City Record, a General Directory of the Citizens, a Special Directory of Trades, Professions, &c. An Almanac from July 1849, to July 1850, with a Variety of Miscellaneous Matter* (Boston: George Adams, 1849), 61, 151, 323; *The Directory of the City of Boston: Embracing the City Record, General Directory of the Citizens, and a Special Directory of Trades, Professions, &c. with an Almanac from July 1850, to July 1851* (Boston: George Adams, 1850), 77, 176, 285. See also "Hale, Luther Holman" in *Craig's Daguerreian Registry*, comp. and ed. John S. Craig (Torrington, Conn.: J. S. Craig, 1994–96), http://www.daguerreotype.com/ (accessed December 1, 2008).

56. For a thoughtful study of the transatlantic community of black and white reformers whose constellated in the pages of Weston's annual, the longest running gift book during the American antislavery movement, see Valerie Domenica Levy's dissertation "The Antislavery Web of Connection: Maria Weston Chapman's *Liberty Bell* (1838–1859)" (PhD diss., University of Georgia, 2002).

57. Fabian, *Unvarnished Truth*, 85.

58. Zackodnik, *The Mulatta*, 47; see also her entire discussion entitled "The White Slave: Slavery's Zero Limit," 43–50.

59. Barbara McCaskill, "William and Ellen Craft in Transatlantic Literature and Life," introduction to William and Ellen Craft, *Running*, xii.

60. "Slave Hunters Arrested—Knight and Hughes Arrested for Slander, at the Suit of William Crafts—Damages Laid at $10,000—Secret Bail—Proceedings of the Vigilance Committee!!" *[Macon] Georgia Telegraph and Messenger*, November 5, 1850; "The Fugitive Slave Case in Boston," *[Macon] Georgia Telegraph and Messenger*, November 6, 1850; "The Boston Slave Hunt and the Vigilance Committee," *[Macon] Georgia Telegraph and Messenger*, November 12, 1850; *Liverpool Mercury*, November 12, 1850; "The Boston Excitement," *[Macon] Georgia Telegraph and Messenger*, November 13, 1850; *Report of the Great Anti-Slavery Meeting, Held April 9, 1851, in the Public Room, Broadmead, Bristol, to Receive the Fugitive Slaves, William and Ellen Craft* (Bristol: James Ackland,

1851), 11–12; "The Boston Slave Hunt—Another History," *New York Tribune*, December 9, 1850, 5; "The Slave Hunt in Boston," *[Boston] Commonwealth*, January 15, 1851; Vincent Y. Bowditch, *Life and Correspondence of Henry Ingersoll Bowditch* (Boston: Houghton Mifflin, 1902), 372.

61. Wilbur H. Siebert, *The Underground Railroad from Slavery to Freedom* (New York: Macmillan, 1898), 132–33, 252; Wilber H. Siebert, *The Underground Railroad in Massachusetts* (Worcester, Mass.: American Antiquarian Society, 1936), 42–43; Priscilla Sawyer Lord and Virginia Clegg Gamage, *Marblehead: The Spirit of '76 Lives Here* (Philadelphia: Chilton Book Company, 1972), 172, 173; National Park Service and Salem Maritime Historical Site, "Abolitionists and the Underground Railroad in the Essex National Heritage Area," http://www.nps.gov/archive/sama/indepth/pdfs/ugrr4.pdf (accessed December 1, 2008).

62. Thomas Wentworth Higginson, "The Romance of History, in 1850," in *The Liberty Bell* (Boston: Prentiss, Sawyer, 1858), 51.

63. Lydia Maria Child, *The Freedmen's Book* (1865; repr. New York: Arno Press, 1968), 204.

64. Timetable, British and North American Royal Mail Steam-Ships, *Liverpool Mercury*, November 1, 1850, 4; "Arrival of the British and North American Royal Mail Steam-Ship, Cambria," *Liverpool Mercury*, December 13, 1850, 2; "The Fugitive Slaves from Boston," *Patriot*, January 16, 1851, 34.

65. In addition to their flight from America and resettlement in England, the time necessarily spent in acquiring literacy and learning and supporting their growing family may have delayed the creation and publication of *Running*. When the narrative was published in 1860, it was well timed, coming on the heels of John Brown's 1859 raid on Harper's Ferry and the heightened debates about slavery that his failed rebellion had precipitated. On the other hand, since the imminence of war may have overshadowed their book, and since the Crafts disclosed little that was different from what they had already said in public venues about their escape from slavery and their two years in the North, their book, though warmly received, failed to achieve the attention and transnational influence of many slaves' narratives published at the height of the genre's production, in the 1840s and 1850s.

66. Sarah Brusky, "The Travels of William and Ellen Craft: Race and Travel Literature in the 19th Century," *Prospects* 25 (2000): 177–91.

67. Daneen Wardrop, "Ellen Craft and the Case of Salomé Muller in *Running a Thousand Miles for Freedom*," *Women's Studies* 33 (2004): 961–84.

68. William and Ellen Craft, *Running*, 67–68.

69. Ellen Craft to William Lloyd Garrison, *Liberator*, December 17, 1852, 207. See also *London Antislavery Advocate* 1, no. 3 (1852): 22; *Pennsylvania Freeman*, December 23, 1852, 207; *National Anti-Slavery Standard*, December 23, 1852; and the discussion of Ellen's letter in McCaskill, "'Yours Very Truly,'" 512–15. Craft is paraphrasing the words of William Cowper, an eighteenth-century British poet and abolitionist, who wrote in his book-length poem *The Task* (1785): "Slaves cannot breathe in England: if their lungs / Receive our air, that moment they are free; / They touch our country, and their shackles fall" (bk. 2, *The Timepiece*, l. 40). She and William also quote these lines of Cowper's as the epigraph for *Running a Thousand Miles for Freedom*.

70. Robert Collins, letter to Pres. Millard Fillmore, *New York Herald*, November 20, 1850, 1; "Southern News," *New York Tribune*, November 19, 1850, 4.

71. P. Gabrielle Foreman, "Who's Your Mama?: 'White' Mulatta Genealogies, Early Photography, and Anti-Passing Narratives of Slavery and Freedom," *American Literary History* 14 (2002): 503–39.

72. William and Ellen Craft, *Running* 79–82.

73. R. J. M. Blackett, "The Odyssey of William and Ellen Craft," in *Beating against the Barriers: Biographical Essays in Nineteenth-Century Afro-American History* (Baton Rouge: Louisiana State University Press, 1986), 121–22; Yellin, *Harriet Jacobs*, 148, 214.

74. Blackett, "Odyssey," 121; Yellin, *Harriet Jacobs*, 214; "Ellen Craft and Her Mother," *Liberator*, August 4, 1865, 122.

75. Blackett, "Odyssey," 123.

76. Yellin, *Harriet Jacobs*, 218. Two of their sons, William Jr. and Brougham, remained to continue their studies (Blackett, "Odyssey," 123).

77. Blackett, "Odyssey," 123–24.

78. William Craft, "Primary Education in Georgia," *Boston Daily Advertiser*, August 22, 1873; "William Craft's Letter," *Christian Union*, July 30, 1873, 9.

79. Ronald E. Butchart, "Freedmen's Education during Reconstruction," in *The New Georgia Encyclopedia*, http://www.georgiaencyclopedia.org/nge/Article.jsp?id=h-634 (accessed December 30, 2008).

80. "The Craft-Naylor Suit: The Third Day of the Georgia Libel Case," *Boston Daily Advertiser*, June 8, 1878.

81. For example, Ellen Samuels understands disability and illness as an effective lens for examining how the cross-dressing Ellen Craft, in her disguise as an invalid planter, manipulates mid-nineteenth century assumptions about identity. See Ellen Samuels, "'A Complication of Complaints': Untangling Disability, Race, and Gender in William and Ellen Craft's *Running a Thousand Miles for Freedom*," *MELUS* 31, no. 3 (2006): 15–47.

# Fanny Kemble and Frances Butler Leigh

## (1809–1893; 1838–1910)

## *Becoming Georgian*

DANIEL KILBRIDE

In a book dedicated to documenting the lives of Georgia women, it may seem impertinent to wonder whether Frances Anne Kemble (Fanny) and her daughter, Frances Butler Leigh (Fan), were Georgians in any meaningful sense of the word. The State of Georgia itself does not seem certain. The historical marker commemorating "Famous Butler Authors" on the site of the family's Butler Island plantation ignores Fanny Kemble altogether, even though that she was, by virtue of her *Journal of a Residence on a Georgian Plantation* (1863), the most influential of the family's writers. Instead the marker pays homage to her daughter, Frances, for authoring *Ten Years on a Georgia Plantation since the War* (1883), "an interesting and valuable account of life in this section during the Reconstruction." Both adjectives are doubtful. For good measure the marker also honors Owen Wister, Fan's nephew, who "also visited Butler Island plantation." Arguably this Georgia connection did not make much of an impression on young Dan (as he was known in the family), since Owen Wister is best known for his novel *The Virginian* (1902). Another marker at the same location does commemorate "Fannie" Kemble, whose *Journal*, the marker reports testily, "is said to have influenced England against the Confederacy." It does little to establish Kemble's Georgian bona fides, though, since it identifies her as a "brilliant English actress" married to "Pierce Butler of Philadelphia."[1]

Fanny Kemble spent only four months in Georgia (late December 1838 through mid-April 1839), though those weeks impressed her deeply and produced what many readers consider to be the best first-person account of antebellum slave life. The family did not tarry in the South after leaving Hampton Point plantation; by May 1 they were in New York. Fanny Kemble never returned to the South. Though she toured much of the country giving her acclaimed readings of Shakespeare in the 1840s and 1850s, she refused to travel into the slave regions. If time of residence builds roots and legitimates one's claim to belong to a place, Fan was far more the Georgian than her mother. But it is important to observe that Philadelphia was her home for most of her life, and she spent more time in Europe than in the South. She was not yet a year old when she arrived on Butler Island that winter of 1838, and those months left no impression on the infant Fan. Her sister Sarah, by contrast, was three years old. She retained quite vivid memories of her time on the coast, including her interactions with slaves.

Fan's first exposure to Georgia may not have shaped her sense of self, but her close relationship to her father, as well as her membership in a strongly pro-southern clique in Philadelphia high society, impressed upon Fan a strong sense of regional identity rooted in her father's holdings on Butler and St. Simon's Islands at the mouth of the Altamaha River, just south of Darien on the southern Georgia coast. She did not see her father's properties again for nearly twenty-two years, until the fateful spring of 1861, when Pierce traveled to Georgia to see to the disposition of a legal dispute regarding his lands. She returned with him in 1866 and again in 1867. During Reconstruction she poured her energies into restoring the lands to their former glory. Though she failed, Fan established a visceral, lasting bond with the land, the people, and their history. Sarah's connection to Georgia was always tenuous, despite the early promise of 1838–39. She returned to Georgia several times after the Civil War, but only for short periods. She published nothing on her Georgia connection. By temperament as well as choice she was emphatically a Yankee.[2]

In short, Frances Butler Leigh was a Georgian because she chose to be. Her mother and sister decided otherwise. Personal identity always involves the element of choice, of course, but in this case it may be useful to point out that discretion, like any other commodity, is usually distributed unequally. The slaves on the Butler plantations were also Georgians. And while a generation of scholarship has demonstrated that slaves possessed some degree of autonomy, their daily bread was constraint.[3] They were Georgians because Pierce and John Butler, backed up by the laws of Georgia and the United States, would not let them contemplate alternatives. Most white Georgians were also southerners by default, in the sense that they lacked the leisure and wealth that would enable them to consider the rather abstract question of regional identity through reading or travel. But planters were a different story. Though most of them were

FANNY KEMBLE

Steel engraving after painting by Alonzo Chappel after painting
by Sir Thomas Lawrence, copyrighted by Johnson Wilson, & Co.
Courtesy of the Library of Congress, LC-USZ62-69903.

**FRANCES AND SARAH, DAUGHTERS OF FANNY KEMBLE**
Courtesy of the Coastal Georgia Historical Society.

hardly the plantation lords of legend—a myth Fanny's Georgia *Journal* went to some pains to debunk—middling and wealthy southern whites could afford subscriptions to *De Bow's Review* and the *Southern Literary Messenger* and join lyceums and debating societies, all forums that welcomed discussions of regional and national identity.[4] The Butlers were at the very top of this heap. An 1849 appraisal made on the occasion of the death of Pierce's brother John (from dysentery, while serving in the Mexican War) counted 840 slaves on the Butler properties, putting them in the very highest echelon of American slaveholders.[5]

Fanny Kemble wrestled with the problem of her national identity all her adult life. She could not decide whether she was American or English. Her obituary in the *Atlantic Monthly* observed, "whichever side of the ocean she sojourned, she was homesick for the other." Whether she was at heart a citizen of the United States or subject of Great Britain may be uncertain, but one thing is not: Fanny

Kemble did not see herself as a southerner. Fan was a Georgian and a south-erner in the most provisional and cosmopolitan sense, though one common among the highest echelons of southern society.[6] The southern identity em-braced by Frances Butler Leigh was a peculiar sort, a self-conscious affectation made possible by privilege, contemporary political and cultural developments, and personal circumstances. Other planters felt the influence of the first two features; the third was the product of the conditions created by the disastrous marriage of her parents, Pierce Butler and Fanny Kemble.

Frances Butler Leigh opted to become a southerner partly because she knew it would displease and even hurt her mother. Fanny and her girls suffered through difficult relations with one another throughout their lives. In 1864 Fanny likened her vexed connection to Sarah and Fan as resembling that between Great Britain and the United States: "mother and daughter though they be, [they] can no more understand each other than I and my children can." Sarah Butler Wister put it more bluntly. "My Mother was the most stimulating companion I have ever known," she recalled. "[S]he was also the most goad-ing."[7] Many roads led to this unsatisfying destination. By her words and deeds, Fanny Kemble did not always endear herself to her daughters. Even her friends characterized her as temperamental to the point of being "antipodal": it is pos-sible that she suffered from a minor bipolar disorder. Henry James, who be-friended her in Rome during the winter of 1872–73, marveled (in 1880) at the "explosions of vitality (I don't mean merely of temper)" that she could still sum-mon at age seventy-one. She was not completely blind to her own defects, as when she called attention to "the Amazon which is both natural and acquired in me."[8]

Sarah and Fan brought along their own baggage as well. The former suf-fered from depression for much of her adult life. Samuel Ward qualified his characterization of Fan as a "*bel esprit*" by noting that she was also an "*esprit fort*." Sarah, and especially Fan, enraged and saddened their mother with the affection they held for their father, a love that evolved into idealization after his death in 1868. The girls can hardly be held responsible for this state of affairs. Both were scarred by the very public and very nasty breakup of their parents' marriage. For Frances Leigh, becoming Georgian was less an organic process than an act of will, a means of taking sides against her mother and in favor of the memory of her father, of favoring the past against the future. So it should not be surprising that her Georgian roots, however loudly proclaimed, were in the end provisional, superficial. Frances Leigh was more Georgian than her mother and sister, but just barely.[9]

Though she seems not to have known it, Fanny Butler's connection to Georgia commenced on June 7, 1834 when she "was married in Philadelphia . . . to Mr. Pierce Butler, of that city," as she put it discreetly forty-five years later.[10] Butler was a Philadelphian who possessed a large fortune of indeterminate provenance, for all she knew. She claimed later that she was unaware that the source of his wealth lay in two Sea Island plantations worked by enslaved gangs of human laborers. In fact, when Pierce married Fanny in 1834, he did not own a single slave. The family patriarch, the first Pierce Butler, once a major of the British army, had died in 1822 after amassing a fortune in land and slaves around the time of the American Revolution. Under the terms of his will, his Georgia properties were to be dispersed to his grandsons—Thomas, John, and Pierce Mease, the sons of his daughter Sarah and James Mease, a Philadelphia physician—upon the death of the executrix, his daughter Frances, a second Frances Butler.

But the Major insisted on one, cruel, condition that reflected his own self regard as much as his disdain for his medical son-in-law: in order to inherit anything, his grandsons had to change their names to Butler by their sixteenth birthdays. Thomas Mease, who was already of age, refused to do so. He died in 1823. John Mease also declined, for the time being. But Pierce Mease, just twelve upon his grandfather's death, made clear his intention to assume the surname Butler at his first opportunity. When Frances Butler died in 1836, Pierce Mease Butler and his brother John became the second largest slaveholders in Georgia. Out of respect to his mother, John had kept the Mease name until her death in 1831. Pierce was legally entitled to the whole of the dispensation but, in a rare display of magnanimity, allowed his brother an equal share. Though it strains credulity to believe that Fanny did not know where Pierce's money came from before 1836—she probably chose not to dwell on it—she could no longer avoid the unpleasant fact that her well-being, social position, and future prospects all depended on two plantations and on the women and men who toiled there.[11]

Predestination does not enjoy the intellectual respectability it once did, but it can hardly be denied that the marriage of Pierce Butler and Fanny Kemble was doomed from the start. First, it turned out that Fanny, who had married one of the largest owners of human property in the United States, hated slavery. Second, it became apparent that they were temperamentally incompatible. Fanny, who was just twenty-three when she began her triumphant tour of the northeastern United States with her father in 1832, was fresh off of two acclaimed seasons at Covent Garden and an equally successful provincial tour. Critics had singled out her performance as Julia in James Sheridan Knowles's *The Hunchback* for special praise. She was not yet a public figure whose opinions on the issues of the day were sought out. But her 1835 *Journal of Frances Anne Kemble* (her American *Journal*) demonstrated that she held strong antislavery views at the time of her initial tour of the United States. Upon hearing Philadelphian Charles Mifflin's testimony that slaves "are kept in the most brutish ignorance, and too often treated with the most brutal barbarity, in order to ensure their subjugation," she anticipated "a fearful rising of the black flood" against "wrong so long endured—so wickedly inflicted." These early opinions did not augur well for her marriage to a slaveholder. Pierce may have hoped he could temper them by exposure to his own holdings, which were widely considered model plantations both for their productivity and for the condition of the slaves. It was not to be. Her vaguely antislavery sentiments hardened into moral convictions during her marriage. That fact alone determined that it would be an unhappy one.[12]

Fanny might have been able to live with Pierce if the only difference between them had been over slaveholding. It proved to be no obstacle to friendship. Among her closest friends in Philadelphia was the staunchly proslavery Elizabeth Fisher, whose father, Henry Middleton, ranked among the largest slaveholders in South Carolina. Pierce and Fanny, however, possessed clashing temperaments and divergent views of marriage that clinched the difference between uneasy cohabitation and divorce. Predictably, they were the same in some of the wrong ways. Both were impulsive, willful, and self-involved—not qualities calculated to foster domestic peace. But they also brought their own vices to the marriage. Fanny was renowned for her irascible temper and impulsiveness. Both she and her closest companions feared that she had inherited from her mother a "positively and greatly diseased" mind that rendered her extremely high strung. Fanny also was far more outspoken than was deemed appropriate for a woman in respectable society. Herman Melville, Charles Sumner, and Sidney George Fisher, the last a Philadelphia gentleman who knew her well, described her as "masculine" (Fisher said "the reverse of feminine"), referring to her disinclination to defer to the opinions of men in mixed company—though she also had the arresting habit of wearing pants when she deemed it appropriate (which, in the minds of those who set the standards in such matters, it never was).[13]

Yet any fair assessment would have to conclude that, for all Fanny's personal faults, Pierce's were by far the greater. His wealth, breeding, and comportment made him a gentleman, entitled to a lofty position in Philadelphia's *beau monde*. Sidney Fisher judged him to be "uneducated, obstinate, prejudiced, & passionate," yet also "handsome, clever, [and] most gentlemanlike in his manners."[14] Selfish, vain, irresponsible, and dissolute, Pierce had little direction in his young adulthood save the pursuit of pleasure. He was also a gambler and a womanizer. The first vice would destroy his fortune; the second, his marriage. Pierce and Fanny also had mutually exclusive concepts of relations between husband and wife. Pierce condemned the "heartlessness and falsity" of the "principal of equal rights in marriage." His idea of marriage was conventional in mid-nineteenth-century American culture, though his insistence that Fanny actually practice this ideal—hardly any wives actually did so—places him on the Neanderthal side of the spectrum. What made this more galling was that he gave no inkling of these convictions during their courtship. Fanny, on the other hand, insisted on spousal equality. She declared that it was "not in the law of my conscience to promise implicit obedience to a human being fallible like myself."[15]

Fanny asked for or threatened separation several times during the early years of their marriage. She felt genuinely isolated in the Butler family, and Pierce turned out to be a kind of domestic tyrant instead of the refined companion it had seemed he would be. He also struggled mightily to stop Fanny from publishing her American *Journal*. Though he failed, the effort profoundly alienated his wife, who felt stifled by the anti-intellectualism of the Butler clan. Pierce developed three responses to her separation demands: he ignored them, he rejected them (a course which always produced epic arguments), or he used his charms to coax his wife back to his fireside. The last was an effective tactic, to judge by the two children to which Fanny gave birth: Sarah, on May 28, 1835, and Frances, born on the same day three years later. The children did little to bind the parents closer to one another. Weeks after giving birth to Sarah, Fanny urged Pierce to allow her to return to England alone. Leaving Sarah as a newborn would be good for mother and child alike, she argued; it would be "as though she had never known me, and to me far less miserable than at any future time." She made precisely the same appeal after Fan's birth in 1838.[16] It is difficult to make firm conclusions about these statements. Callousness was not among Fanny's faults. True, her sister Adelaide never really forgave Fanny for separating herself from her girls just before and after the divorce, with the result that they did not see one another for years at a time.[17] Considering how her marriage disintegrated, however, Fanny's argument that she leave for their own good is not entirely implausible. It is more likely that she suffered from postpartum depression compounded by a profound sense of unhappiness with her marriage. Whatever the case, there is no doubt that the girls did nothing to bring their parents together. They became unwitting agents in their breakup, as Pierce became skilled in using them to hurt and eventually drive away Fanny.

Late in 1839, Pierce Butler made the fateful decision that his family would accompany him on his annual visit to his Georgia properties. Perhaps he thought that first-person exposure to slavery—at its best on his lands, it was said—would dampen Fanny's growing antislavery fervor.[18] He may just have craved the company of his family. The visit had disastrous consequences for the already shaky marriage. Anticipating seeing slavery as it was represented by its defenders—as a reciprocal relationship between master and man, a kind of cradle-to-grave welfare system—Fanny was instead confronted with the mulatto children of the Kings, the supposedly benign overseers of the properties who were soon to move to Alabama to establish their own cotton empire, overworked slaves, desperate conditions in the plantation infirmary, and other horrific spectacles. The effect was magnified because Fanny had come down to Georgia with such high expectations. The inevitable result was to push her ever closer to abolitionism. In her American *Journal*, she had displayed the usual genteel prejudices toward African Americans. In the Georgian *Journal* she appropriated those same stereotypes for antislavery ends. It was a staple of American racism that blacks emitted an offensive odor. Fanny observed this firsthand. Her personal servant on Butler Island, Mary, reeked so badly that "it is impossible to endure her proximity," she recorded. She further observed that white "Southerners . . . insist that it [odor] is inherent with the race, and it is one of their most cogent reasons for keeping them as slaves." But Fanny was having none of it. "I am strongly inclined to believe that peculiar ignorance of the laws of health and the habits of decent cleanliness are the real and only causes of this disagreeable characteristic," she maintained. Masters, and masters alone, were responsible for this and the rest of the vices that afflicted enslaved African Americans. "[S]lavery is answerable for all the evils that exhibit themselves where it exists," she insisted, "from lying, thieving, and adultery, to dirty houses, ragged clothes, and foul smells."[19]

What Fanny saw in Georgia made her fear for slavery's corrosive influence on African Americans' moral and physical health. But slavery also posed a threat to her family life. Observers of southern society had long argued that mastery over other human beings bred in slave owners a habit of command, a despotic temperament.[20] Fanny discerned the taint of slavery in the development of three-year-old Sarah. It was bad enough, for a stickler for elocution like Fanny, when the toddler began to speak with a southern accent, which she believed originated with an imitation of the "Negro jargon" of the slaves. She was more alarmed when she observed slaves following Sarah about, rushing "to obey her little gestures of command." Dictatorial habits learned at such an early age would be hard to efface. "[T]hink of learning to rule despotically your fellow creatures before the first lesson of self-government" had been inculcated, she confided darkly to her journal.[21]

Fanny also took notice of the effect that exercising mastery had on her husband. Ruling over his slaves exposed to Fanny's eyes hitherto unimagined recesses of her husband's character. The first blow came when John Couper, the Scottish-born master of the adjacent Cannon's Point plantation, informed Fanny that the Roswell Kings were something less than the benevolent overlords that Pierce represented them to be. But when a gang of pregnant field-workers appeared one night to appeal to their master of overwork and instead received a lecture on responsibility, Fanny exploded. "Mr. [Butler] seemed absolutely degraded in my eyes," she fumed. She hoped that witnessing her husband playing master would not "lessen my respect for him, but I fear it." In fact, it was too late. "[T]he details of slaveholding are so unmanly . . . that I know not how any one with the spirit of a man can condescend to them." Gradually, since 1834, Pierce's shortcomings had gradually revealed themselves to Fanny. But there is no evidence to suggest she ever lost respect for him before this point. In Georgia, Fanny finally confronted the reality that she had married beneath her station. There was nothing to bind her to Pierce any longer—nothing, rather, than the girls and the law.[22]

Late during their Georgia sojourn Fanny had run off to Darien, hoping to escape her marriage via a steamer to the North. Pierce coaxed her back to Hampton Point. The marriage survived only because Pierce spent much time away from Fanny and the girls over the next year, traveling without them to Georgia and the Virginia Springs. His brother John, learning of some of Fanny's seditious activities (she had told a group of slave women, "though I was the wife of the man who pretends to own them, I was, in truth, no more their mistress than they were mine"), and perhaps learning of her Georgia *Journal*, which was privately circulating in abolitionist circles, sensibly banned her from the properties. She was, her brother-in-law diagnosed, a "danger to the property."[23] On the first day of December 1840, the family boarded the steamer *British Queen* for Liverpool. Fanny had been badgering Pierce for years to return to Britain. Word that Charles Kemble was on his deathbed broke through Pierce's habitual procrastination. Though they planned a short trip, the Butlers spent two and a half years in the Old World. Charles recovered, and Fanny's contacts gained Pierce entrée into fashionable social circles in London. He rented a number of expensive properties so that they could entertain appropriately, and they spent several months on the Continent with Franz Lizst and with Fanny's sister Adelaide.

Pierce spent far beyond his means and went deeply into debt. His financial worries, rumors of his gambling and philandering, and continuing marital tensions became fodder for British gossip mills. Charles Greville observed that

Fanny was "passionately fond" of her daughters. He also faulted her for discovering too late that she had married "a weak, dawdling, ignorant, violent tempered man," who had ruined "himself and his children by his lazy stupid mismanagement of their affairs." These rumors reached Fanny's ears, though she had suspected the worst for some time. She and Pierce went for days "without our exchanging a dozen words," she told Sarah Cleveland early in 1842. He spent "morning to night . . . out in search of amusement." Word that Pierce had seduced a maidservant at their Hartley Street house prompted Fanny to bolt from his household. "[F]or God's sake," she implored him, avoid "unworthy pursuits and pleasures." She feared the girls could not escape the taint of their father's behavior. "[R]emember your children," she pleaded, "as you hope to influence them toward what is noble, virtuous, and excellent." A relapse in Pierce's rheumatism prompted a brief reconciliation early in 1843. On May 4 the Butlers boarded a steamer for the return voyage to America after almost thirty months abroad.[24]

Pierce was so cash-poor that upon returning to America he opted to rent out Butler Place to raise funds. Fanny was mortified that she and the children were forced to endure boarding-house life. The rooms were genteel enough but felt like a prison because, not being able to reciprocate invitations, they could accept none. In October Fanny discovered letters that indicated that Pierce had been involved in a relationship with a woman for at least five years. Retaining Theodore Sedgwick, she sought terms of separation from Pierce that would allow maximum access to the children. Though they reached an agreement quickly, Pierce immediately reneged. Sedgwick then began making inquiries about Pierce's sex life. Suspicion quickly fell on Amelia Hall, the girls' English governess, though there were plenty of other candidates: in March 1844, Pierce had fought a duel with James Schott, a business partner who had discovered his wife engaged with the "knavish" Pierce in "scandalous" behavior in her Astor Place hotel room. Until this time, Fanny had received at least as much of the blame for their well-known marital troubles as Pierce. He had even been able to count on the Sedgwicks as allies in his efforts to tame Fanny's independent streak. But a growing awareness of his debauched behavior—fueled by public scandals like the Schott duel—inaugurated a sudden and permanent turning of the tide in Fanny's favor. Late in 1844 Pierce characterized the Sedgwicks, his erstwhile allies in saving his marriage, as "low-bred, vulgar meddlers."[25]

This sympathy also owed much to a well-founded awareness that Pierce was using his daughters as pawns in his campaign to bend Fanny to his will or, failing that, to inflict emotional harm upon her. In an era that exalted motherhood, such a tactic on his part was seen as nothing short of scandalous; it was also assumed to be exacting a psychological toll on the children. In 1843 and for much of 1844 husband and wife lived under the same roof, dining at the same table, but communicating only though notes. Rebecca Gratz, a well-connected Philadelphia matron who was close to Fanny, observed with considerable understatement that the inevitable tensions could not "last with any advantage to the children." In the summer Pierce took the girls, accompanied only by their governess, to Newport. In the fall Pierce, Sarah, and Fan moved into a new house in downtown Philadelphia. Fanny, unwilling to submit to new, restrictive conditions laid down by Pierce, took up residence in a nearby boarding house. Her access to her daughters was limited to an hour a day, which Pierce—with Amelia Hall's apparent collusion—enforced with sadistic literalness. Encountering Fanny on the street one day, Sarah and her governess passed by their mother without so much as an acknowledgment. Her younger daughter, however, called out to her, upon which "the governess reiterated her command, that they should pass on." Distraught, Fanny overtook the three, asking Sarah "how she could bring herself to insult and would me in so cruel a manner?" Sarah replied that "she had acted in obedience to the governess, whose orders her father told her she was to obey."[26]

Worn down by such behavior, fearing for the damage being done to the girls, Fanny surrendered to Pierce—apparently at his great surprise, for he seems to have believed that his draconian conditions would force her to return to England and the stage, providing him with the foundations for a divorce proceeding based on a claim of abandonment. In any case, Pierce forced the issue when, in April 1845, he handed her a letter written by one of the Sedgwicks. Fanny took it, assuming his action implied approval, even though the terms of her cohabitation included a provision that she not communicate in any way with the Berkshire clan. It was a trap. He forced her to leave the house immediately. Efforts by Fanny and her daughters to see each other that summer only led to further humiliations and emotionally draining scenes. Pierce continued to use them as objects for the manipulation and harm of their mother. "[T]hus he gained the point of separating them from me," Fanny wrote in 1848. She acknowledged that Pierce had used her as "the means of injuring my children." So, "for their own sakes, I forbore all further attempts to see or be with them." In the fall of 1845 she sailed for England. She did not see ten-year-old Sarah and seven-year-old Fan again for three years.[27]

This separation (there would be another, longer one, from 1850 to 1856), and the conditions surrounding it, had important consequences for Fan and Sarah's developing personalities as well as for their relationship to their mother. The self-absorbed Pierce, who was not inclined—to say nothing of qualified—to

raise two young girls, relinquished their day-to-day management to a governess. Sarah and Fan suffered the inevitable handicaps. Rebecca Gratz observed
in 1846 that the girls displayed the absence of "their poor mother's watchful
care," which was necessary to "counteract the injurious tendency of too much
indulgence and the want of maternal direction." Fanny did not forget her girls.
She counted on her American friends to monitor their development and de-
voured every nugget of news they provided. Early in 1847 she thanked her friend
Sarah Cleveland for providing "the greatest, the only service you can render
me . . . the receiving from all who can furnish me with every particle of information of my girls which can be gleaned or gathered." To pay her bills she
returned to the stage. By 1848 she had reprised her most famous performance,
as Julia in Knowles's *The Hunchback*, in London. By March, however, she gave
up stage acting, which she had always disliked, to take over her father's public
readings of Shakespeare. To Fanny, Charles passed on his greatest resource: his
abbreviated, sanitized edition of the plays that provided about two hours' worth
of reading per sitting. It was a lucrative practice, far more profitable and more
flexible than acting with a company. Also in March 1848, Pierce Butler sued for
divorce on the grounds that his wife had abandoned him for two years—the
statutory minimum in Pennsylvania.[28]

Fanny returned to the United States as soon as she received word of her
husband's suit. Financial necessity, as well as the realization that she had the
support of nearly all of her and Pierce's American friends, prompted her to
begin a spectacularly successful American tour soon after she reunited with
her daughters at a Philadelphia hotel in November. Meanwhile she contested
Pierce's abandonment claim, arguing in a "Narrative" filed with the court that
his abuse and dissolute behavior had left her little choice but to leave her household for her daughters' own good. Fanny and her lawyers proved to be adept at
the no-holds-barred sport of divorce contestation. Her "Narrative" was leaked
to the press, appearing in major newspapers throughout the country in July. She
used a threat to exercise her right of dower over the financially strapped Pierce
to secure two months with Sarah and Fan in the Berkshires during the summer
of 1849. In September he accepted Fanny's offer to withdraw her challenge to
his divorce petition in exchange for a $1,500 annuity transferable to the girls at
her death and a guarantee of two months alone with them every summer. On
September 22, 1849, Frances Anne Butler became once again Fanny Kemble.[29]

Fanny anticipated reentering her girls' lives. Two months a year, unob-
structed correspondence, and shorter meetings throughout the year would be
enough to undo the damage inflicted over the past three years and would allow her to shepherd them through their adolescences, she believed. But it was

not to be. In mid-1850 she returned to England upon receiving word that her father was once again gravely ill. Though he died in November 1854, Fanny did not return to the United States for over five years—in May 1856, when Sarah turned twenty-one. It is unclear why she separated herself from the girls for this entire period. She did have an acute family crisis to deal with. In early 1851 her brother Henry, broken by drink and suffering from a psychological disorder, revealed that he was sole parent to a son and infant daughter. Fanny and Adelaide took over the responsibility of raising their niece and nephew and had Henry institutionalized. But these responsibilities hardly absorbed her attention for five years. Her American friends wondered what she was doing across the ocean while Sarah and Fan confronted adolescence without their mother. Her stalwart friend Sarah Cleveland cut off contact with her in disgust. The girls may well have wondered what their mother was up to as well. Their mother's long, voluntary absences likely produced some repressed resentment and a longing for affection. Sarah alluded to some of these feelings when an extended absence from her husband in 1861 brought back "the old vague yearning of my empty heart which I had from a child for some human love to fill my being."[30]

Fanny seems to have decided to earn money giving public readings in Britain and to return to the States only when Sarah reached legal adulthood at age twenty-one. She wrote to Joshua Francis Fisher in 1852 that she had decided to delay her return until Sarah's majority, "which may restore to me some portion of what I have lost." But she was a proven draw in America, and her divorce had rendered everything she earned her own. And if by "restor[ing] to me some portion of what I have lost" she meant to salvage her relationship with her daughters, why risk further alienation and complications by extending their separation unnecessarily? She came back to America in 1856, declaring that her "life now chiefly hangs upon Sarah." She discovered that her daughters' lives no longer hung around her.[31]

The reunion was not without a hitch, a foreshadowing of the difficult, even antagonistic, relations that would mar Fanny's relationships with her daughters, particularly Fan, for the rest of her life. She whisked the girls off to "The Perch," her house in Lenox, Massachusetts, for some time alone. But Pierce showed up uninvited and unexpected, and Fanny's joy at seeing her girls was tempered by the "ill habits" they displayed as a result of the "wretched influences" they had been under since 1850—partially as a result of her negligence. Fanny did what she could to maintain her daughters' financial and social positions. She resisted entreaties from Pierce that she allow the sale of land entrusted to the girls, a decision that hastened his insolvency but did much to ensure the stability of their fortune. In 1859 Pierce was forced to sell his half of the Butler slaves (his brother's estate owned the difference). That Pierce went South to be present at the humiliating event won him some accolades—a sense of responsibility, not legal obligation, compelled his attendance—but Fanny was aghast. Pierce had "ruin[ed] my girls prospects," she raged to Cleveland, by his "insane gambling in the stocks." She took pleasure in maintaining Sarah and Fan at a style Pierce could not sustain. As she wrote smugly to J. Francis Fisher in 1858, "I have had the great happiness of providing them not only with comfortable existences . . . but with many pleasures which they can no longer command under their father's roof."[32]

The late 1850s proved to be a particularly bad time to mend family fences in an intersectional clan. That part of Philadelphia society in which Fanny and her daughters moved had a deservedly prosouthern reputation.[33] Yet Sarah, who all her life was haunted by the memory of being taunted by English children for being the daughter of a slaveholder, opposed slavery's extension and became an enthusiastic supporter of the Union cause.[34] So was Owen Wister, whom she married in 1859. Though she shared these sentiments, Fanny enjoyed only partial success in repairing her relationship with Sarah. The most significant obstacle was the lingering affection both girls held for their father. Years later, Owen Wister Jr. recalled, "I was brought up to revere my grandfather. He did indeed make both his daughters adore him." This regard angered and confused Fanny, the affection being, as she believed, utterly undeserved. Fanny was also responsible. Her personality could alienate as much as ingratiate. "I wish I could say: peace go with her," Sarah exhaled after a tense visit by her mother in 1861, "but that it never will." When a springtime visit to Butler Place that year provoked a rush of nostalgia for the old house, Sarah reflected, "next to Owen, Father & Fan I love it above all things." Her mother was conspicuously missing from that list.[35]

How much more difficult a task Fanny faced, then, in mending ties with her youngest. Fan sympathized with the South. It is not clear why. Her Philadelphia friends certainly oriented her in that direction, though when secession forced their hand all but a few of them chose the Union. She may have done so to distinguish herself from her mother, sister, and brother-in-law, as a declaration of separate identity. She may also have had personal connections with the South. Urging her to accompany him to Georgia in late 1860, her father promised a "warm welcome of the friends you made" in Savannah, possibly alluding to a prior visit for which no records seem to exist. In any case, Fan committed herself to the South during the Civil War and deepened this connection after its defeat. Fanny tried hard to bridge these differences, even taking Fan to England to give her some much-needed polish when she came of age in 1859. Yet when her father traveled to Georgia during the exciting March of 1861, Fan went with him without hesitation.[36]

To Fanny's great frustration, the travails of the Civil War only succeeded in strengthening her daughters' ties to their father. To Sarah's immense relief, Fan and her father were in Georgia when Unionist riots rocked Philadelphia after the Fort Sumter's surrender. Crowds had sought out known southern sympathizers, and had Pierce not been away he would surely have been at the top of their lists. Though he disavowed support for the Confederacy based on a Robert E. Lee–like bond of loyalty "as a born & bred Pennsylvanian," both he and Fan openly expressed disloyal sentiments and associated themselves with known Copperheads—northern Democrats sympathetic to the Confederacy—when they returned to Philadelphia.[37] In mid-August federal officials arrested Pierce on suspicion that he had provided "secession cockades, pistols, etc." to the rebels during his Georgia trip. Sidney George Fisher had heard Butler express "the strongest opinions in favor of the Southern cause" since his return but doubted the more serious charges of treason. Pierce was probably better off in jail, the sardonic diarist supposed, since "it will keep him quiet and out of harm's way." Fanny thought or hoped Pierce was guilty. Knowing his "Southern sympathies," she told a friend, "I think the charge very likely to be true." How galling, then, that Sarah and Fan—the latter suffering from hysterical bouts of crying that left her bedridden—threw themselves into successful efforts to win his release, and that they did so while visiting their mother at her Lenox retreat?[38]

Fearing her Copperhead attitudes might land her in trouble as well, Fanny took Fan to Europe once again in 1862. If she hoped the trip might remove Fan from Civil War tensions, though, Fanny was mistaken. In fact, she was responsible for placing her daughter in the midst of a war-related maelstrom that would shape their relations for the rest of their lives. She was scandalized to discover the depths of prosouthern sympathy in her beloved Britain—"*not* England," she despaired in a letter to Arthur Malkin. Fanny did what she could among her social set to promote the Union cause, though Fan's presence at her side complicated these efforts. At this point she decided to publish the journal she had kept in Georgia, kept in a drawer for two decades in fear of whatever retaliation Pierce might dream up. Fan was back in the States when her mother's *Journal of a Residence on a Georgian Plantation* was published in London in May 1863 to glowing reviews; excerpts from it were even read in the House of Commons. The American edition published later that year enjoyed a similar response in the northern press. Fan opposed the publication of her

mother's journal for obvious reasons, but it seems not to have too deeply damaged their relations, since she sailed back to England to be with her mother in
1864. They were together when news arrived of Lee's surrender at Appomattox.
They both wept "over the news," Fanny told Harriet St. Leger, "I with joy, she
with sorrow."[39]

Given her daughter's stubbornly prosouthern sympathies, Fanny could not
have been surprised when Fan boarded a steamer for the States once the war
ended. The old resentment must have resurfaced, however, when she learned
that Fan had joined her father in his efforts to bring his Georgia properties back
to life in the midst of postwar chaos. The conflict had unhinged Pierce. Always
in frail health, he appeared shrunken, diminished, by 1865. Enraged by his failure to hang his house with black after Lincoln's assassination, a mob threatened
to torch the place; he also challenged a business partner to a duel. Perhaps Fan's
willingness to travel south with her father stemmed partly from a simple desire
to remove him from this atmosphere. If that was her goal, it worked better than
she could have planned: because of their ownership of northern properties, the
Butlers were in sound economic shape. In addition, the freedpeople—including
many who had been sold off in 1859 and returned—welcomed Fan and her
father warmly. Resembling no one so much as her mother in 1838–39, Fan leapt
enthusiastically into plantation affairs. Charged by Pierce with management of
the household, in fact she negotiated with laborers, dispensed medicine, and
oversaw plantation affairs. Her father ordered her back to the North that summer, but she returned in the fall with Sarah and young Dan, answering her
mother's objection with "fanciful words of rebuke." As if to legitimate Pierce's
insistence that she travel North during the summers, Fan fell ill in the early
summer of 1867; she did not arrive in Philadelphia until August. In a month
Pierce Butler was dead.[40]

Fanny, who returned to the States immediately upon hearing of Pierce's
death, was once again witness to the strange magnetism that warped relations,
even in death, between herself, Pierce, and their children. The girls were "in
great grief," observed the prescient Sidney George Fisher, who doubted the
wisdom of Fanny's plan to reside with Sarah in Germantown, Pennsylvania. "I
doubt her being able to live in the same house with either" daughter, he predicted wisely. Sarah sunk into a deep depression which seems to have resulted
as much from her mother's intrusion into her household as from her father's
passing. She would "gladly pass with winter in Siberia if I c[oul]d have solitude
there," she wrote to Fan. The latter was back on Butler Island, stubbornly re-
doubling her efforts to revive its rice culture. She did her best to decipher her
father's accounts with the freedpeople, which caused a good amount of resent-

ment on both sides. Slowly, Fan's early idealism at restoring the lands to profitability and rebuilding relations with the laborers on a paternalistic basis turned to bitterness. She confronted the same depressed postwar conditions, the confusion of labor relations, and the conflict between old attitudes on the part of whites and the freedpeople's new expectations. Bitterness and disillusion were the inevitable harvest. Like Charles Manigault, another planter whose paternalistic views of black character were shattered by Reconstruction, she retreated into rage against Republicans and crude racial stereotypes against African Americans. Without slavery, she opined in 1869, blacks were "going steadily backwards, morally, intellectually, and physically." Her sister and mother looked on, horrified yet mesmerized, as Fan's will to memorialize her father by reviving his estates crashed against the social, political, and economic conditions of the Reconstruction South. Sarah regretted that her sister was "destined to encounter opposition & disappointment in her plans," she predicted in 1867, "but it could hardly be otherwise."[41]

Fan struggled on in Georgia, returning to the North every summer, until 1876. She saw her mother only sporadically, both because Fanny was often away on reading tours and in Europe, and because Fan's devotion to the estates—and, by extension, to her father's memory—remained a thorny point. Prospects for both their relationship and for the lands improved in 1869, when Fan met James Leigh, an Anglican clergyman, while visiting New York. Leigh happened to be in Savannah that winter, and his party made an agreeable visit to Butler Island and its "fair queen resid[ing] among her sable subjects," as it seemed to the smitten Englishman. Her mother liked him almost as much as she did Owen Wister and was overjoyed when, in the spring of 1870, they were married while the sisters were visiting England. It is easy to understand why Fanny liked Leigh: his tenderness with Fan, who shared her mother's stormy temperament, promised that her daughter's marriage would be far happier than her cursed union with Pierce Butler. And while her close relationship to Owen Wister was often a source of tension between Sarah and her husband, Fanny's closeness with Leigh seems to have eased her relations with her youngest daughter.[42]

James Wentworth Leigh proved to be a good match for Fan in other ways as well. He shared her political attitudes toward Reconstruction, having seen northern efforts to preserve the Union as little more than imperial aggression. He proved to be an enthusiastic and able rice planter, despite his complete ignorance of plantation agriculture. In 1874 he doubled the previous year's rice harvest. Still, it was no good. Regardless of how productive the plantations could be made, prices were far too low to return a profit. The Leighs were also frustrated by their failure to restore paternalistic labor relations. The freedpeople proved to be unavailing, unwilling to take instruction or to behave according to the Leighs' expectations. In 1876 they gave up. They tried to sell the lands entirely but found no buyers. Fan and James had to be satisfied with hiring an agent and putting the furniture and other movables up for sale, almost all of which was bought by women and men who had been slaves just over a decade before. During the 1870s Fanny, Sarah, Fan, and their families grew closer, bound by what Fanny's biographer James Furnas called a "habit of transatlantic vibration"—periodic trips to England and the Continent accompanied by increasingly infrequent returns to the States. Fanny, the Wisters, and the Leighs became part of the core expatriate community of Americans in London and Rome that included Henry James, who became Fanny's closest friend during her final fifteen years. "Your mother is the only woman I am in love with," he told Sarah, only half in jest.[43]

"Transatlantic vibration" helped bring Fanny and her daughters closer together, for it called forth all the things that they shared in common—a love of travel, sociability, childrearing—and put distance between divisive affairs and memories in America. Nevertheless, Fan's insistence on reiterating her Georgian identity, as well as Fanny's self-aggrandizing behavior, ensured that tension would remain at the heart of their relationship. Though she and James had moved permanently to England in 1877, Fan fell into the habit of making tactless anti-English comments in company. These were probably aimed less at her unflappable husband than at her mother, who never returned to the United States after 1877. In 1876 and 1879 Fan had given birth to boys. The first died after a day; the second lived nearly a year before succumbing to a skin disease. To her mother's fury, Fan named both boys Pierce Butler Leigh. Fanny refused to attend the christening of the second boy and made clear her displeasure over their names, the pronunciation of which would fill her mouth with "the bitterness of a poison that destroyed my life." In the context of their tragic deaths—which she had to suffer through without her mother's support—Fan found forgiving her mother difficult. Fanny displayed a similar stubbornness when, in 1881, she agreed to extend her remunerative memoirs by publishing *Records of Later Life*, which would cover her marriage and divorce. Fan was aghast. She had never forgiven her mother for publishing the Georgia *Journal*. Fan begged her mother to consider that any mention of their married strife "must be intensely painful to me," warning her that to publish such material inevitably would "alienate my affection from you entirely." *Records of Later Life* appeared in London in 1881. Fanny dismissed her youngest daughter's concerns. "I must myself be the judge of what I think to write and publish," she wrote coldly.[44]

Whether Fan's threats to her mother were empty or not, the publication of *Records of Later Life* did not produce a fatal breach. Quite the contrary. Fanny continued to spend enjoyable weeks at her daughter's house in Leamington, experiencing particular joy in the company of her granddaughter, Alice, among the closest companions of her last decade. In 1888 Fanny moved in to the Leighs' London home. Fan became her primary companion after Sarah moved back to Philadelphia. The publication of Fan's answer to her mother, *Ten Years on a Georgia Plantation since the War* (1883) did little, it seems, to spoil their relationship. Perhaps, as Catherine Clinton suggests, Fanny had accommodated Fan's wishes in *Records* by removing most of the most explicit material pertaining to her marriage and by obscuring personal identities. And Fanny had little to fear from *Ten Years*, which was little more than standard Lost Cause apologia and anti-Reconstruction boilerplate. The book was an exercise in what Eric Hobsbawm called the "invention of tradition"—in this case, the process by which the New South invented the Old South. In literary and historical terms, *Journal of a Residence on a Georgian Plantation* had nothing to fear from Fan's book. Fan and her mother continued to experience difficult relations throughout the 1880s, though these seem to have had more to do with Fanny's increasing debility, accompanied by a souring disposition; she was particularly frustrated by her inability to summer in her beloved Switzerland after 1886. Fanny retained a tender solicitude for her youngest daughter. She especially desired that Fan be "spared the useless pain of seeing me die." She got her wish: when she died on January 15, 1893, it was in the arms of Ellen Brianzoni, her devoted servant of many years. Fan was in Philadelphia, visiting her sister.[45]

Was Frances Butler Leigh more Georgian, more southern, than Fanny Kemble and her sister, Sarah? Certainly. Nationalism, localism, and other forms of identity are not completely contrived sensibilities. Fan did, after all, have real and deep connections to Georgia, while her mother, whose 1838–39 visit established roots that she might have built on, maintained a self-conscious distance from the South throughout her life. Her sister, whose early experience with slavery established a fertile field for the flowering of a southern identity, also rejected the connection. Yet there was a powerful element of imagination in both mother and daughters' choices. Fan had to work hard to become Georgian. The process was anything but natural, but arose from the peculiar conditions of her childhood and young adulthood. Her experience of becoming southern was more tortuous and contrived than it was for most of planter children. Few could match Sarah and Fan's dysfunctional family life. But her blend of localism and cosmopolitanism was not exceptional among wealthy planters. Beneath the few lines devoted to Fanny Kemble and Frances Butler Leigh on U.S. Route 17 lies a complex story about the processes by which the children of privilege in the Civil War era did, or did not, become southern.

## NOTES

1. Both markers are located on U.S. 17, 1.3 miles south of Darien, Georgia. They can be seen at Georgia Historical Markers, GeorgiaInfo Web site, http://www.georgiaplanning.com/hm/ ViewMarker.aspx?DCA_ID=1759 (Famous Butler Authors) and http://www.georgiaplanning.com/ hm/ViewMarker.aspx?DCA_ID=1750 (Butler Island Plantation) (accessed December 3, 2008). Frances Anne Kemble, *Journal of a Residence on a Georgian Plantation in 1838–1839*, ed. John A. Scott (1863; repr., Athens: University of Georgia Press, 1984); Frances Butler Leigh, *Ten Years on a Georgia Plantation since the War* (London: R. Bentley, 1883); Owen Wister, *The Virginian: A Horseman of the Plains* (New York: Macmillan, 1902).

2. Malcolm Bell Jr., *Major Butler's Legacy: Five Generations of a Slaveholding Family* (Athens: University of Georgia Press, 1987), 266–450.

3. This literature is epitomized by John W. Blassingame, *The Slave Community: Plantation Life in the Antebellum South* (New York: Oxford University Press, 1972). Peter Kolchin, "Reevaluating the Antebellum Slave Community: A Comparative Perspective," *Journal of American History* 70 (1983): 579–601, provides a useful assessment of this literature.

4. The *Journal of a Residence* took special aim at planters' self-image regarding gentility and hospitality. Kemble's portrayal of insipid planter-class women in and around Darien rankled contemporary (and some modern) readers, and she punctured the image of southern hospitality with her story of a North Carolina planter who, after offering "ready hospitality" to a party of stranded travelers, presented them with "dirty water—I cannot call it tea—old cheese, bad butter, and day-old biscuits." Before their departure, he charged the men of the party fifty cents each (Kemble, *Journal of a Residence*, 29, 31). On hospitality see Bertram Wyatt-Brown, *Southern Honor: Ethics and Behavior in the Old South* (New York: Oxford University Press, 1982), 331–39. The *Journal's* position toward southern gentility was among the features that angered Margaret Davis Cate, who sought to undermine its credibility with "Mistakes in Fanny Kemble's Georgia Journal," *Georgia Historical Quarterly* 44 (1960): 1–17. Jonathan Daniel Wells, *The Origins of the Southern Middle Class, 1800–1861* (Chapel Hill: University of North Carolina Press, 2003), chap. 2 and 4, traces reading habits and voluntary associations among southerners.

5. Bell, *Major Butler's Legacy*, 312.

6. Henry Lee, "Frances Anne Kemble," *Atlantic Monthly* 71 (May 1893): 669. Fan's cosmopolitan sensibility was mirrored by many of the South's largest slaveholders, as studied by William Kaufmann Scarborough in *Masters of the Big House: Elite Slaveowners of the Nineteenth-Century South* (Baton Rouge: Louisiana State University Press, 2003). See also Robert Manson Myers, *The Children of Pride: A True Story of Georgia and the Civil War* (New Haven: Yale University Press, 1972); Timothy James Lockley, *Lines in the Sand: Race and Class in Lowcountry Georgia, 1750–1860* (Athens: University of Georgia Press, 2001).

7. Kemble quoted in J. C. Furnas, *Fanny Kemble: Leading Lady of the Nineteenth-Century Stage* (New York: Dial Press, 1982), 385; Sarah B. Wister, "The Early Years of a Child of Promise," in *That I May Tell You*, ed. Fanny Kemble Wister (Wayne, Pa.: Haverford House, 1979), 75.

8. Lee, "Frances Anne Kemble," 675; Henry James to Mary Walsh James, October 31, 1880, in

Leon Edel, ed., *Henry James Letters* (Cambridge, Mass.: Belknap Press of Harvard University Press, 1974–84), 2:311; Kemble, *Journal of a Residence*, 218.

9. Wister, "Early Years," 79.

10. Frances Anne Kemble, *Records of a Girlhood* (New York: Henry Holt and Co., 1879), 605.

11. On these complicated proceedings see Bell, *Major Butler's Legacy*, chap. 14. Fanny told Eliza Middleton Fisher that "she was not aware, before her marriage of his [Pierce's] being a Slave holder—or even owning a Southern estate." Eliza M. Fisher to Mary H. Middleton, February 10, 1845, in Eliza Cope Harrison, ed., *Best Companions: The Letters of Eliza Middleton Fisher and her Mother, Mary Hering Middleton, from Charleston, Philadelphia, and Newport, 1839–1846* (Columbia: University of South Carolina Press, 2001), 427.

12. *Journal of Frances Anne Kemble* (Philadelphia: Carey, Lea, and Blanchard, 1835), 2:136. On Kemble and Channing, see Scott, editor's introduction, to *Journal of a Residence*, xxxi–xxxii.

13. Elizabeth B. Sedgwick to Fanny Butler, June 7, 1839, in *Mr. Butler's Statement, Originally Prepared in Aid of his Professional Council* (Philadelphia: J. C. Clark, 1850), 40; Nicholas D. Wainwright, ed., *A Philadelphia Perspective: The Diary of Sidney George Fisher Covering the Years 1834–1871* (Philadelphia: Historical Society of Pennsylvania, 1967), 168 (entry for May 15, 1844); Charles Sumner to Samuel G. Howe, September 11, 1844, in *Memoir and Letters of Charles Sumner*, vol. 2, *1838–1845*, ed. Edward L. Pierce (Boston: Roberts Brothers, 1878), 319; Herman Melville to Evart A. Duycknick, February 24, 1849, in Merrell R. Davis and William H. Gilman, eds., *The Letters of Herman Melville* (New Haven: Yale University Press, 1960), 77–78. In Philadelphia, merchant Thomas Cope had happened upon Fanny fishing, wearing "pantaloons, boots, & man's hat" (Eliza Cope Harrison, ed., *Philadelphia Merchant: The Diary of Thomas P. Cope, 1800–1851* [South Bend, Ind.: Gateway Editions, 1978], 400).

14. Wainwright, ed., *Philadelphia Perspective*, 531 (entry for June 20, 1867). On changing conventions governing romance and marriage in this period, see Ellen K. Rothman, *Hands and Hearts: A History of Courtship in America* (New York: Basic Books, 1984); Anya Jabour, *Marriage in the Early Republic: Elizabeth and William Wirt and the Companionate Ideal* (Baltimore: Johns Hopkins University Press, 1998); and Henrik Hartog, *Man and Wife in America: A History* (Cambridge, Mass.: Harvard University Press, 2000).

15. *Mr. Butler's Statement*, 75–76.

16. Fanny Butler to Pierce Butler, n.d., in ibid., 25.

17. Catherine Clinton, *Fanny Kemble's Civil Wars* (New York: Simon and Schuster, 2000), 247.

18. Roswell King Jr., "On the Management of the Butler Estate, and the Cultivation of the Sugar Cane," *Southern Agriculturist* 1 (December 1828).

19. Kemble, *Journal of a Residence*, 61–62. Clinton, in *Fanny Kemble's Civil Wars*, 123, misreads this passage as evidence of Kemble's lingering racism.

20. This observation was made most famously by Thomas Jefferson, in *Notes on the State of Virginia*, William Peden, ed. (New York: W. W. Norton, 1954), 162: "The whole commerce between master and slave is a perpetual exercise of the most boisterous passions, the most unremitting despotism on the one part, and degrading submission on the other." Abolitionists made much of this argument. See Elizabeth B. Clark, "'The Sacred Rights of the Weak': Pain, Sympathy, and the Culture of Individual Rights in Antebellum America," *Journal of American History* 82 (1995): 463–93.

21. Kemble, *Journal of a Residence*, 280, 93.

22. Ibid., 114; on the Coupers and Kings, 266–67, 285–86.

23. Ibid., 60; Frances Anne Kemble, *Records of Later Life* (London: Richard Bentley and Son, 1882), 2:42.

24. Letter to Cleveland quoted in Furnas, *Fanny Kemble*, 251; *The Greville Diary, Including Passages Hitherto Withheld from Publication*, ed. Philip Whitwell Wilson (Garden City, N.Y.: Doubleday, Page, and Co., 1927), 2:547 (entry for December 8, 1842); Fanny to Pierce, December 15 [1842], Philadelphia *Public Ledger*, December 4, 1848, p. 1, col. 3.

25. *A Statement by James Schott, Jr.* (Philadelphia: n.p., 1844), 3; Pierce Butler to William H. Furness, December 13, 1844, Philadelphia *Public Ledger*, December 4, 1848, p. 1, col. 4.

26. Rebecca Gratz quoted in Furnas, *Fanny Kemble*, 277; Philadelphia *Public Ledger*, December 7, 1848, p. 1, col. 1.

27. Philadelphia *Public Ledger*, December 7, 1848, p. 1, col. 3.

28. Rebecca Gratz to Miriam Cohen, February 24, 1846, Miriam Gratz Moses Cohen Papers #2639 (Manuscripts Department, Southern Historical Collection, Wilson Library, University of North Carolina, Chapel Hill); Fanny Butler to Sarah Cleveland, January 16, 1847, quoted in Clinton, *Fanny Kemble's Civil Wars*, 140.

29. Clinton, *Fanny Kemble's Civil Wars*, 148, argues that Philadelphians were disposed to side with Pierce. This is unlikely. Pierce certainly had the sympathy of the gentlemen tipplers and gamblers of the Philadelphia Club, but the city's genteel society seems to have sympathized broadly with Fanny. Joshua Francis Fisher, a high ranking gentleman, was her chief legal counsel, and she was close with the Biddles and other leading families. Georgians, by contrast, seem to have been partial to Pierce. James Holmes, the doctor retained to care for the Butler slaves and who had met Fanny in 1838–39, thought Pierce had borne a difficult burden patiently (James Holmes, *"Dr. Bullie's" Notes: Reminiscences of Early Georgia and of Philadelphia and New Haven in the 1800s*, ed. Delma Eugene Presley [Atlanta: Cherokee Pub. Co., 1976], 157).

30. Sarah Butler Wister to Owen Wister, September 3, 1861, quoted in Clinton, *Fanny Kemble's Civil Wars*, 174; Ann Blainey, *Fanny and Adelaide: The Lives of the Remarkable Kemble Sisters* (Chicago: Ivan R. Dee, 2001), 250–52. On Cleveland, see Clinton, *Fanny Kemble's Civil Wars*, 157.

31. Fanny Kemble to Joshua Francis Fisher, June 17, 1852, Frances Anne Kemble Papers, Manuscript Division, Library of Congress, Washington, D.C.; Kemble to Sarah Cleveland, June 22, 1856, quoted in Clinton, *Fanny Kemble's Civil Wars*, 157.

32. The first two Kemble quotations are cited in Furnas, *Fanny Kemble*, 373, 375; the third, Kemble to Joshua Francis Fisher, December 12, 1858, Kemble Papers. On the slave sale see Bell, *Major Butler's Legacy*, 326–40.

33. According to George Lathrop, a historian of Philadelphia's Union League, "Philadelphia society had been ruled by rigorous distinctions, often arbitrary, but entirely irreversible; and those who had made the distinctions were in general Southern in their leanings" (quoted in *Chronicle of the Union League of Philadelphia, 1862 to 1902* [Philadelphia: n.p., 1902], 55). The Gilded Age journalist Charles Godfrey Leland recalled that in the Philadelphia of his youth, "everything southern was worshipped and exalted" (Charles Godfrey Leland, *Memoirs* [New York: D. Appleton, 1893], 136).

34. Fanny Kemble Wister, ed., "Sarah Butler Wister's Civil War Diary," *Pennsylvania Magazine of History and Biography* 102 (July 1978): 297 (entry for May 11, 1861).

35. Owen Wister Jr. to Florence Kane, January 2, 1927, quoted in Fanny Kemble Wister, *That I May Tell You*, 3; Wister, "Sarah Butler Wister's Civil War Diary," 289 (entry for April 27, 1861), 281 (entry for April 21, 1861).

36. Pierce Butler to Frances Butler, January 7, 1861, quoted in Bell, *Major Butler's Legacy*, 344.

37. See Frank L. Klement, *The Limits of Dissent: Clement L. Vallandigham and the Civil War* (New York: Fordham University Press, 1998).

38. Wister, "Sarah Butler Wister's Civil War Diary," 304 (entry for June 5, 1861); J. Thomas Scarf and Thompson Westcott, *History of Philadelphia, 1609–1884* (Philadelphia: L. H. Everts, 1884), 1:777; Wainwright, ed., *Philadelphia Perspective*, 400 (entry for August 20, 1861); Fanny Kemble to Arthur Malkin, September 15, 1861, in *Fanny Kemble's Journals*, ed. Catherine Clinton (Cambridge, Mass.: Harvard University Press, 2000), 188.

39. Fanny Kemble to Arthur Malkin, September 15, 1861, in Frances Anne Kemble, *Further Records, 1848–1883* (New York: Benjamin Blom, Inc., 1891), 2:231; Kemble to Harriet St. Leger, n.d., quoted in Furnas, *Fanny Kemble*, 406.

40. Kemble to Harriet St. Leger, 1866, quoted in Clinton, *Fanny Kemble's Civil Wars*, 197. The most comprehensive account of Fan and Pierce's efforts during this time is Bell, *Major Butler's Legacy*, 392–402.

41. Wainwright, ed., *Philadelphia Perspective*, 531 (entry for June 20, 1867); Sarah B. Wister, "Early Years," in Wister, *That I May Tell You*, 75; Leigh, *Ten Years on a Georgia Plantation*, 147–48; Sarah Butler Wister to Owen Wister, November 28, 1867, quoted in Clinton, *Fanny Butler's Civil Wars*, 213. On the tribulations of planters like Fan, see James L. Roark, *Masters without Slaves: Southern Planters in the Civil War and Reconstruction* (New York: W. W. Norton, 1977); Michael Wayne, *The Reshaping of Plantation Society: The Natchez District, 1860–80* (Baton Rouge: Louisiana State University Press, 1983).

42. J. W. Leigh, *Other Days* (London: T. Fisher Unwin, 1921), 114.

43. Furnas, *Fanny Kemble*, 388; James to Sarah Butler Wister quoted in ibid., 435.

44. Henry James to Alice James, December 29, 1877, in Edel, *Letters*, 2:148; Fanny Kemble to Sarah Cleveland, quoted in Furnas, *Fanny Kemble*, 415; Fan to Fanny, May 1, 1881; Fanny to Fan, n.d., both quoted in Clinton, *Fanny Kemble's Civil Wars*, 250.

45. Kemble to Harriet St. Leger, n.d., quoted in Clinton, *Fanny Kemble's Civil Wars*, 260. Clinton suggests that Kemble pulled some punches in *Records of Later Life*, perhaps in response to Fan's distress (251). On Kemble's increasing infirmity and "irresponsible quirks," see Furnas, *Fanny Kemble*, 441. Eric Hobsbawm and Terence Ranger, eds., *The Invention of Tradition* (Cambridge: Cambridge University Press, 1988).

# Susie King Taylor
## (1848–1912)

## *"I Gave My Services Willingly"*

### CATHERINE CLINTON

Like thousands of African American women of her generation, Susie King Taylor was born into slavery in Georgia.[1] Like only a very few of them, she seized her freedom and joined the Union army, and like no others, she left a memoir of her experience, which makes her story compelling. However, Taylor was emblematic of her generation as she, like hundreds of thousands of black Georgians, was liberated by the Civil War, an experience both profound and transformative. Although she would later settle in the North, Taylor's first thirty years were spent in antebellum, wartime, and Reconstruction Georgia— times of enormous struggle and challenge. She served as a laundress, nurse, and teacher to the black troops in the Union army of her husband's regiments. Most black women's wartime experiences went unheralded, unrecorded. Yet the dramatic events of Taylor's life have been preserved in her 1902 account, *Reminiscences of My Life in Camp with the 33rd U.S. Colored Troops, Late 1st South Carolina Volunteers.*

Taylor's memoir remains the only published account by an African American woman who served with the Union army, and one of less than a score of eyewitness black Civil War memoirs. This autobiography remains a significant chronicle of wartime experience for both "contraband" and black troops in the South, as Taylor's matter-of-fact style reveals the life-and-death events for black troops in combat, as well as the camp experiences for black men and women. Her volume preserves vivid details of Taylor's early years in Georgia and her parabolic life.

Most enslaved Africans had no genealogical records for their families, especially during the explosive era of territorial expansion following the American Revolution. But through oral histories, tales have been handed down despite the family strife suffered by those enslaved and scattered across the American continent. As hundreds of thousands of enslaved workers were transported onto the frontier in the eighteenth and early nineteenth centuries, Africans and their descendants endured a forced migration of greater magnitude than the transatlantic diaspora to North America.[2]

Enslaved children born into the plantation world of the coastal South were commonly sold off to populate the borderlands. As a result, many later complained, as did black abolitionist Samuel R. Ward, "Like sources of the Nile, my ancestry, I am free to admit, is rather difficult of tracing."[3]

Yet Susie King Taylor took pride in her ancestry. Primarily tracing her ancestors through the women of her family, she attempted to recapture her roots through her mother's matrilineal line—which she followed back to mixed-race ancestry in the colonial era. She opened her memoir: "My great-great grandmother was 120 years old when she died. She had seven children, and five of her boys were in the Revolutionary war. She was from Virginia, and was half Indian."[4] One of this woman's offspring, Susanna, produced twenty-three daughters and one son, and became a respected midwife within her community. One of Susanna's twenty-three daughters was Dolly, Taylor's maternal grandmother. Although Susie identifies Susanna's husband as Peter Simons and Dolly's husband as Fortune Lambert Reed—only the mention of a name is offered, without any supporting detail.

At the same time, we learn Susanna spent time as a midwife in Savannah, and died from a stroke at the age of one hundred. Dolly, who also spent much of her adult life residing in Savannah, played a central role in young Susie's early life. But Susie's male ancestors, even her father and grandfathers, seem a vague presence in these recollections. Whether it was slavery's perverted imposition (the child followed the status of the mother) or simply Susie's proclivity, only the women in her family are afforded biographical detail.

Taylor's 1902 recollections featured an introduction by Thomas Wentworth Higginson, the Boston aristocrat who commanded a black Union regiment. In 1870 Higginson published his own wartime memoir, *Army Life in a Black Regiment.*[5] Because of his cordiality during their Union service in South Carolina, Taylor sent her manuscript to Higginson for advice and assistance. She had settled in Massachusetts, where Higginson had become a prolific and respected editor and author. Higginson expressed his delight at helping his former comrade, and confessed to offering a light editorial hand. He only corrected a few proper names and then helped her to self-publish the book. Taylor, in gratitude, dedicated her volume to Higginson.

Born at the Grest Farm on the Isle of Wight in Liberty County, Georgia,

SUSIE KING TAYLOR

From the original 1902 edition of *Reminiscences of*
*My Life in Camp* by Susie King Taylor.

southwest of Savannah, on August 5, 1848, Susie was the first child of Hagar and Raymond Baker. Raymond Baker's status remains unknown, while Hagar was owned by Valentin Grest.[6] Hagar was the only surviving child of Dolly Reed, and Grest was a wealthy planter in Liberty County. Liberty had been established out of pre-Revolutionary St. John, St. Andrew, and St. James's parishes. By the time of Susie's birth, the county boasted schools, such as Sunbury Academy, and houses of worship, including the esteemed Midway Church—for whites only. Liberty County was (ironically) a veritable fortress for slaveholding. Its large extended planter families, such as the Charles Colcock Jones clan, had been ensconced and flourishing for generations.[7] But even relative newcomers like Roswell King and his son and namesake, Roswell King Jr., put down roots and reaped vast fortunes from the land—and the expropriation of slave labor.[8]

Susie might very well have spent her life as a house slave, fanning flies from the master's table before graduating to parlor maid or kitchen worker. More likely, she would have been sent into the fields from an early age—as most slave children performed taxing agricultural labor from the age of eight until age or infirmity prevented them from field labor. But Susie followed a different path, one shaped by the exertions of her grandmother, Dolly Reed.

By the time Susie was seven, Reed resided in Savannah, nearly forty miles away from the Grest estate. Reed's status remains unknown, as she may have been an emancipated slave who remained within the state only by the grace of her former owner. Or perhaps she remained Grest's legal property but was granted the "quasi-freedom" denied to all but a few. She lived out—paying her own keep and giving her owner the rest of her earnings. In either case, Reed needed Valentin Grest's guardianship and legal protection to remain within the state and to thrive within urban environs.[9]

She made trips several times a year to and from her Savannah home and the Grest estate, where her daughter's family remained. After her son James died at the age of twelve, Dolly Reed poured her devotion into her only remaining child, Hagar, and Hagar's children. Hagar gave birth to six children—but only three survived infancy, as infant mortality for Georgia blacks remained high during this era.[10]

In 1856, when Susie was only seven years old, Dolly Reed convinced the Grests to send her granddaughter and Susie's younger brother to live with her in Savannah. This, again, was a rare privilege. Susie had been a favorite of Mrs. Grest: chosen to share the mistress's bed, sleeping at its foot when the master was away from home. Perhaps as this "pet slave" aged, her role was supplanted by younger black children. But it was a clear advantage for Susie to

reside with her grandmother in the city rather than to be subjected to plantation labor, or worse—to be sold away, a common fate for enslaved offspring in
antebellum Georgia.[11]

Dolly Reed may have been determined to give her grandchildren what had
been denied her and her own children: education. This precious commodity
was denied by law and in practice to blacks in slave states for generations. At
a time when only 5 percent of Georgia blacks were literate, when a plantation
slave caught writing might have his or her thumbs cut off as a result, underground education was a precious commodity.[12]

Cities such as Savannah provided distinctive opportunities for antebellum
blacks, what scholar Whittington B. Johnson calls "a middle ground" between
slavery and freedom.[13] Schools, churches, burial societies, and fraternal groups,
even "back to Africa" societies marked African American autonomy within the
late antebellum era.[14]

For example in 1859 the Savannah city council "voted to double the size of the
'Colored Cemetery,' and build a dwelling there for a caretaker."[15] Most impressive were the educational institutions, as there were at least six schools open to
blacks in Savannah.[16] Many of these were "underground" efforts.

Reed sent her grandchildren to a "bucket school" run by a free black woman,
Mary Woodhouse. Woodhouse's residence, which stood on Bay Lane between
Habersham and Price, was a haven for her African American pupils. She took
in anywhere from two dozen to thirty children, free and slave, who secretly
made their way to her schoolroom, staggering arrivals and hiding texts in
"buckets" or wrapped in newspapers. The children at the Woodhouse school
were taught the rudimentary basics, their sums and their "ABCs." After they
became proficient at the alphabet, Susie was promoted to a school with a more
advanced curriculum, run by Mary Beasley (who after her widowhood became
the first African American nun in Georgia).

Stealth and disguise were essential at a time when teaching slave children was
a crime. Savannah educator James M. Simmons, a free black running a charity
school, did not turn away enslaved pupils, but taught them alongside his free
black students. This transgression incurred the wrath of white authorities. They
closed his school and put Simmons under arrest—fining him and then publicly
whipping him. Shortly thereafter, Simmons sailed for Boston.[17]

When she was only eleven, Susie Baker had outgrown the underground
schools for African American children. Even after she got all she could from
these black schools, she thirsted for more knowledge. She begged her childhood playmate and white neighbor, Katie O'Connor, to share her books and
lessons. Susie and her grandmother were so persuasive that O'Connor's mother

agreed to this proposal, but *only* if her daughter's role was never revealed. Mrs. O'Connor made Susie promise that Katie's lessons would be held in the strictest confidence, and *especially* hidden from Katie's father. When O'Connor entered a convent four months later, thus ended the deception.

But by now, Susie's appetite had been whetted. She longed to study the books to which white students were entitled, and Susie begged her grandmother to find her another teacher. Dolly Reed sounded out her landlord's son, James Blouis, who was willing to offer the twelve-year-old Susie clandestine lessons. Both O'Connor and Blouis necessarily swore Susie and her grandmother to secrecy, as they might well have been charged for the crime of teaching a slave—if their activities were found out.

Susie's lessons continued until the Civil War intervened. Most of the white South was consumed with rage over the election of "Black Republican" Abraham Lincoln, who had been swept into office with a minority of the vote—as four candidates competed for the White House in November 1860. In December 1860 delegates in South Carolina proclaimed an "Ordinance of Secession." In short order, the Confederate States of America declared their independence and inaugurated former Mississippi senator Jefferson Davis as president in February 1861. Susie's tutor, James, and his brother Eugene were members of the Savannah Volunteer Guards. After the Battle at Fort Sumter in April 1861, the Blouis brothers were called up, and thus ended Susie Baker's tutoring.

Once the war was declared, blacks in Savannah, free and enslaved, engaged in an even more dangerous underground—holding political meetings in deserted buildings and churches, breaking curfew. Susie Baker was drawn into this political intrigue because literacy allowed her to forge passes for those who needed to be out on the streets at night. Although only thirteen at the time, she was in the thick of black resistance and racial intrigue.

Dolly Reed was arrested in a raid on a church. She had been breaking curfew and singing hymns that authorities branded as treasonous, gospels that included such lines as "we shall all be free." Valentin Grest intervened. But in the aftermath, Grest's valuable slave property, Susie, was transported back to his plantation. Susie arrived back in Liberty County on the first day of April 1862—after an absence of nearly six years.

Shortly thereafter, on April 11, Fort Pulaski fell. With the impending invasion of federal troops on the horizon, and with the Confederates caught off guard, many slaves in Liberty County seized the opportunity to escape. Two days later, Susie took off with her uncle and cousins—in search of Union protection along the coast. While whites were openly fleeing the coastal region, black fugitives covertly flocked to the island-dotted coast—in search of Yankee sanctuary.

Susie and a boatload of refugees landed on St. Catherine's Island, one of the northernmost of Georgia's Golden Isles, the barrier islands stretching from South Carolina to the Florida border. Susie Baker joined the thousands of runaway slaves taken into Union custody, soon given the nickname of "contraband."[18]

With the capture of Port Royal on November 7, 1861, the North gained a foothold within the Confederacy, and was most pleased to gain a beachhead in this small corner of South Carolina—the belligerent state that had "started" the war.[19] This port region became a linchpin where Union plots to infiltrate and occupy Rebel territory were hatched. The coastal corridor produced some of the most radical proposals, including Sherman's infamous directive to allow "forty acres" for African American freedpeople (Special Field Order No. 15, January 1865).

In the late fall of 1861, Union troops along coastal Carolina found scores of abandoned plantations and hundreds of slaves left behind. The Atlantic coast between North Carolina and Florida boasted some of the most fertile soil in the region, where Sea Island cotton was grown. The region also boasted rice plantations, fanning out from the Atlantic shore, yielding a crop that became known as Carolina gold. Northern papers reported in December 1861 that "the cotton upon these islands is being picked by contrabands, under the direction of our officers. About two million dollars of cotton has already been secured."[20] By March 1862 the Union had conquered sufficient territory that Secretary of War Edwin Stanton designated Georgia, Florida, and South Carolina as the Department of the South—again, a key milestone in the Union campaign to subdue and recapture Rebel territory.

A flock of New England civilian volunteers migrated South to work with African American refugees. The goal was to help these black refugees become self-sufficient, which would demonstrate their suitability for citizenship. This massive migration southward of black as well as white missionaries was dubbed "the Port Royal experiment" by its sponsors.[21]

Also, South Carolina was one of the locations where the debates over recruiting blacks into the military was most hotly contested. From the war's earliest days, African Americans demanded to take their place on the front lines, in combat. Independent black units, such as the Hannibal Guards in Pittsburgh, rallied round the cause—but initially were not welcome in the Union ranks due to color prejudice. African American leaders such as Frederick Douglass complained that the Union could not fight with one hand behind its back, and championed black enlistment. Douglass saw military service as an important step along the road to black equality. He suggested: "Let the black man get upon his person the brass letters 'U.S.'; let him get an eagle on his button and musket on his shoulder and bullets in his pocket . . . there is no power on earth which can deny that he has earned the right to citizenship in the United States."[22]

The newly appointed military commander of the region, Union general David Hunter, had ambitious ideas about such matters. On May 9, 1862, Hunter declared "the persons in these three States [South Carolina, Georgia, and Florida] . . . heretofore held as slaves are therefore declared free."[23] Hunter directed officers to begin rounding up able-bodied African Americans for federal army use. He was passionate about his dream of "negro regiments" and determined to move ahead, even if the government dragged its feet.[24]

Congress passed a Confiscation Act in July 1862 that "freed all slaves whose masters were rebels" and a Militia Act that allowed these "forever free" blacks to be enlisted by the military as paid laborers. By then Washington brass had finally begun to warm to the idea of stealing away Rebels' slaves—even if they resisted the idea of ex-bondsmen as soldiers. Hunter did not want the army to employ freedmen only as laborers, but wanted them, as Frederick Douglass advocated, with muskets on their shoulders and eagles on their buttons.[25]

This dream looked to become a reality in the wake of Lincoln's preliminary Emancipation Proclamation in September 1862. General Rufus Saxton, appointed Supervisor of Contraband Affairs, was willing to organize former slaves into regiments. This was a signal for which many blacks in the region had been waiting, a chance to don a uniform and join in the fight. This was the heady atmosphere, when fourteen-year-old Susie Baker struck out for freedom in 1862.

Baker and her relatives found refuge with Union soldiers on St. Catherine's Island, where they were given food and shelter until they were put on a boat and shipped to St. Simons Island, a federal stronghold farther south along the coast. When the officer in charge of the evacuation found Susie was literate, articulate, and mature beyond her years, she was drafted to run a school for contrabands on the island. She consented after she was promised books for her pupils—which arrived from the North within a matter of weeks. She taught a total of forty young children by day, and an equally staggering number of adults in night classes. The makeshift school, with Susie Baker at the helm, continued into the late fall of 1862, until the black refugees were relocated to Beaufort, South Carolina.

Susie Baker arrived in South Carolina when the former First South Carolina Volunteers were preparing to officially join the Union army as part of the reconstituted Company E, the Thirty-third Regiment of the United States Colored Troops (USCT). Baker devoted herself to the men of the Thirty-third. Her uncles and cousins joined up, as did a young carpenter from Savannah whom Susie had known before the war, Edward King. King escaped his master and joined up as a black volunteer for the Union. King and Baker were married during this period. Although the exact date is unknown, they were wed late in 1862 or the earliest weeks of 1863. This early marriage followed the pattern of her mother (wed at thirteen) and African American women in general, who generally chose mates and gave birth at earlier ages than southern white women during the era.[26]

Also, Susie Baker's marriage to Edward King came at a momentous time for ex-slaves. The Emancipation Proclamation became law on January 1, 1863, ushering in not just a new year but a whole new era. Official ceremonies organized by General Saxton for soldiers and civilians in occupied South Carolina were both elaborate and poignant. The general anticipated a crowd of thousands— and ordered the roasting of twelve oxen for a celebratory feast. Crowds were ferried in by boat to the former Smith plantation, where the First South Carolina tented at Camp Saxton. Soldiers at the wharf escorted guests to the middle of a large grove where a platform had been set up for speakers. A regimental band played and spirits were high when festivities commenced shortly before noon. This three-hour program of prayer, hymns, and speeches washed over the assembled crowd.

Following the presentation of the regimental flag, a quavering voice from the audience unexpectedly broke into song—"My country 'tis of thee"—and soon the entire crowd joined in for several verses.[27] When the singing ended, Colonel Higginson, flag in hand, was so moved that he confessed it was difficult for him to regain his composure. But after collecting himself, he regained his voice and delivered a stirring speech.[28]

The formal program resumed, and soldiers joined in on their favorite songs, such as "John Brown's Body." For those gathered near Port Royal, it was a turning point on the road to freedom that few would forget.

For Susie Baker King, it was the dawn of a new era as well. As a free black woman, the fourteen-year-old bride took on enormous responsibilities while serving with her husband's regiment. Although primarily enlisted as a laundress, she confessed "I did very little of it, because I was always busy doing other things."[29] The health of men in uniform was a primary focus, as three out of five soldiers who died during the war succumbed to disease unrelated to combat. Although less than 2 percent of black soldiers were killed in combat (compared with 6 percent of white soldiers), death from disease was a deadly 20 percent for black troops—double the rate of whites.[30]

Black troops suffered distinct disadvantage due to the lack of proper medical attention. White doctors rarely served black units, and there were fifty-eight black regiments in the field by October 1863. Medical care fell on the shoulders of nurses—many and mainly heroic black women. Taylor committed herself to the well-being of "our boys" as she called them, although she was not much more than a girl herself.

Taylor became a skilled apprentice to Union surgeons, switching from washing bandages to applying them. During this transformation, she became an eyewitness to war's horrors, as she deftly described: "We are able to see the most sickening sights, such as men with their limbs blown off and mangled by the deadly shell, without a shudder; and instead of turning away, how we hurry to assist in alleviating their pain, bind up their wounds, and press the cool water to their parched lips."[31]

When Clara Barton arrived at Beaufort in the spring of 1863, she was appalled by the primitive conditions suffered by the wounded men, and set about establishing her own independent brand of discipline—for white soldiers only at first. Yet after dining with Colonel Higginson in June, he insisted that she tour General Hospital Number Ten, where colored regiments were housed. She was introduced to Susie King and visited King's black patients in the wards. King enjoyed the older woman's company: "Miss Barton was always very cordial toward me, and I honored her for her devotion and care of those men."[32]

When Union troops were battered and repelled on the parapets of Fort Wagner during their famous assault in July 1863, Susie King stood by to tend to survivors carried into hospital tents. During her travels with the troops, she offered valuable insights into the ways in which black soldiers and white officers interacted.[33]

During this period, Taylor confronted numerous hardships—isolated and anchored within a military stronghold. Her housekeeping duties might include clearing skulls off makeshift paths. At one point she and a Mrs. Chamberlain, the wife of the regiment's quartermaster, were the only women in residence with the troops (when they were stationed on Cole Island). Susie was inventive with her cuisine, making custard from turtle eggs and other substitutes. She recalled the men making "slap jacks," cooking flour into bread on the bottom of a frying pan.

Camp life was fraught with other perils, and she "learned to handle a musket very well. . . . I assisted in cleaning the guns and used to fire them off, to see if the cartridges were dry, before cleaning and reloading each day."[34] In addition, Susie King complained of frequent interruptions of her nighttime slumber. Once, after hearing gunfire, she was forced to dress quickly, preparing to flee as "night was the time the rebels would try to get into our lines."[35]

But life in camp was staid compared to what soldiers faced during their forays. In transit from Augusta, Georgia, to Hamburg, South Carolina, some black soldiers ran into "bushwhackers," Rebels lying in wait. Sleeping black soldiers had their throats cut in sneak attacks. When a Confederate was caught in the act of attempted murder, Susie King reported that his trial and execution were meant to put a stop to deadly raids.[36] She was also haunted by the fate of a deserter, who, after being given a second chance, left his post again. As a consequence, he was put on trial and sentenced to die. The soldier was paraded through the town, accompanied by his own coffin. This public spectacle was meant to serve as a warning to other soldiers: "They drove with him to the rear of our camp, where he was shot. I shall never forget this scene."[37]

Another dramatic incident resulted in a lifelong trauma for Susie King when she was on a boat, being ferried to Beaufort with other passengers. The ship went down and King reported that the passengers "were only saved through the mercy of God. I remember going down twice . . . we were capsized about 8:15 P.M. and it was near midnight when they found us . . . had the tide been going out, we should have been carried to the sea and lost."[38] Although she recovered after a prolonged illness, the drowning death of both a soldier and a baby held in its mother's arms throughout the ordeal was a tragic memory of that night. Susie King suffered a lifelong fear of drowning.

On February 28, 1865, the men of the Thirty-third were able to march into Charleston. But in the wake of Confederate evacuation, flames threatened to raze the entire town. Susie described the chaos: "For three or four days the men fought the fire, saving the property and effects of the townspeople whenever possible, yet these white men and women could not tolerate our black Union soldiers, especially those known to them as former slaves. These brave men risked life and limb to assist residents of the 'Cradle of Secession' in their distress."[39] Angry white Charlestonians resisting the helping hands of black firefighters remains a vivid, symbolic image of the Civil War's contested terrain.

Yet Taylor frequently commented on the cordial attitude of whites—when she interacted with both Union officers and northern ladies. She and the men of the regiment hero-worshiped Lieutenant Colonel C. T. Trowbridge—"no officer in the army was more beloved."[40] She had kind words about Clara Barton, and nearly all mentions of white officers were positive, if not effusive. The feelings were apparently mutual, as many recognized Susie King's extraordinary talents. She was appreciated for her many fine qualities, especially self-sacrifice: King confessed, "I gave my services willingly for four years and three months." However, she added with some disdain: "without receiving a dollar."[41]

Her bitterness over wage discriminations permeated discussions of military life in her memoir over a half century later. She fumed over the army's attempts to pay African American soldiers less than their white counterparts. She supported the protest for equal pay. Susie King Taylor proudly recalled, "I was the wife of one of those men who did not get a penny for eighteen months of their services, only their rations and clothing."[42] These protesting black soldiers broke the will of the United States Army, with a dignity that demanded admiration.

In war's immediate aftermath, Susie and Edward King returned to Savannah with high hopes, even as prejudice remained strong. Although Taylor's memoir mainly concentrated on the wartime years, it is possible to piece together some of the remainder of her life from evidence contained within.

It must have been a disappointment to the couple that King was unable to secure employment in his skilled trade as a carpenter. Instead, he took on contracts as a longshoreman along the city's bustling levees. King may have been one of the dockworkers who protested wages, who joined a Union League branch, which organized to combat racism among Savannah's white employers.[43]

Susie King fought racism in the way she always had: through education and uplift. Knowledge and literacy were viewed as keystones for permanent freedom, and education became a primary focus for southern African Americans of the post–Civil War era. Susie King set up an academy in her own Savannah home.

As early as January 1865, black clergy had founded the Savannah Educational Association, and funded the operation with an eight hundred dollar donation. Louis B. Toomer was the principal teacher, supervising fifteen instructors.[44] When the American Missionary Association (AMA) arrived on the scene in coastal Georgia and discovered this enterprising African American educational operation, the white leadership was amazed. They volunteered to supervise these independent schools, but blacks resisted mightily. King's independent academy charged each of her twenty pupils a modest dollar a month.

Tragedy struck when Edward King was killed in a dock accident in September 1866, leaving behind his pregnant widow. After her son was born in 1867, she tried to run a school in Liberty County, Georgia. But after only a year, Susie King returned to Savannah to live with her widowed mother, who ran a dry goods store. Susie King's father, Raymond Baker, had served on a Union gunboat during the war, but had died in 1867. So the two black women, mother and daughter, struggled together for survival and to raise King's son. Susie King taught an adult school, but when the Beach Institute (a free school run by the AMA) offered rival classes, her students deserted her and she had to close her own school.[45]

Impoverished and devoid of alternatives, Susie King joined the growing ranks of black women in the post–Civil War era forced into domestic service. In 1868 she left her son with her mother while she "lived in" as a household servant.

She was offered positions with a series of southern employers, some of whom took her with them when they went on summer holiday in the North. She found this exposure both eye-opening and thrilling. She became a prize-winning cook and was soon hired by a daughter of the former mayor of Boston. By 1874 Susie King relocated to Massachusetts and worked in the households of several wealthy Boston women, until 1879 when she wed Russell L. Taylor of Boston. Following her remarriage, Susie King Taylor was emancipated from her role as domestic servant at the age of thirty-one.

After her remarriage, Susie King Taylor seized on the role of respected club-woman. In 1886 she organized a women's auxiliary branch of the Grand Army of the Republic (GAR) in Boston. She served in several capacities, and finally assumed the role as president of the group in 1893. In 1896 she organized a GAR survey, compiling a list of war veterans living in Massachusetts. This veterans' census enabled her to link up with old comrades and to have them discover one another again. The project embodied an "official record," and one she undertook with pride, as her list of the Thirty-third Regiment served as an appendix for her published volume.

But the relatively harmonious balance she had achieved as a daughter of the South and a matron of the North was disrupted in 1898 when she received a dire summons from her only child, an actor with a traveling theater company. Taylor's thirty-year-old son lay desperately ill in Shreveport, Louisiana. Her journey to try to rescue him and the obstacles she faced created a dramatic ending for her published reminiscences.

Susie King Taylor had been back to the former Confederacy at least once since her remarriage, making a pilgrimage to see her dying grandmother, Dolly Reed, in Savannah in 1888. Yet she certainly was not unhappy to bid Dixie farewell. When she received word from her son that he needed her help, she most likely had not set foot in the region for nearly a decade.

Taylor's southern journey in 1898, in a post–*Plessy v. Ferguson* era, was jarring and unsentimental. She discovered the region had been even more disfigured by racism's ugly scars. Black men who had served in the Union army were routinely discriminated against. During her train ride south, Taylor was forced to sit in a smoking car, relegated to separate, unequal accommodations. While she was in Shreveport, a black porter was murdered in cold blood for his "saucy" answer to a white man, and the white man got off scot-free.[46]

But racism's horrors hit home when she was unable to secure proper medical care for her son and could not even purchase a ticket for passage in a sleeping car to transport him to vital medical care. In the North he would have been allowed effective medical treatment. But in the segregated South Taylor was forced to nurse her son alone—and then, following his death, to bury him in Louisiana.

On her sad journey home, Taylor witnessed a lynching in Clarksdale, Mississippi. The shock and trauma of the incident exposed a nerve: "In this 'land of the free' we [blacks] are burned, tortured and denied a fair trial, murdered for any imaginary wrong conceived in the brain of the negro-hating white man." She vented anger over the pretense that America reflected "one flag, one nation."[47] She would work with Boston women to supply soldiers with packages for the Spanish American war, but she felt it was a pretense that the nation was reunited—with the return of white supremacists and Klan hegemony in the turn-of-the-century South.

Taylor lashed out at the ladies of the United Daughters of the Confederacy who raised objections to performances of *Uncle Tom's Cabin*, fearing the "bad effect" it might have on children. Where were their objections to lynching? she countered: "Do you ever hear of them fearing this would have a bad effect on their children?" Taylor raged that the white supremacists preached "civilization" while promoting barbarity, while blacks suffered indignities, deprivations, and worse.[48]

Yet rather than sinking into bitter despair, Taylor fought back with her book of memories—she created a written record of black deeds and accomplishments, of interracial cooperation, of proud and not-to-be forgotten heroism. She argued that "the black man is given equal justice" in the North. She commended her hometown of Boston, where in 1897 Colonel Robert Gould Shaw, the white commander who died at Fort Wagner, was commemorated. Shaw's heroism was burnished in bronze when Augustus St. Gauden's gilded statue was dedicated on the Boston Common in 1897.[49] Susie King Taylor made no mention of this ceremony in her reminiscences, although it is likely she would have attended such a veterans' festival, had she been in Boston at the time.

She did not denigrate the role played by whites in the war and declared with forbearance that not all whites should be blamed for the "few of the race" guilty of hatred and racism. She was grateful for those who had lent her a helping hand—and she wanted black and white to remember the true meaning of the Civil War. In her literary effort, she employs Biblical language, comparing her race with the children of Israel and invoking images of Christian redemption. Her memoir contains poetry and power, as she asserts that progress "will come in time, surely if slowly."[50]

Despite her hopeful suggestions, a pervasive air of melancholy hangs over the memoir's conclusion. She was able to escape southern racism and make a new life for herself in the North, yet she felt an ache of sorrow about the losses she had sustained. She maintained a bond with many surviving members of her regiment, but resented that by century's end, too many of the present generation had forgotten the sacrifices of their forefathers and "noble women as well."[51]

The choices facing Susie King Taylor may have been limited by the constraints of race, gender, and region, but the heroism she demonstrated during wartime led to a lifelong vocation to keep the flame burning and to pass the torch. Her own child might have died young, but his tragic demise inspired his mother to compose a tribute, a record of her own life, so that future generations might know the reasons why their ancestors had fought. Taylor's memorialization was a significant response to the counterrevolution of Jim Crow and the rise of lynch law. Her stirring reflections remain insightful. Taylor's clarion call of remembrance reminds us of Georgia women's unsung heroism during the Civil War—of black women's courage and sacrifice to put an end to slavery.

Although Susie King Taylor's death and burial went unheralded in 1912, her powerful hopes for her nation were prophetic: "I hope the day is not far distant when the two races will reside in peace in the Southland, and we will sing with sincere and truthful hearts, 'My country 'tis of thee, Sweet land of Liberty, of thee I sing.'"[52] It would be half a century later that another Georgian would confess similar convictions with his "I Have a Dream" speech in Washington during the summer of 1963. The testimony and example of Susie King Taylor showcases an earlier generation of freedom fighters, veterans whose example continues to inspire and lead the way.

### NOTES

1. This essay has been adapted from the introduction to Susie King Taylor, *Reminiscences of My Life in Camp*, ed. Catherine Clinton, vii–xi (1902; repr., Athens: University of Georgia Press, 2006).

2. See Ira Berlin, *Generations of Captivity: A History of African Americans* (Cambridge, Mass.: Harvard University Press, 2003).

3. Samuel Ringgold Ward, *Autobiography of a Fugitive Negro: His Anti-Slavery Labors in the United States, Canada & England* (London: John Snow, 1855), 4.

4. Taylor, *Reminiscences*, 1.

5. See Christopher Looby, ed. *The Complete Civil War Journal and Selected Letters of Thomas W. Higginson* (Chicago: University of Chicago Press, 2000); and Edmund Wilson, *Patriotic Gore: Studies in the Literature of the American Civil War* (New York: Oxford University Press, 1962), chap. 7.

6. All biographical detail is derived directly from the single source of Taylor's published autobiography.

7. See Robert Manson Myers, ed. *The Children of Pride* (New Haven: Yale University Press, 1972).

8. See Malcolm Bell, *Major Butler's Legacy* (Athens: University of Georgia Press, 1987).

9. Timothy Lockley, *Lines in the Sand: Race and Class in Lowcountry Georgia, 1750–1860* (Athens: University of Georgia Press, 2001), 24.

10. See Catherine Clinton, *Fanny Kemble's Journals* (Cambridge, Mass.: Harvard University Press, 2000), 154–55.

11. Julia Floyd Smith, *Slavery and Rice Culture in Low Country Georgia, 1750–1860* (Knoxville: University of Tennessee Press, 1985), 105–7.

12. Jacqueline Jones, *Soldiers of Light and Love: Northern Teachers and Georgia Blacks, 1865–1873* (Chapel Hill: University of North Carolina Press, 1980), 60.

13. Whittington B. Johnson, *Black Savannah, 1877–1864* (Fayetteville: University of Arkansas Press, 1996), chap. 4.

14. For an excellent discussion of religion, see in Lockley, "Praying Together," chap. 5 in *Lines in the Sand.*

15. Johnson, *Black Savannah*, 141.

16. Ibid., 128.

17. Ibid., 128.

18. See Russell Duncan, *Freedom's Shore: Tunis Campbell and the Georgia Freedman* (Athens: University of Georgia Press, 1986), 20–21.

19. See Katharine Jones, *Port Royal under Six Flags* (Indianapolis: Bobbs-Merrill, 1960).

20. *Christian Recorder*, December 21, 1861.

21. See Willie Lee Rose, *Rehearsal for Reconstruction: The Port Royal Experiment* (Indianapolis: Bobbs-Merrill, 1964)

22. James M. McPherson, *The Negro's Civil War* (New York: Knopf, 1965), 171.

23. General Orders No. 11, May 9, 1862, Department of the South, *Official Records of the Rebellion* 6:224, 240.

24. See Edward A. Miller Jr., *Lincoln's Abolitionist General: The Biography of David Hunter* (Columbia: University of South Carolina Press, 1997).

25. Miller, *Lincoln's Abolitionist General*, 114.

26. See Herbert Gutman, *The Black Family in Slavery and Freedom, 1750–1925* (New York: Pantheon, 1976).

27. Elizabeth Ware Pearson, ed. *Letters from Port Royal* (New York: Arno Press, 1969), 130; and Looby, *Complete Civil War Journal*, 76–77.

28. Looby, *Complete Civil War Journal*, 77.

29. Taylor, *Reminiscences*, 35.

30. Ira Berlin, ed. *A Documentary History of Emancipation, 1861–67*, ser. 2, *The Black Military Experience* (New York: Cambridge University Press, 1982), 633.

31. Taylor, *Reminiscences*, 31–32.

32. Ibid., 30.

33. See Joe Glatthaar, *Forged in Battle: The Civil War Alliance between Black Soldiers and White Officers* (New York: Free Press, 1991), 137–40.

34. Taylor *Reminiscences*, 26.

35. Ibid., 51.

36. Ibid., 43–44.

37. Ibid., 27–28.

38. Ibid., 39.

39. Ibid., 42

40. Ibid., 46.

41. Ibid., 21.

42. Ibid., 51.

43. Jones, *Soldiers of Light*, 61. See also Eric Foner, *Reconstruction: America's Unfinished Revolution, 1863–1877* (New York: Harper, 1988), 281.

44. Jones, *Soldiers of Light*, 73.

45. Donald L. Grant, *The Way It Was in the South: The Black Experience in Georgia* (Athens: University of Georgia Press, 1993), 223.

46. Taylor, *Reminiscences*, 72–73.

47. Ibid., 61.

48. Ibid, 65–66.

49. Thomas J. Brown, Martin H. Blatt, and Donald Yacovone, eds., *Hope and Glory: Essays on the Legacy of the 54th Massachusetts Regiment* (Amherst: University of Massachusetts Press, 2001).

50. Taylor, *Reminiscences*, 75.

51. Ibid., 68.

52. Ibid., 62.

# Eliza Frances Andrews

## (1840–1931)

## "I Will Have to Say 'Damn!' Yet, Before I Am Done with Them"

### CHRISTOPHER J. OLSEN

❀ ❀ ❀

Eliza Frances Andrews was the sort of educated, witty, and independent, stereotype-flouting woman about whom historians seem to love reading and writing. It is easy to be engaged by someone who notes casually that a friend "has lent me *Les Miserables* in French, which I read whenever I can steal a moment during the week." She was also blissfully condescending and a miserable racist. Her published works are filled with the bitterness that a generation of southern whites held toward all things Yankee; when she edited and published her wartime diary in 1908 there was little forgiveness, even forty-three years after Appomattox. In 1865 she expressed nothing but hatred for northerners and almost nothing but contempt for freedpeople. She wished every "wretched Yankee" "had a strapping, loud-smelling African tied to him like a Siamese twin." "Oh, how I hate them!" she concluded, "I will have to say 'Damn!' yet, before I am done with them." Her feelings toward Yankees and African Americans mellowed just slightly with age, although her racism was undiluted. The visceral hatred of northerners, so evident in 1865, evolved into a deeper resentment, even half-pity, over their "arrogance" at believing they could transform the nation and African Americans simply by making them voters. Certainly the two emotions fed each other: she hated Yankees for winning the war and imposing emancipation and the Fifteenth Amendment; free African Americans were a constant reminder of defeat and northern power. The "passion and fury" of Reconstruction, she concluded, had led to the great "fatal mistake" of black

ELIZA FRANCES ANDREWS

From *War-Time Journal of a Georgia Girl.*

Courtesy of UNC University Library.

male suffrage, which "injected a race problem into our national life," and she predicted a race war that would make "the tragedy of the Civil War [seem like] child's play." Certainly some educated white southerners made peace with defeat and worked for reconciliation with the North and a patriotic reunion. Andrews was not one of them.[1]

In so many ways the Civil War shaped her entire adult life, upsetting all the normal expectations for a woman of her class and education, and leaving memories that never faded. The night Georgia seceded from the Union remained a vivid moment, even after forty-eight years. "I shall never forget that night when the news came that Georgia had seceded," she wrote in 1908. "[T]he people . . . were celebrating the event with bonfires and bell ringing and speech making," but her father "shut himself up in his house, darkened the windows, and paced up and down the room in the greatest agitation." He paused occasionally, she recalled, to shout "Poor fools!"[2] Her father's Unionism and her own fanatical Confederate patriotism, the unfiltered excitement of the moment and all of the cataclysmic changes that followed undoubtedly kept those moments so fresh in her mind. The history of Georgia's women in the nineteenth century was dominated by the Civil War and Reconstruction. Unlike its most famous heroine, Scarlett O'Hara, the revolutionary changes of these years simply overwhelmed many whites, who never adjusted to some of the new realities. The war ended slavery and devastated much of the planter class, overturning the traditional hierarchies of race and class. Then the Fifteenth Amendment guaranteed black men the right to vote and in less than a decade whites were faced with slaves-become-Congressmen. The conflict killed more than one-fourth of the white men between seventeen and fifty, and in some areas simply erased the basic structure of society and threw into chaos the most fundamental social and economic relationships. White men also faced the psychological damage that came from losing the war and failing to defend their society or protect and provide for their women and children. The effects of these blows to the South's collective male ego are now being examined seriously by historians, but it may be sufficient simply to consider the impact of these failures on southern gender relations. Southern white women, in turn, took on the task of revitalizing the male psyche for the entire region, in part through the literature and imagery of the "Lost Cause."[3]

The course of these tumultuous years—particularly the emotions and attitudes of southern whites struggling to survive and adapt—can be traced in the pages of hundreds of diaries kept by men and women. The destruction and destitution that civilians faced on the home front was recounted in painstaking detail by nearly all those who put some ink to paper during the war. These tales of suffering constitute a familiar refrain: widespread, prolonged absence of white men leading to fear of slave revolt and growing food shortages; spiraling inflation that crippled the economy and forced civilians to beg and barter for basic necessities; and finally, of course, pervasive death and destruction that accompanied the advancing Union armies and occupation. A much smaller number of more thoughtful, reflective Confederates articulated a succession of less tangible emotions: pride and nationalism, fear and uncertainty, and eventually shock, bewilderment, and hatred. Among this latter group, only a few have left truly insightful, even witty memoirs. Eliza Frances Andrews certainly ranks as one of the most articulate and perhaps underappreciated of Civil War–era diarists. Her straightforward recollections seem less artificial than other memoirs or edited diaries, and she commented on a greater range of topics and issues than most writers.[4]

Eliza Frances "Fanny" Andrews was born August 10, 1840, in Washington, Georgia. Her father, Judge Garnett Andrews, ranked as one of the state's leading citizens. Fanny Andrews grew up in luxury at Haywood plantation, which included "fourteen buildings, besides 'the big house,' on the grounds." It was "a town residence, where there were never more than twenty or thirty servants to be housed, including children."[5] Washington was a favorite for many of Georgia's cotton planters, including Robert Toombs and Alexander Stephens. Andrews attended the Washington Female Seminary before withdrawing over a dispute with one of her teachers. Instead, she graduated from LaGrange College in 1857 with a BA in languages and literature.[6] During her childhood she also developed a keen interest in nature, something that evolved from hobby to career after the war. Andrews writes more of her father than mother, and, based on her diaries, he appears to have been the dominating force in her life; or, at least, he was the most prominent character during the war years, which is probably not surprising considering his political prominence and opinions. Another influential figure seems to have been her cousin Eliza Bowen (twelve years older), who came to live with Fanny's parents when her own died. Eliza Bowen "was a woman of unusual intelligence," remained single like Fanny, and later wrote a "successful school book, 'Astronomy by Observation.'" It was with Eliza that Andrews apparently edited a newspaper in the late 1870s, and the older woman also wrote many articles and taught school after the war.[7] At the very least the two women shared many similarities, and it is not hard to imagine cousin Eliza as a role model of sorts for younger Fanny, particularly as she aged, remained unmarried, and evolved as a professional woman. When the war started Fanny Andrews would have been just the age for marriage, and local men almost certainly considered her a leading belle. As for so many southern women, the war interrupted her probable life of marriage, children, and a plantation household to run. Instead, she found dislocation, defeat, and poverty.

After the war Andrews did not pursue those Old South dreams and conventions. Instead, she became a teacher and writer, and she never married. Drawing on her education and literary background, she published three novels between 1876 and 1882, a serialized novel in the *Detroit Free Press,* and many newspaper and journal articles ranging from light fiction to more serious commentary on current events. Apparently Andrews also edited a newspaper for some time in the late 1870s or early 1880s.[8] In her 1865 "Georgia: The Elections, A Peep behind the Scenes," Andrews expressed the usual white disdain for the notion of emancipation and black suffrage, and the article is a fairly typical expression of Reconstruction thinking. "[I]t is plain, from various indications, that 'getting their rights,' is, in their minds, equivalent to getting their hands into other people's pockets. The only tickets they ever heard of before, were circus and railroad tickets, and they have an idea that the 'Radical ticket' will admit them to something much better than a show of horses, or a ride in a railroad car." She did suggest, however, that African Americans might—"when . . . enlightened by education and experience"—be entrusted with the vote. Two articles about women reveal some of her attitudes about gender and the difficulties of southern women during the war. "A Plea for Red Hair" and "Paper-Collar Gentility" are fun, ranging from witty to sarcastic. The latter, in particular, ridicules superficial "clerks" who worry about appearance but do not develop any "inner grace."[9] Her novels were not distinguished by any great departure from the late nineteenth-century norms for southern romantic literature. The heroes are honorable, if poor, southern gentlemen from "good" families; an occasional Yankee with redeeming qualities makes an appearance, but they invariably have southern connections or have been influenced by living in the South. The women bear some obvious resemblance to Andrews herself—prone to be somewhat independent, even sarcastic—and they embrace and espouse the Lost Cause at every opportunity.[10]

Despite these numerous articles and novels, however, she achieved lasting recognition as a botanist. This childhood fascination eventually grew into a professional career. Andrews began teaching in 1873, the year her father died. She first moved to Yazoo City, Mississippi, but after only one year returned to Washington as superintendent of the Girls' Seminary. According to one former student she was "of medium height, lithe and graceful. She rode her bicycle to and from school 'just like one of us kids.'" She was on the faculty at Wesleyan College in Macon, Georgia, from 1885 to 1898, teaching history and rhetoric, and finally at Washington High School until 1903, where she focused on botany. Andrews published two texts on botany, in 1903 and 1911, and became a member of the International Academy of Science in Italy. Her second text was translated into French and used in public schools in that country. Her basic approach was "hands-on," and the texts were filled with exercises that could be completed using common plants.[11] The texts apparently sold well and earned her a secure income. Throughout her teaching and writing career she used the summers to travel and explore nature. She hiked the Adirondacks and White Mountains, the Yosemite Valley, Mexico, and much of western Europe, including the Alps. She had specimens from all over the world and eventually donated over three thousand specimens to the Alabama Department of Agriculture in 1910.[12] It was these fundamentally "independent" aspects of her professional career that make her stand out in such relief from other elite southern women of her generation. Andrews carved out an international reputation that made her a worldwide figure separate from her family and, perhaps most importantly, from the Civil War and the Lost Cause. In other words, her fame and fortune—quite literally—did not come from writing about the Civil War or the "glorious Old South." If these unusual experiences and travels were not enough to distinguish her, she also became a nationally recognized Socialist in the first two decades of the twentieth century.

Despite her well-deserved reputation as a botanist, and some success and notoriety as a novelist, Fanny Andrews's most important literary legacy are two diaries that chronicled the end of the Civil War and beginning of Reconstruction in Georgia. Throughout the pages of these diaries she comments on the war, slavery and race, gender and the place of women in southern society, and resentment of Reconstruction imposed by the ever-hated Yankees. Most of her opinions were certainly within the mainstream for a southerner of her background, and few passages will surprise readers familiar with other Civil War diaries. But Andrews wrote very well, the diaries filled with long, often vivid descriptive passages, sharp characterizations, and frequently biting sarcasm. Perhaps more striking is what the diaries do not contain. Unlike many women diarists, Andrews spends relatively little time discussing fashion or romance (although there is some of each, and indications that she cut out sections dealing with her own suitors) and pays virtually no attention to religion. Indeed, the nearly total lack of religious language and imagery is startling. There is a welcome absence of those typically dreary summaries of each week's sermon; Andrews barely mentions church attendance at all. Finally, Andrews demonstrates a good understanding of historical memory. She notes that the wartime diary is filled with "expressive animosities of the time" that she would like to erase, but instead they all remain: "not as representing the present feeling of the writer or her people, but because they do represent our feelings forty years ago, and to suppress them entirely, would be to falsify the record."[13]

Her first diary, *The War-Time Journal of a Georgia Girl, 1864–1865*, was published in 1908. Despite its title, most of the diary deals with the months after Appomattox and the Confederate defeat. One of the most interesting aspects of this work is Andrews's own editorial commentary that opens each chapter. Written more than forty years after the diary, these comments allow a reader to compare her opinions on any number of subjects: Yankees; slavery, emancipation, and race; southern class relations; and the place of women in American culture. In particular, certain contrasting passages reveal the impact of defeat and Lost Cause mythology on one thoughtful, articulate southern woman. While the prose is frequently clever and engaging, Andrews is consistently condescending and racist, and frequently arrogant. The second diary, *Journal of a Georgia Woman, 1870–1872*, was just recently discovered in the papers of her brother, Garnett Andrews, who became a successful lawyer and eventually mayor of Chattanooga, Tennessee.[14] It chronicles about two years of her life between 1870 and 1872, ending with the death of her mother. Most interesting is her trip to Newark, New Jersey, to visit her "Yankee kin." In these pages Andrews records general hatred for anything northern, but is partially won over by her cousin's apparently unrelenting hospitality. Still, Andrews refuses to say much positive about northern society or culture, generally denigrating it as superficial and crass. This later diary also reveals her growth as a writer, containing some of the most biting satire and genuinely hilarious passages, as well as moving commentary on the slow decline and death of her mother.

Secession divided the Andrews family along generational lines: Judge Andrews and his wife were staunch Unionists; their children were not.[15] Three of Fanny's brothers served in the Confederate army; the eldest, Garnett, was captured. All three survived. In her wartime diary Fanny discusses her father's position repeatedly, normally in a defensive tone that tries to "justify" his position and highlight the family's sacrifices for the Confederacy despite his Unionism. As noted above, the night Georgia seceded from the Union left Fanny with vivid memories. Her father's gloomy predictions likewise remained vivid, and his Unionism caused the Andrews children—as least the women—to express their Confederate loyalties in secret. Fanny and her sister Metta were bitter that they were not allowed to celebrate in the streets, particularly since Fanny had helped her sister-in-law secretly sew a "Bonnie Blue Flag" to celebrate the much-

anticipated moment. In the diary she frequently noted her father's devotion to
"the Cause" once the war had started. "[H]e is a Southerner and a gentleman,
in spite of his politics, and at any rate nobody can accuse him of self-interest,
for he has sacrificed as much in the war as any other private citizen I know."[16] In
her later comments she also appreciated how much Union men had "suffered
not only the material losses of the war, but the odium their opinions excited."
Also, because her father's Unionism naturally "removed him . . . from all participation in the political and official life of the Confederacy," she thought that
her diary recorded the more ordinary reflections on the sufferings of common
people. After the war these "party divisions" within the household endured,
albeit, apparently, with much good nature as parents and children frequently
discussed secession and the war over dinner.[17]

As to the causes of the war, Andrews articulated at least two different positions. Her 1908 prologue reflects the Socialist thinking that Andrews found
appealing, as well as more typical southern rationalizations about the relative
importance of slavery and other factors in secession and the war. Consider it the
Lost Cause with a twist of Marxism. "It was a pure case of economic determin-
ism," Andrews concluded, "which means that our great moral conflict reduces
itself, in the last analysis, to a question of dollars and cents, though the real issue
was so obscured by other considerations that we of the South honestly believe
to this day that we were fighting for States Rights." She argued that slavery had
become unprofitable, replaced instead by "wage slavery" in the historical evolution of the world's economy.[18] This position, of course, removed morality from
the issues of slavery and emancipation, and reduced the North's claim to be
fighting "in a magnanimous struggle to free the slave" to nothing more than
humanitarian pretense for an economic and political grab for national power
and supremacy. Her devotion to the Lost Cause is evident throughout: if the
Old South "stood for some out-worn customs that should rightly be sent to the
dust heap, it stood for some things, also, that the world can ill afford to lose.
It stood for gentle courtesy, for knightly honor, for generous hospitality." She
also claimed southerners scorned "cunning greed and ill-gotten gain through
fraud and deception of our fellowmen—lessons which the founders of our New
South would do well to lay heart." These passages are, on the one hand, standard
southern fare. But Andrews's Socialism gives them an interesting flavor, setting
her at odds with much New South propaganda and giving an edge to her Lost
Cause romanticizing. She would not have thought much of Scarlett O'Hara's
lumber mills; instead she preferred the genteel poverty of an intellectual and
writer, but one whose attitudes reflected a distinctly atypical ideological perspective.[19]

In the diary itself—before the Lost Cause myth making and her embrace of Socialism—Andrews acknowledges the central role of slavery in secession and the war. This evolution of her thinking, of course, put her in the southern mainstream. Historians have long noted that before and during the war southerners were much more open about the fact that slavery lay at the root of their conflict with the North. Only in defeat did the notions of states' rights or socioeconomic sectional conflict assume center stage. In May 1865 Andrews lamented the Confederate defeat and commented on her father's longtime Unionism. "I used to sympathize with father myself, in the beginning, for it did seem a pity to break up a great nation about a parcel of African savages, if we had known any other way to protect our rights." The next day she wrote similarly that her father was right "in the beginning" that "secession was a mistake, and it would be better to have our negroes freed in the Union, if necessary, than out of it, because in that case, it would be done without passion, and violence, and we would get compensation for them."[20] Andrews's explanations of secession and the causes of the war also manifest the vagaries of history and memory; in this case, the author's views during the event itself seem to be more objective than with the perspective of four decades.

Andrews's wartime experiences and emotions follow a somewhat predictable set of themes: inflation, shortages, and massive disruption to everyday life; disillusionment about the "romance" of war; growing hatred and fear of Yankees; shock and disappointment; anxiety and uncertainty about the future. Because the wartime diary begins in December 1864 it describes some of the worst conditions for Georgians, as Sherman's massive army marched from Atlanta toward Savannah. Andrews recorded her trip (accompanied by younger sister Metta) from the family home at Haywood plantation to her older sister's plantation near Thomasville, traveling "across Sherman's track." The chaotic trip featured encounters with both Confederate troops and Yankee prisoners, a crowded, uncomfortable carriage, broken down railroads, and bug-infested hotel beds. Andrews vividly conveys the effects of nearly four years of conflict: infrastructure in ruins, economic collapse and runaway inflation, and basic services nearly unobtainable. Their first leg by train was eleven miles and took two hours. "Some of the seats were without backs and some without bottoms, and the roadbed so uneven that in places the car tilted from side to side as if it was going to upset and spill us all out." After that came a "little spring wagon" with no top "but was the choice of all the vehicles there, for it had springs, of which none of the others could boast." All the miserable conveyances departing this stop reminded Andrews of "delegations from the old woman that lived in a shoe."[21] At a later stop the two sisters moved rooms to avoid beds so infested with bugs they were afraid the mattresses might crawl away. A previous guest had left a note: "One bed has lice in it, the other fleas, and both bugs." The full effects of Confederate inflation (estimated at 9,000 percent for the war's four years) were also evident: one short ride in a mule cart cost seventy-five dollars for each, and on a later trip they hired "a two-horse wagon for one thousand dollars"; and a silk parasol "that cost four or five hundred dollars."[22]

Throughout the journey of several days Andrews also related stories from the many troops with whom they shared their transportation. Some of the men, perhaps many, likely had deserted from the Confederate army. By the end of 1864 most estimates suggest over one-half of southern troops were absent without leave. Andrews either did not consider that the men might be deserters or chose not to comment on it. Considering her pointed—perhaps brutally honest is more accurate—comments on any number of subjects, it is hard to imagine she would not have had something caustic to say if she had thought about their questionable status. More likely, it seems, is that she simply did not consider the possibility of desertion. Several of the men did seem to delight in telling Andrews and her sister some stories of "losin'" Yankee prisoners. One of the Confederates said, with the proper amount of irony, that when guarding captured Union men our "guns *would* go off an' shoot 'em, in spite of all that our folks could do." Others would try to escape and soon "their heads was caught in a grape vine and they would stand thar, dancin' on nothin' till they died." These grim stories made the women blanch, although the men assured them the prisoners were "thieves and houseburners" who had deserted from Sherman's army. In her 1908 comments, Andrews reaffirmed this opinion, offering that "stragglers and freebooters" "probably got no worse than they deserved when they fell into the hands of the enraged country people."[23]

Andrews also documented the legendary destruction of Sherman's army and the destitution of Georgians left in the Union army's wake. The two sisters traveled just days after Sherman's men, and, if Fanny's diary is an accurate indication, they witnessed the war's effects up close for the first time. She seemed to labor over rich passages that describe the barren countryside. "There was hardly a fence left standing all the way from Sparta to Gordon," she wrote. "The fields were trampled down . . . lined with carcasses of horses, hogs, and cattle . . . the stench in some places was unbearable." There was virtually no food for the "crowds of soldiers . . . tramping over the road in both directions." Further down the road Andrews came across "the poor people of the neighborhood" picking over garbage from a Union campsite. Finally they arrived at the small town of Gordon: "There was nothing left of the poor little village but ruins, charred and black as Yankee hearts." Here the Union troops had practiced their art of making "Sherman neckties," twisting the railroad tracks around tree trunks to make them forever unusable. After seeing and feeling the impact of Sherman's March to the Sea, Andrews concluded that "Yankee, Yankee, is the one detestable word always ringing in Southern ears. If all the words of hatred in every language under heaven were lumped together into one huge epithet of detestation, they could not tell how I hate Yankees." Those were feelings that faded only slightly over the rest of her life.[24]

Andrews's travels during the last months of the war also brought into clear relief her feelings of disillusionment about the "romance" of war. Many southerners, of course, questioned the sacrifices of the war by this point. The post-Sherman landscape evidently affected Andrews, as did the reports from Andersonville prison. The shocking tales from the Confederacy's most notorious prison put southerners on the defensive at the end of the war and for decades after that. Andrews was no exception, and Andersonville appears numerous times in the wartime diary. In January 1865 she related stories from the previous summer, one of many "low points" in the notorious prison. "[P]risoners died at the rate of 150 a day," she wrote. "My heart aches for the poor wretches, Yankees though they are, and I am afraid God will suffer some terrible retribution to fall upon us for letting such things happen." And she feared what would happen when the Union army finally came to Andersonville: "God have mercy on the land!" Later, she witnessed prisoners en route to Jacksonville and, although she expressed the usual hatred for them as "foreigners," admitted that "I couldn't find it in my heart to be angry. They were half-naked, and such a poor, miserable, starved-looking set of wretches that we couldn't help feeling sorry for them in spite of their wicked war against our country."[25]

The legions of wounded and disfigured troops straggling home as the war ended also forced Andrews to consider the folly of war "when stripped of all its 'pomp and circumstance'!" "No more gay uniforms, no more prancing horses, but only a few ragged foot soldiers . . . ready to march—Heaven knows where." These scenes seemed genuinely to haunt Andrews even while she praised the men's glorious struggles in the name of liberty and freedom—preparing herself for the full-blown Lost Cause rhetoric that was to come during Reconstruction. But there were moments of honesty as well, such as when she witnessed "the poor wounded men . . . hobbling about the streets with despair on their faces. There is a new pathos in a crutch or an empty sleeve, now, that we know it was all for nothing." As late as April 19, 1865, while visiting Milledgeville, Andrews watched the young cadets drilling in uniform on the capitol grounds. The "boys" were angry, she said, at Governor Joseph Brown for denying them a chance at Sherman's army; Andrews was more realistic: "The truth is, they ought all to be at home in their trundle beds . . . for they are nothing but children." In her editorial comments she reflected that "[w]e caught the infection of the war spirit in the air and never stopped to reason or to think." Like most southerners of the war generation, Andrews normally buried these moments of honest admission under a mountain of Lost Cause propaganda, but the futility and waste of it all sneaked through occasionally.[26]

When the war ended, southerners like Andrews began to face the realities of defeat, military occupation, and emancipation with the attendant racial revolution. It is in these few years—really a few months after the Confederate surrender—that Andrews wrote the bulk of her diary entries. More than half of the *War-Time Journal* covers the months of May to August, 1865. These pages relate with subtlety and considerable insight the great mixture of emotions that so many whites felt: shock, confusion, and relief; anxiety, fear, and uncertainty; anger, despair, and bitterness; hatred and vengeance. Andrews also captures the day-to-day life struggles for wealthy (or formerly wealthy) whites like herself, and the difficulty of living under the direction of Union officers. But there also were theater productions, dinner parties, and dances, and the diary is not without humor. Despite the cataclysmic changes, peacetime life resumed. In the first week of April 1865 she recorded two dinner parties—one of which included Metta and her efforts at "impromptu couplets" (a favorite nineteenth-century entertainment) celebrating the Confederate troops, of course—and a production of *Richelieu* by the Cuthbert Thespian Corps. By the middle of summer, however, Andrews seemed more infused with a "chronic state of ennui." In addition to the basic theme of "adjustment," Andrews returns again and again to the overriding issues of Reconstruction for most southern whites: contempt for Yankees and racism.[27]

Andrews's family certainly faced economic hardship when the war ended. Eventually her father sold nearly all of his lands, including property in Mississippi. In the spring and summer of 1865 Fanny and her sister began to work in the house, most likely for the first time. "A favorite topic of conversation at this time," she wrote in May, "is what we are going to do for a living." One local acquaintance "has been working assiduously at paper cigarettes to sell the Yankees," and Andrews admitted trying the same without much success. The reality of hard physical labor also made a deep impression. "I was so tired at night that I went to bed as soon as I had eaten my supper," she noted one evening. Of course her privileged background led to some unintentionally humorous lines. "I can hardly believe it is I," she wrote in late May 1865, "plotting with the servants in the pantry to get up a dinner out of nothing, like the poor people I read about in books." And at the same time she commented on their "poverty-stricken" condition and calculated that she should have enough clothes to make it through five or six months, Andrews fretted that "mother's house linen is hopelessly short."[28]

Exactly how the family survived, or what the men were doing, were not topics that Andrews addressed directly. The family had some lands nearby and still a number of servants, although they began to leave by summer 1865. There are some tantalizing suggestions in the diary, however. One is that her father was associated with the Union commandant in some way, perhaps including a business arrangement of some sort. This was undoubtedly a natural assumption that many residents made, considering her father's politics. Whether or not there existed resentment toward the family cannot be determined, although considering her three brothers' military service that would seem unlikely. Perhaps more intriguing is the suggestion that the family survived, at least in part, off the income earned by a former slave. "We live from hand to mouth like beggars," Andrews wrote in early June. Her father had sent to Augusta "for a supply of groceries," but it would not arrive for a week. "[I]n the meantime, all the sugar and coffee we have is what Uncle Osborne [a family slave] brings in. He hires himself out by the day and takes his wages in whatever provisions we need most, and hands them to father when he comes home at night. He is such a good carpenter that he is always in demand, and the Yankees themselves sometimes hire him."[29]

Andrews hated Yankees in 1865, and her opinion softened only slightly over the years. It is a cliché that no other Americans have encountered defeat in quite the same way as southerners; certainly no one else experienced military occupation by a conquering enemy, and in the 1865 diary northerners receive nearly universal scorn. At first there was trepidation at being "captured" or even having to encounter Union troops—stories of rough treatment, even rape were common enough among southern whites. In April Andrews lampooned another local woman (she "was always a great scatter-brain when I knew her at school) for going "into regular hysterics" at the report of nearby Union troops. "Such antics would have been natural enough in the beginning of the war, when we were new to these experiences, but now that we are all old soldiers, and used to raids and vicissitudes, people ought to know how to face them quietly." This stoic resignation struggled to coexist with outbursts of pure hate, often expressed in creative prose. One day she ran into their minister, who was originally from the North. "I used to like him, but now I hate to look at him just because he is a Yankee. What is it, I wonder, that makes them so different from us, even when they mean to be good Southerners! You can't even make one of them look like us." She tried to muster some "Christian charity" for them, but refused to accept "that when Christ said 'Love your enemies,' he meant Yankees. Of course I don't want their souls to be lost, for that would be wicked, but as they are not being punished in this world, I don't see how else they are going to get their desserts." Her bitterness extended to the Stars and Stripes—"their hateful old striped rag"—which she refused to look at. When she tried to move past her emotions, Andrews admitted that the daily reminders of "the humiliations" that southerners "had to endure" only "rouses me up to white heat again.[30] As many historians have argued, southerners moved past losing the war more easily than they dealt with Reconstruction and, of course, particularly the Fifteenth Amendment.[31]

Two factors seemed to have lessened—however slightly—Andrews's harsh opinion of northerners: time and contact with her Yankee relatives. In 1870 Andrews traveled to Newark, New Jersey, and stayed with her cousin Elizabeth Littell Ward ("cousin Lilla," Fanny called her). Richmond Ward, Lilla's husband, was part owner of the Clark Spool Thread Company and was representative of the new "manufacturing elite" rising to power in the North. Andrews's comments about these northern relatives, and northern culture generally, were frequently caustic, but there was also some grudging admiration and at the least acknowledgment of their hospitality. Finally, in her 1908 editorial comments for the *War-Time Journal,* Andrews makes numerous references to Union officers who, in retrospect, dealt honorably and fairly with southerners. Of course these were written long after Reconstruction ended, Jim Crow segregation was nearly perfected, and most black men had been disenfranchised. It was easier for her to be "generous" toward northerners.

Fanny Andrews and her sister Metta arrived in Newark on August 12, 1870. Immediately she noted the Wards' wealth, and their willingness to show it off. "[A]ll that I see confirms my former impressions of Yankee society. Money, flash, and vulgarity. Everybody is so loud and flashy. My cousin is a handsome, lady like person; but she shuts us up in the dark to keep the sun from fading her carpet, and does other little skimpy Yankee tricks at home, while she wears point lace and diamonds." Andrews complained about getting new towels only once a week; Yankees were rich, she conceded, but did not seem to enjoy life: "Everybody seems in a hurry." Although she admired Richmond Ward's mill and manufacturing operation, Andrews spent more time belittling, as she saw it, the northern obsession with "trade." One evening she claimed to have met "the nicest Yankee I have seen yet." "He is not a millionaire, I believe, and has not been in the shoe peg or paper box manufacturing business."[32] Most northern men, however, she dismissed in typically brutal fashion: "The he-Yankees are as contemptible as their females are vulgar: little sniveling, scrubby wretches";

and "Mett and I have noticed what miserable little sniveling specimens of humanity pass along the streets: even Mortimer Ward [a cousin], who is really good looking for a Yankee, is small and stunted, as if he had thought too much about pennies." She faulted northerners for "a stiffness, a want of cordiality," and concluded that "Yankees never joke."[33]

Still, Andrews admitted that she was, perhaps, too critical as she looked back on several pages of her diary: "[T]hese Yankees are overwhelming us with hospitality and attention," and "though they talk a vast deal about money and clothes . . . their actions often belie their words." Most of all Andrews obviously seems torn between her entrenched hatred of anything Yankee and her appreciation for the genuinely gracious treatment from her cousin. She even conceded that most northerners they met expressed real concern over conditions in the South, and sympathy for whites struggling to regain control over their lives and fortunes. No doubt her relatives were winning her over, and even the subconscious acknowledgment of "Yankee hospitality" made Andrews lash out bitterly in the privacy of her journal. Once she left Newark, on the journey back home, she unleashed one more particularly scathing assessment. "They are a nasty, miserable, sniveling, driveling, cheating, swindling, humbugging, vulgar minded set of snobs and skinflints, these Yankees, and if there is another rasping expletive in the language, I wish somebody would tell it to me, for I have exhausted my vocabulary." Naturally, many of her complaints of snobbery masked a real sense of jealousy. Absent the war, of course, Andrews herself would have enjoyed the luxuries and comforts of her northern cousins, a fact she implied rather than explicitly stated.[34]

The passage of time had a greater impact on Andrews's Yankee-hating than the visit to New Jersey. By 1908 she willingly conceded the difficult position in which Union army officers were placed in 1865. "Looking back through the glass of memory," she wrote about a Union commander from Iowa, "I see no reason to dissent from my father's opinion as to the good intentions and general uprightness of this much-berated Federal officer." She complimented another commander by admitting he acted out of "a desire to make his unpopular office as little offensive as possible, and I take pleasure in stating that his efforts were afterwards more fully appreciated by the people."[35] Andrews's personal experiences with these particular Union men, much like with her own northern relatives, forced her to admit their good intentions and reasonable behavior. That did not necessarily translate into a revised opinion of Yankees generally, but perhaps just a more subtle approach to judging people. Certainly some of that can be attributed to maturity: Andrews was twenty-five when she wrote in the wartime diary and nearly seventy when she added the editorial comments for publication. Finally, it should be reiterated that much had changed in the South between 1865 or 1870 and 1908. Personally, Andrews and most of her family had prospered and, if they had not returned to their antebellum wealth and status, they were certainly comfortable. Most importantly, of course, firmer racial hierarchy had been reestablished, alleviating Andrews's primary complaints about northerners who had forced southern whites to accept emancipation and black male suffrage.

Throughout both diaries Andrews commented frequently on race. Generally her views conformed to what most historians would consider the "mainstream" among southern whites, particularly the antebellum elite. She mentioned slaves often and displayed an interest in African American culture. She was universally condescending and racist. If anything, she became more "consciously" racist by 1908, and her opinions reflected what whites considered the disastrous experiments of freedom and universal male suffrage and office holding. Again like many other white southerners, Andrews primarily blamed northerners for the "plight" of free African Americans. Her diaries also confirm the judgment of historians that many, perhaps most Confederates held more bitterness over the course of Reconstruction than they did over losing the war. "Were it not for the bitter wrongs of Reconstruction and the fatal legacy it has left us," Andrews wrote in 1908, "the animosities engendered by the war would long ago have become . . . a mere fossil curiosity."[36]

Andrews often went to "the quarter" to hear slaves sing, both before and during the war. She records several instances in the wartime diary, and her comments suggest these were frequent trips for her. "At their 'praise meetings' they go through with all sorts of motions in connection with their songs, but they won't give way to their wildest gesticulations or engage in their sacred dances before white people, for fear of being laughed at." Andrews seemed interested in the music, although she admitted that it was difficult for her to follow (as slaves often intended, of course). "[T]he tunes are inspiring," she wrote, and "I wish I was musician enough to write down the melodies; they are worth preserving." "The words," however, were for Andrews "a wild jumble of misfit Scriptural allusions." Two weeks after this session, she again visited the Praise House to hear slaves sing. Her comments included the usual mixture of genuine interest and unconscious racism. "I wish I was an artist so that I could draw a picture of the scene. Alfred, one of the chief singers, is a gigantic creature, more like an ape than a man." He was so huge, she continued, that his hands look "as if their weight would crush the heads of the little piccaninnies when he pats them; yet, with all this strength they say he is a great coward, and one of the most docile negroes on the plantation." She also recognized—as many whites failed to do—

that the "chief personages on the plantation are old" slaves, "superannuated and privileged characters."[37] Her attitude and comments were not greatly different from those found in other diaries and letters, although they suggested a greater attention to the details of slave culture. In her April 2, 1865, entry she described a "final" visit to the quarter, during which she said goodbye to many of her family's slaves. "We all went to bed crying," she claimed, "sister, the children, and servants." In the first weeks after the war ended Andrews also complimented the "servants" as "treasures" for their loyalty and support. As late as June 1865 she avowed that their ex-slaves had "acted so well through all these troublous times that I feel more attached to them than ever."[38] When the ex-slaves did finally leave Haywood her attitude became more bitter, although for the most part she ignored their departures.

As to slavery itself, Andrews had difficulty envisioning an alternative. She suggested that if the Confederacy won the war it ought to enact a new policy that allowed slaves to choose their own masters. "Of course they would choose the good men, and this would make it to everybody's interest to treat them properly." And like virtually all southern whites, she found the prospect of emancipation overwhelming. "[W]hat on earth could we do with them, even if we wanted to free them ourselves?" In her 1908 prologue she declared that slavery was indeed better consigned to the dustbin of history, and emphasized that she no longer considered it "just and sacred." This later position also drew on her Socialist thinking, and Andrews discussed slavery as simply a stage "in the evolution of the race." African Americans were then (in 1908) in the stage of "wage slavery," from which they would eventually emerge to "free and independent labor."[39] Her editorial comments, in short, demonstrate a willingness to consider the notion that African Americans could, and would, "progress" toward (if not to) equality in an economic sense.

She gave no indication, however, that she ever considered the possibility that nonwhites could achieve anything like intellectual or cultural equality with whites. Andrews's basic assumption of African Americans as childlike was consistent throughout her nearly fifty years of comments on racial matters. "The negro is something like the Irishman in his blundering good nature, his impulsiveness and improvidence, and he is like a child in having always had some one to think and act for him." In an article she published in the *New York World* in 1865 she similarly wrote that "the negro with his gun, is like a boy with his first tin sword, when he struts out to look big, and attack imaginary dragons in turkey cocks, or giants in gate posts." By the time of her 1908 comments she seemed to have fixed on the notion of African Americans as sexually unrestrained—a by-product of their "innate childishness." Describing the fate of her "dear old

mammy" Andrews concluded that she "shared the weakness of her race in regard to chastity." Interestingly, Andrews wrote that two of her mammy's five
children were "handsome mulattoes" who were purchased by a "wealthy white
man, reputed to be their father." Apparently she never considered the possibility that her mammy's "lack of chastity" was actually her inability to resist
white male "privilege" with black women. Andrews's basic assumptions were
also evident in a scathing indictment of Emily, another family slave. Emily's
family "multiplied like rats," Andrews clucked. One of Emily's children "grew
up a degenerate of the most irresponsible type, and became the mother of five
or six illegitimate children, all by different fathers. One of her sons was hanged
for the 'usual crime,' committed against a little white girl."[40]

The particular events of Reconstruction, of course, fueled Andrews's racism,
as it did for so many other whites. Resentment over the destruction of southerners' carefully maintained racial hierarchy likewise focused hatred on Yankees,
and it is worthwhile to consider these two overriding southern emotions as
interrelated after the war. Not until southern whites reestablished, as they saw it,
proper race relations could most of them begin to consider reconciliation with
the North. The association of Yankee hating and race began even before the war
ended. Andrews acknowledged, like so many Georgians, that Sherman's March
had affected her emotionally: "I would have done justice to Yankee virtues [in
her diary], if they had had any, but since that infamous march of Sherman's and
their insolence in bringing negro soldiers among us, my feelings are so changed
that the most rabid secession talkers . . . are the only ones that satisfy me now."
As the end of the war neared, Andrews was shocked that blacks were allowed to
have ammunition and guns.[41]

After the war, when Union troops physically occupied communities, southern whites experienced firsthand a new racial order. Andrews commented
frequently on the tendency of Union soldiers to "parade" around town with
"negro wenches on their arms." She claimed they held interracial dances and
that Union men encouraged African Americans to "fill the sidewalks," making
it difficult for her to walk around town. "The streets are so full of negroes that I
don't like to go out when I can help it," she admitted in June 1865. These sorts of
complaints, of course, underscored the widespread southern belief that Yankees
were responsible for the end of proper race relations. "Poor darkeys, they are the
real victims of the war, after all. The Yankees have turned their poor ignorant
heads and driven them wild with false notions of freedom," she concluded.[42]
By late June 1865 Andrews was predicting a race war, "and we shall have only
the Yankees to thank for it" because they had encouraged ex-slaves to expect
equality, by "putting into his ignorant, savage head notions it is impossible to

gratify." Yankee ignorance of racial realities, Andrews concluded, would mean only disappointment for African Americans and suffering for southern whites. The presence of a northern missionary ("a miserable, crack-brained fanatic") in Washington caused her again to lash out at both Yankees and ex-slaves, the latter with "poor wooly heads [now] full of all sorts of impossible nonsense." By the end of the summer of 1865 Andrews seemed to lose control of her "polite racism," and her language slipped toward the more vulgar, Ku Klux Klan version: "I wish every wretch of them [Yankees] had a strapping, loud-smelling African tied to him like a Siamese twin, and that Wild [a Union General] had one on both sides. Oh, how I hate them! I will have to say 'Damn!' yet, before I am done with them."[43]

Ultimately, like nearly all whites in her section, Andrews regarded the Fifteenth Amendment "as the greatest of all the evils brought upon us by the war," something which "injected a race problem into our national life." By 1908 Andrews was again firmly in step with the majority of southern whites, adopting the language of racial purity and Anglo-Saxon superiority: "[I]t is good to feel coursing in your veins the blood of a race that has left its impress on the civilization of the world wherever the Anglo-Saxon has set his foot."[44] The evolution of her thinking about Yankees and race, then, seemed to put Andrews in the southern mainstream. At the close of the war, she was disposed toward some fondness for her family's "servants," praising them for "loyalty" and sensible behavior. As they became more "unruly" and "ungrateful," however, she first blamed northerners for encouraging the childlike slaves to think they could become equals, and then turned on African Americans as a group. The war years and Reconstruction, in short, seemed to harden Andrews's racial thinking, leading her, by 1908, to embrace the language of Anglo-Saxon purity of blood.

If the war years hardened Andrews's notions of race, their impact on her understanding of gender is less clear. The Confederate experience and ultimate defeat disrupted traditional gender relationships in the South. White men were gone for months, even years, and women had to run farms and manage slaves; Union victory called southern masculinity into question. Andrews participated fully in the Lost Cause myth-making that was, in part, designed to rehabilitate southern men's collective ego and reestablish the patriarchy so broken by the war. Her public language normally conformed to the traditional notions of "separate spheres," although she did occasionally tweak the public conscience about the place of women in American society. In contrast to the rhetorical support for traditional gender roles, of course, was her own extraordinary professional career. Unfortunately Andrews simply did not write enough, or explicitly enough, about her own feelings, and therefore we are left with these contradictory images. That was hardly unusual for southern women in the nineteenth century.

Even before the end of the war Andrews expressed her intentions for an independent life. "One man grows tiresome unless you expect to marry him, and I am never going to marry anybody," she wrote in February 1865. "Marriage," she concluded, "is incompatible with the career I have marked out for myself." By 1871 Andrews, at thirty-one years old, had tasted some success as a writer, traveled to parts of the United States, and clearly enjoyed her freedom. On the other hand, her family struggled to regain its financial fortunes, and both Fanny and her sister Metta debated marriage to help her parents. Fanny apparently could have married "Old Sam Wynn," a man who lived in Washington, but she concluded he "isn't rich enough to pay" her "price": "It would take a round hundred thousand to make [him] . . . go down with me, to say nothing of his silly daughter. I wish I was like the other girls—willing to marry anybody and be done with it." Of course she wasn't willing to do it, which helped make her so unusual. She noted other local girls who recently married or were pursuing potential wealthy mates, "while I, who am just as poor and needy as any of them, can't make up my mind to take the plunge." "Even school teaching," she continued, "bad as it is, can't bring me to terms." Metta was considering another local bachelor, "a far worse case than old Sam, though he has got more money." Andrews evidently agonized over the position she was in. She was an attractive, well-connected, and educated woman, and her family needed the money, but just as evidently she wanted no part of marriage. "I believe I will ask father if we are so bad off as to make such a sacrifice necessary—though I don't believe starvation itself could drive me to it." She admitted Sam Wynn was "by no means bad looking for a man of fifty, or thereabouts—but I don't know what it is—I can't, and I won't. I am afraid my pen has spoilt me: it has opened such a world to me, and I shudder at any kind of a Marriage."[45] Many elite southern women like Andrews faced this agonizing choice in the years after the war. Of course, most women had no such "problem," and thousands of poor, widowed southerners surely would have liked to choose between an independent career and marriage to a "good," wealthy man.[46]

Andrews's most extended discussion of women's place in America came in an 1869 article in *Scott's Monthly Magazine*, "Professions and Employments Open to Women," which she wrote under her pen name of Elzey Hay. It was generally a defense of her own choices and a definite, although restrained argument for women having greater choices in their lives. She criticized the prevailing attitude that women had "but one vocation": "the rearing of children and fulfillment of household duties." Andrews defended women who worked to support themselves or their families, and lampooned the pressure that society heaped on men who "failed" to earn enough money. Through hypothetical cases she debated the advantages and disadvantages for women who worked in public—her example was a teacher, of course—and those women at home with husbands and children to care for. Andrews tended to side with her theoretical teacher, noting that she had to answer to the general public and not just her husband. "One great difficulty in the way of professional women," she concluded, "arises from the nature of the employments which are considered within the legitimate scope of female efforts." Other than sewing and teaching, not much existed for women to "earn a modest competency for herself," and there was virtually no chance for a public woman to gain "social advantage." Andrews expressed ambivalent sentiments about teaching, in particular: "School-teaching, the most intellectual of [women's occupations], and I suppose the best, as it seems to be much in favor of reduced gentlewomen, is merely a sort of mental tread-mill, and its tendency is to contract and narrow the mind."[47] Presumably, or at least hopefully, her opinion changed, since she taught school for about three decades after this was written. One noteworthy aspect of the article is that Andrews strongly advocated professions that would allow women to develop intellectually and creatively—she cited the stage and literature in particular—rather than emphasizing financial reward. Given her family background, of course, that is hardly surprising, but it also naturally reflected her readership.

Although Andrews expressed some dissatisfaction with women's place in society, her article included a strong defense of men as protectors of the weak. Women were disadvantaged in the careers open to them, true, but "the difference is more than made up to the sex at large by the fact that men have to work for us, and if they possess advantages over us they use them for our good." She was, of course, smart enough to note that this "arrangement" worked well "for the generality of women, [but] it is a little hard upon those few unfortunates who happen to be left out in the cold, and have to take care of themselves." Finally, in this article and elsewhere Andrews vigorously attacked the "school of female radicalism" that advocated political rights. In the *Washington Gazette*, also in 1869, Andrews feared that women's suffrage might actually happen: "A people that have swallowed the camel of negro suffrage will not strain long at the gnat of woman's rights." She asserted that the vast majority of women had no interest in politics and hoped that men would not force the "fairer sex" to accept something they did not want. Interestingly, Andrews argued that women alone should decide the question—itself a fairly advanced notion of equality, of course. She concluded with classic language and imagery from the ideology of "separate spheres": "The responsibilities of social and private life rest almost entirely upon women, and the sensible ones know that they have enough to do without assuming the additional burden of public cares. One who discharges properly her duties as mother of a family, will not have much ambition to figure as the mother of her country." Taken with her Lost Cause rhetoric, these sentiments demonstrated that Andrews supported the broader theme of reinvigorating patriarchy and reestablishing the old rules of gender, no matter how contradictory her own career was to those ideas.[48]

Eliza Frances Andrews almost certainly had her life transformed by the Civil War and Reconstruction. As the privileged daughter of a wealthy slave owner she was educated and trained to be a mother, wife, and plantation mistress. The destruction of her society pushed her to make different choices, although some of her comments suggest she was headed in those directions anyway. After the war she became an independent, professional woman who succeeded as a teacher, writer, and internationally recognized botanist. Throughout the years she also reflected broader social attitudes among white southerners, and in her diaries she recorded the physical and emotional upheavals of the war and Reconstruction. Like so many fellow Georgians and southerners, Andrews expressed most consistently a hatred of Yankees and a mixture of fear and hatred of African Americans. Her attitudes about race tended to harden over time: consistently racist, of course, but also more convinced of the innate weaknesses of nonwhite people and fixed on notions of Anglo-Saxon "purity of blood." And someone of Andrews's background and experiences would never "forgive" Yankees, but by the twentieth century she seemed to accept them again as fellow human beings, if not exactly fellow Americans.

In her words and her own actions she also recorded the dilemmas of gender in the Civil War South, where so many women, mostly by necessity, assumed public roles for the first time. Yet, most women also participated in the regional therapy session that became the "Lost Cause," an elaborate myth designed to justify the war's horrendous human cost and to rehabilitate southern men's sense of pride. From the end of the war into the twentieth century, white southerners worked to reestablish the racial and gender hierarchy that existed before the war. Women were a crucial part of these efforts, and Fanny Andrews lent her rhetorical support. In that sense she remained a "traditional" southern woman, even while her own career took her far from tradition. She and other elite women built the public educational system and molded the New South in very significant ways. What Andrews did at Wesleyan and Washington High

School was not only educate daughters of the elite and new middle class, but model and educate a new role for women out of the household. From the sheltered luxury of an antebellum plantation Andrews became a teacher in several states, an acclaimed author and botanist, and a nationally known Socialist. For a well-bred daughter of privilege from the Old South, it was a long, strange journey. Fanny Andrews died in Alabama in 1931, at age ninety, and is buried in the family plot in Washington, Georgia.

## NOTES

1. Eliza Frances Andrews, *Journal of a Georgia Woman 1870–1872*, ed. S. Kittrell Rushing (Knoxville: University of Tennessee Press, 2002), 50; Eliza Frances Andrews, *The War-Time Journal of a Georgia Girl, 1864–1865* (Lincoln: University of Nebraska Press, 1997), 363, 281, 336 (previous editions were: Eliza Frances Andrews, *Wartime Journal of a Georgia Girl: 1864–1865* [New York: D. Appleton, 1908]; and *Wartime Journal of a Georgia Girl: 1864–1865* [Macon, Ga.: Arvidan Press, 1960]; all page references are to the 1997 edition).

2. Andrews, *War-Time Journal*, 176.

3. The literature on these topics is vast. Among dozens of important studies, see Drew Gilpin Faust, *Mothers of Invention: Women of the Slaveholding South in the American Civil War* (Chapel Hill: University of North Carolina Press, 1996); Andrews does not always fit her interpretation, particularly with regard to religion and spirituality. Also Drew Gilpin Faust, "Altars of Sacrifice: Confederate Women and the Narratives of War," *Journal of American History* 76 (March 1990): 1200–28; George Rable, *Civil Wars: Women and the Crisis of Southern Nationalism* (Urbana: University of Illinois Press, 1989); Laura F. Edwards, *Gendered Strife and Confusion: The Political Culture of Reconstruction* (Urbana: University of Illinois Press, 1997); Anne Firor Scott, *The Southern Lady: From Pedestal to Politics, 1830–1930* (Chicago: University of Chicago Press, 1970); Peter W. Bardaglio, *Reconstructing the Household: Families, Sex and the Law in the Nineteenth-Century South* (Chapel Hill: University of North Carolina Press, 1995). On the roles of women in reconstructing the New South, see especially LeeAnn Whites, *The Civil War as a Crisis in Gender: Augusta, Georgia, 1860–1890* (Athens: University of Georgia Press, 1995); Grace Elizabeth Hale, *Making Whiteness: The Culture of Segregation in the South, 1890–1940* (New York: Pantheon, 1998); Anastasia Sims, *The Power of Femininity in the New South: Women's Organizations and Politics in North Carolina, 1880–1930* (Columbia: University of South Carolina Press, 1997).

4. The closest comparison to Andrews is probably Ella Gertrude Clanton Thomas, from Augusta, Georgia. Thomas graduated from Wesleyan Female College in Macon and had similar wartime experiences, including encounters with Sherman's army. Thomas advocated women's education after the war and knew Andrews as a fellow activist in the United Daughters of the Confederacy. Thomas's own writings contained similar themes, most notably in regard to gender and the role of women and the Lost Cause. Thomas's opinions on race, however, were considerably more liberal than Andrews's, and Thomas was a greater enthusiast for reunification. See Mary Elizabeth Massey, "The Making of a Feminist," *Journal of Southern History* 39 (February 1973): 3–32; Ella Gertrude Clanton Thomas, *Secret Eye: The Journal of Ella Gertrude Clanton Thomas, 1848–1889*, ed. Virginia I. Durr (Chapel Hill: University of North Carolina Press, 1990). See also Faust, "Altars of Sacrifice;" Mary A. H. Gay, *Life in Dixie during the War*, ed. J. H. Segars (1892; repr., Macon, Ga.: Mercer

University Press, 2001); Sarah Morgan Dawson, *A Confederate Girl's Diary*, ed. James I. Robertson (Bloomington: Indiana University Press, 1960); and of course Mary Boykin Chesnut, *A Diary from Dixie*, ed. Ben Ames Williams (1949; repr., Cambridge, Mass.: Harvard University Press, 1989).

5. Andrews, *War-Time Journal*, 180.

6. Andrews, *Journal of a Georgia Woman*, xxii, xxiv; Andrews, *War-Time Journal*, vi.

7. Andrews, *War-Time Journal*, 178; Andrews, *Journal of a Georgia Woman*, xxx–xxxi. For other biographical information on Andrews, see Barbara B. Reitt, "Eliza Frances Andrews," in *Dictionary of Georgia Biography* (Athens, Ga.: University of Georgia Press, 1983), 1:29–31; "Eliza Frances Andrews (Elzey Hay)," in *Southland Writers: Biographical and Critical Sketches of the Living Female Writers of the South*, ed. Mrs. Mary Tardy (Philadelphia: Claxton, Remsen, and Haffelfinger, 1870), 1:512–19; "Miss Eliza Frances Andrews: A Versatile Genius," *Montgomery Advertiser*, April 1911; "Georgia Woman Wins International Honor," *Atlanta Journal*, March 26, 1926. On Judge Garnett Andrews, see Robert M. Willingham Jr., "Garnett Andrews," in *Dictionary of Georgia Biography*, 1:31–32; and Garnett Andrews, *Reminiscences of an Old Georgia Lawyer* (Atlanta: Franklin Steam Printing House, 1870).

8. Andrews, *Journal of a Georgia Woman*, xxx; Andrews, *War-Time Journal*, vii.

9. "Georgia: The Elections" was originally published in the *New York World*, 1865; "Dress under Difficulties; or, Passages from the Blockade Experience of Rebel Women" appeared in *Godey's Lady's Book and Magazine*, 1866; and "Professions and Employments Open to Women" was published under her pen name of Elzey Hay in *Scott's Monthly Magazine*, January 1869. All of these articles, as well as "A Plea for Red Hair" and "Paper-Collar Gentility" are reprinted in Rushing's *Journal of a Georgia Woman, 1870–1872*.

10. The novels are: *A Family Secret* (Philadelphia: J. B. Lippincott, 1876); *A Mere Adventurer* (Philadelphia: J. B. Lippincott, 1879); and *Prince Hal* (Philadelphia: J. B. Lippincott, 1882).

11. Andrews, *War-Time Journal*, vii; Andrews, *Journal of a Georgia Woman*, xxxix; Spencer Bidwell King Jr., 1961 introduction to *War-Time Journal*, xiii.

12. Marie Bankhead Owen, "Miss Eliza Francis Andrews, a Versatile Genius," *Montgomery Advertiser*, April 1911; Charlotte A. Ford, "Eliza Frances Andrews, Practical Botanist, 1840–1931," *Georgia Historical Quarterly* 70 (Spring 1986): 63 and passim for her scientific career, including a bibliography of her botanical publications. See also Laura Davis Holt, "A Naturalist of the Old South and New," *Volta Review* (March 1926): 109–14. Andrews also led tours of Europe for a time. See Andrews, *Journal of a Georgia Woman*, xxxix.

13. Andrews, *War-Time Journal*, 8.

14. According to his own introduction, S. Kittrell Rushing discovered the journal in 1998 among the papers of Garnett Andrews (Fanny Andrews's brother) in the archives and special collections of the University of Tennessee at Chattanooga Lupton Library. See Rushing, introduction to Andrews, *Journal of a Georgia Woman*, xi.

15. Generational divisions over secession were not unusual. According to one of the most careful studies of the movement, age and wealth (closely related factors, of course) were the two most important factors determining whether or not one supported secession or disunion. See William L. Barney, *The Secessionist Impulse: Alabama and Mississippi in 1860* (Princeton: Princeton University Press, 1974).

16. Andrews, *War-Time Journal*, 176, 206.

17. Ibid., 16–17, 3–4.

18. Ibid., 13. See also 12, on the evolution of world economy and South's place in it.

19. Ibid., 14–15.

20. Ibid., 220, 228. On women's narratives and changing perceptions of the war, see Sarah E. Gardner, *Blood and Irony: Southern White Women's Narratives of the Civil War, 1861–1937* (Chapel Hill: University of North Carolina Press, 2004).

21. Andrews, *War-Time Journal,* 23, 23.

22. Ibid., 27, 162 (quotes), 39, 116.

23. Ibid., 31, 31n. According to James McPherson, desertion rates for Union and Confederate armies were about equal until winter 1864–65; see *Ordeal By Fire: The Civil War and Reconstruction,* Third Edition (New York: McGraw-Hill, 2001), 504–5. By early 1865 most estimates place the rate of Confederate soldiers who were absent without leave at near or above 50 percent.

24. Andrews, *War-Time Journal,* 32, 33, 38, 67.

25. Ibid., 78–79, 131.

26. Ibid., 79, 154 (also 138), 154–55, 164, 15.

27. Ibid., 133–41, 311.

28. Ibid., 250, 339, 380 (quote), 272, 271.

29. Ibid., 266, for instance, 286.

30. Ibid., 151, 148–49, 233, 288.

31. On the related themes of sectional reconciliation and southern memory, see David Blight, *Race and Reunion: The Civil War in American Memory* (Cambridge, Mass.: Harvard University Press, 2001); Gary Gallagher and Alan T. Nolan, eds., *The Myth of the Lost Cause and Civil War History* (Bloomington: Indiana University Press, 2000); William C. Davis, *The Cause Lost: Myths and Realities of the Confederacy* (Lawrence: University Press of Kansas, 2003); Gaines M. Foster, *Ghosts of the Confederacy: Defeat, the Lost Cause, and the Emergence of the New South, 1865–1913* (New York: Oxford University Press, 1988); W. Fitzhugh Brundage, ed., *Where These Memories Grow: History, Memory, and Southern Identity* (Chapel Hill: University of North Carolina Press, 2000); and Thomas Connelly and Barbara Bellows, *God and General Longstreet: The Lost Cause and the Southern Mind* (Baton Rouge: Louisiana State University Press, 1982).

32. Andrews, *Journal of a Georgia Woman,* 12, 4, 13.

33. Ibid., 12, 8, 6.

34. Ibid., 19, 25–26. For a classic piece of Andrews sarcasm, read her comments about the feet of a Yankee woman she encountered (27).

35. Andrews, *War-Time Journal,* 266n., 304n.

36. Ibid., 315n.

37. Ibid., 89, 91, 101, 101–2.

38. Ibid., 128, 272, 293. In one hilarious instance, Andrews noted that the slaves seemed to be lampooning her and Metta at one of their evening gatherings (345).

39. Ibid., 127, 13, 14.

40. Ibid., 340, 294n., 378n. The 1865 article is reprinted in Andrews, *Journal of a Georgia Woman,* 69.

41. Andrews, *War-Time Journal,* 314.

42. Ibid., 267, 251, 282, 277; see also 332–34.

43. Ibid., 316, 317, 363.

44. Ibid., 280, 281, 387. See also her 1865 article from the *New York World,* reprinted in Andrews, *Journal of a Georgia Woman,* 74.

45. Andrews, *War-Time Journal,* 96; Andrews, *Journal of a Georgia Woman,* 35, 36.

46. For women, teaching was the only option to earn a "respectable" income. See Ann Short Chirhart, *Torches of Light: Georgia Teachers and the Coming of the Modern South* (Athens: University of Georgia Press, 2005). A contemporary diary that details the struggles of women teachers is Amelia Akehurst Line, *To Raise Myself a Little: The Diaries and Letters of Jennie, a Georgia Teacher 1851–1886,* ed. Thomas Dyer (Athens: University of Georgia Press, 1982).

47. Andrews, *Journal of a Georgia Woman,* 84, 87, 88.

48. Ibid., 88, 89, xxviii, xxix.

# Amanda America Dickson

## (1849–1893)

## *A Wealthy Lady of Color in Nineteenth-Century Georgia*

### KENT ANDERSON LESLIE

One day in the middle of February 1849, a wealthy man named David Dickson rode across his fallow fields. As he rode he spotted a young female slave, whom he knew, playing in a field. The girl not only belonged to his mother but was also a great favorite of hers. Deliberately, he rode up beside her, reached down, and swung her up behind him on his saddle. As one of her descendants remarked years later, "that was the end of that." The enslaved girl's childhood ended as Amanda America Dickson's life began, on the day when her forty-year-old father raped her thirteen-year-old mother.[1]

Amanda America Dickson was born on November 20, 1849, on the Dickson home place in southeastern Hancock County, Georgia. She spent her infancy, childhood, and early adulthood in her white father's household, inside the boundary of his family, as his daughter. She married a white Civil War veteran and had children of her own. She inherited her father's enormous estate and eventually moved to Augusta, Georgia, where she died amid luxury and comfort, at home in the wealthiest section of the city. An exploration of Amanda America Dickson's story from several perspectives will show that her personal identity was ultimately bounded by her sense of class solidarity with her father, that is, by her socialization as David Dickson's daughter,[2] her gender role as a lady, and her racial definition as a person to whom racial categories did not apply. How did these definitions affect the life choices of an elite mulatto lady of color in nineteenth-century Georgia?

**AMANDA AMERICA DICKSON**
Courtesy of Michaele Jean Jackson.

This life provides us with a kaleidoscopic glimpse into a world of conflicting ideologies and expectations where what was forbidden in the abstract existed in reality. This glimpse is afforded by the fascinating story of a woman, born of a slave mother and a white father, whose life engaged the interlocking issues of race, class, and gender in the nineteenth-century South, both before and after the Civil War. Her story reflects light into both the black and white communities in that time and place. It is a story in which the strong wills of an elite white father and a slave mother, coupled with lifelong personal relationships and extensive economic obligations, interacted to mitigate the boundaries of race for the sake of a daughter, not necessarily a family. Amanda America Dickson's story reveals the formation of an identity as raceless and consequently alone, without a nuclear family or an extended family, as a "no nation."[3]

If it is true that public sentiment, not abstract ideology, controlled the amount of miscegenation that took place in the nineteenth-century South, then what factors combined to create a place where an elite white male could rape a slave child and raise the offspring of that act of violence in his own household? If we include the sentiments of the slave community in this observation, we are left with a complex question. A partial answer lies in the geography, history, and socioeconomic arrangements that evolved in Amanda Dickson's place, a place where she was both protected and trapped.[4]

Amanda America Dickson's birthplace, Hancock County, is in the fertile so-called black belt of the state, 125 miles south and east of Atlanta, between the pre–Civil War capital of Milledgeville and the riverport city of Augusta.

Between the establishment of Hancock County in 1793 and the official end of Indian hostilities in 1828, the county emerged from its frontier status and became an "incubator," a place where poor to middling settlers congregated while waiting to move on to land in the middle and western parts of the state. Farmers who had accumulated a surplus of capital bought up the fertile bottomlands of the county and stayed put. The white population of the area reached 9,605 in 1800 and steadily declined thereafter. By 1850 the white population had been reduced to 4,210. Conversely, the slave population increased from 4,835 in 1800 to 8,137 in 1860, 4,242 males and 3,895 females.[5]

By 1830 the county had established itself as a cotton-growing region. A decade later, it produced twice as much cotton as any of its nearest competitors in Georgia. In sharp contrast with the relative wealth of Hancock County as a whole, approximately one-third of its white families owned land but no slaves, and approximately one-third owned neither land nor slaves.[6]

In addition to important social institutions, including churches, schools, and an agricultural club, society in Hancock County was held together by social conventions that evolved along with "civilization" and the plantation regime. Foremost among these was what David Potter has described as personalism. The people who stayed in the county knew one another and what to expect from their neighbors. Some knew one another and their families all of their lives, across racial and class lines. In 1885, during the trial to decide the validity of David Dickson's will, the superior court of Hancock County summoned thirty-seven witnesses to testify. These individuals were Dickson's slaves, employees, business associates, relatives, and friends. Ten of them testified that they had known David Dickson all their lives. The six former slaves who testified declared that they had known Dickson an average of forty-three years. Twenty-nine whites testified that they had known Dickson for an average of twenty-six years. Comments like "ever since I have known myself," "as long as I recollect," and "ever since I was a boy" appeared frequently in the court record.[7]

Manners and a shared sense of what Bertram Wyatt-Brown has termed honor minimized differences in status among whites in the county. According to Wyatt-Brown, individuals of high social status addressed those of lower status with directness and respect as whites and vice versa. In addition, status inequities among whites were minimized by notions of hospitality and generosity, which worked in both directions. Wyatt-Brown found that deviance from the accepted norms could be tolerated only if the offender "somehow conveys a sense of powerlessness, otherwise the nonconformist, whose misdeeds may be real or socially conjured up, faced ostracism or worse." In this system of honor, miscegenation and the formation of a white-mulatto kinship relationship within the elite class would constitute a violation of community norms, a "danger in the margins."[8] The relationship between Amanda America Dickson and her father disproves Wyatt-Brown's assumption that everyone who transgressed racial taboos in the antebellum South was "ostracized or worse." As we shall see, David Dickson sometimes behaved in an imperious manner, and though he may have been ostracized by a segment of the population in Hancock County, he certainly was accepted by other segments of this complex community.

This, then, was Amanda America Dickson's place, a place where black slaves outnumbered white citizens by almost two to one; a place where education, culture, and even luxury were available to a small minority of a ruling race; a place where enough was available for everybody to subsist; a place where people often knew each other all their lives. How did these factors combine across racial and class lines both to impose order on human behavior and to make it possible for the community to tolerate exceptions to that order in the elite class?[9]

David, Julia Frances, and Amanda America Dickson's stories represent threads that intertwine to form a pattern, a pattern distorted by the tensions between racial ideology and family, between paternalism and exploitation, and between power and the control of power in an interdependent community. As a consequence, Amanda America Dickson's life unfolded within the boundaries of her father's social and economic power, her mother's conflicting loyalties, and her own evolving sense of self. The story of this family's struggles spans most of the nineteenth century, bracketing the beginning and the end of the plantation regime in Hancock County; the Civil War and Reconstruction; the New South for some, the nadir for others; and the complete disfranchisement of black male Georgians by 1908.

Close analysis of the pattern of these lives reveals the processes by which David Dickson created a web of interlocking social and economic relationships, accumulating enough power to transgress a fundamental social taboo. Julia Frances Dickson's story shows the conflicting loyalties that are reflected in her relationship with David, with Amanda, and with her own black family. Amanda America Dickson's story is complicated because there are several contradictory versions of it. The African American Dickson family oral history presents a picture of an elite "lady," in the ornamental sense. David Dickson's will, on the other hand, speaks respectfully of his daughter as one possessing "sound judgment." His will case transcript depicts her as a person whose blackness was mitigated by her father's relationships in the community. Finally, contemporary newspaper reports published after David Dickson's death describe Amanda America as an oddity, a contemporary oxymoron, a wealthy black "lady."

By 1845 David Dickson had accumulated an estate worth $25,000 and was in the initial stages of transforming himself from a plowboy to a merchant to a planter. In 1841 he had owned ten slaves and no land. By 1845 he owned forty-five slaves and 1,000 acres of land. By the end of 1849 Dickson owned 2,010 acres of land and fifty-three slaves. In that same year only seven people in Hancock County owned more slaves than he did.[10]

In 1850 David Dickson still lived on the Dickson home place with his mother, Elizabeth, his unmarried sister, and his unmarried brother, each of whom also owned slaves in their own right. One of Elizabeth's slaves was David's infant daughter, Amanda.[11]

In addition, by 1860 David Dickson had become famous as one of Georgia's most innovative and successful farmers. In the early 1850s C. W. Howard, the editor of the widely read *Southern Countrymen*, which later became the *Southern Cultivator*, "discovered" Dickson. Howard praised Dickson in his publications and invited him to publish letters describing the Dickson method of farming in both journals. As a result, by 1861 Dickson was labeled in the agricultural publications of the day as the "Prince of Georgia Farmers" and described as "the person most responsible for agricultural reform in the region."[12]

Amanda was also the daughter of Julia Frances Lewis Dickson, described in the African American Dickson oral history as a small, copper-colored person with soft hair and beautiful teeth, a woman who was "very temperamental and high-strung."[13]

We do not know what reactions the violence of Amanda America Dickson's conception evoked. Years later, David Dickson commented that Julia had been a waiting maid in his mother's house and he had "let his foot slip." According to the African American Dickson oral history, Julia never forgave David for the rape, for forcing her to have sex with him at such an early age. Julia was a "great pet" of Elizabeth Dickson's, so what was Elizabeth's reaction to this violent event?

After Amanda America was weaned, she was taken from her mother, another act of violence against Julia Dickson as tragic as the rape itself. Thereafter the child lived in her white grandmother's room, sleeping in a trundle bed that Elizabeth Dickson had made especially for her. She lived in that same room, in the white Dickson household, until her grandmother's death in 1864.[14]

Later in his life David Dickson reflected on the decision to bring Amanda America into the Dickson household. He declared that he believed it was his duty to care for his daughter and that he wanted her to be with him. Perhaps these feelings prompted Dickson to take the infant into his household. Perhaps Elizabeth Dickson made the decision to separate Amanda America from her mother in an effort to make amends for her son's loss of control, or perhaps she simply wanted the company of her grandchild and could obtain David's co-operation. One of Elizabeth Dickson's grandsons commented that he had "never seen a man in all his life that was as kind to his mother as [David] was; I have never seen any person any kinder; there was nothing he could do for her but what he was ready to do it." Perhaps David and Elizabeth made the decision together to create a "family" that excluded the child's mother.[15]

From her birth in 1849 until her grandmother's death in 1864, Amanda America Dickson remained legally a slave. During this time, it would have been virtually impossible for Elizabeth or David to free Amanda and still keep her with them in Georgia. As early as 1801 the state of Georgia had outlawed manu-mission within the state, except by petitioning the legislature, a process that became more and more restrictive after 1818. Before 1859 masters and mistresses could free their slaves outside the state while they were alive or outside the state via their wills. Amanda Dickson could have been freed in another state, but she could not have legally returned to Georgia as a free person of color. Though Elizabeth and David kept Amanda America with them, the child remained a slave and continually at risk, vulnerable to her grandmother's and father's morality and mortality.[16]

According to both the African American Dickson family oral history and white observers, Amanda America spent most of her childhood and youth in her grandmother's room. Julia Frances Dickson observed that Amanda stayed there night and day, studying her books and doing "whatever she was told to do." Dr. E. W. Alfriend, the Dickson family doctor, observed that Amanda America was "very devoted" to her grandmother and "very comfortably situated" in her grandmother's room.[17]

Some evidence supports the thesis that her white relatives treated Amanda like a servant. For example, one of David Dickson's nephews commented that "she was about the house like any other child would be; helped at sweeping the floor and such as that."[18]

Although she seems to have performed duties that would typically be performed by servants, the evidence suggests that some members of the white Dickson household treated Amanda America as they would a pet, as someone to love and spoil, behavior very much like the care and "loving fascination" with children that Jane Turner Censer argues was common within elite planter families but not possible in relationships between these families and slave children. According to the African American Dickson family oral history, Amanda America was the "darling of David Dickson's heart." He "adored her" and "gave her everything in the world. He had her bathed in sweet milk to lighten her skin. He allowed her to claim newborn slaves as her own and name them whatever she liked." Everyone on the plantation called her "Miss Mandy," including her father, and, one would presume, her mother. "She was his pampered darling." Because Amanda America Dickson was a mulatto and a slave, this description of child rearing seems tragic. It is a picture of a raceless "little princess of the hinter isles" raised in a make-believe world. Curiously, the African American Dickson family oral history does not record this situation with regret.[19]

Another, more practical indicator of David Dickson's affection for Amanda is that she learned to read and write, a luxury for any girl child of the time, and ironically, a skill that Dickson's own mother and sister never acquired. Scholars have observed that antebellum southern fathers often took charge of their daughter's formal education,[20] and it is entirely possible that Dickson's love for his daughter, a concern for her future, led him to willingly assume this role. It is perhaps no accident that Amanda's signature is very similar to that of her father.[21]

David Dickerson may well have assumed the initial responsibility for teaching Amanda to read and write, but he took additional steps to ensure that she received more than the basic literacy that in adulthood would suit her for little more than a servile existence. According to the African American Dickson family history, tutors came to the Dickson plantation specifically to teach Amanda. Her education advanced to the point where, for example, she was reading *Camille*, a play written in 1852 by Alexander Dumas the Younger, himself a mulatto. Ironically, the play deals with a young courtesan in Paris who was doomed to be "ostracized from polite society."[22]

It was while living within the boundaries of the white Dickson household that Amanda America learned the skills and manners appropriate to the family's newly elevated social class. As a child she learned to play the piano; to dress with subdued elegance, including the display of jewelry; and to behave like a "lady," in the educated though ornamental sense. Amanda America Dickson also learned to manage business transactions in the manner of her very successful father and to retain control of her own financial affairs after marriage. We do not know who her friends were as a child or as an adult. We do not know if or how the family of Elizabeth, David, and Amanda protected themselves, especially Amanda, from chance encounters with individuals who were unaware of their unorthodox arrangements. Neither do we know how Julia Frances Dickson reacted to having her mulatto daughter raised as a "lady."

While Amanda America was growing up in the big house, her mother lived a very different life. Julia Frances Lewis Dickson began her life as a slave living in a "nigger" house in the yard with the other servants. It was a large frame building, two stories high, with three to five rooms. By 1857 Julia Dickson was living in another house on the edge of the yard that was "a little better furnished." Julia lived upstairs in this second house, in a room partitioned off from the other servants. Her mother, Rose, had an adjoining room separated from Julia's space by a door.[23] From these residences, Julia Frances Dickson moved in and out of the white Dickson household as a slave with a privileged position.

Slaves and at least one white employee on the Dickson plantation observed a relatively open show of affection between Julia and David. They were present when David lifted Julia down from her horse and kissed her. They also

observed David kissing Julia on other occasions.[24] In addition, other members
of the plantation community and several of David Dickson's relatives spotted
them behaving as intimates, either sitting in the parlor or, rather more suggestive, by the fire in David Dickson's bedroom. Indeed, the relationship between
Julia and Dickson became such that with Elizabeth Dickson's ever increasing
infirmity, the latter promoted Julia together with another mulatto slave, named
Lucy, to stand guard over the plantation keys and to preside over the kitchen. In
effect, Julia became Dickson's housekeeper. There is no evidence to suggest that
Julia's new and influential role in the Dickson household involved, and possibly
stemmed from, a continuing sexual relationship. What we can be sure of, and
possibly this was Julia's motivation for what, at least on the surface, was her close
relationship with the man who had raped her as a child, was that her new position brought her into daily contact with her daughter. How they regarded one
another, what they might have talked about is lost to history.[25]

In 1861, when the war erupted, Amanda America Dickson was twelve years old,
living in a household that consisted of her eighty-four-year-old grandmother
and her fifty-two-year-old father. What she knew about the impending crisis
at the time is hard to say. After all, she lived in the household of a powerful
patriarch-paternalist, a man who had protected her from other ambiguities and
anxieties. Of course, her mother's role and close proximity may have provided
her with a continuing flow of news and opinions from the "outside" world, not
least from the enslaved people's world. By 1865, at the end of the war, the teenage
Amanda must have been aware of her uncertain future.

   What Julia Frances Dickson thought as the war broke out is also unclear. She
was twenty-five years old and also a slave. One of her living daughters had been
taken from her and benefited materially from the slave system while the other,
Julianna Youngblood, had not. In fact, Julianna; Julia's mother, Rose; and her
brothers John C. and Seab Lewis were Dickson slaves. Julia's privileged position
as the Dicksons' housekeeper rested on David Dickson's wealth, which rested
on the backs of his slave labor force, Julia Dickson's kin.

   Four years later, in 1865, Julia was a free woman. She was free to leave the
Dickson household and, assuming that she had been engaged in one, free to
terminate her sexual relationship with David Dickson.[26]

   Julia Frances Dickson chose to stay on the Dickson plantation. Perhaps she
was reluctant to leave the place. She had grown up there, a "special pet" of
Elizabeth Dickson's. Perhaps she stayed because of her position of responsi-

bility in the operation of the Dickson plantation. Perhaps she stayed because David would not allow Amanda America to leave or because Amanda America would not leave. Perhaps she stayed because she did not want to leave David Dickson.

In 1865 Amanda America Dickson was sixteen years old. Her white grandmother had been dead a year. Her father's empire lay in ruins, and she faced the possibility of being poor for the first time in her life. She had always been treated as essentially free from slavery, but she was also trapped in the domain of her white family. The material privileges that she enjoyed were the result of the enslavement of others. She may have been afraid of those others. She may have been afraid of poverty. Or she may have put her trust in the belief that her father was still in control.

Among the returning Confederate soldiers was Charles H. Eubanks, David Dickson's nephew, who had served in the Georgia Volunteer Infantry. Born in 1836, Eubanks, who was exactly the same age as Amanda's mother, had spent all his life in Hancock County, and, unsurprisingly, there is evidence that he spent a good deal of time on the Dickson plantation. Some time in 1865 Amanda America Dickson began an intimate sexual relationship with Charles Eubanks that is not remembered in the Dickson family oral history as "forced." By choosing to marry her first cousin, Amanda America abandoned the slave-sanctioned preference for endogamous marriage and adopted the white convention of consanguine marriage. By May 1865 Amanda America Dickson Eubanks was pregnant with her first child, Julian Henry, born in 1866.[27]

According to the African American Dickson family history, David Dickson gave the couple a plantation on the banks of the Oostanaula River, near Rome in Floyd County, Georgia. In fact, on February 2, 1866, Charles H. Eubanks purchased seventeen and seven-tenths acres of land on the Oostanaula for six hundred dollars. In October 1870 the couple had a second son, Charles Green. Aunt Mary Long, Amanda America Dickson Eubank's personal servant, remembered seeing Amanda and Charles Eubanks with their small sons and their nurses crossing the river on a ferry as they left to go live on their own "plantation."[28]

As Amanda America Dickson Eubanks attempted to establish an existence independent of her father, David Dickson began the process of financial recovery. Initially, Dickson lamented that he was planting "cautiously, not caring to save money until we had a government that would protect us in person and property." On September 4, 1865, David Dickson begged the pardon of the United States.[29] This action was necessary for Dickson to regain control of his property, excluding his slaves, and to be able to vote or run for public office, which he never did.

By 1870 David Dickson was back on his feet financially. From that year until his death in 1885, Dickson's net worth increased each year, from $72,920 in 1870 to $276,030 in 1885.[30] His fame increased with the publication in 1870 of *A Practical Treatise on Agriculture*.

The 1870s were momentous years for Amanda, Julia, and David. According to the African American Dickson family oral history, shortly after giving birth to Charles, Amanda America and her two children returned to the Dickson plantation. Amanda "explained the situation" to her father with the comment, "I want to live with you, 'Papie,'" Charles Eubanks attempted to retrieve his wife and was met with a "stormy" reply. "He never came back."[31] The census of 1870 lists Eubanks as living with his mother, Elizabeth.

According to the African American Dickson oral history, David Dickson loved the little boys, called them "my little men," and slept with them. Dickson "never wanted them to do anything but ride over the plantation with him and see what was going on." When visitors came to the plantation and were invited to eat, they sometimes asked if they had to eat with Amanda and the children, to which David replied, "By God, yes, if you eat here!"[32]

Sometime in 1870 or early 1871 David Dickson began construction of a new house for Julia, Amanda America, and the children. The house was approximately three hundred yards from the Dickson home place. When completed, it was "a very respectable," "comfortable," two-story home, with "a nice room for a parlor." The parlor contained a piano and "had everything that usually constitutes the furniture in that kind of room. . . . Everything was nice and kept in nice order." When one of David Dickson's employees, W. S. Lozier, a carpenter, was asked which was the best of the two houses, the home place or the new house, he replied that the new house was "a good deal the best house. I would rather have had it at the time."[33]

On October 2, 1871, David Dickson drew up a deed selling the new house and 210 acres of land, more or less, with a twenty-foot right-of-way the entire distance between the house lot and the John R. Latimore place. Amanda America Dickson purchased a seven-eighths interest in the property for $1,000 and Julia Frances Dickson purchased one-eighth interest for $125.[34]

After completing the new house and moving his "outside" family into that comfortable dwelling, David Dickson did something that must have shocked everyone who knew him. On October 3, 1871, he married Clara Harris, who was thirty-seven years younger than himself and only three years older than his daughter, Amanda. Born in Hancock County, Clara was the second daughter in a prominent family whose history in the county stretched back to 1800. Both of Clara's parents were younger than David Dickson and probably had known his family all their lives.[35]

What did Julia Frances Dickson think about the match? Much later, when she was asked when she ceased to have a sexual relationship with David, she replied, "We separated before he ever married or thought of it, I reckon." Was Julia secure in her new house and in her position of authority as the housekeeper in the Dickson home? This marriage is not mentioned in the African American Dickson family oral history. Julia Dickson erased it when she retold the family story.[36]

Amanda America Dickson and her sons might also have felt threatened by the arrival of Clara Harris Dickson. The two women were about the same age and lived only three hundred yards apart. Perhaps Amanda America felt secure enough in her relationship with her father to be civil to Clara at a distance or simply to ignore her. Clara, however, entered a situation with a long established set of relationships and consequently was at the greatest disadvantage.

It appears that Clara Harris Dickson took offense at the presence of David Dickson's outside family and tried unsuccessfully to have her husband remove Amanda and her family from the plantation.[37] When forced to choose between his wife and his daughter and grandsons, David Dickson seems not to have hesitated in making his choice. His decision might well have resulted in Clara leaving him and returning to her parents' home in Sparta. This is where she died in August 1879, after less than two years of marriage and at the early age of twenty-seven.[38]

After Clara Harris Dickson's death, Dickson continued to care for Amanda America and her children. Within a matter of weeks, he deeded 1,560 acres of land to her, "in consideration of the sum of ten dollars to him and went on to mention 'the good will and kind regard' in which he held her and her sons, his grandchildren."[39] Significantly though, he said that the boys were "the natural children of Charles E. Eubanks," a legal term that referred to children born out of wedlock. It seems as if by denying both the human and the legal paternity of Eubanks he was attempting to assume those things for himself.

During the same period, Julia Frances Lewis Dickson "spent most of her time at the meeting house." Indeed, Julia was active in the life of her church and the school it supported. In 1874, as a concession to Julia, David Dickson signed an indenture between himself and John C. Lewis (Julia Frances Dickson's brother), Gilbert Castleberry, Boston Dickson, Washington Warthen, and Julia Dickson, all trustees for the Cherry Hill Church and School of the Methodist Episcopal

Church, South. He agreed to sell the Cherry Hill Church three acres of land for five dollars. The trustees were to hold the land as a place of worship and for a schoolhouse and keep the roads in good repair; otherwise, the land would revert back to David Dickson. Through this agreement Julia Frances secured the future of her church and school against the possibility that David might marry again, and David made sure that the use of the land was limited.[40]

In 1876, although David Dickson wanted Amanda and her children around him, twenty-seven-year-old Amanda America Dickson enrolled in Atlanta University, leaving the security of her father's farm and her children, Julian, who was ten, and Charles, who was six. Her program, the normal course, consisted of the ordinary grammar school branches and the work of the two higher normal, or high school, courses. The African American Dickson family did not remember that Amanda ever taught school. According to her mother, she left the university because "she didn't like the discipline." The Atlanta University catalog does not list Amanda America Dickson as a teacher anywhere in Georgia, although she is listed as a onetime alumnae donor of two dollars in 1882.[41]

During the 1870s and early 1880s, Julia Frances Dickson continued to serve as David Dickson's housekeeper and to trade in Sparta. According to a newspaper report, she was perceived by the people of that town as a "very quiet, inoffensive woman," who "never put herself forward." Apparently, when she visited Sparta to trade, she brought "things" to David Dickson's friends, and when they invited her to dinner, "she would always prefer having her dinner sent to the kitchen, where she would eat with the other servants."[42]

During the twenty-two years after the war, David Dickson busily accumulated more and more wealth and prestige. For Julia, her daughter Amanda, and her children, everything was to change with his death at the age of seventy-six on February 18, 1885. According to the African American Dickson family history, Amanda America's reaction was to cling to his body and repeat over and over, "Now I am an orphan; now I am an orphan." Amanda America was an orphan only if she defined herself as a member of a family composed only of herself and her white father. Her mother was alive, her uncle John C. Lewis was alive, and many of her white aunts and uncles were still alive. Nevertheless, Amanda America Dickson defined herself as an orphan with no black relatives and no white relatives, in fact, a kinless "no nation."[43]

On March 2, 1885, David Dickson's will entered the public domain when the executors, T. J. Warthen and Dickson's "personal friend" and lawyer, Charles W. Dubose, submitted the document to the Court of Ordinary of Hancock County. Like a clap of thunder this event shattered the silence that had separated David Dickson's private life from his public life. David Dickson made his mulatto daughter and her children the largest property owners in Hancock County, Georgia. Julia Frances Dickson is not mentioned in the will to avoid the question of undue influence through a long-term sexual relationship.

Scholars have argued that although the power of the master constituted the linchpin of slavery as a social system, no one satisfactorily defined the limits of that power. Theoretically, this tension was resolved in favor of the interest of the ruling class: "the collective conscience of the ruling class must prevail over the individual interests constituting that class." This does not appear to have been the case with David Dickson. This master-father both raised his mulatto daughter inside the boundaries of his family and legally appointed her as his successor, making her, in some sense, an oxymoronic member of the ruling class, a wealthy black "lady." Dickson left the administration of his estate to the "sound judgment and unlimited discretion" of Amanda America Dickson "without interference from any quarter," including "any husband she may have." Before his death, Dickson's community essentially denied the former, and after his death, it endured the latter.[44]

As has been demonstrated, David Dickson spent a lifetime accumulating two fortunes and cultivating a web of obligations within his community. Before the Civil War he and Thomas M. Turner had maintained the only banking business in Hancock County through a network of personal loans. Dickson continued to loan money throughout his life. At the time of his death, 147 individuals owed him approximately $75,000. His debtors included lawyers, judges, the ordinary of Hancock County, friends, business associates, relatives, tenants, and former slaves.[45]

David Dickson did not accumulate wealth and create obligations within his community for the sole purpose of taking care of Amanda America. By the time of her birth in 1849, he already ranked among the eight wealthiest slaveholders in Hancock County. As the battle over David Dickson's will reveals, however, his wealth, generosity, and hospitality mitigated the impact of his family arrangements and made it possible for Amanda America Dickson to walk away from her community with a fortune.

The estate was left Amanda during her lifetime, "clear and exempt from the marital right, power, control or custody of any husband she may have, with full power to her . . . without the aid or interposition of any court." David Dickson charged Amanda America to support and educate her children, "their support to be ample but not extravagant, their education to be the best that can be procured for them with a proper regard to economy," all of which was left to "the sound judgment and discretion of the said Amanda Dickson." When Amanda America died, her children were to inherit the remains of the estate.[46]

Disgruntled white relatives brought suit on several grounds. They argued that the will should not be admitted to probate because it was not the "act and will of David Dickson"; that Dickson was not of sound and disposing mind at the time of writing of the will; that he was unduly influenced by Amanda and Julia Dickson; that Amanda was not David Dickson's child; and that the will was "in its scheme, its nature and tendencies illegal and immoral, contrary to the policy of the state and of the law" and was "destructive and subversive to the interest and welfare of society."[47]

In accordance with their duties as executors, on May 26, 1885, Dubose and Warthen submitted an appraisal of David Dickson's estate to the probate court. The estate contained $81,000 in bonds and 147 notes and accounts due for approximately $75,000. The executors designated 125 of the notes for approximately $25,000, as "bad" or "doubtful." Included among the doubtful notes was one for $575 from Judge R. H. Lewis, the ordinary faced with the responsibility of deciding whether the will should be accepted as David Dickson's will, that is, admitted to probate. Also included in the estate were crops, livestock, and farming equipment; household goods such as silver forks, spoons, and goblets; a bookcase; fifteen thousand acres of land in Hancock County; and forty gallons of whiskey. The executor and appraisers reported that the total value of the estate was $309,543, $281,543 in Hancock County and $28,000 in Washington County.[48]

The Dickson case was scheduled to be tried in the Superior Court of Hancock County in November 1885 before Judge Samuel Lumpkin, judge of the Northern Circuit of Superior Courts. As the Dickson will case trial approached, more lawyers converged on Sparta than normally lived in the county. Many of those who came had statewide, even national, reputations. The caveators, or excluded white relatives, hired nine of Georgia's most eminent lawyers. Amanda Dickson hired five equally prominent Georgia lawyers.[49]

At the special request of C. W. Dubose, who stated that he "felt deeply the responsibility that was upon him as executor" and desired "the aid of the best intelligence of the County," a special slate of grand jurors was drawn. Two of these owed David Dickson's estate money: J. T. Middlebrooks and John Turner. The latter was elected foreman of the grand jury.[50] Although Middlebrooks and Turner were listed as debtors to the Dickson estate in the appraisal that Charles Dubose filed with the Probate Court of Hancock County, a public document, neither man was removed from the grand jury.

After five days of testimony, the jury deliberated "about twenty minutes." John Turner, the foreman of the jury, returned to the court a verdict in favor of the will. Immediately the lawyers for the excluded white relatives filed a motion to grant a stay on all proceedings for sixty days so that they might file an appeal to the Georgia Supreme Court for a new trial.

In March 1886 the Georgia Supreme Court recorded an appeal for a new trial for the Dickson will that listed thirty objections by the excluded white relatives.[51] On October 11, 1886, Chief Justice James Jackson and Associate Justices Samuel Hall and Mark Blanford heard the case on appeal. On June 13, 1887, eight months after the Supreme Court hearing, Judge Hall finally rendered an opinion upholding the ruling of the lower court.

The jury had ruled that David Dickson was of sound mind, that he had not been improperly influenced, and that Amanda was David Dickson's "natural" child. Under the Fourteenth Amendment of the Constitution of the United States, the Superior Court of the United States had ruled that all "colored" persons born in the United States were subject to its jurisdiction and were citizens of the United States and the state in which they resided, and the Georgia constitution declared that all citizens of the United States residing in the state were citizens. Therefore, "all distinctions as to the rights pertaining to citizenship between the two races are abolished, and as to their civil rights, they stand upon the same footing." Justice Hall summed up his opinion with what must have been a startling judgment: "Therefore, whatever rights and privileges belong to a white concubine or to a bastard white woman and her children, under the laws of Georgia, belong also to a colored woman and her children, under like circumstances, and the rights of each race are controlled and governed by the same enactments on principles of law."[52]

The drama was over. The Superior Court in Hancock County and the Georgia Supreme Court had ruled in favor of David Dickson's will—his right to leave his private property to whomever he pleased. In the process, Dickson's community had to acknowledge that one of its most prominent members had maintained a family outside the category of race, a family to whom he was willing to leave his vast fortune even though doing so might "bring him into disrepute and blacken his memory forever."[53]

David Dickson's death created a change of a cosmic order for Amanda America Dickson. She was no longer protected by her white father or controlled by his powerful presence. What choices faced this thirty-six-year-old woman who described herself as an orphan? Her first concern was to address the legal implications of her father's will. Would the excluded white relatives, or caveators, be able to overthrow the will? A second concern must have been for her own safety on the Dickson plantation. David Dickson's gin houses had been burned twice, once in 1871 and once shortly before his death, in October 1884. Would she be safe living nine miles from town, among Dickson's former slaves and tenants?

If she chose to remain, would the white community allow her to take control of the Dickson empire? Would the black community allow her to remain? Should she leave the county, the state, or the country? How could she create a safe place for herself?

Immediately after David Dickson's death, Amanda America Dickson began to make choices. First, she took control of her legal affairs. On July 6, 1885, she personally appeared in court to petition the ordinary to be appointed the legal guardian of her two children and was granted letters of guardianship after she posted an eight-hundred-dollar bond with T. J. Warthen.[54] That same day, David Dickson's excluded white relatives filed their objections to admitting the Dickson will to probate and, after losing their case, appealed to the Superior Court of Hancock County.

After the Superior Court ruled in favor of David Dickson's will in November 1885, and before the Georgia Supreme Court upheld that ruling on June 13, 1887, Amanda America Dickson began preparing to leave Hancock County for good. On July 15, 1886, she purchased a large brick house at 452 Telfair Street in Augusta, Georgia, for $6,098. An *Atlanta Constitution* reporter described this three-story, twelve- to fifteen-room house with a "large yard" as a most desirable residence. Because of the attention the Dickson will case had received in the newspapers of the state, we can safely assume that Amanda America Dickson's fame preceded her to the city of Augusta. As Dr. W. H. Foster, a prominent physician in Augusta, later observed, "Her surroundings were altogether superior to the average colored person and I had always understood for years past that she was very wealthy." The *Atlanta Constitution* also noted: "Amanda A. Dickson, the $400,000.00 heiress from Hancock went to Augusta last Friday. Everybody on the train was anxious to see the richest colored woman in the United States. She created about as much of a sensation as did Henry Ward Beecher when he traveled through the south. She was dressed in deep mourning and had her mother and youngest boy with her." The general populace in Augusta would have known that Amanda America Dickson was wealthy, illegitimate, and a woman of color.[55]

Why did Amanda Dickson choose to move to Augusta? In 1886 Augusta was a relatively cosmopolitan southern city. Gaslights illuminated the main thoroughfares, and as many as four rows of trees on the main streets provided both relief from the heat and a grand promenade. Citizens could purchase ice from the Arctic Ice Company, ready-made clothes, cut flowers, fine French wine and pastry, a newspaper edited by a black editor or a newspaper edited by a white editor. They could also take a ride on a streetcar.[56]

In the elite black community of Augusta, status was based on more than

wealth, either earned or inherited. Community position was more likely to de-
pend on a constellation of attributes, including color, status before the Civil
War, education, manners, family connections, and wealth. According to these
standards, Amanda America Dickson's status in the elite black community of
Augusta would have been enviable. She was a mulatto, specifically a quadroon
(that is, one-fourth black). Although she had not been legally free before the
Civil War, or at least she was not listed in the register of Free Persons of Color in
Hancock County, Amanda Dickson enjoyed material advantages that the individuals who were listed as free in the Hancock County register could never have
afforded. She was literate and had attended Atlanta University for two years.
She could play the piano and dress with impeccable taste, as was expected of
any proper lady, black or white. Before Amanda America Dickson came to Augusta, her African American family connections were not impressive; shortly
thereafter, however, her children married into the city's most prominent black
families. Finally, Amanda America Dickson was the wealthiest black person in
the state of Georgia. That wealth was put on display in Augusta in the place she
chose to live and in the way she chose to furnish her residence in the most elite
section of the city.[57]

According to one of Amanda America Dickson's white neighbors, John M.
Crowley, manager of the local Western Union Telegraph, the Dickson family
was held in high regard in this elite neighborhood. When asked to describe the
wealth, refinement, intelligence, and comforts of Amanda Dickson, Mr. Crowley replied: "It was common report that she was worth one-hundred-thousand
dollars. My family held her family in very high esteem and would exchange
little neighborly acts. I have never heard a word of slander or anything of that
nature against them." Crowley continued in a matter-of-fact tone: "The general
reputation of the Dickson family in the neighborhood [was] very good. From
the reported wealth of the Dickson family they made no ostentatious show nor
did they push themselves forward or out of their way. Whilst they had every
comfort, I never observed any excess of comfort." Amanda America Dickson
displayed what William S. McFeely described in his biography of Frederick
Douglass as "bourgeois values maintained with the staunchest respectability."[58]

Amanda America Dickson furnished her residence handsomely. The house
contained seven bedrooms, including one for a live-in servant, a library, a hall,
a dining room, a parlor, and a kitchen. Thus by 1887 Amanda America Dickson
had purchased a comfortable, safe place for herself in the midst of Augusta's
white elite.[59]

Amanda's life changed dramatically after she moved to Augusta. On September 17, 1887, she gave the new house on the Dickson place to her mother,

acknowledging the "natural love and affection, which she has and bears to her mother." In October of the same year, Amanda Dickson's youngest son, Charles, married Kate Holsey, the mulatto daughter of Bishop Lucius Henry and Harriet Holsey of Augusta. Charles was seventeen at the time of his marriage and Kate was eighteen. Kate had graduated from Paine College, from the normal, or teachers' training course, in 1886. Charles would graduate from the same department at Paine College in 1891. On December 10, 1885, shortly after the Hancock County Superior Court ruled in favor of the will, Julian Dickson married Eva Walton, the mulatto daughter of George and Isabella Walton of Augusta.[60]

While white Georgians were establishing apartheid as the ruling social order, Amanda America Dickson and her family went on about their private and privileged lives. On July 14, 1892, Amanda America married Nathan Toomer of Perry, Georgia. Toomer was also a "wealthy and highly educated" mulatto. The *Houston Home Journal*, Toomer's hometown newspaper, stated at the time that Toomer, "the esteemed colored farmer," had married the "richest Negress in Georgia" and that he "Has many white friends in Houston County who will cordially congratulate him."[61]

After their marriage, Nathan took up residence in Amanda America's house in Augusta. There the Toomers lived amid all the luxury money could buy, including the live-in maid. But Amanda's health was frail, and she was afflicted with an assortment of ailments that required the constant attention of her family physician, Dr. Thomas D. Coleman, a neighbor. Dr. Coleman, a prominent doctor in Augusta, had graduated for the University of the City of New York (now New York University) and retained a position as professor of physiology at the Medical College of Georgia. Dr. Coleman described Amanda as "a woman of delicate constitution," who suffered from chronic bronchitis, uterine trouble, premature menopause, wandering pains, catarrh of the stomach, and muscular rheumatism.[62]

Amanda America Dickson Toomer died on June 11, 1893, from "complications of diseases."[63] Her funeral was held in the Trinity Colored Methodist Episcopal Church, and, according to a tribute written for the *Augusta Chronicle* by "a friend," it was attended by "a very large and respectful gathering of friends and acquaintances." Three ministers of the gospel "officiated," and they paid tribute to Amanda America's "Christian life and character, her exemplary worth, her unostentatious charities, and the beauty of her home life." Scripture passages that she had marked in her own bible were read, and the service ended with a song that Amanda requested to be sung on that occasion, "Shall We Meet beyond the River," which "moved to tears almost the entire audience." The body was buried in Augusta, in the Toomer plot, in the Colored Cedar Grove Cemetery, behind the Magnolia Cemetery for whites.[64]

Amanda America Dickson's obituaries in white newspapers describe her as the "wealthiest colored woman in the world," "the wealthiest Negro in the United States," and "one of the wealthiest, if not the wealthiest, negro woman in the state." Without exception, these obituaries mentioned that Amanda America inherited her wealth from her father, David Dickson, one of the wealthiest planters in Hancock County. The black *Savannah Tribune*'s obituary described Amanda America Toomer "nee Dickson" with no mention of David, as "one of the richest persons in the state." Nathan Toomer was mentioned in the newspaper obituaries as a lawyer from Perry, who was also wealthy and highly educated or who was "immensely rich." In the *Augusta Chronicle* obituary the Dickson family connection to the Holseys was mentioned, and the Holseys were described as one of the best-known and most respected black families in the state. Amanda America Dickson Toomer's only claim to fame and respect in these obituaries seems to be that she was David Dickson's daughter and that she was wealthy by any standard of the day.[65]

Amanda America's obituaries and the tribute by "a friend" reveal something about the way she was perceived by the black and white communities in which she lived. She was described in the *Atlanta Constitution* as "modest, generous, and benevolent, a woman who enjoyed her fortune," and "others shared her pleasure." The article continued, "She was kind-hearted and in no way pompous or assuming on account of her wealth."[66] In the tribute by "a friend" we learn a great deal about the author's perception of Amanda:

> The subject of this notice was well known to the writer as a most amiable, gentle woman. To everyone with whom she came in contact she was always kind, considerate, respectful. Although for years she was very feeble of health, and endured great suffering, she was very patient, submissive, uncomplaining. Possessed of great wealth, she made no display of it, nor did it affect her, as it has so many others. She fully appreciated the true value of riches. She felt that they were given her not only for her own use, but for the use of others. No narrow selfishness marked her possession of means. While she gave them liberally to procure the comforts and many of the luxuries for herself and those of her own household, she never forgot the needy—as was said most tenderly at her funeral services today. She was a devoted and loyal wife, and the tender affection between herself and her husband, Mr. Nathan Toomer, late of Houston County, Georgia, evidenced a union of mutual happiness. For her two children, Mr. Julian H. Dickson and Mr. Charles G. Dickson, the former of Hancock County, Georgia, the latter of Augusta, Georgia, she always

felt the most intense and anxious solicitude and motherly love. To her mother she was all that a dutiful, loving child should be. As she lived, so she died, a gentle, sweet spirit.[67]

The Amanda America Dickson of these obituaries is a fiction not unlike the myths of true womanhood and of the southern lady that were articulated in the nineteenth century for white ladies. In this era, ladies were socialized to accept purity, piety, domesticity, and submissiveness as ideal behavior patterns. Southern ladies were also described a physically weak, timid, modest, beautiful, graceful, innocent, and self-denying. Amanda was not described as beautiful, graceful, innocent, or self-denying in her possession of physical luxury, but she was described as physically weak, respectful, and uncomplaining: a devoted and loyal wife, a loving mother, and a dutiful child.[68]

The Amanda America of the obituaries does not fit the myths of the white lady in several ways. Purity (innocence) and beauty (grace) are not missing by accident. When applied to white ladies, these attributes created the essential symbol used to justify racism. It would have been ideologically untenable, perhaps even dangerous, for whites to describe Amanda America Dickson as beautiful and pure.

If we compare the idealized Amanda America Dickson Toomer of the obituaries with expressed ideals for the behavior of African American ladies of the late nineteenth century, another important imperative is missing: racial uplift. It was not unusual for African American women to aspire to the cult of true womanhood. But they were also encouraged by the ideals of their community to step outside the domestic sphere and engage in community building and racial uplift. The Amanda America Dickson Toomer of these obituaries, with her quiet charities and attention to the needy, appears to have no racial identification, no influence outside the limited sphere of an attractively disabled "lady."[69]

The real Amanda America Dickson Toomer left one husband and refused to return to him, left the security of her father's empire to attend Atlanta University at the age of twenty-seven, endured her father's death, used the legal system to fight for control of a vast fortune, left the security of her own plantation and moved to the city of Augusta, and remarried while retaining control of her estate, giving Nathan Toomer "gifts." The real Amanda Toomer also died of nervous exhaustion, of "something which profoundly shocked her nervous system." Perhaps that shock was the private chaos and turmoil she faced within her family, in addition to deteriorating relations between blacks and whites in Georgia. The behaviors that she so carefully practiced in the public sphere, to be unassuming, amiable, gentle, kind, considerate, respectful, patient, submissive, and uncomplaining, were a prescription for self-destruction in her time and place. The last thing in the world Amanda America Dickson needed to be in an increasingly racist public space was a "gentle, sweet spirit." Amanda America may have escaped the prevailing white myths about being a degraded female African American, described by Drew Gilpin Faust, only to become trapped by a myth of the proper role of an elite white lady.[70]

## NOTES

1. For a lengthy discussion of Amanda America Dickson, see Kent Anderson Leslie's *Woman of Color, Daughter of Privilege, Amanda America Dickson, 1849–1893* (Athens: University of Georgia Press, 1995), esp. Appendix A, "The African-American Dickson Family Oral History." A movie about Dickson, *A House Divided* (Showtime, 2000), starring Sam Waterston, Jennifer Beals, Lisa Gay Hamilton, and Tim Dailey, is available on VHS.

2. Elizabeth Fox-Genovese, *Within the Plantation Household: Black and White women of the Old South* (Chapel Hill: University of North Carolina Press, 1988), 62.

3. Williamson, Joel, *New People: Miscegenation and Mulattoes in the United States* (New York: Free Press, 1980).

4. Edward Byron Reuter, *The American Race Problem: A Study of the Negro* (New York: Thomas Y. Crowell, 1927), 129–30.

5. John Rozier, *Black Boss: Political Revolution in a Georgia County* (Athens: University of Georgia Press, 1982), 197.

6. Rozier, *Black Boss*, 200n.17; James C Bonner, "Profile of a Late Ante-Bellum Community," *American Historical Review* 49 (July 1944): 663–80.

7. David M. Potter, *People of Plenty: Economic Abundance and the American Character* (Chicago: University of Chicago Press, 1954); Dickson Will Case Transcript, Appealed September 1, 1886, Superior Court of Hancock County, Ga., Records of the Georgia Supreme Court, Box 219, Location: 246–10, case 14443, Georgia Department of Archives and History.

8. Bertram Wyatt-Brown, *Southern Honor: Ethics and Behavior in the Old South* (New York: Oxford University Press), xv, xii.

9. Mary Douglas, *Purity and Danger: An Analysis of the Concepts of Pollution and Taboo* (Boston: Routledge and Kegan Paul, 1966), 122.

10. Tax Digest for Hancock County, 1849, Georgia Department of Archives and History.

11. Slave Census for Hancock County, 1850, Georgia Department of Archives and History.

12. Willard Range, *A Century of Georgia Agriculture, 1850–1950* (Athens: University of Georgia Press, 1954), 24; *Southern Cultivator* 17 (December 1852): 367; 18 (April 1861): 113.

13. A Dickson family oral history was collected from Kate Louise Dickson McCoy-Lee, the granddaughter of Amanda America Dickson. Kate Dickson McCoy-Lee was born in 1894, the year after Amanda America Dickson died. She was the third child of Amanda America's son Charles Green Dickson and his wife, Kate Holsey Dickson. Kate Dickson's sources of information on the Dickson family history included her great-grandmother Julia Frances Lewis Dickson, who lived in Sparta until at least 1914; her mother, Kate Holsey Dickson; other family members; and Aunt Mary Long, Amanda America Dickson's lifelong personal servant, who later worked for Kate Dickson.

14. Dickson Will Case Transcript, testimony of Julia Frances Dickson, 160–88.

15. Dickson Will Case Transcript, Henry Harris, for the propounders, 90; Augustus E. Eubanks, for the propounders, 147.

16. For the relevant sections of the 1901 legislation see Oliver H. Price, ed., *A Digest of Laws of the State of Georgia* (Athens, Ga.: privately published, 1837), 787. See also Lucius Q. C. Lamar, ed., *A Compilation of the Laws of the State of Georgia, 1810–1819* (Augusta, Ga.: W. S. Hannon, 1821), 811–12.

17. Dickson Will Case Transcript, testimony of Julia Frances Dickson, for the propounders, 161; testimony of Dr. E. W. Alfriend, for the propounders, 129.

18. Ibid., testimony of A. E. Eubanks, for the propounders, 148.

19. Jane Turner Censer, *North Carolina Planters and Their Children, 1800–1860* (Baton Rouge: Louisiana State University Press, 1984), 135; W. E. B. DuBois, "Princess of the Hinter Isles," in *Darkwater: Voices from Within the Veil* (New York: Schocken Books, 1969), 75–80; Leslie, *Woman of Color, Daughter of Privilege*, appendix 2.1.

20. Fox-Genovese, *Within the Plantation Household*, 111.

21. U. S. Census, 1840; David Dickson's signature, *Practical Treatise on Agriculture, to Which Is Added the Author's Published Letters* (Macon: Burke, 1870); Amanda America Dickson's signature, Hancock County, Probate Court, records of the Probate of David Dickson's Will, Acknowledgment that Melinda Warthen was Melinda Johnson, May 10, 1888.

22. Dickson Will Case Transcript, testimony of Judge J. C. Simmons, for the propounders, 156; Leslie, *Woman of Color, Daughter of Privilege*, appendix 2.1.

23. Dickson Will Case Transcript, testimony of J. M. Eubanks, for the caveators, 57–58.

24. Ibid., testimony of Julia Frances Dickson, for the propounders, 160–66, 175; W. H. Matthews, for the caveators, 37; Washington Printup, for the caveators, 40; Joe Brooken, for the caveators, 32. Matthews was an employee, and the other two men were David Dickson's slaves.

25. Lucy Dickson is listed in the U.S. Census of 1880 as a mulatto female, twenty-seven years old, living in the house with David Dickson and T. J. Warthen (David's nephew) as a servant. Lucy Dickson is mentioned in the Dickson Will Case Transcript as "the most important servant" (Henry Harris, 91). Lucy Dickson died on June 19, 1884. John C. Lewis, Julia's brother, was the administrator of the estate. Dickson Will Case Transcript, testimony of Lozier, for the caveators, 20, 29; Printup, for the caveators, 41, Barry for the propounders, 85; Harris for the propounders, 91; testimony of Dr. E. W. Alfriend, for the propounders, 130.

26. Leslie, *Amanda America Dickson*, appendix 2.1; Fox-Genovese, *Within the Plantation Household*, 64.

27. Herbert George Gutman, *The Black Family in Slavery and Freedom, 1750–1925* (New York: Vintage, 1976), 88; Censer, *North Carolina Planters*, 7; Lillian Henderson, comp., *Roster of the Confederate Soldiers of Georgia, 1861–1865* (Hapeville, Ga.: Longino and Porter, 1959), 2:476.

28. Leslie, *Woman of Color, Daughter of Privilege*, appendix 2.2; Deeds between S. C. Johnson and Charles H. Eubanks, Floyd County Courthouse, Rome, Ga.

29. Dickson, *Practical Treatise*, 242; Pardon, a "Special Pardon" by Andrew Johnson, petitioned for on August 9, 1865, National Archives, Washington, D.C.

30. Tax Digest for Hancock County, 1870–85.

31. Leslie, *Woman of Color, Daughter of Privilege*, appendix 2.1.

32. Ibid.

33. Dickson Will Case Transcript, testimony of Lozier, for the caveators, 18–19.

34. This deed was not recorded until June 11, 1885, Deed Book W, 298–99, Clerk of the Superior Court, Hancock County Courthouse.

35. Marriage Certificate, Marriage Records, no. 106, 1871, Hancock County Courthouse; Elizabeth Wiley Smith, *The History of Hancock County, Georgia* (Washington, Ga.: Wilkes, 1974), 1:128, Historical Activities Committee of the National Society of Colonial Dames of America in the State of Georgia, comp., *Early Georgia Portraits, 1718–1870* (Athens: University of Georgia Press, 1975), 92–95.

36. Dickson Will Case Transcript, testimony of Julia Frances Dickson, for the propounders, 162.

37. Ibid., testimony of S. D. Rogers, for the caveators, 55.

38. Deborah Gray White, *"Ain't I a Woman?" Female Slaves in the Plantation South* (New York: Norton, 1985), 41; *Milledgeville Union Recorder*, August 6, 1873, 2, col. 6.

39. Book of Deeds, "U," 137–38, Hancock County Courthouse.

40. Dickson Will Case Transcript, Lozier, for the caveators, 17; Book of Deeds, "U," 595–96, registered July 31, 1877.

41. *Atlanta University Catalogue*, 1876–77, 19, Special Collections, Woodruff Library, Atlanta University.

42. *Sparta Ishmaelite and Times Planter*, August 1, 1885, 1, col. 6.

43. Leslie, *Woman of Color, Daughter of Privilege*, appendix 2.1; James Kinney, *Amalgamation! Race, Sex, and Rhetoric in the Nineteenth-Century American Novel* (Westport, Conn.: Greenwood Press, 1970), 100.

44. Fox-Genovese, *Within the Plantation Household*, 326; Eugene Genovese, *The World the Slaveholders Made* (New York: Vintage Books, 1971), 215; David Dickson's will, March 2, 1885, Probate Court Records, Drawer "D." Hancock County Courthouse.

45. Smith, *History of Hancock County*, 1:122; Inventory of David Dickson's Estate, May 26, 1885, 66–70, Hancock County Probate Court Records, Inventory of Estates, 1885, Drawer "D," Hancock County Courthouse.

46. *Atlanta Journal*, August 1, 1885, 1, col. 6; David Dickson's will, item 7.

47. Dickson Will Case, Legal Records, 117, Objections to the Probating of the Will in Solemn Form addressed to the Ordinary, R. H. Lewis, July term, 1885.

48. David Dickson's Estate Records, Office of the Ordinary, Hancock County, 65–75, the Appraisal of David Dickson's Estate; *Sparta Ishmaelite*, June 10, 1885, 3, col. 2.

49. Candler and Evans, *Georgia*, 2:188–89, 272–73, 1:404–6. Nathaniel Harris was Clara Harris Dickson's first cousin (Candler and Evans, *Georgia*, 3:116, 166–67); Inventory of David Dickson's Estate, Office of the Ordinary, Hancock County, 66–67. E. H. Pottle owed David Dickson's estate $2,180 and Frank Lightfoot Little owed the estate $147.25.

50. Inventory of David Dickson's Estate, 66. J. T. Middlebrooks owed David Dickson's estate $1,500 and Turner owed $5,012.68 (*Supreme Court of Georgia Reports*, 78 Ga. 446).

51. Dickson Will Case Records, 8.

52. *Sparta Ishmaelite*, December 17, 1887, 2, col. 3; *Georgia Supreme Court Reports*, 78 Georgia, 442, 414.

53. Leslie, *Woman of Color, Daughter of Privilege*, 91; Dickson Will Case Transcript.

54. Records of David Dickson's Estate, Probate Court Records, Drawer "David Dickson," Hancock County Courthouse.

55. *Atlanta Constitution*, July 19, 1887, 6, col. 1; *Sparta Ishmaelite*, March 18, 1885, 3, col. 2; *Nathan Toomer v. Pullman Palace Car Company*, Court of Common Pleas of the City of Baltimore, Deposi-

tion of Dr. W. H. Foster, who lived one block over from Amanda America Dickson at 320 Greene Street, January 10, 1894, Maryland Department of Archives and History, Annapolis.

56. *Augusta City Directory*, 1888 (Atlanta: R. L. Polk, 1888). According to the *Augusta City Directory* for 1886, the bridges in Augusta charged tolls: buggies and one horse, each way $.20; carts each way $.25; with wood, $11.25; "loose" cattle $.10; horse and rider $.10; sheep, goats, and hogs, each way $.05.

57. According to Anne R. Lockhart Hornsby, "Shifts in the Distribution of Wealth among Blacks in Georgia, 1890–1915" (PhD diss., Georgia State University, 1980), 200, 37 percent of wealthy black Georgians in 1890 had inherited their wealth, whereas in 1915 only 1 percent of the same group had inherited their wealth. See also E. Franklin Frazier, *Black Bourgeoisie: The Rise of a New Middle Class in the United States* (New York: Macmillan, 1957); Willard B. Gatewood Jr., "Aristocrats of Color, North and South: The Black Elite, 1890–1920," *Journal of Southern History* 54 (February 1988): 3–20; Murray, *Proud Shoes: The Story of an American Family* (1956; repr., New York: Harper and Row, 1978). The U.S. Census of 1890 lists the total black population of Georgia as 858,815, broken down as 773,682 blacks, 72,072 mulattoes, 8,795 quadroons, and 470 octoroons. Julian and Charles Dickson would have been classified as octoroons. In 1900, 67.3 percent of the black population of Georgia was still illiterate (Hornsby, "Shifts," 105, 118–20).

58. *Nathan Toomer v. Pullman Palace Car Company*, Deposition of John M. Crowley, January 4, 1894; William S. McFreely, *Frederick Douglass* (New York: Norton, 1991).

59. *Nathan Toomer v. Julian Dickson, Charles G. Dickson, and Julia Dickson*, Hancock Superior Court, filed July 18, 1899.

60. Deed Book W, 510–11, Hancock County Courthouse; *Sparta Ishmaelite*, July 29, 1887, 3, col. 2; U. S. Census of 1900; Paine College Alumni Association listings in the *Annual Catalogue* of 1912, 56–57. George and Isabella Walton are buried in the Toomer family plot in the Cedar Grove Cemetery in Augusta. George died October 15, 1908, and Isabella died on February 15, 1909.

61. Horace Calvin Wingo, "Race Relations in Georgia, 1872–1908" (PhD diss., University of Georgia, 1969); *Houston Home Journal*, July 21, 1892, 2, col. 3.

62. *Nathan Toomer v. The Pullman Palace Car Company*, deposition of Dr. Thomas D. Coleman.

63. Death Certificate of Amanda D. Toomer: forty-three years old; color—colored; nativity—Georgia; occupation—housewife; married, in Richmond County Courthouse, Augusta, Ga.

64. *Atlanta Constitution*, June 12, 1893, 2 col. 2; Tribute paid by "A Friend," *Augusta Chronicle*, June 13, 1893, 2, col. 6. I am grateful to Gordon B. Smith for this reference. The entrance to the Cedar Grove Cemetery is on Watkins Street in Augusta. According to the *Savannah Morning News*, "Amanda Toomer (or Dickson), the wealthy colored woman who was buried in the colored cemetery of Augusta last week was buried with some valuable jewelry on her person. A policeman is guarding the grave to prevent robbery" (June 19, 1893, 6, col. 1).

65. *Houston Home Journal*, June 15, 1983, 2, col. 2; *Atlanta Constitution*, June 2, 1893, 2, col. 2, June 12, 1893, 2, col. 1; *Savannah Morning News*, June 13, 1893, 6, col. 1; *Savannah Tribune*, June 17, 1893, 2, col. 1; *Atlanta Constitution*, June 12, 1893, 2, col. 1; *Augusta Chronicle*, June 12, 1893, 5, col. 1.

66. *Atlanta Constitution*, June 12, 19893, 3, col. 2; *Augusta Chronicle*, June 13, 1893, 2, col. 6.

67. *Augusta Chronicle*, June 13, 1893, 2, col. 6.

68. Barbara Welter, *Dimity Convictions: The American in the Nineteenth Century* (Athens: Ohio University Press, 1976); Kent Anderson Leslie, "A Myth of the Southern Lady: Proslavery Rhetoric and the Proper Place of Woman," *Sociological Spectrums* 6 (1986): 31–49; Ann Firor Scott, *The Southern Lady: From Pedestal to Politics, 1830–1930* (Chicago: University of Chicago Press, 1970).

69. Beverly Lynn Guy-Sheftall, "Daughters of Sorrow: Attitudes toward Black Women, 1880–1920" (PhD diss., Emory University, 1984), 155–56.

70. *Nathan Toomer V. the Pullman Palace Car Company*, deposition of Nathan Toomer, deposition of Dr. William H. Foster; Drew Gilpin Faust, "Culture, Conflict and Community: The Meaning of Power on an Antebellum Plantation." *Journal of Social History* 14 (Fall 1980): 83–89.

# Mary Gay
## (1829–1918)

## Sin, Self, and Survival in the Post–Civil War South

MICHELE GILLESPIE

❀ ❀ ❀

In most respects, Mary Ann Harris Gay was an ordinary nineteenth-century white southern woman. Born on a slaveholding farm in Jones County, Georgia, in 1829, she never married, survived wartime hardships, and endured a succession of personal tragedies during her eighty-nine long years. But she also published three books over her lifetime, and from the time of the Civil War until her death in 1918 her contemporaries hailed her as a true daughter of the South. She was celebrated for her heroism on the Civil War home front, her single-handed fundraising efforts to rebuild her war-ravaged church, her ever-present Christian devotion, and her sustained commitment to the southern cause. During the last years of her life she was famous for wearing mourning clothes in honor of her Civil War dead. Although children were frightened by her appearance, their parents sang the strange old woman's praises. Walter McCurdy's father repeatedly told him, "She was a fighter for freedom. She lost everybody she had and everything she had fighting for our Lost Cause and you must always respect her."[1] Historians have documented the important role white southern elite and middle-class women played in advancing the memorialization of the Civil War in the late nineteenth and early twentieth centuries, and the role this memorializing played in the institutionalization of white supremacy in the Jim Crow South. Mary Gay's life and work complicates that story because it suggests some white women were at least as invested in peddling the memory of the Civil War dead to serve their own very real needs, as in romanticizing the

**MARY GAY**

Courtesy of Georgia Archives,
Vanishing Georgia Collection, dek418-85.

white past to secure cultural authority, perpetuate racist ideologies, and pursue political ends.[2]

Mary Gay has slipped in and out of southern memory throughout the twentieth century. Margaret Mitchell, creator of Scarlett O'Hara, perhaps the most enduring female figure in southern fiction, was influenced by at least one of Mary Gay's books, *Life in Dixie during the Civil War* (1892). Certain scenes in *Gone with the Wind* (1936) are drawn directly from Gay's memoir.[3] In Decatur, Georgia, during the 1970s, where Mary Gay had lived for much of her long life, the old guard resurrected her memory as a last stand against white flight. This time the Junior League moved Gay's rotting house, set square in the path of urban redevelopment, to a side road where it could be lovingly preserved and her story retold.[4] In a widely publicized event local residents, including the Agnes Lee Chapter of the United Daughters of the Confederacy and the Gate City Guard and Sons of Confederate Veterans, remembered Mary Gay during their observance of Confederate Memorial Day with a flag-raising at the Confederate Memorial at Courthouse Square in Decatur on April 26, 1979. That same year the DeKalb Historical Society funded a new edition of *Life in Dixie*, the first in eight decades.[5] Three years later, Kathryn L. Helgeson, a history student at Agnes Scott College, attracted local interest when she produced a well-researched honor's thesis on Gay.[6] Then in 1997 Gay received statewide recognition when she was inducted into the Georgia Women of Achievement Hall of Fame.[7] As a result, Mary Gay is perceived by many as a local hero, and remains a fixture in the history of the Civil War in Atlanta for scholars and Civil War buffs alike.[8]

Still, over the past decade or so, the need to remember Mary Gay's alleged heroics in order to preserve a dying white community and its traditions has declined. The once bedraggled town of Decatur has transformed itself into a shrewd investor's Shangri La, replete with high-end condos, Starbucks, and boutique shopping, all courtesy of speedy light rail into downtown Atlanta only a few miles away. Mary Gay's quaint home, along with the Courthouse Memorial to the Confederacy at whose 1908 unveiling Gay was honored, is passé in this bedroom community composed increasingly of hip cosmopolitan professionals.

Mary Gay's memory probably would not merit resurrecting today if it were not for her work as a writer and bookseller. Her three books, including *Life in Dixie*, do not constitute great literature, or even sustained good reads, though parts of all three of her books are certainly compelling. Nor were her efforts to raise funds for religious causes and Confederate memorials uncommon pursuits for women of her race and social class in the postwar South into the late nineteenth century. Yet an examination of her writing along with a cache of family letters offers a more complex picture of this celebrated guardian of Confederate heritage. Indeed, what makes her interesting to us in the twenty-first century is not so much her lifelong devotion to the southern cause, but what she gained for herself out of this pursuit, and how she stretched well-heeled white southern women's freedoms in doing so. As one reviewer of the 1979 edition of *Life in Dixie* observed, "[T]he book is an unconscious uncovering of self."[9]

Mary Gay's dual advocacy of religious piety and "the ghosts of the confederacy" allowed her literally to take to the road as a fundraiser and bookseller for some four decades. This role freed her from the burden of running an impoverished household comprising three grown women and a fatherless boy in the postwar South. Some white southern women secured newfound political influence through social reform, preservation work, and writing about their southern heritage during the late nineteenth and early twentieth centuries (including Mary Gay's half sister, Missouria Stokes, who worked for the Women's Christian Temperance Union). Other white southern women experienced new autonomy through their entry into paid work as teachers and store clerks (and Missouria worked as a teacher too), although marriage and childbearing often returned them to the household. Mary Gay pursued both paths as a reformer and a wage earner, but she moved beyond them by acting as a kind of traveling salesperson in the South, one who was in some respects peddling the memory of death. While her writing and fundraising gave her a political voice, and a measure of financial independence too, her physical mobility as an author/advocate peddling first the Bible, then her war-ravaged church, and then her books and the southern cause gave her personal and economic freedom permitted few women of her time and place. It is important to note that throughout this career, she was selling the painful memory of southern loss as measured by deaths in one southern city after another, to one church group after another.

In doing so, Mary Gay took on the identity of the traditional male as household breadwinner *and* cultural commentator. She could justify her frequent absences, which she clearly enjoyed, through her role as traveling agent on the road sending funds home to put food on the table. What made her actions acceptable, despite the fact that she was a single white woman journeying alone, were her "wares." She peddled prevailing religious and cultural values developed in her books and spun through the causes for which she sought support. That she herself had lost a beloved family member made her actions and her public identity all the more legitimate. These values, which turned on memorializing the Confederacy as the Lost Cause, were not uniquely her own by any stretch of the imagination. They had been increasingly championed by white women in the last quarter of the nineteenth century. Mary Gay broke new ground, how-ever, by literally selling those beliefs and values in the public marketplace, in those spaces where elite women in the South generally did not go, and among people she usually did not know. Lower-class white and black women had sold garden produce, eggs and fowl, cloth and baskets, not to mention their bod-ies on southern city streets and in city markets since colonial days, but few elite white women in the South had ever before literally sold beliefs from door to door in one neighborhood after another. How Mary Gay "hawked" these ideas, and the personal freedom she gained through her gendered role reversal, deserves greater appreciation, as does her crafting of her identity as a female victim of Civil War devastation. Her story begins with her childhood.

Mary Gay's early years were tumultuous. She was born the daughter of Wil-liam and Mary Stevens Gay on March 18, 1829, on the Gay family farm in Jones County, Georgia, to her newly widowed mother.[10] Mary Stevens Gay quickly left her in-laws, with her infant in tow, to return to her own family's plantation in Baldwin County, a few miles from the state capital of Milledgeville.[11] Here Mary Gay lived under the roof of her grandfather, Thomas Stevens, immortalized in the historical record by his former slave, John Brown, who lived for twelve years on the Stevens plantation around the 1820s. Subsequently bought and sold sev-eral times over, Brown eventually escaped to Canada and then journeyed to En-gland, where he dictated his life story to Louis Alexis Chamerovzow, secretary of the British and Foreign Anti-Slavery League. Their collaboration resulted in the 1855 publication of *Slave Life in Georgia: A Narrative of the Life, Sufferings, and Escape of John Brown.*[12]

John Brown's autobiography describes Mary Gay's grandfather as a raging man who exerted utter dominion over his chattel. Brown's account, much of which has been verified in state and county records, provides a crucial founda-tion from which to grapple with Mary Gay's lifelong racist assumptions about slavery, slaves, and race relations. Her later insistence on the benevolence with which she and her mother and sister acted as slaveholders during the Civil War may mark an implicit acknowledgment of her grandfather's cruel treatment of his slaves, as well as a pained reaction to John Brown's published portrait of her grandfather as a brutal master.[13]

Thomas Stevens, Gay's grandfather, had been an itinerant carpenter as a young man, but not content to make wage labor his career, he soon built a still, which he turned into a successful distillery. The earnings from this endeavor allowed Stevens, whom Brown described as "a great rogue," to buy a plantation and slaves.[14] By resorting to extreme punishments, he forced his slaves to steal corn from his neighbors to cut whiskey-making costs. Brown himself received beatings from Stevens that left "the blood . . . trickling down [his] back." He told how others were "flogged with switches and the cowhide, until the blood ran down in streams and settled under [them] in puddles." Stevens made all his slaves attend his tortures, and insisted many of them deliver the whippings.[15]

We do not know what Mary and her mother witnessed, but one has to presume they were aware of these horrific acts and the pain and terror they unleashed in the slave quarters. Meanwhile, Thomas Stevens, like so many other men on the make in this time and place, was not only selling whiskey and growing crops, but purchasing land throughout middle Georgia, including in DeKalb County, where he had become active in local politics by 1829. Sometime in the early 1830s Mary and her mother moved to the brand new courthouse town of Decatur, the county seat of DeKalb, where Mrs. Gay married local lawyer Joseph Stokes, who worked on legal concerns for Thomas Stevens and his sons. The multigenerational Stevens and Stokes families moved again to Cassville, in north Georgia, the source of many of Mary's childhood memories. While her grandfather pursued more moneymaking ventures in their new home, sending his slaves to the Allatoona gold mines to sell bacon, Mary recalled an idyllic youth. She cherished the beauty of her wild surroundings and the warmth of the Cherokees she met, and was delighted when the little Stokes family moved further north to a farm near Calhoun they named Oak Grove that adjoined the newest Stevens plantation. Here Mary's mother gave birth to Thomas (Thomie) J. Stokes in 1837 and Missouria Horton Stokes a year later. Mary and her half-siblings were raised in a manner befitting genteel southern families. The Stokes family library contained Shakespeare, Byron, Milton, and other classic authors as well as popular reading. The family relished music, and Missouria and Thomas both played the piano. Mary received some formal education as a young girl at the Hannah More Female Institute while in Decatur, and later spent "the four happiest years of my life . . . in school days in Nashville," thanks to a special provision in her grandfather's will.[16]

Mary treasured poetry while growing up, and like many young ladies of her time she penned her own verse. Unlike most other southern belles, who consigned their personal writings to their diaries, Mary published hers. When she was seventeen, "My Valley Home" appeared in print, albeit anonymously, in nearby Marietta, and was probably her first published piece. She wrote many more poems in the years preceding the Civil War, all on the themes of truth and beauty, Christian faith and virtue, and love. Victorian in sensibility, and unremarkable in style, Mary took her identity as a writer seriously, and encouraged her sister, nine years her junior, to do likewise. In 1858, at the age of twenty-nine, Mary published her first book, *Prose and Poetry by a Southern Lady*, anonymously, using the nom de plume of "A Georgia Lady." Her volume contained a number of pieces penned by Missouria too, filling perhaps as much as half the book.[17]

. We know little about Mary's romantic life, although multiple poems in *Prose and Poetry* hint at a special love interest. In addition, several lines in her 1907 semiautobiographical novel, *The Transplanted*, suggest she had had a special beau in her youth. The young man in question, a "splendid man, handsome and bright, . . . graduated with honor from the university [probably Emory College in nearby Oxford]." His reading of Voltaire and Rousseau had compelled him to reject Christianity, he wrote her, which caused Mary to reject him. "I could read no more. . . . I fainted. . . . I nearly died."[18] Her heartbreak was furthered by his subsequent marriage to her friend. While much of her early poetry turned on her love for this young man, her "spirit groom," her love for God proved much greater. Her faith would serve as the touchstone for her heart and soul, as well as her muse, throughout her long life.

In 1850 Mary's stepfather died, and Mary's now twice-widowed mother and the three children, eleven-year-old Missouria, ten-year-old Thomas, and twenty-one-year-old Mary, moved back to Decatur, settling with their six slaves into a small house on Marshall Street, on a large lot with a livestock barn and a big vegetable garden. Meanwhile, as sectionalism reshaped the political landscape, Mary continued to write. She paid for the publication of four more editions of *Prose and Poetry*, retitling the 1860 edition *The Pastor's Story and Other Tales* and including new poems as well.[19] At the same time she presumably aided her mother, cared for her younger siblings, visited kin, and led a relatively independent life.

By the time the Civil War broke out, Mary was a thirty-two-year-old spinster. A strong advocate for the South's right to self-determination, this southern patriot traveled to Montgomery, Alabama, with her aunt and cousin, to witness Jefferson Davis's inauguration as President of the Confederate States of America.[20] Meanwhile, her brother Thomas had departed for Texas to find his fortune. He had married there and settled down, and then he enlisted like so many other young men of his generation.[21] Back in Decatur during the summer of 1861, townspeople attended parties and dances in honor of their enlisting men, and Mary and Missouria joined in all the festive departures for the new soldiers, who so reminded them of their own brother.[22] They spent the following months knitting and sewing for the troops, penning them letters, and looking forward to the South's swift victory.[23] They also eagerly awaited word of Thomie's whereabouts. After joining the army as a private in the Tenth Regiment Texas Infantry, Granbury's Brigade, Cleburne's Division, Hardee's Corps, he served under General Joe Johnson's army in the western theater. He rose to sergeant, and then commissioned lieutenant, but was captured in Arkansas on January 11, 1863, and exchanged for Union prisoners of war at City Point, Virginia, in April. That summer, he visited his sisters in Decatur, thin almost beyond recognition, departed for Texas to see his wife, and then returned, largely on foot, to his regiment in Dalton, Georgia. By the spring of 1864 Thomie, like so many other war-weary and disillusioned soldiers around him, had become increasingly religious and then spent the next months of his life embracing God. He had discovered a gift for preaching, which he practiced before whole brigades eager for his message of faith and love.[24]

Thomie stayed in touch with his Decatur family throughout the spring, summer, and fall of 1864, and indeed put them in grave danger by sending nine large dry-goods boxes filled with Confederate blankets and coats to store in their house. Over the course of the summer, Atlanta remained a key supply center for the Confederacy as skirmishes with Union forces continued just to the north. Thomie saw much action at Kennesaw and around the Chattahoochee River, and he witnessed the devastation of the family farm, Oak Grove. He received news that he was the father of little Thomas H. Stokes and dreamed of going home to Texas. After recuperating from exhaustion at a Macon hospital, Thomie returned to the front in September and fought throughout the fall, until November 30, 1864, when he was killed on the battlefield in Franklin, Tennessee, with the majority of his regiment.[25]

As the only man in the family, Thomie's death brought inconsolable grief to the Gay-Stokes women. Indeed, his life, letters, and heroics form one of the two centerpieces around which Mary Gay constructed her Civil War memoir. (Mary's own role on the home front marks the other centerpiece of the book.) Missouria, who had taught school off and on before the war, spent most of the war years with cousins in Madison, or even further east in Augusta, where she seems to have taught a bit as well. With Missouria away, Mary cared for her mother, who grew increasingly feeble, and their two domestic slaves, a young woman named Telitha, who was deaf, and a youth named Toby. The family had hired out several other slaves in Atlanta, while "Uncle Mack," their elderly blacksmith, was living independently in Decatur.

Mary threw herself into the thick of the fray during the war, and if her memoir is accurate, not only did she hold her own fragile household together and prove heroic in her support for the Confederate cause, but she saved the ragtag residents of war-torn Decatur from starvation during its occupation in 1864. Throughout *Life in Dixie*, Mary insisted she was as much a bona fide soldier as any man enlisted in the Confederate army. Wartime has always allowed women to step into new situations previously deemed unorthodox for them. Mary Gay, fueled by southern nationalism and love for her family, understood the opportunities presented her, and took pride in her execution of them. She consistently used her class and gender privileges to support the Confederacy, whether by hiding blankets and coats to aid the soldiers, working as a spy, or resisting Union occupation and its demands. Although she was unable to halt the course of the war, and its particular manifestations in northern Georgia, like any good soldier she never completely acquiesced to the demands of Union officers or accepted the inevitability of Confederate defeat.

Hiding Thomie's company's blankets and coats marks one such example of her Confederate patriotism. Upon learning from Uncle Mack that Sherman's troops were headed straight for Decatur on July 18, 1864, and knowing that possession of these items could cost her her home and freedom, Mary locked up the house, and assisted by Telitha, climbed up on her dining room table, then on to a wardrobe, and hammered enough plaster and lathe out of the ceiling to shove the contraband into the crawl space.[26] That same evening, Mary and Toby took prized possessions to friends in Atlanta by train for safekeeping, only to find on their return that Union troops had torn up part of the track. Intent on welcoming the Confederate troops to Decatur, she and Toby, who was now quite ill, walked the five miles back home in the night. She then cooked breakfast for Wheeler's cavalry that morning. By midday Sherman's troops had arrived under the watchful eye of Decatur's mere six hundred residents, almost all white women and children, free blacks, and slaves. Mary Gay reported she stood tall and fixed a cold stare on the Union men. But when a group of soldiers stopped in front of her house, with her mother, Telitha, and a very ill Toby standing beside her, she could do nothing to stop them from breaking in. They looted through their dressers and cupboards, taking what they deemed valuable and destroying the rest, including her beloved books. Garrard's cavalry, on the heels of these troops, then selected the Stokes-Gay home for its headquarters, tore down the barn to put up makeshift huts, and killed the Stokes-Gay family's cow, calves, hogs, and poultry to produce an enormous feast. The officers spread the family furniture over the lawn for seating and fed their horses corn from the dresser drawers, while Mary, her mother, and their servants locked themselves into the two rooms permitted them, and listened to their stomachs growl. Toby died shortly thereafter, probably of measles.[27]

But Mary Gay did not accept the limitations of her confinement, and instead used her status as an elite woman to defy her jailors. Having wheedled Union newspapers from them to occupy her time, she received word that an ill relative near Atlanta had requested her help. Southern ladies always come to the aid of their relatives in need, she explained to the provost marshal, and so she requested special permission to visit. Little did he know that once she had secured his authorization, Mary lined her petticoat and made a bustle with the newspapers, before walking with Telitha and a military escort to her kin's home a mile and a half away. Upon the escort's overnight departure, she and Telitha slipped out of the house, walked fifteen miles through the lines to deliver the Union papers to Confederate leaders, and then returned to the aunt's home by daybreak to meet the escort. The newspapers, filled with valuable news about Union troop movements and the war in general, were warmly received by Confederate officers. At least this is what Mary Gay relates in her memoir.[28]

When Atlanta fell on September 2, 1864, Mary finally realized, as did so many other white southerners, that the Confederacy was in trouble. That fall, as Sherman prepared to bring total war to the heart of Georgia and South Carolina, he ordered all Decatur and Atlanta residents to evacuate. Once again, Mary foiled the Union forces. She and her family avoided joining the hundreds of refugees thronging south to Jonesboro by concocting a laundry and sewing business, which fooled the provost marshal into letting them stay in their home, since they were allegedly self-supporting. Penniless, for Mary's mother had invested all her money in Confederate bonds, the family's only possession of any real value remained the Marshall Street property, and they were loath to abandon it, regardless of the danger.[29]

Mary Gay's southern nationalism remained largely undimmed throughout these trials, or so she tells her readers, even though the war's bad outcome seemed ordained. That fall before Thomie's death, as the weather turned cold, Mary realized her brother's company needed the blankets and coats she had hidden so effectively. In a bold move, she begged burlap sacks from Union soldiers, filled them with the contraband, sewed them tight, and then persuaded the guileless provost marshal to secure a wagon to take her to the train station. Her daring exploits ended when she arrived in Jonesboro and sent word to the Confederate troops nearby, who brought Mary and the contraband to their encampment. When Thomie discovered his sister there, he expressed great pleasure, as much at the discovery of his warm wool overcoat as at her presence. "Had a bombshell exploded at his feet," Mary recalled, "the effect could not have been more electrical."[30]

Mary's patriotic exploits did not end there. On discovering that her neighbor and her children were starving, but that this woman had a sister-in-law in Madison who would take the family in, Mary instructed the mother to pack up, and then persuaded Uncle Mack to rig together a wagon from the leavings of the Union army. She found an abandoned horse at the edge of town, skinny as a rail, riddled with saddle sores, and branded with the letters "U.S." on his rump. Calling him Yankee, she hitched him to the makeshift wagon, loaded up the hungry family, and drove them for two days across enemy lines to Social Circle. She then bought food for the return trip and headed back alone. Thwarted by Yankee's collapse in his traces, a scene familiar to devotees of *Gone with the Wind*, she found overnight shelter with ex-slaves in a former plantation home, in a world she now understood to be truly turned upside down, and escaped raiding parties to arrive home unscathed. On reaching Decatur, so many women and children raced to her wagon clamoring for food that she had nothing left for her mother, Telitha, or herself by the time she turned into her own yard.[31]

Mary tells her audience she was resourceful as well as brave, and there is no reason to doubt her. When she learned that a Confederate commissary in Atlanta would trade food for minie balls and lead, Mary organized munitions hunts. Although it was freezing cold, Mary, Telitha, and the remaining children in Decatur walked south of the train tracks to a battlefield where they pried the shot from the freezing ground with hands bleeding from the cold and ice. They carried their heavy baskets to the city, and much to their delight received flour, sugar, coffee, meal, and some meat in return, repeating their efforts for some weeks until the commissary closed. Mary never let the boundaries of traditional southern femininity stop her from searching for solutions to the enormous problems she encountered in occupied Decatur. She consistently assumed a special role as leader and caretaker of the woebegone collection of largely female Decatur residents eking out their existence in this ravaged place. Unlike those Confederate women who gave up the southern cause when the scale of loss became too enormous, as historian Drew Faust has argued, Mary Gay tells us some thirty years later that she never despaired.[32]

But then, in late January 1865 Mary and her family learned that Thomie had died in battle nearly two months earlier. Mary's mother never recovered from her grief, suffering more and more debilitating strokes until she fell into a coma and died in the spring of 1866 at the age of fifty-nine. Mary's war memoir essentially ends with the news of Thomie's death, although the war itself would drag on for two and half more months. We know that Mary mourned her brother's and her mother's deaths, but she also recalled her promise to Thomie to care for his wife and child in the event of his demise. As the oldest daughter, it was up to Mary to keep the remnants of their family together, through war's end and into the future.[33]

The postwar task of rebuilding was as daunting for Mary as it was for most southerners. Not only must she and her sister reconstruct their lives without their brother and their mother, but they must shore up their home, and add two people whom they did not know. Although the Stokes-Gay family had been comfortable enough despite the death of Thomas Stokes Sr. before the war, their investment in bonds during the war, and the inflated costs of provisions and supplies, had left Mary, Missouria, and Telitha in a sorry state like so many others by the spring of 1866. The sisters had also lost their human property, with the exception of Telitha, who continued to live with them immediately after the war.[34]

Mary's ability to survive the challenges posed by her tumultuous Civil War experiences had to have prepared her for the difficult world she faced in the postwar era. By early 1867 her sister Missouria had taken the safe route as tutor to her cousin's daughter in Madison. Mary, however, was pursuing an unlikely path for a genteel southern lady nearing forty without resources caught in the chaos of early Reconstruction. She took to the road as a seller of Bibles, supporting herself with the small commissions she secured as an agent. She even traveled to Texas, where she persuaded her sister-in-law to move east to Georgia.[35]

By the summer of 1867 Mary and Missouria had both returned to Decatur and were joined by their sister-in-law Mary Stokes and her three-and-a-half-year-old son, Thomie Junior. This female-headed household would subsequently hold together for some twenty years, although the adult women often found themselves disagreeing on how to raise and educate Thomie, how to handle money, and how to run the household. While Mary Gay and Missouria Stokes were acting out of the kindness of their hearts, and out of a sense of duty to their dead brother according to the memoir, the letters exchanged among the three women during much of this period convey significant tensions, especially because money remained a constant struggle for all of them.

Mary Gay and Missouria Stokes seem to have left the management of the house and garden to the widowed Mary Stokes for much of the time. Missouria worked off and on as a teacher, and then as a dedicated temperance advocate. Both pursuits meant she was away from the Marshall Street house for long periods. Mary Gay was absent for even more extended periods than Missouria. Although both sisters adored their nephew, and in many respects invested all their hopes and dreams in him, the challenge to find adequate financial resources to support their household, and to deal with Thomie's mother, proved difficult.[36]

Faith appears to have been the cornerstone of both sisters' lives. Missouria belonged to the Presbyterian Church, as had their mother, and Mary belonged to the Baptist Church. Both Missouria and Mary had been dedicated to the Union Sunday School organized by Decatur churches in 1866. Mary, in particular, developed such a powerful commitment to her congregation that when her fellow Baptists, a mere twenty-three of them, admitted defeat at raising enough money to build a new church (their original building had been burned by Sherman's troops), she decided to tackle the problem herself. People in Kentucky and Tennessee, she stated at a meeting of the congregation, had not suffered on the home front as badly as Georgians. Because she had connections in these places as a Bible-seller, she offered to travel to these states to solicit funds. The members agreed to this "generous offer" and prepared credentials for her journey. Mary spent August through December 1867 soliciting small amounts of money, generally from twenty-five cents to a dollar or two, in twenty-three different towns in these two states, collecting nearly a thousand dollars. The following spring, Mary journeyed through middle Georgia to the coast, gathering enough additional support to begin financing the construction. As late as 1870, when "The Little Red Brick Baptist Church" had been completed, Mary was still seeking monies for it.[37]

Mary's travels had taken her through Franklin, Tennessee, where she had stopped to find her brother Thomie's grave. The Union forces at the Battle of Franklin had pressed surviving Confederates to flee for their lives, leaving their dead behind them. John McGavock, who lived near the battle site, collected 1,496 Confederate bodies, burying the corpses on his own property adjoining his family cemetery. When Mary visited the site, she was disturbed to find cows grazing on the makeshift graves. She headed to Texas, the home of the majority of these fallen Confederates, and raised approximately five thousand dollars, enough money to enclose the cemetery with an iron fence and a gate, the latter bearing a silver plaque engraved with her name.[38]

Once the cemetery fence was completed, and the Baptist Church built, Mary was probably without income, but was now an experienced traveler and fundraiser. She had supported herself and her household by siphoning off a small amount of money from the donations she raised as her agent's fee, which amounted to one or two dollars a night for her board, money for her train travel, and a little money to send home, never a large amount, perhaps five dollars or so. Mary clearly stated in her letters how she wanted Missouria and Mary Stokes to distribute the cash she sent them, directing them when to purchase food or clothing, or pay for repairs, and she always indicated which creditors needed payment the soonest.[39]

By 1870 Mary Gay was forty-two, and Missouria thirty-one. Both officially shared in "keeping house" at Marshall Street. The value of their real estate, which was listed in Mary's name, amounted to one thousand dollars, while their personal property totaled four hundred dollars, but their letters to each continued to reference their debt.[40] Besides their sister-in-law, Mary M. Stokes, thirty-one, and their nephew, now six, their household contained one other resident at this time, a sixteen-year-old named William Kendrick (whose identity is not clear). The Stokes-Gay family lived in a neighborhood sprinkled with homeowners like themselves, but increasingly made up of boarding houses, not surprising given the poverty of postwar Decatur and its environs.[41]

The next year Mary ordered a seventh edition of her *Pastor's Story* printed in Memphis. She had had a tough time convincing publishers to take it on themselves, and ultimately paid for the printing out of her own pocket. She may also have tried to secure income through financing the publications of other would-be authors. Orie S. Vendery wrote Mary Gay to take advantage of her offer to publish and sell Gay's book in the fall of 1870.[42] We do know Mary Gay was well aware of the high commission booksellers demanded, as much as a third of the book's price, so she chose instead to sell her books herself at $1.50 a copy, earning 65 cents for each.[43] Her correspondence with Orie S. Vendery may mean she was selling others' books too. Regardless, throughout the 1870s and 1880s, Mary took to the road to sell her reprinted book.[44] She traveled in Georgia and her old haunts to the west, but also north through the Carolinas and into Virginia. Her book was published in four more editions over this period.[45] There is no question that Mary worried constantly about money to support the Stokes-Gay family. Her letters to Missouria are filled with these concerns. "Would come home but for the necessity of doing something to reduce my indebtedness. . . . In the interest of the familys demands [necessitates] exertion on my part, and I am willing to make that exertion, believing that the work I am engaged in will be blessed," she wrote to explain her continued absence.[46] Another letter relates her ever-present anxiety about finances but assures Missouria she will hold to her promise to send five dollars each week.[47]

*The Pastor's Story* must have circulated widely, for it came to Mark Twain's attention. In his inimitable style, Twain poked fun at the sentimentalism of her poetry in a memorable scene in *The Adventures of Tom Sawyer* (1876). Tom's classmates were to recite original compositions before an audience, wrestling their words into some sort of morally uplifting message, an expectation Twain considered an affront to the English language. To bring home his point, the wily author provided several examples of this mawkish genre in his novel, which were thinly disguised pieces drawn straight from Mary's book.[48] She responded to this mean jab by enlisting William Cullen Bryan's opinion of her poetry, and then cited part of his letter in the preface to subsequent editions of *The Pastor's Story*.[49]

It was not until 1892, at the age of sixty-one, however, that Mary Gay finally secured relative fame with the publication of *Life in Dixie*. Part memoir, part romance, part pantheon to the Lost Cause, it fitted neatly into the already developing genre of women's writing that memorialized Confederate soldiers and the Civil War.[50] Gay stated in the introduction that this book was intended for her nephew, so that he could learn the heroic story of the father he had never met, but this statement is misleading. While *Life in Dixie* certainly lionized Thomas Stokes as a beloved brother and husband, brave soldier and lay preacher in wartime, it also celebrated Mary Gay as a dedicated sister and daughter, and a brave soldier and pious Christian in wartime too. Published in Atlanta, the book received good reviews and sold quite well. Perhaps Mary had taken Mark Twain's dismissal of her writing to heart, for her style in *Life in Dixie*, as Joel Chandler Harris confirmed in 1879, was surprisingly "unpretentious. . . . It has the charm and the distinction of absolute verity. Here, indeed, is one of the sources from which history must get its supplies." The *Atlanta Journal* reviewer opined that "*Life in Dixie* was one of the truest pictures of the life of our people that has yet been drawn."[51] Although she was now advanced in age at sixty-three, the book's good reception induced Mary to return to the road as a traveling saleswoman once again, and she peddled it throughout the 1890s. She also brought out three more editions of her book, in 1894, 1897, and 1901, that included expanded accounts of local wartime drama as well as the latest positive reviews, almost doubling its original length of 255 pages to 404.

Meanwhile, Missouria had sought out teaching positions that brought in income and allowed her to live elsewhere. Her sister-in-law rented out her room to boarders to help pay household accounts in her absence, and may have done the same when Mary Gay was traveling too. Tensions about what constituted an adequate budget for clothes percolated throughout the three women's exchange of letters, and identified Mary Stokes as a bit of a spendthrift and clotheshorse compared to her more frugal sisters-in-law.[52] The conflicts over wardrobe suggest the emotional turmoil beneath the surface that characterized their relationships. Missouria resigned from her post at a private school in Dalton in 1877 to come home to teach Thomie. Never a good student, he did not appreciate his aunt's sacrifice, and Mary Stokes did not appreciate her sister-in-law's intrusion. Missouria bemoaned this situation, until she found work as head of a mission school in Marietta, and then joined the temperance movement in Atlanta. In fact, she became an important and longtime leader in both the Atlanta and state chapters of the WCTU.[53] Mary Gay likewise regretted this situation, and while she appreciated Missouria's hard work as house manager, she had no desire to replace her. Upon returning home in Missouria's absence, she wrote her sister, "I daily regret coming home. I feel no interest in this place nor anybody except Tommy." For Mary, this was a "house of heart loneliness" and she would sooner be on the road than live there.[54]

By the late 1880s Thomie was a young adult and had moved to Atlanta to run a grocery store with an old friend of his father's. His mother, Mary Stokes, followed him there. Thomie wrote his aunts at this time, conveying his love for them, his respect for how hard they had always worked to support him, and his desire to support them in their old age. Unfortunately, he died suddenly of unknown causes in 1891. Neither Missouria nor Mary left anything in print conveying their heartache, but Missouria immediately resigned from her WCTU office, receiving confused letters from her colleagues begging explanation for her sudden departure.[55] It was perhaps fortunate that Mary's latest book was about to win the public's heart, for Mary immediately took to the road to sell it, while Missouria handled the financial arrangements and visits the two received as a result of the book's fine reception.

In 1901 a group of young women in Decatur formed the Agnes Lee Chapter of the United Daughters of the Confederacy. One of their first acts was to induct seventy-two-year-old Mary Gay as a charter member and appoint her Historian, a duty she actively pursued. They also titled a chapter of the Children of the Confederacy after her as well. At this point, Mary finally stopped peddling her books, relying on subscriptions for income instead. She also held scripture lessons in her home for Decatur children on Sunday afternoons. Whether it was the enjoyment she had gleaned from her fame as author of *Life in Dixie* or the nostalgia that can come with growing old, Mary Gay picked up her pen once more. In 1907 Walter Neale's New York publishing house put out her third and final book, *The Transplanted: A Story of Dixie before the War*. In the preface Neale heralded Gay for writing "intimately and lovingly" about the South of the past and the present, and for having lived through the "happiness" of the prewar past and "the dark days of Reconstruction." He added that her characters in *The Transplanted*, set in the 1840s, "are very charming people. Their traditions and customs are very much the same today as they were one hundred years ago."[56]

Like *Life in Dixie*, which fully embodied the developing genre of women's Civil War memoirs in the late nineteenth century, *The Transplanted* too resonated with the latest themes in southern women's writing, and particularly the romanticization of the Old South and the Civil War. Like other novels in this early twentieth-century form, it explored the idea of national reconciliation through intersectional marriage and therefore rewrote the southern story as a national one.[57] In Gay's book, a handsome bachelor planter in Mississippi unknowingly weds a Bostonian adventuress, and despite his travails, proves honest, true, and redeemed in the end. Thus, it is hard not to read *The Transplanted* as anything other than semiautobiographical wish fulfillment by an elderly southern white woman convinced of the righteousness of the southern cause. Yet she also understood the present-day need for reunion with the North.[58]

There is another important dimension to Mary Gay's novel and most southern women's writing in this genre as well. Books like Gay's *The Transplanted* embraced the idea of a mythical southern past as balm for the wounds of the war, but at the same time such books served to bind contemporary white southerners together as the regional economy began to industrialize, and the southern social order broadened and changed.[59] While Mary Gay wrote about a romanticized past in her novel, and romanticized some aspects (but by no means all) aspects of her Civil War experience in her earlier memoir, she also lived in the present. Indeed, the very life she chose to lead in the four decades after the war resulted as much from the impact of modernization as the setbacks of the South's impoverishment. Gay took full advantage of the national rise in commercial publishing, and the accompanying growing national interest in southern women's writing, that enabled her to have her books printed and reprinted so she could market them on the road.

Mary Gay's insistence on her own independence was facilitated greatly by the spread of trains throughout the region. Indeed, Gay was among the first generation of Victorian women in the South to defy cultural sanctions against train travel for elite women. Despite public images of the train as a masculine space, where danger for women predominated, Mary Gay remained undaunted by the alleged risks. Her sister feared Mary's travels, urging her to come home regardless of the finances. "You ought to be very careful—I often think of your danger of being murdered in hope of gain."[60] Mary remained undaunted, worrying more about the impropriety of mixed social contact, especially across race, than her own physical safety.[61]

Mary Gay was an adventuress, a devotee of the southern cause, and a moderate racist. She remained sympathetic to the tenets of white supremacy, like so many other white southerners of her time, even as those tenets crescendoed into Jim Crow segregation late in her life. Her postwar world was a biracial one in which freedpeople had been granted political and civil rights. Her attitude about black southerners was complex, however, and did change somewhat over time. In *Life in Dixie*, Mary Gay described her household servants during the Civil War as childlike dependents, and underlined her devotion to their well-being. After the war, when so many African Americans broke away from white churches, Mary's beloved Baptist Church, where she was such a dominant figure, appears to have been biracial, at least for a short period.[62] In 1866 Mary Gay described herself recoiling in disgust while awaiting a train at the Atlanta station when she and her companion witnessed young northern white women entering the cars escorted by black men behaving with too much familiarity. But her scorn was for the young white women, whom she believed were acting without propriety and indeed had encouraged the young freedmen in their attentions.[63] Mary wrote her sister in 1870 about freedmen "revolting" in Albany, but blamed their employers, the Albany and Brunswick Railroad Company, for failing to pay them.[64] A decade later, and after some years of performing domestic work without servants, Mary Gay bemoaned the high prices black laundresses charged in the town, and elected to do the washing herself.[65]

There are no black people, slave or free, in the poems and stories in *The Pastor's Story*, and the only blacks who get any real attention in *Life in Dixie* are Mary's own servants, for whom she is a ministering angel. Near the end of her life, having adapted to the transformation of race relationships since the Civil War, she painted a portrait in *The Transplanted* of a Mississippi bachelor planter who is benevolence personified on racial matters. His slave quarters were actually described invitingly, with their "majestic water oaks, furnished homes and playgrounds for children that they might be coveted by many an Anglo-Saxon in colder latitudes."[66] She also inserted plenty of all-too-familiar stereotypes of slave life, including dance scenes and banjo playing. At the same time, she was alert to social differences within the black community, as represented by clothes and deportment for example. With national figures like Charles Nelson Page and Thomas Dixon Jr. writing novels that turned on grossly drawn caricatures of African Americans as either "Uncle Toms" or rapacious mulattoes, and the recent Atlanta race riot fresh in her mind, it is not surprising that Mary Gay's black characters in *The Transplanted* were often little more than cardboard figures. Esther the cook was sneaky, mean, and at times downright diabolical—"this Afro-American woman with the malignity of Satan"—although her dislike of her master's northern wife, whom she described as "poor white trash" from Boston, turned out to be well-placed.[67] Thus Mary Gay's rendering of antebellum black life also suggests that her understanding of the black experience had undergone some revision during her adulthood, even as she remained committed to preserving manufactured memories of slaveholder benevolence and slave deviousness in the end.

Taken as a whole, Mary Gay's life after the Civil War paints a new image of postwar white women's experience. Here is an elite woman who traveled by train all around the South, staying sometimes in the homes of friends and kin, but more frequently in boarding houses where she knew no one. She spent her days asking for contributions from churchgoing, comfortable people, and in the process she assessed the inhabitants of the town she was visiting, its tourists, the place's beauty and purpose, even its investment possibilities.[68] All the while, Mary Gay left her sister-in-law, and oftentimes her sister, at home to do the daily work of keeping house, paying bills, shopping for bargains, arranging for repairs, raising a fatherless boy, and maintaining integral community relationships, none of which were easy to accomplish in a financially strapped female-headed household. It is clear that Mary Gay justified her absence from her home through her peddling of good deeds on behalf of her family and southern values. While this rationale was not untruthful, it is also accurate to state that Mary Gay gained great physical and personal freedom, and real stimulation, through her journeys and through the people she met.[69] She prided herself on her ability to sell large numbers of her books in new places to new people.[70] Perhaps her heroic adventures during the Civil War, if they in fact were not all imagined, had shown her a dimension of herself she had not known as a young woman. The postwar decades, with all their hardships, actually enabled her to continue challenging herself, in a way that keeping house or writing pious poetry never could.

Unlike her sister, Mary Gay did not see the value in joining reform associations. She did not seek out membership in the Agnes Lee Chapter of the UDC, although she received an honorary induction. She did convey interest in developing the state's role in paying homage to the Confederate generation, as in pressing for the establishment of the Alexander H. Stephens Monument in Crawfordville, but did not make such pursuits her life.[71] She was certainly pleased to be connected with key memory-makers of the Lost Cause. In what had become a frequent occurrence throughout the urban South, a group of men, women, and children unveiled a draped obelisk in front of the county courthouse in the center of Decatur in 1908.[72] Mary Gay, nearly seventy years old, wearing "widow's weeds," stood with the Corps of Cadets from the Donald Fraser School for Boys, philanthropist Rebeka Candler, and Civil War hero General Clement A. Evans, in front of the memorial while photographers captured the moment. Except for the notable absence of any mention about women's roles in the war, Mary Gay could have penned the inscription on the monument herself:

> To the memory of the soldiers and sailors of the Confederacy . . . to whose virtue in peace and in war we are witnesses, to the end that justice may be done and that the

truth perish not. . . . After forty two years another generation bears witness to the
future that these men were of a covenant keeping race who held fast to the faith as
it was given by the fathers of the republic. . . . How well they kept the faith is faintly
written in the records of the armies and the history of the times.

Mary Gay worked to carve the faith of these southern men, and the faith of
the southern women who supported them, into southern memory. She also
carved out an independent personal life and a well-known public identity for
herself through her commitments to her religious faith and to the preservation of the memory of the Civil War, most obviously as the author of three
books, but also through her work as a seller of the Lost Cause, peddling the
memory of the Confederate dead and the attendant suffering. She was like many
other women of the period, and yet in one sense she was not. Few elite white
southern women born in the antebellum period could reinvent themselves to
adapt so neatly with each successive generation of southern women into the
twentieth century. She is significant to historians less for her public work and
ideology, however, which is not so unique in the end, than for her construction of a special role for herself as sales agent, breadwinner, and independent
woman through her marketing of the memory of the Civil War dead. By seeking
funds for her church and for Confederate memorials, and by selling her books
across six decades, four of them as a traveling salesperson, Mary Gay was able
to defy the confines of the new domesticity of postwar southern white women.
Her life on the road allowed her to escape the pettiness and frustrations of
running a household on a shoestring without the help of servants, as expected
of so many white women of her class in the postwar South. Traveling meant
she could flee from the inevitable conflicts and competition in her own home
where three adult women attempted to raise a child on whom they had heaped
all their love and hopes, under difficult circumstances they had never expected
to find themselves in. Mary Gay enjoyed the stimulation of her travels and the
autonomy they offered her. She convinced people whom she had never met
that her cause was legitimate because she herself had suffered the terrible loss
of a loved one during the war, and they owed her for that loss, which shaped
their own identity. They bought her books for the memories of death they contained as well as the distinctly southern values they extolled. Little about her
upbringing as a genteel southern lady had prepared her for this life, yet she was
surprisingly talented at it. Moreover, by the end of her life, she was celebrated
for it.

In the wake of Missouria's death in 1909, Mary Gay slipped increasingly into
dementia. The following year she was judged an imbecile by the court of ordi-

nary and assigned a guardian. She was committed to the Georgia State Sanitarium by court order on February 14, 1915, where she died three years later.[73] Mary Gay's life story, and the suggestive mention she provides in her letters and books of other women on the road doing likewise, indicates that we have overlooked a fascinating group of women peddling sadness and loss, and securing autonomy in the process. Such women, even more than the female reformers, political activists, writers, and teachers we have just begun to recognize in the late nineteenth and early twentieth centuries, not only stretch our knowledge of women's roles in the New South, but begin to transform them.

### NOTES

1. Interview with Walter McCurdy Jr., DeKalb Historical Society, July 5, 2000.

2. Indeed, many Confederate organizations made her a cause célèbre. See, for example, "A Study in Gray—Miss M. A. H. Gay," *Confederate Veteran* 16 (1908): 633–35; "A Noble Georgia Woman," *Confederate Veteran* 27 (1919): 113; "Mary Gay: Confederate Hero," *The United Daughters of the Confederacy Magazine*, May 1951, 15, 18.

3. When she came across Stephen Vincent Benet's glowing review of her book in *The Saturday Review*, with its praise for her command of historical sources, Margaret Mitchell wrote him. "Do you know, you're the only reviewer who has picked up the diaries and memoirs out of my background? Of course, I used everybody from Myrta Lockhart Avary to Eliza Andrews and Mary Gay" (Letter dated July 9, 1936, in Richard Harwell, ed., *Margaret Mitchell's Gone with the Wind Letters, 1936–1949* [New York: Macmillan, 1976], 34–36).

4. See the undated typescript of the "Mary Gay House" presentation that docents provide interested visitors, the 1991 "Tour of the Mary Gay House" typescript, and the 1999 brochure titled *The Junior League of DeKalb County, Inc. Welcomes You to the Home of Mary Ann Harris Gay*, available at the Junior League of DeKalb County, Inc., 716 Trinity Place, Decatur, Georgia. See also Howard Pousner, "DeKalb Junior League Restoring Mary Gay House," *Atlanta Constitution*, May 13, 1982.

5. Although *Life in Dixie* went out of print in the early twentieth century, it has been reprinted by two different publishing houses in the last twenty-five years. Mary A. H. Gay, *Life in Dixie during the War: 1861–1862–1863–1864–1865*, 5th ed. (1897; repr., Atlanta: Darby Printing Company for the DeKalb Historical Society, 1979); and Mary A. H. Gay, *Life in Dixie during the Civil War*, ed. J. H. Segars (Macon, Ga.: Mercer University Press, 2000); "*Life in Dixie* Selling Well All Over," *DeKalb New Era*, November 22, 1979.

6. Kathryn L. Helgeson, "A Singular Rebel: Mary Ann Harris Gay" (Senior Thesis, McCain Library, Agnes Scott College, 1982).

7. Georgia Women of Achievement Web site, Honorees, Mary Ann Harris Gay, http://www .georgiawomen.org/_honorees/gaym/index.htm# (accessed December 1, 2008).

8. A description of Mary Gay as author in the Miscellaneous File on Mary Gay at the DeKalb County Historical Society, Decatur, Georgia, states, "As a source book of DeKalb County and greater Atlanta's history there is nothing in print that describes the cultural and geographic detail of DeKalb and Atlanta as does *Life in Dixie during the War*." On the institutionalization of Mary Gay's memory consider that the Decatur Holiday Inn has even named one of its conference rooms after her.

9. Elizabeth Stevenson, "Surviving the Civil War Years," Review Essay, *Georgia Historical Quarterly* 64 (Spring 1980): 86.

10. This conclusion is based on the invaluable research notes historian Kenneth H. Thomas Jr. of the Historic Preservation Division, State of Georgia, provided me on the genealogies of the Gay and Stevens families (in the Thomas's possession), as well as letters Thomas exchanged with F. N. Boney on the Stevens family genealogy.

11. Lilly Reynolds, "A Georgian: Mary A. H. Gay and Her Books," c. 1930s, unpublished essay, copy in the Dekalb Historical Society Archives, original at the Atlanta Historical Society; Helgeson, "A Singular Rebel," 1; see also the notes of Gordon M. Midgette, in preparation for the republication of *Life in Dixie* in 1979, copy in file in Mary Gay Papers, DeKalb Historical Society, Decatur, Ga.

12. John Brown, *Slave Life in Georgia: A Narrative of the Life, Sufferings, and Escape of John Brown, a Fugitive Slave*, ed. F. N. Boney (Savannah, Ga.: Beehive Press, 1972, 1991); F. N. Boney, "Thomas Stevens, Antebellum Georgian," *South Atlantic Quarterly* 72, no. 2 (Spring 1973): 226–42.

13. F. N. Boney shows readers that the manuscript sources "allow the scholar to verify in detail most of Brown's narrative." He adds it is "a story which becomes increasingly convincing as it is increasingly investigated and analyzed." See Boney's introduction to Brown, *Slave Life in Georgia*, xv.

14. Stevens owned more than twenty slaves by the early 1820s, and over forty by his death in the late 1830s (Brown, *Slave Life in Georgia*, 22–23n.5); on ambitious young men in antebellum Georgia, see Michele Gillespie, *Free Labor in an Unfree World: White Artisans in Slaveholding Georgia, 1789–1860* (Athens: University of Georgia Press, 2000).

15. Brown, *Slave Life in Georgia*, 34–38.

16. Brown, *Slave Life in Georgia*, 46; Helgeson, "A Singular Rebel," 4–5; see also the notes of Gordon M. Midgette, in preparation for the republication of *Life in Dixie* in 1979, copy on file in Mary Gay Papers, DeKalb Historical Society, Decatur, Ga., 3.

17. A Georgia Lady [Mary A. H. Gay], *Prose and Poetry* (Nashville: South-Western Publishing House, 1858).

18. Mary Gay, *Transplanted: A Story of Dixie before the Civil War* (New York: Neale Publishing Company, 1907), 48–50.

19. *Prose and Poetry*, 2nd ed. (Nashville: South-Western Publishing House, 1859); *Prose and Poetry* (Nashville: Graves: Marks and Co., 1859); and *Prose and Poetry* (Nashville, South-Western Publishing House, 1860). She listed herself as Mary A. H. Gay on each of these subsequent volumes, no longer willing to be anonymous.

20. Gay, *Life in Dixie*, 1897 ed., 17.

21. Ibid., 15, 58–71.

22. Ibid., 36–47.

23. Ibid., 42–43.

24. Ibid., 15, 58–71, 77; James M. McPherson, *For Cause and Comrade: Why Men Fought in the Civil War* (New York: Oxford University Press, 1997), 75–76; Gay, *Life in Dixie* (2000), 243–50.

25. Gay, *Life in Dixie* (2000), 92, 97, 99, 104–5, 161, 165, 167, 174, 176, 184–85, 192, 272.

26. There is significant evidence that the story Mary Gay relates in *Life in Dixie* actually occurred. Mary Gay showed an interviewer from the *Confederate Veteran* the patched hole in the ceiling in 1908, and the DeKalb Junior League documented its existence some eight decades later when doing renovation work.

27. Gay, *Life in Dixie* (2000), 113–45.

28. Ibid., 156–67.

29. Ibid., 156–67.

30. Ibid., 168–93.

31. Ibid., 207–25

32. Ibid., 255–67; Drew Gilpin Faust, *Mothers of Invention: Women of the Slaveholding South in the American Civil War* (Chapel Hill: University of North Carolina Press, 1996), 234–46.

33. Gay, *Life in Dixie* (2000), 272, 274–81.

34. Neither sister ever mentioned their former slaves who had been hired out in Atlanta during wartime, and who must have used the chaos of occupation to secure their own de facto freedom, in any of their subsequent letters. Nor is Uncle Mack's fate known. In 1867, almost two years after the war had ended and emancipation enacted, Telitha apparently died of some "sad fate" while both sisters were out of town. Telitha's name does not appear in any extant family document until the publication of *Life in Dixie*, where Mary put significant emphasis on portraying the kindly, loving, and familial nature of master-servant relationships in the Gay-Stokes household, including their nursing of Toby through his illness and their care of the disabled Telitha, in telling contrast with Brown's depiction of master-servant relationships on the Gay plantation in *Slave Life in Georgia*.

35. Missouria H. Stokes to Mary Gay, February 4, 1867, Missouria H. Stokes Personal Correspondence, 1856–1924, Special Collections, Duke University Library, Durham, N.C. (hereafter Stokes Correspondence).

36. S. S. Moreland to Missouria, undated, Stokes Correspondence, recognizes that Missouria is tending house for herself, her sister-in-law, and her nephew while Mary is away, and Moreland bemoans the fact that all families must teach their children to work, which is all parents can do for them in this new world. Mary Stokes to "My Dear Sister," March 28, no year, conveys her reliance on Mary and Missouria for support and money.

37. The First Baptist Church of Decatur keeps Mary Gay's "Account Book of Contributions" in the Walter and Louise McCurdy Reading Room. She seems to have collected 15 percent of the contributions for herself. She maintained a list of contributions, divided by city. Each entry was numbered, followed by a name and an amount, and the column usually tallied at the bottom of each two-column page. On the history of this church, see Hettie Pittman Johnson, *The Church Expanding: The Story of the First Baptist Church, 1862–1987, Decatur, Georgia* (Decatur, Ga.: First Baptist Church, 1987).

38. Tennessee Historical Marker, Confederate Cemetery, 3D 45, Tennessee Historical Commission; Colonel James G. Bogle, Memo for the Record, June 10, 1983, Mary A. H. Gay Files, DeKalb Historical Society. Older sources indicate that Mary Gay discovered that farmers were eager to plow up a hastily dug mass gravesite of Confederate dead, prompting her to seek funds in Texas for buying land, reburial, gravesite markers, and the iron fence enclosure. That the graves are neatly laid out in rows and each marked with a number and the initials of the deceased, and that records are maintained with full names of the dead, belies the older, more dramatic story.

39. Letter Fragment, Mary Gay to Missouria Stokes, March 16, 1870, Brunswick, Ga., Stokes Correspondence.

40. Missouria H. Stokes to Mary Gay, Decatur, Ga., Feb. 5, 1869; Mary Gay to Missouria Stokes, Brunswick, Ga., March 13, 1870; Stokes Correspondence.

41. U.S. Federal Census, 1870, DeKalb County, Georgia, 52.

42. Orie S. Vendery to Mary Gay, October 8, 1870, Cartersville, Ga., Stokes Correspondence.

43. Turnbull Brothers Publishers to Mary A. H. Gay, April 14, 1873; Reynolds, 2–3.

44. The Stokes Correspondence abounds with receipts from the Turnbull Brothers in Baltimore during the 1870s and 1880s for copies of *The Pastor's Story* shipped directly to Mary Gay.

45. The eleventh and final edition of Mary A. H. Gay, *The Pastor's Story, and Other Pieces; or,*

*Prose and Poetry*, was published by Southern Methodist Publishing House in Nashville in 1881; Mary Gay to Missouria Stokes, 187?, Greenville, S.C., describing her travels by train and how hard she works to send the family money, Stokes Correspondence.

46. Mary Gay to Missouria Stokes, no date, Stokes Correspondence.

47. Mary Gay to Missouria Stokes, March 27, 1872, Stokes Correspondence.

48. Kristina Simms, "Mark Twain and the Lady from Decatur," *Atlanta Journal and Constitution*, November 12, 1972, magazine section, 48. William Cullen Bryan, for his part, noted "the imagination and feeling" of her poetry, but added "in several instances the rhyming could be improved," prompting Mary to rework some of her lines, as duly noted by her publisher in the tenth edition. Identifying him in the preface only as "that renowned Bohemian," Mary included her own barb at Twain in her newest foreword: "The criticism of the greatest literary humbug, who could not himself produce a work equal in merit to the one criticized, is always the most virulent."

49. Mary Gay, *The Pastor's Story, and Other Pieces; or, Prose and Poetry*, 11th ed. (Nashville: Southern Methodist Publishing House, 1881), iv–vi.

50. Sarah Gardner, *Blood and Irony: Southern White Women's Narratives of the Civil War, 1861–1937* (Chapel Hill: University of North Carolina, 2003), chap. 5.

51. Quotes reprinted in *The Dekalb News/Sun*, April 25, 1979, 10A.

52. Missouria Stokes to Mary Stokes [?], June 2, 1876, Dalton, Ga.; Mary Stokes to Missouria Stokes, December 11, 1876, and especially Mary Gay to Missouria Stokes, July 30, 1877, Stokes Correspondence.

53. On Missouria's work with the Georgia Women's Christian Temperance Union consult her correspondence as well as the Georgia Woman's Christian Temperance Union Records, 1888–1982, Collection #647, in Manuscripts, Archives, and Rare Book Library, Emory University.

54. Mary Gay to Missouri Stokes, July 30, 1877, Stokes Correspondence.

55. Letter Fragment to Missouria H. Stokes, no date; J. E. Sibley to Missouria H. Stokes, March 6, no year, both letters in Stokes Correspondence.

56. Walter Neale, preface to *The Transplanted: A Story of Dixie before the War*, by Mary A. H. Gay (New York: Neale Publishing Company, 1907), 5–6.

57. Gardner, *Blood and Irony*, chap. 5.

58. David W. Blight, *Race and Reunion: The Civil War in American Memory* (Cambridge, Mass.: Harvard University Press, 2001), 338–80.

59. Gaines Foster, *Ghosts of the Confederacy: Defeat, the Lost Cause, and the Emergence of the New South, 1865 to 1913* (New York: Oxford University Press, 1987), 5–7.

60. Missouria Stokes to Mary Gay, no date, Stokes Correspondence.

61. Amy G. Richter, *Home on the Rails: Women, The Railroad, and the Rise of Public Domesticity* (Chapel Hill: University of North Carolina Press, 2005), 1–9.

62. Entry for September 3, 1871, Decatur Baptist Church Minutes, 1867–1871, Walter and Louise McCurdy Reading Room, First Baptist Church of Decatur, Decatur, Georgia.

63. Mary Gay to Missouria H. Stokes, June 1868, Winchester, Tenn., Stokes Correspondence.

64. Mary Gay to Missouria Stokes, March 13, 1870, Brunswick, Ga., Stokes Correspondence.

65. Mary Gay to Missouria Stokes, August 3, 1877, Stokes Correspondence.

66. Gay, *The Transplanted*, 58.

67. Gay, *The Transplanted*, 106–10.

68. Mary Gay to Missouria Stokes, October 25, 1881, Atlanta, Ga.

69. See for example Mary Gay to Missouria Stokes, March 16 and 30, 1870, Brunswick, Ga., Stokes Correspondence.

70. Mary Gay to Missouria Stokes, August 12, 1873, Farmville, Va., Stokes Correspondence.

71. Karen Cox, *Dixie's Daughters: The United Daughters of the Confederacy and the Preservation of Confederate Culture* (Gainesville: University Press of Florida, 2004), 72; on Mary Gay's work to establish this monument see Gay biographical works and Mary Gay to Missouria Stokes, January 25, 1885, Jackson, Ga., Stokes Correspondence.

72. Cox, *Dixie's Daughters*, 50.

73. December 8, 1910, Letters of Guardianship, Book B, DeKalb County; December 5, 1910, Guardian Bonds, Book A, DeKalb County; February 15, 1915, Lunacy Book C, DeKalb County; Administration of Mary A. H. Gay Estate, Minute Book P, 330, Court of Ordinary, DeKalb County, DeKalb County Courthouse, Decatur, Ga.

# Rebecca Latimer Felton

## (1835–1930)

## *The Problem of Protection in the New South*

### LEEANN WHITES

❀ ❀ ❀

On November 21, 1922, women packed the galleries of the U.S. Senate. Delegations from every women's organization in Washington were present for the introduction of the first woman senator ever. Hale and hearty despite her eighty-seven years, the new junior senator from Georgia rose to give her maiden speech. "The women of the country have reason to rejoice," she asserted. "This day a door has been opened to them that never was opened before."[1] Rebecca Latimer Felton had particular reason to rejoice, and to be proud, for not only was she the first woman to be so honored but, equally important to her, she was a woman of the South, from Georgia. As she later wrote, "It meant that a woman reared in the sheltered security of an antebellum plantation was to be the first of her sex to sit in the U.S. Senate. It was hard to realize. . . . Who in that day would have had the hardihood to predict that the time would come when Georgia women would hold public office?"[2]

Who would have had the hardihood to predict it even two years earlier, when the South, almost to a state, refused to ratify the Nineteenth Amendment? And who would have looked to the state of Georgia, whose legislators had rushed to be the first to go on record in opposition to the amendment?[3] Perhaps only Rebecca Felton herself, long a power in state Democratic circles, even without the vote, and savvy in the ways of southern politics and southern gender relations. Having grown up in the antebellum South, she understood the intensity of planter-class men's commitment to the protection and the subordination of their women. Having endured the hard years of Civil War and Reconstruction, she also understood the personal and economic necessities that had led to the new public roles that women took on during those years.[4] How to reconcile the old values of protection and seclusion with the new realities of independence and public status for women? This was a critical problem of elite southern gender relations in the late nineteenth-century South. It was in this context that Felton carved out a new role for herself. In negotiating these contradictory crosscurrents, she found a place for herself and for women of her class and race. She emerged as one of the preeminent new women of the New South.[5]

At first glance, Rebecca Latimer Felton's early life course gives little indication of her eventual emergence as a leading spokesperson for women's rights.[6] Born in 1835 on her family's plantation in DeKalb County, she grew up in a prosperous planter family. The oldest of the four Latimer children, she was particularly close to her father. A sister, Mary Latimer, was five years younger and later became active in women's reforms as well. Eventually, Rebecca's father sent her to live with kinfolk in the town of Madison so she could attend the Female College there and acquire the best higher education then available to women in the state. Upon graduating at age seventeen, Rebecca Latimer promptly married the graduation speaker, William Felton, a man of many talents: medical doctor, minister, planter, and politician.

For Rebecca Latimer Felton, the role of the plantation mistress, which she took up at eighteen, was one to which she had been reared. It was the life of her mother and her grandmother before her and the one she assumed her daughters would occupy after her. Even toward the end of her long life, in what had become a much different South, she continued to see the antebellum plantation mistress as a feminine ideal. "The mother of eleven children," she wrote of her grandmother, "her industry, her management and her executive ability in caring for and carrying out her household affairs are still wonderful memories." Such women presented, in Felton's estimation, *the* model for womanly endeavor and as such provided her with "examples in my own extended life."[7]

By the same token, Rebecca Latimer Felton's male ideal remained in many ways one from the antebellum planter class, men like her grandfather and father, whom she described as being as hardworking and as industrious as their wives. Her grandfather ran a grain mill and sawmill along with his plantation, and her father combined plantation work with management of a tavern and local store. In Felton's recollection, these men cast a long shadow, a shadow that kept their women in the shade of the plantation, sheltered from the outside world. "The wife and mother," she wrote, "were like plants in the deep forest. Their softness and dependence were derived from the shade. A woman's home was the center as well as the circumference of her efforts for civilization or humanity."[8]

In her book *The Southern Lady*, Anne Scott discussed the apparently contradictory role of the antebellum plantation mistress, caught between her authority

REBECCA LATIMER FELTON
Courtesy of Hargrett Rare Book and Manuscript
Library, University of Georgia Libraries.

and responsibility within the plantation and her subordination to the planter within both the household and the public arena.[9] Although some planter-class women expressed their discontent with this role through private outpourings in their diaries, Felton, at least in retrospect, understood that elite women's subordination was the price they paid for their class and race privileges. Few women anywhere, Felton argued, could lay claim to such a retinue of "servants," to such an extended domestic place. "No wonder," she concluded, "matrimony was the goal of the average woman's existence." The only acceptable alternative was that of the schoolmistress, and even she "usually married some man with slaves to wait on her." Better to be subordinate but wealthy, in Felton's view, than to be independent and poor.[10]

The planter's public power redounded to the private advantage of the lady. Her public subordination to him not only signified her recognition of his public position but also announced the extent of her own private domain. Through her exaggerated deference and public incapacity, the lady expressed the extent of her own domestic authority. To violate one's place in this world was to break an unspoken agreement, an implicit social balance of power. Only through a studied acceptance of one's place and a strict delineation of its limits could harmony reign. Precisely because elite women's class and racial authority was so substantial within the confines of the plantation, gendered proscriptions against activities outside of it were necessarily all the more intense. As George Fitzhugh so aptly put it in analyzing the nature of "women's rights" in the antebellum South, "In truth, woman, like children, has but one right, and that is the right to protection. The right to protection involves the obligation to obey. . . . If she be obedient, she is in little danger of maltreatment; if she stands upon her rights, is coarse and masculine, man loathes and despises her, and ends by abusing her."[11]

According to Rebecca Felton, women of the planter class rarely broke their end of this agreement. They "obeyed," that is, they minded their place. The rupturing of elite gender relations was the result of the hubris of planter-class men rather than the insubordination of planter-class women.[12] It was planter men who refused to compromise on the issue of slavery, who masterminded secession, and who thereby set in motion a series of events that would forever undermine their ability to offer "protection" to their dependents. It was the wholesale destruction wrought by the Civil War, especially the death and crippling of so many fighting men and the loss of their property in slaves, that eroded the privileged option of planter-class women, rendering them vulnerable to the forces that had long molded the lives of most southern women.

For women of the planter class, the decline of male protection and women's exposure to economic hardship was inextricably fused through the crucible of the Civil War. Rebecca Felton repeatedly described the impact of the war in terms of her own unprotected "exposure" to the elemental forces of nature. "The War," she wrote, "broke on the South like a thunder clap from an almost clear sky" and brought with it a "four year hail storm."[13] The location of the Felton plantation, outside Cartersville in north Georgia and near a major railroad line, did indeed put them in the center of the storm. A main supply line for the army of the West, the railroad brought the war to Cartersville early through an almost constant stream of soldiers and supplies and, increasingly, through the return of the wounded and dead. Felton suddenly found herself in the public arena, not as a result of any rejection of her domestic status but in an effort to protect it. There was now an entire army to care for, and a woman's place was where the hungry, ill clad, and wounded were. Felton helped organize the local Ladies Aid Society and became its first president. Members met the trains, provided food, and took in wounded soldiers who would not survive the rest of the trip. She cut up her dresses for uniforms and ended the war in homespun. Running out of coffee, sugar, and salt, she found substitutes.

Eventually, the strategic location of the Felton plantation made it necessary for Rebecca herself to find refuge. Her husband, who was then serving as a Confederate surgeon, was able to secure an old farm outside Macon. Here Rebecca, her two children, and what remained of their slaves lived out the last year of the war. What began with the loss of her private domestic status and the stripping of her household to support the war effort would finally end with the virtual destruction of life on the plantation as she had known it. Invading troops razed the buildings, the slaves were emancipated, and her two surviving children died in the last year of the war from tainted water supplies and epidemic disease.[14]

To rehabilitate their plantation after the war, Rebecca and William Felton opened a school. Their neighbors were so impoverished that they frequently paid their children's tuition by working to rebuild the Felton's plantation. In the context of their common struggles, Rebecca Felton came to understand and in some sense to identify with the experience of her yeomen neighbors. She particularly identified with the plight of the women, perhaps widowed and most certainly rendered destitute by the war, who faced an even harder lot than she, "forced to work in the field," as she wrote, "or worse."[15]

The bonds forged with other Confederate women in the heat of battle were thus strengthened in the lingering misery of the postwar era; they would come to form the basis for Felton's political activities for the rest of her life. Left to their own devices, women like Rebecca Felton had become a "wonder to themselves."[16] Not only could they support themselves, but they could also aspire to make a vital contribution to the well-being of the less advantaged members of their own sex. As much as Felton came to value this new independence among women, however, she feared with a passion the economic necessity, the threat of "exposure" that drove it on. More than ever she valued her own domestic privilege—what was left of it.

Rebecca Latimer Felton was of two minds. Like other women throughout history, she agonized over the trade-offs between freedom and protection.[17] That which was "progressive" in her looked to the expansion of her own autonomy and that of other women as well. That which was fearful and threatened looked back longingly to the old days when protection and seclusion had been the experience of women of her race and class. She railed at those she held responsible for its decline. And *who* was responsible? Felton never answered this question in a consistent fashion, any more than she ever made a clean break with the desirability of male "protection." As the years passed and elite women emerged more securely as public figures in their own right, Felton did begin to argue with mounting forcefulness that it was the men of her class who were responsible, because they were the ones who had allowed the profitability of slavery and the lure of the market to override their sense of responsibility to domestic dependents. The domestically responsible course, according to Felton, would have been to compromise with the North and agree to gradual and compensated emancipation. Instead, having grown "overblown" with their own self-importance, slave-owning men recklessly threw the entire plantation world into the crucible of war.[18]

At her most independent and outspoken, Felton was inclined to expound on the shortcomings of male dominance at great length. When confronted with the economic vulnerability that these shortcomings had created for women, however, she concluded that some male protection was preferable to none at all. To salvage what little remained of antebellum "protection," she was inclined to limit her criticism of patriarchal social relations, or at least to exempt those few individual men, like her father and husband, who initially opposed secession. In her dependent, vulnerable persona, she was inclined to criticize not patriarchy per se but those individual men whom she regarded as inadequate or downright dangerous. Gingerly criticizing hotheaded secessionists, she reserved her greatest ire for those two-faced scalawags who supported Reconstruction governments and the empowerment of black freedpeople. To Felton, the very existence of free blacks, not to mention their assumption of political authority, was a constant reminder of all the ways in which the planter patriarchy had failed.

Indeed, it was freedpeople who engendered Felton's most intense feelings of animosity in the postwar context. Unable to confront fully the white man's failure to live up to his domestic responsibilities, she became preoccupied with the freedman's failure to live up to his. In her view, the decline of plantation life and the loss of the protected status it afforded plantation mistresses came to rest squarely on the shoulders of the ex-slaves, whose insubordination and refusal to work were safer targets for her frustrated outrage than were the men of her own class. Indeed, Felton's racial politics reflected her own experience of class power and gendered subordination. When the ownership of slaves had enabled the planter to shelter the women of his family on the plantation, Felton had perceived black slaves as diligent and loyal members of her world. In her reminiscences, the typical slave was the female domestic, who symbolized not only the planter's authority but the authority of the mistress as well. When the fall of slavery left her husband and others of his class economically and politically exposed, the prototypical black became the shiftless male laborer—a dangerous, threatening, foreboding figure, whom she envisioned as fundamentally out of his place in the postwar world, plundering her fields rather than laboring diligently in them.[19]

The collapse of the slave-based plantation economy created a virtually irreconcilable tension for Felton. Her desire for gender equity was countered by the devastating economic vulnerability she witnessed among the women around her, particularly among those who were without male "protection." It was this tension that drove her into the political arena. In the summer of 1874 William Felton entered the race for the U.S. Congress as an Independent, committed to representing the interests of the yeoman farmer in his upcountry county, Bartow. Rebecca Felton began her political career in support of her husband's candidacy, by acting as his campaign manager, scheduling his speaking engagements, arranging to have others speak for him, and writing numerous letters to the local press in response to attacks on his positions. For the Feltons, one legacy of the new womanly roles opened during the war was the possibility for a new kind of partnership in postwar politics. William Felton not only accommodated himself to his wife's new public activities but also actively facilitated her further political development. It was widely rumored, for instance, that Rebecca Felton not only wrote newspaper editorials in the doctor's defense, which she signed "Plowboy" or "Bartow," but wrote parts of his speeches as well.[20]

If this partnership reflected the possibilities created for more equitable relations between the sexes in the postwar South, the hostile public response reflected the larger social limitations imposed on couples that assumed such relative gender equality. Widespread derision of Rebecca Felton's participation in her husband's campaign reflected the fact that although new roles for women created the opportunity for more equitable gender relations, they were even more certain to create a gender backlash, particularly among economically and psychologically diminished men. Having been forced by the exigencies of the period to give up some aspects of their former dominance, many southern men clung with increased insistence to those forms that remained. The political sphere was the one arena to which women had virtually no entree in the 1870s and 1880s, and most southern white males, defeated and defensive, intended to maintain their sexual prerogatives there. As Rebecca Felton herself recalled, "I was called a 'petticoat reformer' and subject to plenty of ridicule, in public and in private."[21] Her husband was subject to ridicule as well. One local paper went so far as to entitle the announcement of William Felton's reelection to the U.S. Congress in 1878, "Mrs. Felton and Doctor Reelected."[22]

Beyond a certain point, the hostility Rebecca Felton's political assistance engendered became a liability to her husband and outweighed the benefits that her intelligence, argumentative skill, and political savvy brought. There were real limits to the degree to which William Felton's private acceptance and public support of her work could counteract the impact of a hostile public. Gender norms in the larger society thus set limits on the extent of equity between even the Feltons. Rebecca Felton could contribute her prodigious pen to her husband's speeches, but she had to mask her contributions and certainly could not speak for herself. She could write flaming editorials in defense of his campaign for the "plow boys" of Bartow County, but she could not sign those editorials in her own name. The Feltons' partnership was necessarily based on supporting the development of William Felton's career and the interests of William Felton's yeoman constituency. The emergence of Rebecca Felton's own political career awaited the development of a new political constituency in Georgia, a constituency that was shortly to take form throughout the New South.

It was the Woman's Christian Temperance Union (WCTU) that would provide Felton with an audience of her own for the first time. In 1881 Frances Willard, president of the WCTU, made her first southern organizing tour. Friends and supporters tried to dissuade her from making the trip in the first place. As one friend counseled, "It will be a most disastrous failure, for there are three great disadvantages under which you will labor—to go there as a woman, a Northern woman, and a Northern temperance woman."[23] Willard was therefore pleased at the warm reception her plea for home protection received from southern audiences. She was particularly heartened when Rebecca Latimer Felton joined the WCTU in 1886. Felton was a great asset to the fledgling organization, and the benefits were more than reciprocated. Regularly touring the state, she gave rousing speeches for the cause, holding forth against public ridicule and demonstrating that her powers as a speaker, if anything, exceeded her abilities in cold print. By the end of the decade, she had become one of the organization's most prominent orators.[24]

As important as the WCTU was for Felton's development as a public political figure, it was even more important for the way it allowed her to address the gender issue at the center of her concerns—the question of home protection. For Felton, the "drink demon" became a metaphor for the social consequences that the decline of the power of the individual planter and of agricultural life in general in the South had unleashed. In the burgeoning anonymity of the city and with the expansion of free labor, Felton found a threatening world, one full of the "glow of factory furnaces" and the "whirl of machinery." This was a world where a woman could not walk down a street in safety and where her children were particularly exposed and vulnerable. "Tonight," as she told one temperance audience, "there is not a city in Georgia where a decent woman's child can go, and be safe in its streets from the danger and temptation of liquor saloons."[25]

While the Civil War had dealt a crippling blow to the power of white southern men to protect their women, Felton now argued that the "drink demon" constituted an even more formidable threat. Drink promised to destroy what little protection remained to women and children by turning their fathers, husbands, and sons into useless drunkards. According to Felton, the temperance issue revealed the continuing, and in some ways increasingly critical, gap between the rightful place of domesticity in society and its subordinated second-class status in actuality. For a few "sin-cursed dollars, contended Felton, state legislators were even willing to bargain away the well-being of the entire younger generation." "I see them sell a license," she told her audience, "which says to the liquor dealer, you can for such a length of time destroy every man you can reach—not excepting my own son." "Friends, neighbors, citizens," queried Felton in one temperance speech, "what is this curse that walks in darkness and wastes at noonday? . . . Is it not the unholy gain that follows liquor selling—and the eternal loss that follows liquor drinking? . . . Oh Men of Georgia, when your hearts prompted you to legislate for hound dogs, and sand hill gophers—why haven't you protected your own offspring? It is this failure to protect that has raised the outcry of temperance women."[26]

As with the issue of slavery, the lure of profit continued to override and undercut men's allegiance to the domestic interests of their families and society as a whole. Now, though, matters were far worse. At least under slavery, the subordination of elite women's domestic sphere had been in some measure balanced by the extraordinary profitability of the planter's economic system. Class privilege had served to soften the impact of domestic subordination. In the face of their declining economic position, Felton insisted that elite men now needed to legislate domestic "protection" through the agency of the state. No longer capable of simply controlling their own plantations as relatively self-contained social worlds, they were now called upon to actively represent the domestic interests of their women and children in the political arena. In her temperance speeches around the state, Felton encouraged men to cast their votes for properly "feminized" candidates: "Vote for true men—men who will do your will—men pledged to your protection. Oh Men of Georgia! Your votes will either make or unmake the boys of this generation. This is a crisis. Stand to your homes and vote for no man who will not pledge himself to save these boys."[27]

Insofar as men had failed to take up her challenge and represent women's domestic interests politically, they had, according to Felton, "impeached their own manhood." Women were left with no alternative but to enter the political arena themselves and lobby for a policy of prohibition in defense of their maternal roles. As in the case of women's wartime organization into Ladies Aid Societies, public organizational activity under such circumstances did not constitute a rejection of motherhood. Quite the contrary, according to Felton, it manifested the reemergence of a similar kind of militant commitment to domestic defense, an "organized mother love," "*Mother love . . .* stung to desperation," a "Mother love grown bold in its agony."[28]

The wctu's politics of empowering motherhood brought elite southern women like Rebecca Felton to the threshold of an exciting but paradoxical new world. Achieving a free and independent motherhood required a precarious balancing act for female politicians with gender as the key to their agenda. While history had taught elite women of Felton's generation that they had to be prepared to earn their own living, the meager prospects for real autonomy for women in the straitened postwar economy led them back to the desirability of access to male income. Felton therefore hesitated to advocate that young women set their sights on the acquisition of a career. She was more eager to see the basic structure of the family, especially the white farm family, reformed along more gender equitable lines.

In the 1890s she took up speaking to rural audiences on the critical but undervalued role of women on the family farm. She urged farmers to recognize the contributions their wives made to farm operation. "In this day of scarce labor, I'd like to know what a farm in Georgia would amount to, as a home, unless there was a woman on it." Farmers, according to Felton, should discard the old adage "A dog, a woman and a walnut tree: The more you beat them the better they be" and replace it with greater respect and appreciation for wives and mothers. Rather than devote all his time and energy to his marketable crops, the farmer should realize that "the best crop a man ever raised in all his life was a crop of good obedient children."[29]

In 1891 Felton proposed a program to the state agricultural society that she called the "Wife's Farm." In recognition of the wife's contribution to the family farm, every farmer in the state should pledge himself to work a portion of his land as his "Wife's Farm." While the wife cooked the husband's breakfast, Felton suggested to her rural audiences, the husband should be out laboring in her fields. Felton assumed that the product of the "Wife's Farm" would be crops for home consumption rather than market production. In this way, the farmer could confront the "vexed question of commercial independence" while promoting the "contentment and happiness of the household."[30] A more balanced relationship between the interests of the family and the demands of the market would be the ultimate result of an agricultural system grounded in gender equity.

Felton claimed that the underlying message of domestic gender equity she offered her farmer audiences of the 1890s was similar to the advice she would have given the men of the antebellum planter class some thirty years earlier, had they asked. Confronted with the specter of a mounting agricultural depression, Felton herself saw the same dark vision: a vision in which southern agriculture and domesticity were undermined by white men's determination to pursue profit in the market at any human cost. Like the antebellum planter, the postwar farmer continued to orient himself toward a fickle market economy at the expense of the more solid and enduring interests of his family. Just as the planter's war had rendered him unable to protect his dependents, so the persistence of a market-oriented culture was once again threatening the very perpetuation of the farm family, leaving lower-class women and children unprotected and exposed.

In the aftermath of Civil War, when Felton herself felt overwhelmingly threatened, she focused her own fears onto the freedperson. Unable to blame the husband who could no longer support her as he once had been able to do, she displaced her anger on the *freedperson* who refused to return to his or her "place" in the postwar order of things. Once again, in the serious agricultural depression of the 1890s, her efforts to seek the roots of the problem in a diagnosis of gender imbalance and a program of domestic reform ended in race baiting. Felton was ultimately reduced to holding the black population, especially black men, responsible for the dire condition of white farm life. Since the most pressing need of the farm population was a "feeling of security in the homes we inhabit, where wives and daughters can be safely protected," it was all too easy to absolve the farmer for his failure to provide these and to visualize danger in terms of the threat of assault and rape on the part of black men: "I know of no evil, which more unsettles farm values and drives farmers to towns and other occupations than this lurking dread of outrage upon their helpless ones—in their homes and on the highways."[31]

Just how far out of balance Felton perceived southern gender relations to be in the 1890s can be seen in the lengths to which she took this argument. Poor white farm women in the 1890s were considerably more "vulnerable" and "exposed" than women of Felton's class had ever been, even in the darkest days of Reconstruction. During the 1890s it seemed to Felton that poor white women were losing their economic security and that their very lives and physical safety were in jeopardy. In the image of the rape of a poor farm woman on an isolated and desolate country road or homestead, Felton found a graphically explicit and emotionally explosive symbol to express the intensity of her fears for the sanctity of motherhood and the necessity for domestic reform.

Despite her best efforts to promote the elevation of motherhood and the realm of reproduction within the farm family, the condition of farm women and children appeared only to deteriorate in the 1890s. If farm men would not or could not sustain their wives and children in a progressive fashion, who or what could? In fact, the failure of gender reform in the countryside caused Felton to appeal with ever more conviction and intensity to the membership of elite women's voluntary organizations. Both because of their dedication to empowering motherhood and because of their commitment to the supremacy of their race, elite white women should throw themselves into reform efforts to improve the lot of rural women and children. The best vehicle to achieve such reform, Felton argued in speech after speech, was to be found in the expansion of educational opportunities for poor youth, especially poor white girls. "Why do I particularly mention poor white girls?" she questioned an audience of the United Daughters of the Confederacy. "Because," she answered, "these girls are the coming mothers of the great majority of the Anglo-Saxon race in the South. The future of the race for the next fifty years is in their hands."[32]

By raising the specter of "race degeneration" in the impoverishment and powerlessness of white motherhood, and by pointing to elite women as the only group likely to carry out the reforms necessary to improve the status of these women, Felton lent increased urgency and larger social significance to the organizational activities of elite white women. Should gender reform fail among the mass of the white population, the threat to the entire social structure was so critical that even the voluntary activities of elite women's organizations were not sufficient to the task at hand. Government intervention was required to place a floor below which white motherhood could not be allowed to sink. As much as elite women were the critical actors in voluntary familial reform activity, they were, like the WCTU before them, even more important as the key political pressure group that would move the government to regulate the family in the interests of an improved domestic life. In particular, women's organizations had to pressure the state government to pass compulsory education laws. It was not enough to improve the quality of rural schools. Children must be required to attend them. Furthermore, the ability of men and women to enter the familial relationship in the first place must be regulated by raising the age of consent and requiring marriage licenses and health certificates: "It will always be the intelligent home life of the nation which will hold our ship of state to its moorings as a republic and we can all appreciate the necessity of protecting home life and domestic interests. I believe as a method for the prevention of crime and for the protection of the helpless and innocent safeguards should be thrown around the issuance of marriage permits, known as marriage licenses. . . . A health certificate should have been required a hundred years ago—for the protection of the unborn."[33]

Ultimately, Felton was prepared to go so far as to demand sterilization for those women who were, in her opinion, incapable of maintaining a respectable family life. "Perhaps you may decide that my plan is too radical, but I do believe that a criminal woman should be made immune to childbearing as a punishment for crime," Felton asserted to her audience. Although she did not single out black women explicitly here, it would appear that Felton did have them particularly in mind when she proposed this scheme. Although she desired to "throw around another woman's daughter the safeguards which that less fortunate child needs" if the child was white, in the case of "erring" black women, she advocated compulsory curtailment of all reproductive capacity.[34] If the basis for racial superiority was grounded in an empowered white motherhood, as Rebecca Felton assumed, then the supposed racial inferiority of the black population must be reflected in a highly disorganized black motherhood and family. As she concluded in this speech,

> We have a problem to work out in this country—as to the best methods for the intelligent education of the colored race amongst us. That it is a serious problem no one will deny. Until we can find clean living, as a rule, and not simply as an exception in the colored homes of this country, we are simply walking over a hidden crater which may do as much general damage as Mt. Pelee did in the island of Martinique. The plan of prevention of crime, by making criminals immune to the

propagation of their own species, would go very far towards shutting off influx of infanticides and brazen prostitution among the ignorant and shameless.[35]

Government intervention to protect white women and children and the actual elimination of some black women's ability to reproduce would, according to Felton, create the kind of motherhood that was critical to the larger economic, social, and political well-being of the South. It was precisely at this juncture of class, race, and gender relations in the late 1890s that Felton came to commit herself publicly to suffrage for white women.

Instead of supporting suffrage for women out of a recognition of the common interests of all women, regardless of race, or the desirability of autonomy for women for its own sake, Felton advocated the enfranchisement of white women precisely because she perceived them to be so vulnerable and threatened in a world where they could only rely on themselves to protect their own domestic interests. She quickly became one of the most prominent spokespersons for the movement in the state. Like so many others in the North and South, her arguments in favor of the vote for women were not explicitly racist, but they were clearly exclusionary, couched in terms of empowering native-born white women to defend the greater interests of their motherhood.[36]

Indeed, Felton's commitment to white women's suffrage was a result of what she perceived to be a lifetime of failure on the part of white men to protect their wives and daughters and to give them sufficient space to discharge their maternal role. In Felton's view, when offered a choice between the interests of motherhood and the family or of profit and the market, most southern men had consistently chosen the latter, even when womanhood had been "exposed" as a result. The issue of woman suffrage offered southern men one last opportunity to redress the failure of their fathers and grandfathers by empowering their wives and daughters to represent directly the interests of domesticity. Although the "failure of statesmanship" that led to the Civil War was a result of white southern men's inability to recognize that "the time had come in the Providence of God to give every human life a chance for freedom," Felton hoped that the intervening generation of men had learned a lesson and would not engage in another "vain effort to hold . . . property rights," this time by continuing to control women rather than slaves.[37]

Fathers, according to Felton, should give their daughters the vote because they recognized the limits of their own ability to protect them and saw that they would be most effectively protected when empowered politically to protect themselves, especially against the power of an abusive mate.[38] Indeed, making

women into citizens would create the basis for a more equitable and companionate relationship between husband and wife. Political gender equity would
underwrite the construction of the family in its "best form," as a "school for
tenderness—for sympathy—for self-sacrifice—for forgetfulness of self—and
honest dealing as to privileges between husband and wife." The days of the "fox-
hunting, hard drinking—high playing—reckless living country squire," who
"played the tyrant in his home," were gone. They were as gone as the days of
"our great-grand-mothers," who were "too busy with the spinning wheel and
the loom to trouble their minds with elections and taxes."[39]

Rebecca Felton's hopes for a progressive politics of gender in the New South
were to be disappointed when Georgia's legislators revealed themselves to be
singularly recalcitrant. Even after the national Democratic party adopted
woman suffrage as a part of its presidential platform in 1916, Georgia legislators continued to object almost to a man. In Felton's mind, this behavior was
reminiscent of that manifested by their fathers and grandfathers over fifty years
before. By turning their backs on the national Democratic party, Georgia legislators had once again, Felton declared, "become a law unto yourself." History was apparently repeating itself. Prominent Georgia anti-suffragist Mildred
Rutherford testified before the legislature that a vote for the Nineteenth Amendment was tantamount to a vote for the Fifteenth, because granting the franchise
to black women would serve to reopen the whole question of enfranchising
black men. Nothing could be further from the truth, Felton countered before
the state legislative committee. Instead of contributing to the decline of white
supremacy by politically empowering the black population, the vote for women
would make a critical contribution to it by empowering white motherhood.[40]

As elsewhere in the South, it was anti-suffragists who first introduced racist arguments into the suffrage campaign, and as elsewhere, Georgia's representatives supported the anti-suffrage position by an overwhelming majority.
According to Felton, this failure of state legislators to grant the vote to white
women actually constituted a refusal to treat them as other than slaves. Although southern representatives tried to argue that they opposed the passage
of the Nineteenth Amendment because of their "steadfast belief in states rights—
their exalted and virginal devotion to the principle—handed down from father
to son—ever since the Civil War," the real reason Georgia legislators refused
to support suffrage for women, according to Felton, had nothing to do with
defending states' rights or even white supremacy. The real reason was because
these men were committed to their grandfathers' gender politics, which had
now become hopelessly obsolete: "The truth of the whole business lies in their
determination to hold the whip hand over the wives and mothers of the South!"

These men, however, would learn the same lesson that their grandfathers had before them: "I predict that woman suffrage will come to the South—despite the drastic and frantic opposition of nine-tenths of the Southern Democrats in Congress—at this time. They seem to be the lineal and legal heirs to all the *political debris of secession*. . . . They forget that the world is enfranchising its women as an act of right and justice. . . . It is their ignorance of what the world is doing—that now obsesses them."[41]

Knowledge of what the world was doing was to come to the state legislators of Georgia sooner than perhaps even Rebecca Latimer Felton could have hoped. On August 26, 1920, the Nineteenth Amendment to the U.S. Constitution was finally ratified. That which Georgia state legislators had claimed to fear most, the forcible arrival of woman suffrage through a federal amendment, had come to pass. The response of the entrenched political powers was a curious one. The state that had rushed to go on record first in opposition to the passage of the Nineteenth Amendment made even better speed in moving to be the first state to place a woman in the U.S. Senate. When Tom Watson, a longtime political ally of the Feltons, died with his term in the U.S. Senate unfinished in 1922, it provided Governor Thomas Hardwick of Georgia with the requisite opportunity. He initially offered the appointment to Watson's wife, Georgia Durham Watson, but she declined the honor. He then offered the appointment to Rebecca Latimer Felton, who accepted.

Felton was immediately flooded with congratulatory mail, not only from the state of Georgia but from across the country as well. One correspondent wrote that the appointment had "taken New York by surprise and has electrified her. Men and women alike are thrilled and enthusiastic."[42] Not only was the appointment "well earned," concluded a second correspondent, but it also constituted an honor to all women. It was "one of the signs of the times; the hand-writing is on the wall. Women are rapidly coming into their own."[43] The newly formed National Woman's Party responded to the appointment by asking Rebecca Felton to join their list of "eminent women" and to accept the honorary chairmanship of their political council. As Alice Paul, the vice president of the party, concluded, "Now that you are the first woman Senator your name has exceedingly great weight and we hope you will be willing to lend it to this campaign to secure a better lot for all women."[44]

For all her justified pride in the honor, Rebecca Latimer Felton must have been of two minds regarding the appointment. It reflected a due recognition of her political contributions to the state, and perhaps more important the changed status of women that had been effected as a result, but it was only a temporary, symbolic appointment, and her first Senate speech was also to be her last. As one correspondent pointed out, "Mr. Hardwick knows that Mrs. Felton has a following and Power in Georgia Superior to any Woman in the State, This Bunch of Flowers that He has tossed at your Feet does not cost Him anything yet, Since Women have been given the Franchise, his little Stunt is a Ballot winner." "Now Mrs. Felton, Why not you run for the U.S. Senate?"[45] Why not, indeed? The appointment was in fact a half gesture of the sort that Felton had come to expect from the southern male establishment over a long and active political life. As such, it reflected the ambiguous state of southern gender relations, even after sixty years of crisis and change. The secluded status of elite white women had indeed ended, and nothing marked that fact more clearly than Rebecca Felton's rising to give her acceptance speech on the floor of the U.S. Senate. Nevertheless, the purely symbolic nature of her appointment also reflected the reality that no clear-cut public position or power for women had yet emerged in the South.[46]

Just as the South was forever remaining old while becoming new, so, ever since the collapse of the traditional order during the Civil War and Reconstruction, had the new southern woman remained subordinate while becoming liberated. The ambivalent and contradictory story of Rebecca Latimer Felton should give us some idea of why this was the case. The life of this archetypal woman reformer reveals the dynamic of progressive self-assertion and reactionary resistance characteristic of the larger social order that she steadfastly sought to change. The very forces spurring the development of independence and autonomy among elite white women in the postwar South were at the same time frequently the bedrock of conservatism and reaction that impelled them backward to nostalgia for the hierarchies of patriarchy and race. The decline of the social and economic power of the planter class, which opened the door for the emergence of greater equity between the sexes, simultaneously reinforced the value of home "protection" and thus the ideal of gender dominance by men. White southerners' commitment to the "supremacy" of their race could be enlisted by gender reformers like Rebecca Felton to support the politics of empowering white motherhood. The larger consequence of the rigid racial hierarchy that emerged after the collapse of slavery was to deny the rights of black women as citizens and as mothers. Nevertheless, it was this denial that served to rationalize state legislators' opposition to granting the vote to white women as well. Ironic as it may appear in light of the Georgia legislature's refusal to ratify the Nineteenth Amendment less than three years earlier, the token appointment of Rebecca Felton as the first woman to sit in the U.S. Senate was perhaps the most fitting expression of the pattern of elite white gender relations that had developed in the postbellum South. As an honor graciously bestowed on her by her governor, not a right that Felton herself had earned, it marked the end, not the beginning, of a notable political career.

## NOTES

1. Rebecca Latimer Felton, *The Romantic Story of Georgia's Women* (Atlanta: Atlanta Georgian and Sunday American, 1930), 44.

2. Ibid., 45.

3. See A. Elizabeth Taylor, "Development of the Woman's Suffrage Movement in Georgia," *Georgia Historical Quarterly* 62 (December 1958): 339–54, and "The Last Phase of the Women's Suffrage Movement in Georgia," *Georgia Historical Quarterly* 63 (March 1959): 11–28.

4. For a discussion of the centrality of protection to antebellum white gender relations, see Bertram Wyatt-Brown, *Southern Honor: Ethics and Behavior in the Old South* (New York: Oxford University Press, 1982). For the ways in which the Civil War stressed the quid pro quo of white southern gender relations, see Victoria E. Bynum, "War within a War: Women's Participation in the Revolt of the North Carolina Piedmont, 1863–1865," *Frontiers* 4, no. 3 (1987): 43–49; Drew Faust, "Altars of Sacrifice: Confederate Women and Narratives of War," *Journal of American History* 76, no. 4 (1990): 1200–28; Donna D. Krug, "The Folks Back Home: The Confederate Homefront during the Civil War" (PhD diss., University of California, Irvine, 1990); and LeeAnn Whites, *The Civil War as a Crisis in Gender: Augusta, Georgia, 1860–1890* (Athens: University of Georgia Press, 1995).

5. The outcome of this wartime rupturing of antebellum gender roles is contested. In her pathbreaking study, *The Southern Lady: From Pedestal to Politics, 1830–1930* (Chicago: University of Chicago Press, 1970), Anne Scott argued that the Civil War "opened every door" for elite white southern women. More recently, historians have argued in a more pessimistic vein. Suzanne Lebsock, *The Free Women of Petersburg: Status and Culture in a Southern Town, 1784–1860* (New York: W. W. Norton, 1984), suggests that impoverished and defeated white men were not inclined to tolerate increased gender equity with any more equanimity than they greeted the prospect of racial equity. Jean Friedman, *The Enclosed Garden: Women and Community in the Evangelical South, 1830–1900* (Chapel Hill: University of North Carolina Press, 1985), and George Rable, *Civil Wars: Women and the Crisis of Southern Nationalism* (Urbana: University of Illinois Press, 1989), have carried this line of argument further and suggested that the autonomous roles women took up in the context of war had little lasting impact on postwar gender relations. More attention to the experience of individual women whose experience spanned the period may help sort out the nature of the relationship between persistence and change in women's roles and gender relations as well. See Kathleen Berkeley, "Elizabeth Avery Merriwether, 'An Advocate for Her Sex': Feminism and Conservatism in the Post Civil War South," *Tennessee Historical Quarterly* 43 (Winter 1984): 390–407; Joan Cashin, "Varina Howell Davis," in *Portraits of American Women: From Settlement to Present*, ed. C. J. Barker-Benfield and Catherine Clinton, 259–75 (New York, St. Martin's, 1991); and Nell Irvin Painter, "The Journal of Ella Gertrude Clanton Thomas: An Educated White Woman in the Eras of Slavery, War, and Reconstruction," in *The Secret Eye: The Journal of Ella Gertrude Clanton Thomas, 1848–1889*, ed. Virginia Ingraham Burr, 1–67 (Chapel Hill: University of North Carolina Press, 1990).

6. Treatments of Rebecca Latimer Felton's political career focus almost exclusively on her work in the male political arena. See John E. Talmadge, *Rebecca Latimer Felton: Nine Stormy Decades* (Athens: University of Georgia Press, 1960). See also Josephine Bone Floyd, "Rebecca Latimer Fel-

ton, Political Independent," *Georgia Historical Quarterly* 30 (March 1946): 14–84, and "Rebecca Latimer Felton, Champion of Women's Rights," *Georgia Historical Quarterly* 30 (June 1946): 81–104. This focus ignores both the domestic impetus for Felton's participation in the formally constituted male political arena and the interrelated emergence of a whole world of female political activity on Felton's part in the Ladies Aid Societies, Ladies Memorial Association, the United Daughters of the Confederacy, the Woman's Christian Temperance Union, the General Federation of Women's Clubs, as well as the Georgia Woman's Suffrage Association. Anne Scott first outlined this move from "pedestal to politics" among elite white southern women in *The Southern Lady*. See also Friedman, *The Enclosed Garden*, 110–30; Kathleen Berkeley, "The Ladies Want to Bring Reform to the Public School?: Public Education and Women's Rights in the Post Civil War South," *History of Education Quarterly* 44 (Spring 1984): 45–58; LeeAnn Whites, "The Charitable and the Poor: The Emergence of Domestic Politics in Augusta, Georgia, 1860–1880," *Journal of Social History* 17 (Summer 1984): 601–15; and Anastatia Sims, "Feminism and Femininity in the New South: White Women's Organizations in North Carolina, 1888–1980" (PhD diss., University of North Carolina at Chapel Hill, 1985).

7. Rebecca Latimer Felton, *Country Life in Georgia in the Days of My Youth* (Atlanta: Index Printing, 1919), 29.

8. Rebecca Latimer Felton, "Impact of the Civil War on Women," May 20, 1892, Felton Papers, Special Collections, University of Georgia, Athens, Ga.

9. Scott, *The Southern Lady*, 3–22. See also Catherine Clinton, *Plantation Mistress: Woman's World in the Old South* (New York, Pantheon Books, 1982).

10. Felton, *Country Life*, 25. See also Felton, "Impact of the Civil War on Women." For a more general discussion of the ways race and class position tended to override gender identification, see Jacqueline Jones, *Labor of Love, Labor of Sorrow: Black Women, Work and the Family, from Slavery to the Present* (New York, Basic Books, 1985); and Elizabeth Fox-Genovese, *Within the Plantation Household: Black and White Women of the Old South* (Chapel Hill, University of North Carolina Press, 1989).

11. George Fitzhugh, *Sociology for the South or the Failure of Free Society* (New York: L. 8. Franklin, 1966), 218–14.

12. Felton, *Country Life*, 79–94.

13. Ibid., 104.

14. In her recollections Felton gives a graphic description of the state in which she found her plantation upon returning home: "I never saw the home any more until August, 1865. When I reached the gate I picked up the springs that had been a part of my dead child's fine baby carriage, also the arm of a large parlor mahogany chair that had also burned. Desolation and destruction everywhere, bitter, grinding poverty—slaves all gone, money also" (Felton, *Country Life*, 89).

15. Rebecca Latimer Felton, "Education of Veteran's Daughters," 1893, Felton Papers. The fact that Felton came to identify with lower-class white women in the context of her own class fall does not mean that the sentiment was reciprocated. For a discussion of the difference class location could make in the political commitments of Southern women, see Jacquelyn Dowd Hall, "O. Delight Smith's Progressive Era: Labor, Feminism, and Reform in the Urban South," in *Visible Women: New Essays on American Activism*, ed. Nancy A. Hewitt and Suzanne Lebsock, 166–98 (Champaign: University of Illinois Press, 1993); Dolores Janiewski, *Sisterhood Denied: Race, Gender, and Class in a New South Community* (Philadelphia: Temple University Press, 1985); and Stephanie McCurry, "Their Ways Were Not Our Ways" (paper delivered at the Southern Historical Association Meeting, Houston, Tex., 1985).

16. Felton, "Impact of the Civil War on Women." See also Rebecca Latimer Felton, "Southern Womanhood in Wartimes," n.d., Felton Papers.

17. For a further discussion of this dilemma in the particular context of the nineteenth-century South, see Suzanne Lebsock's analysis of the position of free black women in antebellum Petersburg in *The Free Women of Petersburg*, 87–111. For a similar discussion in a different time and place, see Judith Bennett, "History that Stands Still: Women's Work in the European Past," *Feminist Studies* 14 (Summer 1988): 269–83.

18. Felton, *Country Life*, 88.

19. Felton was inclined to use the same incidents from her life over and over again to illustrate her arguments. In the case of displacing responsibility for the decline of the planter-class onto black men, her favorite example was a story of crop theft. See Felton, *Country Life*, 57–59.

20. Talmadge, *Rebecca Latimer Felton*, chap. 5.

21. Felton, *Romantic Story*, 227.

22. Talmadge, *Rebecca Latimer Felton*, 83.

23. Frances Willard, *Woman and Temperance or the Work and Workers of the* WCTU (Hartford, Conn.: Park Publishing, 1883), 570.

24. Lula Barnes Ansley, *History of the Georgia Woman's Christian Temperance Union from Its Organization, 1883–1907* (Columbus, Ga.: Gilbert, 1914), 58. For a further discussion of the Georgia Woman's Christian Temperance Union in the nineteenth century, see Henry Anseim Scamp, *King Alcohol in the Realm of King Cotton* (Chicago: Blakely, 1888), 677–78; and, more generally, Ruth Bordin, *Woman and Temperance: The Quest for Power and Liberty, 1873–1900* (Philadelphia: Temple University Press, 1981).

25. Rebecca Latimer Felton, "Temperance," 1892, Felton Papers.

26. Ibid. For a discussion of the centrality of drink to southern male culture, see Ted Ownby, *Subduing Satan: Religion, Recreation, and Manhood in the Rural South, 1865–1920* (Chapel Hill: University of North Carolina Press, 1990).

27. Felton, "Temperance."

28. Ibid.

29. Rebecca Latimer Felton, "Southern Women and Farm Life," n.d., Felton Papers.

30. Rebecca Latimer Felton, "The Before Breakfast Club," 1891, Felton Papers.

31. Felton, "Southern Women and Farm Life." Joel Williamson, *The Crucible of Race: Black White Relations in the American South since Emancipation* (New York: Oxford University Press, 1984), discusses this atmosphere. For a further discussion of race, gender, and the lynching of black men, see Jacquelyn Dowd Hall, *Revolt against Chivalry: Jessie Daniel Ames and the Women's Campaign against Lynching* (New York: Columbia University Press, 1979).

32. Felton, "The Education of Veteran's Daughters." See also "The Duty and Obligation that Lies on Southern Women," n.d., Felton Papers.

33. Rebecca Latimer Felton, "Rescue Work," n.d., Felton Papers. See also "The Problems that Interest Motherhood," in Felton, *Country Life*, 279–83.

34. Felton, "Rescue Work."

35. Ibid.

36. See, e.g., Rebecca Latimer Felton, "Votes for Women," n.d., Felton Papers, and "Why Am I a Suffragist? The Subjection of Women and the Enfranchisement of Women," in Felton, *Country Life*, 246–60.

37. Felton, "Votes for Women," In retrospect, clear parallels can be drawn between southern black women's efforts to organize to protect themselves against abusive white men or against debilitating

stereotypes in their own communities and the organizing efforts of southern white women like Felton, even though white women rarely recognized the similarities between them at the time. See Darlene Clark Hine, "'We Specialize in the Wholly Impossible': The Philanthropic Work of Black Women," in *Lady Bountiful Revisited: Women, Philanthropy and Power*, ed. Kathleen McCarthy, 70–93 (New Brunswick: Rutgers University Press, 1990); and Anne Firor Scott, "Most Invisible of All: Black Women's Voluntary Organizations," *Journal of Southern History* 61 (February 1990): 3–22.

38. Felton, "Votes for Women."

39. Ibid.

40. Rebecca Latimer Felton, "Southern Congressman Opposing Equal Suffrage," n.d., Felton Papers. For a further discussion of the relationship between the woman suffrage movement and the politics of white supremacy in the South, see Marjorie Spruill Wheeler, *New Women of the New South: The Leaders of the Woman Suffrage Movement in the Southern States* (New York: Oxford University Press, 1993).

41. Felton, "Southern Congressman Opposing Equal Suffrage."

42. Corinne Stecker Smith to Rebecca Latimer Felton, October 7, 1922, Felton Papers.

43. Henrietta Grossman to Rebecca Latimer Felton, October 3, 1922, Felton Papers.

44. Alice Paul to Rebecca Latimer Felton, October 27, 1922, Felton Papers.

45. F. A. Powell to Rebecca Latimer Felton, October 7, 1922, Felton Papers. For a further discussion of the ways in which political expediency would momentarily elevate white women's political status in the South, see Judith McArthur, "Democrats Divided: Why the Texas Legislature Gave Women Primary Suffrage in 1918" (Paper delivered at the Southern Historical Meeting, Fort Worth, Tex., 1991).

46. As one correspondent described the situation, "Woman is not what she once was, pure and good, and bless her, the fault is not hers that she has changed. Time was when man was her sword and her provider and she, perforce, was above the ten commandments, but man failed, and she was compelled to become her own sword and provider so man and woman instead of being one, became competitors. . . . Alas! The race of Toombs, of Webster and of Calhoun has run out. That is the reason that Women feel impelled to go into politics. Why don't you say it?" H. L. Trisler to Rebecca Latimer Felton, October 27, 1922, Felton Papers.

# Mary Latimer McLendon
## (1840–1921)

## *"Mother of Suffrage Work in Georgia"*

STACEY HORSTMANN GATTI

Mary Latimer McLendon, like her better-known sister, Rebecca Latimer Felton, was raised in an antebellum slaveholding Georgia family and supported the Confederacy during the Civil War as a loyal daughter of the Old South. Following the war and Reconstruction, both Latimer sisters reacted to the end of their antebellum society by creating a new identity for white women of the New South that included bringing women into politics as both activists and voters. Mary, unlike her sister, however, did not move into politics through her role as political wife, but rather as a consequence of facing the challenges of urban life in the New South. As a resident of the rapidly growing city of Atlanta during the late nineteenth century, McLendon faced the struggles of maintaining the values of white womanhood she learned as a young woman. As an elite white Southern woman, although interested in listening to political discussions, McLendon initially accepted politics as men's domain. She also believed that white women should bear the responsibility for sustaining and protecting the moral development of their families and communities, but by the end of the nineteenth century, after managing an urban household, raising three children, and serving as an active church member and temperance reformer, she became convinced that white women could no longer properly fulfill their responsibilities without moving into politics. As McLendon explained to her sister members of the Georgia Woman's Christian Temperance Union in 1910, "To do her duty nobly and well, the woman of today must take her place at the ballot box beside her husband, father and brothers, and use the ballot, not as a toy or plaything, but as a tool with which to carve out for the children of the race a better and brighter future."[1] McLendon thus advocated the enfranchisement

MARY LATIMER MCLENDON
Courtesy of Manuscript, Archives, and Rare Book Library,
Emory University.

of white women in her state, and throughout her adult life she would work to bring the voices of white women into politics.

McLendon's experience as a wife, mother, and community leader in Atlanta during and following the Civil War illustrates the changing roles of urban white southern women adjusting to the demands and realities of the New South and creating a new political and social identity for themselves. This identity continued to connect women to family, church, and community but also propelled women into moral reform and political activism. Thousands of other white southern women joined McLendon as they swelled the ranks of the Woman's Christian Temperance Union, but fewer women shared in her enthusiastic support for woman suffrage through the National American Woman Suffrage Association. McLendon's story of the struggle for white women to define the parameters of their participation in the political and social world of the New South illuminates trends followed by other white women in Georgia, the South, and, albeit with some substantial modifications, throughout the United States as the nation moved from its agrarian, rural roots to a more industrial, urban country during the years following the Civil War. Women who grew up in leading plantation families found themselves adjusting to new economic, social, and political conditions by engaging in political activism on their own behalf.[2]

During her childhood, Mary Latimer's family provided the financial, educational, and emotional support that made possible her adult activism. By the time Mary entered their lives on June 24, 1840, her parents, Charles Latimer and Eleanor Swift Latimer, and her five-year-old sister, Rebecca, were already well-established residents of DeKalb County. The family, descendants of Maryland and Virginia planters, owned a plantation, a general store, and a tavern, and they ran the local post office on Covington Road ten miles south of Decatur. Charles Latimer's devotion to the cause of his children's education, even when it required personal and financial sacrifice, initially ensured his children's status as members of the southern elite, but ultimately this education prepared his daughters to reinterpret their role in society. The year Mary was born her father coordinated efforts to improve the educational opportunities for the community by helping to build a quality school. He donated land and money, hired its first teacher, and immediately enrolled his eldest daughter in the school.[3] When this initial venture of maintaining a quality neighborhood school on his own property failed, Charles Latimer remained committed to providing an education for his children. In 1845, as Mary approached school age, he sold his Covington Road businesses and moved the family to the city of Decatur, where his children could attend school, while he remained on the South River plantation ten miles away, visiting his family only on Sundays. When his daughters finished their primary school education, Latimer sent both Rebecca and Mary to female academies, Madison Female Academy and Southern Masonic Female College at Covington, respectively. Both young women graduated with first honors and prepared to take their places as part of the antebellum plantation elite.[4]

The Latimer family embraced the religious revivals that swept through Georgia during Mary's childhood, and both Latimer daughters joined the Methodist Church as young women. Through the moral teachings of these revivals and the churches that followed, they joined their first temperance clubs. These early reform efforts, however, did not bring them into public work at this point. The Methodist Church still forbade women from praying aloud in church beyond the level of a whisper at a mourning bench, but it provided them with the moral foundation that eventually led both women into a public advocacy that would include public speaking.[5]

Soon after they completed their formal education, both of the Latimer sisters embraced traditional roles for women. They married, established their own households, and began to bear and raise their children. At this point their stories diverge. For Rebecca, marriage took her away from the city, to a plantation in Cartersville, where she lived out the rest of her life as the wife of a doctor and politician, eventually becoming a prominent public figure and even a politician in her own right, and throughout her life she identified herself as a "country" woman.[6] For Mary, Atlanta beckoned, and she spent most of the rest of her life as a resident and eventually a leading citizen of that city. Even though Mary and Rebecca remained close during their adulthood, championing the same political causes and reform movements, including temperance, prison reform, improvements in education, and woman suffrage, Mary embraced a city life and urban character that would shape her own personal and political growth and that would be reflected in the particular arguments she used to defend women's political activities.

On January 29, 1860, Mary Latimer married Nicholas A. McLendon of Atlanta at her parents' plantation, after which the young couple established their new home in a two-story stone house at the corner of Peachtree and Baker Streets in the heart of Atlanta. Nick McLendon, six years her senior, had moved to the young city of Atlanta in 1848 while still a teenager, and sought his fortune as a member of that city's growing merchant class. After working as a clerk for a prominent merchant and cotton buyer, A. Dulin, Nick opened up his own wholesale business and joined the city's first military organization, the Gate City Guards. On the eve of the Civil War the young couple's lives seemed quite promising. In a letter Eleanor Latimer wrote to her daughter Rebecca, dated April 1861, she reported that Mary and Nick were making plans to visit relatives throughout the state. Mary had purchased a new silk dress for the occasion, and her parents were looking forward to the opportunity to spend time with their new grandson, Charles Latimer McLendon.[7]

Despite the obvious turmoil of the Civil War, the young McLendon family fared relatively well. They remained in Atlanta for most of the war. Nick McLendon served the Confederacy as a member of Major Dillard's Quartermaster Department while Mary bore her second son, Edgar H. McLendon, and occupied herself with domestic responsibilities.[8] They remained in town through the siege of Atlanta, during which their cement basement provided refuge for them and many of the neighbors who shared its shelter until they could dig and reinforce their own cellars. The McLendons finally evacuated the city under the orders of General Hood, fleeing to Crawfordville, where Mary and her family stayed for the duration of the war.[9]

During Reconstruction the young family returned to Atlanta and purchased a "small brick cottage" on Washington Street. The McLendon family welcomed a new addition with the birth of their third child, their only daughter, Mary Eleanor McLendon.[10] While the family adjusted to the new house and the new baby, Nick McLendon struggled to find his place in this New South city. As the city of Atlanta sought to rebuild after the war, its leaders and promoters recognized that the fundamental structure of the Old South collapsed with the end of the Confederacy and the subsequent abolition of slavery through the Thirteenth Amendment. New South boosters sought to create a new society by expanding the economic base of the region. Henry Grady and Atlanta boosters encouraged and developed industrial and commercial interests, which included improving the city's education and transportation systems, and actively promoted Atlanta as the center of the New South to potential investors from outside the region. Nick McLendon, who had already explored his mercantile interests, worked in various different New South occupations throughout the postbellum years, including schoolteaching and working in a livery stable before he finally found his way to the position as the superintendent of the new Metropolitan Street Car Company. The McLendons, thus, found themselves in the center of the booster spirit that pervaded Atlanta during the postbellum years.[11]

As Nick worked to find a new role in the bustling city of Atlanta, the rise of the New South also impacted Mary McLendon's life. Between 1868 and 1880 Mary McLendon devoted most of her time to traditional women's pursuits—caring for her growing family, keeping house, and attending church—but while embracing her traditional roles she simultaneously paved the way for an increasingly public life as she reacted to changing circumstances in her own city. She took her first steps into public action early in her marriage. Soon after arriving in Atlanta, Mary McLendon joined Trinity Methodist Church. Through her membership in this urban church McLendon would deepen her devotion to moral reform, and the church would provide her with an acceptable outlet in the public domain for her energy in those issues, especially temperance.[12]

During the early 1880s throughout Georgia, especially in Atlanta and other urban areas, the increasingly visible effects of alcohol and debates over prohibition laws intensified. Methodist churches had long provided institutional support to the temperance cause. Georgia's Methodist ministers regularly promoted temperance not only from their pulpits but also by allowing temperance organizations to meet in their facilities. Most of these organizations were run by and for men, and there were few women's temperance organizations in the South prior to 1880. Additionally, southern Methodist women had previously been constrained by their church's belief that women should not speak in public. Nevertheless, new social and political conditions and positive role models from other regions of the country would soon usher in the winds of change that would propel faithful Methodist women, like Mary McLendon, into public reform activities.[13]

Prior to the Civil War, southern women rejected reform organizations that had been initiated in the North. By the 1880s, however, southern women recognized shared concerns and values with northern women on the issue of temperance and now put aside sectional prejudices to join a national organization that would fight for a common cause. In 1873 a group of women in Hillsboro, Ohio, conducted a "Crusade" of prayer against their local saloons. The reaction to those demonstrations led to the creation of the Woman's Christian Temperance Union the following year. By the end of the 1870s the movement had spread throughout much of the nation, and the WCTU had successfully recruited members from the ranks of churchgoing women, especially from Methodist and Baptist churches. Members were originally attracted to the prayerful crusade, but in 1881 WCTU president Frances Willard expanded the tactics of the WCTU, admonishing the women to "Do Everything." By "everything," Willard explained, women should engage not only in such traditionally accepted activities as prayer and moral suasion but also with education, publicity, press, and political action. The women, consequently, used a socially acceptable cause to move into the world of politics.[14]

Willard and the WCTU soon set out to spread their message to the South. The organization sent the National WCTU Chairman of Southern Work, Eliza Stewart, on a speaking tour, and in April 1880 she delivered a public temperance speech at McLendon's own Trinity Methodist Church. After the address Stewart helped the women organize their own local union of the WCTU, and within a few days two hundred women had joined the organization. Women in other Georgia cities soon formed local WCTU unions, and in 1883 they joined together to form the Georgia WCTU. Middle class and elite white women throughout the state began to recognize that they could exert a positive influence over their society by participating in this national movement.[15]

In their efforts to recruit white southern members into their organization, the National WCTU carefully crafted its agenda and organizational structure to meet southern needs and concerns. Recognizing that white southerners had shunned northern reform organizations prior to the Civil War at least in part due to the connection between northern moral reformers and abolitionism, the National WCTU quickly allowed state and local unions to determine their own membership criteria and to select their own departments of work. The only required line of work was some aspect of temperance reform. Frances Willard and other national leaders encouraged all white WCTU members to join with black women in their communities, but how, when, and on what terms this work took place was left to the discretion of the local unions. The Georgia WCTU formed as a white woman's organization. White women in Atlanta did work with local black women's temperance groups during the 1880s, before black men were disenfranchised, but those efforts were infrequent. The Georgia WCTU also operated a department of "Work Among Colored People," but that work, which was usually reported on with a missionary tone rather than as collaborative efforts, was only undertaken sporadically. Throughout the late nineteenth and early twentieth centuries, the Georgia WCTU remained a white women's organization and was overwhelmingly concerned with protecting the interests of the white community.[16]

Mary McLendon enthusiastically embraced this new organization. She joined the Atlanta WCTU in 1880 and attended the temperance prayer meetings held at Trinity Methodist Church and public meetings held throughout the city. She assumed the office of president of the newly formed South Side Union in 1887. As president of this local union, McLendon conducted weekly meetings at Trinity Methodist Church, initially leading women in prayer and Bible readings, then expanding their educational duties to include sponsoring Sunday School programs, and ultimately bringing the women out of the confines of the church to deliver their message to prisons and schools.[17]

Throughout its first decade the WCTU enjoyed the support of Methodist and Baptist ministers, including those who had previously preached against women speaking in public. Recognizing temperance reform as an acceptable line of work for their women members, southern ministers welcomed national WCTU speakers into their churches and encouraged women to hold meetings in church

facilities and to speak in public to audiences of both sexes. When women temperance reformers pushed their work into other, more clearly political, work,
however, southern ministers would withdraw their support, causing the southern members of the WCTU necessarily to engage in an extended debate over
the extent to which women should engage in public and political work. Mary
McLendon would find herself in the center of this debate.

National WCTU organizers, propelled by Frances Willard's "Do Everything"
admonition in 1881, had grown increasingly frustrated in their efforts to accomplish their political aims as citizens without the vote, and thus they embraced
the cause of woman suffrage in 1887 as a means to an end. As news spread of
the National WCTU's decision to embrace woman suffrage, a cause endorsed
prior to the Civil War by abolitionists, southerners reconsidered their support
for this organization. When the Georgia WCTU gathered in Savannah for their
annual meeting, they found all the churches in the city closed to them. The
Masonic Temple provided them with an alternate meeting site, but the mayor
responded by refusing to deliver his usual welcoming address. The Georgia
WCTU clearly believed that this new hostility to their organization related to
the National WCTU's suffrage position, so the following year the Georgia WCTU
drafted a carefully worded response in which they declared "it to be the duty
of this Convention to adopt *only* those principles espoused and plans devised
by the National Woman's Christian Temperance Union as are best suited to the
needs of our Southern work."[18] This response seemed to quell the criticism, and
the churches again opened their doors to the Georgia WCTU.

That compromise, however, would prove to be short lived, because discussions of woman suffrage continued in Georgia, and some Georgia women, including McLendon and other members of the Georgia WCTU, began to embrace
this cause of votes for women. In 1890 Mary McLendon attended the National
WCTU annual convention, which was held in Atlanta. WCTU president Frances
Willard delivered her annual address to a large audience and presented a strong
defense of women's participation in public work, including politics. Speaking
specifically to the men in her audience, Willard explained, "My brothers, do
not misunderstand us, we are not overstepping our sphere, we are only laboring to get to one end of the line while you stand at the other, to help you lift the
burdens of the world."[19] Willard did not directly address the issue of woman
suffrage, but left that responsibility up to Mrs. Zeralda Wallace of Indiana,
mother of General Lew Wallace, the famed author of *Ben-Hur*. Mrs. Wallace
spoke on a Sunday, and according to Georgia WCTU historian Lula Ansley, the
large crowd that gathered demonstrated their approval through a standing ova-
tion of waving handkerchiefs. Those in attendance were persuaded. Georgia

WCTU president Jane Sibley left a reception promoting establishment of franchise departments proclaiming, "Now, for the first time I publicly declare myself in favor of woman's ballot, and I will do my best to get the Georgia WCTU to adopt a franchise department." Even though the Georgia WCTU had not yet endorsed woman suffrage, the issue was clearly gaining some attention.[20]

The growing intensity of women's reform efforts and the reconsideration of women's roles within these movements corresponded to a transitional time in Mary McLendon's personal life. Her youngest child, Nellie, was graduated with top honors from Atlanta's Girls' High School in 1885. Thereafter, although Nellie and her two older brothers occasionally resided at the family home, they steadily pursued their own occupations, primarily in clerical and sales jobs. The McLendon marriage apparently entered a new phase as Nick moved out of the family residence. With her husband out of the house and her children pursuing their own careers, Mary was able to devote her time to her public work.[21]

Mary McLendon responded to these changes in her personal life and to the recent developments in white southern women's public activities by beginning what would become a lifelong pursuit to convince white southern women reformers to embrace political activism, including woman suffrage. In 1890 McLendon wrote a paper for the annual meeting of the Georgia WCTU, providing a rationale for women's entry into politics and basing her argument on women's traditionally accepted roles and responsibilities as mothers and homemakers. Through this paper, which principally described the effects of the 1887 repeal of Atlanta's 1885 prohibition law, McLendon presented a female-centered critique of the social and economic effects of alcohol and introduced her proposals for a multifaceted approach to reform, including both education and political activism. In effect, she adopted the arguments Frances Willard had made and shaped them for a southern audience. McLendon's fundamental concern with intemperance stemmed from its impact on the family, especially on dependent women and children. In condemning the actions of the anti-prohibitionist Mayor Glenn, she wrote, "If he will only assure us that . . . our men will be sober and virtuous, to accompany sober and virtuous women, and decent enough to set a correct example to the children we give them, we will forgive him . . . [because] a drunken man can bring greater anguish and distress to a household than anything in the world."[22] McLendon argued that because women were directly affected by alcohol abuse, they were justified in using any means necessary to protect themselves, including entering the political realm, especially when men would not engage in this fight. In closing she pledged, "We will do our best to bring men, women, and children of Atlanta to a knowledge of the great blessing accruing from right living by totally abstaining from the sin of liquor selling and drinking."[23] Through her use of a "home protection" argument, McLendon had not only justified women's participation in the public reform work, but also began to outline her arguments in favor of women's political work.[24]

From this point on McLendon increased her involvement in the activities of the Georgia WCTU, beginning with the quest to publicize temperance while also educating school-age children about the dangers of alcohol and the virtues of temperance. While attending the National WCTU convention in Atlanta in 1890, McLendon was appointed to the newly created position of Superintendent of the Demorest Medal Contest for the Georgia WCTU, which annually awarded medals for the best student essays on temperance. When this appointment was approved at the Georgia WCTU convention a few months later, Mary McLendon began an endeavor that she would continue throughout the rest of her life, and through it she would devote her time and energy to promoting temperance education both within the schools and at public meetings. McLendon explained that Frances Willard had encouraged members of the WCTU to take up this work "[to drill] Prohibition into the brains of young people, and through them [penetrate] the craniums of the voters of this and other nations," and argued that this line of work "exceeds any one method of which I have cognizance."[25]

For the rest of her life McLendon would continue to promote and coordinate the work of the Georgia WCTU's medal contests as a means of educating all Georgians, especially children. This work, she believed, served the WCTU's long-term strategy of promoting temperance support among the general population. The medals themselves were donated by William Jennings Demorest, a wealthy prohibition proponent, but the local chapters of the WCTU bore the cost of publicity, postage, and other miscellaneous expenses. During years in which the Georgia WCTU experienced financial difficulties, Mary McLendon paid some of those costs out of her own pocket. She devoted her own time, energy, and money to this work because she believed, as she stated repeatedly, that this work was indispensable if temperance supporters were to win additional converts to the cause, both children and their parents along with neighbors. Her continued interest in these programs demonstrated the seriousness with which she continued to view women's connections with children even while her interest in politics grew.[26]

Despite McLendon's genuine enthusiasm for both education and publicity as a means of stirring up temperance support, she grew frustrated with the limitations of these tactics. The children she might successfully influence could not immediately end the problems brought about by alcohol abuse, and McLendon believed that other methods must be employed to win legislative battles. Moral reformers needed to increase their direct influence over political decisions by speaking to elected officials, but even that influence would not be sufficient. Ultimately, she believed politicians would only respond to appeals brought by women if women had the vote.

McLendon soon moved beyond general statements about women's political influence, publicly embraced the cause of woman suffrage, and began her efforts to promote that cause in Georgia. In 1892 she joined the Georgia Woman Suffrage Association, an organization founded in 1890 by Augusta and Claudia Howard of Columbus, Georgia, and affiliated with the National American Woman Suffrage Association, and two years later McLendon and Margaret Chandler formed an Atlanta branch of the GWSA whose initial membership of forty men and women more than doubled the size of the state organization.[27] McLendon and the other leaders of the Georgia Woman Suffrage Association were encouraged by that rapid growth. They also recognized that support for woman suffrage in Georgia was not widespread, and they continued to believe that greater exposure to pro-suffrage advocates and their arguments would win converts. Consequently, they believed that an indispensable opportunity presented itself when the National American Woman Suffrage Association decided to hold its annual convention in Georgia in 1895. Surely, they argued, Georgians would support the cause when they saw and heard national leaders, such as Frances Willard's friend and fellow temperance advocate Susan B. Anthony and the Methodist minister Anna Howard Shaw, explain that woman suffrage was both a matter of equal justice and political expediency for moral reform movements.[28]

In late January 1895 McLendon delivered the official welcome address on behalf of the GWSA to the ninety-three delegates from twenty-eight states and their invited guests who gathered in DeGive's Opera House in Atlanta for the first NAWSA convention held outside of the nation's capital. In her speech, McLendon decried the injustice of women's subordinate legal status in Georgia and highlighted the necessity of the vote for women's self-protection. She stated, "It is with difficulty that women can secure a hearing before a legislative committee to petition for laws to ameliorate their own condition, or to secure compulsory training in the public schools, that their children may be brought up in the way they should go, and become sober, virtuous citizens." The argument that women, including Georgia women, both deserved and needed the vote was repeatedly echoed throughout the convention as Susan B. Anthony, Anna Howard Shaw, and numerous southern politicians spoke before standing-room-only crowds, thus giving the suffrage advocates the publicity they sought.[29]

Just as the National WCTU recognized that if they hoped to recruit white southern women into their organization, they would have to allow their southern unions to remain racially segregated, the national suffrage association, NAWSA, well understood the challenges they faced in the South on racial matters. The first woman suffragists in the country were abolitionists, and those early members continued to lead NAWSA at the end of the nineteenth century. Some of these former abolitionists, however, would soon modify their stance and even went so far as to employ race-based arguments in a direct appeal to the white South. In an 1890 article in the *Woman's Journal*, Henry Blackwell crafted an argument in favor of woman suffrage as "A Solution to the Southern Question." He argued that "The evils of an illiterate suffrage are felt and deplored alike North and South," but that the solution rested with woman suffrage rights, whether qualified by literacy or not. Other suffrage restrictions, he argued, would not be necessary "if educated Southern women were enfranchised, [because] there would no longer be a Negro majority of voters in any State."[30] Blackwell repeated these sentiments in a speech at the 1895 NAWSA convention in Atlanta, highlighting data for Georgia, where, he argued, "there are 149,895 white women who can read and write, and 143,471 negro women, of whom 116,516 are illiterates." He concluded his speech with support for free schools, but in the meantime, he acknowledged the current challenges of illiteracy to democracy and proposed enfranchising women, because "In every State, save one, there are more educated women than all the illiterate voters, white and black, native and foreign."[31] NAWSA would continue its appeal to white southern women by excluding black members from attending the 1903 convention in New Orleans, at which time they issued an official statement allowing all state associations to restrict their membership to white women.[32]

The suffragists hoped that by drawing more attention to their cause and by incorporating white supremacist arguments into their speeches, they would recruit supporters, but the publicity itself actually undermined the progress the WCTU had made in gaining acceptance for women's engagement in political causes. Some members of the Georgia WCTU and other citizens throughout the state were persuaded to support woman suffrage as a consequence of the 1890 National WCTU convention and the 1895 NAWSA convention, but the vast majority of Georgians rejected this cause. The state's newspapers covered the proceedings of both conventions, yet only the Atlanta-based weekly *Sunny South* endorsed woman suffrage.[33] Other Georgians, including the influential Methodist and Baptist ministers who had helped nurture the fledgling Georgia WCTU during the 1880s, began to condemn the organization for its pro-suffrage leanings. McLendon and other pro-suffrage members of the Georgia WCTU served as lightning rods for clerical criticism, and the public controversy that ensued would nearly destroy the Georgia WCTU. These crises revealed that even among those Georgia women who sought moral reform, many were not ready, willing, or able to join the ranks of suffragists. Some ministers and women may have been concerned about the prospect of enfranchising black women or at least with allying themselves with former abolitionists, but the specific critique that emerged from the Georgia ministers focused not on racial issues but rather on appropriate gender roles. The message from the male church authorities was clear. Women could enter the public arena to agitate for temperance, but advocating woman suffrage violated conventional understandings of biblically proscribed gender roles and as such threatened to undermine society.

Leading ministers in Georgia's Baptist and Methodist churches argued that the northern women who led the National WCTU had exerted undue and perhaps dangerous influence over the women of the Georgia WCTU. In 1892 both Dr. J. B. Hawthorne of the First Baptist Church in Atlanta and Methodist bishop Dr. Warren A. Candler sharply denounced the Georgia WCTU for its increasing support of women's rights. Both men were strong temperance advocates and early supporters of the Georgia WCTU. Hawthorne struck first, publishing several articles criticizing National WCTU president Frances Willard's recent statements in favor of ordaining women into the ministry. He charged that her statements ran "contrary to the teachings of the preachers and leaders, contrary to the Scriptures," and would so disrupt the social system as to create "a subversion of the relations between women and marriage."[34]

Candler's condemnations were leveled directly against the Georgia WCTU itself, especially at Mary McLendon and other woman suffrage supporters from its ranks. In 1892 Candler wrote to Georgia WCTU president Jane Sibley expressing his concern about the growing suffrage sentiment among members of the WCTU and warning her that unless the state union severed its ties from the national union he and his wife, both of whom had been active supporters of the Georgia WCTU, would break ties with the organization.[35] Sibley refused to comply, and the following year Candler struck back. At a meeting of the North Georgia Conference of the Methodist Episcopal Church, Candler proposed that the conference withhold their usual endorsement for the Georgia WCTU. Atticus Haygood and many other Methodist leaders supported Candler's position and expressed concern that over time even well-intentioned women within the Georgia WCTU would be influenced by the national union. Following that meeting Candler continued his public denunciations from the pulpit and in the press, and Mary McLendon, despite her long devotion to the Methodist church, protested his actions with letters to the press.[36]

As a consequence of these heated debates and the negative publicity that ensued, the Georgia WCTU suffered. In 1893 Jane Sibley discussed the controversy in her annual address to the Georgia WCTU convention and encouraged the members to "take it all to God in prayer" and keep discussion "carried on quietly and calmly."[37] The convention responded with a resolution addressing the perception that the Georgia WCTU "is regarded as a body of woman suffragists" by reaffirming both their loyalty to the national union and their own right "to adopt only those principles espoused and plans devised by the National WCTU that are best suited to the needs of our southern work," thereby concluding, "we hereby believe that woman's suffrage is not conducive to the best interests of temperance work in Georgia."[38] Despite that carefully crafted compromise, the following year attendance at the annual convention decreased by nearly half, and only thirty-two out of fifty-two local unions sent reports.[39]

As one of the more controversial members of the Georgia WCTU, Mary McLendon reported frequent frustrations that year. In her report on medal contests she stated, "One minister in Atlanta is so opposed to women's work, except in church societies, that he thinks it is not the correct thing to read the notice of a coming [medal] contest from his pulpit." The problem was not restricted to Atlanta. In Milledgeville the medal contest was held in the courthouse because no church would admit them. In her capacity as president of the Fifth District of the Georgia WCTU, McLendon reported that the district conference in Conyers was forced to meet in an abandoned Baptist church because the local Methodist minister would not allow the meeting to be held in the usual church. The local women did an admirable job of decorating the old building with vines, flowers, and lamps, but few WCTU members bothered to attend the meeting.[40]

By the turn of the century these public controversies between Georgia's ministers and the WCTU led many WCTU members to abandon the organization. In 1898 McLendon brought the woman suffrage issue to the floor of the annual meeting of the Georgia WCTU, making a formal motion to establish the franchise department as part of the state's official work, but many WCTU members had clearly understood the statements and actions of ministers. Additional suffrage activity would not be tolerated. A three-hour debate ensued, and although the motion failed by a vote of seventeen to thirty-one, the official press statement suggests that their vote primarily reflected practical concerns. The Georgia WCTU reported, "while there was no good reason why women in particular should not be allowed to vote . . . at present time it would be inexpedient for them to assert the right to that privilege."[41] Even though the Georgia WCTU failed to endorse woman suffrage, Bishop Warren Candler again publicly denounced the organization, and many local unions disbanded. The following year the Georgia WCTU had so few active members that it did not even bother to hold its annual convention.[42]

Despite this dramatic decline, a few loyal workers held the Georgia WCTU together until the controversy passed and the reform spirit resurged with the national trend toward progressive reform, which in the South primarily focused on prohibition, drawing new recruits into the struggling organization. In the meantime, Georgia WCTU historian, Lula Ansley, credited a small band of a dozen women with holding the organization together and gave special mention to Mary McLendon for continuing to work on educational and legislative issues.[43]

Even in the face of the obvious disapproval of her own church, McLendon had not been deterred. She had continued to embrace both temperance reform and woman suffrage, believing, as Frances Willard had, that women must "Do Everything" necessary to protect women and children. McLendon led her local WCTU union and prodded other members of the state organization not only to continue to pursue aggressively their early agenda of prohibition, temperance education, and prison reform, but also to endorse legislation to raise the legal age of consent, to abolish prostitution, to prohibit child labor, and to expand educational opportunities for children and career opportunities for women. She also expanded her focus to include both state and federal legislation. After the state legislature passed a statewide prohibition law in 1907, McLendon and other prohibitionists rejoiced at the success but also recognized that they must remain vigilant to ensure that the law would be enforced. The struggle to enforce prohibition in the state further convinced them that measures passed on the state level were not sufficient; consequently, despite the South's persistent concerns with states' rights principles, the Georgia WCTU and other southern prohibitionists turned to the federal government for national legislation and ultimately for a constitutional amendment prohibiting the manufacture and sale of alcohol.[44]

For the rest of her life, McLendon would devote her time to both the Georgia WCTU and the Georgia Woman Suffrage Association, and just as she encouraged the WCTU to endorse suffrage, she also ensured that the GWSA would work for reform legislation. To McLendon woman suffrage was both a right and a means to secure moral reform legislation. As president of the GWSA, from 1906 through 1921, she encouraged the members of that organization to pursue not only their women's rights agenda but also to support the moral reform and educational issues promoted by the Georgia WCTU. Consequently, the petitions that the GWSA sent to the state legislature included not only demands for woman suffrage and expanding legal rights for women, including allowing women to serve on boards of education and to practice law, ensuring mothers' rights to coguardianship of their children, and providing greater educational opportunities for women, but also included support for prison reform, raising the age of legal consent, and stricter child labor laws.[45]

With her slogan, "Do Everything," Frances Willard encouraged women reformers to expand their reform agenda and to become more aggressively involved in politics. Throughout the last two decades of her life, McLendon followed both suggestions, and in the process she helped to open up spaces for white women in the political arena prior to women's enfranchisement. As the president of the local union located nearest to both Atlanta's City Hall and the Georgia State House, she coordinated the municipal and state legislative efforts. The members of her union continued their earlier tactics of circulating petitions throughout their neighborhoods, distributing literature on the issues along the way, and then delivering those petitions to legislators, but during the 1900s they also added some new tactics to their arsenal. Taking advantage of their close proximity to the legislative bodies, they made their presence known. Beginning in 1900, whenever a bill on prohibition was announced, delegations from McLendon's union appeared at the capitol building wearing white ribbons as a symbol of their support for prohibition, and then they distributed ribbons to supportive politicians. As support for statewide prohibition rose, the Georgia WCTU increased their efforts. In 1907 their lobbying efforts contributed to the successful passage of that law, and the women of the Georgia WCTU filled the galleries in the capitol building to celebrate their victory.[46]

McLendon joined the other members of the Georgia WCTU in these gatherings, but she also worked on her own as well. She carried out a regular correspondence with Georgia's elected officials on local, state, and federal legislation and sent in frequent contributions to the state's newspapers. By the 1910s she had gained so much prominence that two newspapers, the *Atlanta Georgian* and the *Atlanta Constitution*, assigned her a weekly column. Her prominence and persistence led politicians to invite her to testify before legislative committees. By 1912 her appearances became so frequent that she registered as "a lobbyist without compensation" on behalf of both the Georgia WCTU and the GWSA, and regularly testified on behalf of child labor laws, creation of free kindergartens, licensing women lawyers, and on several well-publicized occasions in favor of woman suffrage.[47]

As McLendon juggled her commitments to the Georgia WCTU and the GWSA, she sought not only to represent the interests of both organizations, but also to unify the two movements by continuing to emphasize the home protection argument for woman suffrage. McLendon had long believed that as moral guardians of their families and their communities, women needed greater political power, and as she attempted to influence legislation, she grew increasingly frustrated with the limitations of lobbying politicians who were not dependent on women's votes. Due to the damage the suffrage debates had inflicted on the Georgia WCTU during the 1890s, many WCTU leaders wished to avoid the issue, but McLendon persisted. Her local union, the Atlanta Frances Willard Union, had endorsed woman suffrage, established the "franchise department," and despite the opposition of the local clergy they never abandoned it. In 1905 the national woman suffrage association, seeking to expand support for woman suffrage, suggested that their state affiliates send "fraternal greetings" to other women's organizations. Since McLendon was a member of the Georgia WCTU, she not only wrote and delivered those annual messages but also used that opportunity to encourage the Georgia WCTU to reconsider their official stance on woman suffrage. Through these letters she pointed to such role models as the late Frances Willard and a few women of Georgia who supported woman suffrage, to the fact that the majority of other state WCTU organizations had taken up this work, to their sense of pride by explaining that as disenfranchised people women were categorized with "lunatics, criminals and idiots," and to arguments of simple justice, but more than any other argument she stressed that if mothers were to successfully protect their own children, they simply needed the vote.[48] Accepting that women owed their primary devotion to the care of their families, she explained, "Not only has politics invaded the home but it is creeping in and influencing every relation and phase of home life, until today men and women are coming to realize that a new element is needed in public affairs, that in the politics of the present time the mothers['] element is necessary to foster and safeguard the growth and development of our boys and girls in an age when the spirit of commercialism runs rampant."[49] McLendon's arguments seemed to be gaining some support in 1912 when her motion to adopt the franchise department finally received a seconder and a debate ensued. The discussion focused not on the merits of woman suffrage itself but on the advisability of the WCTU taking an official position. Ultimately, the motion failed, but the convention passed a resolution allowing local unions to take up this work if they so desired. This scene was repeated several more times before 1920, but despite McLendon's persistent efforts, the Georgia WCTU never officially endorsed woman suffrage.[50]

McLendon did manage to win some support for woman suffrage. In 1912 a second local union, the Atlanta Patterson Union, also adopted the franchise department, and three years later the Union Point organization would follow suit. Beginning in 1912 several prominent Georgia WCTU leaders, including both the president and the superintendent of legislative work, expressed their own public support for, or at least sympathy with, the woman suffrage movement. During the next few years support for woman suffrage would increase, especially among those women in the Georgia WCTU who worked most directly with politicians.[51]

As support for woman suffrage increased both within Georgia and, more dramatically, throughout the nation, Mary McLendon devoted more of her time to this cause, and her prominence in the state began to rival that of her sister. Her columns appeared regularly in two Atlanta papers, and she made frequent contributions to other Georgia papers as well. She coordinated public meetings and rode in public parades to promote woman suffrage, including the 1914 Harvest Festival parade in which she rode in a car that the government had confiscated from Anna Howard Shaw when she refused to pay taxes in protest of the injustice of women's taxation without representation. When the Georgia legislature held the first hearings on woman suffrage during the summer of 1914, Mary McLendon joined her sister to testify on its behalf. Mary and Rebecca repeated their performances again in 1915 and 1917, and even though the legislation never received a floor vote, these debates were well covered by the local press, keeping McLendon's public life in the spotlight.[52]

Concerns about race relations pervaded virtually every political discussion in Georgia and the South, especially issues related to the franchise, during the early twentieth century. McLendon and other advocates of woman suffrage both shared and understood the concerns of the white southern community and addressed them in their arguments. Despite Henry Blackwell's earlier suggestion that female enfranchisement would counterbalance any ill effects of the illiterate "Negro" vote, Southern states, including Georgia, chose to disenfranchise African American men rather than to grant the franchise to women. By 1908 Georgia had adopted the white primary, a poll tax, and finally a literacy test requirement, with a grandfather clause to protect the voting rights of the poor white population; enfranchising white women was not only unnecessary, but would perhaps even risk disrupting a precarious balance of political power.[53]

These developments changed the situation so that Blackwell's argument was no longer immediately relevant; nonetheless, both woman suffragists and antisuffragists continued to use race-based arguments to support their positions, and it was clear that both sides sought to preserve white supremacy. At a 1914 hearing of the Georgia Assembly's committee on constitutional amendments, three of the four speakers testifying in favor of woman suffrage, including both McLendon and Rebecca Felton, and both of the speakers opposing woman suffrage addressed racial concerns. McLendon and Felton expressed both their frustration with the enfranchisement of African American men, ignoring the provisions that made a mockery of that right, and their corresponding outrage that white southern women lacked that right. McLendon proclaimed, "The negro men, our former slaves, have been given the right to vote and why should not we southern women have the same right?" Leonard Grossman, president of the Georgia Men's League for Woman Suffrage, reassured the legislators that woman suffrage would not disrupt black disfranchisement, arguing that "There is no possibility of Negro women ever getting to vote in Georgia with our white primary." The opposition, represented by Mrs. Walter B. Lamar and Miss Mildred Rutherford, warned that if woman suffrage measures were approved in the South, a national law would soon follow, and that law would enfranchise black women.[54]

As the decade progressed, however, racial arguments seemingly became an unwanted distraction to woman suffragists. In a 1915 internal report on the status of suffrage work in Georgia, McLendon wrote, "Last year we introduced a bill in the Legislature to submit to the voters an amendment to the Constitution allowing women to vote upon the exact bases that men were allowed. This satisfactorily disposed of the Negro woman's vote."[55] Throughout the rest of the campaign, when racial issues were introduced by the Antis, McClendon would respond to them, but when given the opportunity to present her own arguments, she avoided the topic; instead, she continuously stressed that her goal was for white women to win the right to vote. At a 1915 hearing of the Georgia Senate's committee on constitutional amendments, the anti-suffragists were not present, and McLendon did not discuss race but rather the injustice of women being classed with "lunatics, idiots, paupers, criminals, and aliens." In 1917, when McLendon and other suffrage leaders visited Georgia governor Harris, they presented arguments based on justice and women's contributions to moral reform efforts, particularly prohibition, but did not mention race, other than to emphasize their goals to "uplift the human race."[56]

Although McLendon and other white southern woman suffragists used a variety of arguments to promote woman suffrage, including both justice and the preservation of white supremacy, she devoted most of her attention to arguments based on women's interests in preserving the sanctity of their homes and the moral purity of their communities. While Mary McLendon's public work intensified during the 1910s, however, her personal life went through another period of transition, and both her identity and actual role as mother became more symbolic than real. Between 1910 and 1915 Mary McLendon's two sons died and her daughter married, leaving McLendon alone for the first time in her life.[57] McLendon never mentioned her own family in her public statements, but while she delivered addresses laced with references to motherhood as a justification for women's increased political activity, her public life seemed to fill the void left as her familial responsibilities declined. In effect, she transformed her own role from mother of the children she bore and nurtured to a woman who could mother other women's children through legislation.

World War I and the worldwide epidemic of Spanish influenza temporarily disrupted the work of the GWSA and the Georgia WCTU, but as the crises eased, both organizations enjoyed major victories. World War I propelled Congress to pass constitutional amendments for both prohibition and woman suffrage. The Georgia legislature wasted no time in ratifying prohibition, doing so on June 26, 1918, and Mary McLendon observed the vote from the galleries, sitting alongside her fellow white ribboners.[58] Less than a year later, McLendon celebrated two woman suffrage victories. On May 3, 1919, Atlanta's City Democratic Executive Committee gave Georgia's white women suffragists a surprise victory when, by a vote of twenty-four to one, they gave women the right to vote in the party's white primary elections in Atlanta.[59] No sooner did McLendon finish celebrating that victory than word reached Georgia that the majority of Congress appeared ready to pass the Susan B. Anthony Amendment for woman suffrage. Mary McLendon and Rebecca Felton boarded a train so that they could witness the historic events in the United States Capitol on May 21 and June 4, 1919.[60]

McLendon returned to Atlanta to receive hearty congratulations from her friends and supporters within the Georgia WCTU and continued resistance from the Georgia legislature. Even though the Georgia WCTU had never officially endorsed woman suffrage, Lella Dillard, president of the Georgia WCTU, praised the congressional vote in her column in the *Georgia Bulletin*, thanking the two members of the congressional delegation from Georgia who supported the cause. Dillard reserved special honors for Mary McLendon, "that brave pioneer who has dared to stand true to her convictions in the face of what to the ordinary woman would have been fearful odds." She also encouraged the members of the Georgia WCTU to "let our legislators know we wish Georgia to be just progressive enough to ratify the Suffrage Amendment as soon as the Legislature convenes."[61]

Georgia's suffragists were under no illusions that the Georgia legislature would ratify the amendment. They hoped, instead, that the legislature would take no action at all, but they were to be disappointed, again. The legislators took up the constitutional amendment within days of convening for the simple purpose of rejecting it, which they did before the summer was over.[62]

While Mary McLendon waited for other states in the country to provide her with a constitutionally guaranteed right to vote, she eagerly embraced the limited suffrage she had, at last, won, the right to vote in Atlanta's Democratic Party primary. She explained, "It is only a crumb, but when one is hungry even a crumb contains some nourishment, . . . I am so proud [of my state taking its first step toward equal suffrage] that I am addressing my male friends as 'my fellow citizens.'"[63] On primary election day Mary McLendon arrived at the polls before they opened, carrying her six-year-old grandson. For a woman who had long argued that women needed to vote to protect their children, it was certainly fitting that she cast her first vote with a child in her arms.[64]

In August 1920 neighboring Tennessee became the thirty-sixth state to ratify the Susan B. Anthony Amendment, and McLendon believed her work was done. The Georgia legislature, however, had one more challenge to present. They argued that since women had not registered to vote before the deadline for the primary election, they were not entitled to vote in either the primary or the general elections that fall. McLendon fought this decision with her usual vigor, but she did not succeed, and most of Georgia's women had to wait another year to cast their first ballots.[65] As a white Democrat in Atlanta, however, she was able to vote again in Atlanta's white primary in 1920. That year she intensified her commitment by working as manager in the Second Ward precinct, where she worked from seven o'clock in the morning until seven o'clock at night. She only earned six dollars, but her motive was not salary, but principle.[66]

By 1921 Mary Latimer McLendon saw her major life's work accomplished. Neither organization claimed that its work was finished. The Georgia WCTU would continue to work for enforcement of prohibition, for temperance education to safeguard its future, and for the expanding slate of reform issues they supported. The GWSA would soon disband and encourage its members to join the newly formed League of Women Voters, but McLendon left that work for younger women. McLendon's eighty-one-year-old body suddenly grew tired. In the fall of 1921 her health suddenly declined and on November 20, 1921, Mary McLendon died.[67]

Georgia honored McLendon and recognized the invaluable contributions she had made in creating a new role for white women in the New South. Her death was reported on the first page of the *Atlanta Constitution*.[68] Members of the Georgia Woman Suffrage Association and the Georgia WCTU worked together to find a fitting tribute to the woman who had spent half her life helping to carve out a place for white southern women in the world of politics. In October 1923 the two organizations placed the first memorial to a woman in the Georgia Capitol, erecting a white marble fountain with the head of Mary Latimer McLendon carved in bas relief in honor of the work she did to make "a wider world for women, a safer world for mankind."[69] It seems a fitting tribute that the likeness of the woman who claimed that "she could not remember the time when she was not interested in listening to the men discuss politics" and who devoted her adult life to bringing women's perspective into those discussions should find itself in the Georgia Capitol building.[70]

## NOTES

1. "Fraternal Greetings from the Georgia Woman Suffrage Association to the Georgia Woman's Christian Temperance Union," *Report of the Twenty-eighth Annual Convention of the Woman's Christian Temperance Union of Georgia, Held in the Baptist Church, Madison, Ga., October 11th to 14th, 1910* (Columbus, Ga.: Gilbert Printing Co., 1910), 30. All annual reports and convention minutes of the Georgia WCTU are located in the Georgia Woman's Christian Temperance Union Records, Special Collections Department, Robert W. Woodruff Library, Emory University.

2. See, in particular, Anne Firor Scott, *The Southern Lady: From Pedestal to Politics, 1830–1930* (Chicago: University of Chicago Press, 1970); Mary Martha Thomas, *The New Woman in Alabama: Social Reforms and Suffrage, 1890–1920* (Tuscaloosa: University of Alabama Press, 1992); Glenda Gilmore, *Gender and Jim Crow: Women and the Politics of White Supremacy in North Carolina, 1896–1920* (Chapel Hill: University of North Carolina Press, 1996); Elizabeth Hayes Turner, *Women, Culture, and Community: Religion and Reform in Galveston, 1880–1920* (New York: Oxford University Press, 1996); Anastatia Sims, *The Power of Femininity in the New South: Women's Organizations and Politics in North Carolina, 1880–1930* (Columbia: University of South Carolina Press, 1997); Judith N. McArthur, *Creating the New Woman: The Rise of the New Woman: The Rise of Women's Progressive Culture in Texas, 1893–1918* (Urbana: University of Illinois Press, 1998). Historians of the New South, in general, have also recently begun to incorporate the perspective of white women into their narratives; see, in particular William A. Link, *The Paradox of Southern Progressivism, 1880–1930* (Chapel Hill: University of North Carolina, 1992).

3. Rebecca Latimer Felton, *Country Life in Georgia in the Days of My Youth* (Atlanta: Index Printing, 1919), 16–28, 54–58; Rebecca Latimer Felton, *The Romantic Story of Georgia's Women* (Atlanta: Atlanta Georgian and Sunday American, 1930), 17; John Talmadge, *Rebecca Latimer Felton: Nine Stormy Decades* (Athens: University of Georgia Press, 1960), 2–6.

4. Felton, *Country Life*, 58–62, 71; Felton, *Romantic Story*, 17; Talmadge, *Rebecca Latimer Felton*, 5–9; Katie Lee Reeves, "Life Sketch of Mary Latimer McLendon," Georgia Woman's Christian Temperance Union Records, 3; "Her Two Ambitions Realized, Mrs. McLendon Goes to Reward," *Atlanta Constitution*, November 21, 1921. See Christie Anne Farnham, *The Education of the Southern Belle: Higher Education and Student Socialization in the Antebellum South* (New York: New York University Press, 1994); Amy Thompson McCandless, *The Past in the Present: Women's Higher Education in the Twentieth-Century American South* (Tuscaloosa: University of Alabama Press, 1999), 1–82. For a contrasting argument, see Eleanor Boatwright, *Status of Women in Georgia, 1783–1860* (1940; repr., Brooklyn, N.Y.: Carlson Publishing Inc., 1994), 5–24.

5. Felton, *Country Life*, 34, 41–42, 58, 60–61, 65; Felton, *Romantic Story*, 17; Talmadge, *Rebecca Latimer Felton*, 100; Boatwright, *Women in Georgia*, 111–12. For a discussion of the Methodist church and Georgia women, see Naomi L. Nelson, "She Considered Herself Called of God: White Women's Participation in the Southern Methodist Episcopal Church, 1820–1865" (PhD diss., Emory University, 2001).

6. LeeAnn Whites, "Rebecca Latimer Felton and the Wife's Farm: The Class and Racial Politics of Gender Reform," *Georgia Historical Quarterly* 76 (Summer 1992): 354–72, and "Rebecca Latimer Felton and the Problem of 'Protection' in the New South," in *Visible Women: New Essays on American Activism*, ed. Nancy A. Hewitt and Suzanne Lebsock, 41–61 (Urbana: University of Illinois Press, 1993).

7. Ted O. Brooks, ed., *Fulton Country, Georgia, Marriage Records* (Cummings, Ga., 1922), 223, 569; Felton, *Country Life*, 54; *Pioneer Citizens' History of Atlanta 1833 to 1902* (Atlanta: Byrd Printing, 1902), 378; Thomas H. Martin, *Atlanta and Its Builders: A Comprehensive History of the Gate City of the South* (Atlanta: Century Memorial Publishing, 1902), 2:607; Reeves, "Life Sketch," 3; Letter from Eleanor Swift Latimer to Rebecca Latimer Felton, dated April 1861, Rebecca Latimer Felton Papers, Hargrett Library, University of Georgia.

8. *Pioneer Citizens*, 378. National Archives and Records Administration, *1870 United States Federal Census*; National Archives and Records Administration, *1880 United States Federal Census*.

9. Reeves, "Life Sketch," 3; "Her Two Ambitions Realized"; "Funeral Tuesday for Mrs. McLendon," *Atlanta Journal*, November 21, 1921.

10. *1870 U.S. Federal Census; 1880 U.S. Federal Census*; Reeves, "Life Sketch," 3–4.

11. "Her Two Ambitions Realized"; "Funeral Tuesday for Mrs. McLendon"; *1870 U.S. Federal Census; 1880 U.S. Federal Census; Atlanta City Directory, 1889* (Atlanta: R. P. Polk and Co., 1889). On the New South and Atlanta "Boosterism," see Paul Gaston, *The New South Creed: A Study in Mythmaking* (Baton Rouge: Louisiana State University Press, 1970); Numan V. Bartley, *The Creation of Modern Georgia* (Athens: University of Georgia Press, 1983); James Michael Russell, *Atlanta, 1847–1890: City Building in the Old South and the New* (Baton Rouge: Louisiana State University Press, 1988).

12. Mary McLendon was a member of the Trinity Methodist Church for over sixty years. "Trinity Methodist Episcopal Church, South: A Compilation of Her History, 1854–1935" (1935) and "Membership/guest rolls and statistics, 1912," included in records of Trinity Methodist Church (Atlanta, Ga.), Archives and Manuscript Department, Pitts Theology Library, Emory University.

13. Henry Scomp, *King Alcohol in the Realm of King Cotton or, A History of the Liquor Traffic and other Temperance Movements in Georgia from 1773–1887* (Chicago: Blakey Print Company, 1888), 473–74; Russell, *Atlanta, 1847–1890*, 207–8. For other discussions of the connection between temperance and Methodism, see Ruth Bordin, *Women and Temperance: The Quest for Power and Liberty, 1873–1900* (Philadelphia: Temple University Press, 1981); Scott, *The Southern Lady*; Anne Firor Scott, *Natural Allies: Women's Associations in American History* (Urbana: University of Illinois Press, 1992).

14. Bordin, *Women and Temperance*, 169. Nancy Hardesty, "'The Best Temperance Organization in the Land': Southern Methodists and the W.C.T.U. in Georgia," *Methodist History* 28, no. 3 (1990): 187.

15. Scomp, *King Alcohol*, 679–87; Lula Barnes Ansley, *History of the Georgia Woman's Christian Temperance Union* (Columbus, Ga.: Gilbert Printing Company, 1914), 38–58, 84–85; Bordin, *Women and Temperance*, 78–79; Hardesty, "Best Temperance Organization," 187–90; Talmadge, *Rebecca Latimer Felton*, 79–80; Russell, *Atlanta, 1847–1890*, 209–10.

16. Scomp, *King Alcohol*, 693; Ansley, *History of the Georgia WCTU*, 84–88, 101. For other discussions of the extent and limits of interracial cooperation within the WCTU in the South, see Glenda Gilmore, "'A Melting Time': Black Women, White Women and the WCTU in North Caroline, 1880–1900," in *Hidden Histories of Women in the New South*, ed. Virginia Bernhard, Betty Brandon, Elizabeth Fox-Genovese, Theda Perdue, and Elizabeth H. Turner, 153–72 (Columbia: University of Missouri Press, 1994); and Gilmore, *Gender and Jim Crow*, 45–59.

17. Reeves, "Life Sketch," 4; *Minutes of the Sixth Annual Convention of the Woman's Christian Temperance Union of Georgia, Held in Atlanta, Georgia, May 29, 30, & 31, 1888* (Augusta, Ga.: J. M. Richards, Book and Job Printer, ca. 1888), 20; *Proceedings of the Eighth Annual Convention of the Woman's Christian Temperance Union of Georgia, Held May 6th, 7th and 8th at Rome, Georgia* (Atlanta: Constitution Publishing Company, 1889), 22; *Proceedings of the Tenth Annual Convention of the Woman's Christian Temperance Union of Georgia*, 18–19, found in the Georgia Woman's Christian Temperance Union Records, Special Collections Department, Robert W. Woodruff Library, Emory University.

18. Ansley, *History of Georgia* WCTU, 97–119; *Minutes of the Sixth Annual Convention of the Georgia* WCTU, 12.

19. Ansley, *History of the Georgia* WCTU, 130.

20. Ansley, *History of Georgia* WCTU, 130; Hardesty, "Best Temperance Organization," 190. Sibley quote from "Temperance and Suffrage," *Woman's Journal* 22 (November 28, 1891): 383.

21. Although the existing sources do not provide an explanation for the change of residency, we know that Nick, who had been listed as the home owner and head of household in the 1880 federal census report and in the *Atlanta City Directory* of 1892, was no longer listed as a resident beginning in 1893; instead, the head-of-household status was transferred to Mary. Beginning in 1893 Mary was also occasionally listed as a widow, but Nick McLendon did not die until 1912. She remained at the same residence until her death in 1921, and her children are occasionally listed as residents of that home. Given the existing evidence, it is difficult to determine precisely what happened in the marriage. See *Atlanta City Directory* (Richmond, Va.: R. L. Polk 1893), unpag.; *Atlanta City Directory* (Richmond, Va.: R. L. Polk 1896), 938; *Atlanta City Directory* (Richmond, Va.: R. L. Polk 1897), 955; *Atlanta City Directory* (Richmond, Va.: R. L. Polk 1898), 921; *Atlanta City Directory* (Richmond, Va.: R. L. Polk 1899), 956; *Atlanta City Directory* (Richmond, Va.: R. L. Polk 1902), 1038; *Atlanta City Directory* (Richmond, Va.: R. L. Polk 1903), 937; *Atlanta City Directory* (Richmond, Va.: R. L. Polk 1913), 1194; *Atlanta City Directory* (Richmond, Va.: R. L. Polk 1921), 594. For information on the McLendon children, see "The Girls' High School," *Atlanta Constitution*, June 27, 1885; "Many Matters Serve to Enliven the Legislature as It Gets Down to Work," *Atlanta Constitution*, July 26, 1895; *Atlanta Constitution*, November 2, 1898; *1880 U.S. Federal Census*; *Atlanta City Directory* (Richmond, Va.: R. L. Polk, 1892), 893.

22. *Proceedings of the Eighth Annual Convention of the Georgia* WCTU, 55–56.

23. *Proceedings of the Eighth Annual Convention of the Georgia* WCTU, 60.

24. *Proceedings of the Eighth Annual Convention of the Georgia* WCTU, 9; Ansley, *History of the Georgia* WCTU, 121. See also Aileen Kraditor, *The Ideas of the Woman Suffrage Movement, 1890–1920* (New York: Columbia University Press, 1965); Scott, *The Southern Lady*; Bordin, *Women and Temperance*; Marjorie Spruill Wheeler, *New Women of the New South: The Leaders of the Woman Suffrage Movement in the Southern States* (New York: Oxford University Press, 1993).

25. *Proceedings of the Ninth Annual Convention of the Woman's Christian Temperance Union of Georgia, Held April 11th, 12th, 13th, 14th and 15th, 1891 at Thomasville, Georgia* (Atlanta: Constitutional Publishing Company, 1891), 2, 7; Mary McLendon's report printed in *Proceedings of the Tenth Annual Convention of the Georgia* WCTU, 35.

26. Reeves, "Life Sketch," 4–5; *Proceedings of the Eleventh Annual Convention of the Woman's Christian Temperance Union of Georgia, Held April 25th, 26th, 27th 28th, 1893 at Macon, Georgia* (Atlanta: Southern Christian Printing and Publishing, 1893), 24; *Report of the Twenty-second Annual Convention of the Georgia Woman's Christian Temperance Union, Held in the First Methodist Church, Eastman, Ga., October 7–11, 1904* (Macon, Ga.: T. A. Coleman Book and Printing, 1904), 48.

27. A. Elizabeth Taylor, "The Origin of the Woman Suffrage Movement in Georgia," *Georgia Historical Quarterly* 28 (June 1944): 63–65; Mary L. McLendon, "Georgia," in *History of Woman Suffrage*, vol. 4, *1883–1900*, ed. Susan B. Anthony and Ida H. Harper (Rochester, N.Y.: Charles Mann Printing, 1902), 581–88.

28. A. Elizabeth Taylor, "Woman Suffrage Activities in Atlanta," *Journal of the Atlanta Historical Society* (Winter 1979): 45; Taylor, "Origin of the Woman Suffrage Movement," 66; McLendon, "Georgia," 4:581; Martin, *Atlanta and Its Builders*, 600. For discussions of the WCTU's impact on the woman suffrage movement, see Scott, *The Southern Lady*; Bordin, *Women and Temperance*; Wheeler, *New Women of the New South*, Elna C. Green, *Southern Strategies: Southern Women and the Woman Suffrage Question* (Chapel Hill: University of North Carolina Press, 1997).

29. Taylor, "Origin of the Woman Suffrage Movement," 68–79; "Woman Suffrage Activities," 45–47; "The National-American Convention of 1895," *History of Woman Suffrage*, 4:236–51.

30. Henry Blackwell, "A Solution to the Southern Question," *Woman's Journal*, September 27, 1890.

31. Quoted in "The National-American Convention of 1895," 4:246.

32. Green, *Southern Strategies*, 10; Wheeler, *New Women of the New South*, 100–125; Kraditor, *Ideas of the Woman Suffrage Movement*, 163–216.

33. Taylor, "Origin of Woman Suffrage Movement," 77–78; Taylor, "Woman Suffrage Activities," 47; McLendon, "Georgia," 4:581–82.

34. Quoted in Ansley, *History of the Georgia WCTU*, 140.

35. J. E. Sibley to Warren Candler, April 29, 1892, and Warren Candler to J. E. Sibley, May 2, 1892, Warren Candler Papers, Special Collections Department, Robert W. Woodruff Library, Emory University.

36. Hardesty, "Best Temperance Organization," 192; Ansley, *History of the Georgia WCTU*, 142–43; Letter of Mary McLendon to the *North East Georgian* (1893), Warren Candler Papers; Articles from *Atlanta Constitution*, January 14, 1893, and January 16, 1893, contained in Warren Candler Papers.

37. *Proceedings of the Eleventh Annual Convention of the Georgia WCTU*, 17–18.

38. *Proceedings of the Eleventh Annual Convention of the Georgia WCTU*, 14.

39. Ansley, *History of the Georgia WCTU*, 148. See also Green, *Southern Strategies*, 73–74, 200; Wheeler, *New Women of the New South*, 10–11.

40. Quoted in *Report of the Twelfth Annual Meeting of the Woman's Christian Temperance Union of Georgia, at Rome, May 25th, 26th, 27th, 28th, 1894* (Atlanta: The Foote and Davies Co., 1894), 30–31 and 26–27.

41. Press statement quoted in Ansley, *History of the Georgia WCTU*, 174.

42. Ansley, *History of the Georgia WCTU*, 177–81. A decade later Warren Candler would publicly endorse the Georgia Antisuffrage Association. Green, *Southern Strategies*, 73.

43. Ansley, *History of Georgia WCTU*, 177–81.

44. *Report of the Twenty-second Annual Convention of the Georgia WCTU*. For background on the prohibition movement in Georgia, see Bartley, *Creation of Modern Georgia*, 153–54; and Alton DuMar Jones, "Progressivism in Georgia, 1898–1918," (PhD diss., Emory University, 1963), 183–207. For a discussion of southern reformers' acceptance of and justification for increased government restrictions and regulations, see Link, *Paradox of Southern Progressivism*, 48–51, 95–112; and Dewey Grantham, *Southern Progressivism: The Reconciliation of Progress and Tradition* (Knoxville: University of Tennessee Press, 1983), 172.

45. McLendon, "Georgia," 4:583–88; McLendon, "Georgia," *History of Woman Suffrage*, vol. 6, *1900–1920*, ed. Ida H. Harper (New York: National American Woman Suffrage Association, 1922),

121, 133; *Minutes of the Georgia Woman Suffrage Association Convention, 1899*, Georgia Woman Suffrage Collection, Georgia Department of Archives and History; letters from Mary McLendon to Mary Sumner Boyd, June 2, 1916, and September 22, 1917, Georgia Woman Suffrage Collection; A. Elizabeth Taylor, "Revival and Development of the Woman Suffrage Movement in Georgia," *Georgia Historical Quarterly* 62 (1958): 339–54.

46. *Proceedings of the Seventeenth Annual Convention of the Georgia wctu, Held April 25th, 26th and 27th, 1900, at Augusta, Ga.* (Atlanta: The Byrd Print Co., 1900), 28; "Miss Griffin's Account of the Georgia Vote in 1907," manuscript, Georgia wctu Records.

47. *Report of the Twenty-eighth Annual Convention of the Georgia wctu*, 37, 52; *History of Woman Suffrage*, 4:127; "Georgia Suffragists to Have Department in Constitution," *Atlanta Constitution*, June 15, 1913; *Report of the Twenty-first Annual Convention of the Georgia Woman's Christian Temperance Union, Held in the First Methodist Church, Griffin, Georgia, October 6–8, 1903*, 31–32; *Report of the Thirtieth Annual Convention of the Woman's Christian Temperance Union of Georgia, Held at Sam Jones Memorial Church, Cartersville, Georgia, September 24–27, 1912* (Columbus, Ga.: Gilbert Printing Co., 1912), 42–43; Taylor, "The Last Phase of the Woman Suffrage Movement in Georgia," *Georgia Historical Quarterly* 43 (1958): 17–28.

48. McLendon, "Georgia," 6:123; Taylor, "Last Phase," 14; *Report of the Twenty-third Annual Convention of the Georgia Woman's Christian Temperance Union, Held in the First Baptist Church, Americus, Georgia, October 16–20, 1905* (Macon, Ga.: Anderson Printing Co., 1905), 23–24; *Report of the Twenty-fourth Annual Convention of the Woman's Christian Temperance Union of Georgia, Held in the First Methodist Church, LaGrange, Georgia, September 25–28, 1906* (Columbus, Ga.: Gilbert Printing Co., 1906), 24–25; *Report of the Twenty-fifth Annual Convention of the Woman's Christian Temperance Union of Georgia, Held in St. Luke Methodist Episcopal Church, Columbus, Georgia, October 22–25, 1907* (Columbus, Ga.: Gilbert Printing Co., 1907), 22; *Report of the Twenty-sixth Annual Convention of the Woman's Christian Temperance Union of Georgia, Held in The Methodist Church, Albany, Georgia, October 1st to 5th, 1908* (Columbus, Ga.: Gilbert Printing Co., 1908), 27, 108–9; *Report of the Twenty-seventh Annual Convention of the Woman's Christian Temperance Union of Georgia Held in the Mulberry Street Methodist Episcopal Church, Macon, Georgia, October 5th to 8th, 1909* (Columbus, Ga.: Gilbert Printing Co., 1909), 117–18; *Report of the Twenty-eighth Annual Convention of the Georgia wctu*, 107–8; *Report of the Twenty-ninth Annual Convention of the Woman's Christian Temperance Union of Georgia, Held in the First Presbyterian Church, Savannah, Georgia, October 10–14, 1911* (Columbus, Ga.: Gilbert Printing Co., 1911), 121; *Report of the Thirtieth Annual Convention of the Georgia wctu*, 114; *Report of the Thirty-first Annual Convention of the Woman's Christian Temperance Union of Georgia, Held in Bainbridge, Georgia, November 18th to 22nd, 1913* (Columbus, Ga.: Gilbert Printing Co., 1913), 123–25, 135; *Report of the Thirty-third Annual Convention of the Woman's Christian Temperance Union of Georgia, Held at Covington, Georgia, October 26–29, 1915*, 174; *Report of the Thirty-fifth Annual Convention of the Woman's Christian Temperance Union of Georgia, Held at Dawson, Georgia, October 16, 1917 in the Methodist Episcopal Church*, 126.

49. *Report of the Thirty-first Annual Convention of the Georgia wctu*, 124.

50. *Report of the Thirtieth Annual Convention of the Georgia wctu*, 114, 130; *Report of the Thirty-first Annual Convention of the Georgia wctu*, 137; *Report of the Thirty-third Annual Convention of the Georgia wctu*, 174; *Report of the Thirty-fourth Annual Convention of the Woman's Christian Temperance Union of Georgia, Held at Waynesboro, Georgia, October 17–20, 1916*, 145, 154 (located in the Georgia Woman's Christian Temperance Union Records, Special Collections Department, Robert W. Woodruff Library, Emory University); *Report of the Thirty-fifth Annual Convention of the Georgia wctu*, 126.

51. *Report of the Twenty-ninth Annual Convention of the Georgia* WCTU, 69; *Report of the Thirtieth Annual Convention of the Georgia* WCTU, 42, 56–57, 130; *Report of the Thirty-third Annual Convention of the Georgia* WCTU, 117, 153; "A Great Convention," *Georgia Bulletin*, October 1912.

52. Taylor, "Revival and Development," 350–52; Taylor, "Last Phase," 17–23.

53. Bartley, *Creation of Modern Georgia*, 149; Dewey Grantham, *Hoke Smith and the Politics of the New South* (Baton Rouge: Louisiana State University Press, 1958), 131–79.

54. Testimony quoted in "Suffrage Bill Is Lost by One Vote," *Atlanta Constitution*, July 8, 1914; and Taylor, "Last Phase," 17–18.

55. "Report on the Status of Suffrage Work in Georgia," unpublished, located in Georgia Woman Suffrage Collection, GDAH.

56. Taylor, "Last Phase," 21; *Woman's Journal*, August 7, 1915; "Governor Harris Gets 'A Dose of Suffrage' at Extra Session Hearing," *Atlanta Journal*, March 6, 1917. For recent discussions of the relationship between white supremacy and the woman suffrage movement, see, in particular, Wheeler, *New Women of the New South*; Gilmore, *Gender and Jim Crow*; and Green, *Southern Strategies*.

57. *Atlanta Constitution*, February 27, 1910; *Atlanta Constitution* July 19, 1915. Nick McLendon had not lived at the family home since 1892, but his departure from Mary's life did not become final until he died in 1912. Their estrangement continued in death. Mary was not mentioned by name in his obituary, and he was buried in the Oakland Cemetery in Atlanta rather than in her family plot in Decatur. See his obituary, *Atlanta Constitution*, March 31, 1912.

58. "A Great Day for Georgia," *Georgia Bulletin*, June–July 1918.

59. Taylor, "Last Phase," 23.

60. Talmadge, *Rebecca Latimer Felton*, 108; McLendon, "Georgia," 6:131.

61. "President's Letter," *Georgia Bulletin*, June 1919.

62. Taylor, "Last Phase," 24–28;

63. Quoted in *Atlanta Journal*, May 4, 1919.

64. Reeves, "Life Sketch," 5.

65. Taylor, "The Last Phase," 28; McLendon, "Georgia," 6:132–33.

66. Reeves, "Life Sketch," 5; "Funeral Tuesday for Mrs. McLendon."

67. Reeves, "Life Sketch," 7.

68. "Her Two Ambitions Realized."

69. "Marble Foundation Erected in Honor of Mrs. M'Lendon," *Atlanta Constitution*, October 19, 1923; "President's Report," *Georgia Bulletin*, November–December 1923.

70. "Funeral Tuesday for Mrs. McLendon."

# Mildred Lewis Rutherford

(1851–1928)

## The Redefinition of New South
## White Womanhood

SARAH CASE

Mildred Lewis Rutherford, club woman and educator, was one of the best-known Georgian women of the early twentieth century.[1] Mostly remembered for her work in the United Daughters of the Confederacy (UDC), Rutherford was also an educator and principal of one of the state's most prestigious schools for young women. Through these and other activities, Rutherford took part in the redefinition of race relations and southern white womanhood in the New South era.[2] Although her justification of secession, support for the Confederacy, and romanticization of slavery might make Rutherford appear out of touch with early twentieth-century modernity, she played an active role in the economy and politics of the New South. Although she taught her students to emulate the modesty of the southern belle, she sought publicity for her own writings and waged an aggressive fundraising campaign for her school. Rutherford carefully monitored the behavior and social activities of students, but at the same time she taught them how to support themselves. A leading anti-suffrage activist and advocate for women's domesticity, she nonetheless carved out a public role for herself, writing and speaking widely on political issues affecting not only her hometown of Athens, but Georgia and the nation. Indeed, her idealization of the Old South helped create national support for modern methods of racist control such as state-sponsored segregation and disenfranchisement. As a historian, club woman, and educator, Rutherford represented the New South quest to mediate modernity with allegiance to conservative understandings of race and gender hierarchies.

Born in 1851 in Athens, Mildred Rutherford lived most of her life in the "clas-sic city." Athens, founded in 1802 as the site for Franklin College (which became the University of Georgia), sat on the northern edge of the state's plantation belt. By midcentury it had become the population center of Clarke County. The town's development depended on that of the college, and despite the school's struggles to maintain adequate funding, retain faculty, and keep enrollment high, Athens succeeded in drawing settlers into rural north Georgia. In keeping with the town's name, the university built impressive Greek Revival buildings that signaled what would become the town's architectural ideal. Following this classical style, the elite of Athens built large, stately white homes with columns, large porches, high ceilings, and plenty of windows.[3]

Although the fortunes of Athens were closely tied to those of the university, agriculture drove the economy of surrounding Clarke County. In 1840, 80 per-cent of the county's whites worked the land or supervised slaves who farmed for them. North of Georgia's cotton belt, the county still boasted a few large plantations, and both the area's rate of slave holding and its concentration in a few hands increased over time. Clarke County, however, did not remain entirely dependent on agriculture, and even boasted some industry before the Civil War. Thanks to the presence of local men in its corporate hierarchy, the Georgia Railroad passed through Athens, reaching the town in 1841. The railroad al-lowed Athens to become a major trade center for agricultural goods, especially cotton, and also encouraged the development of cotton processing in Athens.[4]

Rutherford's maternal grandfather, Colonel John Addison Cobb, took advan-tage of the county's economic opportunities, becoming one of the area's wealthi-est men. Cobb profited from investment in agriculture, the railroad, and real estate in Athens and the surrounding area. In addition to owning a plantation and 209 slaves by 1840 (only one other man in the county owned more than 200), Cobb served on the board of the directors of the Georgia Railroad and owned property in an area, still known as Cobbham, that became the site of Athens's most desirable addresses.[5]

Cobb's elder son, Howell, made a career as a politician, serving as a Demo-cratic congressman for six terms (and briefly as Speaker of the House), as gov-ernor of Georgia, and as secretary of the treasury in President James Buchanan's cabinet. Howell's younger brother, Thomas, or T. R. R., was an influential lawyer who helped found the law school at the University of Georgia, codified Geor-gia's state laws, and wrote the wartime state constitution of 1861. His work as a proslavery propagandist brought him national attention, particularly his well-regarded study of 1858, *An Inquiry into the Law of Negro Slavery*. In 1860 the Cobb brothers were instrumental in securing Georgia's secession vote, despite

**MILDRED LEWIS RUTHERFORD**
Courtesy of Hargrett Rare Book and Manuscript
Library, University of Georgia Libraries.

the congressman's past efforts as a Unionist. The brothers also participated in Confederate politics, Thomas by writing the Confederacy's constitution and Howell by serving as the first speaker of its Congress. Both men served in the war as generals; Thomas Cobb lost his life at Fredericksburg. Howell Cobb remained in politics after the war, resisting Reconstruction and supporting the Democratic Party until his death in 1868.[6]

Thomas and Howell Cobb's sister, Laura, married Williams Rutherford, a mathematics professor at the University of Georgia. A local historian described Williams Rutherford as a religious and "kind hearted" man, and a popular professor at the university, recognizable from the long hair and beard that earned him the nickname "Wild Man of Borneo."[7] Williams Rutherford's family, although not as prominent in politics, was also part of Georgia's slaveholding elite. His father owned a plantation in Culloden, and he and Laura received a section of it as a wedding gift, which they maintained as a winter residence. Although they viewed the plantation as their link with their planter-class lineage, the couple spent most of their married life in Athens. Five of their children survived childhood: John, born 1842; Mary Ann, born 1848; Mildred, born 1851; Bessie, born 1855; and Laura, born 1859.[8]

Laura Cobb Rutherford had been a strong student herself and had a long interest in expanding access to education for white women.[9] In 1857 she anonymously wrote to the *Athens Watchman*, deploring the lack of educational opportunities for the girls of Athens, especially shameful in light of the town's association with higher learning. Her brother Thomas read the article without knowing its author, and moved by its plea, responded by founding the Athens Female Academy. Before the school opened in the fall of 1859, Lucy Cobb and Sarah Rutherford, daughters of both Thomas Cobb and Laura Rutherford, died. To honor Cobb's loss, the board of the new school changed its name to Lucy Cobb Institute. Laura Rutherford enrolled her surviving school-age daughters, including eight-year-old Mildred, in the school's first session.[10]

Lucy Cobb remained open throughout the Civil War years, but the Rutherford women endured unfamiliar hardships. Although Athens did not experience the devastation of other Georgia towns, the family suffered from the destruction of Howell Cobb's plantation and the closing of the university. Like other southern women, Laura Rutherford faced new difficulties during the war, including scarcities of food and supplies, and new responsibilities with the absence of her husband. In addition, she actively participated in the "war work" effort to aid the Confederate cause. As the cofounder and second president of the Volunteer Aid Society (later the Soldiers' Aid Society), she supervised the collection of clothes and other supplies, and even took wounded Confederate soldiers into her own home. The experiences of financial hardship, deaths of family members (including Thomas Cobb), and the suffering of the young soldiers Laura Rutherford nursed in their home left a deep psychological imprint on the Rutherford children. The later writings of Mildred, especially, attest to an abiding bitterness over wartime loss.[11]

Mildred Rutherford enrolled at her uncle's Lucy Cobb Institute as soon as it opened and graduated in 1868. Although contemporary accounts of Rutherford's life always stress her popularity with young men, she did not marry, and on reaching her twentieth birthday took a job teaching in Atlanta. She remained there for eight years, living with a cousin and enjoying the sense of accomplishment (and steady salary) that teaching and living in the city offered. In 1880, however, Rutherford's parents beseeched her to return to Athens to become principal of her alma mater. Enduring declining enrollment, indifferent leadership, and financial difficulties, Lucy Cobb began to face an uncertain future. Only a keen sense of family responsibility led a reluctant Mildred to leave Atlanta to lead Lucy Cobb. The decision led her to more than fifty years of involvement in the school as director and teacher of literature, history, and the Bible.[12]

As principal of Lucy Cobb in the 1880s and 1890s, Rutherford created a school with a serious academic program that also sought to create properly modest and moral southern "ladies." Thomas Cobb had founded the school to offer young women a more academically challenging education than had been available in Athens, yet the school also integrated some of the antebellum tradition of southern women's schools. For young southern women in the mid-nineteenth century, education, especially knowledge of French, music, and art, served as a marker of class status rather than as preparation for a career or public life. "French schools," as they were called, created cultivated young "ladies" who were accomplished but not ambitious. Still, many schools offered advanced courses in languages, literature, sciences, and mathematics. Elite southern women had greater access to higher education than did northern women in the antebellum era, as southern schools' emphasis on gentility strengthened rather than weakened gender hierarchies as the vocational training northern women sought might have done. In its blending of subjects such as Latin grammar and "Wax Fruit and Flowers," in its first years Lucy Cobb fit squarely into the tradition of the antebellum "French school."[13]

Rutherford took over a struggling institution and rebuilt it into one of the most prestigious schools for young women in Georgia. She immediately went to work improving its academic standards, beautifying the physical plant, and increasing enrollment. In agreeing to head the school, Rutherford had insisted that the all-male board of directors cede to her its control of the budget and power to hire and fire staff. One of her first hires was her widowed older sister, Mary Ann Rutherford Lipscomb, who had been living in Washington, D.C. Her younger sister Bessie also taught at Lucy Cobb before her marriage in 1884, and was credited with making law and mathematics interesting and accessible to female students. The faculty remained primarily female, but by 1890, their areas of expertise had greatly expanded. Several faculty members had earned advanced degrees from northern colleges. Lipscomb and Rutherford oversaw remarkable growth in the school's enrollment, from 26 in 1880 to 104 just two years later.[14]

These students continued to take the art, music, and French classes demanded by southern parents, and the extra tuition required for these courses benefited the school's bottom line.[15] Yet Rutherford also emphasized academics. She organized the "collegiate" program into a five-year class system (freshman, sophomore, and so on, with the freshman course spread out over two years) and required five years of Latin, five of higher mathematics, and several years of the sciences, logic, rhetoric, philosophy, and literature (including history). This plan of study was based on the traditional "male" liberal arts curriculum that emphasized ancient languages and higher mathematics. Women's colleges typically either adopted a less rigorous approach to traditional subjects, or substituted modern languages for either Latin or Greek, or both. Lucy Cobb in part followed this pattern; Rutherford included five years of Latin and math, but did not offer Greek and saved more difficult Latin texts for the optional postgraduate year.[16]

In addition to improving academic offerings and faculty, Rutherford also improved the buildings and grounds of the school, dubbed by an alumna "'run down at the heel,' so to speak."[17] Rutherford added several new buildings, including an infirmary, a new schoolroom, and new boarding rooms, and, most significantly, the Seney-Stovall Chapel. A woman of strong Baptist faith, Rutherford believed that religion ought to be the cornerstone of education, and wanted a beautiful and substantial building for the school.[18] Unable to raise funds for a new chapel locally, she assigned members of a composition class to write letters to nationally known philanthropists with interests in education. Nellie Stovall's letter caught the attention of George Seney, a New Yorker with ties to Georgia, who agreed to give ten thousand dollars if the town could raise another four thousand. Rutherford accepted the challenge, and by 1883 the new chapel was completed and named for Seney and Stovall. The center of religious and social life for the school, it housed performances, commencements, and community events, cementing Lucy Cobb's place as an important Athens institution.[19]

Along with her attention to improving the academics and architecture of Lucy Cobb, Rutherford put high priority on cultivating womanly virtue in all of her students. Like other directors of boarding schools for women, Rutherford needed to protect the reputation of students attending the school and imposed very strict rules on the "Lucies" (as they were dubbed) under her guardianship.[20] Students were not allowed to spend the night away from the school; entertain male visitors other than brothers, fathers, and uncles; receive food other than fruit as gifts; dress "extravagantly" or wear silk or satin; or venture on their own beyond the stately magnolia tree in front of the main building.[21] Although Rutherford hoped to ensure that rumors of impropriety did not discourage parents from enrolling their children in Lucy Cobb, her chief concern—and that of her pupils' parents—lay in creating students who conformed to the social ideal of the southern lady.

Southern schools for girls had always instilled notions of correct and ladylike behavior in students, but the concern with proper manners became even more acute in the postwar era when once-prominent planter families faced serious economic losses.[22] In the New South era, the chief indication of proper feminine propriety remained sexual purity and modesty. The tie between sexual reputation and women's class identity extended back to the antebellum era.[23] With emancipation, industrialization, and urbanization, sexual propriety became even more central to maintaining class identity for women in the New South. Lucy Cobb's association with the antebellum elite, as well as the emphasis on feminine manners and decorum, appealed to parents from the urban middle class. Lucies typically were granddaughters of planters but the daughters, and later wives, of businessmen or professionals.[24] With the rise and fall of family fortunes, and constant contact with strangers in cities, women had to prove their elite status through dress, language, and behavior. By regulating students' interactions with males, manner of dress, and speech patterns, Rutherford created young women who could be clearly identified as elite even in the ever-changing circumstances of the New South.

Her several textbooks, on English, American, French, southern, and Biblical literature, published between 1890 and 1906, reflected Rutherford's deep preoccupation with propriety and morality.[25] All five criticized authors who openly portrayed sexuality or themselves lived in ways Rutherford found immoral.[26] The books gave particular attention to how writers depicted female characters. Rutherford most severely castigated male authors for personally acting cruelly towards or neglecting their duty to their families. In this way, Rutherford extended her judgment of proper social behavior to men, especially in regard to their actual and literary treatment of women. She commended Richard

Steele, for example, for having "an intense admiration for woman, appreciating her nobler and finer qualities of mind and heart" while she censured Charles Dickens for tending to portray women as "weak, simpering and affectionate."[27] *American Authors*, published in 1894, also introduced themes of the South and southern history that would inform Rutherford's later historical writing and activism as a leader of the United Daughters of the Confederacy. Not only did the textbook favor southern authors, it repeatedly defended the worthiness of the Confederate cause and glorified southern literary achievement.[28] All four textbooks championed female writers, particularly those who conformed to her ideal of feminine propriety in their work and personal lives.

Rutherford's deep concern with propriety and feminine modesty should not obscure the fact that the school prepared women for more than traditional domestic roles. Lucy Cobb recognized that many of its alumnae would seek employment, and by teaching students marketable, and at the same time, respectable, skills, as well as genteel decorum and dress, Lucy Cobb created a new image of elite white single womanhood, distinguished both from leisured antebellum ladies and contemporary women of the working class. In this way, Lucy Cobb invented a modern version of womanhood that combined aspects of the new woman and the southern belle, what I call the "new belle."[29] As early as 1885, a Lucy Cobb commencement speaker argued that women ought to be allowed into more professions. Noting that many women worked, John Whitner pointed out the hypocrisy of a chivalry that restricted women to the backbreaking work of the needle trades.[30] By the 1920s the school offered an optional business course that included bookkeeping, stenography, and typing, preparing students for a job market that increasingly hired young single women as clerks.[31]

There is evidence that at least some Lucies did seek employment in the respectable female professions, despite the widespread assumption that elite white southern women never entered the labor market.[32] Lucies took jobs that signified their education and class standing; none worked in the textile mills then springing up across the South. Nonetheless, their work was economically as well as symbolically significant; in the new circumstances of the urban New South, families might depend on the income of women, particularly unmarried daughters or "maiden aunts," to help maintain trappings of class. The most obvious examples of employed Lucies are Rutherford and her sisters themselves. Although financial need was never directly acknowledged, it is striking that all four of the Rutherford sisters taught at Lucy Cobb, and that the school continued to offer a major source of employment for its own graduates throughout its history. Other professional graduates of Lucy Cobb included the librarian for the state of Georgia, the first two deans of women at the University of Georgia, and a New York congresswoman.[33] The extent of income earning among Lucy Cobb alumnae may seem at odds with the school's emphasis on socializing southern ladies, a role that suggested domesticity and leisure, but in fact they are intimately related—the school's concern with manners made the paid work of its alumnae more respectable. Rutherford, along with the school's other teachers, offered students a model of modern elite white womanhood that included employment.

Rutherford's blend of academic rigor, practical skills, and conservative morality at Lucy Cobb won praise from observers around Georgia and elsewhere in the South. Local businessmen praised the "atmosphere of refinement, of gentle, sweet dignity, of natural and easy culture" and called the Lucy Cobb ideal a "perfection of sacred womanhood."[34] Others also noted the school's academic excellence. In a letter to the editor of the *Atlanta Constitution*, a "learned gentleman" referred to Lucy Cobb Institute as "the most thorough and ideal [women's seminary] in this country," and observers routinely called Lucy Cobb the leading school for women in the South.[35] Even given the propensity for exaggeration among the press of the period, Rutherford succeeded in carefully balancing intellectually rigorous education with proper social and moral training for ladies. Students and alumnae remembered their time at Lucy Cobb fondly. Alumnae particularly noted in reminiscences their deep admiration and respect for Rutherford as a teacher, principal, and mentor.[36] Even young women who did not attend Lucy Cobb revered Rutherford, such as the State Normal School students who named their literary club the "Mildred Rutherford Society" in honor of "the strong personality of our beloved Miss Millie."[37]

In 1895 Rutherford stepped down from her post as principal in order to care for her ailing father, and turned the school's leadership over to Lipscomb. During her tenure, Lipscomb expanded the school further, adding a preparatory department and hiring more instructors with advanced degrees. She also added several Lucy Cobb graduates to the faculty, creating both a sense of tradition and community within the school and respectable employment for graduates. Rutherford continued to teach at Lucy Cobb and remained closely associated with the school. She took on the leadership of the school in 1907 for its fiftieth anniversary year before turning it over to her handpicked successors, both Lucy Cobb grads. Enjoying her freedom from the everyday oversight of the school, Rutherford traveled with students to Europe and the Middle East, and gave more attention to her writing.[38]

Over the course of the next ten years, the school continued to improve academically but never achieved financial stability. In 1917 Elizabeth Avery Colton of the Association of College Women wrote in her extensive report on southern higher education for women that "a diploma from Lucy Cobb Institute, which does not pretend to be a college, is preferable to a degree from any of the nominal nine colleges [in Georgia]."[39] The following year, the University of Georgia began to accept Lucy Cobb graduates into its junior class.[40] But the economic uncertainty of the war years hurt the school. In 1917 Rutherford again resumed leadership of Lucy Cobb, this time with the title of "president," signaling the school's college-level ambitions. Five years later, citing exhaustion, Rutherford convinced her niece and namesake, Mildred Rutherford Mell, to take the position.[41]

Mell was particularly well qualified to run Lucy Cobb. After Rutherford's younger sister Bessie Rutherford Mell died in 1894, leaving behind three young children, Mildred Rutherford took on the task of helping to raise and educate her nieces and nephew, becoming particularly close to her namesake, Mildred Rutherford Mell. Mell graduated from Lucy Cobb at the top of her class in 1907 and assisted her aunt at the school, traveling with her to Europe in 1910. After receiving a bachelor's degree from the University of Wisconsin and teaching for two years at Lucy Cobb, Mell took on the presidency of the school in the early 1920s and did her best to improve its academic standards and financial situation. Mell faced a school much hurt by the boll weevil devastation of cotton production of the early 1920s, which hurt the finances of parents and donors alike, and by new competition from public high schools and better-funded women's colleges. In 1925, after turning the leadership of the school back to her aunt, Mell taught elsewhere and later earned a PhD in economics and sociology from Howard Odum at the University of North Carolina, the academic center of southern progressivism. Like her aunt, Mell became an educator of southern women, teaching for twenty-two years at Agnes Scott College in Decatur.[42]

Rutherford spent a final year, 1925–26, as Lucy Cobb president. Along with another niece, she threw herself into an effort to raise a substantial endowment and earn the school accreditation as a junior college in order to retain the school's independence from the University of Georgia and the city of Athens.[43] Failing to establish a secure endowment and completely worn out, however, she finally retired for good in 1926. Her family worried that her commitment to saving Lucy Cobb had taken its toll on her physical and mental health. Even so, she did not save Lucy Cobb; the school struggled on a few more years before closing in 1931.[44]

The close association of Rutherford and Lucy Cobb attests to her dedication to the school, but Rutherford also gave considerable energy to her work as a club woman and historian. Well known in Athens, Rutherford earned the affectionate nickname "Miss Millie." Her public lectures in the Seney-Stovall

Chapel on everything from southern history to her visit to the Middle East drew large crowds. Much praised as a speaker, Rutherford had a commanding presence and an ability to inspire admiration among men and women alike.[45] Her most outstanding physical feature may well have been her ramrod-straight posture. One former student remembered that whenever she passed through a room, people instinctively straightened themselves.[46] Rutherford used her powerful presence to achieve leadership positions in many of the women's clubs popular at the time. She held state, regional, and national offices in the YWCA, the Daughters of the American Revolution (DAR), and the Women's Christian Temperance Union (WCTU). But Rutherford was best known for her work with Confederate memorial associations, particularly the UDC.[47]

Mildred Rutherford had been introduced by her mother to the movement to commemorate the Confederacy. With the Confederate surrender, Laura Rutherford turned the soldiers' aid organization she had headed into the Athens chapter of the Ladies' Memorial Association (LMA).[48] After her mother's death in 1888 Mildred Rutherford became president for life of the Athens chapter of the LMA, but the UDC gave her more opportunity for broader historical activity. Created in 1894, the United Daughters of the Confederacy took part in the late nineteenth-century fascination with memorializing the past.[49] The Civil War received particular attention from groups attempting to create meaning from the still-recent bloody conflict.[50] Veterans had been the first to commemorate the Civil War, but by the turn of the century these groups had lost numbers and influence. The UDC became the largest and most significant of the Confederate memorial organizations in the new century.[51] Whereas the United Confederate Veterans (UCV) gave their attention primarily to annual reunions and parades that helped restore masculine pride damaged by defeat, the UDC focused on determining how the South—and the nation—remembered and understood the Civil War, the Confederacy, and the antebellum South. Through their work sponsoring monuments, creating archives, and regulating textbooks used in schools and universities, the women of the UDC popularized a pro-Confederate historical memory of the Civil War and prewar southern society designed to win northern acceptance of segregation and disenfranchisement.

Rutherford played a key role in how the organization defined and disseminated its version of southern history. In 1896, the year after she ended her first term as principal of Lucy Cobb Institute, Rutherford created an Athens branch of the UDC and named it for her mother. Remaining president of the Laura Rutherford chapter for ten years, she served as Georgia's historian general for life, and held the state presidency from 1901 to 1903.[52] As state historian, Rutherford pushed local chapters to have active historical programs. She sent each chapter a form requesting that they report the number of pages written, number of war relics collected, number of meetings held, and other activities related to their historical activities. Chapter historians sent back a wide range of replies, some admitting to lack of attention to the subject, but most claiming to have fairly active programs.[53]

Because Rutherford had established a reputation as a historian and southern patriot through her work in the Athens and Georgia UDC and her textbooks, she was appointed historian general of the national UDC in 1911. Rutherford's popularity led the UDC to amend its constitution twice, overturning two-year term limits, in order to allow her to remain its national historian until 1916. Rutherford used the office to broaden her prominence as a historian and conservative activist. As UDC historian general, she created an archive of Confederate memorabilia, set the agenda for the UDC historical program, and gave an annual speech, often in full antebellum dress. She published her speeches in pamphlet form and promoted them as part of the "Mildred Rutherford Historical Circle" series, a sort of correspondence course for adults on southern history.[54] The titles of her speeches, such as *The Civilization of the Old South: What Made It: What Destroyed It: What Has Replaced It* and *The South Must Have Her Rightful Place in History,* make clear their messages.[55]

Although Rutherford's speeches and pamphlets echoed standard UDC themes such as the heroism of southern soldiers, her writings also took on more ambitious goals: establishing the South's contribution to United States history, legitimizing secession, and idealizing the antebellum plantation.[56] After becoming historian general, Rutherford lectured on the importance of southerners and slaveholders in the early American republic.[57] The South, Rutherford argued, was not a backward, separatist region; rather, it was integral to the nation itself. Like other postbellum southern advocates, the UDC historian defended the legality of Confederate secession and asserted that the true cause of the war had been not slavery, but "a different and directly opposite view as to the nature of the government of the United States."[58] In doing so, she sought to justify the extensive segregation and disenfranchisement laws that had been passed by southern state legislatures in the 1890s and early 1900s in direct violation of the Fourteenth and Fifteenth Amendments.[59]

Rutherford not only defended secession, she also glorified the plantation system and slavery itself. Toward this end much of her writing portrayed slavery as a benign institution that aided and uplifted African Americans in bondage.[60] In *Civilization of the Old South,* she wrote that "the servants were very happy in their life upon the old plantation" and in other writings quoted approvingly from an English traveler who described joyful slaves singing, dancing, and laughing. Claiming to "love everyone in Athens, white and black," Rutherford reported that she gave "every one of the old time negroes in Athens" a gift at Christmas "in appreciation of their faithfulness of the long ago."[61] Despite her "love" for everyone in Athens, Rutherford's glorification of plantation slavery implied that contemporary African Americans did not behave with the servility that she expected. Like contemporary writers such as Thomas Nelson Page and Joel Chandler Harris, she suggested that African Americans had fared better on the antebellum plantation than in the New South city.[62] Several of her writings asserted that slaves had been unprepared for freedom, and that emancipation had caused their moral and physical corruption.[63]

The belief that white southern women benefited from conservative gender roles and white supremacy associated with the southern plantation, although not as prominent in Rutherford's UDC speeches and pamphlets as her attempts to justify secession or prove slavery benign, emerged as a major part of her worldview in her overall activism, teaching, and writing. In this way, she highlighted the gendered aspects of the plantation legend.[64] In one UDC speech, for example, she assured her listeners that antebellum life had been "a picture of contentment, peace, and happiness," where ladies received respect and honor. Unfortunately, she lamented, modern women no longer enjoyed the reverence of the belle; "old time chivalry" was fading away. Rutherford's descriptions of chivalry suggest that when southern men lost the war, and along with it their wealth and way of life, they had failed their women, leaving them unprotected and vulnerable.[65]

Yet Rutherford had strong criticism not only for the shortcomings of white men, but also for unfeminine behavior on the part of white women. Women, she believed, must prove themselves worthy of men's protection. Modern women and girls had become so much "bolder and less modest," Rutherford lamented, that they allowed men and boys to address them by their first names, declined to discourage men from smoking in their presence, and, worst of all, pursued men "instead of making the men seek them." In experimenting with new social and sexual behavior, she implied, women acted "so as to not deserve anything better" and therefore endangered their claim to deference and protection.[66] Acting on these sentiments, Rutherford tried to suppress any hint of immodest behavior in her students at Lucy Cobb. Talking to boys, wearing makeup, and venturing alone beyond the magnolia tree in the school's front yard remained prohibited well into the 1920s. Rutherford continued to measure each girl's skirt before group outings to make sure that it fell below the ankle.[67]

Not only did young women in southern cities experiment with bold new fashions and behavior, they also, to Rutherford's dismay, sought to expand women's direct participation in politics and, in particular, gain access to the vote. By 1910 significant numbers of southern women had embraced the woman suffrage campaign.[68] In 1912 Rutherford expressed her disapproval by asserting, "If there is a power that is placed in any hands, it is the power that is placed in the hands of the southern woman in her home. That power is great enough to direct legislative bodies—and that, too, without demanding the ballot." Three years later, Rutherford argued on the floor of the Georgia House of Representatives that "the glare of public life" had made modern woman "an unsexed mongrel, shorn of her true power" and suffrage only endangered women more. Suffrage, she continued, was not a step toward equality, but rather a way of robbing women of the only power that they truly held—that of feminine influence and persuasion within their families.[69] Rutherford never reconciled this view with the fact that she herself was one of Georgia's most publicly active and well-known women of her time.

Like other "antis," Rutherford also feared that a constitutional amendment granting voting rights for women would open the way for more federal scrutiny of voting and civil rights.[70] Invoking the specter of Reconstruction in a 1914 speech at the University of Georgia, Rutherford argued: "If we today yield our state rights, whether for National prohibition or for National Woman Suffrage or for any other causes . . . we will have a Reconstruction Period worse than that which followed the War Between the States," linking expansion of the constitution with military occupation and the mythic "Negro rule" of the postwar years. Southern antis like Rutherford commonly asserted that woman suffrage would enfranchise a huge population of African American women, despite the disenfranchisement measures in state constitutions. In addition, new constitutional amendments, they alleged, would give the federal government an excuse to assert control over local affairs.[71] Indeed, Rutherford opposed *all* constitutional amendments, including prohibition, despite her anti-alcohol sentiments, on the basis of limiting federal power.[72] Rutherford reserved her strongest resistance for the suffrage amendment, believing that it would strengthen national oversight of the internal political processes of the states.

Even more deeply, suffrage and feminism threatened the South's racial, sexual, and political hierarchies. Rutherford recognized the interconnectedness of southern racial and sexual ideologies, and in calling for a return to chivalry, she reminded white men and women of their racial duty to conform to sexual stereotypes.[73] Although Rutherford did not make the connection directly, modest behavior by white women was essential to the political power of the white southern elite. Even the appearance of immodesty (a quality often attributed to suffragists) by white women brought into question one of the key justifications for segregation, disenfranchisement, and Democratic hegemony: the protection of white women's virtue.[74] Protection of white women from black men served as the basis of Democratic Party platforms throughout the South, especially when party hegemony faced internal or external threats.[75] In Georgia, Governor (and later senator) Hoke Smith freely used anti-black propaganda to win elections in the early 1900s. In 1906, one month after a particularly racist campaign for the Democratic nomination for governor, rumors of rapes of white women by black men ignited a riot in Atlanta that by one account left 25 blacks dead and over 150 people injured.[76] Three years later, Governor Smith helped pass a new state constitution that significantly reduced the number of both blacks and whites eligible to vote.[77] Hoke Smith, married to Rutherford's cousin and a member of Lucy Cobb's board of directors in the 1920s, proved the political success of racist appeals.[78]

Rutherford's speeches and writings suggest that she understood the racialized and gendered notion implicit in these racist policies: white women must prove their worthiness of the protection offered by disenfranchisement and segregation in order for the racist rhetoric of politicians like Smith to resonate with voters. If white women were promiscuous, acted carelessly in public, or campaigned for the vote, they endangered a key rationale for the early twentieth-century southern racial and political hierarchy. Despite the contradictions in her own life, Rutherford genuinely believed that elite white women benefited most from gender relationships that promised protection in exchange for submissiveness and sexual purity.[79] Rutherford's belief in social hierarchy—a hierarchy that gave her an exalted place as a white woman from a socially prominent family— led her to believe that gender, as well as race, was immutable. Further, Rutherford's strong Baptist faith supported a worldview that saw social difference as God-ordained, not manufactured; for her, resisting one's place in the social order defied not only biology, but even God's will. And of course, her own life attests to the possibilities of political influence for women without, as she put it, "demanding the ballot." Like other prominent women who rejected feminism and suffrage, Rutherford truly believed that women like her held more power through feminine "influence" than through a spurious equality.

Rutherford sought to influence not just contemporary morality, race relations, and politics but economic development as well. Despite her conservative impulses on matters of sexual propriety and racial hierarchy, Rutherford did not seek to prevent economic development or national unification. Rather, her sentimental portraits of antebellum life were intended to have the opposite effect; they served to *promote* southern industrialization and sectional reunification. Like her contemporaries, Rutherford traced a tradition of industrial production back to the antebellum era and promoted industry as essential to contemporary southern strength. In a speech of 1912, sounding like the New South promoters, she pointed to the productivity of the region with respect to cotton, sulfur, oil, marble, and coal; boasted of the South's lumber, saw, and cotton mills; and claimed the world's largest fertilizer and sulfuric acid plants for southern states. These were hardly the words of the nostalgic agrarian that at first glance she appeared to be.[80]

Rutherford was not alone in lauding the Old South yet welcoming the new. Other authors in the plantation tradition, including Thomas Nelson Page and Joel Chandler Harris, also supported New South development. In addition, the New South boosters associated particularly with Henry Grady's *Atlanta Constitution*, painted idyllic portraits of antebellum plantation life. Harris, the author of the Uncle Remus stories, also wrote for Grady's paper. Grady himself, the best-known New South promoter and Rutherford's childhood classmate, praised the comfort and grace of the plantation in his speeches and articles. Honoring the Old South reminded southerners of a worthy past, one they could take pride in despite subsequent defeat. Memorializing the Confederacy reassured southerners that economic development would not destroy their regional distinctiveness or identity.[81] Although she shared the New South boosters' pro-southern boosterism, Rutherford's especially strong interest in gender and women's roles distinguished her writing from that of Grady and others.

Rutherford herself played an active role in the New South economy and displayed a sharp, even aggressive, business sense. In many ways, her career as a historian depended on the expansion of publishing and advertising and on the improvements in travel of the early twentieth century.[82] Rutherford energetically raised money for her Confederate work and for the Lucy Cobb Institute through public speaking, fundraising letters, and print ads. Her own "scrapbooks" carried prominent ads for Lucy Cobb and for the "Mildred Lewis Rutherford Historical Circle," and she used her own textbooks extensively. In correspondence with her publishers, she proves to be aware and quite interested in the sales numbers of her books and in their promotion.[83] Rutherford took full advantage of the New South economy to publicize her vision of an idealized antebellum era.

Not only did Rutherford personally take part in the new economy, but her sentimental portrayal of the antebellum era and the Confederacy actually served to support the economic, political, and social changes associated with the New South. By romanticizing, but containing, the memory of the Old South, Rutherford and other members of the UDC helped alleviate their husbands' and fathers' guilt over moving away from the culture and values associated with the plantation myth. Their identity as women was key: in the mouths of women, the celebration of the Confederacy seemed harmless, even charming, since voteless women could hardly be taken seriously as political actors. Women represented the nostalgia for the antebellum past and the spirit of the Confederate revolt, keeping it in public consciousness while containing it as a political threat.

Rutherford's pro-Confederate work had another ironic consequence: helping to bring about sectional reconciliation. Northerners also romanticized the Old South, identifying it with the gentility and stability they believed were missing from their own competitive, acquisitive, and diverse society.[84] The mutual celebration of the antebellum South, like the shared military success of the Spanish-American War, helped to begin the psychological reunification of the sections.[85] Rutherford constantly identified her purpose in writing history as creating peace through truth, and she infused her writing with American, not just southern, patriotism. As she wrote, the South "desires that the truth be told in such a way that peace between the sections shall be the result."[86] The romanticization of the antebellum plantation further brought the North and South together over the issue of race. Although writers such as Rutherford conceded that slavery's demise was inevitable, her benevolent, harmonious, and peaceful view of the institution aided the South in "winning the peace"— that is, implementing segregation, disenfranchisement, and other forms of racial control.[87] The sentimentalization of slavery helped ease northern guilt about allowing states to control racial policy.[88] Rutherford's pro-Confederate rhetoric, far from rekindling sectional tension, justified local control of racial issues in a reunited nation.

Rutherford remained active as a historian of the Confederacy and Old South up until her death in 1928. In 1922, when Rutherford again resigned as president of Lucy Cobb Institute, she cited a wish "to spend her remaining life in the devotion of her literary work in Southern history." Yet her support that year for H. W. Johnstone's *Truth of the War Conspiracy of 1861*, a stridently anti-Lincoln book, embroiled her in one of the biggest controversies of her career.[89] Her endorsement of the volume at a United Confederate Veterans convention led to criticism from the press and even members of the veteran's group.[90] Although still respected in pro-Confederate circles, Rutherford's views appeared extreme to Americans celebrating the dedication that year of the Lincoln memorial.[91]

Unswayed by the controversy, in the early 1920s Rutherford continued to work on Confederate causes and become a leading fundraiser for the Stone Mountain monument, a sort of Confederate Mount Rushmore carved on the rocky hillside outside of Atlanta, where the Ku Klux Klan had been reborn in 1915.[92] By 1926 both the failure of the Lucy Cobb endowment campaign and the

Lincoln controversy had taken their toll. In June of the following year, Rutherford became seriously ill while attending a convention of the Children of the Confederacy and was hospitalized. On Christmas night that year a fire in her home destroyed most of her private collection of Confederate artifacts; a joke went around Athens that her incendiary comments on Lincoln had caused "spontaneous combustion." She never fully recovered from the illness and the shock of the fire and died August 15, 1928.[93]

To the end, Rutherford remained committed to telling the "truths," as she viewed them, of southern and Confederate history. Yet her waning influence was not just the result of lack of diplomacy on her part. By the mid-1920s the Confederate celebration had begun to fade. Most of those who could personally remember the war had died by this time, and the memories of defeat were less raw. There were political changes as well. With the election of Woodrow Wilson, southerners gained both national influence and political self-confidence. The South seemed to have won its battle to keep its region free from federal interference, and laws restricting African American voting and movement remained in place. In addition, World War I, even more than the Spanish-American War, marked a turning point in sectional reconciliation.[94] Finally, the woman suffrage amendment brought neither the full-scale destruction in gender roles anticipated by some anti-suffragists nor the large numbers of black women to the polls feared by white southerners.[95]

Rutherford may have lost some of the esteem in which she was held before 1920, but the UDC historian's version of Confederate history and antebellum life had lasting influence. Not only did the history she promoted remain southern orthodoxy for almost another half-century, but the hierarchical social and political structure that she favored also remained in place. Her work writing history helped create a culture that legitimized control by traditional southern elites. Glorifying antebellum life and Confederate heroism, Rutherford actually lent legitimacy to economic and social shifts that privileged whites used to their advantage. By inventing a mythical Old South, Rutherford aided a reinvented elite in asserting its hegemony over New South society and politics.

## NOTES

1. Studies of Rutherford include Hazelle Beard Tuthill, "Mildred Lewis Rutherford" (master's thesis, University of South Carolina, 1929); Virginia Pettigrew Clare, *Thunder and Stars* (Oglethorpe, Ga.: Oglethorpe University Press, 1941); Margaret Anne Womack, "Mildred Lewis Rutherford: Exponent of Southern Culture" (master's thesis, University of Georgia, 1951); and Fred Arthur Bailey, "Mildred Lewis Rutherford and the Patrician Cult of the Old South" *Georgia Historical Quarterly*

77 (Fall 1994): 509–35; Grace Elizabeth Hale, "'Some Women Have Never Been Reconstructed': Mildred Lewis Rutherford, Lucy M. Stanton, and the Racial Politics of White Southern Womanhood, 1900–1930," in *Georgia in Black and White: Explorations in the Race Relations of a Southern State, 1865–1950*, ed. John C. Inscoe, 173–201 (Athens: University of Georgia Press, 1994). The author would like to thank Jane Sherron De Hart, Carl Harris, John Majewski, Beverly Schwartzberg, and Jay Carlander for their suggestions on this essay.

2. Marjorie Spruill Wheeler, *New Women of the New South: The Leaders of the Woman Suffrage Movement in the Southern States* (New York: Oxford University Press, 1993); Glenda Gilmore, *Gender and Jim Crow: Women and the Politics of White Supremacy in North Carolina, 1896–1920* (Chapel Hill: University of North Carolina Press, 1996); Anastatia Sims, *The Power of Femininity in the New South: Women's Organizations and Politics in North Carolina, 1880–1930* (Columbia: University of South Carolina Press, 1997); Elna Green, *Southern Strategies: Southern Women and the Woman Suffrage Question* (Chapel Hill: University of North Carolina Press, 1997); Elizabeth Hayes Turner, *Women, Culture, and Community: Religion and Reform in Galveston, 1880–1920* (New York: Oxford University Press, 1997); Jane Turner Censer, *The Reconstruction of White Southern Womanhood, 1865–1895* (Baton Rouge: Louisiana State University Press, 2003).

3. Ernest C. Hynds, *Antebellum Athens and Clarke County Georgia* (Athens: University of Georgia Press, 1974), 2–5, 7–8, 22; Frances Taliaferro Thomas, *A Portrait of Historic Athens and Clarke County* (Athens: University of Georgia Press, 1992), 39–40.

4. Hynds, *Antebellum Athens*, 25, 29, 33.

5. Hynds, *Antebellum Athens*, 27, 30, 32, 174; Thomas, *Portrait of Historic Athens*, 46.

6. Hynds, *Antebellum Athens*, 63–67, 76, 170–71; Numan V. Bartley, *The Creation of Modern Georgia* (Athens: University of Georgia Press, 1983), 29, 45; Lewis Nicholas Wynne, *The Continuity of Cotton: Planter Politics in Georgia, 1865–1892* (Macon, Ga.: Mercer University Press, 1986), 56, 64; Thomas, *Portrait of Historic Athens*, 71–78.

7. Augustus Longstreet Hull, *Annals of Athens, Georgia, 1801–1901* (Athens, Ga.: Banner Job Office, 1906; repr., Danielsville, Ga.: Heritage Papers, 1978), 412.

8. Clare, *Thunder and Stars*, 10–11, 22, 52, 82; Womack, "Mildred Lewis Rutherford," 1–2, 4.

9. Clare, *Thunder and Stars*, 16–17.

10. Womack, "Mildred Lewis Rutherford," 12–13; Phyllis Jenkins Barrow, "History of Lucy Cobb Institute, 1858–1950" (master's thesis, University of Georgia, 1951; repr. in *Higher Education for Women in the South: A History of Lucy Cobb Institute, 1858–1994*, ed. Phinizy Spalding [Athens, Ga.: Georgia Southern Press, 1994]), 11–12.

11. Womack, "Mildred Lewis Rutherford," 6–7, 14–15; Clare, *Thunder and Stars*, 73–74, 82, 89, 99, 107–8; Thomas, *Portrait of Historic Athens*, 101; Drew Gilpin Faust, *Mothers of Invention: Women of the Slaveholding South in the American Civil War* (Chapel Hill: University of North Carolina Press, 1996); Laura F. Edwards, *Scarlett Doesn't Live Here Anymore: Southern Women in the Civil War Era* (Urbana: University of Illinois Press, 2000).

12. Mildred Lewis Rutherford, "The Early History of the Lucy Cobb," *The Lightning Bug* (March/April 1926): 9–28; Womack, "Mildred Lewis Rutherford," 16–17; Clare, *Thunder and Stars*, 130–35; Barrow, "History of Lucy Cobb Institute," 25.

13. "Announcement of opening of Lucy Cobb Institute, 1859," folder 15, box 30, E. Merton Coulter Historical Manuscripts Collection, Hargrett Library (hereafter Coulter Manuscripts); Rutherford, "Early History of the Lucy Cobb," 9; Barrow, "History of Lucy Cobb Institute," 13, 18; Christie Anne Farnham, *The Education of the Southern Belle: Higher Education and Student Socialization in the Antebellum South* (New York: New York University Press, 1994), 14–17.

14. "Catalogue of the Lucy Cobb Institute," 1883, in the Georgia Room, Hargrett Rare Book and Manuscript Library, University of Georgia, Athens, Georgia (hereafter Hargrett Library); "Announcement of Lucy Cobb Institute, Athens, Georgia," 1890, Lucy Cobb Institute Scrapbook, 1858–1908, box 4, Mildred Lewis Rutherford Scrapbooks, Hargrett Library (hereafter Lucy Cobb Institute Scrapbook); Rutherford, "Early History of the Lucy Cobb," 12–13; Barrow, "History of Lucy Cobb Institute," 25–26; "Mrs. George A. Mell," folder 1, box 1, Mell-Rutherford Family Papers, Hargrett Library (hereafter Mell-Rutherford Papers).

15. "Catalogue of the Lucy Cobb Institute," 1883, 3, 7–9, 14–15; Amy McCandless, *The Past in the Present: Women's Higher Education in the Twentieth-Century South* (Tuscaloosa: University of Alabama Press, 1999), 30–31; Farnham, *Education of the Southern Belle*, 86–88.

16. "Catalogue of the Lucy Cobb Institute," 1883, 10–11, 15–16; "Announcement of Lucy Cobb Institute," 1890; Farnham, *Education of the Southern Belle*, 23.

17. Florida Orr, "The Lucy Cobb: Reminiscence by an 'Old Pupil,'" *Athens Banner-Watchman*, June 1887, in Lucy Cobb Institute Scrapbook, 1858–1908.

18. Lucy Cobb was officially nondenominational. Rutherford required all students to attend services at a church of their parents' choice every Sunday. "Lucy Cobb Institute Annual Announcement, 1904–1905," 33, Georgia Room, Hargrett Library.

19. Rutherford, "Early History of the Lucy Cobb," 13–14; Barrow, "History of Lucy Cobb Institute," 27–28.

20. McCandless, *Past in the Present*, 56.

21. "Announcement of Lucy Cobb Institute," 1890; Tuthill, "Mildred Lewis Rutherford," 37; Clare, *Thunder and Stars*, 141.

22. Wynne, *Continuity of Cotton*, 179–84; Bartley, *Creation of Modern Georgia*, 103–6; Thomas, *Portrait of Historic Athens*, 103–4.

23. Victoria Bynum, *Unruly Women: The Politics of Social and Sexual Control in the Old South* (Chapel Hill: University of North Carolina Press, 1992), 9–10.

24. John E. Drewry, "Some of our Lucy Cobb Girls," and "The Old Fashioned Women, Atlanta, Ga.," *The Lightning Bug* (January 1926): 36–37; Lucy Cobb Alumnae Association, scrapbook of clippings, box 4, Lucy Cobb Institute Collection, Hargrett Library; *Women of Georgia: A Ready and Accurate Reference Book for Newspapers and Librarian[s]* (Atlanta: Georgia Press Reference Association, 1927), 39, 67, 124, 137, 150–51, 155, 156, 127.

25. Mildred Lewis Rutherford, *Bible Questions With Reference in the Old Testament* (Athens, Ga.: MacGregor Co. [?], 1890); Mildred Lewis Rutherford, *English Authors: A Handbook of English Literature from Chaucer to Living Writers* (Atlanta: Constitutional Book Co., 1890); Mildred Lewis Rutherford, *American Authors* (Atlanta: Franklin Printing and Publishing Co., 1894); Mildred Lewis Rutherford, *French Authors* (Atlanta: Franklin Printing and Publishing Co., 1906); Mildred Lewis Rutherford, *The South in History and Literature: A Hand-book of Southern Authors from the Settlement of Jamestown, 1607, to Living Writers* (Atlanta: Franklin Printing and Publishing Co., 1906).

26. For example, Rutherford condemns George Eliot for her common law marriage with a married man: "We must condemn in unqualified terms the weakness of moral character that allowed her to defy God's law" (*English Authors*, 560).

27. Rutherford, *English Authors*, 149 (first quotation), 411 (second quotation).

28. Rutherford, *American Authors*, 14–15, 79–85, 108–18.

29. Sarah H. Case, "Renegotiating Race and Respectability in the Classroom: Women and Education in the New South" (PhD diss., University of California, Santa Barbara, 2002), 19.

30. Jno. C. Whitner, "Woman: God-made. Her true culture, and her sphere of work," commence-

ment address, Lucy Cobb Institute, Athens, Georgia, June 17, 1885, pamphlet in Lucy Cobb Institute Scrapbook, 1858–1908.

31. "Lucy Cobb Institute Sixty-sixth Annual Announcement, 1858–1923," 1923, 21, Georgia Room, Hargrett Library.

32. McCandless, *Past in the Present*, 60.

33. List of Faculty, Lucy Cobb Institute File, Athens–Clarke County Heritage Foundation, Athens, Georgia (hereafter Athens–Clarke County Heritage Foundation); Barrow, "History of Lucy Cobb Institute," 50; "What the Lucy Cobb Stands for in the State," *Lucy Cobb Dots* 1 (October 3, 1917): 1–2; "Address of Mrs. May Hull Pope" [1922], folder 4, box 1, Mildred Lewis Rutherford Papers, Hargrett Library (hereafter Rutherford Papers). Lucy Cobb graduate Caroline Goodwin O'Day became a Progressive activist in New York and a close friend of Eleanor Roosevelt. She served in Congress from 1934 to her death in 1943. See "Atlanta Women to Hear Address by Mrs. Carolina O'Day Tomorrow" [1936]; and "Mrs. Caroline O'Day, N.Y Congresswoman, to Pay Visit to Athens," unidentified newspaper clippings, Lucy Cobb Alumnae Association, scrapbook of clippings.

34. D. G. Bickers, "Spirit of Lucy Cobb," 10–11.

35. "Constitutionals: General Gossip and Editorial Short Stops Caught on the Run," *Atlanta Constitution*, n.d., Lucy Cobb Institute Scrapbook, 1858–1908. See also other newspaper clippings collected in the Lucy Cobb Institute Scrapbook, 1858–1908.

36. Anne Bates Windship, Memorial letter, 1928; and "Letters from H + H," folder 1, box 1, Rutherford Papers; "Miss Mildred Rutherford Paid Tributes By Former Lucy Cobb Girls," unidentified newspaper clipping, 1928, folder 3, box 4, Rutherford Papers; Katherine Trussell Wilson, LaGrange Trussell DuPree, and Phyllis Jenkins Barrow, compilers, "Interview with Bessie Mell Lane," in Spalding, *Higher Education for Women in the South*, 266.

37. "Outline of Work, 1908–1909, Mildred Rutherford Literary Society, State Normal School, Athens, Georgia"; and "Mildred Rutherford Society, 1916–1917, State Normal School, Athens, Georgia," box 1, State Normal School Records, Administrative Subject Folder, Senior Essays and Microfilm, 1904–33, University Archives, Hargrett Library. I thank Rebecca Montgomery informing me of these clubs.

38. "Lucy Cobb Institute Annual Announcement, 1902–1903," 4, Georgia Room, Hargrett Library; Rutherford, "Early History of the Lucy Cobb," 16; Barrow, "History of Lucy Cobb Institute," 33–34, 36, 41. The anniversary was dated from the school's incorporation in 1857.

39. Colton called Agnes Scott the only true college for women in Georgia. Mildred Lewis Rutherford, "Sketch of Lucy Cobb Institute," in Rowe, *History of Athens and Clarke County*, 77; "A Word to the Alumnae of Lucy Cobb and to the Citizens of Athens," 1, folder 9, box 2, Rutherford Papers. The report took Colton seven years, and was generally critical of the 142 institutions that it surveyed. See McCandless, *Past in the Present*, 36–37.

40. Lucy Cobb Institute Announcement, 1923, 15–16. Women could enter the College of Education or the College of Agriculture (for the home economics degree) as juniors. See Thomas, *Portrait of Historic Athens*, 177.

41. Board of Trustees, Minutes, April 9, 1917, July 5, 1917, and June 11, 1918, Minute Book, Lucy Cobb Institute Stock Books, Hargrett Library (hereafter Lucy Cobb Institute Stock Books); Womack, "Mildred Lewis Rutherford," 113.

42. "Mrs. George A. Mell"; "Report of Miss Mildred Mell, President Lucy Cobb Institute" [1923], folder 4, box 1, Rutherford Papers; Barrow, "History of Lucy Cobb Institute," 46; Bessie Mell Lane, "Mildred Rutherford Mell, 1889–1982," in Spalding, *Higher Education for Women in the South*, 256–57.

43. Womack, "Mildred Lewis Rutherford," 131–33. See the several articles in the fundraising circular "A Word to the Alumnae of Lucy Cobb and to the Citizens of Athens."

44. Minutes, Board of Trustees, April 22, 1925, Minute Book, Lucy Cobb Institute Stock Books; George Mell to Annie Laurie Mell Poats, April 15, 1926 and April 20, 1926, folder 12, box 1, Mell-Rutherford Papers; Barrow, "History of Lucy Cobb Institute," 49.

45. Womack, "Mildred Lewis Rutherford," 85–86, 91, 97, 102.

46. Wilson, DuPree, and Barrow, "Interview with Mrs. Bessie Mell Lane," in Spalding, *Higher Education for Women in the South*, 266.

47. Mildred Lewis Rutherford, "Life Sketch of Miss Mildred Rutherford," in H. J. Rowe, *History of Athens and Clarke County* (Athens, Ga.: McGregor Co., 1923), 105–107; Womack, "Mildred Lewis Rutherford," 79–82, 85, 87; Bailey, "Mildred Lewis Rutherford," 516, 521–22.

48. Womack, "Mildred Lewis Rutherford," 6–7. On the LMA, LeeAnn Whites, "'Stand by Your Man': The Ladies Memorial Association and the Reconstruction of Southern White Manhood," in *Women of the American South: A Multicultural Reader*, ed. Christie Anne Farnham, 133–49 (New York: New York University Press, 1997).

49. See David Glassberg, *American Historical Pageantry: The Uses of Tradition in the Early Twentieth Century* (Chapel Hill: University of North Carolina Press, 1990); Michael Kammen, *Mystic Chords of Memory: The Transformation of Tradition in American Culture* (New York: Random House, 1991); and John Gillis, ed., *Commemorations: The Politics of National Identity* (Princeton: Princeton University Press, 1994).

50. See Gaines Foster, *Ghosts of the Confederacy: Defeat, the Lost Cause, the Emergence of the New South* (New York: Oxford University Press, 1987); Nina Silber, *The Romance of Reunion: Northerners and the South, 1895–1900* (Chapel Hill: University of North Carolina Press, 1993); and David W. Blight, *Race and Reunion: The Civil War in American Memory* (Cambridge, Mass.: Harvard University Press, 2001).

51. Karen L. Cox, *Dixie's Daughters: The United Daughters of the Confederacy and the Preservation of Confederate Culture* (Gainesville: University of Press of Florida, 2003).

52. List of Athens Chapter UDC, folder 4, box 4, Rutherford Papers; Rutherford, "Life Sketch of Miss Mildred Rutherford," 105–6; Womack, "Mildred Lewis Rutherford," 7, 73–74.

53. Mildred Rutherford, State Historian, and Lillian Martin, Assistant State Historian, Letter to All Chapter Historians, Georgia Division,UDC, folder 4; Historical Reports for 1924, folder 18; and Mildred Rutherford, handwritten list of each state chapter and their historical activities, folder 18, all box 4, Rutherford Papers.

54. Bailey, "Mildred Lewis Rutherford," 520–21; Womack, "Mildred Lewis Rutherford," 85, 93, 104; "The Mildred Lewis Rutherford Historical Circle," 1915, folder 7, box 4, Rutherford Papers.

55. Mildred Lewis Rutherford, *Civilization of the Old South: What Made It: What Destroyed It; What Has Replaced It* (Athens, Ga.: McGregor Co., 1917); Mildred Lewis Rutherford, *The South Must Have Her Rightful Place in History* (Athens, Ga.: McGregor Co., 1923). Other published speeches include Mildred Lewis Rutherford, "The South in the Building of the Nation" (1912), "Thirteen Periods of United States History" (1912), "Wrongs of History Righted" (1914), and "Historical Sins of Omission and Commission" (1915) in Rutherford, *Four Addresses by Mildred Lewis Rutherford* (Birmingham, Ala.: Mildred Lewis Rutherford Historical Circle Printers, [1916]); Mildred Lewis Rutherford, *Truths of History: A Fair, Unbiased, Impartial, Unprejudiced, and Conscientious Study of History* (Athens, Ga.: McGregor Co., [1920]).

56. Rutherford, "The South in the Building of the Nation," 7–9; Rutherford, "Wrongs of History Righted," 49–51; Rutherford, *Civilization of the Old South*, esp. 6–17; Mildred Lewis Rutherford,

"Memories of Christmas on a Southern Plantation," in Spalding, *Higher Education in the South*, 211–16.

57. Rutherford, "The South in the Building of the Nation," 7–8; Rutherford, "Thirteen Periods," 21–28.

58. Rutherford, "Historical Sins of Omission and Commission," 113 (quotation); Rutherford, "Wrongs of History Righted," esp. 49–50; Rutherford, *Truths of History*, 1–7. Rutherford's views echo the ex-Confederates discussed in Foster, *Ghosts of the Confederacy*, 53–61.

59. Mildred Lewis Rutherford, *What the South May Claim, or Where the South Leads* (Athens, Ga.: McGregor Co., [1916 ?]), 17; Rutherford, "Historical Sins of Omission and Commission," 108–11; Rutherford, *Truths of History*, 19–21.

60. Rutherford, *Civilization of the Old South*, 6–7; Rutherford, *The South Must Have Her Rightful Place in History*, 18–19; Rutherford, "Memories of Christmas," 213, 216. Her description of slavery and race resemble those analyzed in George M. Fredrickson, *The Black Image in the White Mind: The Debate on Afro-American Character and Destiny, 1817–1914* (New York: Harper and Row, 1971); John David Smith, *An Old Creed for the New South: Proslavery Ideology and Historiography, 1865–1918* (Westport, Conn.: Wesleyan University Press, 1985); and Joel Williamson, *Rage for Order: Black-White Relations in the American South Since Emancipation* (New York: Oxford University Press, 1986).

61. Rutherford, *Civilization of the Old South*, 6; Rutherford, "Life Sketch of Miss Mildred Rutherford," 105; Rutherford, "Memories of Christmas," 216.

62. Paul Gaston, *The New South Creed: A Study in Southern Mythmaking* 2nd ed. (New York: Vintage, 1973), 181–83; Fredrickson, *Black Image in the White Mind*, 205–8, 211.

63. Rutherford, "Wrongs of History Righted," 61–63; Rutherford, *The South Must Have Her Rightful Place in History*, 16–17; Rutherford, *Civilization of the Old South*, 6–7, 30–31, 33; Rutherford, "Historical Sins of Omission and Commission," 110–11.

64. Male writers in the plantation tradition also celebrated the southern lady, but Rutherford offered a more pointed criticism of contemporary gender roles. See Silber, *Romance of Reunion*, 113, 117–19.

65. Rutherford, *Civilization of the Old South*, 7, 15, 40–42; Rutherford, "Thirteen Periods," 40; Hale, "'Some Women Have Never Been Reconstructed,'" 183; Cox, *Dixie's Daughters*, 45–46.

66. Rutherford, *Civilization of the Old South*, 40.

67. "Memories of a Lucy Cobb Girlhood" *Athens Observer*, October 13, 1986; and John Toon, "Lucy Cobb," *Athens Observer*, December 28, 1978, Lucy Cobb Institute File, Athens–Clarke County Heritage Foundation; Lucy Cobb Institute Catalogue, 1925, 38–40, Georgia Room, Hargrett Library.

68. Green, *Southern Strategies*, 13–14.

69. Rutherford, "The South in the Building of the Nation," 4; Womack, "Mildred Lewis Rutherford," 97–99, 102.

70. Suzanne Lebsock, "Woman Suffrage and White Supremacy: A Virginia Case Study," in *Visible Women: New Essays on American Activism*, ed. Nancy A. Hewitt and Suzanne Lebsock (Urbana: University of Illinois Press, 1993), 62–100, esp. 73–74; Jane Jerome Camhi, *Women against Women: American Anti-Suffragism, 1880–1920* (Brooklyn, N.Y.: Carlson Publishing, 1994), 129–32; Green, *Southern Strategies*, 86–87.

71. Lebsock, "Woman Suffrage and White Supremacy," 73; Green, *Southern Strategies*, 86–87.

72. Womack, "Mildred Lewis Rutherford," 82, 85, 97; Clare, *Thunder and Stars*, 172–73.

73. Elna Green found that southern antis believed in a "triangular structure" of society in which hierarchies of race, class, and gender reinforced and were dependent on one another (Green, *Southern Strategies*, 90).

74. Camhi, *Women against Women*, 64–66; Susan E. Marshall, *Splintered Sisterhood: Gender and Class in the Campaign against Woman Suffrage* (Madison: University of Wisconsin Press, 1997), 121, 191.

75. Green, *Southern Strategies*, 87–91; Williamson, *Rage for Order*, 186–91; Gilmore, *Gender and Jim Crow*, 95–99.

76. This was a 1969 report cited in Williamson, *Rage for Order*, 150.

77. Dewey W. Grantham Jr., *Hoke Smith and the Politics of the New South* (Baton Rouge: Louisiana State University Press, 1958); Bartley, *Creation of Modern Georgia*, 151–53; Williamson, *Rage for Order*, 141–151.

78. Smith married "Birdie" Cobb, Lucy Cobb's sister. Lamar Rutherford Lipscomb to Hoke Smith, March 23, 1925 and other correspondence in folder 15, box 30, Coulter Manuscripts.

79. Rutherford, *Civilization of the Old South*, 39–40, 42–43; Rutherford, "The South in the Building of the Nation," 4; Womack, "Mildred Lewis Rutherford," 99, 102; Clare, *Thunder and Stars*, 172–73.

80. Rutherford, "Thirteen Periods," 40–43; Rutherford, *Where the South Leads and Where Georgia Leads* (Athens, Ga.: McGregor Co., 1917), 41.

81. Womack, "Mildred Lewis Rutherford," 14; Gaston, *New South Creed*, chap. 5, esp. 159–60, 167–68, 173–75, 180, 185–86.

82. Pamela Walker Laird, *Advertising Progress: American Business and the Rise of Consumer Marketing* (Baltimore: Johns Hopkins University Press, 1998); Edward L. Ayers, *The Promise of the New South: Life after Reconstruction* (New York: Oxford University Press, 1992), 9, 10–11 (map), 18–20.

83. Ginn and Company, Publishers, to Mildred Rutherford, January 4, 1924; and other correspondence in folder 16, box 1, Rutherford Papers. Examples of publications by Rutherford that carry ads for having other books or for the Lucy Cobb include Rutherford, *What the South May Claim*, 37, 42, and "The Mildred Lewis Rutherford Historical Circle." The Lucy Cobb Annual Announcements indicate that the school used Rutherford's textbooks; in the Georgia Room, Hargrett Library.

84. Gaston, *New South Creed*, 172–73, 180–83; Silber, *Romance of Reunion*, 108–9.

85. Silber, *Romance of Reunion*, 178–85; Rutherford, "The South in the Building of the Nation," 14; Rutherford, "Thirteen Periods," 41.

86. Rutherford, *The South Must Have Her Rightful Place in History*, 2; Rutherford, "The South in the Building of the Nation", 14–15; Rutherford, "Wrongs of History Righted," 81–82; Rutherford, "Historical Sins of Omission and Commission," 113; M. Rutherford, "New America," in *Where the South Leads*, 21.

87. Rutherford, *The South Must Have Her Rightful Place in History*, 16.

88. Gaston, *New South Creed*, 181–83; Fredrickson, *Black Image in the White Mind*, 204–9; Silber, *Romance of Reunion*, 124, 135, 139–41; Rutherford, "Memories of Christmas," 211–16; Rutherford, *Civilization of the Old South*, 7.

89. Womack, "Mildred Lewis Rutherford," 122, 123–24; H. W. Johnstone, *Truth of the War Conspiracy of 1861* (Athens, Ga.: MacGregor Co., 1921); Mildred Lewis Rutherford, speech to UCV Reunion in New Orleans, 1923, folder 4, box 4, Rutherford Papers.

90. "Degrading Her Talent," *Wilkes-Barre (Pa.) Evening News*, December 1922; "The Voice of a Lost Cause: Two Writers Cling to a Dead Illusion," *Boston Evening Transcript*, August 30, 1922;

"Slur on Lincoln a 'Lie' Says Speakers," *New York Times*, June 26, 1922; all in Lucy Cobb Institute Scrapbook, 1858–1908; Mildred Lewis Rutherford, letter to editor, *Atlanta Constitution*, n.d., folder 2, box 3, Rutherford Papers.

91. Merrill D. Peterson, *Lincoln in American Memory* (New York: Oxford University Press, 1994), 195–97, 214–15.

92. Jno. Goolrick to Mildred Lewis Rutherford, April 12, 1924; and David Webb to Rutherford, April 29, 1924, folder 16, box 1, Rutherford Papers.

93. Wilson, DuPree, and Barrow, "Interview with Mrs. Bessie Mell Lane," 265; Womack, "Mildred Lewis Rutherford," 143.

94. C. Vann Woodward, *Origins of the New South, 1877–1913* (Baton Rouge: Louisiana State University Press, 1951), 480–81; Dewey W. Grantham, *The South in Modern America: A Region at Odds* (New York: Harper Collins, 1994), 63–64, 68; Cox, *Dixie's Daughters*, chap. 8.

95. Camhi, *Women against Women*, 231–32; Green, *Southern Strategies*, 175–77; Rosalyn Terborg-Penn, *African American Women in the Struggle for the Vote, 1850–1920* (Bloomington: Indiana University Press, 1998), 151–55.

# Nellie Peters Black

## (1851–1919)

## *Georgia's Pioneer Club Woman*

CAREY OLMSTEAD SHELLMAN

In 1868 seventeen-year-old Nellie Peters wrote in her school diary, "I slept and dreamed that life was beauty; I woke and found that life was duty."[1] Adhering always to this precept, Nellie Peters Black, Georgia's "Pioneer Club Woman," dedicated her life to organizing women for the purposes of benevolence, self-improvement, and social and civic reform. Holding powerful positions in both the Georgia Federation of Women's Clubs (GFWC) and the Woman's Auxiliary of the Episcopal Diocese of Georgia, Black became one of the most public examples of white female activism in early twentieth-century Georgia. Whether working to expand the Episcopal church in Georgia, increase educational opportunities, institute civic and agricultural reforms, or provide war relief, she invariably epitomized "the power of organized womanhood."[2] Born into a socially prominent family in antebellum Atlanta, Mary Ellen "Nellie" Peters Black (1851–1919) represented the continuity between the myths of the Old South and the progressive paradoxes of the New South.[3] A product of her time and place, she was active in the traditional female reform venues of education and religious outreach. Yet as an independent thinker with a keen business sense, Black also supported causes such as civic reform and agricultural diversification.

Nellie Peters's progressive attitudes can be attributed in part to her father, Richard Peters, a civil engineer who came to Georgia from Pennsylvania in 1835 to survey railroad lines. Within two years he had risen through the ranks of management, eventually becoming a shareholder and officer in the Western and Electric Railroad. Known as "the Georgia Yankee," Peters quickly amassed a fortune in real estate and became a civic leader and one of the power elite in the new town of Atlanta. In 1848 he married Mary Jane Thompson, daughter of a

NELLIE PETERS BLACK
Courtesy of Hargrett Rare Book and Manuscript
Library, University of Georgia Libraries.

Decatur physician and hotelier. Richard Peters busied himself with the business of business while his wife directed the household and participated in church work, charitable endeavors, and social clubs. The second of nine children born to the couple, Nellie spent a reportedly comfortable and happy childhood in Atlanta.[4]

Life changed, however, for the Peters family when the Civil War reached Atlanta. Although Richard Peters had not favored southern secession, he contributed to the Confederate cause by providing supplies for both the troops and the home front. Because Peters's investments in a blockading enterprise proved successful, his family did not suffer the deprivation that many Atlantans were forced to endure. However, as faithful believers in social Christianity, the Peters family shared what they had with friends and neighbors, as well as others in need—of whom there were plenty.[5] Atlanta was besieged with wounded soldiers and refugees from all parts of the Confederacy fleeing the encroaching Yankees. On daily visitations to the various makeshift hospitals, Nellie and her mother delivered biscuits, soup, chicken, buttermilk, and coffee to the wounded soldiers. Although her efforts were limited to the white sons of the South, young Nellie learned firsthand that the true meaning of Christian charity was to relieve suffering.[6]

Shortly before the siege of Atlanta, the Peters family safely evacuated to Augusta, only to return six months later to find their home destroyed and the city they had known basically in ruins. Although his fortunes vacillated, Richard Peters managed to enter the Reconstruction period financially solvent. He aligned himself with other New South boosters such as Henry Grady, who alleged that it made good business sense to put the animosity of the war aside and rebuild Atlanta as quickly as possible. Peters and Grady shared an interest in both urban development and agricultural diversification. Their friendship no doubt influenced Nellie Peters Black, who, through her later urban and rural activism, became the feminine embodiment of Grady's New South ideal. Peters, Grady, and Black understood that the economic success, as well as the social stability of the region depended upon both industrial and agricultural development and cooperation.[7]

After the war, Nellie attended finishing school at the prestigious Brooke Hall in her father's home state of Pennsylvania. By all accounts, she was popular with both the administration and her fellow students. While away at school, Nellie developed her leadership skills, offering spiritual guidance, as well as friendship, to her classmates. It was also at school that Nellie developed a personal philosophy that centered on Christian dedication and hard work. Disciplining herself for the rigors of a future serving others, she repented of her "sinful ways of mis-spending time," which included daydreaming, procrastination, and "spending time in reverie which ought to be spent in prayer."[8]

Returning to Atlanta after graduation, Nellie began to put her training for Christian duty into practice. She declined her father's graduation gift of a diamond ring and chose instead a horse, which she named Black Diamond. As a child, Nellie had developed a lifelong love of animals, horses in particular. According to family legend, she began her career of benevolence while riding the horse around the environs of Atlanta and visiting the white underprivileged.[9] Concerned with the welfare of horses who stood for long hours in the hot, dusty Atlanta streets while their owners conducted business or shopped, Nellie persuaded the city council to erect six ornamental drinking fountains (donated by the Society for the Prevention of Cruelty to Animals) so that "citizens and strangers" could refresh their animals.[10] She also joined her mother and other society ladies in organizing creative fundraising events to alleviate the widespread poverty prevalent in postwar Atlanta. In 1871 she helped coordinate a fashionable "calico ball," to which ladies wore calico dresses and gentlemen calico scarves. Afterward, the participants donated their garments, along with money and supplies, to the relief effort.[11] Nellie's quick wit and persuasive personality ensured the success of any fundraising effort she undertook. Having to decline an invitation to one of Nellie's charity dances, one admirer wrote: "Can't you give another charity party? It would be genuine charity to me."[12] By this point in her life, Nellie understood well that social prominence and feminine influence could prove useful in obtaining her charitable goals.

While Nellie Peters enjoyed the social aspect of her charity work, family responsibilities and church work consumed most of her time. Like many of her female contemporaries, she gained her early reform experience through organized religion. Having come from a staunch Episcopal family, Richard Peters was disappointed to find only a small struggling Anglican community when he arrived in Georgia. He helped organize Atlanta's first Episcopal church, and over the years he served on the vestry and provided much-needed financial support. As a small child, Nellie saw many prominent Episcopal leaders pass through her home, including Leonidas Polk, Stephen Elliott, and Charles Todd Quintard (who later wrote that he was impressed with Nellie's "prompt and proper and answers" to religious questions).[13] Obviously influenced by her family's support of the Episcopal church, Nellie Peters helped to organize Holy Innocents, the city's first mission. Since she had persuaded her father to donate the land for the mission and worked so hard to get it started, it soon became known as "Miss Nellie's Mission." She hammered, nailed, painted, and plastered alongside other volunteers constructing the chapel. Although a deaconess administered the mission, Nellie personally supervised daily activities and taught Sunday school classes. Her dedication and hard work yielded results when the mission was officially recognized by the Episcopal Diocese of Georgia.[14]

In 1877, at the age of twenty-six, Nellie Peters married forty-five-year-old George Robison Black, the son of a wealthy south Georgia planter. A lawyer, Confederate officer, and legislator, Black was also a widower with four children. The marriage of Nellie Peters and George Black personified the ideal consolidation of the urban and country elite, a powerful liaison in the New South. Although planter politicians dominated state politics, their financial security depended on the marketing and distribution networks established through the towns and cities. Maintaining the social and economic status quo in Georgia required a cooperative relationship between town and country.[15] Possessing both urban and rural prominence, Nellie Peters and George Black represented the ultimate political power couple of their day.

Nellie Black approached her marital responsibilities with the same sense of duty she applied to her charity work. Perceiving marriage to be the only acceptable alternative to the life of service she had planned for herself, Nellie viewed her role of wife and mother as a transfer of duty. She explained her feelings in a letter to her fiancé: "I feel that my new life will be full of *duty* else I should not be happy in it. Is it really possible that I am to be a private in the ranks so soon— but my darling you'll be General. As you say, even the poor have given me to you. You have come and undermined all of my grand noble resolve of a self sacrificious [sic] devoted life and I instead have installed your grand noble self."[16] Even though she advocated that "a woman's noblest truest sphere is at home," Nellie hoped to maintain some of her independence after marriage by continuing her charity work. Preparing George for that possibility, she contended that ministering to the "cheerless firesides" of orphans and widows was too serious a responsibility to place on the immature shoulders of young women. Nellie argued that this work should be undertaken by "married women who should only try not to be so selfish about their home life."[17]

Marriage did not weaken Nellie Black's resolve to perform her Christian duty. On the contrary, her new role as wife and mother provided her the social status and financial resources she needed to broaden her attempts at both Christian outreach and community improvement. Like her father many years earlier, Nellie Black was distressed at the absence of an Anglican community in her new hometown of Sylvania, in rural south Georgia. If no Episcopal church existed there, she would establish one. Black donated a lot in the middle of town and had a small wooden church constructed. Members of the parish consisted primarily of Black's family and friends.[18] Nellie Black managed to create a comfortable, if somewhat rustic, lifestyle for her growing family, to which over the next few years, she added two daughters and a son.[19] Tragically, a mere five years into the marriage, George Black suffered a paralytic stroke. Nellie nursed him at their home in Sylvania until his death in 1886.

Nellie Black returned to Atlanta as a financially comfortable widow with three small children. Though she had been away from Atlanta for fewer than ten years, the city her father helped build had increased dramatically in size and population. By the mid-1880s electricity lit the city and ran the streetcars, some carrying passengers out to the new suburbs populated by whites seeking to escape the problems associated with urbanization. With miles and miles of paved streets, Atlantans no longer had to stroll through mud or dust.[20] It was an exciting time and place in which to live. Purchasing a small cottage across the street from her parents' large home on Peachtree Street, Nellie poured most of her energies into educating and raising her children. She also spent a great deal of time helping her father write his memoirs. Following his death and the publication of the biography they had worked on together, Black resumed her career of benevolence.[21]

In terms of charitable activities and philanthropic endeavors, widowhood proved the busiest period in Nellie Black's life. Although she no longer had to devote time to wifely duties, as a widow she possessed the same moral authority accorded to wives and mothers. Like most of her contemporaries, Black's career as a club woman and reformer can be traced through three distinct phases: religious outreach, self-improvement, and social reform. Although women in the antebellum South had been relatively isolated from one another, urban development and increased communication facilitated the development of women's clubs during the 1880s and 1890s. Atlanta, in particular, offered both white and black middle-class women a variety of clubs that provided outlets for altruistic service and self-improvement. Women of Black's age and class were expected to join clubs that reflected their social standing and patriotic heritage, such as the Colonial Dames of America, Daughters of the American Revolution, and the obligatory Daughters of the Confederacy. Although Nellie Black joined these clubs, she did not hold executive positions in them, choosing instead to focus her energies on self-improvement, religious outreach, and community service.[22]

As the study of culture was considered an appropriate activity for upper-class women seeking to improve their minds, Nellie Black joined the Every Saturday History Club. Organized in 1894, it was one of the earliest study clubs for women in Atlanta. Although an entertainment for the ladies, the club served a much larger purpose. As women during that period had limited access to formal education, the club became an informal "school" where members took their scholarship very seriously. Their research offered a feminine perspective of history not commonly available at the time, and presenting papers to fellow club members provided the women with valuable public speaking experience or, as one historian has written, an opportunity to "become accustomed to the sound of their own voices."[23] Nellie Black presented her first paper (a study of the Russian author Leo Tolstoy) a scant two months after joining. Her subsequent papers reflected her interest in literature, philosophy, and history. Black enjoyed the intellectual stimulation and companionship provided by the club, and it became an Every Saturday tradition to celebrate the last meeting of the year at her home.[24]

Accurately described by one historian as "the quintessence of matronage," most of Nellie Black's secular charitable activity focused on her role as a mother, both to her family and within her community.[25] As Atlanta became home to more mills and factories, Black became increasingly interested in improving the quality of life for the city's burgeoning white working class and associated with organizations that specifically aided that portion of the population. Particularly concerned about public health, Black helped organize the King's Daughters Hospital, the first free hospital in Atlanta. She also served as vice president of the Home for the Friendless, a group that established and maintained a home for unemployed, white working-class women. Members furnished childcare, provided health care, and helped the women find employment. As vice president of the Associated Charities Conference, Black spoke out in the press against the city council's "olfactory crusade" to "bar persons who carry odors" from the streetcars, a move obviously intended to segregate poor whites and blacks from middle-class whites. In a bold statement against class prejudice, Black stated publicly that "some people prefer the good honest guano odor to odors that emanate from our belles and beaus."[26] Many reformers of the day, including Black, equated increased poverty with the spread of disease, particularly tuberculosis, which had become widespread in urban areas throughout the country. Yet Black also understood that the successful containment of disease depended not upon social segregation, but on medical care for the afflicted. In addition to serving several terms as vice president of the Atlanta Anti-Tuberculosis and Visiting Nurse Association (a group that administered free testing and treatment for both blacks and whites), Black spearheaded a variety of social service projects to help meet the educational and medical needs of Atlanta's indigent population.[27]

Also during this period, Nellie Black renewed her interest in Episcopal outreach ministries and reestablished Holy Innocents Mission, as the first had been destroyed by a windstorm. She raised the funds for the construction of a new church building by selling a piece of property her father her given her and persuaded family members and friends to donate money, labor, pews, crosses, alms basins, and an organ. Supposedly with no help from an architect, she designed the church with a tabernacle-shaped roof in hopes of making it more resistant to windstorms. Nellie enlisted the aid of her three children in helping run the mission. Her son kept the fire stoked, and her daughters played music, taught sewing, and entertained the children. The mission thrived under Nellie Black's supervision, operating a free kindergarten and a mothers' club. With auxiliary duties and club work demanding more and more of her time, Nellie turned the administration of the mission over to a deaconess in 1912.[28]

When the Episcopal Diocese of Georgia formed a Woman's Auxiliary to provide support for the all-male Board of Missions in 1889, Nellie Black became the secretary of the Atlanta Archdeaconry.[29] In 1905 she became the diocesan secretary, a time-consuming position that required her to travel throughout the state and to national conventions. To make oversight of the large diocese more manageable, she persuaded the bishop to increase the number of archdeaconries from five to seven. In addition to supporting foreign missions and schools in Japan, China, and Cuba, Black insisted that the auxiliary continue to support domestic projects, including parish schools in rural areas and missions for "the colored people."[30] As diocesan secretary of the auxiliary was the most powerful administrative position a woman could assume in the Episcopal church, Nellie Black became quite possibly the most influential woman in the Diocese of Georgia. In 1907 the Episcopal Diocese of Georgia split into two separate dioceses, and Nellie became secretary of the new Diocese of Atlanta.

Atlanta's Cotton States and International Exposition in 1895 provided an unprecedented opportunity to spotlight the progressive New South and offered both white and (in a much more limited sense) black women the unique opportunity to interact with one another on a national and international level. Like the Board of Lady Managers of the 1893 International Columbian Exposition and World's Fair in Chicago, white Atlanta middle-class women planned their own building, raised most of the construction funds, and even sponsored a national competition to select an architect to design the building that would "represent the delicacy of southern womanhood."[31] They wanted the building to reflect not only their heritage and traditional values, but also their new role as the moral and social engineers of the New South. As such, the women's buildings contained not only artistic and historical exhibits, but also meeting rooms, an assembly hall, a model school, demonstration kitchens, a library, science exhibits, and a hospital and day nurseries. As chair of the hospital, Nellie organized a large group of nurses and volunteers to staff the facilities. She solicited supplies from merchants all over the country, including cots, medicine, drugs, linens, soap, food, baby supplies, milk, and wine and whiskey (for medicinal purposes only). Displaying characteristic thrift and economy, she arranged to have all leftover supplies sent to the children's ward of Grady Hospital. In a post-exhibition newspaper interview, Black described enthusiastically the various emergencies treated at the hospital: burns, bruises, bear bites, broken noses, falls, insect stings, electric shocks, lost children, and a severed finger. She claimed proudly that "black and white Americans and foreigners alike came for relief from pain and were all cared for kindly and skillfully."[32]

Encouraged by their success at the Cotton Exposition, the members of the Board of Lady Managers decided to "organize a body worthy of Atlanta's progressive and independent spirit." That same year a group of "thinking women" (including Nellie Peters Black) formed the Atlanta's Woman's Club—"a representative, but conservative . . . association for the advancement of women." Charter members agreed that they would be "broad minded" in approaching club issues, but they "opposed using sensational methods" in their "pursuit of culture and human advancement." Essentially a self-improvement club, members of the Atlanta Woman's Club were well read in world history and interested in current events. Perhaps understanding the correlation between knowledge and power, the club women delighted in the fact that "the sun never set on Queen Victoria's empire, Queen Wilhelmina sat on the throne in Holland, and the Empress Dowager Tuen-Tson-Hsi ruled China."[33]

Although Atlanta had many organizations and clubs for white women in the 1880s and 1890s, no unified efforts existed among the participants. Realizing the importance of unification, Nellie Black helped incorporate the Atlanta Woman's Club into the Atlanta Federation of Women's Clubs, and ultimately into the Georgia Federation of Women's Clubs (GFWC) in 1896. Shortly thereafter, the GFWC affiliated with the General Federation of Women's Clubs, founded in 1868.[34] Membership in these organizations provided women with unprecedented public influence. Nellie Black was elected to positions of leadership in all of these organizations, culminating in her three-term presidency of the GFWC. Her club activities began to center around social welfare and municipal housekeeping. As a widow with grown children, she turned her mothering duties toward the community. Believing that "civic beauty encourages civic righteousness," she urged her fellow white club members and politicians to pay closer attention to "parks, public squares, and above all, the cleanliness of court houses, jails, depots, and all buildings open to the public."[35]

It was at the 1895 Cotton States Exposition that Nellie Black saw an exhibit based on the German method of early childhood education—the *Kindergarten* or "children's garden." Not only did the idea of preparing young children for formal schooling greatly appeal to Black's maternal sensibilities, but she also viewed such training as a foundation for good citizenship. As women (mothers in particular) were perceived as the moral compass of Victorian society, it seemed natural for them to extend their moral influence outside of the home to counteract the destabilizing effects of modernization on the traditional southern way of life. Concerned about the moral welfare of poor and working-class whites and blacks, progressive reformers in both the North and South hoped that kindergarten teachers would be able to instill a sense of order and discipline into the families of their students. Although it developed more slowly in the less industrial and more economically depressed South, the kindergarten movement eventually gathered momentum in cities such as Atlanta and provided urban club women with a socially acceptable space within which to transform their domestic authority into public reform.

In 1895 Nellie Black helped organize the Atlanta Free Kindergarten Association (AFKA) for white children, and she served as its president for almost twenty years. Black's "sterling credentials as a southern blueblood and Christian humanitarian" provided the AFKA with a social prestige and moral authority that not only attracted benefactors, but also helped deflect criticism. Answering critics who identified kindergartens as merely another form of charity for the poor, Black argued that the practical work of the schools was to teach students to help themselves. Theoretically, Black claimed, the kindergarten classes would "implant noble thoughts and moral traits before the powers of evil [could] exert their influence" over the child.[36] With funds donated by the Atlanta Woman's Club and several wealthy individuals, the first "free" kindergarten in Atlanta opened on Magnolia Street to serve the children of workers at the Atlanta Cotton Mill. The AFKA raised operating funds through membership dues, Christmas appeals, and charity "entertainments" such as balls, musicals, and dinners. Once again, utilizing her social prominence, motherly image, and network of club women, Black organized an effective fundraising campaign. By 1910 the Association maintained and supported ten kindergartens for white children throughout the city, as well as a school to train the teachers. In addition to their regular school-day duties, kindergarten teachers offered after-school story hours, and sewing and cooking lessons for older children. They also visited the homes of their students. Nellie Black explained "through the door of the kindergarten we enter the home of the little ones and extend the influence of our law of love which strives to raise the standard of future citizenship through raising the standard of parenthood."[37] Teachers supervised regular medical clinics and "mothers clubs." Members of the AFKA viewed the kindergartens as centers of the community where parents, as well as their children, could benefit from educational opportunities.

As all of these activities required additional funding, Black lobbied the Georgia state legislature on several occasions for support of the program but was unsuccessful in getting them to assume financial responsibility. However, in 1908 the City Council of Atlanta began subsidizing the kindergarten association, supplying approximately one-third of the AFKA's annual budget. They steadily raised their level of support as the number of kindergartens increased. Regardless of the fact that the push for public kindergartens originated as a class-based reform movement, municipal and state governments eventually recognized their social and educational value. The Atlanta Free Kindergarten Association disbanded in 1923 when the Atlanta Board of Education added kindergartens to the school system.[38] Although she did not live to see state-funded kindergartens, Black remained an ardent education advocate, arguing in favor of admitting women to the University of Georgia, as well as the Georgia Bar.[39]

Aside from her many club duties and charitable activities in Atlanta, Nellie Black also enjoyed spending time on the family "farm," a 1,500-acre plantation in Gordon County in northwest Georgia. Although Richard Peters had sons, it was Nellie who inherited his avid interest in agriculture. Hoping to keep the property in the family, Black assumed management of the farm after her father's death in 1888. Quickly making administrative changes, she promoted a long-time fieldhand as overseer and herself as manager. Identifying herself only as "N. B. Black, Manager," Black transferred the business address of the farm to her residence in Atlanta. Most customers believed they were conducting business with a man, and Black willingly perpetuated the pretense so that her business would not suffer. With good humor, "Mr. Black" graciously accepted masculine gifts such as cigars from appreciative customers.[40] Although Nellie Black ran most of the affairs of the farm from Atlanta, she visited Calhoun at least once a month and maintained frequent communication with the overseer. She proved to be an efficient farm manager, personally keeping the account books and maintaining all records of farm transactions. Although she constantly battled high freight rates and labor shortages, most months Black produced a profit through crop sales, the rental of pasture land, the sale of stock animals, and the sale of by-products such as eggs and butter—which was occasionally churned by the manager herself.[41] Nellie Black considered herself a farmer.

Although life on the farm was less formal, Nellie Black maintained the lifestyle to which she was accustomed in Atlanta. At the farm, she continued to enjoy her regular social activities, such as entertaining, attending to club matters, and teaching Sunday school. As there was great interest among the towns-people of Calhoun in the Peters family, invitations to the farm were highly sought after, and Nellie Black often obliged them. Near the main house, Black had a wooden platform constructed in the cool woods overlooking a stream. She named the spot "Buzzard's Roost," and when weather permitted she entertained guests there with afternoon tea. Dressed in a white coat, the butler Tom would set the tea table with a white linen tablecloth, silver tea service, and china—just as if they were in the parlor on Peachtree Street.[42]

In private, Nellie Black was the feminine version of a "gentleman farmer," but in public she became an ardent proponent of practical and businesslike ap-proaches to agriculture, declaring it to be "both a science and an industry" that could lay our children at "Mother Nature's feet."[43] During a trip to the market to buy vegetables for dinner, Black realized how dependent Georgians had become on imported foodstuffs. She lamented that other states, and even some foreign countries, supplied the variety of fruits and vegetables found on Georgia's din-ner tables. She complained to the press that, "for her own children's consump-tion," the state of Georgia supplies only "a few turnip greens."[44] To Black, this "food for the stomach" was "food for thought." Angry that merchants imported mass quantities of food products that could be procured locally from farm sur-plus, she suggested that Georgia farmers and merchants work together to make the South more self-sufficient.

Black used her powerful position in the Georgia Federation of Women's Clubs to carry her personal crusade for agricultural diversification into the public arena. In 1914 she chaired a series of agricultural rallies sponsored by the federation that were intended to benefit the women of the more isolated clubs and address issues relevant to their more rural lifestyle. As chair of the federa-tion's Country Life Committee, Black toured each of the congressional districts of Georgia publicizing her "Live at Home" campaign and touting the advantages of a diversified home garden and pantry. Over a three-year period she addressed nearly twenty thousand white people, traveled over five thousand miles, and wrote more than fifty newspaper articles about the rallies—all the while keeping meticulous records of rally attendance.[45]

Capitalizing on the willingness of public agencies to cooperate, in 1916 Black enlisted the Georgia Department of Agriculture and the State Agricultural School at the University of Georgia to support her efforts. At each rally she shared the podium (albeit sometimes reluctantly) with their representatives, as well as members of the Georgia Chamber of Commerce. Traveling by car and train, Black maintained a rigorous rally schedule and seemingly handled with ease any unforeseen changes to the rally agendas. In the more populous areas, the rallies sometimes spanned several days. Advertised in local newspapers as an "institute" or "school," the coordinators offered a diverse program that they assumed would be most helpful to the farmer and his family. Audiences were always welcomed by local government officials and the district president of the Georgia Federation of Women's Clubs. Following the opening invocation from a local minister, Black or another prominent GFWC officer took the podium and explained the purpose of the rallies. Always quick to emphasize the success of their rural reform campaigns, the urban women highlighted in particular their efforts to increase educational opportunities in rural areas through such projects as the Tallulah Falls School. Established by the Georgia Federation of Women's Clubs to help the poor white children living in the Blue Ridge Mountains of north Georgia, the school, like the agricultural rallies, represented the southern progressive trend to help poor whites, while basically ignoring African Americans.[46]

Although the rallies represented a collective effort, Black carefully kept the club women in the forefront. Maintaining a cooperative relationship between the club women, government officials, rural inhabitants, and newspaper reporters required striking a delicate balance between the aims of the farmers with the rhetoric of the agricultural reformers. Black understood that the support of the press was crucial to the success of the rallies. At an address in Tifton in 1919 she explained their relationship: "at first some of the newspapers were indifferent and a few inclined to be funny, but now they are nearly in line with club women and the objects for which they strive."[47] For the most part, Black's claim of a cordial relationship with the press was accurate. However, smaller rural newspapers were not always favorable to her activities. In 1916, for example, former Populist politician Tom Watson criticized her labors in his county newspaper, the *Jeffersonian*. Watson, an outspoken critic of Henry Grady's New South creed, portrayed Black's work as evidence of the encroaching control over rural areas by urban elites. Commenting on the rallies, he wrote: "I notice that these city farmers carry some ladies along in their rotary movement; and that these benevolent Atlanta ladies are endeavoring to lift the farmer's wives to a higher plane. . . . Us country folk have no pride and no self-respect and no sense and no experience; and therefore we gladly welcome these city folks who modestly take it upon themselves to come out into the country and teach us how to farm, and our wives how to keep house."[48] Although he did not mention anyone by name, there is little doubt that Watson's sarcastic remarks were aimed directly at Black and the agricultural rallies. Realizing that tact and good manners could be powerful weapons, Black refrained from responding publicly to the criticism, which represented the growing divide between urban elites and rural whites.

On the local level, the rallies represented a goodwill venture between public agencies and private organizations. As coordinator of the rallies, Black had to work amicably with not only newspaper editors, but also politicians and local club women. She planned the rallies as if she were hosting a social function or chairing a club meeting. Often, as an incentive to boost attendance and participation from local club women, the meetings included picnics or luncheons. Black and her fellow club women worked with federally funded and state trained demonstration agents whose job it was to teach rural women improved methods for accomplishing their diverse chores. Black also needed the cooperation of the politically powerful state Commissioner of Agriculture, who controlled issues that affected the everyday existence of both the town and country, such as the inspection of crops, animals, and fertilizer, as well as the regulation of freight rates. In March 1917 Black wrote to Commissioner J. J. Brown requesting that he grant members of local women's clubs the authority to serve as assistant food inspectors. Additional inspectors would increase the speed and efficiency of getting crops to market. Not long after Black's request, the first local assistant food inspector appointed by a woman's club was commissioned at an agricultural rally in Waynesville.[49] Although the rallies did not produce tangible solutions for most of the problems Georgia farmers faced, they did help increase the awareness of those who lived in the city to the plight of those in the country. For example, in 1920 the influential Atlanta Woman's Club opened a curbside market that provided an accessible place for regional farmers to sell their wares. Due in part to the persistent lobbying of the club women, the city council joined in the endeavor, and the Atlanta Municipal Market opened in 1924.[50]

Within the national context, Black's rallies became part of a focused campaign to encourage Georgia farmers help feed victims of war and famine in Europe. With patriotic zeal, Nellie Black tried to push her fellow Georgians into accepting their national responsibility. She claimed that "when the soil of Georgia is made to produce what it ought to yield, after scientific and preserving methods are used, she can feed not only her own people but many others besides."[51] Her "Grow at Home" campaign complemented President Wilson's wartime call for "Victory Gardens." Known to the Georgia Federation of Women's Clubs as the "War President," Nellie Black considered it her personal responsibility to rally the Georgia home front. Her patriotic appeals became even more urgent when America officially entered World War I. Although the GFWC was supposedly a nonpolitical organization, President Black enthusiastically supported Wilson's domestic and foreign agendas. Believing him to be the "finest man in the world," she defended Wilson's programs and publicly chastised his critics in speeches and newspaper articles. In a 1919 speech to women's club members in Tifton, Black characterized Wilson's critics in the Senate as "spoiled children." Accusing the "misfit senators" of attempting to "handicap the president's work," she declared that she was ashamed to "have sent such men to misrepresent us."[52]

To complement the wartime campaign of conservation and thrift, the Georgia Federation of Women's Clubs encouraged member clubs to send canned food donations to military hospitals in Georgia, such as Fort McPherson and Camp Gordon. Fastidious about details, President Black insisted that each district send her detailed "canning accounts" that specified not only the amount of foodstuffs preserved, but also a breakdown of the particular fruits, vegetables, jellies, and jams.[53] Always encouraging club women to take credit when it was due them, Black arranged for the jars to be marked with club labels. To encourage competition, Black tracked the canning numbers of each district. She also monitored merchants to determine which stores did or did not carry adequate canning supplies. Those who demonstrated their patriotism by complying with the canning campaign received public accolades. Those who did not risked being reported to the Chamber of Commerce and condemned by Black in local newspapers and club publications.[54]

Unlike its strategy in World War II, during World War I the federal government chose not to institute mandatory food rationing among the civilian population, but did urge citizens to observe voluntary "meatless" and "wheatless" days each week and to limit sugar consumption. Although Nellie Black understood the seriousness of the food conservation campaign, she approached it with wit and humor. At a luncheon in Augusta, a club member who knew of Black's famous love of sweets questioned her about the government's intention to limit the candy supply. Black's face immediately clouded and she responded that all of this talk of rationing and self-sacrifice "should not be carried too far."[55]

Black answered more calls to serve both the state and federal governments. In 1917 President Wilson appointed her a "Dollar a Year" woman for her volunteer service to the war effort. The following year, Georgia governor Hugh Dorsey chose her to be a delegate to the "Win the War for Permanent Peace" convention in Philadelphia. Always a staunch supporter of Wilson, she also served as a delegate to the Southern Conference for a League of Nations in Atlanta during February and March of 1919. Viewing the uplifting of the South as a moral obligation, Black attended several annual meetings of the Southern Sociological Congress, a loosely configured organization of civic and religious leaders, sociologists, and educators that sought remedies for the social and economic problems of the South. While these conventions and meetings may not have resulted in immediate changes in government policies, they certainly helped to bring the region into line with goals of progressives throughout the country.[56] Southern progressives, like those throughout the country, were calling for reform and bureaucratic intervention for problems concerning public health, child welfare, labor conditions, education reform, as well as a multitude of moral issues. Black and other reformers realized, however, that the rest of the nation perceived the South, in and of itself, as a particular problem. The Southern Sociological Congress was an attempt by southern progressives to fix their own problems, thus averting outside interference.

With the same ease that they had adopted Wilson's war relief agenda, the Georgia Federation of Women's Clubs adjusted their postwar reform efforts to suit the social and economic needs of their region. Although the GFWC continued to champion agricultural development as a cure for Georgia's economic ills, the call for diversification was muffled by their land reclamation campaign. A champion of this new project, President Black claimed that only one-tenth of Georgia's available land was under cultivation. Specifically identifying the swamp lands of middle and south Georgia as targets for drainage, Black insisted that land reclamation would eradicate the breeding grounds of the malarial mosquito. She appeared in a public service film to demonstrate how "quickly and economically swamp and stumpy land could be transformed into profitable and healthful acreage." As the GFWC distributed the film to movie theaters all over the state, Black's name and face became familiar to a group of Georgians that may not have been aware of her work.[57]

Named director for life during her presidency, Nellie Peters Black secured her place in the history of the Georgia Federation of Women's Clubs. While still very much involved in her reform work, Black died of heart failure in August 1919 at the age of eighty-six. In obituaries and memorials throughout the state, she was praised for her "essential womanliness, high type of motherhood, broad-minded citizenship, and devotion to the up-building of that which is holiest and best in her state." One newspaper editor even claimed that "had Mrs. Black been a man, she would have been in the United States Senate from Georgia."[58] Public acclaim continued long after death. In 1976 she was honored as one of "Georgia's 25 Historic Mothers" for her "gift of persuasion" and "knack for public speaking." That same year, the Atlanta branch of the American Association of University Women featured her in their publication *Georgia Women: A Celebration*. Proclaiming Black "A Woman for All Seasons," they wrote that her "energy and dedication fairly took one's breath away."[59] Commending her efforts to reform education, medicine, religion, and agriculture, the Georgia Women of Achievement honored Black at their annual induction ceremony in 1997.

Although her name is no longer widely recognized, Nellie Peters Black played a significant role in shaping the social and religious life of the Atlanta that exists today. She bridged the gap between the religiously grounded activism of the Victorians and the state-focused activism of the progressives. As the world in which she lived changed, so did her reform goals. Where there were no Episcopal churches, she established missions, and in the process she expanded the role of women in the church. Where there were no schools for young children, she created kindergartens and brought the need for government-supported schools to the public's attention. When Georgia farmers were caught in a cycle of dependence on a one-crop economy, she rallied for diversification, lower freight rates, and local markets. And when her country faced world war, she brought the full force of the Georgia Federation of Women's Clubs to bear on the crisis. During her lifetime, the state of Georgia experienced some of the most turbulent political and social crises in its history: race riots, populist revolts, the rise of Tom Watson, the institution of Jim Crow laws, the scourge of lynching, and the struggle for women's suffrage. Yet she did not march in the streets for prohibition, suffrage, or social justice. In fact, Black was conspicuously silent on most of these volatile issues. Her silence speaks volumes and reveals that she understood the social limitations of her place and time and devised a strategy to work within the existing power structures to accomplish her goals. By compelling the early club-woman movement forward, enlarging the role of women in the Episcopal church, and expanding the boundaries for women in reform politics, Nellie Peters Black skillfully negotiated the gendered boundaries of her day, thus challenging the patriarchal society in which she lived and initiating social change.

## NOTES

1. Entry from Nellie Peters's school scrapbook, Black Papers, Hargrett Rare Book and Manuscript Library, University of Georgia, Athens (hereafter cited as Black Papers, UGA).

2. In her speeches Black referred to the influence exerted by the Georgia Federation of Women's Clubs as "the power of organized womanhood." Over the last two decades, scholars have focused on various women's groups (secular and religious) that exerted political and social influence during this period. A sampling includes Karen Blair, *The Clubwoman as Feminist: True Womanhood Defined, 1868–1914* (New York: Holmes and Meir Publishers, 1980); Anastatia Sims, *The Power of Femininity in the New South: Women's Organizations and Politics in North Carolina, 1880–1930* (Columbia: University of South Carolina Press, 1997); Glenda E. Gilmore, *Gender and Jim Crow: Women and the Politics of White Supremacy in North Carolina* (Chapel Hill: University of North Carolina Press, 1996); and Elizabeth Hayes Turner, *Women, Culture and Community: Religion and Reform in Galveston, 1880–1920* (New York: Oxford University Press, 1997).

3. William Link explains these paradoxes "of democracy and hierarchy, of humanitarianism and

coercion, and of racism and paternalistic uplift" in his *The Paradox of Southern Progressivism, 1880–1930* (Chapel Hill: University of North Carolina Press, 1992), 323–24. For additional information on the curious relationship between progressivism and paternalism and how it influenced gender and race relations in the South, see Numan V. Bartley, *The Creation of Modern Georgia* 2nd ed. (Athens: University of Georgia Press, 1990); Dewey Grantham, *Southern Progressivism: The Reconciliation of Progress and Tradition* (Knoxville: University of Tennessee Press, 1983); and Glenda E. Gilmore, *Gender and Jim Crow.*

4. The most comprehensive source of information on Richard Peters is Royce Shingleton's *Richard Peters: Champion of the New South* (Macon, Ga.: Mercer University Press, 1985). See also Jane Bonner Peacock, "Nellie Peters Black: Turn of the Century 'Mover and Shaker,'" *Atlanta Historical Journal* 22, no. 4 (1979–80): 7–15. According to the slave schedules for the 1860 census, Richard Peters kept five slaves at his home in Atlanta and sixteen on the plantation in Gordon County.

5. This type of social Christianity would later be known as the social gospel. Reform-minded social gospelers sought Christian remedies for the social and economic problems of the day. Susan Curtis has described the social gospel as "the religious expression of progressivism." See Susan Curtis, *A Consuming Faith: The Social Gospel and Modern American Culture* (Baltimore: Johns Hopkins University Press, 1991), 2. For additional information on the social gospel in the South, see Ralph E. Luker, *The Social Gospel in Black and White: American Racial Reform, 1885–1912* (Chapel Hill: University of North Carolina Press, 1991).

6. Civil War Reminiscences, Nellie Peters Black, Atlanta History Center, Atlanta (hereafter cited as AHC).

7. See Shingleton, *Richard Peters*. For information on Grady's New South vision, see Henry Grady, *The New South: Writings and Speeches of Henry Grady*, (Savannah, Ga.: Beehive Press, 1971); and Paul M. Gaston, *The New South Creed: A Study in Southern Mythmaking* (New York: Alfred A. Knopf, 1970).

8. Scrapbook, Black Papers, UGA.

9. Nellie Rucker Walter, *Grandmother Nellie's Stories* (Longmeadow: By the author, 1979), 17.

10. *Annual Reports of the Committees of Council, Officers and Departments of the City of Atlanta,* 1877, Book 8, 566, AHC.

11. Eula Turner Kuchler, "Charitable and Philanthropic Activities in Atlanta during the Reconstruction," *Atlanta Historical Bulletin* 10, no. 4 (1965): 48–50.

12. The same young man also professed his desire to renew the couple's "long dissolved engagement." See G. E. Radcliff to Nellie Peters, February 20, 1871, Black Collection, Georgia Department of Archives and History, Morrow (hereafter cited as GDAH.)

13. Alex M. Hitz, *History of the Cathedral of St. Philip* (Atlanta: Cathedral Chapter, 1947), 27–30. See also Charles T. Quintard, *Nellie Peters Pocket Handkerchief and What It Saw* (Sewanee, Tenn.: University Press, 1907), 3.

14. Helen C. Smith, "She Helped Found City's First Mission," *Atlanta Journal and Constitution,* January 25, 1976.

15. For information about the political and economic tensions that existed between urban and rural areas in Georgia during this period, see Bartley, *Creation of Modern Georgia,* 75–127.

16. Nellie Peters to George Black, March 11, 1877, Black Papers, UGA.

17. Nellie Peters to George Black, March 18, 1877, Black Papers, UGA.

18. Unfortunately, Nellie proved to be the driving force of the church, and when she left Sylvania in 1887, the parish slowly disintegrated (Dixon Hollingsworth, *The History of Screven County, Geor-*

*gia* [Sylvania, Ga.: Screven County History Project, 1989], 102). See also Instrument of Donation for All Saints Church, Episcopal Church, Diocese of Georgia (1750–1942), Georgia Historical Society, Savannah (hereafter cited as GHS).

19. Three children were born to Nellie Peters Black and George Black: Nita Hughes Black (1878), Louise King Black (1879), and Ralph Peters Black (1881).

20. For statistical information about Atlanta during these years, see Franklin M. Garrett, *Atlanta and Environs: A Chronicle of Its People and Events*, vol. 2 (New York: Lewis Historical Publishing Co., 1954).

21. Nellie Peters Black, *Richard Peters: His Ancestors and Descendants* (Atlanta: Foote and Davies Co., 1904).

22. Black joined several altruistic organizations and social clubs, including the Every Saturday [Study] Club, Pioneer Club of Atlanta, Colonial Dames of America, Daughters of the American Revolution, and Daughters of the Confederacy. For Nellie Peters Black's resume of club work, see Darlene R. Roth, *Matronage: Patterns in Women's Organizations, Atlanta, Georgia, 1890–1940* (Brooklyn, N.Y.: Carlson Publishing Inc., 1994).

23. For information on women's cultural clubs of the period, see Theodora Penny Martin, *The Sound of Their Voices: Women's Study Clubs, 1860–1910* (Boston: Beacon Press, 1987); and Anne Ruggles Gere, *Intimate Practices: Literary and Cultural Work in U. S. Women's Clubs, 1880–1920* (Urbana: University of Illinois Press, 1997).

24. When the curriculum was expanded to include the sciences and current events, she presented papers with such diverse titles as "Agencies for the Assimilation of Immigrants" and "The Growth and Function of Trees" (Club records, Every Saturday Club, AHC).

25. Roth, *Matronage*, 73.

26. "An Olfactory Crusade" *New York Times*, May 14, 1903. In 1900 Atlanta, along with several other southern cities, passed a municipal ordinance requiring the racial segregation of streetcars. Until the 1906 race riot, "Atlanta streetcars exhibited a flexible system of segregation, with mixed smoking sections at the back of the cars, and some Negroes sitting with whites in the middle part." See August Meier and Elliott Rudwick, "The Boycott Movement against Jim Crow Streetcars in the South, 1900–1906," *Journal of American History* 55, no. 4 (1969): 758.

27. Annual Report, The Atlanta Anti-Tuberculosis and Visiting Nurse Association, 1909, GDAH.

28. "Holy Innocents Mission, Atlanta" William C. Granberry Collection, GHS. See also "Women Painting Little Church in Valley of Pines," *Atlanta Journal*, December 8, 1916.

29. *Handbook of The Woman's Auxiliary to the Board of Missions of the Domestic and Foreign Missionary Society of the Protestant Episcopal Church in the United States of America* (New York: Church Mission House, 1897).

30. "Woman's Auxiliary of Savannah Archdeaconry," *Savannah Morning News*, December 16, 1905.

31. Darlene R. Roth and Louise E. Shaw, *Atlanta Women: From Myth to Modern Times* (Atlanta: Atlanta Historical Society, 1980), 24–32. See also *Official Guide to the Cotton States and International Exposition* (Atlanta: Franklin Printing and Publishing Co., 1895).

32. "Was a Great Work," *Atlanta Journal*, January 6, 1896. Black continued to contribute to local fairs and served as Woman Commissioner of the State of Georgia to the Centennial Exposition of Tennessee in 1896.

33. Scrapbook, Atlanta Woman's Club, AHC. Also see Mrs. J. C. Croly, *The History of the Women's Club Movement in America* (New York: H. G. Allen, 1898).

34. Although not as numerous, clubs for African American women also existed. A thorough study of the white women's club movement in Atlanta is Roth's *Matronage*. See also Croly, *History of the Woman's Club Movement*, 365–66.

35. Report of the President, Yearbook 1918–1919, Georgia Federation of Women's Clubs.

36. Report of the President, Annual Meeting, Atlanta Free Kindergarten Association, April 25, 1910, Black Papers, UGA.

37. Report of the President, Annual Meeting, Atlanta Free Kindergarten Association, April 28, 1908, Black Papers, UGA.

38. Sarah Judson, "Cultivating Citizenship in the Kindergartens of Atlanta, 1890s–1920s," *Atlanta History* 41, no. 4 (1998): 17–30. Judson's article explains the beginnings of the movement in both the black and white communities. Black club women established the Gate City Free Kindergarten Association in 1905.

39. Women were first admitted to the university in 1911 for summer sessions, but admission as full-time students came in 1919, the year Nellie Black died. Kenneth Coleman, *History of Georgia* (Athens: University of Georgia Press, 1977), 328.

40. "Management of Peters Farm Is Told by Mrs. Lamar Rucker," *Atlanta Constitution*, October 18, 1925.

41. Belle Bayless, "Mrs. Black's Home," *Calhoun Times*, October 23, 1919. When Black died in 1919, eight tenant families lived on the farm. Labor on the farm was a mix of tenants and wage laborers, white and black. See also Terry Brumlow, "Peters Plantation," *Southwind: A Reminiscence of Local History and Culture* (Calhoun, Ga: Calhoun High School, 1982), 17; and Farm Scrapbook, Black Papers, UGA.

42. Nellie Rucker Walter, *Grandmother Nellie's Stories*; and Belle Bayless, "Mrs. Black's Home," *Calhoun Times*, October 23, 1919.

43. Address, Southern Conference of Education and Industries, New Orleans, April 19, 1916, Black Papers, UGA.

44. Unidentified newspaper clipping (n.d.), Black Papers, UGA.

45. Jane Bonner Peacock, "Nellie Peters Black: Turn of the Century 'Mover and Shaker,'" *Atlanta Historical Journal* 22, no. 4 (1979–80): 14. See also Scrapbook of Agricultural Rallies, Black Papers, UGA.

46. For information on the GFWC and the Tallulah Falls School, see Vera Connelly, "The Light in the Mountains," n.d., Heyward-Howkins Collection, GHS; and Roth, *Matronage*, 115–17.

47. "Mrs. Black's Tifton Address," *Atlanta Constitution*, April 13, 1917.

48. Unidentified newspaper clipping, Scrapbook of Agricultural Rallies, Black Papers, UGA. Black wrote on the clipping, "I am one of these ladies." For more on urban-rural cooperation, see Bartley, *Creation of Modern Georgia*, 103–26; and Rebecca Montgomery, "Lost Cause Mythology in New South Reform: Gender, Class, Race, and the Politics of Patriotic Citizenship in Georgia, 1890–1925," in *Negotiating Boundaries of Southern Womanhood: Dealing with the Powers That Be*, ed. Janet Coryell, Thomas H. Appleton, Anastatia Sims, and Sandra Gioia Treadway, 174–98 (Columbia: University of Missouri Press, 2000).

49. Walter J. Brown, *J. J. Brown and Thomas E. Watson: Georgia Politics, 1912–1928* (United States: Walter J. Brown, 1988), 14–15. See also "Plant Food Crops, Urges J. J. Brown," *Augusta Chronicle*, March 20, 1917; and J. J. Brown to Black, March 13, 1917, Black Papers, UGA.

50. John R. Hornady, *Atlanta Yesterday, Today, and Tomorrow* (USA: American Cities Book, 1922), 368; and Garrett, *Atlanta and Environs*, 2:802.

51. "History of Agricultural Rallies Told by Mrs. Rucker," *Atlanta Constitution*, September 20, 1925.

52. "Mrs. Black's Tifton Address," *Atlanta Constitution*, April 13, 1919.

53. Canning accounts from various clubs in the GFWC, Black Papers, UGA.

54. "War Affects Federation," *Savannah Morning News*, April 25, 1918. To help meet wartime shortages, Black also organized towel drives for the hospitals.

55. "Complexity of Club Leaders," *Atlanta Constitution*, November 11, 1917.

56. The most thorough sources of information on the Southern Sociological Congress are the published convention reports, edited by the General Secretary of the ssc, James McCulloch: *The Call of the New South* (1912), *The South Mobilizing for Social Service* (1913), *Battling for Social Betterment* (1914), *The New Chivalry-Health* (1915), *Democracy in Earnest* (1918), and *"Distinguished Service" Citizenship* (1919). The ssc did not publish proceedings in 1916 and 1917.

57. "Mrs. Black in the Movies," *Atlanta Constitution*, July 27, 1919. The film was sponsored by Southern Bell Telephone Company and Dupont Powder Company.

58. "In Memoriam—The Georgia Federation of Women's Clubs—Mrs. Nellie Peters Black," *Atlanta Constitution*, August 17, 1919. This special supplement featured obituaries from around the state. See also obituary clippings, Every Saturday Club, AHC.

59. Barbara Reitt, ed., *Georgia Women: A Celebration* (Atlanta: American Association of University Women, 1976), 28–29.

# Lucy Craft Laney and Martha Berry

## (1855–1933; 1866–1942)

*Lighting Fires of Knowledge*

JENNIFER LUND SMITH

In one of the great changes that occurred after the Civil War, southerners, both black and white, redefined the meaning of education in the South. Southern states had not created public educational systems during the antebellum period; hence, possession of an education was reserved for the elite who could afford tutors and private schools. In the antebellum—and postbellum—South education signified power. After the war, however, the freedpeople made education a priority and essentially forced the issue of public education, for children of all races and all classes.

In the dissemination of education, women played an enormous role. During the unsettled years after the war, and for decades after, teaching was essentially the only acceptable career choice for a southern woman. But for many southern women, it became both a means of earning a living and a point of entry into the public sphere.

Martha Berry and Lucy Craft Laney were two of these women who dedicated their lives to teaching in the late nineteenth and early twentieth centuries. In many ways they have much in common with each other and with other women of the Progressive Era: they both established and taught in private schools, they addressed the issue of local poverty, and their work reflected a national movement that promoted reform and women's activism during the Progressive Era. Progressive reformers aspired to transform the values, behaviors, and morals of the working class, immigrants, and those in poverty to reflect those of white, Protestant, middle-class America. They referred to this conversion as the "uplift" of the masses. Nationally, they pursued this process by means of both assistance and coercion, and each sought to educate only their own race. In Georgia, Lucy Craft Laney and Martha Berry joined those who viewed education as a means of "uplift," for people living in the margins of American society.[1]

As female educators, Martha Berry and Lucy Craft Laney shared several characteristics in common. They were independent women who challenged the stereotypes of female behavior of the era by devoting themselves not to a husband and family, but instead to their work. They established large schools and remained in firm control of these institutions rather than defer to male authority. Through their schools they challenged the Old Order of the South that had reserved education for the elite. And they both embraced the middle-class ideology of the Progressives that stressed Protestant Christian values, hard work, and a responsibility to their communities. Yet as a white woman and an African American woman, respectively, their missions were quite different. Martha Berry hoped to instill middle-class values into her white students and help them conquer the poverty in which they lived, but as a member of the southern elite, she embraced the paternalism that Lucy Craft Laney hoped to eradicate by teaching her African American students racial pride and skills that would allow them to defy white supremacy and assimilate into white society as equals.

Lucy Craft Laney's parents had the ability to offer her a childhood that allowed her luxuries unknown to the majority of African Americans in the antebellum South. Her father, David Laney, had been born a slave in South Carolina and worked for his owners as a carpenter. His master allowed him to use his skill to earn his own wages on his own time, which enabled him to buy his freedom, and eventually he made his way to Macon, Georgia. There, the white Presbyterian Church recognized his gifts as a preacher by ordaining him a minister, a position that denoted a great deal of status in black communities. David Laney also met his wife, Louise, in Macon.[2]

When she was a young girl, Louise Laney's owners, the Campbells, had purchased her from an itinerant group of Native Americans. Her mistress must have been fond of Louise, as she broke Georgia law to teach her how to read and write. When Louise was thirteen, David Laney purchased her freedom and they married. Together they had ten children; Lucy was the seventh, born in 1855. Although not all the children survived, as Lucy grew up the Laney house was full of children, their own and others they took in.[3]

After her marriage, Louise continued to work for the Campbells, and often she brought Lucy to work with her. The Campbells' home contained a sizeable library, and at a very young age, Lucy demonstrated a precocity for reading. Her

**LUCY CRAFT LANEY**

Courtesy of Lucy Craft Laney Museum of Black History and Delta House, Inc.

**MARTHA BERRY**

Courtesy of Oak Hill and the Martha Berry Museum.

mother had taught her to read, and Miss Campbell took an interest in Lucy's education as well, allowing her access to her library and helping to choose books for her to read.[4]

When Robert E. Lee surrendered to the Union in the spring of 1865, Lucy had just turned ten. The defeat of the Confederacy allowed northern missionaries to move southward to assist African Americans in their transition to freedom. One of these groups, the American Missionary Association (AMA), organized by northern Congregationalists, opened schools for African Americans across the South. When they established Lewis School in Macon, Lucy Laney attended a formal school for the first time. Lucy's informal antebellum education surely made her stand out in the classroom.[5]

In 1869 the AMA opened Atlanta University to offer African Americans a higher education in the liberal arts. The school's founders carefully culled its first class of eighty-nine scholars from the best students attending the various AMA schools in the state; twenty-seven of those students were female. Lucy Laney had the honor of becoming one of the members of that class. She was approximately fifteen years old when she moved away from home to begin her studies in "algebra, geometry, natural science, drawing, English literature, elements of Latin, the theory and practice of teaching, and mental and moral philosophy."[6]

As a student in the AMA schools, Laney learned not only the fundamentals of a liberal arts education, but also the values of the northern missionaries who staffed the schools. Northern teachers taught their students, many of whom had not gained freedom until the end of the war, values and behavior they hoped would help them assimilate into middle-class American society: responsibility, "thrift, temperance, cleanliness, and free labor ideology."[7] In 1872 the AMA opened a Normal Department to train teachers. The university assumed that these teachers would disseminate both the knowledge and the values they learned at Atlanta University to freedpeople across the South. Lucy Laney graduated in 1873 and she did just that. During these peripatetic years she taught not only in her hometown of Macon, but also in Milledgeville and Savannah.

In her own school Laney demanded that her students adopt a code of behavior similar to that in the AMA schools. She hoped that it would protect them from reproach and racist perceptions. She required neatness, cleanliness, and attendance at daily prayers, and she did not allow students to return home during the term without her permission.[8]

In 1883 Laney was in her early twenties and living in Savannah when a representative from the Board of Missions for Freedmen of the Presbyterian Church convinced her to return to Augusta to open a much-needed school for African

Americans. Despite her close association with the Congregationalists of the AMA, Laney retained close ties to the Presbyterian Church, of which her father was an ordained minister. The Mission for Freedmen had offered no pecuniary support, but Laney embraced this challenge as mission work. She exhausted her own meager savings and appealed to friends and family to obtain the finances to open the school. The room she rented in Christ Presbyterian Church proved ample space for the five students who enrolled when she opened her doors. But as her reputation grew, so did the size of the school. By the end of the first year it had grown to seventy-five students, and at the end of its second year Laney had attracted over two hundred pupils.[9]

The expansion of the school necessitated both assistance and a new location. Several women provided particularly critical aid to Laney in the early years of the school. Miss Freeman was the first teacher to join Laney at her school. Tragically, she died of typhoid fever, as did so many, following a violent flood in 1888. For a time, Laney's younger brother Frank taught at the school. Beginning in 1895 Mary Jackson, Laney's close friend for over a decade, served as Laney's associate principal. Jackson left when she married, as most female teachers did at the time. As the faculty and student body expanded, so too did the physical necessities of the school. When it grew out of the room in Christ Presbyterian Church, the school moved to a building on Gwinnett Street, but quickly it too faced overcrowding. A sympathetic white undertaker offered Laney the use of a two-story house with a barn on Calhoun Street; Laney filled both the house and the barn with black students.[10]

Funding the school became a constant struggle for Laney. A supporter of Laney's remembered that during the first three years of the school's existence she "lived on the supplies carried in from nearby farms by her pupils and on the very few contributions given her."[11] Needing resources, in 1886 she gambled and traveled to Minnesota by train to attend the General Assembly of the Presbyterian Church to beg for aid. Exhausted, she fell asleep during the meeting; fellow participants had to wake her up to speak. Sensing that she would not convince the assembly to assist her financially, she changed tactics and merely explained her school's needs. The assembly provided her with a ticket home. But the trip did not prove futile. In time, the Board of Freedmen of the church took the school under its wing and extended financial help, albeit never enough. More importantly, she piqued the interest of Mrs. F. E. H. Haines, the president of the Women's Department of the Presbyterian Church U.S.A., and an advocate of church mission work both at home and abroad. Though Mrs. Haines passed away later that year, her encouragement had so affected Laney that she named her school Haines Normal and Industrial Institute. Northern benefactors, presumably introduced to Laney's work through Mrs. Haines, became interested in the school and sent substantial donations, which enabled her to erect new buildings. As a result, the school moved yet again, this time back to Gwinnett Street where it added several buildings that served as dormitories, classrooms, a library, and a chapel. The grueling trip to Minneapolis ultimately allowed Laney's school to expand to nine hundred students and thirty-four faculty members by 1913. Despite generous assistance, in 1927 a friend noted that the school's needs continued to require Laney to make strenuous trips "about the state of Georgia, begging for help from the colored churches, [and] occasionally [traveling] North" to solicit funds to keep the school running.[12]

From her parents, Miss Campbell, and her years at Atlanta University, Lucy Laney learned to appreciate the importance of a liberal arts education to prove oneself equal in a society dominated by white people who deemed African Americans intellectually inferior. But economic realities led Laney to offer her students vocational skills as well, a decision that invoked a great deal of controversy. Black educators at the turn of the century engaged in a fierce debate about the merits of a liberal arts education versus a vocational education. Booker T. Washington, the founder of Tuskegee Institute, articulated the argument that African Americans needed vocational skills above all, to gain economic power and independence. W. E. B. DuBois, who earned degrees at Fisk University and Harvard, and who taught economics and history at Atlanta University from 1897 to 1910, forcefully disagreed. He contended that intellectual parity would empower black Americans. In refusing to reject vocational education, Laney "mixed idealism and pragmatism."[13] Furthermore, philanthropists tended to fund vocational schools, which they considered less threatening, more generously than liberal arts schools for black students, and the intense competition for benefactors' money most likely influenced Laney's decision to include vocational classes for her students.[14]

Despite the fatiguing work of fundraising a private school required, Laney believed Haines Institute could give her students a "broader [education] than that offered to them in the public schools."[15] At Lucy Laney's school that education included a strong dose of racial pride and religious instruction. Her friend Mary White Ovington, a white woman whose Unitarian background and abolitionist parents had laid the foundations for her work in progressive movements at the turn of the century and who had become one of the founding members of the National Association for the Advancement of Colored People (NAACP), noted, too, that the public schools "did not give full swing to her virile personality." Ovington added, "Lucy Laney never toadies," as a female teacher in the public schools often had to do.[16] Mary McLeod Bethune spent a year at Haines

Institute before she later opened her own school for African American girls in Florida. Bethune later enthused that she was "impressed with [Laney's] fearlessness, her amazing touch in every respect, an energy that seemed inexhaustible and her mighty power to command respect and admiration from her students and all who knew her."[17]

Indeed, Lucy Laney's energy and dedication to the school seemed indefatigable. She never assumed the position of a lofty administrator; throughout her life she maintained an intimate relationship with all details of running the school. In fact, Laney literally lived at Haines Institute. In her later years some of her former students, seeking to make her more comfortable, built a house for her, right across the street from the school. But she refused to move, preferring to remain with her students instead. At Haines, not only did she teach and administer, she made biscuits, raked leaves, and went to battle with the furnace when necessary.[18]

Running her own private school also allowed Laney to establish a curriculum that surpassed that offered in the public schools. Haines Institute offered its students, both male and female, the study of foreign languages; Laney herself taught the Latin courses "with the greatest enthusiasm."[19] She also focused a great deal on character building in her students—a point in which her white benefactors at the Board of Missions took great delight—and always Laney taught racial pride.

For pragmatic purposes Haines Institute taught female students "laundering . . . darning. . . mending . . . sewing," and cooking, while male students learned "cobbling, printing, carpentry, broom-making, [and] rug-weaving."[20] Always on the cutting edge, Laney added a kindergarten to the school in 1890; it was the first to appear in Augusta. While Laney maintained a belief in self-help for African Americans, she did not hesitate to work with white people who benefited the school. Hence she hired a northern white woman with the pedagogical skills to teach young children when the kindergarten opened. Two years later Laney opened a nursing school, the Lamar School of Nursing, calling in a white nurse from Canada to help launch the program.[21]

Ultimately Lucy Laney envisioned her pupils as a means of outreach. As students graduated from Haines Institute they supplied black communities with their skills as teachers and nurses, many of them staying in Augusta to address the needs there. As her trained nurses healed bodies, Lucy Laney trusted that the teachers who graduated from her school could instill dignity and self-esteem in their students, whom southern whites challenged constantly. Laney eventually added Negro Studies to the curriculum, ensuring that her graduates would do what white teachers would not, instill a sense of pride in their African heritage as well as a sense of responsibility to those who shared it.[22]

By the twentieth century Lucy Laney and Haines Institute drew national attention. Atlanta University, Lincoln University, South Carolina State College, and Howard University had all awarded her with honorary degrees. In January 1909 Laney arranged for William Howard Taft, who was president-elect at the time, to visit Haines Institute. He reportedly stated that "He had seen nothing in the South in the way of efficiency and of self-sacrifice that could compare with the work of Miss Laney at Haines Institute." Locally, she received praise as well. In 1928 Lawton Evans, the Superintendent of Public Schools in Augusta, noted that "[the] graduates of her school have stood high in the business and professional life of this city. The teachers I get from her school are capable, well trained, [and] upright."[23] Additionally, her students regularly went on to study at prestigious universities, such as "Atlanta, Brown, Lincoln and Yale."[24]

Laney persistently served as a model to her students, many of whom would become teachers and establish their own schools, in demonstrating responsibility to the community, not only through the programs she initiated at her school, but through her own outreach. In the 1890s Laney and Mary McLeod (Bethune) established a mission Sabbath school in Augusta. Sabbath schools arose in abundance in the South in the years following the Civil War. Especially for African Americans, these schools aimed not only to teach religion, but also reading and writing. Sabbath schools had the unique ability to reach out to children who did not have the opportunity to attend school regularly. Augustus Griggs, a student and later a colleague of Lucy Laney's, wrote after her death that many Augustans remembered her for the ubiquitous tuning fork she used when teaching them hymns in churches that had no other musical accompaniment. Laney participated in efforts to improve the quality of life for Augustans living in the "Territory," or the "Terri" for short, the slums of Augusta where the poorest African Americans lived. As a member of the Augusta Interracial Committee she convinced white citizens of the need to improve the unsanitary sewage system in the Terri and fought, unsuccessfully, to fund more schools for black children. She joined the local Urban League, a group launched to help rural people adjust to life in urban areas.[25]

The turn of the century witnessed a growing concern with urban poverty that issued in the Progressive Era. Progressives formed groups to force legislation to benefit urban laborers, warn immigrants of the dangers of alcohol, enforce morality on new forms of entertainment, such as the movies, and teach sanitation, health care, cleanliness, and middle-class values in an attempt to alleviate indigence. Yet white progressives ignored black Americans, many of whom constituted the poorest and the least protected people in the nation.

During the years following Reconstruction, the tenor of race relations in the United States plummeted. It was during these years that the Supreme Court upheld segregation laws in *Plessy v. Ferguson* in 1896, which institutionalized separation of the races but clearly did not enforce equality; lynching of black men became epidemic; and prison chain gangs targeted black prisoners. The year after the *Plessy v. Ferguson* decision the Richmond County Board of Education voted to close Ware High School, the only black high school in Augusta. The board announced that it would instead use the money that had been allotted to the high school to hire more teachers to focus on black students at the grammar school level. Recognizing that the board of education was attempting to deny black citizens education above the elementary level, the black elite in the county sued the school board and originally won the case. But the board of education appealed the decision. The case held ramifications for black education on the national level, and ultimately it wound up at the United States Supreme Court, which decided in favor of the Richmond County School Board. Interestingly, Lucy Laney, a champion of education for African Americans, did not lend her support to the lawsuit initiated by black Augustans. Most argue that she preferred not to have the competition Ware High School presented. Another historian who has studied Laney posits that her decision also may have reflected her belief that the county-run high school did not provide a rigorous enough classical education for black students.[26]

As the courts turned their backs on African Americans, middle-class black activists realized that it was up to them to address inequality and the needs of black people in destitution. In 1909 a group of African Americans and sympathetic white Americans formed the NAACP, a group that concentrated on challenging discriminatory laws through the court system. In February 1917 Lucy Laney hosted the organizational meeting of the Augusta chapter of the NAACP. She also served as president of the Federation of Colored Women's Clubs, Augusta, Georgia, a middle-class organization grounded in the idea that women constituted the agents for social change.[27]

The club movement nationalized in 1895 in reaction to a letter sent to *The Women's Era*, a journal catering to black women engaged in social reform, that claimed, "Negroes are wholly devoid of morality, the women are prostitutes and all Negroes are thieves and liars." Enraged, Lucy Laney attended the first meeting of the National Federation of Afro-American Women, which later merged with the League of Colored Women to form the National Association of Colored Women (NACW). Membership in the NACW allowed black women reformers to form networks and share concerns on a national level. Among the issues for which they fought were the need for orphanages and day cares, an end to miscegenation laws, and a federal law against lynching. Moreover, Laney belonged to several state and national organizations that focused on education and community responsibility. She joined the State Teachers' Association and served as its secretary.[28]

Black women who engaged in social reforms did so not only to alleviate the suffering of the poor, but also as an attempt to gain respect for themselves. They realized that white Americans did not recognize the class and cultural differences that existed among African Americans. They hoped that by reaching out to the less fortunate and "raising up the race" they could erase the stereotypes of degenerate and wanton black women that had endured since the slave era and counter white society's belief in the intrinsic inferiority of black people. Following Emancipation, most white Americans held fast to racial stereotypes that deemed black men and women as intellectually inferior and inherently unable to resist the lures of alcohol, gambling, and sexual promiscuity. In an era when middle-class Americans held a regard for female purity that bordered on obsessive, black women felt a great deal of pressure to disprove the prevailing beliefs about the behavior and morals of black people. Yet if white Americans reduced all African Americans to a stereotype, the black elite feared that the behavior of all African Americans would have to adhere to white middle-class standards before white society accepted them as equals. Hence, as Audrey Thomas McCluskey states of Laney and other black women engaged in reform, they "considered the adoption of middle-class habits, not as acquiescence to racism, but as an effort to subvert it."[29] Ann Short Chirhart further notes that black women astutely used "an existing cultural form of authority, evangelical Protestantism, to legitimate their public roles while challenging racist assumptions about black women's inferiority."[30]

One of the middle-class assumptions Laney championed was the moral superiority of mothers and the importance of their role. At the Women's Meeting of the Atlanta University Conference on Negro Problems in 1898, she gave a lecture highlighting a mother's duty. Yet in her speech Laney empowered women to a degree not usually conferred on nineteenth-century women: "Motherhood, honored by our blessed Master, is the crown of womanhood. This gives her not only interest in the home and society, but also authority. She should be interested in the welfare of her own neighbors' children. To women has been committed the responsibility of making the laws of society, making environments for children."[31] In placing such authority in the hands of women, Laney openly challenged the assumption that women, notably black women, had no role in politics.

Lucy Laney, unconsciously it seems, further challenged gender assumptions at the turn of the century. She did not marry or become a mother. She was an intelligent, independent woman who operated a large school that gained national attention for its success. She did not dress the part of a successful woman, putting most of her money back into the school rather than spending it on clothes. She wore her hair cut close to her head.[32]

While she never bore a child, Laney did see herself as a mother figure to all her students. And her students and supporters evinced a great deal of affection for, and loyalty to, her and Haines Institute. In 1905 supporters founded a Lucy Laney League to help the school. Its first contribution consisted of twenty-one dollars, but by 1924 the league had about 150 members and had sent approximately eight thousand dollars to Augusta to assist Lucy Laney operate her school. The league was centered in Harlem, the center of black intellectual life following World War I. During the war countless southern African Americans had relocated to northern cities, pushed out of the South by the boll weevil and drawn to the North with the promise of jobs opened up by World War I. The Harlem Renaissance of the 1920s produced brilliant black writers, artists, and musicians, and Haines Institute had produced many of the individuals taking part in this movement. In the spring of 1924 the league hosted its nineteenth annual Reception and Vaudeville for the benefit of Haines Institute, featuring musicians and singers, including Florence Mills, one of the singing and dancing sensations of the Harlem Renaissance.[33]

As Laney reached her seventies her health began to decline. Although she continued to work for the school, her niece Margaret Laney took on the role of principal. Suffering from kidney ailments and hypertension, Lucy Craft Laney died in the fall of 1933. Her funeral, a testimony to her influence, drew an estimated crowd of five thousand, and the *Augusta Chronicle* described it as "more like a coronation than a funeral."[34]

The same year Lucy Laney died, a contemporary of hers on the other side of the state struggled with the most public challenge to her image as the head of a well-known school when some male students accused her of taking advantage of students who worked on campus. Martha Berry and Lucy Laney both established renowned institutions of learning as a means of uplift for those who had little access to education, but their backgrounds were profoundly different.

Martha Berry enjoyed a truly privileged upbringing. Her father, Thomas Berry, in his mid-forties when she was born, owned a successful "grocery and cotton commission." Born in Virginia, he had moved with his family to Chattanooga, Tennessee, but the newly "opened" lands of north Georgia, available after the brutal removal of the Cherokees, had lured him to the settlement of Rome, Georgia, as a young man. He left Rome to serve the United States in the Mexican-American War and the Confederacy during the Civil War. In between the two he married Frances Rhea, an educated Alabama belle seventeen years his junior. In 1866, when Martha was born, Thomas Berry had an advantage that many of his Confederate neighbors did not. Due to speculative foresight or a sense of moral obligation, perhaps both, he had settled his debts with northern creditors before joining the Confederacy. Ultimately, his actions enabled him to obtain credit from those same men when the war ended. The loans enabled him to rebuild his plantation and his assets. Hence, Martha grew up in a very wealthy family.[35]

In 1871 Thomas Berry bought Oak Hill, a large home overlooking his land, and moved in his family and black house servants. Martha grew up with a house full of playmates that included five biological siblings and two adopted cousins. She loved riding her horse in the woods with her father, with whom she was very close. Later in life she stated, "The greatest influence in my life was having a father who praised and encouraged me whenever I did anything well and who taught me to love animals, birds, and flowers and take care of every living thing."[36]

Thomas left home for business trips frequently, so quite often the women at hand (Martha had two brothers) took charge of the plantation. The Civil War had given Frances some experience in surviving without her husband, and she was not without help in the postbellum years. Enoch and Martha Freeman, recently freedpeople, came to work at Oak Hill. "Aunt Marth," in particular, became essential to the family as its cook and general household assistant.[37]

Several governesses and teachers aided Frances with the children. Public schools did not appear in Rome until 1884, so Thomas hired teachers to ensure his children had the education befitting their status. Miss Ida McCullough taught the Berry children not only lessons from books, but also about the natural world surrounding them, taking them on nature walks in the area. As the children got older their parents sent them to boarding schools to continue their education. All the girls, save Jennie, the eldest, attended Madame LeFebvre's Edgeworth Finishing School in Baltimore while the boys furthered their education at Bingham Military Academy in North Carolina and Sewanee, an Episcopalian school in Tennessee.[38]

Martha entered Madame LeFebvre's in 1882, but later that year her father suffered a debilitating stroke. As a result, Martha never returned to finishing school. She chose instead to stay at home to nurse her father and help in his cotton brokerage business. Thomas Berry never fully recovered from the stroke, and five years later, in 1887, he died. Martha's oldest sister, Jennie, had already married by the time of her father's death, and so Frances and Martha took on the jobs of managing the business and the plantation. Later, Martha's brother Tom, younger than her by five years, joined them.[39]

Martha's youngest sister, Frances, wrote years after Martha's death that she had had many beaux as a young woman, but that "[t]here was only one love in her life." Frances did not reveal the identity of the man with whom Martha had an understanding, nor did she know why they had not married. But she did say that their father had purchased a house that he anticipated the couple would live in once they married. For undisclosed reasons, the engagement ended and Martha "went off to Europe" in the aftermath.[40] Ultimately, she poured her energy into her work rather than a marriage.

During her life, Martha Berry retold the story of how she started teaching countless times to prospective benefactors. As she sat reading in a cabin that she used as a personal retreat, she noticed some white children looking in at her. She managed to coax the waifs into the cabin and, since it was Sunday, she narrated Bible stories for them. Her surprise at their ignorance of these Bible stories, and their apparent eagerness to hear more, prompted her to invite them back the next week along with an invitation to bring their brothers and sisters as well. They did, and eventually they brought their parents too. The Berry family had belonged to the Episcopal Church, but Martha gravitated toward a non-denominational position. She began holding, in essence, a Sunday school for white families in her cabin each week, playing an old melodeon to accompany their hymn singing.[41]

Martha began visiting the homes of her students. The conditions in which they lived disturbed her. She described her stops at "cabin homes . . . built of rough logs" with dark interiors that she found "none too clean." The cabins allowed for "small window openings, but with cracks and crevices large enough for a dog of fair size to leap through." These windows illuminated rooms in which "pots and pans are usually scattered about the floor." Witnessing the conditions in which her students lived stirred Martha to devote herself to "teach them the way to help themselves." She aimed to "make them useful and successful men and women by teaching them how to scrub, to cook, to care for their rooms, to dress neatly, to farm, to build houses, [and] to save money."[42]

To this end, Berry organized four private schools at the turn of the century in which to educate rural children. One of them she housed on land that her father had bequeathed to her, the others she located in places that made them more accessible to distant students. To ensure the students felt invested in the venture, and to cut costs, Berry made certain that they and their parents took part in building and repairing the buildings they used for schools. Martha Berry did not teach in the schools herself; she provided buildings and then appealed to the county for the funds to hire a teacher for a five-month term. She then extended the term to six months by paying for the extra month herself.[43]

Martha Berry's image has been fiercely protected by the school and those who knew her, hence virtually all sources that cite her effort universally applaud it. But as historian Ann Short Chirhart points out, many rural parents maintained a suspicion of education beyond the household and the church and hence hesitated to send their children to school. Berry may have included parents in the building projects to ensure that they too had a stake in the school and would give their blessing to the enterprise.[44]

The people who attended Martha's makeshift schools were poor, illiterate, rural Georgians who lived outside of Rome's relative prosperity. In the late nineteenth century, "New South" boosters such as Henry Grady pressed the South to industrialize and diversify its economy. With three rivers and a railroad making it easy to transport goods to and from the city, postwar Rome experienced an expansion of business, construction of new factories, and an expanding population. But businesses wanted workers who had skills and a different kind of work ethic than the rural subsistence farmers possessed. As public schools took root in the South, cities often created a school system independent of the county system, draining funds from the county schools. Such was the case in Rome, and as a result too few schools existed in rural areas to absorb the number of prospective students. Moreover, by the turn of the century progressives, both northern and southern, viewed the expansion of education as a means of uplift to wrestle with the South's relative poverty. They began concerted efforts to tap into the pockets of interested northern philanthropists to help establish schools in underfunded areas. In addition to teaching an academic curriculum, they hoped to instill in students the middle-class "values of thrift, cleanliness, and hard work." Many of these private schools included an emphasis on agricultural and industrial education to train their students for employment once they graduated. Berry's focus reflected these ideals.[45]

Martha Berry and Lucy Laney both adopted industrial education in their schools to prepare their students for employment. Martha Berry envisioned her graduates as the future working class in the South, who would provide the foundation for southern economic success even though her school's curriculum was grounded in some collegiate programs that led to the creation of Berry College. Lucy Laney, on the other hand, not only hoped to teach her students employable skills for economic gain—even as these jobs became increasingly circumscribed by Jim Crow laws—but also to foster their intellectual skills to garner self-respect as well as the respect of white Americans.

Martha became concerned that her students' home lives interfered with their ability to learn new habits, and hence she made plans to open a boarding school where rural boys could live, work, and learn while separated from the influence of their families and friends. She believed that her students' contact with their families only encouraged them to revert to their former manners of speaking and behavior that had led to poverty. In 1902 she opened Berry Boys' Industrial High School. The next year it became incorporated as Boys' Industrial School, and Berry deeded eighty-three acres of the land her father had left her to the school. By this time she had engaged the assistance of Elizabeth Brewster, a college graduate with a degree in botany, who taught virtually all the classes in the school's early years. She became a close friend to Martha and they worked together to make Berry's dream a reality.[46]

Berry's students could not afford tuition outright, but she did not envision her institution as a charity. Her attitude toward charity and education paralleled that of the Southern Education Board, formed in 1901 to promote education in the southern states. An article in its biweekly newsletter addressed the issue, quoting the position of the *World's Work*, which stated: "It is worth while to help those who help themselves, and only those." At the Boys' Industrial School students paid the equivalent of five dollars a month for tuition and board in work done for the school. They paid for their clothes and donated to the school with work they did on holidays. During the regular term, for two hours a day they "cleaned, cooked, washed, farmed and did carpenter's work, much of which was new to them." It was student labor that built most of the buildings on the campus, giving the students a proprietary interest in the Berry Schools—the name that was adopted in 1908.[47]

The school grew quickly; in the spring of 1909 the trustees reported that too many students had been allowed to enroll the previous fall, causing overcrowding. They responded by limiting the number of students they accepted for the spring term. Despite that, in 1909, in a seemingly unilateral move that went against the advice of her associates, Berry opened a girls' school. The school operated under the same premise as the boys' school. The only substantial difference between the boys' and girls' school was the work assigned to each group, which followed the gender conventions of the period. As in Laney's school, girls performed tasks that would teach them to become wives and mothers while the boys took on more masculine tasks. The following May the board of trustees reported rather tersely, "Miss Berry reported the establishment of a

Girl's School, and an attendance of twelve boarders. The Board ratifies any steps Miss Berry has taken in this matter."[48]

The academic curriculum at the Berry School contained all the elements of a liberal arts education of the day, which at the time included Latin, Cicero's Orations, botany, geography, Greek, physics, and a course on Caesar or physiology. Recitations were held five times a week. Classes on the Bible were mandatory. An Episcopalian herself, Berry chose to declare the school a nondenominational institution in its charter. Nevertheless, the school affirmed a belief in Christianity, and the charter did deem that teachers "shall be members of some protestant church."[49]

To ensure that students behaved in a manner appropriate to the image of the school, they had to follow a strict set of rules set out by Martha Berry and the board of trustees that limited their mobility and contact with their families and the city of Rome. Students had been allowed to visit home once a month. Finding that homesick scholars often did not return from these visits, or that parents who needed help at home discouraged their children from returning, in 1913 the administration limited trips home to once a term. A dress code determined that students dressed simply and practically with clothes made by Berry students; young women were cautioned to wear only "low heel, common sense shoes." Female students could not correspond with males without their parents' consent. In fact, the school placed great emphasis in keeping males and females separated on campus as well. They could not smoke or drink, and they could not leave the school's grounds without the permission of the dean. The administration did not want visitors wandering onto the campus either. Berry was horrified in the fall of 1924 to learn that the gates had been left open one Sunday, leading to "a carload of 'flappers' on the campus."[50]

Both Laney and Berry regulated their students' behavior to safeguard their reputations. Women, particularly, faced judgment if their morals appeared "loose." To many people in the 1920s "flapper" dress represented the modern woman who symbolized not only a break from middle-class tradition, but a woman of questionable purity. For the young women in Laney's school, purity took on a heightened meaning as black women attempted to counter the stereotypes of black promiscuity.[51]

Over the years Martha Berry worked closely with her board of trustees, a group of men she chose to help run her schools, but she retained effective control of the school itself. Many members of the board were both friends or family and had connections that could serve the school. Her brother, Tom, served on the board early on, as did Moses Wright, her brother-in-law and a judge. Controversial Governor Hoke Smith, who favored educational reform while simultaneously stirring up racial tension and playing a leading role in disfran-chising black Georgians, but who had the political clout that could help the school, served on the board as well. But it was John Eagan, the president of the board, "an Atlantan with large real estate holdings and owner of the American Cast Iron Pipe Company in Birmingham" whom she relied on most heavily for advice and support. He was also a confidant who received letters full of frustration regarding potential donors and requests for help that reflected the personal side of a woman who was seemingly unflappable in public.[52]

Fundraising became a constant task for Martha Berry. Like Lucy Craft Laney, she always had too many students and not enough money. There existed a lim-ited number of philanthropists and a seemingly limitless number of private schools that competed with one another for their donations. In 1915 Berry ap-parently attended an event at Tuskegee that also included prospective donors. Booker T. Washington wrote to Berry after the affair, apologizing for "not call-ing on you to speak before you left," insisting that he had "fully meant to do so" but had been unaware of her plans to leave early. To compensate, he sent her the names and addresses of the "visitors," so she could contact them and per-haps "interest them in [her] work." And while he also invited her to attend any further functions at Tuskegee, one has to wonder whether the slip might have been intentional; they were, after all, competitors.[53]

In her fundraising efforts, Berry displayed almost superhuman energy, a characteristic she shared with Laney. Both women campaigned publicly for their schools in a way that stretched and challenged the boundaries of the tra-ditional roles of southern women. She wrote letters and pamphlets on behalf of the school, of which *Uplifting Backwoods Boys in the South* is an example. She issued invitations to visit the school to anyone she thought could help by either donating funds or finding people who could. And she made frequent trips to the North. Berry worked hard at this part of her job. Using southern charm and her knowledge of upper-class mores, she was able to woo funds from many wealthy benefactors. But she often pushed herself and wore herself down physically in the effort. While she did face many disappointments, she also had enormous successes in her fundraising efforts, successes that Laney could only dream about.[54]

Emily Vanderbilt Sloan Hammond, an heir to both the Sloan and Vander-bilt fortunes, and her husband, John Henry Hammond, became longtime sup-porters of Martha Berry and the Berry Schools. Berry impressed Theodore Roosevelt, and he introduced her to wealthy friends from whom she solicited funds. In the spring of 1909 the board of trustees noted that Andrew Carnegie and Mrs. Russell Sage had offered to donate "$25,000 each toward an $100,000

Endowment." That left Berry to raise the other half on her own, which she determinedly accomplished. Other gifts came in, sometimes in monetary form, others as "a building or an electric plant or a herd of cows." But it was Henry Ford who became Berry's biggest donor.[55]

Berry began courting Henry Ford and his wife, Clara, in the 1920s. Eventually they agreed to visit the school, and it impressed them. They made several subsequent visits to the school. The Fords not only helped purchase land for the school, which allowed it to expand, but they built a group of imposing stone buildings for the girls' school.[56]

By the 1920s Berry School and its founder had gained national attention and accolades. She received an honorary doctorate from the University of Georgia in 1920. In 1924 the Georgia Assembly made her a Distinguished Citizen of the State. The following year the Roosevelt Memorial Association awarded her the Roosevelt Medal, which was presented by President Calvin Coolidge. Journalist Ida Tarbell listed her among America's Fifty Greatest Women in 1930, and in 1931 *Good Housekeeping Magazine* named Berry as one of the America's Twelve Greatest Women. In 1932 her reputation earned her an appointment to the Board of Regents of the University System of Georgia. Numerous honorary degrees followed.[57] Lucy Laney, too, received accolades during her lifetime from the black community, but it was not until after her death, indeed the last half of the twentieth century, that Lucy Laney gained recognition from white Americans.

Berry College did have detractors, however, and the school faced its most serious crisis during the Depression. By the 1930s the Berry Schools had grown considerably and encompassed a college as well as high schools. In 1933 the boys' school became the focus of conflict over how much (or how little) the school paid the male students for their work. The ensuing dispute garnered embarrassing national publicity for the school's administrators and Martha Berry in particular.

The administrators of the Berry Schools blamed Don West, a former Berry student, for the havoc. West was a poet of some renown, and also one of the cofounders of the Highlander Folk School. The Highlander Folk School, which opened in November 1932 in Monteagle, Tennessee, aimed to train "leaders . . . for the conservation and enrichment of the indigenous cultural values of the mountains,"[58] and as "one instrument to build a new social order."[59] Don West returned to Georgia in the spring of 1933 as the Depression worsened despite the initiation of the New Deal. At the time, West's nephew Willis Sutton was attending Berry. In the summer of 1933 Berry Schools had lowered the "wages" students received as credit toward tuition. Don West saw this as an injustice, as did some of the students, and they organized a protest strike in August. While most of the students went back to work after a short time and professed loyalty to the school, a few remained unrepentant and sought Don West's help. He enlisted the help of the radical National Student League, and its members across the country began sending letters of protest not only to the Berry Schools, but to its benefactors as well. Moreover, the *New Republic* newsmagazine printed a letter by West that criticized the school for raising tuition and lowering wages at the same time. He charged that the strike ended only when the administration had threatened participants with expulsion.[60]

Martha Berry adamantly defended the image of her school. After the letter appeared in the *New Republic* the Berry administrators initiated a public relations defense and launched an offensive against Don West as well. Berry began writing letters ensuring her donors that her students remained loyal and branding Don West and his supporters as active "Reds" and communists who threatened to "destroy the School." Many of the letters sent out asked the recipients to write a letter of protest to the *New Republic*. Robert Alston, president of the board of trustees at the time, even contacted the Bureau of Investigation, the forerunner of the FBI, to look into the incident. The bureau reported back that "at the present time there is no Federal statute violation of communism or radicalism," but did agree to have an agent call on him.[61]

As the perceived threat faded, the school suffered no threat to its image, nor did it lose loyal benefactors. Martha Berry had painstakingly cultivated the school's image to encourage donations and cull loyalty from its students, who were potential future contributors. The carefully constructed history of the school, with a focus on the sacrifices and spunk of its founder, the enduring struggles it faced, its faith in prayer, and its ultimate success in molding successful, productive, and loyal students, was retold time and again to prospective donors. Founder's Day became an official celebration of the school's history and endurance, in which all the students were made to feel a part of something unique and special. Berry, the administrators, and most of the students fiercely protected this image.

Berry's story of encouraging underprivileged young people to help themselves succeed through hard work and thrift captured the imaginations of Americans. It was the epitome of the American "success story." And Martha Berry was its architect. In 1939 she received the prestigious Medal of the National Institute of Social Sciences. At a lavish dinner at the Waldorf-Astoria, Emily Vanderbilt Hammond gave a speech honoring Berry.[62]

By 1941, now in her early eighties, Martha Berry became seriously ill. Throughout her life she had had bouts of pneumonia; later in life a heart condition and high blood pressure threatened her health, sending her to a hospital in Atlanta. She died in February 1942.[63]

Both Lucy Craft Laney and Martha Berry dedicated their lives to educating young Americans who did not have access to public education. The admiration and devotion of their students demonstrates how much they affected their lives. Both women were posthumously recognized by the state of Georgia by having their portrait hung in the state capitol and received the honor of being inducted into the Georgia Women of Achievement. And yet the differences in their experiences reflect the racism and segregation that existed in the late nineteenth and early twentieth centuries. Americans are drawn to success stories that involve hard work and struggles, but they found it harder to respond to the needs, and applaud the successes, of Laney's black children than they did Berry's white children.

## NOTES

1. Ann Short Chirhart, in *Torches of Light: Georgia Teachers and the Coming of the Modern South* (Athens: University of Georgia Press, 2005), compares black and white female teachers in the South and illuminates the empowering and subversive nature of teaching in the Progressive era. Glenda Elizabeth Gilmore's *Gender and Jim Crow: Women and the Politics of White Supremacy in North Carolina, 1896–1920* (Chapel Hill: University of North Carolina Press, 1996) looks at the role of women, including teachers, during this era. On Progressivism in the South see Dewey Grantham, *Southern Progressivism: The Reconciliation of Progress and Tradition* (Knoxville: University of Tennessee Press, 1983); and William A. Link, *The Paradox of Southern Progressivism, 1880–1930* (Chapel Hill: University of North Carolina Press, 1997). Robyn Muncy discusses the importance of female institutions in the early twentieth century and the continuation of the work of female progressives and those they mentored beyond the 1920s in *Creating a Female Dominion in American Reform, 1890–1935* (New York: Oxford University Press, 1991).

2. A. C. Griggs, "Lucy Craft Laney," *Journal of Negro History* (January 1934): 97; Ninth Census of the United States, Population Schedules, Georgia, 1870 (hereafter cited as Ninth Census).

3. Griggs, "Lucy Craft Laney"; Mary Ovington, "From Portraits in Color," 53–64, a typed copy of part of the book sent in to the Harmon Foundation to support Laney's nomination for the Harmon Foundation's Distinguished Achievement among Negroes Award, Harmon Foundation Papers, Collection of the Manuscript Division, Library of Congress (hereafter cited as Harmon Foundation), 3.

4. Griggs, "Lucy Craft Laney," 97.

5. Ibid., 98.

6. Jennifer Lund Smith, "The Ties That Bind: Educated African-American Women in Post-Emancipation Atlanta," in *Georgia in Black and White: Explorations in the Race Relations of a Southern State, 1865–1950*, ed. John C. Inscoe (Athens: University of Georgia Press, 1994), 94. See also James D. Anderson, *The Education of Blacks in the South, 1860–1935* (Chapel Hill: University of North Carolina Press, 1988).

7. Anderson, *The Education of Blacks.*

8. Ibid.; Griggs, "Lucy Craft Laney," 98. Mary Magdalene Marshall, "'Tell Them We're Rising!': Black Intellectuals and Lucy Craft Laney in Post Civil War Augusta, Georgia" (PhD diss., Drew University, 1998), 138.

9. Griggs, "Lucy Craft Laney," 98; Kent Anderson Leslie, "No Middle Ground: Elite African Americans in Augusta and the Coming of Jim Crow," in *Paternalism in a Southern City: Race, Religion and Gender in Augusta, Georgia*, ed. Edward J. Cashin and Glenn T. Eskew (Athens: University of Georgia Press, 2001), 126; Gloria T. Williams-Way, "Lucy Craft Laney—The Mother of the Children of the People: Educator, Reformer, Social Activist" (PhD diss., University of South Carolina, 1998), 171.

10. Griggs, "Lucy Craft Laney," 98; *Augusta City Directory* (Atlanta: R. L. Polk and Co., 1888), 273. See also *Augusta City Directory*, 1888–1910, various publishers.

11. Dr. J. M. Gaston, Secretary Treasurer, Board of National Missions of the Presbyterian Church, Recommendation for the Harmon Award, August 8, 1930, Harmon Foundation.

12. *The Church at Home and Abroad* (Philadelphia: Presbyterian Board of Publication, 1887), 1:17–18. Mrs. Haines's father had been a New York merchant and the first president of the American Tract Society. Her husband, also a merchant, served on the Board of Union Theological Seminary In New York City. Having entertained the idea of becoming a missionary herself when young, she turned instead to supporting them as an organizer of the Home Missions Board of the Presbyterian Church, U.S.A. Laney may have named the institute after Mrs. Haines as attempt to keep Haines attention on the school in order to secure more funds, but Haines died later that year. See Griggs, "Lucy Craft Laney," 98–99; Leslie, "No Middle Ground," 126; and Ovington, "From Portraits in Color," 7.

13. Audrey Thomas McCluskey, "'We Specialize in the Wholly Impossible': Black Women School Founders and Their Mission," *Signs: Journal of Women in Culture and Society* 22 (Winter 1997): 407.

14. Ibid.; James D. Anderson, *The Education of Blacks in the South, 1860–1935* (Chapel Hill: University of North Carolina Press, 1988), 109; Chirhart, *Torches of Light*, 21–23, 30–31, 113–14, 124–36; Gilmore, *Gender and Jim Crow*, 158–161.

15. Leslie, "No Middle Ground," 126.

16. Ovington, "From Portraits in Color," 2, 5.

17. McCluskey, "'We Specialize in the Wholly Impossible,'" 406.

18. Ovington, "From Portraits in Color," 5, 15; Lucy Lilian Notestein, *Nobody Knows the Trouble I See* (New York: Board of National Missions of the Presbyterian Church in the U.S.A., n.d.), 9, Harmon Foundation; *Augusta City Directory* 1888, 273; See also *Augusta City Directory*, 1888–1910.

19. Notestein, *Nobody Knows the Trouble I See*, 11.

20. Ibid, 8.

21. Ibid, 8–9; Leslie, "No Middle Ground," 124, 127; Williams-Way, "Lucy Craft Laney," 184–85. For examples of the Board of Missions tributes to Lucy Laney, see William Hallock Johnson, "A Friend of Boys and Girls," *Women and Missions* 3 (April 1926): 1–14; and Anes Bell Snively, "A Sketch of Lucy C. Laney" *Women and Missions* 3 (April 1926): 14–16, both in Harmon Foundation.

22. Leslie, "No Middle Ground," 127.

23. George E. Haynes, New York, to Lawton B. Evans, September 1928. Haynes sent Evans a questionnaire to fill out regarding Laney. She had been put forward as a nominee for the Harmon Award for Distinguished Achievement among Negroes in the Field of Education. See Harmon Foundation.

24. Dr. Gaston, Secretary and Assistant Treasurer of the Board of National Missions, Presby-

terian Church in the U.S.A., Division of Missions for Colored People, August 8, 1830, "Information about Lucy Laney," Harmon Foundation; Griggs, "Lucy Craft Laney," 101; Leslie, "No Middle Ground," 127.

25. On Sabbath schools and their importance in the South, see Sally G. McMillen, *To Raise Up the South: Sunday Schools in Black and White Churches, 1865–1915* (Baton Rouge: Louisiana State University, 2001); Griggs, "Lucy Craft Laney," 100; Leslie, "No Middle Ground," 126; Bobby J. Donaldson, "Standing on a Volcano: The Leadership of William Jefferson White," in *Paternalism in a Southern City: Race, Religion and Gender in Augusta, Georgia*, ed. Edward J. Cashin and Glenn T. Eskew (Athens: University of Georgia Press, 2001), 144–48.

26. Leslie, "No Middle Ground," 123–34; Chirhart, *Torches of Light*, 30; Marshall, "'Tell Them We're Rising!'" 227–29.

27. Williams-Way, "Lucy Craft Laney," 306, 31–12.

28. Williams-Way, "Lucy Craft Laney," 312–14; Richard R. Wright, *A Brief Historical Sketch of Negro Education in Georgia* (Savannah: Robinson Printing House, 1894), 47.

29. McCluskey, "'We Specialize in the Wholly Impossible,'" 405–8.

30. Chirhart, *Torches of Light*, 9. See also Gilmore, 31–59.

31. Lucy Laney, "Address before the Women's Meeting, Delivered by Lucy Laney at the Atlanta University Conference on Negro Problems, Atlanta, Georgia, 1898," reprinted in Williams-Way, "Lucy Craft Laney," 363.

32. Ovington, "From Portraits in Color," 5.

33. Pamphlet announcing the "Nineteenth Annual Reception & Vaudeville of the Lucy Laney League," Harmon Foundation.

34. Quoted in Williams-Way, "Lucy Craft Laney," 323.

35. Susan Asbury, "The Berry Family: An Evolution of a Southern Family Living in the Reconstruction and New South Eras" (unpublished paper, 1997), 6–9; Martha McChesney Berry Papers, Berry College Archives, Memorial Library, Berry College, Rome, Georgia (hereafter cited as Berry Papers); Doyle Mathis and Ouida Dickey, eds., *Martha Berry: Sketches of Her Schools and College* (Atlanta: Wings Publishers, 2001), 5–6; Harnett T. Kane with Inez Henry, *Miracle in the Mountains* (Garden City, N.Y.: Doubleday, 1956), 10–11.

36. Asbury, "The Berry Family," 11; Ninth Census; Eighth Census of the United States, Population Schedules, Georgia, 1860; Martha Berry, "Comments by Martha Berry," in Mathis and Dickey, *Martha Berry*, 32, Frances Berry Bonnyman, "Some of Martha's Activities," in Mathis and Dickey, *Martha Berry*, 33.

37. Asbury, "The Berry Family," 11–13; Kane, *Miracle in the Mountains*, 18.

38. Kane, *Miracle in the Mountains*, 15–16; Asbury, "The Berry Family," 14.

39. Asbury, "The Berry Family," 16–17; Mathis and Dickey, *Martha Berry*, 7; Carol Anne Guthrie, "Education and the Evolution of the South: A History of the Berry Schools, 1902–1970" (PhD diss., University of Tennessee, 1994), 15.

40. Frances Bonnyman, "Reminiscences of Childhood by Frances Bonnyman," Berry Papers.

41. Martha Berry, *Uplifting Backwoods Boys in the South*, copy from the World's Work 1904, Berry Papers.

42. Berry, *Uplifting Backwoods Boys*, 5, 6.

43. Ibid., 6–7.

44. Chirhart, *Torches of Light*, see especially 55–62.

45. Asbury, "The Berry Family," 2–5; Guthrie, "Education and the Evolution of the South," 15–22.

46. Berry, *Uplifting Backwoods Boys*, 8; Guthrie, "Education and the Evolution of the South," 53–54.

47. Berry, *Uplifting Backwoods Boys*, 8–9; *Southern Education Notes* 9 (June 30, 1902): 5; Mathis and Dicky, *Martha Berry*, 70.

48. "Annual Report of the Principal to the Trustees of the Berry School for the School Year, 1908–1909," Berry Papers; "Annual Meeting of the Board of Trustees Held at the Berry School," April 27, 1910, Berry Papers.

49. Catalogue and Historic Sketch, Boys Industrial School, 1903–1904 and 1905–1906, Berry Papers; Asbury, "The Berry Family," 14; Board of Trustees Minutes, January 10, 1903, Berry Papers.

50. Berry School Bulletin, April 1913, Berry College Archives; *Berry School Bulletin: Catalogue and Announcements of the Marth Berry School for Girls*, 1914, Berry College Archives; Guthrie, "Education and the Evolution of the South," 78; Martha Berry to Miss Wingo, 29 September 1924, Berry Papers.

51. Chirhart, *Torches of Light*, 58–61. Page 58 includes a fabulous description of a female student who bobbed her hair.

52. Berry, *Uplifting Backwoods Boys*, 14; Guthrie, "Education and the Evolution of the South," 38. For examples of letters from Berry to Eagan, see, in the Berry Papers, Martha Berry to John J. Eagan, January 20, 1923, February 27, 1923, April 4, 1923. Their correspondence is extensive.

53. Booker T. Washington to Miss Martha Berry, February 26, 1915, reprinted in Mathis and Dickey, *Martha Berry*, 247.

54. For a discussion of the way teachers created a professional status for themselves, see Chirhart, *Torches of Light*, esp. 133–38.

55. "Annual Meeting of the Board of Trustees Held at the Berry School," April 27, 1909, Berry Papers; Mathis and Dickey, *Martha Berry*, 60–70.

56. Mathis and Dickey, *Martha Berry*, 73.

57. Ibid., 8–9.

58. Guthrie, "Education and the Evolution of the South," 84.

59. Myles Horton, The Highlander Fold School, Monteagle, Tenn., undated statement of purpose sent to the Berry Schools, quoted in Guthrie, "Education and the Evolution of the South," 84.

60. Guthrie, "Education and the Evolution of the South," 85–91.

61. Martha Berry to Mr. and Mrs. George Listor Carlisle, October 7, 1933, Martha Berry to Mrs. John Henry Hammond, October 16, 1933, unsigned copy of letter to Mrs. Henry Ford, October 7, 1933, J. H. Hanson, Acting Special Agent in Charge to Mr. Robert C. Alston, October 7, 1933, Berry Papers.

62. From a loose clipping of the *Southern Highlander*, 1939, Berry Papers.

63. Kane, *Miracle in the Mountains*, 294, 206–7.

# Corra Harris

## (1869–1935)

## *The Storyteller as Folk Preacher*

### DONALD MATHEWS

❀ ❀ ❀

Corra White Harris is largely forgotten now, although an Evangelical publishing house did publish her most famous book a few years ago under a slightly modified title. For the first decade of the twentieth century, however, she was a famed reviewer of books for the *Independent* magazine of New York City. In 1910 she published her "circuit rider" stories between hard covers and for the next decade was one of the most famous popular storytellers in the magazines of the middle-brow middle classes, with a readership that spanned the continent despite the fact that she was an unapologetic southern partisan from Elberton, Georgia. She was also an unapologetic champion of wives and mothers, telling their stories and celebrating their courage in homely, small-town settings that were being threatened by the ravages of fast-growing cities, swift industrialization, foreign ideologies, and rapidly changing morals. Born in 1869 to a Confederate veteran, Colonel Tinsley White, and his wife, Mary Mathews White, Corra Mae White married at seventeen a fellow teacher, Lundy Howard Harris, who had just become a Methodist preacher. The shock of a newly imposed piety would provide this clever and witty young woman with the marrow of her first book, but she had not been aware of the opportunities offered her at the time. Gradually, as she followed her husband from country churches into academic life, she kept her sanity by observing the humor in the lives of sometimes humorless people and practicing her narrative skills in private.[1]

It was not humor, however, that launched her literary career. Corra Harris was dead serious when she wrote a letter to the *Independent* in May 1899. She had penned witty pieces for the *Atlanta Constitution* earlier,[2] but her good humor had fled as she described the cultural climate within which a crowd

**CORRA HARRIS**

Courtesy of Hargrett Rare Book and Manuscript
Library, University of Georgia Libraries.

of white men had lynched Sam Hose in Newnan, Georgia, on April 23. Although the *Independent* was based in New York City, it had always reported news from the suspect South. In the issue of May 11, a black army chaplain had condemned Hose's burning, and Harris's friend, the Reverend William P. Lovejoy, had lamented the "mob spirit" of white savages, even though he believed it a clear response to the restless politics of unruly blacks.[3] Harris's letter, printed a week later, condemned African Americans as brutish men and sluttish women who had cloaked the region in sexual danger. This premise helped Harris understand "facts which do not mitigate the atrocious conduct of the Newnan mob, but which do explain its savage fury." We live, she insisted, "next door to a savage brute, who grows more intelligent and more insolent in his outrages every year." No southern white woman, Harris accused, was safe from the "insults" of this creature, reared as he was, in a "cesspool of vice" and "brutal lust" that enabled him to accept the repeated seduction of women closest to him as a matter of course. Neither the "savage's" family, nor his religion, nor his women could civilize him; even the performances of African American prophetic women in the transports of the Spirit were, she shuddered, "lewd and blasphemous." If southern white women shrank from mob violence "with alarm and horror," she added, swift and sure draconian punishment was nonetheless reasonable under the hovering sexual peril that enveloped them all. When you condemn our men, she protested to Yankees, you side with those who threaten us. "This cannot be true."[4]

That the *Independent* published Harris's letter was mildly surprising. The magazine had been launched by abolitionists and in the 1890s remained a consistently hostile critic of most white southerners; but there was something about Harris's style and energy that captivated the editor. He was critical of the Georgian's reasoning and prejudices, to be sure, but he asked her to write again, which she did a month later, this time on "Negro Womanhood." And once again, Harris attacked the source of vice among black men, which she believed was "the debased motherhood of the negro [*sic*] race in the South." The "victim of savage moods and brutal chastisements from infancy," the black woman was "prey to the first wretch who approaches her with deceitful kindness." She did not mention that this situation existed in her own household. Harris could not excuse the white seducers of black women, she wrote in passing, but they did not invite her fury, at least in public. She believed that black women had an almost miraculous power to attract white men to their beds with an inviting capacity for exciting sexual adventure. If the moral integrity of the white race resulted from its virtuous women, Harris believed, the moral degeneration of the black man had resulted from the fact that his own women became "any man's mistress, every man's victim,"[5] and in their own sexual predation was the source of the white South's alarm and ferocity. In other words, African American women were ultimately responsible for the lynching of Sam Hose.

Imagining a myth of sexual danger explained by the lustful predation of black women came easily to Corra Harris. Understanding why this was so helps to fathom how she became a storyteller, why she told the tales that so delighted a national audience, and how she became a religious critic during a time when religion and women and public commentary were changing in sometimes bewildering ways. Like most writers, Harris imagined narratives that flowed from her own experience. Like the Methodist preachers she had heard and observed all her life,[6] she believed that authentic solutions to the daily problems of living were embodied in ordinary people who may not have understood the complexities of doctrine or managed to memorize the right proof texts, but who nonetheless exhibited a recuperative spiritual power based on Christian Faith (her daughter's name) and Hope (her sister's name). If this power was strengthened by pain and personal victory and frequently expressed in delightfully good humor, it was all the more authentic. Her talent for "preaching" through recounting moral dramas became apparent after she had served an apprenticeship at the *Independent* as an insightful and witty, if prudish, reviewer of books, but her earliest essays erupted from an existential pain and the frailties, betrayals, confusions, and fantasies that inflicted it. As so many evangelists did, she began by publicly attacking the evil that assailed her—as she understood it. African American lust, she believed (or at least pretended to do so), had driven her husband, and thus her family, from Eden.

That storied garden was the village of Oxford, Georgia, where Methodists had built an institution of higher learning named for a dead bishop. Emory College's fame, such as it was, had flowed from the prestige of an early president, Augustus Baldwin Longstreet; the labors of its New South leader, Atticus Green Haygood; and one of its most legendary alumni, Senator Lucius Quintus Cincinnatus Lamar II of Mississippi.[7] Corra entered the Wesleyan Paradise when in 1888 President Warren Akin Candler appointed her husband, Lundy, to an adjunct professorship of Greek after two years as a probationary member and local preacher in the north Georgia annual conference of the Methodist Episcopal Church, South. In 1894 Candler named Lundy as Seney Professor of Greek, and in 1896 Bishop Haygood ordained him to the diaconate. In Lundy, Candler believed he would have a loyal, congenial, and valued colleague. In Corra, Mrs. Candler found a young and devoted friend whose infectious wit could make her laugh and whose understanding of the staid and sanctimonious community in which they lived was refreshing. Much later in life Corra would remember her life in Oxford as idyllic,[8] but in 1898, a year before she wrote to the *Independent*, she had remembered it as an education in uncertainty, irrationality, fantasy, and grief. She had lived under the "shadow" of a "madman" for over a decade, she confessed to intimates; her domestic nightmare had been sufferable only through remembering the Cross of Christ, a mental ritual that she had enacted in silence, tortured constantly by the fear that one day she would find the depressed and self-destructive Lundy bloodied and dead by his own hand.[9] Then everything changed when she could not find him at all. He abruptly disappeared, leaving wife, children, colleagues, friends, calling, and honor to seek "the Spirit." In that crisis of June 1898 Corra let loose "the pent up unspeakable sorrow of the years" that would one day be repeated over and over in her stories. "To suffer is my nature," she confessed to the newly elected Bishop Candler, "it is the birthright of my married life." She had endured her husband's darkest moods, his terrible struggles with doubt, his almost catatonic withdrawal from her—all in silence; but now he had disappeared and she was completely demoralized. "I am frightened," she told Candler, as the first torrential expressions of her grief and terror subsided for the moment. She did not know what to do: "I have suffered passively so long."[10]

Corra would eventually tell an adoring public that Lundy's weaknesses had welled up from within his hyperreligious sensibility that demanded a spiritual perfection he could never realize. His intensity in this quest became a leitmotif in her representations of him, while she also encouraged those who did not know him to believe that he had been ignored by an ungrateful church because he was not sufficiently "political" to earn the handsome rewards of a successful Methodist ministry. She described him as principled, scholarly, overly idealistic, and ill-equipped psychologically to live in the "real" world. She wanted her readers to think he had been a well-read and substantial scholar of Greek— he had, after all, occupied an endowed chair. But her very real terror that he would one day take his own life suggested that she knew he lived in constant contempt of his own failings despite the fact that he could be charming, entertaining, witty, and appropriately reflective. He was, it seems, a popular and respected teacher. But Corra sensed trouble in May of 1898 even if she did not know its source.[11] She did not know that Lundy had been shamed by exchanges with a new professor of Latin. Andrew Sledd had recently arrived from Harvard Graduate School after a brief stint at Vanderbilt University in Nashville, where he had been appalled by lax academic standards. Emory was even worse, he discovered, and the prize example of this wretched fact was that the professor of Greek knew nothing of Pindar or Sappho, which he excused by having preferred to focus on Plato. When Sledd learned that Harris relied on a "pony" to

help him read the ancient philosopher, the young Harvard graduate's contempt
was boundless, and it must have been obvious, too. Sledd was determined to do
everything in his power to establish standards of excellence at Emory. To com-
pound the anxiety induced by Lundy's remarkable deficiency and deception,
Corra, much to her horror and dismay, had felt morally compelled to report
plagiarism by a young professor whom authorities quietly permitted to resign.
Her husband would have been profoundly affected by his wife's outrage at the
affair because of his own guilty secret. One can imagine his shame and con-
sternation. He had felt that way before. In 1882 he had publicly confessed to the
entire Methodist church in Oxford that he had disgraced himself, the church,
and the college by drunkenly celebrating his darker side at a brothel in nearby
Covington. He had then resigned his position as teacher in Emory's preparatory
school and accepted Warren Candler's help in finding other employment. In
the spring of 1898, Lundy Harris was once again overcome by shame and guilt.
After he and Corra had given a highly successful garden party for sixty-five
guests, and after the board of trustees had praised the faculty as "cultured" and
honorable men, Lundy Harris ran away to Texas to find salvation. He woke up
with a hangover in an Austin whorehouse.[12]

Corra was stunned by successive waves of cruel discovery. First she endured
the shock of being abandoned, then the shock of leaving Oxford in shame,
then the shock of facing her family's poverty and then the shock of Lundy's
public confessions. All these things were prelude. She gingerly received him
back. She reached out, but he could not bear her touching him until he had
confessed everything. She did not want to hear everything, she replied. He had
already told friends, colleagues, former students, and relatives all the "details,"
but in deference to her he relented. Corra of course learned the details anyway;
she learned he had been intimate with many unmarried and married African
American women in Oxford. She must have wondered if the servants in her
own household had been involved, and then as she thought about what she had
just discovered, she began to worry about what she did not yet know of her husband's life and began to fear that he had bedded white women whom he might
disgrace by confessing publicly as he had his exploits with black women—
giving out specific names, dates, and places. Corra was once again afflicted, this
time—and for the rest of his life—by fear of what he might have done, and what
he might yet do. After Lundy confessed to her in abjection and shame, Corra
had cradled him like a child in her arms. He was now a profoundly sad, desperately contrite, and terribly weakened man who was ill "in some strange and
secret way," she wrote. She turned to Candler once again, as she had the day
Lundy left. The Bishop had "never failed" her; he was the source of strength and

hope for a better future; Lundy was her cross. As he became a fragile man-child in her mind, he seemed also to become a victim. She thought he was not a "deliberately unchaste man," she told Candler. "Lundy's weakness is not unchastity, it is madness." She wanted to shield him.[13] Weak as he was, vulnerable as he was, "mad" as he was, he had been ensnared in the sexual traps that others had set for him. As she would later insist in her stories, predatory adventuresses lay in wait for such susceptible men as he and the morally feeble antiheros of her imagination. Thus when she wrote to the *Independent*, in the wake of a horrific lynching, she wasn't thinking of Sam Hose, but—even as she shielded him— Lundy Harris.

If one man's frailty and joblessness demanded that Corra begin to write in earnest, other men's strength, approval, and support made it possible for her to do so. She soon learned that Hamilton Holt, the twenty-seven-year-old managing editor of the *Independent*, liked her spirit and style, and she wanted desperately to write for him. She didn't want to write about race necessarily, but she did want somehow to enter the "literary" world to exercise and expand her creative power.[14] She wanted to earn enough money to allow the family once again to live together,[15] to be sure, but practical necessity soon yielded to the exhilarating experience of being birthed anew quite beyond the imagination of a dutiful academic wife in a remote southern village. Soon she was writing essays, short (short) stories, and reviews; she was telling other people what she thought as if her ideas actually counted for something. More important still, she was learning so many new things. She found that Yankees—even those from the abolitionist tradition, could be supportive of her even as they censured her prejudices. The welcome and amazing sympathy of Dr. William Hayes Ward, editor-in-chief, released a torrential eruption of delight that quashed the terrible agony of the previous twenty-one months. His compassion had been so healing that she could even endure, she laughed, his comments with "tails of yellow jackets in them about us here in the South." Ward had respected her enough to send her something he had written; he had also written in appreciation of the South's poet laureate, Sidney Lanier, and had sympathized with Corra when she was damaged by the cruel pieties of "consecrated" Christians after Lundy had confessed his sins. "The public," she wrote—meaning the *good Christian public*, "has a vulture's stomach for scandal. And nobody ever forgives the seriously self-confessed sinner but God." To be sure, "a sinner's friends . . . . will poke sympathy and a few rags of advice to him through the keyhole of the outer gates, but as for opening to him again the doorway of life and honor, O Lord! they are 'consecrated' and must not be contaminated, you know, by contact with a self confessed sinner." Ward's generosity had allowed her to open up far more honestly and profoundly than she ever could have to the good Bishop Candler, and she offered the editor her own confession as "an unconscious pharisee myself." Chastened by this knowledge, she would remind herself that God loved those people who had ostracized her husband; and, better yet, she could begin to realize that she did not relish a return to Eden. She had once thought that in turning Adam and Eve from their garden, God had "cursed them. But now," she wrote, "I know He blessed them." Ward had blessed her, too. She knew she had taken advantage of his kindness by writing as she had, but he had to know that he had resurrected her from grief. "I have less of sorrow in me everyday," she told him. "I feel that I am on the verge of a great discovery."[16]

And indeed she was. With the help of Paul Elmer More, the scholarly book review editor, she discovered herself. For over four years he blue-penciled her work; he pushed, encouraged, and showed her how to think and how to write reviews in her own voice. In doing so he ignited a joy that transformed her. Not that Corra would ever be completely free of sorrow, but she learned from More now how to soar, how to "stretch the wings of my spirit, and take flight." She found it difficult indeed to shed her moralistic outrage and chatty interest in the personalities of authors and subjects—and she never completely succeeded; but she tried, for she knew that she had much to learn about the artistry of the books she reviewed. She needed to learn the "vocabulary" of successful reviewing; she needed to pay more attention to style; she needed to learn what she did right as well as what she did wrong. She knew that sometimes she could write with "phenomenal stupidity"—no one else could make her admit that—and she knew she lacked self-control. But she had great faith in her mentor, who, she understood, appraised each book a "measuring line" from every point of the literary compass; and "if any part is put off plumb—goodbye praise." It was an achievement she beheld in awe: "the author not only sees himself crucified but he sees how you do it." The skill and the effect impressed her. If Holt was her "disciplinarian," she wrote, More was her "inspiration."[17]

 She awaited every piece of mail from him as a possible "chastisement" and then eagerly embraced his comments from which she was determined to learn through her own "masculine persistence." She loved writing to him: she found it hard to put her pen down once she had taken it up to be with him; her long letters to him were "essential to my peace of mind," she confessed, "they leave me unburdened." He gladdened her heart when he told her she was improving;[18] and he obviously found in her letters to him something more than friendly chit chat between editor and writer, for by the spring of 1902 they were conspiring to write an epistolary novel together. *The Jessica Letters* appeared in 1904 and allowed Corra to tell a story based on her relationship with More. The subtitle was *An Editor's Romance*, but it allowed Corra to play with themes she would develop later: religion, love, loss, and renewal. The young woman Corra imagined herself to be (Jessica) became a "certain, poor little Eve [who] escaped from her garden in the South . . . and brazened her way into the office of a certain literary editor in New York." She had left her preacher-father (a blending of all the preachers Corra had ever known), whom she called the "good shepherd, but," she described herself as "a small black sheep determined not to be made white according to his plan."[19] She was euphoric; and then—suddenly and without warning, once again she was banished from Eden! Before the book's publication, Corra learned that More was leaving the *Independent*. She was almost terrified. "My heart is aching," she blurted out. "Anybody can get along without me, but I need everybody that I have ever touched hands with and learned to love. These are the only riches I have ever cared for, and they seem to elude me. . . . This is a sorry letter, if you don't know it. And I need comforting." She had to relate to a new editor from whom she could not receive the cherished mentoring and intellectual relationship she prized with More. It was for the best, perhaps, but she lost something intensely and intimately satisfying when she lost More. It was an emotional loss possibly even more cruel than the expulsion from Oxford. When More told her later that "the bowels of human feeling had died" within him, she wondered coldly and unfairly if he had ever had any. She saw him later that year in New York, and wrote a note: "[May you] recall one Jessica, then Mrs. Harris, then wonder whatever became of the latter."[20] The affair was over.

Corra Harris's education was not yet complete, of course, but she was becoming a well-known reviewer, essayist, and short-story writer, a special feature of the *Independent*. Her chatty style, frequently outrageous comments,[21] and capacity for writing pithy little stories about southern country folk caught the attention of George Lorimar of the *Saturday Evening Post*. In 1908 she began to write a series of tales that would make her famous among those people for whom the *Post* was published. No longer Jessica, she slipped into a persona and found a medium that fit her much better. In 1910 the serial was published as *A Circuit Rider's Wife*, and Harris became much better known among people who, like herself, were struggling to find a meaningful and gratifying place in a society that was moving away from country life and small-town values and gratefully sloughing off the rigid sectarianism of traditional folk Protestantism. Such gratitude was tinged, however, with a nostalgic appreciation for the self-sacrifice of saints who may have been easier to honor in memory than to live with in practice. The stories Harris spun from her experiences and her husband's mercifully brief career as a Methodist "circuit-rider" in the north Georgia

hills helped white Protestants remember fondly the range of pieties—religious
and otherwise—that shaped the everyday dramas of their youth.[22] Yankees as
well as southerners responded warmly to the gentle, "sacred and devotional
humor" that permeated stories about the lives of a country Methodist preacher
and his wife.[23] In a publishing market that thrived on "uplift books, therapeutics,
optimism . . . and new thought,"[24] there was apparently also room for what readers thought was the sacred memory of more rigorous times graced by a simple
and authentic faith. Harris's ability to write wittily about the commonplace dramas of country folk brought approval from people who could remember such
stories in their own lives and honor such faith-driven men as the Circuit Rider.[25]
She even encouraged some of them to think that their own lives were worthy
of such loving and imaginative telling.[26] She never forgot the warm personal
responses she received from readers of A Circuit Rider's Wife. They made the
Wife her hallmark; it became her identity. Although she wrote nineteen books,
the Wife was the one that sustained her sense of who she was. For the rest of
her life she would think of herself as "a Circuit Riders Wife," although it was
never clear which "circuit rider" she meant: Lundy or William Thompson, the
minister in the story. She had a small following, but large enough to encourage
the publication of one autobiography in 1924, another in 1925, and personal reflections on life, religion, and immortality in 1927.[27] Wife is the most important
of her works for students of the American South not because of the excellence
of Harris's writing nor the quality of her stories, but because it helps us understand the nature of religious faith in the lives of unexceptional southern people
when their "leaders" were attempting to make them New Southerners.

As a series of homely episodes, A Circuit Rider's Wife reveals life in the Georgia countryside as expressed in religion with all its perplexity, delusion, ba-
nality, beauty, and humanity. In commonplace vignettes Harris describes in a
leisurely cadence the lives of country folk whose vision was always simple and
unsophisticated but frequently "eternal." In the sacred ambience of a lost past
and in people's wrestles with everyday tragedy, absurdity, and blandness described in the author's chatty banter and commentary, we see religion not only
as remembered in the historical past's past, but also as "lived" as she thought—
in a few cases at least—it should still be lived. In the stories are believers who
suffocate the spirit and fallen women who demonstrate its healing power; there
is birth and death, strength and weakness, sentiment and hardness of heart.
There is an embarrassing revivalist with huckstering instincts, and there are
revivals—certainly important for understanding southerners; there are repentant and saintly backsliders and flawed, vexatious saints. Despite the fact that
Harris can be thought of as defending traditional religion, she could be vicious

in revealing certain aspects of it, and if she at last is disillusioned by the urbanity of modernist religion, she is disgusted with the traditional churches' obsession with doctrine and their failure to sustain Christian sympathy and respect. One woman from Billings, Montana, got it right when she observed in admiration that Corra Harris was not "just a church Christian."[28]

Harris's suspicion of churches included "saints," too. She thought dramatic and intensely driven "saints" were what was wrong with the church—both the saints who sought perfection too ardently, and those who professed it too hypocritically. She exposed the contradictions, triviality, and self-delusion of saintliness, although she was incapable of probing the paradoxes of her own life and thought. She concealed even in her most candid moments the many ways in which her husband was not—even though he wanted to have been—the strong and martyr-like William Thompson of her first book. She polished the manuscript at Lundy's bedside after he had attempted suicide by slashing his throat with a pair of scissors. The conjunction of his act with the final touches to his fictionalized ministry was but one of the many twists in the lives of the Harrises, but it was nonetheless sadly appropriate. The self-destructiveness of the Reverend Mr. Harris's fictional alter ego, while not so dramatic as that inflicted by the real-life man, is nonetheless easily inferred from his wife's characterization. And in many ways it was just as devastating. But since it was conducted in the name of God, clad in the garments of self-sacrifice, and pursued through prayer instead of whiskey and sexual adventure, it was praiseworthy. Thompson's self-denying and rigorous quest for perfection that seemed to damage him seemed also to symbolize an admirable discipleship and spiritual rigor during a time when many men in urban America were thought to be afflicted not by the Holy Spirit but by civilization. A neurasthenic depletion of energy among the male population of the United States seemed to spread like an invisible epidemic wherever men surrendered to the enervating life of bureaucracy and bourgeois pursuits.[29] The Circuit Rider's hard and demanding quest for perfection that ended in a quiet martyrdom stood in judgment of the flaccid and nervous wrecks of civilization. Yet, however much her readers seemed to admire such rectitude, and however much she sentimentalized it, it still seemed to Corra Harris to be tragic because it promised salvation but produced destruction.

The Circuit Rider stories had little but the two main characters to hold them together. There was little plot and little complexity. But sometimes Harris could capture a moment of eternity, as when a young country woman laid her baby on the pew in the middle of Sunday worship and whirled in ecstatic expression, squealing in sharp animal sounds her almost inexpressible sense of the Divine—or her reach for it—"as if she had been sent from God." For the moment she wrenched the congregation from the preacher who willingly conceded her ephemeral yet undeniable authority. For the moment, something he had said—something she was thinking of when he had said it—lifted her beyond herself to dance her salvation in a brazen piety. In such an episode could Corra Harris capture the power of God to speak through a woman who had nothing to commend her save her openness to the Divine. In such a moment may students of religion and the South surely capture the humanity of their subjects. But religion was not only a moment's public expressiveness, it was also the context within which one gave birth, lost faith, and died. If the young mother sang hymns to her worldly husband all the way home after epiphany, she could later fall into disbelief and terror when dying in her now believing husband's embrace. Then at last with the preacher's hushed but forceful assurances, she could "repent" once again and pass "like a sudden gleam into the darkness of the coming night."[30] The scenes and the phrasing were characteristic of Corra Harris, who was as much a critic of religion as a believer and as much commentator as storyteller. The young woman's death in Harris's story came within the context of her commentary on the soft side of her husband's religion that understood all the dying to have departed "in the faith." Such universalist largesse offended Corra's moral sense in the Circuit Rider stories, but later she relinquished a belief in damnation and condemned a religion that was less forgiving than the God it preached. She damned religion that sustained her fictional as well as her actual husband's insistent quest for a steady and subjectively confirmed assurance of "salvation" that broke through his doubt, but ended in failure. She was angered by her husband's self-condemning piety that forced him to the edge of the abyss with such terrifying regularity: denying hell for others, embracing it for himself, and thus so unjustly inflicting it on her.

Then Lundy liberated Corra by killing himself in September 1910. He had tried to do it twenty-nine months earlier as the only way, he wrote, to end his struggle with alcoholism. Then he had told Corra that she had been "the noblest of all wives—the most faithful, the most loving—the most forebearing."[31] Now he told her, "I shall love you [and Faith, their daughter,] both eternally—if love is hereafter permitted."[32] Corra was shocked, stunned, and enraged. She had long lived with the possibility of his suicide in an agony intensified by his melancholia, spiritual torment, and alcoholism. In the aftershock of his death for the next several months every day at dusk she would relive the years of "agony and suspense" and think about him in terms of scandal, shame, and defeat. Her awful torment made her contemplate haven in an asylum or of going "the way that Lundy went,"[33] for his suicide was not merely his failure, she believed, but her own. She had been his Providence—or at least she had tried to be—but "in the end," Faith told her, "he did what he had been pre-ordained" to do. You tried, she told her mother, to "control and direct his life but it was impossible to save him."[34] It is *not*, Faith was saying, *your* fault; but Corra had for almost twenty-four years succored a man who continually flirted with disaster. She had borne his depression and his drinking, his fall from grace, his professional failure, his strange religious obsessions, and his adultery with grace, grit, and dignity. If at last he had seemed to be healed it was probably because she had willed it, but he had defied her; and she deeply resented the way in which he did it. She must have raged—in those dark hours when day turned into night—at Lundy's perverseness for taking his life from her after she had paid such a high price to save it. Why all the planning, pleading, cajoling, supporting, bargaining, and accepting: why all the reserved pretense at a tortured respectability? Why such struggle and commitment wasted on someone of whom it was asked only that he remain alive? Corra resisted such anger in public, where she turned her fury upon the church and imagined that Lundy had been martyred because when Christians give their lives it must somehow be in martyrdom! But in her "heart"—this was her metaphor for the self: in her "heart" she retained her anger at the pain inflicted by the act that freed her.

Nashville, where they lived after Lundy had taken a position in the Methodist bureaucracy, must have been abuzz with rumors and knowing expressions of people who knew the *real truth* about his death—poor thing. Those who knew him well would have remembered his previous attempt at suicide and his terrible drinking problem. Church bureaucrats would have known that he had just resigned as assistant to the Secretary of the General Board of Education of the Methodist Episcopal Church, South, after having defied the hierarchy by siding with Vanderbilt University trustees when they seceded from the Church.[35] Corra hinted that Lundy was a casualty of warfare over the independence of the university, but she preferred to transform him into the Circuit Rider. He had been, she insisted, a scholar whose "deepest piety" had been exemplified in a disregard for worldly wealth. When he died he had $2.16 in his pocket; $116.00 in the bank; four hundred books in his library; and a coffin worth $85.00 in the ground. His character could be inferred from the fact, Corra claimed, that he had given his entire income to charity. He had pensioned an "outcast" woman and an old soldier; he had sent two African American boys to school and supported "a family of 5," race not indicated. His wife added that he had been "persecuted" (cause and source unspecified) for three years prior to his death.[36] She must have been profoundly gratified by reading her version of his life printed in the *Philadelphia Public Ledger* on September 25, 1910. The *Ledger* devoted an entire page exclusively to Lundy's suicide, printing stories that would surely have evoked a sardonic grimace from him, for they did not capture himself so much as the man Corra imagined. The articles were dominated by Corra's handsome likeness and punctuated by engravings from her book that helped illustrate a series of pleasant little stories that became in her mind and on this page a condemnation of the ways in which the Church treated its minor clergy. True, there was also the leitmotif of theological failure attributable to the New Theology,[37] and there was a muddled report of Lundy's own theological confusion followed by the last story in *A Circuit Rider's Wife*. In it, Corra (Sister Thompson) had lamented preachers who made "orphans" of believers by depriving them of "their Heavenly Father." The whole effect of reading such reports could have made one pause in respect for the poverty-stricken and extraordinarily pious preacher who had taken his own life because his ministry could not be achieved in a cruel world where ecclesiastical machinery was hideously lubricated by politics and ambition.[38] The sentimentality may have cautioned readers; but it was clear that Corra's fictionalized husband, William Thompson, was about to be confirmed in popular culture by Lundy's very real suicide.

If Thompson could no longer preach the Gospel and if Lundy had had paralyzing doubts he could not resolve save through death, their chief interpreter had no qualms about becoming the preacher neither of them could be.[39] Harris's "preaching" was not systematic, to be sure, and she was not burdened by consistency: "I Thank God," she wrote, "[that] I can be as inconsistent as is necessary to feminine peace of mind."[40] Her inconsistency resulted from the fact that she found things to attack in both the traditions that shaped her and in the bourgeois religious modernism that frequently nauseated her. For example, she despaired of fundamentalists who were frenzied by the Darwinian hypothesis and who lacked the cleverness and "courage to welcome every discovery of science as confirmation of their faith." She was equally dismissive of ministers who spent a sermon lecturing on evolution instead of preaching Jesus Christ. She knew that expressing her contempt for dogma and the seemingly interminable conflict over the divinity of Christ was dangerous among some "malicious saints" who would make her "a liar and an atheist, for they are good at that." But she did cling to her one consistent theme that the God who loved his creation was safer to worship "than the pinch faced deity handed down to us in some heinous theology." Her ideal sermon was a "simple message of the love and will of God, recited with tenderness and awe"; it came from working with people who "knew how far and how near we all are to God." When she was struck down by illness twice in California and had to revise her plans to visit Australia via Samoa in 1925, she was inspired to reflect on what she valued most in her life in a book that became *The Happy Pilgrimage*. Whereas she had once been cavalier about deathbed repentance, she embraced it now, she confessed, because she was more clearly focused. The agony of Lundy's suicide fifteen years earlier had become a martyrdom to cherish rather than a dark experience to resent; and her daughter's tragic death at a young age was transformed by her resurrection in a painting by Ella Hergesheimer included without comment between pages 24 and 25 of *The Happy Pilgrimage*. The book became a testament to her ability to survive through her own "temper and tenacity," and paradoxically, through realizing that there was nothing more she could do to shape her destiny. "No better imitation of meekness ever existed in the humblest Christian soul," she wrote, "than I now practiced."[41] Thus was Corra Harris suspended between a staunch individualism and a commonsense trust in God.

That trust made her detest an intense and exaggerated piety and a cold and rigid dogmatism. The piety came in two forms. One was the familiar sanctimoniousness of traditional religion in which believers were more interested in dramatizing their faith than in doing good. Revivals represented the evil because they focused on momentary feelings as indicative of true religion. "What we call a revival," insists one of her characters, "is often a false stimulation of the spiritual life, it is not only injurious but blasphemous."[42] Suspicious of the religion of religion, she observed that few people actually lived as if they truly believed in God;[43] the "satisfaction of saints in their piety has always seemed to me despicable. It is a form of deceit never justified by the facts. And the gratified air they give themselves is not to be confounded with simple honest human happiness. We are entitled to that whether we miss the glory of God or not."[44] It was easy to forgive sinners, she thought, but much more difficult to forgive "saints their perverse, hard-headed virtues."[45] In the same spirit she wrote that if saints would not make moonshine whiskey, they all too often would "distill scandals at the expense of helpless people."[46] These are familiar clichés; and so was her despair at believers who lashed themselves to specific Bible verses, restricted doctrine, and literalistic, unimaginative thinking; "it is not easy to interpret a winged mood to a man who has literal-minded damnation ideas," she thought.[47] If these were clichés, however, they were such partially because they were the complaints of a generation that had brought what it thought was a new "winged mood" to the reinterpretation of Christian life.

The other piety she condemned was theoretically modeled on that of her husband. In both fiction and fictionalized autobiography she dramatized how "literally" he attempted to live "the life of Jesus Christ—and could not do it."[48] He seemed to live in a constant struggle with his inability to receive the "witness of God's spirit" that he was a child of God. The subjective confirmation

of salvation was indeed Lundy's frequent obsession, but it was affected by an
angst that imagined God's confusion at His incarnation in a brothel and Lundy's contemplation of his own sexual power as a means of grace.[49] Corra could
never have imagined these things—nor have been sympathetic to a man who
did so. In her writings Lundy seemed to be an impractical, driven ascetic who
dared not relent in a quest that could only end in suicide. It was gravely difficult
for her to live with such a man; but note that it was his religion about which
she complained—that was what she wanted to be remembered, and not his
alcoholism, depression, and adultery—she dealt with those flaws elsewhere! If
you "like human beings better than you do saints," she wrote, "it is a queer feeling to know that you are forever involved in a medieval religion of asceticism,
sacrifice and sufferings." She had written the circuit rider stories, she would say,
to honor her husband's memory as a martyr to his own faith; but she also emphasized that when he died, she became free.[50] Such attempts as his to achieve
perfection seemed as barren as the lives of those who thought they had achieved
it. Her anger had been clear: "I hate perfection. It is worse than damnable; it is
finished, dead!"[51]

She also despised dogmatism as a disease of the spirit, a restraint of imagination, and the negation of true religion. The woman from Billings had understood this when she approved Harris as "not just a church Christian."[52] Dogma
(creeds), by relying on the restricted meaning of specific words and phrases,
was dangerous; they had led to crimes against humanity, "heresy trials and the
stake."[53] In one of her novels she has an activist insist that "so long as we think
of the life of Christ in the terms of doctrines and creeds we shall never discover
what religion is."[54] Creeds were an easy substitute for living a Christian life; the
divinity of Jesus was not to be believed as doctrine but beheld as a miracle in
that people who accepted him as the truth did "become divinely good."[55] The
creed, like the law "consists in mystifying the simple public,"[56] and she called on
her readers (she assumed they were women) to reject the passivity of assenting
to creeds written by someone else and parent, instead, their own scriptures and
creeds through their own sacred creativity. All her heroines seemed to do this—
to create themselves anew in private spiritual pilgrimages. In this, she identified
creeds and literal interpretations of the Bible as the same deadening things. "If
I had had the courage to interpret them [creeds and Bible] according to my
own good senses, provided especially by the Lord for that purpose, I should
have known the doctrine precisely as He promises."[57] "I prefer to write out my
own scriptures," she would tell audiences, and "interpret them according to my
own case" and that is how she preserved "an archaic and astounding faith in the
Word as a mirror of the Mind of the Almighty."[58] The scriptures were made for

us, she argued, "we are not created victims to fulfill them."[59] We were meant to find ourselves in them, not according to others' view of the text, but *our own*, without apology and with the "courage of an honest mind. Such people are safe citizens in this world and the next one. But they are not safe under doctrines, creeds, and laws arbitrarily imposed, whether they get them from the Bible or the Bolsheviks."[60] For the record, she could concede that "everything in the Scriptures is true, if you adjust yourself to the way [in which] it is true."[61] For example, take miracles: "If I cannot swallow them literally I turn them inside out and swallow them spiritually."[62] Hers was an infuriating if witty simplicity, which shared with more self-consciously liberal interpreters an appreciation for the delicious and liberating multivalence of language. A text was sacred when a reader could find herself in it and be transformed according to her own needs— not the demands of others (men) who insisted on certain condensed meanings that cramped the soul and grounded the spirit that was yearning to fly!

Harris was adept at using the familiar metaphors of Christianity to fuse religion and life in ways that transcended a dispirited and recalcitrant folk fundamentalism. She had, she said, been born again three times: when she adjusted to heaven, when she adjusted to her husband's ministry, and when he died. This last experience was the most important: "I had to be born again to the world, capable of dealing with it sensibly and honorably." This required "more divine inspiration than being a private Christian protected by all the defenses that marriage and religion raise about a woman's life."[63] The comment was in part sarcastic because she did not believe that women were "protected" in marriage: men were incapable of fulfilling their part of the bargain. Marriage was a sacrament that men turned into sacrilege, but which women could reclaim through their own redemptive assertiveness and refusal to be victimized. She called this redemption "love." Women were to find their strength through faith in love, and "love" meant women's ability to respect themselves and remain true to an ideal of love, even when their husbands were not. In this act of will they would demonstrate their true strength and find their own happiness through exercising their responsibilities, finally to be "worthy of [their] own admiration at the very least."[64] This is what she herself had done. It is not what one believed beyond the self in creeds and specific Bible verses that constituted religious vocation, she believed, but what we have internalized of "such Scriptures as the Ten Commandments, the twenty-third psalm, and the Sermon on the Mount" and used creatively. "Every man," she wrote of women, "is entitled to his own God, which is the same God no man can escape."[65]

Like those who had written liberal religious texts before her, she could not believe in a literal hell. It was something she seemed to have absorbed during a "sunny childhood" and perhaps from her father's happy hedonism. We wrongly impute our own ideas of punishment to God, she thought—reflecting on her mother's fierce divinity; but she could never believe anything that reflected badly "upon the goodness and mercy of my Lord."[66] Perhaps the punishment she observed and imagined in women's lives, and the incredible and surprising strength she felt welling up within her during the personal tragedies of her own life were subjective confirmation of the fitness of rejecting hell. Such optimism in the midst of sorrow led her to profess belief in an immortality that reflected little of a traditional heaven and much of her own romantic musing about a God whose "faith in us" could not be shaken. Her "Happy Pilgrimage," she firmly believed, would continue after she had returned to dust. This was not an argument or theory so much as a vision that emerged both from her incredible grit and the almost supernatural kindness of people whom she had never before met. In 1934, as she lay helpless from a failing heart, fluttering on the edge of life, she affirmed her happiness among strangers whose kindness and care encouraged her to believe that even after death she would somehow continue to grow into "life more abundant."[67]

In this rejection of hell, distrust of creeds, embrace of cosmic evolution, and the existential interpretation of biblical texts, Harris betrayed the imprint of individualistic liberalism upon her faith. She exalted her right to interpret sacred texts—even to write sacred texts—even to make of her own life a sacred text. If what she said made sense to people, that fact was authentication enough, and for about thirty-five years she did in fact make sense to many people.[68] She was not thought of as a "liberal" in religion, however, despite her own confessions to "heresy," because she presented herself as defending traditional religion.[69] She could express herself in the mood of conventional religiosity even when she denied conventionality. She could recall—and it is just such recollections that probably elicited such positive responses from readers—going down to the altar during revival and returning with an "air of augmented excellence."[70] This result was probably not the intention of furious revivalists, but she could appreciate the importance of harvest revivals, when "religion became a sublime intoxication, to which the wildest excesses of a bacchanalian feast cannot be compared." They were an "ineffable reincarnation of souls, this spiritual upheaval of the highest from the lowest in a rural humanity."[71] And yet she could, as we have seen, think of revivals as "blasphemous" if made the primary goal of religion. If she was critical of the bigotry of small-town saints, she could still throw away a line defending the "tough fibre of righteousness and bigotry" without which there would be no civilization.[72] The toughness and determination of righteousness (bigotry) meant concrete achievement, but religious intensity that prevented the enjoyment of achievement (happiness) was self-defeating. She could betray, but she could not reflect upon the paradoxes in which she delighted.

Despite the fact that she accepted higher biblical criticism and evolution, and despite her disregard for creeds so typical of liberal Christianity, Harris did write a book celebrating that "old time religion." Her indictment of Protestant modernism was that it lacked mystery, sin, guilt, and redemption. The gist of its message, as she understood it, was that "we" believers "should all get together, practice sanity, health, decency and honor and enjoy our virtues"—goals she herself sometimes seemed to prize. Its ministers, she thought, "absolved [their] people from both their sins and the Holy Spirit," and encouraged them improperly to prosper along lines similar to the marketplace; theirs was a "light and easy ministry" all activity and no "hallelujah."[73] The evangelical command, to "be born again," yielded in sermons to scholarly quotations, "salvation by prosperity," and the "science of human duty."[74] There was nothing holy in any of these. Only during the Great War did she sense a religious intensity in modernist eloquence, but since it blended Christianity with American history to make hatred "an international term of inspiration,"[75] she despised it. The minister in her antimodernist novel, *My Son*, reaches a crisis when his reforming religion is revealed as nihilistic radicalism; his crisis is intensified by conflict within his church and reaches meltdown when he confronts the shenanigans of a mischievous feminine spiritualist.[76] The hero's mother hands him his dead father's sermons, and, chastened, enlightened, and renewed, he preaches Jesus as the "way, the truth, and the life," and brings the church together in sacred harmony. He thus repudiates a modernism whose hustling champions did not take seriously the religious needs of people living the tragedies of everyday life in fear, pain, and betrayal. Elsewhere she would write that ministers who believed in evolution should preach Christ, those who believed in higher criticism should preach Christ, and those who gave their lives to reform should preach Christ. As she thought about how this could be done, she concluded that the preacher would be both scientist and saint combining in his person an authority to satisfy both tradition and modernity so that when he preached the symbolic Christ, believers could recognize him as the way just as they "recognize any other law [sign] posted for our safety."[77] She was reaching for a way to "preach Christ" through interpretive strategies similar to those of religious liberalism. "We move through this world according to symbols, illusions, ideals," she wrote, "every one of them designed to indicate something invisible in reality upon which no man can put his finger and say, 'That is it.'" Christianity was her symbolic means. "Let me kneel at an altar," she wrote, "which I submit is a symbolic idea, and pray, not because the Lord would fail to do his duty by me if I did not pray, but because prayer is an instinct of religious faith."[78]

The final scene of *My Son* was not only about religion, but also the confidence, strength, and authority of women. Lundy Harris's suicide, which freed Corra to become the "preacher" he could never have been, also freed her to tell stories of clever women who resurrected themselves from the ashes of male betrayal and failure. Moving beyond the Harrises' brief lives on circuit, which she fictionalized into forty years of dedicated service, she would now write about men and women out of her experiences with a weak, addicted, and adulterous husband. The repentant modernist in *My Son* is brought to his knees by two women: his mother and a "pretty little saint" whom the minister promises to make happy. "Well, he won't" says his mother to the prospective bride. "Because no man ever did or can make a woman happy. They only make us patient and long-suffering, and, maybe, good" through that same suffering.[79] If evangelical preaching could evoke spiritual renewal it was not the moving force, and neither was divine grace. Harris was more pragmatic; salvation came from women. "Men are children," she writes at the end of the novel. "You can never let up on them."[80] And she never did. Children though they might have been in terms of emotional maturity, men nevertheless ruled, and she described that fact in terms that later feminists would have understood as patriarchal. Men, she pointed out, had "made the world what it is, written all the scriptures, defined all the virtues for their own convenience, even set the Lord himself up to be feared and served more particularly by women [than men] with their heads covered." She could even clinch the point with what should have been feminist hyperbole: "We are the trained automatons of an order of things we did not invent!"[81] But she—like many feminists—did believe that women were nonetheless changing things for the better by their own efforts. "We are migrating out of the imaginary into the real," one of her suffragist heroines says. "We are passing from sentiment and romance into history. And we have arrived! Nothing can stop us. You can only shame yourselves," she says to male opponents, "your manhood, and your honor if you oppose us. We must succeed because we are right!"[82] Her solution to male domination, however, was not to raise the banner of gender revolution, because such an act would ignite social chaos—perhaps the fearful cosmic projection of her own experience of domestic pandemonium. Rather, she imagined women fighting within their own households for self-respect, authority, and command with the weapons of unassailable moral responsibility, cleverness, inventiveness, courage, iron will—and deception where needed.

The field of battle for women was within the bonds of matrimony or between those destined to be wed—she was after all writing for middle-aged married women. Male protagonists had the advantages of history, power, tradition, habit, law, and public opinion. They also had women's empathetic concern for the male ego. Harris could remember having blurted out during a walk with Lundy that women "were the victims of the whole social and domestic order of mankind," and he was so startled and defensive that she decided the solution was not a frontal assault but subversion and manipulation. Through knowledge of men's weaknesses, the cleverness to exploit them, and a kind of domestic will to power, women could command an appropriate deference from husbands that would secure sporadic marital faithfulness between domestic crises, which she believed to be the most important of all battles in gendered conflict. The beginning of wisdom was women's learning "how weak and unworthy men have always been of the confidence we have reposed in them."[83] This lesson should teach women to break the patterns of obedience inherited from the past and sustained by the illusions spun by men's self-serving protestations of eternal love. Love itself, she wrote, is the one "everlasting illusion" in every woman's life[84] that "plays havoc with hopes and happiness."[85] To be sure, the naïve, sometimes reckless love of men and women in small-town romantic situations drives Harris's plots, but so does masculine weakness, deceit, perfidy, and (frequently) adultery. Once alluring "maidens" become in her stories middle-aged "ribs" of their work-driven husbands, who are seduced by "flashy" "adventuresses," one of whom is a dark beauty who contemptuously flaunts her erotic power over the husband of a wife unable to bear children. The scene is so powerful that one wonders if Harris were thinking of the African American women whom Lundy had bedded in Oxford. But even in this shaming exchange, divorce was not an option; divorce was never an option for Harris, even though she did allow one desperate, and momentarily crazed heroine to rid herself of a brutal husband by justifiable homicide.[86] Vows made under the illusion of love are nonetheless binding, a moral commitment so fierce in its intensity that errant husbands are (usually) humbled, (briefly) chastened, or (sometimes) broken by it—and brought home. The woman who understood the ways in which men held power through language, scripture, law, and custom, and who derided masculine arrogance and encouraged women to self-respect and self-reliance could not embrace feminism. Instead, she fell back on the moral power she had wielded over her own husband as a model for all women; her preaching came from the scripture of her own life.

The enemy of women with whom Corra Harris identified had many faces, but they were all feminine. She was sometimes an "adventuress" who flaunted her sexuality, or a divorcee who entranced other women's husbands, or the troubled little saint who confessed her deepest desires and longings to a sympathetic

minister until she entrapped him in emotional quicksand. She was a spiritualist, a socialist, a feminist ensnared by the utopian writings of Charlotte Perkins
Gilman, who imagined an impossible world that seemed to spurn love between
men and women and pour contempt on the things that ordinary women held
dear. If Gilman encouraged women to broaden their loyalties beyond the family
according to the dictates of reason and their universal citizenship in humanity, Harris asked them to trust their emotional ties to a loving family life as the
nursery of that very citizenship.[87] That Harris believed love an illusion did not
lead her to renounce it, for illusions were as necessary to human life as a soar-
ing imagination. Their power to guide human action was obvious, and love
between a man and woman—illusion though it may have been—was nonetheless sacramental in that it conveyed through human sentiment the fact and
meaning of God's love. "Love," she once wrote in passing, "is the one perfect
illusion which clothes life and protects it."[88] She believed that betraying love was,
within her blending of religion, obligation, and gender, the unforgivable sin.[89]
The marital relation, which she so ruthlessly dissected for signs of masculine
selfishness, hypocrisy, weakness, and perfidy, was the basis of human civilization, so that if married women, through skilled negotiation with their husbands, were to become the family's emotional center of gravity, wives would
have to be alert to all rivals—including her husband's memory of her as a young
woman. The combat between good and evil with which she and possibly all
Christians were chastened as children was not between the demonic and the
divine, but between wives and the other woman, even if the latter were merely
dangerous illusions in the daydreaming minds of their husbands.

By the 1920s, when Harris wrote her three autobiographical books, she was
winding down. Her serials in the *Saturday Evening Post* and other magazines
had attracted a substantial following,[90] and her essays in the *Independent* had
once made her a reviewer to be reckoned with. Editors had known they could
receive outrageous, sweeping, and often witty and folksy essays about anything from current fiction and European suffragists to New York City and the
South. Explaining why editor Edward Carmack was killed by a political rival in
1908, she began by saying that Tennesseans were ready to "kill a man with less
provocation than any other Southerner" and concluded by insisting that "all
the psychic forces of the state tended toward fury, disorder, and destruction."[91]
She contrasted Babylonian New York City with her idyllic agrarian retreat in
Georgia, warning that "Cleverness is one of the commonest crimes" in the me-
tropolis that had helped her perfect her own cunning. She could then confess
that the longer she remained in the city that taught her what little sophistication
she possessed, "the more charms I discover in it."[92] She went to Europe twice

on assignment, in 1911 and 1914, and she maintained a healthy enough professional life to live comfortably on a two-hundred-acre farm in north Georgia near where Lundy had taken his life. The comfort was financial. Her personal life continued the patterns that had long ago made her believe that love and sorrow were aspects of the same emotion. Her daughter, Faith, married shortly after Lundy's suicide, and the new widow feared that her son-in-law's prospects were not good; he certainly was not the aggressive and romantic hustler that Harris imagined in a few of her heroes. For nine years Harris's relationship with daughter and son-in-law resembled an erratic roller coaster ride, until just as Faith seemed to be coming into her own as a writer, she died. Harris lost her only companion and confidant. Her farm, the Valley, remained, she wrote, the "only dear and living interest I have."[93] For a few years she sustained her creativity. Her first autobiography, *My Book and Heart*, was well received, but after that triumph, editors began to return her manuscripts as not appropriate for their readers. She published a second series of autobiographical essays, *As a Woman Thinks*, which was less popular than *My Book and Heart*, and her *Happy Pilgrimage* was a huge disappointment. A Boston newspaper dismissed *Happy Pilgrimage* as a "series of lay sermons," and indeed it was, but anyone interested in what women of a certain age thought and valued in the 1920s would find it a revelation as to just how heretical and spiritually independent a woman thought to be a traditional Christian could be as she contemplated her life and death. She wondered how she might have fared under the piety of earlier days, shuddering perhaps as she confessed being "temperamentally opposed . . . to being burned at the stake for my religious convictions."[94]

As for that stake associated with the racial inquisition of white mobs, Harris never repeated the tantrums of 1899. She believed the self-serving myths of Reconstruction sung by the balladeers of redemption, white supremacy, and disfranchisement but she could not ride with Thomas Dixon's Klansmen. Neither could she stand with W. E. B. DuBois's John Jones as he awaited the lynch mob after avenging his sister's rape. Yet DuBois may have arrested her for a moment. She sensed the power inherent in his meditation on a people so intimately associated with sacrifice, but she could not wonder why the struggles of a people woven into the "very warp and woof of this nation" should not have been as significant as those of white folk. She was unimpressed by Dixon's celebration of the "American mob spirit" and the "blood curdling imagination" that "lacked aesthetic veracity," but she didn't know exactly what to make of *The Souls of Black Folk*. Having read DuBois's masterpiece, she did think that Booker T. Washington was wrong to say that African Americans' opportunity lay in the "industrial world," for it lay rather in the "realm of art." There, when one is transfixed by a painting or sculpture, the color of the artist, she believed, was irrelevant. She never followed up on this insight. At the end of her life in a reflective mood, however, she wrote that it no longer seemed important that she was the descendant of "very white men"—and then she crossed out "very." She thought her "Nordic conceit" was fading, but the stereotypes lingered still. She had changed, to be sure; Senegalese soldiers she saw in 1914 were almost magnificent to her startled gaze. She had thought of them when writing about a black preacher she respected, and she could comment on the "regrettable renaissance of lynchings" in the 1920s and '30s. She could also praise Julian Peterkin's writing about African Americans but still think of them as primitives who were more children of nature than of civilization. African Americans were deeply religious, to be sure—she had always believed that—and were true disciples of "Jesus, who was also [like black people] a man of sorrows and acquainted with grief." Who it was that had surrounded them with grief she could not say and never carried on the conversations necessary from which to learn. She could hope that whites would not try to remake African Americans in their own image—whites are not God, she pointed out—but she could never engage African Americans and their culture with the empathy in which she prided herself when it came to poor whites.[95] She was of course not unique in this.

In 1932 Harris received the first George Fort Milton Prize, given by the University of Tennessee in honor of the Chattanooga publisher to "the Southern Woman writer accomplishing most for her sex."[96] She was still trying to accomplish even more, but she was failing. Her heart was enlarged; she frequently gasped for breath; she walked with a cane. She was becoming even more difficult for the young women who cared for her to live with. Harris had always been difficult: she was hypersensitive to any perceived slight; she could sometimes transform compliments into insults and drive the person she loved most—Faith—to tears. She had resigned from the Authors' League after Jack London (whom she thought of as a ruffian genius) saw her name tag at a dinner and loudly professed his love for her. He then told her—in response to her well-known capacity for "preaching" in her reviews, that he did not believe in God. Harris replied that God could undoubtedly survive his disbelief, but London kept writing her notes until Harris fled the banquet hall completely unnerved.[97] She did better with friendly exchanges, for example, with students at Rollins College where she taught a course on evil. Naming her Professor of Evil was a public relations stunt by Hamilton Holt, her longtime friend from the *Independent*, who had just been named president of the new college. Class notes from papers in the college library suggest no proof texts, no depth, and much chatter at the level of high tea: "Evil is the medieval part of us."[98] The class gave her an excellent opportunity to practice her homiletic skills, but she soon gave up that pulpit for one closer to home. Her last homilies were printed in the "Candlelight Column" of the *Atlanta Journal Magazine* even after she died in February of 1935. They were not terribly profound, but they did celebrate the same ordinary people with whom she had populated *A Circuit Rider's Wife*. In her essays, she recalled the courage of a woman during a hurricane, the humor of people who had "lost everything," the energetic good works of a woman working with the poor, and (in one printed after she died), regarding those who had "striven against the powers and principalities of their own darkness. They fill me with reverence and a peculiar admiration," she had written, "which better balanced men and women who have made the grade with less effort never do."[99] Their creed did not matter. As she had written a few years earlier, "every man is entitled to his own God, which is the same God no man can escape."[100] Gendered conventions restricted her expression. She was writing, as usual, about herself— but on behalf of women.

## NOTES

1. The reissue is Corra Harris, *The Circuit Rider's Wife* (Wilmore, Ky.: Bristol Books, 1988). John E. Talmadge, *Corra Harris: Woman of Purpose* (Athens: University of Georgia Press, 1968): 1–2, 9. Charles Dobbins, "Life of Corra Harris," *Atlanta Journal Magazine*, October 18, 1931; Karen Coffing, "Corra Harris and the Saturday Evening Post: Southern Domesticity Conveyed to a National Audience, 1900–1930," *Georgia Historical Quarterly* 79 (Summer 1995): 367–93. Corra Harris to John Paschall, January 29, 1935. Box 54.7, Corra Mae White Harris Papers, University of Georgia (hereafter cited as Harris papers, UGA).

2. Corra Harris to John Paschall, January 29, 1935, Box 54.7, Harris papers, UGA. She thought it was November 1895 when she wrote her first article: "I was a funny tacky little wife of a Methodist preacher with the gleaming blade of a thin bright wit in my mind, which did not belong to the Methodist itinerancy and an adventurous spirit which did not belong there either. So, having come to Atlanta that day and hearing the Georgia legislature was in session, I went to see the mighty turbines of law at work and wrote my impressions."

3. T. G. Steward, "The Reign of the Mob," *Independent*, May 11, 1899, 1296–97; W. P. Lovejoy, "Georgia's Record of Blood," *Independent*, May 11, 1899, 1297–300.

4. Mrs. L. H. Harris, "A Southern Woman's View," *Independent*, May 18, 1899, 1354–55.

5. Mrs. L. H. Harris, "Negro Womanhood," *Independent*, June 22, 1899, 1687–89.

6. There is a long history of Methodist preachers using biography as theology. See Robert E. Cushman, *John Wesley's Experimental Divinity* (Nashville: Kingswood Books, 1989).

7. Longstreet was a humorist and lawyer who became president of Emory after his surprising conversion and ordination to the Methodist ministry; Lamar was a famous Mississippi politician who became a reconciler between northerners and southerners in the U.S. Senate, 1877–85. Bishop Haygood attempted to elicit sympathy from whites to blacks. See John Donald Wade, *Augustus Baldwin Longstreet: A Study of the Development of Culture in the South* (New York: Macmillan, 1924); Harold W. Mann, *Atticus Greene Haygood: Methodist Bishop, Editor, and Educator* (Athens: University of Georgia Press, 1965); James B. Murphy, *L. Q. C. Lamar: Pragmatic Patriot* (Baton Rouge: University of Louisiana Press, 1973).

8. Corra Harris to George Lorimar, March 27, 1923, microfilm copy of letters in the George Lorimar papers in the Historical Society of Pennsylvania, prepared for John E. Talmadge in the University of Georgia Library (hereafter cited as Lorimar papers, HSP/UGA).

9. Corra Harris to Mrs. [Nettie Curtright] Candler, May 17, 1898; Harris to Bishop Warren Akin Candler, June 17, 1898; Harris to Candler, July 15, 1898, Warren Akin Candler Papers, Emory University (hereafter cited as W. A. Candler papers EU).

10. Corra Harris to Warren Akin Candler, June 22, July 1, July [15], 1898, W. A. Candler papers EU.

11. Corra Harris to Nettie Candler.

12. R. F. Burden to Warren Akin Candler, April 21, 1882; Corrie Harris to Warren Akin Candler, Thursday [1898], undated letters Box 3, W. A. Candler papers EU; Terry Lee Matthews, "The Emergence of a Prophet: Andrew Sledd and the 'Sledd Affair of 1902'" (PhD diss., Duke University, 1989), 87–89, 90, 91, 94; Wesleyan Christian Advocate, June 15, 1898, front page; Emory Phoenix, June 1898, 371.

13. Corrie Harris to Warren Akin Candler, June 24, July 1, July 5, July [15], July 22, July 27, 1898, June 29, 1899, October 26, 1899; Corra Harris to Bishop and Mrs. [Nettie] Candler, July 15, 1898; Henry Harris to Candler, June 26, 1898, W. P. Lovejoy to Candler, July 27, 1898; Corrie to Mrs. Candler, February 1899, October 29, 1899; Lundy Harris to Candler, October 31, 1899, W. A. Candler papers EU.

14. Corrie Harris to Warren Akin Candler, June 27, 1899, W. A. Candler papers EU.

15. Corrie Harris to Warren Akin Candler, October 26, 1899. She had had to live apart from Lundy to take a teaching position. Her toddler son, Lundy Jr., was also very ill and would soon die.

16. Corra Harris to William Hayes Ward, March 17, 1900, Corra Harris Papers [9638], University of Virginia.

17. Corra Harris to Paul Elmer More, May 30, June 3, June 7, June 24, July 2, July 23, 1901, microfilm of Paul Elmer More Papers in Princeton University Library, at the University of Georgia (hereafter cited as PEM papers PU/UGA).

18. Corra Harris to More, May 16, May 30, June 7, July 2, 1901, March 3, 1902, PEM papers PU/UGA.

19. Paul Elmer More and Mrs. L. H. Harris, The Jessica Letters: An Editor's Romance (New York: G. P. Putnam's Sons, 1904), 312, 328.

20. Corra Harris to Paul Elmer More, October 29, 1903, January 14, December 7, 1905, PEM papers PU/UGA.

21. In reviewing a translation of Fyodor Dostoyevsky's The Brothers Karamazov, an anonymous writer mentioned Harris's style as an example of "disturbing frankness. Mrs. Corra Harris, a purely domestic product has learned to use a shocking freedom in telling things which in Mrs. Harris's set (and ours) used not to be mentioned even in a whisper" (New York Times Book Review Supplement, June 30, 1912).

22. See, for example, Frederick W. McCullody to Corra Harris, February 26, 1910, and Fabius Clarke to Harris, March 14, 1910, Box 20:18; and G. A. Johnston Ross to Harris, August 10, 1910, Box 21:1, in Harris papers UGA.

23. Joel B. Fort to Corra Harris, February 28, 1910, Box 20:17, Harris papers UGA.

24. Edwin E. Slosson to Corra Harris, October 9, 1909, Box 20:13, Harris papers UGA.

25. See for example, Eugene Lawrence to Corra Harris, March 1, 1910, Box 20:18; Margaret Campbell Dunsmore to Harris, March 2, 1910, Box 20:18; J. S. Wightman to Harris, March 3, 1910, Box

20:18; John Hobart Egbert to Harris, March 15, 1910, Box 20:18; Charles O. Wright to Harris, September 20, 1910, Box 21:1; J. H. McNeil to Harris, April 5, 1910, Box 21:1, Harris papers UGA.

26. See for example, E. W. Gardner to Corra Harris, March 30, 1910, Box 20:18, Harris papers UGA.

27. Corra Harris, *My Book and Heart* (Boston: Houghton Mifflin, 1924); Harris, *As a Woman Thinks* (Boston: Houghton Mifflin, 1925); Harris, *The Happy Pilgrimage* (Boston: Houghton Mifflin, 1927).

28. Sarah M. Patterson to Corra Harris, February 5, 1912, Box 22:1, Harris papers UGA.

29. George Miller Beard, *American Nervousness, Its Causes and Consequences: A Supplement* (1881; repr., New York: Arno Press edition, 1972).

30. Corra Harris, *A Circuit Rider's Wife* (1910; repr., New York: Houghton Mifflin Co, 1933), 36–40, 75.

31. See suicide note from Lundy Howard Harris on stationery of the Board of Education of the Methodist Episcopal Church, South, and several bills for the Nashville Sanitorium, where he convalesced thereafter in Harris papers, Box 1.5 UGA; also Talmadge, *Corra Harris*, 38.

32. Lundy Howard Harris to Corra Harris, Saturday, September 17, 1910, Harris papers Box 1.14 UGA.

33. Susan Leech to Harry Leech, February 28, 1911, Harris papers Box 2.03, UGA.

34. Faith Harris to Corra Harris, February 7, 1911, Harris papers Box 2.2, UGA.

35. Paul K. Conkin, *Gone with the Ivy: A Biography of Vanderbilt University* (Knoxville: University of Tennessee Press, 1985), xxx. Talmadge, *Corra Harris*, 51–58; *Nashville Christian Advocate*, May 27, 1910, 12–13, June 3, 1910, 5, July 22, 1910, 9; Lundy Howard Harris to Corra Harris, Wednesday [September 9, 1910 according to archives staff notes, but actually Wednesday and Thursday, September 7 and 8, 1910], Harris papers, Box 1.14, UGA.

36. Newspaper clippings Box 110:19, Harris papers, UGA.

37. See William R. Hutchison, *The Modernist Impulse in American Protestantism* (Cambridge, Mass.: Harvard University Press, 1976).

38. *Philadelphia Public Ledger*, September 25, 1910, full page in the feature section. Box 110.19, Harris papers, UGA. See also Harris, *Circuit Rider's Wife* (1910), 335.

39. In *My Book and Heart*, 77, Harris wrote: "I have often wanted to flare up and preach, but I never have felt the call. My skirts seem to be in the way."

40. Harris, *Circuit Rider's Wife* (1910), 329.

41. Harris, *Happy Pilgrimage*, 48, 56, 80,109, 228–31, 295, 297.

42. Harris, *Circuit Rider's Wife* (1910), 190–91.

43. Harris, *My Book and Heart*, 213.

44. Harris, *As a Woman Thinks*, 206.

45. Harris, *A Circuit Rider's Widow* (Garden City, N.Y.: Doubleday, Page and Co., 1916), 74.

46. Ibid., 136.

47. Ibid., 135.

48. Harris, *As a Woman Thinks*, 81.

49. Lundy Harris, incidental notebook in Box 99.2 and 3, Harris papers UGA.

50. Harris, *As a Woman Thinks*, 81.

51. Harris, *Happy Pilgrimage*, 111.

52. Sarah M. Patterson to Corra Harris.

53. Harris, *As a Woman Thinks*, 194.

54. Harris, *Circuit Rider's Widow*, 190–91.

55. Ibid., 15.

56. Harris, *Justice* (New York: Heart's International Library, 1915), 53.

57. Harris, *As a Woman Thinks*, 177.

58. Typescript Harris papers Box 102:18 UGA.

59. Harris, *As a Woman Thinks*, 177.

60. Ibid., 90–93.

61. Harris, *House of Helen* (New York: George H. Doran Co., 1923), 206.

62. Harris, *Circuit Rider's Widow*, 15.

63. Harris, *As a Woman Thinks*, 77.

64. Ibid., 244; Harris, *In Search of a Husband* (Garden City, N.Y.: Doubleday, Page and Co., 1913), 244. See also *My Book and Heart*, 105, and *Circuit Rider's Widow*, 290–97.

65. Harris, *As a Woman Thinks*, 90–95, 194.

66. Harris, *My Book and Heart* 28, 32; *Happy Pilgrimage*, 235–38.

67. Harris, *Happy Pilgrimage*, 235–38.

68. See, for example, Fabius M. Clarke to Corra Harris March 14, 1910, Harris papers Box 20:18, UGA.

69. Unidentified MS, Harris papers Box 102: 18; also MS in Box 102:15, UGA.

70. Harris, *My Book and Heart*, 23–25.

71. Harris, *In Search of a Husband*, 162.

72. Harris, *My Book and Heart*, 54.

73. Harris, *My Son* (New York: George H. Doran Co., 1921), 55–65, 84.

74. Ibid., 90.

75. Ibid., 113–15.

76. Ibid., 139–64, 199–239.

77. Harris, *Happy Pilgrimage*, 297.

78. Harris, *A Daughter of Adam* (New York: George H. Doran Co., 1923), 265.

79. Harris, *My Son*, 239, 242, 255–60, 270–71.

80. Ibid., 271.

81. Harris, *In Search of a Husband*, 226–27.

82. Harris, *The Co-Citizens* (New York: Grosset and Dunlap, 1915), 193.

83. Harris, *As a Woman Thinks*, 100, 101, 237.

84. Harris, *Making Her His Wife* (London: Thomas Nelson Sons, n.d.), 55.

85. Harris, *House of Helen*, 67.

86. Ibid.; and Harris, *Justice*.

87. Charlotte Perkins Gilman and Mrs. L. H. Harris, "The Future of the Home," *Independent*, October 4, 1906, 788–98.

88. Harris, "New York as Seen from the Valley—Seventh Paper," *Independent*, March 30, 1914, 442.

89. Harris, *In Search of a Husband*, 244.

90. Other magazines she published in included *Good Housekeeping, Harpers, Pictorial Review, Metropolitan, Country Gentleman*; see Talmadge, *Corra Harris*, 71–73, 96.

91. "The Willipus-Wallipus in Tennessee Politics," *Independent*, February 6, 1914, 622–26.

92. "If You Must Come to New York," *Independent*, April 6, 1914, 29–32.

93. Talmadge, *Corra Harris*, 74–102.

94. The quotation is from *Happy Pilgrimage*, 107. See also Talmadge, *Corra Harris*, 129.

95. See Mrs. L. H. Harris, "Our Novelists," *Independent*, November 11, 1905, 1172, 1175; Corra Harris, "Black and Whites," essay in Box 74.12; Harris, "Making a Preacher" essay in Box 78.16; *Atlanta Journal*, March 31, 1929, in Box 110.1, Harris papers, UGA. Reference to John Jones and "warp and woof" from William Edward Burghardt DuBois, *The Souls of Black Folk*, in W. E. B. Du Bois, *Writings* (New York: Literary Classics of the United States, 1986), 535, 545.

96. Clipping from the *Nashville Banner*, March 18, 1932, Box 110:22, Harris papers, UGA.

97. Corra Harris to Dear Miss [Adelaide W.] Neall, February 14, 1914. Box 22:17 Harris papers UGA.

98. Classnotes from the Class on Evil, Rollins College Library.

99. Corra Harris, "Candlelight Column," *Atlanta Journal Magazine*, June 25, 1933, August 6, 1933, January 4, 1935, March 10, 1935 (Harris died in February).

100. Harris, *As a Woman Thinks*, 194.

# Juliette Gordon Low

## (1860–1927)

## *Late-Blooming Daisy*

### ANASTATIA HODGENS SIMS

Ask any Girl Scout, "Who was Juliette Low?" and she will almost always respond, "Founder of the Girl Scouts of the United States." More than eighty years after her death, Low remains a beloved figure among present and former Girl Scouts. The movement she launched in Savannah in 1912 has become an integral part of American girlhood; since its inception, more than fifty million girls and women have joined its ranks.[1]

Low was one of the most influential women ever to live in the state of Georgia, yet few people outside the Girl Scouting community recognize her name, and many within it know only a few essential facts about her. Most women's history textbooks gloss over her achievements, probably because Juliette Gordon Low defies categorization. She was an anomaly among the elite women of her social circle and an anomaly among the reformers working to redefine women's roles. Reared to accept the strictures of Victorian femininity, she never embraced feminism and seemed destined to lead the conventional life of an upper-class lady. But a combination of personality, circumstance, and coincidence took her down an unconventional path and led her to establish an organization dedicated to developing "girls of courage, confidence, and character, who make the world a better place."[2]

Low's story is usually presented to Girl Scouts as a tale of romance, adventure, and triumph. The daughter of a privileged southern family grew from a skinny child into a beautiful woman. A pair of accidents when she was in her twenties severely impaired her hearing, but she never let her deafness bother her or interfere with her life. She married a wealthy, handsome man, lived on an English country estate, mingled with the rich and famous on both sides of the Atlantic, and traveled the globe. After her husband's death she discovered new meaning and purpose in the international movement of Girl Guiding and Girl Scouting. She started the Girl Scouts of the United States in 1912 and devoted the rest of her life to building the organization and promoting international ties of friendship between girls. She was known for her artistic talent, her love of animals, her kind heart, her charm, her wit, and her sense of whimsy. When she died, she was praised by prominent men and women from around the world and mourned by thousands of Girl Scouts.

This synopsis of Juliette Low's biography, while true in its essentials, is only a snapshot of a life. Like a carefully posed still photograph, it casts its subject in a favorable light, foregrounds success, and has been cropped to eliminate most vestiges of struggle, conflict, sorrow, and failure. It blurs the details of the rich and varied life Low led before Girl Scouting and reveals little about the complexities of her character. Moreover, it obscures the most intriguing question about her: how did a fifty-one-year-old socialite—a woman who was more accustomed to luxury hotels than campsites and who had no experience in women's organizations, childhood education, or social reform—start from scratch and build the most successful voluntary association for girls and women in the United States?

Little in her background or upbringing foreshadowed the work that would dominate the last fifteen years of her life. Juliette Magill Kinzie Gordon was born in Savannah on October 31, 1860. She was the second of the six children of Eleanor (Nelly) Kinzie and William (Willie) Washington Gordon II. The Gordons were a distinguished family. Willie Gordon's father, William Washington Gordon I, was a founder of the Central of Georgia Railroad and served as mayor of Savannah; a statue of him stands in one of the city's squares. Nelly Gordon's family, the Kinzies, were among the first settlers of Chicago. Juliette was named after her maternal grandmother, an author and amateur historian, who insisted that her namesake should be called Daisy. Daisy was both a popular name and a common slang term; it meant "any excellent, remarkable, or admirable person or thing." The nickname was appropriate and it stuck. For the rest of her life, friends and family knew her as Daisy.[3]

A few days after Daisy's birth, Abraham Lincoln won the presidency, and within six months the United States had plunged into civil war. This cataclysmic event transformed the nation and touched almost every household in the country, including the Gordons', but Daisy was too young to remember much about the hardships the conflict imposed on Georgians in general or her family in particular. After the war ended, her father, a cotton broker and commission merchant, quickly rebuilt his business. The firm prospered and, although the

**JULIETTE GORDON LOW**
Courtesy of the Girl Scouts of the USA and the Birthplace
and the National Historic Preservation Center.

Gordons' wealth never approached that of the Vanderbilts or the Rockefellers, the family enjoyed a higher standard of living than most southerners knew.

Nelly and Willie Gordon were determined to give all of their children the best education they could afford, and that meant sending them to private schools outside of Georgia. When Daisy was thirteen, she spent a few months at a boarding school in New Jersey. She then attended two different female academies in Virginia before completing her formal education at a finishing school run by two French women in New York City. She studied history, literature, French, music, and art, and acquired the social graces that prepared her to become the cultured wife of a prosperous man. Although Daisy grew up during an era of expanding opportunities for women, no one she knew expected a girl to aspire to anything other than marriage and motherhood.

Daisy was, for the most part, a happy child who was comfortable with the role she was expected to play. Early on she began to display the enduring, if not always endearing, traits that would characterize her until the end of her life. She was clever, witty, and likable, the sort of person to whom others gravitated. She made friends easily, and frequently took the lead in games and activities. At the same time, however, she could be stubborn and willful. Facts and logic would not move her. An incident that occurred when she was eighteen was typical. She was traveling by train to meet her mother in Marietta. She knew that her father's position on the board of the Central of Georgia railroad entitled her to free passage on that line, and, in her mind, one railroad was the same as another. When the conductor asked for her fare, she refused to pay. Instead, she handed him her Central pass. He examined it, then tried to explain to her that the pass was not valid because she was not on a Central of Georgia train. Nelly Gordon described what happened next in a letter to her husband:

> "My Father," returned Daisy with dignity, "is a Director *on all the Roads!*"
> "But," remonstrated the Conductor, "this pass is signed by the General Superintendent of the *Central Rail Road.*"
> "Well *I* can't help *that!*" retorted Daisy.
> So the non-plussed Conductor passed on, & passed *her* on.

The bewildered conductor was not the first person to surrender rather than argue, and he would not be the last. Daisy's stubborn persistence in the face of opposition exasperated the people around her and sometimes became a liability, but it would serve her well in her work with Girl Scouting.[4]

A few months after her encounter with the conductor, Daisy made her debut in Savannah society. The interlude between girlhood and marriage was supposed to be a carefree time, but Daisy's life during these years was marked by sorrow and loss along with happiness and romance. In December 1880 her sister Alice died of scarlet fever while away at school in New York. Alice was three years younger than Daisy, and the two had always been close. They had attended school together in Virginia, and Daisy was visiting her when she became ill. Alice's death was the first profound grief Daisy had known.

Four years later, Daisy suffered another kind of loss when she sustained an injury that permanently damaged her hearing. From childhood onward, she had been plagued with painful ear infections. In January 1885, once again troubled by an earache, she went to her doctor in Savannah. The meeting unfolded in much the same way as her dispute with the conductor on the train to Marietta, but this time Daisy would pay for her willfulness for the rest of her life. She asked the doctor to try a new treatment she had read about, an injection of silver nitrate. The doctor hesitated; Daisy insisted; the doctor capitulated. It became apparent almost immediately that the experiment had gone awry. For the next few days, she endured intermittent pain and had difficulty hearing with the inflamed ear. Her family and physicians hoped that her hearing would improve when the swelling in her ear subsided, but it did not. The partial deafness in that ear was permanent.[5]

In the days following the silver nitrate injection, one of the people who comforted Daisy was William (Willie) Mackay Low, "a strikingly handsome fellow" with a "joyous boyish manner." Willie's father, Andrew, had immigrated to Savannah from Scotland when he was in his teens. He made a fortune trading cotton and built a mansion on Lafayette Square before retiring to England after the death of his second wife, Willie's mother. Daisy and Willie had known each other as children but had not seen each other for several years when they met again in 1882. They fell in love almost immediately, but tried to keep their romance secret and broke off the relationship several times because they feared parental opposition. Their courtship lasted for nearly five years. Finally, both families bestowed their blessings. Daisy and Willie were married in a lavish wedding at Savannah's Christ Church on December 21, 1886.

Unfortunately, the joyous occasion ended ominously. As was customary, the newlyweds departed amid a shower of rice tossed at them by guests. A grain of rice became embedded in Daisy's ear. The ear became infected, and she and Willie had to interrupt their honeymoon so that she could seek treatment. The infection healed, but further impaired her hearing. Although she always retained some auditory ability—she attended concerts and the opera, and went to great lengths to acquire a Victrola—for the rest of her life she would search for a cure. Occasionally she experienced periods of improvement, but she never again heard well.

Daisy found ways to compensate for her deafness. She tended to monopolize conversations and became known as a splendid raconteur, because she found it easier to talk than to strain to listen to others; she also wanted to avoid the embarrassment of responding inappropriately when she misunderstood what was said. She rarely complained or indulged in self-pity. Still, her disability was a source of great frustration. "I *cannot* stand this deafness—& being *so* helpless! Life is too hard for me!" she once cried to her mother. Afterward, Nelly "could hear her sobbing late into the night."[6] Deafness imposed a sense of isolation that reinforced preexisting traits of Daisy's personality. She had always tended to ignore admonition and advice, along with facts and logic, when they were contrary to what she wanted to do. Now physically unable to hear criticism or contradiction, she became more inclined than ever to view the world as she wanted to see it rather than as it was. At the same time, because she could not hear praise or reassurance, feelings of insecurity, self-doubt, and fears of being unloved that had been with her since childhood also intensified.

In 1887 Juliette Low—aged twenty-six and newly married—faced major changes in her life. In addition to assuming the responsibilities of a matron in charge of her own household and coping with a permanent disability, she had to adapt to the customs of a different social circle in another country. Although she had expected to live in Savannah and had refurbished the Low house on Lafayette Square before the wedding, Willie Low was more comfortable in England, and within a year the couple moved across the Atlantic. They bought an estate, Wellesbourne House, in Warwickshire and settled into the life of English gentry. They belonged to an exclusive circle of wealthy and titled men and women surrounding the Prince of Wales, who would eventually become King Edward VII. They hosted house parties at Wellesbourne, spent time in London, and summered in Scotland. Although she probably expected that motherhood would follow soon after marriage, the couple had no children. As years passed, they spent more and more time apart. Willie hunted wild game, caroused with his chums, and drank heavily. Daisy found solace in her art—she studied painting and sculpting and learned ironwork as well—in her own travels, and in visits with family and friends. In 1900 she admitted to a young friend who aspired to find a wealthy spouse that while "Willie Low has other charms besides money. . . . he was a very bad husband."[7]

A year later, the marriage disintegrated. Willie fell in love with a young widow named Anna Bateman. He decided he wanted to marry her and began trying to goad Daisy into divorcing him. The next five years were the most difficult of Daisy's life. At first she refused to consider dissolving the marriage. Like many scorned wives, she hoped that the affair was a passing infatuation. Moreover, she wanted to avoid the scandal and publicity that would have inevitably accompanied the divorce of a couple of the Lows' social standing. But as her hopes for reconciliation faded, she changed her mind. She resolved to emerge from the crisis with her dignity intact and her financial future secured, and she retained the services of one of the best attorneys in Great Britain.

She soon learned that divorce was a lengthy and cumbersome process. Because of the requirements of English law and complicated negotiations over a financial settlement, the divorce suit was still pending when Willie Low died in June of 1905. His demise should have ended Daisy's troubles, but he stunned his widow and her lawyers from beyond the grave by leaving behind a will that bequeathed the bulk of his estate to his mistress, Anna Bateman. Daisy, his wife of nearly twenty years, had to sue for her rightful inheritance.

The final settlement of Willie Low's estate made Daisy a wealthy woman. She received all of his Georgia property, including the house on Lafayette Square, along with a substantial quantity of British stocks and bonds. Although she still considered herself an American and maintained close ties with her relatives and friends in her native country, she made her home in London and leased the Savannah house to various tenants. Unencumbered by family responsibilities or the necessity of earning a living, she continued to do the things she had always enjoyed. She maintained a busy social schedule—teas, luncheons, parties, the opera—worked on her art intermittently, and traveled extensively. She made annual visits to the United States and spent part of each summer in Scotland. She went to Paris to study sculpting and to a German spa to seek a cure for her deafness. She toured India and Egypt. Often she invited a niece, a nephew, or the child of a friend to accompany her on her journeys, but she demonstrated no inclination to organize children into groups or to join voluntary associations herself. Furthermore, she gave no thought to the status of women or to how women's lives might be improved. She appeared to be just another socialite, someone who enjoyed the advantages that accompanied wealth and social status and who harbored no ambition to engage in any large-scale social movement or reform.

Yet Daisy felt that something was missing from her life. Despite her talents, her charm, her many friends, and her wealth, by the standards of the day, she was a failure. Widowed and childless, filling her time with social engagements, artistic projects, and travel, she was neither a "true woman" devoting herself to home, husband, and family nor a "new woman" pursuing a cause or a career. Her notorious lack of punctuality and her inability to manage money—even after Willie's estate was settled, she still occasionally had to make urgent appeals to her father when she found herself overdrawn at the bank—had convinced her family that Daisy, while lovable, was not very competent. When Juliette Low celebrated her fiftieth birthday on October 31, 1910, she seemed fated to spend the rest of her days as a dilettante and an object of pity, a woman who had been both unlucky and unwise in love and who lacked a serious purpose.

Six months later, a chance meeting with Sir Robert Baden-Powell changed her life. Baden-Powell, a military hero who had begun the Boy Scout movement in England in 1908, was one of the most celebrated men in Great Britain. Scouting was wildly popular. When girls clamored to join, Baden-Powell's sister, Agnes, started a separate organization, called the Girl Guides. Daisy and Sir Robert instantly became friends. They were frequent companions in the weeks after they met and, unlike most of the people she knew, he assured her that it was not too late for her to find meaningful work. She organized a Girl Guide troop in Scotland that summer and two more in London in the fall. When she sailed to America in January 1912 she found that, by chance, Baden-Powell was aboard the same ship. Although no record exists of how often they conversed during that voyage or what they discussed, they most likely used the unexpected time together to plan for the launch of Girl Guiding in the United States.

When their ship arrived in New York, Baden-Powell immediately embarked on a tour of the United States and Canada to promote the benefits of Scouting for boys and Guiding for girls. The Chief Scout, as he was known, drew large audiences and widespread media coverage. Local newspapers in the cities he visited ran stories about him and the organizations he led. In addition, in March 1912 at least two newspapers published the same feature story, datelined London, about plans to bring Girl Guiding to the United States. The article did not mention Juliette Low, but it is evidence of a coordinated campaign from Girl Guide headquarters in England to transplant the movement to America.[8]

Because Baden-Powell had started Boy Scouting in Great Britain and had seen it spread to other countries, he knew how much effort would be required to build a national voluntary association from the ground up, and Low relied on him for advice and guidance as she made her plans. The first requirement was publicity, to introduce the public to Girl Guiding and win support for it. The Boy Scouts of America had been in existence since 1910, and there had been several attempts to start similar groups for girls, but the concept of an organization exclusively for girls, devoted to their development and their interests, was still new. Parents had to be convinced that membership would benefit their daughters. Women had to be coaxed to serve as leaders, and girls had to be persuaded to join. Second, a program would have to be created. The Girl Guide handbook provided a blueprint, but it had to be adapted to suit American circumstances. Third, American Girl Guides needed an institutional structure—a headquarters, procedures, bylaws, a budget, a reliable source of income—all the apparatus necessary to sustain a national organization.

Juliette Low faced a daunting task, and it was not a foregone conclusion that she would succeed. In fact, people who knew her were skeptical. Her family regarded her as "most erratic." They compared her to a grasshopper, because "one never knows in which direction she will jump next."[9] In addition to her tendency to embrace projects enthusiastically only to abandon them soon thereafter, she was also stubborn and accustomed to having her own way. Her deafness had intensified these characteristics, and her relationships with people she loved were punctuated with arguments, misunderstandings, and emotional outbursts. Her family must have wondered how she would function in an enterprise whose success depended on cooperation, but for the most part, they kept their doubts to themselves and supported her as she embarked on this latest endeavor.

Family support was just one of the advantages Daisy had as she set out to bring Girl Guiding to the United States; there were others as well. A combination of circumstances and attributes made Juliette Low uniquely qualified to establish the Girl Guides in America. First, her status as an independently wealthy, childless widow meant that she was more autonomous than the vast majority of women. Second, she could draw on a wide network of influential friends and relatives. Several chums from her schooldays in New York were linked by birth and marriage to America's social and financial elite in the Northeast. Her mother, Nelly Gordon, still had contacts in Chicago, the preeminent city in the Midwest. Her older sister, Eleanor, was married to a Republican congressman from New Jersey, and a male cousin from Savannah was active in Democratic politics at the national level, so Daisy had connections to leaders of both political parties and, through them, to their wives, who had their own networks in Washington and in their home states. Third, she possessed personality traits that offset her weaknesses. Time and again, she had demonstrated that once she made up her mind, nothing would deter her from reaching her goal. Although she could be domineering and insensitive at times, she could also be very charming and extremely persuasive. A member of one of the first troops in Savannah recalled, "Mrs. Low had the unique gift of immediately interesting others in whatever subjects [with which] she herself was vitally concerned."[10] Her boundless enthusiasm and her ability to imbue others with the same zeal contributed immeasurably to the movement's success.

In early February 1912 Daisy arrived in Savannah, settled into her parents' home on Oglethorpe Avenue, and set to work. She told friends and family about the Girl Guides and enlisted adults to serve as troop leaders. She prepared a circular to be sent out nationwide. She wrote a "manual of training" based on Boy Scout procedures and the British Girl Guide handbook, and she began organizing girls into Savannah's first troops. By March 12 the officially designated birthday of Girl Scouting in America, the work was well underway. On that day, she sent her sister Mabel a draft of the manual and told her, "You must not be bored with G.G.s [Girl Guides] as I can't write of any thing else." Girl Guiding had become her full-time occupation. Her mother complained that she monopolized the telephone and that visitors eager to discuss Girl Guides rang the doorbell all day long.[11]

In the weeks that followed, she continued to recruit girls and women for the movement, established a headquarters in an outbuilding behind the house she owned on Lafayette Square, and hired a secretary. Within two months of her arrival in Savannah, there were four troops in the city. Members were learning the Girl Guide laws and working on badges. They went on daylong hikes and competed against one another in basketball. Low's sister Eleanor observed, "No one but Mamma (when she was Daisy's age) could have accomplished so much in so short a time."[12]

Daisy was wholeheartedly committed to making the American Girl Guides a success, but she saw no reason why this project should disrupt her usual routine. She would continue to make her home in England, to travel when and where she pleased, and to spend only a few months of each year in the United States. Members of her family urged her to reconsider. If she was serious about Girl Guiding, they said, she would have to reside permanently in America. With the same obstinacy that had enabled her to prevail over the conductor who insisted that her rail pass was not valid and to persuade her doctor to try a risky treatment with which he was not familiar, Daisy ignored their advice. From 1912 until America's entry into the world war in 1917 forced her to curtail her trans-Atlantic travel, she directed the movement largely in absentia, making brief visits to headquarters and handling most business through correspondence. She made all the decisions and paid attention to every detail; still, her prolonged absences could have doomed the new organization to failure. Fortunately, she was able to hire a succession of secretaries who admired her and who shared her devotion to the cause. As one wrote in 1914, "The more I think of what you are doing *alone* for the American girls my admiration grows deeper and deeper, and I hope with all my heart your fondest dreams may be realized." Inspired by Daisy's enthusiasm and commitment, loyal subordinates willingly put in the long hours necessary to carry out Low's orders and manage day-to-day operations.[13]

When Daisy departed Savannah in May 1912 she instructed the newly hired secretary to keep the organization going and left money with her brother to cover expenses. She customarily spent August and September in Scotland, and she did not plan to return to the United States until October. In August, however, her plans changed abruptly when her father became seriously ill. She immediately sailed to America. Over the next few weeks, Willie Gordon's condition fluctuated, and during the times when he appeared to be recovering, she took care of Girl Guide business. But the short-term improvements in Willie's health were temporary; on September 11, he died.

Willie Gordon's death was a devastating loss for the entire family, but it was especially difficult for Daisy. She had always been close to her father, and their relationship had become increasingly important to her after the dissolution of her marriage. Daisy believed that he had been "the only human being who was indulgent to my faults & took my part in all ways." Her grief for him was deep and lasting; she sometimes wondered how she could survive without his unconditional love.[14]

She found consolation by trying to live by the precepts that had guided her father's life. Devotion to duty had been one of the hallmarks of Willie Gordon's character, and in the months following his death, duty sustained Daisy—duty to her mother and duty to Girl Guides. When she returned to England in October, Nelly Gordon went with her. In addition to tending to her mother's needs, Daisy continued her work with the two troops she had formed in London in the fall of 1911 and she supervised the American Girl Guides from afar.

From the beginning, her vision for Girl Guiding had stretched beyond the city limits of Savannah, and in 1913 she moved forward with plans to expand nationwide. She adopted an entrepreneurial strategy that included attempted mergers and acquisitions, marketing, and program development. With Baden-Powell's help, she began contacting leaders of other girls' organizations in an attempt to combine them under one banner. Between 1910 and 1912, several national groups had been created, all claiming that their programs for girls were comparable to Scouting for boys. The two that were most problematic, as far as Low was concerned, were the Camp Fire Girls and the Girl Scouts of America. The Camp Fire Girls had been organized in 1910 by Dr. Luther Gulick and his wife, Charlotte. Dr. Gulick worked for the YMCA and had close ties to the leaders of the American Boy Scouts. Like Girl Guiding, the Camp Fire movement stressed the importance of exercise and outdoor activities. However, while Daisy and the Baden-Powells envisioned a program that would encourage girls to become proficient in a wide variety of fields, ranging from cooking and sewing to aviation and marksmanship, the Gulicks focused exclusively on preparing girls for traditional roles as wives and mothers. Luther Gulick declared that Camp Fire girls displayed "renewed devotion and enthusiasm . . . in their domestic duties and home opportunities." Low promised the Gulicks that the Camp Fire mission and emphasis would remain intact if the organizations united, but insisted that Camp Fire Girls accept the Girl Guide laws, the ten precepts that were the heart of the Scouting movement. Luther Gulick flatly—and rather smugly—refused, boasting that Camp Fire had already attracted 36,000 members and continued to grow. At the time he wrote, in January of 1913, Low's organization had only 100 members, all in Savannah, so Gulick probably regarded the Girl Guides as an upstart group that would soon fail. In public, Low was always gracious about Gulick and the Camp Fire Girls. Privately, however, she believed that their program was less substantial and less appealing to girls than Girl Guiding. She told Baden-Powell, "letters come pouring into headquarters saying that after the first ceremonies the girls find nothing to interest them & camp after camp is breaking up." Furthermore, she felt that rivalry was detrimental to both groups and distracted from their true purpose of developing character and preparing girls to live useful, fulfilling, and happy lives.[15]

The Girl Scouts of America had been founded in Des Moines, Iowa, in 1910 by Clara Lisetor-Lane, a Chicago native who, like Daisy, dreamed of transplanting the Girl Guide idea to the United States. Lisetor-Lane published a handbook modeled on the British Girl Guide handbook in 1911. Because the groups were so similar, Daisy believed that they could be melded together easily. She soon learned differently. Lisetor-Lane accused Low of stealing her idea and threatened to sue. As time passed and Low's organization grew, Lisetor-Lane charged that Daisy had employed deceitful tactics to lure troops away from the Girl Scouts of America. In fact, Lisetor-Lane lacked the financial resources and social connections necessary to sustain a national movement, and her organization never grew beyond a few troops. The Girl Scouts of America withered and died, but Lisetor-Lane continued to pester officials at Girl Scout headquarters until her death in 1960. She went to her grave convinced that Juliette Low had robbed her of the acclaim and recognition she deserved.[16]

If Daisy could not absorb the competition, she would ensure that her group surpassed them. In June 1913 a national headquarters was established in Washington, D.C., and the organization's name was officially changed to Girl Scouts of the United States (GSUS). Several factors prompted the switch. First, according to Girl Scout historians Mary Degenhardt and Judith Kirsch, "the girls themselves requested the change." Second, individual troops and patrols, many calling themselves Girl Scouts, had sprung up on their own in communities throughout the nation. Daisy wanted to make her association attractive to the independent groups, and many of them ultimately chose to affiliate with GSUS.

Finally, she wanted to capitalize on the name recognition already enjoyed by the Boy Scouts—much to the dismay of the leaders of the Boy Scout organization, who believed that the term Scout was unwomanly and attempted for several years to persuade Daisy to revert to the Girl Guide designation. She listened politely to their entreaties but held firm in her decision.[17]

The new name was part of a marketing strategy that included securing endorsements from prominent individuals. Low assembled an honorary advisory committee of more than fifty women in fifteen cities. The list included Mabel T. Boardman (Clara Barton's successor as director of the American Red Cross), Mina Miller Edison (wife of inventor Thomas Alva Edison), Edith Ogden Harrison (author of children's books and wife of the mayor of Chicago) and Fanny Gordon (no relation; the widow of Confederate general John B. Gordon), along with the wives of the postmaster general, a United States Supreme Court justice, an Episcopal bishop, and other leaders in government, education, and business. Daisy's mother, sister, and closest friend were also included. Members of the committee had no assigned tasks or responsibilities and were not expected to make financial contributions, but by allowing Low to link their names to Girl Scouts they helped to draw attention to the fledgling organization and establish its legitimacy.[18]

Daisy used her family connections in Washington and Savannah to obtain an invitation to the White House in the spring of 1913. She hoped to persuade Ellen Axson Wilson, wife of newly inaugurated President Woodrow Wilson and a Savannah native, to accept the position of honorary president. The first lady's prestige, Low believed, would certify the credibility and respectability of Girl Scouting and aid in the recruitment of new members. Moreover, her official sanction might convince Gulick to reconsider his refusal to merge with the Girl Scouts. Although Mrs. Wilson declined the honorary office, she praised Low's work and agreed to host a meeting at the White House to discuss the movement.[19]

At the same time that Daisy was arranging for the opening of Washington headquarters and recruiting members for the honorary advisory committee, she was also supervising the completion and publication of the first full-length handbook for American Girl Scouts. She had turned revision of the book over to Walter J. Hoxie, a naturalist who worked with Girl Guides in Savannah, but she carefully reviewed the manuscript before it went to press. Modeled on Agnes Baden-Powell's British Girl Guide handbook, *How Girls Can Help to Build Up the Empire*, the American version, entitled *How Girls Can Help Their Country*, was a how-to book for girls and women interested in establishing Girl Scouting in their communities. It explained the Girl Scout promise and laws, and covered practical topics such as procedures for starting a troop, the agenda for the first meeting, and the requirements for proficiency badges. It also outlined the fundamental components of the Girl Scout program; chapter headings included "Camping," "Home Life," "Hospital Work," and "Patriotism." Girls were instructed to "be womanly" and were given information about housekeeping, first aid, and child care. But the handbook also told them to "be strong" and "be handy" and incorporated material unlikely to be found in a home economics textbook. Girl Scouts learned how to tell time by the stars, how to signal in semaphore, how to stop a runaway horse, and how to tie up a burglar with eight inches of rope. They could earn badges that demonstrated mastery of the domestic arts—such as Laundress, Child Nurse, Needlewoman, and Matron Housekeeper—but they could also work for recognition in less traditional fields. The Flyer badge, for example, required a Girl Scout to understand air currents and weather, show "some knowledge of engines," and either "have made an aeroplane to fly for 25 yards (or have a certificate for driving an aeroplane)." Implicit in the program outlined in *How Girls Can Help Their Country* was the belief that girls could do or be almost anything they chose. Girl Scouting affirmed domesticity and acknowledged its centrality in most women's lives at the same time that it allowed girls to try on roles that would have been unthinkable a generation earlier. Although troops undertook many group projects, each Girl Scout decided which badges she wanted to complete and thus had some latitude to set her own agenda based on her particular interests and aptitudes. "No unreasonable restraint is placed on the girls," an Atlanta journalist reported. "Rather, they are given more liberty and taught how to use it, as is the policy of the Boy Scouts."[20]

With national headquarters established and a handbook in print, Low spent the next few years building the movement and doing what she did best—sharing her enthusiasm about Girl Scouting with others. Although she continued to divide her time between Great Britain and the United States and to make only brief visits to the Girl Scout offices when she was in America, she oversaw every operational detail and worked tirelessly to promote the organization. When she was in England, she penned hundreds of letters and worked on leaflets, a leader's manual, and other publications. When she was in the United States, she traveled extensively, making speeches, giving interviews, and meeting with influential women and men everywhere she went.

In private conversations, public addresses, and in her writings, Low emphasized the same theme again and again: Girl Scouting was all about girls. The focus was on their interests and their development. Programs were designed to be fun at the same time that they fostered cooperation and nurtured self-reliance.

Girl Scouts played basketball, tag, and other games. They hiked, cooked out-
doors, and told stories around campfires. They learned by doing rather than by
listening, and from enjoyment rather than coercion. "THE IDEA IS NOT TO HAVE
A SCHOOL; THE SCHEME IS PLAY," she admonished troop leaders. At the same
time, she reminded adults that Girl Scouting was play with a purpose. Through
their activities, girls acquired practical knowledge and skills and cultivated the
character traits listed in the Girl Scout laws: "truth, loyalty, helpfulness, friend-
liness, courtesy, kindness, obedience, cheerfulness, purity, and thrift." Daisy was
certain that girls who absorbed these values when they were young would grow
into confident, resourceful women who possessed a deep love of country, a
lasting commitment to helping others, and a strong sense of individual responsibility.[21]

Daisy believed that Girl Scouting would benefit poor girls as well as those
in the middle and upper classes and, from the beginning, insisted that money
(or lack thereof) should not be a barrier to membership—although she took
care to assure parents that their daughters would be in troops with girls from
similar backgrounds. Within the first year, a troop was formed for Savannah's
"business girls," and the local secretary persuaded city officials to light the vacant lot where Girl Scouts held their basketball games so that girls who worked
for wages during the day could play at night. When Savannah's first Girl Scouts
took daylong excursions, Low paid for streetcar fares and food. She also reached
out to daughters of immigrants, perhaps believing that Girl Scouting, with
its patriotic emphasis, would hasten assimilation. In 1914 she met with Jane
Addams and persuaded her to start a Girl Scout troop at Hull House; other
settlement houses sponsored troops as well. As the association expanded, Daisy
worked to keep the costs of membership low in order to reach as many girls as
possible. During the first few years the national organization charged no dues;
Low herself paid all expenses, including rent, salaries, printing costs, and inci-
dentals. Girls were expected to purchase handbooks, badges, and uniforms, but
Daisy negotiated with publishers and manufacturers to maintain reasonable
prices and gave girls the option of making their own uniforms if they couldn't
afford ready-made outfits.[22]

Daisy's vision for Girl Scouting was inclusive up to a point, but she still held
the biases absorbed during her southern upbringing, her lengthy residence in
Great Britain and close association with the aristocracy, and her travels to outposts of the British empire. When a New Yorker inquired about forming a troop
of African American girls in January 1917, Low wavered. She knew all too well
that what was acceptable in Manhattan would not pass muster in Savannah.
She warned that white southern girls would resign if African Americans joined

the organization and that white parents would object to the presence of black Girl Scouts at rallies "for they can & do corrupt other children." Still, she stopped short of mandating a "whites only" policy, which might have angered northern whites at the same time it placated white southerners. Instead, she looked for a compromise. "The Negro question . . . is sure to arise," she wrote when she received a second inquiry about African American Girl Scouts a few months later. "Just let each state vote for it, & never let it be obligatory to have Negroes in all parts of the National organization." In the 1920s African American troops were organized in a few cities, mostly in the Northeast and Midwest, but comprised only a small fraction of the total Girl Scout membership. In 1931 national headquarters reported that of more than eleven thousand registered troops, only forty-four were black and only one was integrated.[23]

Under Low's guidance, the Girl Scouts of the United States grew steadily — from a thousand members in June 1914, to five thousand at the end of 1915, to thirteen thousand in early 1917. In 1915 Daisy moved national headquarters to New York. She brought faculty and administrators from Columbia Teachers College onto the executive board to share their expertise on programs appropriate for girls. She also secured contributions and pledges from philanthropists to guarantee the organization's financial security. The donations, along with increased revenues from the sales of uniforms, badges, and handbooks, enabled the Girl Scouts to hire more staff at national headquarters and additional field organizers to work with troops at the local level. By the time the United States entered World War I in 1917 GSUS was poised for substantial growth, and the war proved to be a boon to Girl Scouting. With its emphasis on patriotism as well as training in practical skills such as first aid, the Girl Scout program promised girls the opportunity to serve their country during wartime. Girl Scouts planted victory gardens, sold war bonds, and assisted the Red Cross. More than twenty thousand girls joined between 1917 and 1918, and by the end of 1919 GSUS boasted a membership of more than forty thousand.[24]

Daisy witnessed the organization's expansion firsthand; however, as in 1912, her enthusiasm was tempered by grief. Nelly Gordon became seriously ill in January 1917, and Daisy traveled to Savannah to be with her. Nelly died in February, and by the time Daisy was ready to return to England, the German policy of unrestricted submarine warfare and America's entry into the world war prevented her from making the voyage across the Atlantic. She remained in the United States until after the armistice was signed in November 1918 and spent much of her time speaking and writing on behalf of the Girl Scouts. Her presence during this crucial period contributed to the movement's success.

Growth changed the organization and Low's role within it. In the early years, she underwrote all expenses and established all policies and procedures. The staff was small—a few office workers at headquarters and a couple of field organizers—and knew that their continued employment depended on Juliette Low's good will. The board was composed entirely of people Daisy recruited, all of whom understood that arguing with her was futile. She knew what she wanted, and she almost always got her way. But after headquarters moved to New York in 1915 the professional staff grew, the board expanded, and a cadre of dedicated and experienced volunteers emerged. Moreover, the Girl Scouts no longer relied exclusively on Daisy for financial support. Although she continued to hold the office of president, board members, staff, and volunteers increasingly questioned her decisions, and some came to see her as an impediment to future progress. During a dispute over proposed revisions to the handbook in the fall of 1918, a board member complained to Daisy that she was difficult to work with and told her that meetings were more productive without her. She reminded Low that GSUS had grown too large to be subject to the sole authority of one person, then concluded, "Your child is grown up and has a will of its own."[25]

Those words must have cut Daisy deeply. The Girl Scout movement in the United States *was* her child; she had conceived it, nurtured it, guided it. The organization she had started in Savannah six years earlier was thriving and reaching more girls than ever before, yet she was being told that she wasn't needed any more. When the war ended, she returned to England and remained there for most of 1919. In 1920 she resigned as president of the Girl Scouts, accepted the title of founder, and increasingly devoted herself to the international Girl Guiding movement.

Daisy continued shuttling between the United States and Great Britain and remained actively involved with Girl Scouts and Girl Guides, despite serious problems with her health; she was diagnosed with breast cancer in 1923. Typically, she kept up with her customary routine as much as possible and remained as stubborn and willful as ever. In 1925 she insisted that American Girl Scouts offer to host the biennial international encampment of Girl Scouts and Girl Guides the following year. Jane Deeter Rippin, the executive director of GSUS, argued that preparations could not be completed in time, but Daisy was adamant. As Rippin recalled, Low demonstrated "the same indomitable purpose, the same refusal to yield to difficulties which she had shown, when, alone, she brought Girl Guiding to this country." Rippin and the executive board gave in, as so many others had when faced with Daisy's intransigence. In May 1926 delegates from thirty countries met at the hastily constructed Camp Edith Macy in Briarcliff Manor, New York. Chief Scout Sir Robert Baden-Powell attended, along with his wife, Olave, who had assumed leadership of the international Girl

Guide movement. For Daisy, hosting the world conference on American soil was a crowning achievement.[26]

She returned to England that summer to put her business affairs in order. In December she crossed the Atlantic for the last time. She spent Christmas at a hospital in Richmond, then traveled to Savannah. She died on January 17, 1927, in her home on Lafayette Square. A large public funeral was held in Savannah, and tributes and condolences poured into Girl Scout headquarters from around the world. At her request, she was buried wearing her Girl Scout uniform.

Juliette Gordon Low had followed an unusual path to find her life's work in Girl Scouting, but then, she was an unusual woman. She did not participate in the vast network of women's organizations that developed in the late nineteenth and early twentieth centuries or in any aspect of the women's movement, yet she founded the most successful voluntary association for girls and women in the United States. Neither philosophical nor reflective, she frequently acted on impulse and intuition. In 1912 and after, her intuition served her well. She understood that girls born in the twentieth century faced options and responsibilities that she had never imagined when she was growing up. Moreover, she knew from her own experience that life does not always unfold as planned: a girl who expected to achieve happiness and fulfillment as wife and mother might one day find herself alone, an independent woman by circumstance rather than by choice. Low saw in Girl Scouting a program that was both appealing and beneficial, a program that offered fun and excitement at the same time that it gave girls the skills, strength of character, and self-confidence to meet any challenge the future might hold. Once she made up her mind to transplant Girl Guiding from Great Britain to the United States, she would not be deterred. Her legacy endures in the organization she established and in the lives of millions of girls and women who have found in Girl Scouting a place to call their own.

## NOTES

Special thanks to the Girl Scouts of the USA for research assistance and permission to use materials located at the Juliette Gordon Low Birthplace in Savannah, Georgia, and the National Historic Preservation Center, Girl Scouts of the USA Headquarters in New York, New York.

1. In 2008, there were 3.7 million Girl Scouts in the United States; Girl Scouts of the USA, "Facts," http://www.girlscouts.org/who_we_are/facts/ (accessed November 16, 2008). Although the majority of members are girls, troop leaders and other adult volunteers are included in the membership statistics.

2. Girl Scouts of the USA, "About Girl Scouts," http://www.girlscouts.org/who_we_are/ (accessed November 16, 2008).

3. Juliette Kinzie to Nelly Gordon, November 2, 1860; Gordon Family Papers, Georgia Historical

Society, Savannah, Ga. (hereafter cited as GFPGHS); Juliette Kinzie to Nelly Gordon, November 20, 1860, Gordon Family Papers, Southern Historical Collection, Manuscripts Department, University of North Carolina Library, Chapel Hill (hereafter cited as GFPUNC); Harold Wentworth and Stuart Berg Flexner, *Dictionary of American Slang*, 2nd supplemental ed. (New York: Thomas Y. Cromwell and Co., 1975).

4. Nelly Gordon to W. W. Gordon, June 22, 1879, GFPUNC.

5. W. W. Gordon to Nelly Gordon, January 19, 1885, GFPGHS. See also W. W. Gordon to Nelly Gordon, January 20, 1885; January 21, 1885; January 24, 1885; January 28, 1885, GFPGHS.

6. Gladys Denny Shultz and Daisy Gordon Lawrence, *Lady From Savannah: The Life of Juliette Low* (1958; repr., New York: Girl Scouts of the USA, 1988), 198–99; Nelly Gordon to W. W. Gordon, August 21, 1904, GFPUNC.

7. Juliette Gordon Low (hereafter cited as JGL) to Arthur Gordon, October 23, 1900, GFPUNC.

8. "Girl Guides Organizing Tour Planned for Two Continents," *Los Angeles Times*, March 10, 1912; "Girl Guides an Auxiliary to Boy Scouts Organization to Be Taken Up in United States," *Portland Oregonian*, March 17, 1912.

9. "Response to Welcome," n.d. , Juliette Gordon Low Speeches and Writing, National Historic Preservation Center, Girl Scout Headquarters, New York, N.Y. (hereafter cited as GSHQ).

10. "History of the 'White Rose' Troop, compiled by the First Troop Captain, Mrs. J. Randolph Anderson, and her daughter, Page Anderson (Mrs. Henry N. Platt, Philadelphia) Savannah, February 1937," Girl Scout First Headquarters Museum and Program Center, Savannah, Ga. (hereafter cited as GSFHM).

11. JGL to Mabel Gordon Leigh, March 12, 1912, GFPUNC; Eleanor Gordon Parker to W. W. Gordon, May 9, 1912, GFPUNC; Nelly Gordon to Eleanor Gordon Parker, May 5, 1912, GFPUNC.

12. Mabel Gordon Leigh to W. W. Gordon, April 12, 1912, GFPUNC; "Re-Chronological History—Girl Scouts. per—Inez F. Oliveros, Savannah, Ga.," GSFHM; Edith D. Johnston, "Early History of the Girl Scouts in Savannah and Washington," GSFHM; Sallie Margaret McAlpin to "My dear Mrs. Espey," October 29, 1936, GSFHM; Eleanor Gordon Parker to W. W .Gordon, May 9, 1912, GFPUNC.

13. Cora Neale, Washington to JGL, July 7, 1914, GSHQ.

14. JGL to Arthur Gordon, December 1, 1912; ibid., October 9, 1912, both in GFPUNC.

15. Alice Marie Beard, "Historical Origins of Camp Fire," http://www.alicemariebeard.com/campfire/history.htm (accessed November 16, 2008); Luther H. Gulick to JGL, January 17, 1913; JGL to Robert Baden-Powell, February 9, 1913, both in GFPGHS; "Girl Guide Headquarters. Report for December. From Dec. 1st 1912 to Jan. 1st 1913," GSHQ. See also Helen Buckler, Mary F. Fiedler, Martha F. Allen, *Wo-he-lo: The Story of Camp Fire Girls, 1910–1960* (New York: Camp Fire Girls, Inc., 1961); and Susan A. Miller, *Growing Girls: The Natural Origins of Girls' Organizations in America* (New Brunswick: Rutgers University Press, 2007).

16. JGL to Robert Baden-Powell, October 19, 1913, GSHQ; Clara Lisetor-Lane file, GSHQ.

17. Mary Degenhardt and Judith Kirsch, *Girl Scout Collector's Guide* (Lubbock: Texas Tech University Press, 2005), 81; "Mrs. Low's Report May 1914," GSHQ; JGL to James E. Russell, May 19, 1917, GSHQ; Edward L. Rowan, *James E. West and the History of the Boy Scouts of America* (privately printed, 2005), 68–71; Mary Ackin Rothschild, "To Scout or to Guide? The Girl Scout–Boy Scout Controversy, 1912–1941," *Frontiers* 6 (1982): 115–21.

18. Nelly Gordon to Mabel Gordon Leigh, May 5, 1913, GFPGHS.

19. JGL to Mabel Gordon Leigh, April 27, 1913; Nelly Gordon to Mrs. Axson, May 8, 1913; Ellen A. Wilson to JGL, May 21, 1913, all in GFPGHS.

20. W. J. Hoxie, *How Girls Can Help Their Country: The 1913 Handbook for Girl Scouts* (Bedford, Mass.: Applewood Books, n.d.), 12–13, 132, and passim; Tarleton Collier, "Dixie's Daughters as Girl Scouts Rival Boys for Outdoor Life," *Hearst's Sunday American* (Atlanta, Ga.), August 10, 1913, Girl Scout News Clippings, Juliette Gordon Low Birthplace and National Girl Scout Center, Savannah, Ga. (hereafter cited as JGLBP).

21. Juliette Low, "Leaders' Manual Girl Scouts," (n.p.: n.p., 1915), 10, 3; "Dixie's Daughters as Girl Scouts Rival Boys for Outdoor Life" and "Why Your Daughter Should Be a Girl Scout," JGLBP.

22. "Report of the Savannah Organization of Girl Scouts for Eight Months. From Oct. 15, 1912 to June 15, 1913," GSHQ; Sallie Margaret McAlpin to "My dear Mrs. Espey," October 29, 1936, GSFHM; Nelly Gordon to Mabel Gordon Leigh, April 28, 1914, GFPGHS; Executive Board Minutes, November 14, 1918, GSHQ.

23. JGL to Montague Gammon, January 19, 1917, GSHQ; Lillian S. Williams, *A Bridge to the Future: The History of Diversity in Girl Scouting* (New York: Girl Scouts of the United States of America, 1996), 11.

24. "Appendix D, Girl Scout Membership from 1912 to 1933," Laureen Ann Tedesco, "A Nostalgia for Home: Daring and Domesticity in Girl Scouting and Girls' Fiction, 1913–1933" (PhD diss., Texas A&M University, 1999), 337.

25. Helen Storrow to JGL, October 15, 1918, GSHQ.

26. Jane Deeter Rippin, "Her Dream Comes True," in *Juliette Gordon Low and the Girl Scouts: The Story of an American Woman, 1860–1927*, ed. Anne Hyde Choate and Helen Ferris (1928; repr., New York: Girl Scouts of the United States of America, 1949), 161–79 (quotation on 165).

# Selected Bibliography

## PRIMARY SOURCES

Andrews, Eliza Frances. *Journal of a Georgia Woman, 1870–1872.* Edited and with an introduction by S. Kittrell Rushing. Knoxville: University of Tennessee Press, 2002.

———. *The War-Time Journal of a Georgia Girl, 1864–1865.* Introduction by Jean V. Berlin. Lincoln: University of Nebraska Press, 1997.

Chesnut, Mary Boykin. *A Diary from Dixie.* Edited by Ben Ames Williams. Cambridge, Mass.: Harvard University Press, 1989.

Dawson, Sarah Morgan. *A Confederate Girl's Diary.* Edited by James I. Robertson. Bloomington: Indiana University Press, 1960.

Felton, Rebecca Latimer. *Country Life in Georgia in the Days of My Youth.* Atlanta: Index Printing, 1919.

———. *The Romantic Story of Georgia's Women.* Atlanta: Atlanta Georgian and Sunday American, 1930.

Gay, Mary A. H. *Life in Dixie during the War.* Edited by J. H. Segars. Macon: Mercer University Press, 2001. Originally published 1892.

Kemble, Fanny. *Journal of a Residence on a Georgia Plantation in 1838–1839.* Edited and with an introduction by John A. Scott. Athens: University of Georgia Press, 1984.

Leguin, Magnolia Wynn. *A Home-Concealed Woman: The Diaries of Magnolia Wynn LeGuin, 1901–1913.* Edited by Charles A. LeGuin. Athens: University of Georgia Press, 1990.

Leigh, Frances Butler. *Ten Years on a Georgia Plantation since the War.* London: R. Bentley and Son, 1883.

Lines, Amelia Akehurst. *"To Raise Myself a Little": The Diaries and Letters of Jennie, a Georgia Teacher, 1851–1886.* Edited by Thomas Dyer. Athens: University of Georgia Press, 1982.

Thomas, Ella Gertrude Clanton. *The Secret Eye: The Journal of Ella Gertrude Clanton Thomas, 1848–1889.* Edited by Virginia Ingraham Burr. Introduction by Nell Irvin Painter. Chapel Hill: University of North Carolina Press, 1990.

## SECONDARY SOURCES

Anderson, James D. *The Education of Blacks in the South, 1860–1935.* Chapel Hill: University of North Carolina Press, 1988.

Ayers, Edward L. *The Promise of the New South: Life after Reconstruction.* New York: Oxford University Press, 1992.

Bardaglio, Peter W. *Reconstructing the Household: Families, Sex, and the Law in the Nineteenth-Century South.* Chapel Hill: University of North Carolina Press, 1995.

Bartley, Numan V. *The Creation of Modern Georgia.* Athens: University of Georgia Press, 1990.

Blair, Karen J. *The Clubwoman as Feminist: True Womanhood Redefined, 1868–1914.* New York: Holmes and Meier, 1980.

Blassingame, John W. *The Slave Community: Plantation Life in the Antebellum South.* New York: Oxford University Press, 1972.

Bleser, Carol K., and Lesley J. Gordon, eds. *Intimate Strategies of the Civil War: Military Commanders and Their Wives.* New York: Oxford University Press, 2001.

Blight, David. *Race and Reunion: The Civil War in American Memory.* Cambridge, Mass.: Harvard University Press, 2001.

Boatwright, Eleanor M. *Status of Women in Georgia, 1780–1860.* Brooklyn, N.Y.: Carlson, 1994.

Bordin, Ruth. *Women and Temperance: The Quest for Power and Liberty, 1873–1900.* Philadelphia: Temple University Press, 1981.

Brundage, W. Fitzhugh, ed. *Where These Memories Grow: History, Memory, and Southern Identity.* Chapel Hill: University of North Carolina Press, 2000.

Bryant, Jonathan M. *How Curious a Land: Conflict and Change in Greene County, Georgia, 1850–1885.* Chapel Hill: University of North Carolina Press, 1996.

Butchart, Ronald E. *Northern Schools, Southern Blacks, and Reconstruction: Freedmen's Education, 1862–1875.* Westport, Conn.: Greenwood, 1980.

Bynum, Victoria. *Unruly Women: The Politics of Social and Sexual Control in the Old South.* Chapel Hill: University of North Carolina Press, 1992.

Camp, Stephanie M. H. *Closer to Freedom: Enslaved Women and Everyday Resistance to Slavery in the Plantation South.* Chapel Hill: University of North Carolina Press, 2004.

Carey, Anthony Gene. *Parties, Slavery, and the Union in Antebellum Georgia.* Athens: University of Georgia Press, 1997.

Carter, Dan T. *When the War Was Over: The Failure of Self-Reconstruction in the South, 1865–1867.* Baton Rouge: Louisiana State University Press, 1985.

Cashin, Edward J., and Glenn T. Eskew. *Paternalism in a Southern City: Race, Religion, and Gender in Augusta, Georgia.* Athens: University of Georgia Press, 2001.

Cashin, Joan E. *A Family Venture: Men and Women on the Southern Frontier.* Baltimore: Johns Hopkins University Press, 1991.

———. *Our Common Affairs: Texts for Women in the Old South.* Baltimore: John Hopkins University Press, 1996.

———, ed. *The War Was You and Me: Civilians in the American Civil War.* Princeton: Princeton University Press, 2002.

Censer, Jane Turner. *North Carolina Planters and Their Children, 1800–1860.* Baton Rouge: Louisiana State University Press, 1984.

——. *The Reconstruction of White Southern Womanhood, 1865–1895.* Baton Rouge: Louisiana State University Press, 2003.

Chirhart, Ann Short. *Torches of Light: Georgia Teachers and the Coming of the Modern South.* Athens: University of Georgia Press, 2005.

Clinton, Catherine. *Fanny Kemble's Civil Wars.* New York: Simon and Schuster, 2000.

——. *The Plantation Mistress: Woman's World in the Old South.* New York: Pantheon, 1982.

Clinton, Catherine, and Michele Gillespie, eds. *The Devil's Lane: Race and Sex in the Early South.* New York: Oxford University Press, 1997.

Clinton, Catherine, and Nina Silber, eds. *Divided Houses: Gender and the Civil War.* New York: Oxford University Press, 1992.

Coleman, Kenneth. *History of Georgia.* Athens: University of Georgia Press, 1977.

Cox, Karen. *Dixie's Daughters: The United Daughters of the Confederacy and the Preservation of Confederate Culture.* Gainesville: University of Florida Press, 2003.

Dailey, Jane, Glenda Elizabeth Gilmore, and Bryant Simon, eds. *Jumpin' Jim Crow: Southern Politics from Civil War to Civil Rights.* Princeton: Princeton University Press, 2000.

Daniel, Pete. *Standing at the Crossroads: Southern Life in the Twentieth Century.* New York: Hill and Wang, 1986.

Dittmer, John. *Black Georgia in the Progressive Era, 1900–1920.* Urbana: University of Illinois Press, 1977.

Drago, Edmund L. *Black Politicians and Reconstruction in Georgia: A Splendid Failure.* Athens: University of Georgia Press, 1992.

Edwards, Laura. *Gendered Strife and Confusion: The Politics of Reconstruction.* Urbana: University of Illinois Press, 1996.

——. *Scarlett Doesn't Live Here Anymore: Southern Women in the Civil War Era.* Urbana: University of Illinois Press, 2000.

Fairclough, Adam. *A Class of Their Own: Black Teachers in the Segregated South.* Cambridge: Harvard University Press, 2007.

Farnham, Christie Anne. *The Education of the Southern Belle: Higher Education and Student Socialization in the Antebellum South.* New York: New York University Press, 1994.

——. *Women of the American South: A Multicultural Reader.* New York: New York University Press, 1997.

Faust, Drew Gilpin. *Mothers of Invention: Women of the Slaveholding South in the American Civil War.* Chapel Hill: University of North Carolina Press, 1998.

Fields, Barbara Jeanne. "Ideology and Race in American History." In *Region, Race, and Reconstruction: Essays in Honor of C. Vann Woodward,* edited by J. Morgan Kousser and James McPherson, 143–77. New York: Oxford University Press, 1982.

Flynn, Charles L. *White Land, Black Labor: Caste and Class in Late Nineteenth Century Georgia.* Baton Rouge: Louisiana State University Press, 1983.

Foner, Eric. *Reconstruction: America's Unfinished Revolution, 1863–1877.* New York: Harper and Row, 1988.

Foster, Gaines. *Ghosts of the Confederacy: Defeat, the Lost Cause, and the Emergence of the New South.* New York: Oxford University Press, 1987.

Fox-Genovese, Elizabeth. *Within the Plantation Household: Black and White Women of the Old South.* Chapel Hill: University of North Carolina Press, 1988.

Fredrickson, George M. *The Black Image in the White Mind: The Debate on Afro-American Character and Destiny, 1817–1914.* New York: Harper and Row, 1971.

Friedman, Jean E. *The Enclosed Garden: Women and Community in the Evangelical South.* Chapel Hill: University of North Carolina Press, 1985.

Gallagher, Gary, and Alan T. Nolan, eds. *The Myth of the Lost Cause and Civil War History.* Bloomington: Indiana University Press, 2000.

Gardner, Sarah. *Blood and Irony: Southern White Women's Narratives of the Civil War, 1861–1937.* Chapel Hill: University of North Carolina Press, 2003.

Gaston, Paul M. *The New South Creed: A Study in Modern Mythmaking.* Baton Rouge: Louisiana State University Press, 1970.

Genovese, Eugene D. *The Political Economy of Slavery.* New York: Vintage, 1967.

———. *Roll, Jordan, Roll: The World the Slaves Made.* New York: Vintage, 1976.

*The Georgia Historical Quarterly* 76 (Summer 1992) and 82 (Winter 1998).

Gillespie, Michele. *Free Labor in an Unfree World: White Artisans in Slaveholding Georgia, 1789–1860.* Athens: University of Georgia Press, 2000.

Gilmore, Glenda E. *Gender and Jim Crow: Women and the Politics of White Supremacy in North Carolina, 1896–1920.* Chapel Hill: University of North Carolina Press, 1996.

Glymph, Thavolia, Harold Woodman, Barbara Jeanne Fields, and Armstead Robinson, eds. *Essays on the Postbellum Southern Economy.* College Station: Texas A&M University Press, 1985.

Goodson, Steven. *Highbrows, Hillbillies, and Hellfire: Public Entertainment in Atlanta, 1880–1930.* Athens: University of Georgia Press, 2002.

Goodwyn, Lawrence. *Democratic Promise: The Populist Moment in America.* New York: Oxford University Press, 1976.

Grant, Donald L. *The Way It Was in the South: The Black Experience in Georgia.* Athens: University of Georgia Press, 1993.

Grantham, Dewey. *Hoke Smith and the Politics of the New South.* Baton Rouge: Louisiana State University Press, 1958.

———. *Southern Progressivism: The Reconciliation of Progress and Tradition.* Knoxville: University of Tennessee Press, 1983.

Green, Elna C. *Before the New Deal: Social Welfare in the South, 1830–1930.* Athens: University of Georgia Press, 1999.

———. *Southern Strategies: Southern Women and the Woman Suffrage Question.* Chapel Hill: University of North Carolina Press, 1998.

Gutman, Herbert G. *The Black Family in Slavery and Freedom, 1750–1925*. New York: Pantheon, 1976.

Hahn, Steven. *The Roots of Southern Populism: Yeoman Farmers and the Transformation of the Georgia Upcountry, 1850–1890*. New York: Oxford University Press, 1983.

Hale, Grace Elizabeth. *Making Whiteness: The Culture of Segregation in the South, 1890–1940*. New York: Vintage, 1998.

Hall, Jacquelyn Dowd. *Revolt against Chivalry: Jesse Daniel Ames and the Women's Campaign against Lynching*. New York: Columbia University Press, 1979.

Harlan, Louis R. *Separate and Unequal: Southern School Campaigns and Racism in the Southern Seaboard States, 1901–1915*. New York: Atheneum, 1968.

Harris, J. William. *Plain Folk and Gentry in a Slave Society: White Liberty and Black Slavery in Augusta's Hinterlands*. Middletown: Wesleyan University Press, 1985.

Hartog, Henrik. *Man and Wife in America: A History*. Cambridge, Mass.: Harvard University Press, 2000.

Harvey, Paul. *Redeeming the South: Religious Cultures and Racial Identities among Southern Baptists, 1865–1924*. Chapel Hill: University of North Carolina Press, 1997.

Hawks, Joanne V., and Skemp, Sheila L., ed. *Sex, Race, and the Role of Women in the South*. Jackson: University Press of Mississippi, 1983.

Hewitt, Nancy A., and Suzanne Lebsock, eds. *Visible Women: New Essays on American Activism*. Urbana: University of Illinois Press, 1993.

Hickey, Georgina. *Hope and Danger in the New South City: Working-Class Women and Urban Development in Atlanta, 1890–1940*. Athens: University of Georgia Press, 2003.

Higginbotham, Evelyn Brooks. *Righteous Discontent: The Women's Movement in the Black Baptist Church, 1880–1920*. Cambridge, Mass.: Harvard University Press, 1993.

Hine, Darlene Clark. *Hine Sight: Black Women and the Re-Construction of American History*. New York: Carlson, 1994.

Hunter, Tera W. *To 'Joy My Freedom: Southern Black Women's Lives and Labors after the Civil War*. Cambridge, Mass.: Harvard University Press, 1997.

Inscoe, John C. *Georgia Black and White: Exploration in Race Relations of a Southern State, 1865–1950*. Athens: University of Georgia Press, 1994.

Jabour, Anya. *Marriage in the Early Republic: Elizabeth and William Wirt and the Companionate Ideal*. Baltimore: Johns Hopkins University Press, 1998.

Johnson, Michael P. *Toward a Patriarchal Republic: The Secession of Georgia*. Baton Rouge: Louisiana State University Press, 1977.

Jones, Anne Goodwyn. *Tomorrow Is Another Day: The Woman Writer in the South, 1859–1936*. Baton Rouge: Louisiana State University Press, 1981.

Jones, Jacqueline. *Labor of Love, Labor of Sorrow: Black Women, Work, and the Family from Slavery to the Present*. New York: Basic Books, 1985.

———. *Soldiers of Light and Love: Northern Teachers and Southern Blacks, 1865–1873*. Chapel Hill: University of North Carolina Press, 1980.

Kammen, Michael. *Mystic Chords of Memory: The Transformation of Tradition in American Culture.* New York: Random House, 1991.

Kirby, Jack Temple. *Darkness at Dawning: Race and Reform in the Progressive South.* Philadelphia: Lippincott, 1972.

Kolchin, Peter. *American Slavery: 1619–1877.* New York: Hill and Wang, 2003.

Lebsock, Suzanne. *The Five Women of Petersburg: Status and Culture in a Southern Town, 1784–1860.* New York: W. W. Norton, 1984.

Leslie, Kent Anderson. *Woman of Color, Daughter of Privilege: Amanda America Dickson, 1849–1893.* Athens: University of Georgia Press, 1995.

Link, William A. *The Paradox of Southern Progressivism, 1880–1930.* Chapel Hill: University of North Carolina Press, 1992.

Litwack, Leon F. *Been in the Storm so Long: The Aftermath of Slavery.* New York: Knopf, 1979.

———. *Trouble in Mind: Black Southerners in the Age of Jim Crow.* New York: Knopf, 1998.

Lockley, Timothy James. *Lines in the Sand: Race and Class in Lowcountry Georgia, 1750–1860.* Athens: University of Georgia Press, 2001.

Luker, Ralph E. *The Social Gospel and Modern American Culture.* Chapel Hill: University of North Carolina Press, 1991.

MacLean, Nancy. *Behind the Mask of Chivalry: The Making of the Second Ku Klux Klan.* New York: Oxford University Press, 1994.

Marsh, Ben. *Georgia's Frontier Women: Female Fortunes in a Southern Colony.* Athens: University of Georgia Press, 2007.

Mathews, Donald G. *Religion in the Old South.* Chicago: University of Chicago Press, 1977.

McCandless, Amy Thompson. *The Past in the Present: Women's Higher Education in the Twentieth-Century American South.* Tuscaloosa: University of Alabama Press, 1999.

McPherson, James M. *Battle Cry of Freedom: The Civil War Era.* New York: Oxford University Press, 1988.

Montgomery, William E. *Under Their Own Vine and Fig Tree: The African-American Church in the South, 1865–1900.* Baton Rouge: Louisiana State University Press, 1993.

Myers, Robert Manson. *The Children of Pride: A True Story of Georgia and the Civil War.* New Haven: Yale University Press, 1972.

*The New Georgia Encyclopaedia.* Available at http://www.georgiaencyclopedia.org/nge/Home.jsp.

Ownby, Ted. *Subduing Satan: Religion, Recreation, and Manhood in the Rural South, 1865–1920.* Chapel Hill: University of North Carolina Press, 1990.

Rable, George C. *Civil Wars: Women and the Crisis of Southern Nationalism.* Urbana: University of Illinois Press, 1989.

Range, Willard. *A Century of Georgia Agriculture, 1850–1950.* Athens: University of Georgia Press, 1954.

Reidy, Joseph P. *From Slavery to Agrarian Capitalism in the Cotton Plantation South: Central Georgia, 1800–1890.* Chapel Hill: University of North Carolina Press, 1992.

Roark, James L. *Masters without Slaves: Southern Planters in the Civil War and Reconstruction.* New York: W. W. Norton, 1977.

Rothman, Ellen K. *Hands and Hearts: A History of Courtship in America.* New York: Basic Books, 1984.

Rozier, John. *Black Boss: Political Revolution in a Georgia County.* Athens: University of Georgia Press, 1982.

Sant, Claudio. *A New Order of Things: Property, Power, and the Transformation of the Creek Indians, 1733–1816.* Cambridge: Cambridge University Press, 1999.

Scarborough, William Kaufman. *Masters of the Big House: Elite Slaveowners of the Nineteenth-Century South.* Baton Rouge: Louisiana State University Press, 2003.

Schwalm, Leslie. *A Hard Fight for We: Women's Transition from Slavery to Freedom in South Carolina.* Urbana: University of Illinois Press, 1997.

Schweiger, Beth Barton, and Donald G. Mathews, eds. *Religion in the American South: Protestants and Others in History and Culture.* Chapel Hill: University of North Carolina Press, 2004.

Scott, Anne Firor. *The Southern Lady: From Pedestal to Politics, 1830–1930.* Chicago: University of Chicago Press, 1970.

Silber, Nina. *The Romance of Reunion: Northerners and the South, 1865–1900.* Chapel Hill: University of North Carolina Press, 1993.

Sims, Anastatia. *The Power of Femininity in the New South: Women's Organization and Politics in North Carolina, 1880–1930.* Columbia: University of South Carolina Press, 1997.

Sweet, Julie Anne. *Negotiating for Georgia: British-Creek Relations in the Trustee Era.* Athens: University of Georgia Press, 2005.

Turner, Elizabeth Hayes. *Women, Culture, and Community: Religion and Reform in Galveston, 1880–1920.* New York: Oxford University Press, 1997.

Wayne, Michael. *The Reshaping of Plantation Society: The Natchez District, 1860–1880.* Baton Rouge: Louisiana State University Press, 1983.

Weiner, Marli F. *Mistresses and Slaves: Plantation Women in South Carolina, 1830–1880.* Urbana: University of Illinois Press, 1998

Wells, Jonathan David. *The Origins of the Southern Middle Class, 1800–1861.* Chapel Hill: University of North Carolina Press, 2003.

Wheeler, Marjorie Spruill. *New Women of the New South: The Leaders of the Woman Suffrage Movement in the Southern States.* New York: Oxford University Press, 1993.

White, Deborah Gray. *"Ain't I a Woman?": Female Slaves in the Plantation South.* New York: W. W. Norton, 1985.

Whites, LeeAnn. *The Civil War as a Crisis in Gender: Augusta, Georgia, 1860–1890.* Athens: University of Georgia Press, 1995.

Williamson, Joel. *The Crucible of Race: Black and White Relations in the American South since Emancipation.* New York: Oxford University Press, 1984.

———. *Rage for Order: Black-White Relations in the American South since Emancipation.* New York: Oxford University Press, 1986.

Wood, Betty. *Gender, Race and Rank in a Revolutionary Age: The Georgia Lowcountry, 1750–1820.* Athens: University of Georgia Press, 2000.

———. *Slavery in Colonial Georgia, 1730–1775.* Athens: University of Georgia Press, 1984.

———. *Women's Work, Men's Work: The Informal Slave Economies of Lowcountry Georgia.* Athens: University of Georgia Press, 1995.

Woodward, C. Vann. *The Burdens of Southern History.* 3rd ed. Baton Rouge: Louisiana State University Press, 1993.

———. *The Origins of the New South, 1877–1913.* Critical essay by Charles B. Dew. Rev. ed. Baton Rouge: Louisiana State University Press, 1971.

Wyatt-Brown, Bertram. *Southern Honor: Ethics and Behavior in the Old South.* New York: Oxford University Press, 1982.

Wynne, Lewis Nicholas. *The Continuity of Planter Politics in Georgia, 1865–1892.* Macon: Mercer University Press, 1986.

# Contributors

SARAH CASE is Assistant Professor of History at Salisbury University in Maryland. Her work has been published in the *Journal of Southern History*. Currently, she is completing a manuscript on southern women and educational reform in late nineteenth- and early twentieth-century Georgia.

ANN SHORT CHIRHART is Associate Professor of History at Indiana State University in Terre Haute. She is the author of *Torches of Light: Georgia Teachers and the Coming of the Modern South* (2005) and articles that have appeared in the *Georgia Historical Quarterly, Journal of Family History,* and *The New Deal and Beyond: Social Welfare in the South since 1930* (2002). She is the coeditor of *Georgia Women: Their Lives and Times,* vol. 2 (forthcoming), and is also working on a manuscript about African American activism in the urban South before 1954.

CATHERINE CLINTON is Professor of United States History at Queen's University Belfast. She is the author of numerous publications, including *The Plantation Mistress: Woman's World in the Old South* (1982), and the editor of, among others, *Battle Scars: Gender and Sexuality in the American Civil War* (2006) and *Susie King Taylor's Reminiscences of My Life in Camp: an African-American Woman's Civil War Memoir* (2006).

STACEY HORSTMANN GATTI is Assistant Professor of History at Long Island University in Brooklyn, New York. Her current research projects focus on the political activities of women's organizations in Georgia and New York during the Progressive era and the 1920s.

MICHELE GILLESPIE is Kahle Associate Professor of History at Wake Forest University in Winston-Salem, North Carolina. She is the author of *Free Labor in an Unfree World: White Artisans in Slaveholding Georgia* (2000) and coeditor of numerous books, most recently *Thomas Dixon Jr. and the Birth of Modern America* (2006).

DANIEL KILBRIDE is Associate Professor of History at John Carroll University in University Heights, Ohio. He is the author of *An American Aristocracy: Southern Planters in Antebellum Philadelphia,* from the University of South Carolina Press (2006). He is writing a book on European travel among Americans from colonial times through the 1870s.

KENT ANDERSON LESLIE is an independent scholar living in Georgia. She is the author of *Woman of Color, Daughter of Privilege: Amanda America Dickson, 1849–1893* (1995). She is working on a manuscript on Lucy Craft Laney.

BEN MARSH is a lecturer of history at the University of Stirling in Scotland. His most recent publication is *Georgia's Frontier Women: Female Fortunes in a Southern Colony* (2007). He has published numerous articles in historical journals such as the *Georgia Historical Quarterly*. His recent scholarship focuses on family relationships on southern plantations and the colonial silk industry.

DONALD MATHEWS is Professor of History at the University of North Carolina at Chapel Hill. His numerous publications include *Sex, Gender, and the Politics of ERA: A State and a Nation* (1990), *Religion in the Old South* (1977), and *Slavery and Methodism: A Chapter in American Morality 1780–1845* (1965). His articles have been published in numerous journals, including the *Journal of Southern History.*

BARBARA MCCASKILL is Associate Professor and General Sandy Beaver Teaching Professor at the University of Georgia. She has recently coedited *Post-Bellum—Pre-Harlem: African American Literature and Culture, 1877–1919* (2006) and authored *Running 1,000 Miles for Freedom: The Escape of William and Ellen Craft from Slavery* (1999). Her essays appear in journals such as *African American Review* and *Signs: Journal of Women in Culture and Society.*

CHRISTOPHER J. OLSEN is Chair and Associate Professor of History at Indiana State University in Terre Haute. He is the author of *Political Culture and Secession in Mississippi* (2000) and *The American Civil War* (2006), and is currently working on a study of political culture in antebellum America.

JOHN THOMAS SCOTT is Professor of History at Mercer University in Macon, Georgia. He has recently published scholarly articles in *The Georgia Historical Quarterly* and *Fides et Historia* and has made presentations to the Society for the History of the Early American Republic and the Southern Historical Association. His current research centers on religion in Trustee-era Georgia.

CAREY OLMSTEAD SHELLMAN is an Instructor of History at Armstrong Atlantic State University in Savannah, Georgia. She completed her PhD at the University of Florida. Her dissertation, "Nellie Peters Black and the Practical Application of the Social Gospel in the New South, 1890–1919," focuses on the role of organized women in the promotion of the social gospel in the South through progressive reform.

ANASTATIA HODGENS SIMS is a Professor of History at Georgia Southern University in Statesboro. She received her PhD from the University of North Carolina at Chapel

Hill. She wrote *The Power of Femininity in the New South: Women's Organizations and Politics in North Carolina, 1880–1930* (1997), coedited *Negotiating the Boundaries of Southern Womanhood: Dealing with the Powers That Be* (2000), and published several articles in journals and anthologies. She is currently working on a biography of Juliette Gordon Low.

JENNIFER LUND SMITH is Associate Professor of History at North Georgia College and State University in Dahlonega. Her publications include chapters in *Georgia in Black and White: Explorations in the Race Relations of a Southern State, 1865–1950* (1994), *Appalachians and Race: The Mountain South from Slavery to Segregation* (2005), and *Intimate Strategies of the Civil War: Military Commanders and Their Wives* (2007).

JULIE ANNE SWEET is Associate Professor of History at Baylor University in Waco, Texas. She is the author of *Negotiating for Georgia: British-Creek Relations in the Trustee Era, 1733–1752* (2005) and has written numerous articles for the *Georgia Historical Quarterly* on a wide variety of colonial Georgia topics.

LEEANN WHITES is a Professor of History at the University of Missouri–Columbia, where she teaches courses on the Civil War era, and gender and sexuality in the nineteenth century. She is the author of *The Civil War as a Crisis in Gender* (1995) and *Gender Matters: Civil War, Reconstruction and the Making of the New South* (2005), and coeditor with Alecia Long of the forthcoming volume *Occupied Women: Reconsidering the Field of Battle in the U.S. Civil War.*

BETTY WOOD is Reader in American History at the University of Cambridge and a Fellow of Girton College, Cambridge. She has authored several books and articles on the history of eighteenth- and early nineteenth-century Georgia, beginning with *Slavery in Colonial Georgia, 1733–1775* (1984) and, more recently, *Gender, Race and Rank in a Revolutionary Age: The Georgia Lowcountry, 1750–1820* (2000), and *Mary Telfair to Mary Few: Selected Letters, 1802–1844* (2007).

# Index

abolitionists: American, 83, 88–89, 90–96, 97, 98–99; British, 96, 97–98

African American men, 2; and the Civil War, 6, 136–41; disenfranchisement of, 160, 177, 251; enfranchisement of, 149, 262–63; escape from slavery, 83–90, 138; lives as slaves, 87, 88; as teachers, 98–99, 134, 135, 141; white stereotypes of, 89, 95, 326, 327; white women's views on, 234–35, 286

African Americans: and the American Revolution, 69–70; in colonial period, 61–64; daguerreotypes of, 91–94; identities of, 2; lives as slaves, 82–89, 130–35, 173, 174, 178–81, 203–4; manumission of, 178–79; political empowerment of, 238; as proportion of Georgia population, 3; purchase freedom, 319; West and West Central African origins of, 2; white women's views on, 3, 5, 63–64, 147–51, 162–65, 168, 215–16, 229–30, 234–36

African American women, 2; and the Civil War, 5, 6, 130, 135–41; club women, 326–28; daguerreotypes of, 91–94; flee from slavery, 3, 5, 82–90, 95–96; form temperance groups, 251; and Girl Scouts, 384–85; literary output of, 82, 87, 93, 96–97, 130, 142, 143; lives as slaves, 3–4, 82–89, 130–35, 173, 174, 178–81, 321–25; rape of, 6, 82, 83, 86, 88, 173, 174, 178, 181; as teachers, 4, 6, 8, 98–99, 130, 134,

137, 141, 185, 318–19, 321, 322, 323–24; white stereotypes of, 89, 326, 327; white women's views on, 5, 111–14, 343–44

Agnes Scott College, 201, 281

agricultural reform: antebellum, 177–78; postbellum, 8, 233–34, 297, 299, 308–11, 312, 313

alcohol, abuse of, 250, 253–54, 345–47, 352–53, 354, 355, 360, 363. See also Georgia Women's Christian Temperance Union; moral reform; National Women's Christian Temperance Union

Almon, William, 74

Alston, Robert, 336

American Association of University Women, 312

American Missionary Association, 141, 321

American Revolution, 2, 3, 59, 63, 111. See also Hart, Nancy; Johnston, Elizabeth Lichtenstein

American Revolution, The (Coleman), 48

Andersonville, Ga., 157

Andrews, Eliza Frances, 4, 6, 7, 8–9; birth of, 150; as a botanist, 150, 151, 152, 168, 169; Civil War experiences of, 149; death of, 169; education of, 150; literary output of, 147, 151, 152–54, 158, 163, 166–69; views of, 66, 147–48, 151, 152, 153, 156–57, 158, 161–65, 166–69

Andrews, Garnett (son), 153

Andrews, Judge Garnett, 150, 151